Inside

Microsoft® Windows® 2000
Third Edition

David A. Solomon
Mark E. Russinovich

PUBLISHED BY
Microsoft Press
A Division of Microsoft Corporation
One Microsoft Way
Redmond, Washington 98052-6399

Library of Congress Cataloging-in-Publication Data
Solomon, David A.
 Inside Microsoft Windows 2000 / David A. Solomon, Mark Russinovich.
 p. cm.
 ISBN 0-7356-1021-5
 1. Microsoft Windows (Computer file) 2. Operating systems (Computers) I.
Russinovich, Mark. II. Title.

QA76.76.O63 S6285 2000
005.4'4769--dc21 00-031888

Portions previously published in *Windows NT Magazine* and *Windows 2000 Magazine*. Copyright © 1997, 1998, 1999, 2000 by *Windows 2000 Magazine*. Reprinted and modified with permission.

Printed and bound in the United States of America.

1 2 3 4 5 6 7 8 9 WCWC 5 4 3 2 1 0

Distributed in Canada by Penguin Books Canada Limited.

A CIP catalogue record for this book is available from the British Library.

Microsoft Press books are available through booksellers and distributors worldwide. For further information about international editions, contact your local Microsoft Corporation office or contact Microsoft Press International directly at fax (425) 936-7329. Visit our Web site at mspress.microsoft.com. Send comments to *mspinput@microsoft.com*.

Acquisitions Editor: Ben Ryan
Project Editor: Sally Stickney
Technical Editor: Jean Ross

To my wife, Shelly, my partner in life. I'll always love you.
—D.S.

For Susan, my soul mate.
—M.R.

CONTENTS

CHAPTER THREE

System Mechanisms **89**

CHAPTER FOUR

Startup and Shutdown **177**

CHAPTER FIVE

Management Mechanisms **215**

CHAPTER TEN

Storage Management 607

CHAPTER THIRTEEN

Networking **779**

HISTORICAL PERSPECTIVE

It is a pleasure to be able to write a few words about such a significant work as this book, and I thank the authors for providing me the opportunity to do so.

I first met David Solomon when I was working at Digital Equipment Corporation on the VMS operating system for VAX and he was only 16. Since that time he has been involved with operating system development and teaching operating system internals. I met Mark Russinovich relatively recently but have been aware of his expertise in the area of operating systems for some time. He has done some amazing work, such as his NTFS file system running on Microsoft Windows 98 and his "live" Microsoft Windows 2000 kernel debugger that can be used to peer into the Windows 2000 system while it is running.

The beginnings of Microsoft Windows NT started in October 1988 with a set of goals to produce a portable system that addressed OS/2 compatibility, security, POSIX, multiprocessing, integrated networking, and reliability. With the advent and huge success of Windows 3.0, the system goals were soon changed to natively address Windows compatibility directly and move OS/2 compatibility to a subsystem.

We originally thought we could produce the first Windows NT system in a little over two years. It actually ended up taking us four and a half years to the first release in the summer of 1993, and that release supported the Intel i386, the Intel i486, and the MIPS R4000 processors. Six weeks later we also introduced support for the Digital Alpha processors.

The first release of Windows NT was larger and slower than expected, so the next major push was a project called Daytona, named after the speedway in Florida. The main goals for this release were reducing the size of the system, increasing the speed of the system, and of course trying to make it more reliable. Six months after the release of Windows NT 3.5 in the fall of 1994, we released Windows NT 3.51, which was an updated version containing support for the IBM PowerPC processor.

The push for the next version of Windows NT was to update the user interface to be compatible with Windows 95 and to incorporate the Cairo technologies that had been under development at Microsoft for a couple of years. This system took two more years to develop and was introduced in the summer of 1996 as Windows NT 4.0.

(Left to right) David Solomon, David Cutler, and Mark Russinovich

That brings us to the Windows 2000 system and what this book is about. Windows 2000 is built on the same Windows NT technology as the previous versions and introduces significant new features such as Active Directory. Windows 2000 took three and a half years to produce and is the most tested and tuned version of Windows NT technology produced to date. Windows 2000 is the culmination of over eleven years of development spanning implementations on four architectures. The Windows 2000 code base is currently being ported to the new Intel IA-64 architecture. Windows 2000 is by far the best version of Windows NT technology we have produced to date, but there's more to come and we are busy working on the next release.

This book is the only definitive work on the internal structure and workings of Windows 2000. The authors have done a remarkable job of assimilating the details of the Windows NT code base and producing examples and tools that help the reader understand how things work. Every serious operating system developer should have a copy of this book on his or her desk.

David N. Cutler
Senior Distinguished Engineer
Microsoft Corporation

FOREWORD

We began in earnest on Microsoft Windows 2000 in August 1996. About three and a half years later, on December 15, 1999, we released Windows 2000 Professional, Windows 2000 Server, and Windows 2000 Advanced Server to manufacturing. With more than 5000 people contributing in one way or another, Windows 2000 represents the single largest operating system effort ever within Microsoft and probably within the entire industry. It also presents the most reliable and comprehensive system we have ever produced. It was quite a journey.

Today, Windows 2000 runs some of the largest Internet Web sites and enterprises in the world and is quickly becoming the standard client operating system for businesses and even some homes. Windows 2000 includes an amazing amount of technology. It can be used for desktop or laptop systems, and an astonishing array of servers, including file, print, Web, database, transactioning, dial-in, routing, streaming media, line-of-business applications, and many others. Understanding all these pieces is a daunting task. But if you start at the core concepts of the system and work out, the puzzle fits together a lot easier.

If you're like me, you like to figure out how things really work. Reading "how to use" books or standard Help information has never been sufficient for me. If you understand how something works internally, you know how to better use it, maximize performance and security, diagnose failures, and frankly have more fun. That's what this book is about.

David and Mark have done an outstanding job detailing the real "inside" technical story of Windows 2000. And the tools that are highlighted (or included) are a great resource for direct hands-on training and diagnostics work. After you read this book, you'll have a much greater understanding of how the system fits together, the improvements done as part of this release, and how to get the most out of the system.

I know Windows 2000 pretty well, but reading this book taught me a few things about the system that I didn't know. So open the book and open the hood on one of the most impressive operating systems ever created.

Jim Allchin
Group Vice President, Platforms
Microsoft Corporation

ACKNOWLEDGMENTS

This book wouldn't contain the depth of technical detail or the level of accuracy it has without the review, input, and support of key members of the Microsoft Windows 2000 development team. Therefore, we would like to jointly thank the following people from Microsoft for both their technical review as well as the time they spent with us explaining the rationale for the myriad details that comprise this world-renowned operating system:

- First and foremost, Dave Cutler, Senior Distinguished Engineer and the original architect of Microsoft Windows NT. Dave originally approved David Solomon's source code access and has been supportive of his work to explain the internals of Windows NT through his training business as well as during the writing of *Inside Windows NT*, second edition. Besides reviewing the chapter on processes and threads, Dave answered many questions on the kernel architecture of the system and wrote a historical perspective for this edition.

- Jim Allchin, for writing the Foreword to this book and for prodding us to add a chapter on networking.

- Lou Perazzoli, Distinguished Engineer (previously director of the Windows 2000 Base Team and author of the original memory manager for Windows NT). Lou was the primary champion for *Inside Windows NT*, second edition (he wrote the Foreword) and continued this role during the initial phases of the development of Windows 2000.

- Rob Short, vice president of the Windows 2000 Base Team, who made sure we had the resources we needed as well as access to the relevant people. Rob also provided direction on the overall content of the book.

- Landy Wang, lead developer for the memory manager, for making us feel welcome on the numerous times we stopped by and interrupted him to ask questions. Landy was always willing to take time to review chapter drafts as well as provide the rationale for the intricacies of this very complicated part of the system, even when others were waiting in line in the hallway to see him!

- Mark Lucovsky, Distinguished Engineer and architect in the Windows 2000 Base Team, for answering technical questions about many areas of the system.

- Richard Ward, for reviewing multiple drafts of the security chapter as well as the section on services. Richard also met with us more than once to provide technical review input.

- John Vert, who reviewed the sections on interrupt handling, the HAL, and the registry. John was also a key source for the rationale behind early Windows NT design decisions.

- Neil Clift, whose intimate knowledge of the Windows 2000 kernel components helped us iron out several details about the object manager and other areas.

- Dan Lovinger, for reviewing the cache manager, storage management, and file systems chapters.

- Adrian Oney and Nar Ganapathy, for reviewing the I/O chapter and helping to make the presentation of Plug and Play more lucid. Adrian was especially generous with his time and clarified some of the trickier aspects of the I/O system.

- Tom Fout, who guided the content of the networking chapter and coordinated the chapter's review by the key developers.

- Dragos Sambotin, for reviewing the registry section.

- Praerit Garg and Robert Reichel, for reviewing the security chapter.

- Michael Maston and Alan Warwick, for reviewing the WMI section.

- Keith Kaplan, for reviewing the storage and file systems chapters.

- Catharine van Ingen for reviewing the storage chapter.

- David Golds, Brian Andrews, and Mark Zbikowski, for reviewing the file systems chapter.

- Tim Moore, Ryszard Kott, Mario Goertzel, Yun Lin, Steven Nelson, Ilan Caron, Gurdeep Singh Pall, David Orbits, and the other networking developers, who improved the accuracy and organization of the networking chapter.

- Andre Vachon, for helping us with facets of the kernel debuggers (and for building a new set!).

- Jon Schwartz, who reviewed the most chapters of any single Microsoft employee—thanks for your excellent comments!

- Joseph Joy, for reviewing the first two chapters from the reader's point of view.

We also want to thank the following people from Microsoft Press (two of whom have since left) for their contribution to this book:

- Eric Stroo, previously acquisitions manager (but now enjoying the spoils of life after Microsoft), who, as with the previous edition, maintained a stern but supportive stance in regard to the book schedule.

- Ben Ryan, previously acquisitions editor (but now with another publisher), who took the reins from Eric but was gentler in his prodding for chapter deliveries.

- Sally Stickney, project editor, whose art and skill with the English language combined with her dogged attention to detail yet again amazed us throughout the whole process. Sally: you were kinder this time.

- Jean Ross, technical editor, who strove to catch each and every technical inconsistency. Jean continually amazed both of us with her tenacious verification of technical details.

We also want to thank Mark Smith, Karen Forster, Dianne Russell, and the rest of the staff of Windows 2000 Magazine (*www.win2000mag.com*) for granting us permission to draw content from Mark's "Internals" columns for the book. Finally, the following external reviewers also merit special thanks:

- Jamie Hanrahan, of Azius Developer Training (*www.azius.com*), who coauthored the Windows NT/Windows 2000 Internal Architecture class from which this book was based. Jamie, who has a real knack for explaining complicated concepts in a simple and practical fashion, developed several of the explanations and a number of the diagrams and figures.

- Brian Catlin, also of Azius Developer Training, for reviewing Chapters 2, 3, and 9 and for providing both technical input as well as excellent suggestions that improved the clarity of presentation.

- Jeffrey Richter, of Wintellect (*www.wintellect.com*), who, as with the previous edition, reviewed several chapters and cajoled the authors throughout the entire process. All those dinners in Bellevue with Jeff at the end of long hard days of writing kept us going.

- Rich Neves, of ReefEdge Inc. (*www.reefedge.com*), for reviewing the I/O and networking chapters.

- Andrew Tanenbaum, of the University of Amsterdam, who provided us with a slew of suggestions for improving the file systems chapter's organization and presentation.

- John Tracey, of IBM Research, for reviewing the networking chapter.

- Keith Moore, previously of Microsoft, for reviewing the networking chapter.

There were others who answered questions in the hallway or cafeteria and provided technical material—if we missed you, please forgive us!

The next two sections contain the authors' individual acknowledgments.

Acknowledgments from David Solomon

When Mark Russinovich first approached me about collaborating on this third edition, I was both excited and nervous. Would Microsoft accept such a notorious hacker of Windows NT to work on the official book about the internal architecture of their premier operating system? Would I be able to meet the technical challenge of working with such a Windows NT expert?

Fortunately, the answer to both questions was yes, and Mark and I had a ball working together on this project. Although Mark didn't look at the source code (only I did), I was constantly amazed at how quickly he could solve technical questions using his disassembled binary of Ntoskrnl.exe in combination with SoftICE. I know my knowledge of Windows 2000 has deepened. (We even kept track of "dumb things learned" for the times we would say to each other "I can't believe you didn't know that!")

I have to thank Mark for much of the new content in this third edition: Chapters 4, 5, 10, and 13 were completely new chapters based on his original content. Mark also made significant contributions to the detail in Chapters 3, 8, 9, and 12.

I also want to thank Mark's wife, Susan, for putting up with me on the long work days at Mark's house and for providing such yummy lunches and dinners (and the strong coffee!).

I thank Frank Artale for originally asking me to write *Inside Windows NT*, second edition, and for all the support from Windows NT Development (especially from Lou Perazzoli and Dave Cutler) while it was being written back in 1997 and 1998.

I want to thank my Mom and Dad for bringing me up and for giving me the support, guidance, and opportunities that molded me into who I am today.

Last but not least, I want to thank wife, Shelly, and our three children, Daniel, Rebecca, and Sarah, for going through the pain of *another* book project. This time, I got less sympathy for being late on deadlines—and rightly so. Thanks for bearing up.

Acknowledgments from Mark Russinovich

When I picked up a copy of *Inside Windows NT*, second edition, I was suitably impressed. Dave had done a fantastic job of detailing the operation of Windows NT, while at the same time making the description accessible through interesting experiments and lucid writing. I was working on my own Windows NT internals book but was quickly realizing the enormous effort required to pull off something like Dave had. On the off chance that he would agree, I e-mailed Dave with the suggestion that we work together on the third edition. I was thrilled when he brought me on board, and I thank him for the opportunity.

As Dave has said already, we learned a tremendous amount from each other and had a great time. There are as many "dumb things Mark learned from Dave" as "dumb things Dave learned from Mark" (well, not quite as many), which just highlights how our different perspectives made the book better. Often, neither of us would know the answer to a complex question about Windows NT behavior one of us had pondered for years, triggering furious multihour research efforts in which only our combined resources met the challenge. I look forward to working with him on future editions.

I also have to thank Bryce Cogswell and Edwin Brasch of Winternals Software for their patience and support while I devoted several months to the book.

I owe Rich Neves thanks for being a good friend and for enabling my effort on the book to be part of my official responsibilities while I worked at IBM Research.

My parents, Nicholas and Vera Russinovich, provided unlimited support and encouragement through my educational years, instilling in me the desire to learn as much as I can. My father, who passed away while I was writing this book, would have been especially proud of this achievement.

Finally, I want to thank my wife, Susan, who is the most important person in my life. She not only sacrificed the many nights and weekends that I devoted to this book by keeping me company, but she also encouraged me through the whole process. Her tolerance of my omnipresent computers without a doubt merits a medal.

INTRODUCTION

The third edition of *Inside Microsoft Windows 2000* is intended for advanced computer professionals (both developers and system administrators) who want to understand how the core components of the Microsoft Windows 2000 operating system work internally. With this knowledge, developers can better comprehend the rationale behind design choices when building applications specific to the Windows 2000 platform. Such knowledge can also help developers debug complex problems. System administrators can benefit from this information as well because understanding how the operating system works under the covers facilitates understanding the performance behavior of the system and makes it easier to troubleshoot system problems when things go wrong. After reading this book, you should have a better understanding of how Windows 2000 works and why it behaves as it does.

Structure of the Book

The first two chapters (Concepts and Tools, and System Architecture) lay the foundation with terms and concepts used throughout the rest of the book. The next three chapters—System Mechanisms, Startup and Shutdown, and Management Mechanisms—describe key underlying mechanisms in the system. The remaining chapters—Processes, Threads, and Jobs; Memory Management; Security; I/O System; Storage Management; Cache Manager; File Systems; and Networking—explain the core components of the Windows 2000 operating system.

Differences in the Third Edition

This new edition of *Inside Microsoft Windows 2000* covers many topics that weren't in the second edition of *Inside Windows NT,* such as startup and shutdown, service internals, registry internals, file system drivers, and networking. It also covers the kernel-related changes and enhancements in Windows 2000, such as the Windows Driver Model (WDM), Plug and Play, power management, Windows Management Instrumentation (WMI), encryption, the job object, and Terminal Services.

For the first time, the book includes a companion CD with useful tools for exploring Windows 2000 system internals. Also included on the CD is a searchable electronic version of the book. Also, many new hands-on experiments have been added to the book that show how to use tools such as the kernel debugger to examine internal Windows 2000 system state.

Hands-on Experiments

When a tool can be used to expose or demonstrate some aspect of Windows 2000 internal behavior, the steps necessary to try the tool yourself are listed in "Experiment" boxes. These appear throughout the book, and we encourage you to try these as you're reading—seeing visible proof of how Windows 2000 works internally will make much more of an impression on you than just reading about it. Many of the experiments use the kernel debugger. The live kernel debugger tool (LiveKd) included on the book's companion CD makes these experiments easy and safe to try.

Topics Not Covered

Windows 2000 is a large and complex operating system. This book doesn't cover everything relevant to Windows 2000 internals but instead focuses on the base system components. For example, this book doesn't describe COM+, the foundation of the Windows distributed object-oriented programming infrastructure.

Because this is an internals book and not a user, programming, or system administration book, it doesn't describe how to use, program, or configure Windows 2000.

A Warning and Caveat

Because this book describes the internal architecture and operation of Windows 2000, much of the information is subject to change between releases (although external interfaces, such as the Win32 API, are not subject to incompatible changes). For example, we refer to internal Windows 2000 system routines, data structures, and kernel variables as well as to algorithms and values used internally to make resource-sizing and performance-related decisions. These details, by definition, can change between releases.

By "subject to change," we don't necessarily mean that details described in this book *will* change between releases—but you can't count on them not changing. Any software that uses these undocumented interfaces might not work

on future releases of Windows 2000. Even worse, software that runs in kernel mode (such as device drivers) that uses these undocumented interfaces might result in a system crash when upgrading to a newer release of Windows 2000.

Using the Companion CD

The CD included with this book contains the complete contents of the Sysinternals Web site (*www.sysinternals.com*)—the Web site maintained by Mark Russinovich (this book's coauthor) and Bryce Cogswell—as well as other helpful tools. The CD also includes a fully searchable electronic version of the book as well as debugging tools and symbols. (See the Readme.txt file on the CD for information on using the debugging tools and the symbols.)

To view the contents of the CD, insert the CD into your CD-ROM drive. If you have the autorun feature in Windows enabled, a splash screen will automatically appear on your screen that will provide you with viewing options. To start this screen manually, run StartCD from the root directory of the CD.

Sysinternals

The contents of the Web site *www.sysinternals.com* have been included on this CD for your convenience. You can find the tools from this Web site that are used in the experiments in this book in the \Sysint folder. You can run these tools from the CD, or you can install them onto your hard drive by selecting Run Setup from the autorun splash screen and following the instructions in Setup.

You can also browse the CD version of the entire Web site by selecting Browse CD Sysinternals from the autorun splash screen or by opening Ntinternals.htm from the \Sysinternals-WebSite folder. You can copy the entire Web site to your hard disk by selecting Run Setup from the splash screen and following the Setup instructions.

For the most up-to-date versions of the Sysinternals Web site and tools, visit *www.sysinternals.com* (which you can do from the splash screen by selecting Browse Online Sysinternals).

Tools

Additional tools have been provided on this CD and are located in the \Tools folder. Among the tools is a performance monitor DLL extension (KVarPerf) that allows you to monitor internal Windows 2000 kernel variables from the Performance tool. Another tool is LiveKd, a special tool that allows use of the standard Microsoft kernel debugger tools (such as Kd.exe, Windbg.exe, I386kd.exe, and so on) on a live system with no special debugging options enabled.

To install the tools, select the Run Setup option from the autorun splash screen (or run Setup.exe in the \Setup folder) and follow the Setup instructions. You can also run these tools directly from the CD, although LiveKd must be run from the \Debuggers directory on the CD rather than the \Tools directory. See the Readme.txt file in the root of the companion CD for more information on running LiveKd from the CD and on setting up your system for kernel debugging.

System Requirements

The following is a list of system requirements necessary to use the contents of the companion CD:

- Any supported Microsoft Windows 2000 Professional, Server, Advanced Server, or Datacenter Server configuration.

- To install the tools needed for the experiments from the Tools and Sysint folders, approximately 5 MB of disk space is required. If you choose to install the copy of the *www.sysinternals.com* site, approximately 30 MB of disk space is required. Installing the contents of the Debuggers folder requires approximately 20 MB of disk space, and the full contents of Symbols requires 20 MB.

- Some of the experiments in this book require the use of tools from the Windows 2000 Support Tools, debugging tools, and resource kit (Professional or Server edition). These tools and their locations are listed in Chapter 1.

E-book

This CD contains an electronic version of the book. This e-book allows you to view the book text on screen and to search the contents. For information on installing and using the e-book, see the Readme.txt file in the \Ebook folder.

Support

Every effort has been made to ensure the accuracy of this book and the contents of the companion CD. Should you run into any problems or issues, please refer to the following sources.

From the Authors

This book isn't perfect. No doubt it contains some inaccuracies; or possibly, we've omitted some topics we should have covered. If you find anything you think is incorrect or if you believe we should have included material that isn't here, please feel free to send e-mail to *insidew2k@sysinternals.com*. Updates and corrections will be posted on the page *www.sysinternals.com/insidew2k*.

From Microsoft Press

Microsoft also provides corrections for books through the World Wide Web at the following address:

http://mspress.microsoft.com/support/

In addition to sending feedback directly to the authors, if you have comments, questions, or ideas regarding the presentation or use of this book or the companion CD, you can send them to Microsoft using either of the following methods:

Postal Mail:

Microsoft Press
Attn: Inside Microsoft Window 2000 Editor
One Microsoft Way
Redmond, WA 98052-6399

E-mail:

mspinput@microsoft.com

Please note that product support isn't offered through the above mail addresses. For support information regarding Microsoft Windows 2000, go to *www.microsoft.com/windows2000*. You can also call Standard Support at (425) 635-7011 weekdays between 6 a.m. and 6 p.m. Pacific time, or you can search Microsoft's Support Online at *support.microsoft.com/support*.

ntkrnlmp!Ki386CheckDelayedNpxTrap+...

0432255 5e pop esi 80432256 5b pop ebx 8
20800 ret 0x8 8043225b cc int 3 ntkrnlmp!
95150 or [ecx+0x50],edx 8043225f 8b4158
ush ebx 80432263 56 push esi 80432264 8b
b10 mov edx 80432269 8916 mov [esi
edx+0x4] 804010 mov eax,[ea
ax,[ecx 80432 jnz ntkrnlmp!
043227 5160 mov e cx+0x60] 8043
043227 902 mov [ed x 8043227e 895
0b9eb00 400 r [ecx+0xeb]
ax,[ecx 804 cmp byte 40f jz ntkrnlmp!
0432290 800 804 byte ptr [eax+0x3],
dx,[eax+0x18] 80432297 8b401c mov eax,[e
eax],edx 8043229c 894204 mov [edx+0x4],
ax,[ecx+0xe0] 804322a5 85c0 test eax,eax
tkrnlmp!KiUnwaitThread+0x50 (804322ac) 8
eax+0x18] 804322ac 8a5133 mov dl,[ecx+0x
[ecx+0x44] 804322b2 80fa10 cmp dl,0x1
rnlmp!KiUnwaitThread+0xc2 (804323le)
[ecx+0x6a] 804322ba 84db test bl,bl
rnlmp!KiUnwaitThread+0x96 (804322f2)
0x1af] hl 804a9008 4d dec ebp 804a9
5f pop esi

CHAPTER ONE

Concepts and Tools

In this chapter, we'll introduce the key Microsoft Windows 2000 concepts and terms we'll be using throughout this book, such as the Microsoft Win32 API, processes, threads, virtual memory, kernel mode and user mode, objects, handles, security, and the registry. We'll also introduce the tools that you can use to explore Windows 2000 internals, such as the Performance tool, the kernel debugger, the special tools on the companion CD, and the various add-on tool packages such as the Windows 2000 Support Tools, Windows 2000 debugging tools, Windows 2000 resource kits, and the Platform Software Development Kit (SDK). In addition, we'll explain how you can use the Windows 2000 Device Driver Kit (DDK) as a resource for finding further information on Windows 2000 internals.

Be sure that you understand everything in this chapter—the remainder of the book is written assuming that you do.

Foundation Concepts and Terms

In the course of this book, we'll be referring to some structures and concepts that might be unfamiliar to some readers. In this section, we'll define the terms we'll be using throughout. You should become familiar with them before proceeding to subsequent chapters.

Win32 API

The Win32 application programming interface (API) is the primary programming interface to the Microsoft Windows operating system family, including Windows 2000, Windows 95, Windows 98, Windows Millennium Edition, and Windows CE. Although we don't describe the Win32 API in this book, we do explain the internal behavior and implementation of key Win32 API functions. For a comprehensive guide to programming the Win32 API, see Jeffrey Richter's book *Programming Applications for Microsoft Windows* (fourth edition, Microsoft Press, 1999).

Each operating system implements a different subset of Win32. For the most part, Windows 2000 is a superset of all Win32 implementations. The specifics of which services are implemented on which platforms are included in the reference documentation for the Win32 API. This documentation is available for free viewing on line at *msdn.microsoft.com* and is on the MSDN Library CD-ROMs. The information in this documentation is also detailed in the file \Program Files\Microsoft Platform SDK\Lib\Win32api.csv (a comma-delimited text file) installed as part of the Platform SDK, which comes with MSDN Professional or can be downloaded for free from *msdn.microsoft.com*. (See the section "Platform Software Development Kit (SDK)" later in this chapter.)

> **NOTE** MSDN stands for Microsoft Developer Network, Microsoft's support program for developers. MSDN offers three CD-ROM subscription programs: MSDN Library, Professional, and Universal. The content of MSDN Library is also available for free on line at the MSDN Web site. For more information, see *msdn.microsoft.com*.

For the purposes of this book, the Win32 API refers to the base set of functions that cover areas such as processes, threads, memory management, security, I/O, windowing, and graphics. The Win32 API is included as part of the Platform SDK. The internals of the other major categories in the Platform SDK, such as transactions, databases, messaging, multimedia, and networking services, are not covered in this book.

Although Windows 2000 was designed to support multiple programming interfaces, Win32 is the primary, or preferred, interface to the operating system. Win32 has this position because, of the three environment subsystems (Win32, POSIX, and OS/2), it provides the greatest access to the underlying Windows 2000 system services. As we'll explain in Chapter 2, application programs on Windows 2000 don't call native Windows 2000 system services directly—rather, they must use one of the APIs provided by an environment subsystem.

History of the Win32 API

Interestingly, Win32 wasn't slated to be the original programming interface to Microsoft Windows NT. Because the Windows NT project started as a replacement for OS/2 version 2, the primary programming interface was the 32-bit OS/2 Presentation Manager API. A year into the project, however, Microsoft Windows 3.0 hit the market and took off. As a result, Microsoft changed direction and made Windows NT the future replacement for the Windows family of products as opposed to the replacement for OS/2. It was at this juncture that the need to specify the Win32 API arose—before this, the Windows API existed only as a 16-bit interface.

Although the Win32 API would introduce many new functions that hadn't been available on Windows 3.1, Microsoft decided to make the new API compatible with the 16-bit Windows API function names, semantics, and use of data types whenever possible to ease the burden of porting existing 16-bit Windows applications to Windows NT. So those of you who are looking at the Win32 API for the first time and wondering why many function names and interfaces seem inconsistent should keep in mind that one reason for the inconsistency was to ensure that the Win32 API is compatible with the old 16-bit Windows API.

Services, Functions, and Routines

Several terms in the Windows 2000 user and programming documentation have different meanings in different contexts. For example, the word *service* can refer to a callable routine in the operating system, a device driver, or a server process. The following list describes what certain terms mean in this book:

- **Win32 API functions** Documented, callable subroutines in the Win32 API. Examples include *CreateProcess*, *CreateFile*, and *GetMessage*.

- **System services (or executive system services)** Native functions in the Windows 2000 operating system that are callable from user mode. (For a definition of native functions, see the section "System Service Dispatching" in Chapter 3.) For example, *NtCreateProcess* is the internal system service the Win32 *CreateProcess* function calls to create a new process.

- **Kernel support functions (or routines)** Subroutines inside the kernel-mode (defined later in this chapter) part of the Windows 2000 operating system. For example, *ExAllocatePool* is the routine that device drivers call to allocate memory from the Windows 2000 system heaps.

- **Win32 services** Processes started by the Windows 2000 service control manager. (Although the registry defines Windows 2000 device drivers as "services," we don't refer to them as such in this book.) For example, the Task Scheduler service is a user-mode process that supports the *at* command (which is similar to the UNIX commands *at* or *cron*).

- **DLL (dynamic-link library)** A set of callable subroutines linked together as a binary file that can be dynamically loaded by applications that use the subroutines. Examples include Msvcrt.dll (the C run-time library) and Kernel32.dll (one of the Win32 API subsystem libraries). Windows 2000 user-mode components and applications use DLLs extensively. The advantage DLLs provide over static libraries is that applications can share DLLs, and Windows 2000 ensures that there is only one in-memory copy of a DLL's code among the applications that are referencing it.

Processes, Threads, and Jobs

Although programs and processes appear similar on the surface, they are fundamentally different. A *program* is a static sequence of instructions, whereas a *process* is a container for a set of resources used by the threads that execute the instance of the program. At the highest level of abstraction, a Windows 2000 process comprises the following:

- A private *virtual address space,* which is a set of virtual memory addresses that the process can use

- An executable program, which defines initial code and data and is mapped into the process's virtual address space

- A list of open handles to various system resources, such as semaphores, communication ports, and files, that are accessible to all threads in the process

■ A security context called an *access token* that identifies the user, security groups, and privileges associated with the process

■ A unique identifier called a *process ID* (internally called a *client ID*)

■ At least one thread of execution

A *thread* is the entity within a process that Windows 2000 schedules for execution. Without it, the process's program can't run. A thread includes the following essential components:

■ The contents of a set of CPU registers representing the state of the processor

■ Two stacks, one for the thread to use while executing in kernel mode and one for executing in user mode

■ A private storage area called thread-local storage (TLS) for use by subsystems, run-time libraries, and DLLs

■ A unique identifier called a *thread ID* (also internally called a *client ID*—process IDs and thread IDs are generated out of the same namespace, so they never overlap)

■ Threads sometimes have their own security context that is often used by multithreaded server applications that impersonate the security context of the clients that they serve

The volatile registers, the stacks, and the private storage area are called the thread's *context*. Because this information is different for each machine architecture that Windows 2000 runs on, this structure, by necessity, is architecture-specific. In fact, the CONTEXT structure returned by the Win32 *GetThreadContext* function is the only public data structure in the Win32 API that is machine-dependent.

Although threads have their own execution context, every thread within a process shares the process's virtual address space (in addition to the rest of the resources belonging to the process), meaning that all the threads in a process can write to and read from each other's memory. Threads can't reference the address space of another process, however, unless the other process

makes available part of its private address space as a *shared memory section* (called a *file mapping object* in the Win32 API) or unless one process opens another process and uses the *ReadProcessMemory* and *WriteProcessMemory* functions.

In addition to a private address space and one or more threads, each process has a security identification and a list of open handles to objects such as files, shared memory sections, or one of the synchronization objects such as mutexes, events, or semaphores, as illustrated in Figure 1-1.

Figure 1-1
A process and its resources

Every process has a security context that is stored in an object called an *access token*. The process access token contains the security identification and credentials for the process. By default, threads don't have their own access token, but they can obtain one, thus allowing individual threads to impersonate the security context of another process—including processes running on a remote Windows 2000 system—without affecting other threads in the process. (See Chapter 8 for more details on process and thread security.)

The virtual address descriptors (VADs) are data structures that the memory manager uses to keep track of the virtual addresses the process is using. These data structures are described in more depth in Chapter 7.

Windows 2000 introduces an extension to the process model called a *job*. A job object's main function is to allow groups of processes to be managed and manipulated as a unit. A job object allows control of certain attributes and provides limits for the process or processes associated with the job. It also records basic accounting information for all processes associated with the job and for all processes that were associated with the job but have since terminated. In some ways, the job object compensates for the lack of a structured process tree in Windows 2000—yet in many ways is more powerful than a UNIX-style process tree.

You'll find out much more about the internal structure of jobs, processes and threads, the mechanics of process and thread creation, and the thread-scheduling algorithms in Chapter 6.

Virtual Memory

Windows 2000 implements a virtual memory system based on a flat (linear) 32-bit address space. Thirty-two bits of address space translates into 4 GB of virtual memory. On most systems, Windows 2000 allocates half this address space (the lower half of the 4-GB virtual address space, from x00000000 through x7FFFFFFF) to processes for their unique private storage and uses the other half (the upper half, addresses x80000000 through xFFFFFFFF) for its own protected operating system memory utilization. The mappings of the lower half change to reflect the virtual address space of the currently executing process, but the mappings of the upper half always consist of the operating system's virtual memory. Windows 2000 Advanced Server and Datacenter Server support a boot-time option (the /3GB qualifier in Boot.ini) that gives processes running specially marked programs (the large address space aware flag must be set in the header of the executable image) a 3-GB private address space (leaving 1 GB for the operating system). This option allows applications such as database servers to keep larger portions of a database in the process address space, thus reducing the need to map subset views of the database. Figure 1-2 shows the two virtual address space layouts supported by Windows 2000.

Figure 1-2
Address space layouts supported by Windows 2000

Although 3 GB is better than 2 GB, it's still not enough virtual address space to map very large (multigigabyte) databases. To address this need, Windows 2000 has a new mechanism called *Address Windowing Extensions* (AWE), which allows a 32-bit application to allocate up to 64 GB of physical memory and then map views, or windows, into its 2-GB virtual address space. Although using AWE puts the burden of managing mappings of virtual to physical memory on the programmer, it does solve the immediate need of being able to directly access more physical memory than can be mapped at any one time in a 32-bit process address space. The long-term solution to this address space limitation is 64-bit Windows.

Recall that a process's virtual address space is the set of addresses available for the process's threads to use. Virtual memory provides a logical view of memory that might not correspond to its physical layout. At run time the memory manager, with assistance from hardware, translates, or *maps,* the virtual addresses into physical addresses, where the data is actually stored. By controlling the protection and mapping, the operating system can ensure that individual processes don't bump into one another or overwrite operating system data. Figure 1-3 illustrates three virtually contiguous pages mapped to three discontiguous pages in physical memory.

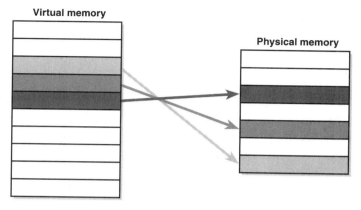

Figure 1-3
Mapping virtual memory to physical memory

Because most systems have much less physical memory than the total virtual memory in use by the running processes (2 GB or 3 GB for each process), the memory manager transfers, or *pages,* some of the memory contents to disk. Paging data to disk frees physical memory so that it can be used for other processes or for the operating system itself. When a thread accesses a virtual address that has been paged to disk, the virtual memory manager loads the information back into memory from disk. Applications don't have to be altered in any way to take advantage of paging because hardware support enables the memory manager to page without the knowledge or assistance of processes or threads.

Details of the implementation of the memory manager, including how address translation works and how Windows 2000 manages physical memory, are described in detail in Chapter 7.

Kernel Mode vs. User Mode

To protect user applications from accessing and/or modifying critical operating system data, Windows 2000 uses two *processor access modes* (even if the processor on which Windows 2000 is running supports more than two): *user mode* and *kernel mode.* User application code runs in user mode, whereas operating system code (such as system services and device drivers) runs in kernel mode. Kernel mode refers to a mode of execution in a processor that grants access to all system memory and all CPU instructions. By providing the operating system software with a higher privilege level than the application software has, the

processor provides a necessary foundation for operating system designers to ensure that a misbehaving application can't disrupt the stability of the system as a whole.

NOTE The architecture of the Intel x86 processor defines four privilege levels, or *rings,* to protect system code and data from being overwritten either inadvertently or maliciously by code of lesser privilege. Windows 2000 uses privilege level 0 (or ring 0) for kernel mode and privilege level 3 (or ring 3) for user mode. The reason Windows 2000 uses only two levels is that some of the hardware architectures that were supported in the past (such as Compaq Alpha and Silicon Graphics MIPS) implemented only two privilege levels.

Although each Win32 process has its own private memory space, kernel-mode operating system and device driver code share a single virtual address space. Each page in virtual memory is tagged as to what access mode the processor must be in to read and/or write the page. Pages in system space can be accessed only from kernel mode, whereas all pages in the user address space are accessible from user mode. Read-only pages (such as those that contain executable code) are not writable from any mode.

Windows 2000 doesn't provide any protection to private read/write system memory being used by components running in kernel mode. In other words, once in kernel mode, operating system and device driver code has complete access to system space memory and can bypass Windows 2000 security to access objects. Because the bulk of the Windows 2000 operating system code runs in kernel mode, it is vital that components that run in kernel mode be carefully designed and tested to ensure that they don't violate system security.

This lack of protection also emphasizes the need to take care when loading a third-party device driver, because once in kernel mode the software has complete access to all operating system data. This vulnerability was one of the reasons behind the driver-signing mechanism introduced in Windows 2000, which warns the user if an attempt is made to add an unauthorized (unsigned) driver. (See Chapter 9 for more information on driver signing.) Also, a mechanism called Driver Verifier helps device driver writers to find bugs (such as memory leaks). Driver Verifier is explained in Chapter 7.

As you'll see in Chapter 2, user applications switch from user mode to kernel mode when they make a system service call. For example, a Win32 *ReadFile* function eventually needs to call the internal Windows 2000 routine that actually handles reading data from a file. That routine, because it accesses internal system data structures, must run in kernel mode. The transition from

user mode to kernel mode is accomplished by the use of a special processor instruction that causes the processor to switch to kernel mode. The operating system traps this instruction, notices that a system service is being requested, validates the arguments the thread passed to the system function, and then executes the internal function. Before returning control to the user thread, the processor mode is switched back to user mode. In this way, the operating system protects itself and its data from perusal and modification by user processes.

> **NOTE** A transition from user mode to kernel mode (and back) does *not* affect thread scheduling per se—a mode transition is *not* a context switch. Further details on system service dispatching are included in Chapter 3.

Thus, it's normal for a user thread to spend part of its time executing in user mode and part in kernel mode. In fact, because the bulk of the graphics and windowing system also runs in kernel mode, graphics-intensive applications spend more of their time in kernel mode than in user mode. An easy way to test this is to run a graphics-intensive application such as Microsoft Paint or Microsoft Pinball and watch the time split between user mode and kernel mode using one of the performance counters listed in Table 1-1.

Table 1-1 Mode-Related Performance Counters

Object: Counter	Function
Processor: % Privileged Time	Percentage of time that an individual CPU (or all CPUs) has run in kernel mode during a specified interval
Processor: % User Time	Percentage of time that an individual CPU (or all CPUs) has run in user mode during a specified interval
Process: % Privileged Time	Percentage of time that the threads in a process have run in kernel mode during a specified interval
Process: % User Time	Percentage of time that the threads in a process have run in user mode during a specified interval
Thread: % Privileged Time	Percentage of time that a thread has run in kernel mode during a specified interval
Thread: % User Time	Percentage of time that a thread has run in user mode during a specified interval

EXPERIMENT: Kernel Mode vs. User Mode

You can use the Performance tool to see how much time your system spends executing in kernel mode vs. in user mode. Follow these steps:

1. Run the Performance tool by opening the Start menu and selecting Programs/Administrative Tools/Performance.

2. Click the Add button (+) on the toolbar.

3. With the Processor performance object selected, click the % Privileged Time counter and, while holding down the Ctrl key, click the % User Time counter.

4. Click Add, and then click Close.

5. Move the mouse rapidly back and forth. You should notice the % Privileged Time line going up when you move the mouse around, reflecting the time spent servicing the mouse interrupts and the time spent in the graphics part of the windowing system (which, as explained in Chapter 2, runs primarily as a device driver in kernel mode). (See Figure 1-4.)

6. When you're finished, click the New Counter Set button on the toolbar (or just close the tool).

You can also quickly see this activity by using Task Manager. Just click the Performance tab, and then select Show Kernel Times from the View menu. The CPU usage bar will show user-mode time in green and kernel-mode time in red.

Figure 1-4
Performance tool showing time split between kernel mode and user mode

To see how the Performance tool itself uses kernel time and user time, run it again, but add the individual Process counters % User Time and % Privileged Time for every process in the system:

1. If it's not already running, run the Performance tool again. (If it is already running, start with a blank display by pressing the New Counter Set button on the toolbar.)

2. Click the Add button (+) on the toolbar.

3. Change the Performance Object to Process.

4. Select the % Privileged Time and % User Time counters.

5. Select all processes in the Instance box (except the _Total process).

6. Click Add, and then click Close.

7. Move the mouse rapidly back and forth.

8. Press Ctrl+H to turn on highlighting mode. This highlights the currently selected counter in white.

9. Scroll through the counters at the bottom of the display to identify the processes whose threads were running when you moved the mouse, and note whether they were running in user mode or kernel mode.

You should see the Performance tool process (look in the Instance column for the mmc process) kernel-mode *and* user-mode time go up when you move the mouse because it is executing application code in user mode and calling Win32 functions that run in kernel mode. You'll also notice kernel-mode thread activity in a process named csrss when you move the mouse. This activity occurs because the Win32 subsystem's kernel-mode raw input thread, which handles keyboard and mouse input, is attached to this process. (See Chapter 2 for more information about system threads.) Finally, the process named Idle that you see spending nearly 100 percent of its time in kernel mode isn't really a process—it's a fake process used to account for idle CPU cycles. As you can observe from the mode in which the threads in the Idle process run, when Windows 2000 has nothing to do, it does it in kernel mode.

Objects and Handles

In the Windows 2000 operating system, an *object* is a single, run-time instance of a statically defined object type. An *object type* comprises a system-defined data type, functions that operate on instances of the data type, and a set of object attributes. If you write Win32 applications, you might encounter process, thread, file, and event objects, to name just a few examples. These objects are based on lower-level objects that Windows 2000 creates and manages. In Windows 2000, a process is an instance of the process object type, a file is an instance of the file object type, and so on.

An *object attribute* is a field of data in an object that partially defines the object's state. An object of type *process,* for example, would have attributes that include the process ID, a base scheduling priority, and a pointer to an access token object. *Object methods,* the means for manipulating objects, usually read or change the object attributes. For example, the *open* method for a process would accept a process identifier as input and return a pointer to the object as output.

> **NOTE** Although there is a parameter named *ObjectAttributes* that a caller supplies when creating an object using either the Win32 API or native object services, that parameter shouldn't be confused with the more general meaning of the term as used in this book.

The most fundamental difference between an object and an ordinary data structure is that the internal structure of an object is hidden. You must call an object service to get data out of an object or to put data into it. You can't directly read or change data inside an object. This difference separates the underlying implementation of the object from code that merely uses it, a technique that allows object implementations to be changed easily over time.

Objects provide a convenient means for accomplishing the following four important operating system tasks:

- Providing human-readable names for system resources
- Sharing resources and data among processes
- Protecting resources from unauthorized access
- Reference tracking, which allows the system to know when an object is no longer in use so that it can be automatically deallocated

Not all data structures in the Windows 2000 operating system are objects. Only data that needs to be shared, protected, named, or made visible to user-mode programs (via system services) is placed in objects. Structures used by only

one component of the operating system to implement internal functions are not objects. Objects and handles (references to an instance of an object) are discussed in more detail in Chapter 3.

Security

Windows 2000 supports C2-level security as defined by the U.S. Department of Defense Trusted Computer System Evaluation Criteria (DoD 5200.28–STD, December 1985). This standard includes discretionary (need-to-know) protection for all shareable system objects (such as files, directories, processes, threads, and so forth), security auditing (for accountability of subjects, or users, and the actions they initiate), password authentication at logon, and the prevention of one user from accessing uninitialized resources (such as free memory or disk space) that another user has deallocated.

Windows NT 4 was formally evaluated at the C2 level and is on the U.S. government Evaluated Products List. (Windows 2000 is still in the evaluation process.) Also, Windows NT 4 has met the European organization ITSEC (IT Security Evaluation Criteria) at the FC2/E3 (functional level C2 and assurance level E3, something normally associated only with B-level systems) security level. Achieving a government-approved security rating allows an operating system to compete in that arena. Of course, many of these required capabilities are advantageous features for any multiuser system.

Windows 2000 has two forms of access control over objects. The first form—discretionary access control—is the protection mechanism that most people think of when they think of protection under Windows 2000. It's the method by which owners of objects (such as files or printers) grant or deny access to others. When users log in, they are given a set of security credentials, or a security context. When they attempt to access objects, their security context is compared to the access control list on the object they are trying to access to determine whether they have permission to perform the requested operation.

Privileged access control is necessary for those times when discretionary access control isn't enough. It's a method of ensuring that someone can get to protected objects if the owner isn't available. For example, if an employee leaves a company, the administrator needs a way to gain access to files that might have been accessible only to that employee. In that case, under Windows 2000, the administrator can take ownership of the file so that you can manage its rights as necessary.

Security pervades the interface of the Win32 API. The Win32 subsystem implements object-based security in the same way the operating system does; the Win32 subsystem protects shared Windows objects from unauthorized access by placing Windows 2000 security descriptors on them. The first time an application tries to access a shared object, the Win32 subsystem verifies the application's right to do so. If the security check succeeds, the Win32 subsystem allows the application to proceed.

The Win32 subsystem implements object security on a number of shared objects, some of which were built on top of native Windows 2000 objects. The Win32 objects include desktop objects, window objects, menu objects, files, processes, threads, and several synchronization objects.

For a comprehensive description of Windows 2000 security, see Chapter 8.

Registry

If you've worked at all with Windows operating systems, you've probably heard about or looked at the registry. You can't talk much about Windows 2000 internals without referring to the registry because it's the system database that contains the information required to boot and configure the system, systemwide software settings that control the operation of Windows 2000, the security database, and per-user configuration settings (such as which screen saver to use).

In addition, the registry is a window into in-memory volatile data, such as the current hardware state of the system (what device drivers are loaded, the resources they are using, and so on) as well as the Windows 2000 performance counters. The performance counters, which aren't actually "in" the registry, are accessed through the registry functions. See Chapter 5 for more on how performance counter information is accessed from the registry.

Although many Windows 2000 users and administrators will never need to look directly into the registry (since you can view or change most of the configuration settings with standard administrative utilities), it is still a useful source of Windows 2000 internals information because it contains many settings that affect system performance and behavior. (If you decide to directly change registry settings, you must exercise extreme caution; any changes might adversely affect system performance or, worse, cause the system to fail to boot successfully.) You'll find references to individual registry keys throughout this book as they pertain to the component being described. Most registry keys referred to in this book are under HKEY_LOCAL_MACHINE, which we'll abbreviate throughout as HKLM.

For further information on the registry and its internal structure, see Chapter 5.

Unicode

Windows 2000 differs from most other operating systems in that most internal text strings are stored and processed as 16-bit-wide Unicode characters. Unicode is an international character set standard that defines unique 16-bit values for most of the world's known character sets. (For more information about Unicode, see *www.unicode.org* as well as the programming documentation in the MSDN Library.)

Because many applications deal with 8-bit (single-byte) ANSI character strings, Win32 functions that accept string parameters have two entry points: a Unicode (wide, 16-bit) and an ANSI (narrow, 8-bit) version. The Windows 95, Windows 98, and Windows Millennium Edition implementations of Win32 don't implement all the Unicode interfaces to all the Win32 functions, so applications designed to run on one of these operating systems as well as Windows 2000 typically use the narrow versions. If you call the narrow version of a Win32 function, input string parameters are converted to Unicode before being processed by the system and output parameters are converted from Unicode to ANSI before being returned to the application. Thus, if you have an older service or piece of code that you need to run on Windows 2000 but this code is written using ANSI character text strings, Windows 2000 will convert the ANSI characters into Unicode for its own use. However, Windows 2000 never converts the *data* inside files—it's up to the application to decide whether to store data as Unicode or as ANSI.

In previous editions of Windows NT, Asian and Middle East editions were a superset of the core U.S. and European editions and contained additional Win32 functions to handle more complex text input and layout requirements (such as right to left text input). In Windows 2000, all language editions contain the same Win32 functions. Instead of having separate language versions, Windows 2000 has a single worldwide binary so that a single installation can support multiple languages (by adding various language packs). Applications can also take advantage of Win32 functions that allow single worldwide application binaries that can support multiple languages.

Digging into Windows 2000 Internals

Although much of the information in this book is based on the Windows 2000 source code, you don't have to take *everything* on faith. Many details about the internals of Windows 2000 can be exposed and demonstrated by using a variety

of available tools, such as those that come with Windows 2000, the Windows 2000 Support Tools, the Windows 2000 resource kits, and the Windows 2000 debugging tools. These tool packages are briefly described later in this section.

To encourage your exploration of Windows 2000 internals, we've included "Experiment" sidebars throughout the book that describe steps you can take to examine a particular aspect of Windows 2000 internal behavior. (You already saw one of these sections earlier in this chapter.) We encourage you to try these experiments so that you can see in action many of the internals topics described in this book.

In addition, this book comes with a CD-ROM that contains the latest version of the tools from *www.sysinternals.com* (a popular site for 32-bit Windows internals-related tools and information), as well as tools that are available only with this book.

Table 1-2 shows a list of the tools used in this book and where they come from. Although the capabilities of many of these tools overlap quite a bit in terms of the information that they can display, each of them shows at least one unique piece of information not available in any other utility.

Table 1-2 Tools for Viewing Windows 2000 Internals

Tool	Image Name	Origin
Dependency Walker	DEPENDS	Support Tools, Platform SDK
Dump Check	DUMPCHK	Support Tools, debugging tools, Platform SDK, Windows 2000 DDK
EFS Information Dumper	EFSDUMP	*www.sysinternals.com**
File Monitor	FILEMON	*www.sysinternals.com*
Get SID tool	GETSID	Resource kits
Global Flags	GFLAGS	Support Tools, Platform SDK, Windows 2000 DDK
Handle/DLL Viewer	HANDLEEX, NTHANDLE	*www.sysinternals.com*
Junction tool	JUNCTION	*www.sysinternals.com/misc.htm*
Kernel debuggers	I386KD, WINDBG, KD	Debugging tools, Platform SDK, Windows 2000 DDK
Object Viewer	WINOBJ	Platform SDK, *www.sysinternals.com*
Open Handles	OH	Resource kits
Page Fault Monitor	PFMON	Resource kits, Platform SDK

Tool	Image Name	Origin
Performance tool	PERFMON	Windows 2000
PipeList tool	PIPELIST	*www.sysinternals.com/tips.htm*
Pool Monitor	POOLMON	Support Tools, Windows 2000 DDK
Process Explode	PVIEW	*www.reskit.com*
Process Statistics	PSTAT	Platform SDK, *www.reskit.com*
Process Viewer	PVIEWER (in the Support Tools) or PVIEW (in the Platform SDK)	Support Tools, Platform SDK
Quantum	QUANTUM	companion CD
Quick Slice	QSLICE	Resource kits
Registry Monitor	REGMON	*www.sysinternals.com*
Service Control tool	SC	Resource kits
Task (Process) List	TLIST	Support Tools
Task Manager	TASKMAN	Windows 2000
TDImon	TDIMON	*www.sysinternals.com*

* All tools from *www.sysinternals.com* are also included on the companion CD.

Tools on the Companion CD

The companion CD contains the following unique tools that will assist you in exploring the internals of Windows 2000:

- **LiveKd** This tool allows you to use the standard Microsoft kernel debuggers, I386kd.exe and Windbg.exe (as well as the new Kd.exe, which replaces both of these tools in newer versions of the debugging tools), to display internal information from the currently running system, without requiring a second computer to act as the host (via a null modem cable). This tool is explained in the section "Kernel Debugging Tools" later in this chapter.

- **Kernel variable performance counter extension DLL** This extension to the Windows 2000 Performance tool allows you to examine the value of any exported kernel variable from the core kernel image, Ntoskrnl.exe.

Many of the experiments throughout this book use the kernel debugger because it can easily display many internal Windows 2000 data structures and other details not available from any user-mode utility. Therefore, LiveKd will make trying these experiments much easier because it allows the kernel debugger to be used on a live system without requiring a second computer.

Whereas LiveKd displays internal kernel variables, the kernel variable performance counter extension DLL monitors the values of these variables over time. For example, these variables can contain numeric values of interest that might not be accessible through any of the Windows 2000 performance counters.

For more information about these tools, see the documentation provided on the CD as part of the tools installation. As a reminder, only people who buy this book can install and use these tools. They can't be further distributed. (See the license agreement in the back of this book for details.)

Performance Tool

We'll refer to the Performance tool found in the Administrative Tools folder on the Start menu (or via Control Panel) throughout this book. The Performance tool has three functions: system monitoring, viewing performance counter logs, and setting alerts. For simplicity, when we refer to the Performance tool, we are referring to the System Monitor function within the tool.

The Performance tool can provide more information about how your system is operating than any other single utility. It includes hundreds of counters for various objects. For each major topic described in this book, a table of the relevant Windows 2000 performance counters is included.

The Performance tool contains a brief description for each counter. To see the descriptions, select a counter in the Add Counter window and click the Explain button. Or open the Performance Counter Reference help file in the resource kit. For information on how to interpret these counters to detect bottlenecks or plan capacity, see the section "Performance Monitoring" in the *Windows 2000 Server Operations Guide,* which is part of the Windows 2000 Server Resource Kit. These chapters provide an excellent description to anyone seriously interested in understanding Windows 2000 performance.

Note that all the Windows 2000 performance counters are accessible programmatically. The section "HKEY_PERFORMANCE_DATA" in Chapter 5 has a brief description of the components involved in retrieving performance counters through the Win32 API.

Windows 2000 Support Tools

The Windows 2000 Support Tools consist of about 40 tools useful in administering and troubleshooting Windows 2000 systems. Many of these tools were formerly part of the Windows NT 4 resource kits.

You can install the Support Tools by running Setup.exe in the \Support\ Tools folder on any Windows 2000 product distribution CD. (That is, the Support Tools are the same on Windows 2000 Professional, Server, and Advanced Server.)

Windows 2000 Resource Kits

The Windows 2000 resource kits supplement the Support Tools, adding some 200 additional tools. Besides including many tools useful for displaying internal system state, they contain useful internals documentation, such as the Registry Reference and Performance Counters help files.

There are two editions of the resource kits: the Windows 2000 Professional Resource Kit and the Windows 2000 Server Resource Kit. Although the latter kit is a superset of the former and can be installed on Windows 2000 Professional systems, none of the experiments in this book use the tools that are included only with the Windows 2000 Server Resource Kit. Be sure you visit *www.reskit.com* for updates to tools as well as for new tools.

Kernel Debugging Tools

Kernel debuggers are tools that device driver developers use to debug their drivers and support personnel use to troubleshoot hung systems and examine crash dumps (a copy of system memory saved in a file that can be analyzed to try and determine the cause of the system crash). Although a kernel debugger is used mainly for analyzing crash dumps or debugging device drivers, it is also a useful tool for investigating Windows 2000 internals because it can display internal Windows 2000 system information not visible through any standard utility. For example, it can dump internal data structures such as thread blocks, process blocks, page tables, I/O, and pool structures. Throughout this book, the relevant kernel debugger commands and output are included as they apply to each topic being discussed.

Microsoft Kernel Debuggers

There are two versions of the Microsoft kernel debuggers: a command-line version (I386kd.exe for x86 systems*) and a graphical user interface (GUI) version (Windbg.exe). There is also a new version, Kd.exe, that replaces both of these. These tools are part of the debugger tools package, which is shipped in three places:

- Windows 2000 Customer Support Diagnostics (downloadable from *www.microsoft.com*)

* Even though Windows 2000 doesn't run on the Intel 80386 processor (early versions of Windows NT did), for historical reasons, the x86 directories on the Windows 2000 distribution media are still called i386. Thus, the x86 kernel debugger is called I386kd.exe.

■ Platform SDK (part of MSDN Professional and Universal, and downloadable from *msdn.microsoft.com*)

■ Windows 2000 DDK (Device Driver Kit—also part of MSDN and freely downloadable from *www.microsoft.com/hwdev*)

NOTE New versions of the debugging tools package are released independently of new versions of Windows 2000. Hence, you should occasionally check the Download section of Microsoft's Web site for the latest versions of these three packages. The debugging tools include a package called the OEM Support Tools, which is updated independently of the debugging tools and therefore might have newer versions of debugging-related tools (such as Kdex2x86.dll, a kernel debugger extension DLL with additional debugging commands).

The debugging tools help file, provided with each of the three packages just mentioned, explains how to set up and use the kernel debuggers (as well as other debugging and support tools that are part of the package). Additional details on using the kernel debuggers that are aimed primarily at device driver writers can be found in the Windows 2000 DDK documentation. There are also several useful Knowledge Base articles on the kernel debugger. Search for "debugref" in the Windows 2000 Knowledge Base (an online database of technical articles) on *support.microsoft.com*.

The kernel debugger has two modes of operation:

■ Open a crash dump file created as a result of a Windows 2000 or Windows NT 4 system crash. (See the section "System Crashes" in Chapter 4 for more information on crash dumps.)

■ Connect to a live, running system and examine the system state (or set breakpoints, if you're debugging device driver code). This operation requires two computers—a target and a host. The target is the system being debugged, and the host is the system running the debugger. The target system can be either local (connected to the host via a null modem cable) or remote (connecting to the host via a modem). The target system must be booted with the /DEBUG qualifier (either by pressing F8 during the boot process and selecting Debug Mode or by adding a boot selection entry in C:\Boot.ini).

Detailed setup instructions can be found in the debugging tools documentation referred to previously.

LiveKd Tool

The companion CD contains a tool called LiveKd that allows the use of the standard Microsoft kernel debugger on a live system, without needing two computers. LiveKd can be used for most of the experiments in the book and thus will be a helpful tool in exploring Windows 2000 internals.

You run LiveKd just as you would I386kd, Windbg, or Kd. LiveKd passes any command-line options you specify through to the debugger you select. By default, LiveKd runs the new command-line kernel debugger (Kd). If Kd is not found in the current directory, LiveKd tries I386kd. To run the GUI debugger (Windbg), specify the –w switch. To see the help on the switches for LiveKd, specify the –? switch.

LiveKd presents a simulated crash dump file to the debugger, so you can perform any operations in LiveKd that are supported on a crash dump. Because LiveKd is relying on physical memory to back the simulated dump, the kernel debugger might run into situations in which data structures are in the middle of being changed by the system and are inconsistent. Each time the debugger is launched, it gets a snapshot of system state, so if you want to refresh the snapshot, quit the debugger (with the "q" command) and LiveKd will ask you whether you want to start it again. If the debugger gets in a loop in printing output, press Ctrl+C to interrupt the output, quit, and rerun it. If it hangs, press Ctrl+Break, which will terminate the debugger process and ask you whether you want to run the debugger again.

SoftICE

Another debugging tool that doesn't require two machines for live kernel debugging is a third-party kernel debugger called SoftICE, which you can buy from Compuware NuMega. (See *www.numega.com* for details.)

Symbols for Kernel Debugging

To use any of the kernel debugging tools listed previously to examine internal Windows 2000 data structures (such as the process list, thread blocks, loaded driver list, memory usage information, and so on), you must have the correct symbol files for at least the kernel image, Ntoskrnl.exe. (The section "Architecture Overview" in Chapter 2 explains more about this file.) The symbols are part of the Customer Support Diagnostics package (which, as mentioned earlier, is downloadable from *www.microsoft.com*). They are installed separately from the debugging tools and by default reside in the \Winnt\Symbols folder.

Later in the book, you'll see how you can use these symbol table files to display the names of internal Windows 2000 system routines and global variables.

NOTE Symbol table files must match the version of the image they were taken from. For example, if you install a Windows 2000 Service Pack, you must obtain the matching, updated symbol files for at least the kernel image; otherwise, you'll get a checksum error when you try to load them with the kernel debugger. These updated symbol files are *not* typically included or installed when you download and install a Service Pack from *www.microsoft.com*—they must be downloaded separately. (If you receive MSDN Professional or TechNet, they're included on the Service Pack CD-ROMs.)

Platform Software Development Kit (SDK)

The Platform SDK is part of the MSDN Professional (and Universal) subscription and can also be downloaded for free from *msnd.microsoft.com*. It contains the C header files and libraries necessary to compile and link Win32 applications. (Although Microsoft Visual C++ comes with a copy of these header files, the versions contained in the Platform SDK always match the latest version of the Windows operating systems, whereas the version that comes with Visual C++ might be an older version that was current when Visual C++ was released.) From an internals perspective, items of interest in the Platform SDK include the Win32 API header files (\Program Files\Microsoft Platform SDK\Include) as well as several utilities (Pfmon.exe, Pstat.exe, Winobj.exe). Some of the tools in the Platform SDK also come with the resource kits. Finally, a few of these tools are also shipped as example source code in both the Platform SDK and the MSDN Library.

Device Driver Kit (DDK)

The Windows 2000 DDK is part of the MSDN Professional (and Universal) subscription, but it is also available for free download at *www.microsoft.com/hwdev*. Although the DDK is aimed at device driver developers, the DDK is an abundant source of Windows 2000 internals information. For example, the DDK documentation contains a comprehensive description of the Windows 2000 I/O system in both a tutorial and reference form, including the internal system routines and data structures used by device drivers.

Besides the documentation, the DDK contains header files that define key internal data structures and constants as well as interfaces to many internal system routines (in particular, Ntddk.h). These files are useful when exploring Windows 2000 internal data structures with the kernel debugger because although the general layout and content of these structures are shown in this book, detailed field-level descriptions (such as size and data types) are not. A number of these data structures (such as object dispatcher headers, wait blocks, events, mutants, semaphores, and so on) are, however, fully defined in the DDK. In addition, the *!dso* command in the kernel debugger displays the format of many internal Windows 2000 data structures that are not defined in the DDK header files.

Systems Internals Tools

Many of the experiments in this book use freeware tools that you can download from *www.sysinternals.com*. Mark Russinovich, coauthor of this book, wrote most of these tools. Copies of these tools are in the \Sysint directory on the companion CD. In addition, a complete copy of the Web site *www.sysinternals.com* is also on the CD. (Keep in mind that although the version of *www.sysinternals.com* on the companion CD has the latest versions of tools available when this book was published, it won't have any new tools or updates that have been added to the live site later.) Many of these utilities involve the installation and execution of kernel-mode device drivers and thus require administrator privileges.

Conclusion

In this chapter, you've been introduced to the key Windows 2000 technical concepts and terms that will be used throughout the book. You've also glimpsed at the many useful tools available for digging into Windows 2000 internals. Now we're ready to begin our exploration of the internal design of the system, beginning with an overall view of the system architecture and its key components.

ntkrnlmp!Ki386CheckDelayedIpxIfBfaptzt:
0432255 5e pop esi 80432256 5b pop ebx 80
20800 ret 0x8 8043225b cc int 3 ntkrnlmp!
95150 or [ecx+0x50],edx 8043225f 8b4158
ush ebx 80432263 56 push esi 80432264 8b
b10 mov edx,... 8916 mov [esi
edx+0x4] ... mov eax,[ea
ax,[ecx... ntkrnlmp
0432276...60 mov ...cx+0x60] 8043 2
0432276...02 mov [edx...x 8043227e 8950
0b9eb00... or [ecx+0xeb],dx
ax,[ecx... cmp byte... jz ntkrnlmp!
0432290 80... byte ptr [eax+0x3].
dx,[eax+0x18] 80432297 8b401c mov eax,[e
eax],edx 8043229c 894204 mov [edx+0x4],e
ax,[ecx+0xe0] 804322a5 85c0 test eax,eax
tkrnlmp!KiUnwaitThread+0x50 (804322ac) 8
eax+0x18] 804322ac 8a5133 mov dl,[ecx+
si,[ecx+0x44] 804322b2 80fa10 cmp dl,0x1
krnlmp!KiUnwaitThread+0xc2 (8043231e)
l,[ecx+0x6a] 804322be 84db test bl,bl 80
krnlmp!KiUnwaitThread+0x94 (804322f2)
ecx+0x18],1 804322cb 4d dec ebp 804a90
5e pop edi 8

CHAPTER TWO

System Architecture

Now that we've covered the terms, concepts, and tools you need to be familiar with, we're ready to start our exploration of the internal design goals and structure of Microsoft Windows 2000 (originally Windows NT). This chapter explains the overall architecture of the system—the key components, how they interact with each other, and the context in which they run. To provide a framework for understanding the internals of Windows 2000, let's first review the requirements and goals that shaped the original design and specification of the system.

Requirements and Design Goals

The following requirements drove the specification of Windows NT back in 1989:

- Provide a true 32-bit, preemptive, reentrant, virtual memory operating system

- Run on multiple hardware architectures and platforms

- Run and scale well on symmetric multiprocessing systems

- Be a great distributed computing platform, both as a network client and as a server

- Run most existing 16-bit MS-DOS and Microsoft Windows 3.1 applications

- Meet government requirements for POSIX 1003.1 compliance

- Meet government and industry requirements for operating system security

- Be easily adaptable to the global market by supporting Unicode

To guide the thousands of decisions that had to be made to create a system that met these requirements, the Windows NT design team adopted the following design goals at the beginning of the project:

- **Extensibility** The code must be written to comfortably grow and change as market requirements change.

- **Portability** The system must be able to run on multiple hardware architectures and must be able to move with relative ease to new ones as market demands dictate.

- **Reliability and robustness** The system should protect itself from both internal malfunction and external tampering. Applications should not be able to harm the operating system or other applications.

- **Compatibility** Although Windows NT should extend existing technology, its user interface and APIs should be compatible with older versions of Windows and with MS-DOS. It should also interoperate well with other systems such as UNIX, OS/2, and NetWare.

- **Performance** Within the constraints of the other design goals, the system should be as fast and responsive as possible on each hardware platform.

As we explore the details of the internal structure and operation of Windows 2000, you'll see how these original design goals and market requirements were woven successfully into the construction of the system. But before we start that exploration, let's examine the overall design model for Windows 2000 and compare it with other modern operating systems.

Windows 2000 vs. Consumer Windows

Windows 2000 and Consumer Windows (Windows 95, Windows 98, and Windows Millennium Edition) are part of the "Windows family of operating systems," sharing a common subset API (Win32 and COM) and in some cases operating system code. Windows 2000, Windows 98, and Windows Millennium Edition also share a common subset device driver model called the Windows Driver Model (WDM), which is explained in more detail in Chapter 9.

From the initial announcement of Windows NT, Microsoft has always made it clear that this operating system was to be the strategic platform for the future—not just for servers and business desktops but eventually for consumer systems as well. The following list highlights some of the architectural differences and advantages that Windows 2000 has over Consumer Windows:

- Windows 2000 supports multiprocessor systems—Consumer Windows doesn't.

- The Windows 2000 file system supports security (such as discretionary access control). The Consumer Windows file system doesn't.

- Windows 2000 is a fully 32-bit operating system—it contains no 16-bit code, other than support code for running 16-bit Windows applications. Consumer Windows contains a large amount of old 16-bit code from its predecessors, Windows 3.1 and MS-DOS.

- Windows 2000 is fully reentrant—significant parts of Consumer Windows are nonreentrant (mainly the 16-bit code taken from Windows 3.1). This nonreentrant code includes the majority of the graphics and window management functions (GDI and USER). When a 32-bit application on Consumer Windows attempts to call a system service implemented in nonreentrant 16-bit code, the application must first obtain a systemwide lock (or mutex) to block other threads from entering the nonreentrant code base. And even worse, a 16-bit application holds this lock *while running*. As a result, although the core of Consumer Windows contains a preemptive 32-bit multithreaded scheduler, applications often run single threaded because so much of the system is still implemented in nonreentrant code.

- Windows 2000 provides an option to run 16-bit Windows applications in their own address space—Consumer Windows always runs 16-bit Windows applications in a shared address space, in which they can corrupt (and hang) each other.

(continued)

Windows 2000 vs. Consumer Windows *continued*

■ Shared memory on Windows 2000 is visible only to the processes that are mapping the same shared memory section. (In the Win32 API, a shared memory section is called a *file mapping object*.) On Consumer Windows, all shared memory is visible and writable from all processes. Thus, any process can write to any file mapping object.

■ Consumer Windows has some critical operating system pages that are writable from user mode, thus allowing a user application to corrupt or crash the system.

The one thing Consumer Windows can do that Windows 2000 will never do is run *all* older MS-DOS and Windows 3.1 applications (notably applications that require direct hardware access) as well as 16-bit MS-DOS device drivers. Whereas 100 percent compatibility with MS-DOS and Windows 3.1 was a mandatory goal for Windows 95, the original goal for Windows NT was to run *most* existing 16-bit applications while preserving the integrity and reliability of the system.

Operating System Model

In most multiuser operating systems, applications are separated from the operating system itself—the operating system code runs in a privileged processor mode (referred to as *kernel mode* in this book), with access to system data and to the hardware; application code runs in a nonprivileged processor mode (called *user mode*), with a limited set of interfaces available, limited access to system data, and no direct access to hardware. When a user-mode program calls a system service, the processor traps the call and then switches the calling thread to kernel mode. When the system service completes, the operating system switches the thread context back to user mode and allows the caller to continue.

Windows 2000 is similar to most UNIX systems in that it's a monolithic operating system in the sense that the bulk of the operating system and device driver code shares the same kernel-mode protected memory space. This means that any operating system component or device driver can potentially corrupt data being used by other operating system components.

Is Windows 2000 a Microkernel-Based System?

Although some claim it as such, Windows 2000 isn't a microkernel-based operating system in the classic definition of microkernels, where the principal operating system components (such as the memory manager, process manager, and I/O manager) run as separate processes in their own private address spaces, layered on a primitive set of services the microkernel provides. For example, the Carnegie Mellon University Mach operating system, a contemporary example of a microkernel architecture, implements a minimal kernel that comprises thread scheduling, message passing, virtual memory, and device drivers. Everything else, including various APIs, file systems, and networking, runs in user mode. However, commercial implementations of the Mach microkernel operating system typically run at least all file system, networking, and memory management code in kernel mode. The reason is simple: the pure microkernel design is commercially impractical because it's too inefficient.

Does the fact that so much of Windows 2000 runs in kernel mode mean that it's more susceptible to crashes than a true microkernel operating system? Not at all. Consider the following scenario. Suppose the file system code of an operating system has a bug that causes it to crash from time to time. In a traditional operating system or a modified microkernel operating system, a bug in kernel-mode code such as the memory manager or the file system would likely crash the entire operating system. In a pure microkernel operating system, such components run in user mode, so theoretically a bug would simply mean that the component's process exits. But in practical terms, the system would crash because recovering from the failure of such a critical process would likely be impossible.

All these operating system components are, of course, fully protected from errant applications because applications don't have direct access to the code and data of the privileged part of the operating system (though they can quickly call other kernel services). This protection is one of the reasons that Windows 2000 has the reputation for being both robust and stable as an application server and as a workstation platform yet fast and nimble from the perspective of core operating system services, such as virtual memory management, file I/O, networking, and file and print sharing.

The kernel-mode components of Windows 2000 also embody basic object-oriented design principles. For example, they don't reach into one another's data structures to access information maintained by individual components. Instead, they use formal interfaces to pass parameters and access and/or modify data structures.

Despite its pervasive use of objects to represent shared system resources, Windows 2000 is not an object-oriented system in the strict sense. Most of the operating system code is written in C for portability and because C development tools are widely available. C doesn't directly support object-oriented constructs, such as dynamic binding of data types, polymorphic functions, or class inheritance. Therefore, the C-based implementation of objects in Windows 2000 borrows from, but doesn't depend on, features of particular object-oriented languages.

Portability

Windows 2000 was designed to run on a variety of hardware architectures, including Intel-based CISC systems as well as RISC systems. The initial release of Windows NT supported the x86 and MIPS architecture. Support for the Digital Equipment Corporation (DEC) Alpha AXP was added shortly thereafter. Support for a fourth processor architecture, the Motorola PowerPC, was added in Windows NT 3.51. Because of changing market demands, however, support for the MIPS and PowerPC architectures was dropped before development began on Windows 2000. Later Compaq withdrew support for the Alpha AXP architecture, resulting in Windows 2000 being supported only on the x86 architecture.

> **NOTE** The next architecture to be supported by a future version of Windows 2000 is the new Intel Itanium processor family, the first implementation of the 64-bit architecture family being jointly developed by Intel and Hewlett-Packard, called IA-64 (for Intel Architecture 64). The 64-bit version of Windows will provide a much larger address space for both user processes and the system. Although this is a major enhancement that extends the scalability of the system significantly, to date, moving Windows 2000 to a 64-bit platform hasn't necessitated major changes in the kernel architecture of the system (other than the support in the memory manager, of course). For information on preparing applications now so that they can be ported to 64-bit Windows more easily later, see the section of the Platform SDK documentation entitled "Win64 Programming Preview" (also available online at *msdn.microsoft.com*). For general information on 64-bit Windows, search for the keyword "64-bit" on *www.microsoft.com/windows*.

Windows 2000 achieves portability across hardware architectures and platforms in two primary ways:

■ Windows 2000 has a layered design, with low-level portions of the system that are processor-architecture-specific or platform-specific isolated into separate modules so that upper layers of the system can be shielded from the differences between architectures and among hardware platforms. The two key components that provide operating system portability are the kernel (contained in Ntoskrnl.exe) and the hardware abstraction layer (contained in Hal.dll). (Both these components are described in more detail later in this chapter.) Functions that are architecture-specific (such as thread context switching and trap dispatching) are implemented in the kernel. Functions that can differ among systems within the same architecture (for example, different motherboards) are implemented in the HAL.

■ The vast majority of Windows 2000 is written in C, with some portions in C++. Assembly language is used only for those parts of the operating system that need to communicate directly with system hardware (such as the interrupt trap handler) or that are extremely performance-sensitive (such as context switching). Assembly language code exists not only in the kernel and the HAL but also in a few other places within the core operating system (such as the routines that implement interlocked instructions as well as one module in the local procedure call facility), in the kernel-mode part of the Win32 subsystem, and even in some user-mode libraries, such as the process startup code in Ntdll.dll (a system library explained later in this chapter).

Symmetric Multiprocessing

Multitasking is the operating system technique for sharing a single processor among multiple threads of execution. When a computer has more than one processor, however, it can execute two threads simultaneously. Thus, whereas a multitasking operating system only appears to execute multiple threads at the same time, a multiprocessing operating system actually does it, executing one thread on each of its processors.

As mentioned at the beginning of this chapter, one of the key design goals for Windows NT was that it had to run well on multiprocessor computer systems. Windows 2000 is also a *symmetric multiprocessing* (SMP) operating system. There is no master processor—the operating system as well as user threads can be scheduled to run on any processor. Also, all the processors share just one memory

space. This model contrasts with *asymmetric multiprocessing* (ASMP), in which the operating system typically selects one processor to execute operating system code while other processors run only user code. The differences in the two multiprocessing models are illustrated in Figure 2-1.

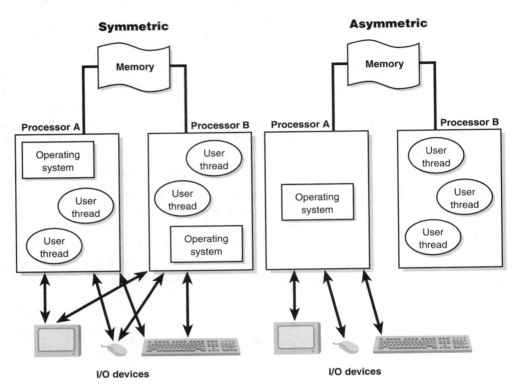

Figure 2-1
Symmetric vs. asymmetric multiprocessing

Although Windows NT was originally designed to support up to 32 processors, nothing inherent in the multiprocessor design limits the number of processors to 32—that number is simply an obvious and convenient limit because 32 processors can easily be represented as a bit mask using a native 32-bit data type.

The actual number of supported processors depends on the edition of Windows 2000 being used. (The various editions of Windows 2000 are described in the next section.) This number is stored in the registry value

HKLM\SYSTEM\CurrentControlSet\Control\Session\Manager\Licensed-Processors. Keep in mind that tampering with that data is a violation of the software license and will likely result in a system crash upon rebooting because modifying the registry to allow use of more processors involves more than just changing this value.

Scalability

One of the key issues with multiprocessor systems is *scalability*. To run correctly on an SMP system, operating system code must adhere to strict guidelines and rules. Resource contention and other performance issues are more complicated in multiprocessing systems than in uniprocessor systems and must be accounted for in the system's design. Windows 2000 incorporates several features that are crucial to its success as a multiprocessor operating system:

- The ability to run operating system code on any available processor and on multiple processors at the same time

- Multiple threads of execution within a single process, each of which can execute simultaneously on different processors

- Fine-grained synchronization within the kernel as well as within device drivers and server processes, which allows more components to run concurrently on multiple processors

In addition, Windows 2000 provides mechanisms (such as I/O completion ports—described in Chapter 9) that facilitate the efficient implementation of multithreaded server processes that can scale well on multiprocessor systems.

Multiprocessor synchronization is described in Chapter 3. Multiprocessor thread scheduling details are covered in Chapter 6.

Architecture Overview

With this brief overview of the design goals and packaging of Windows 2000, let's take a look at the key system components that comprise its architecture. A simplified version of this architecture is shown in Figure 2-2. Keep in mind that this diagram is basic—it doesn't show everything. The various components of Windows 2000 are covered in detail later in this chapter.

Figure 2-2
Simplified Windows 2000 architecture

In Figure 2-2, first notice the line dividing the user-mode and kernel-mode parts of the Windows 2000 operating system. The boxes above the line represent user-mode processes, and the components below the line are kernel-mode operating system services. As mentioned in Chapter 1, user-mode threads execute in a protected process address space (although while they are executing in kernel mode, they have access to system space). Thus, system support processes, service processes, user applications, and environment subsystems each have their own private process address space.

The four basic types of user-mode processes are described as follows:

- Fixed (or hardwired) *system support processes,* such as the logon process and the session manager, that are not Windows 2000 services (that is, not started by the service control manager).

- *Service processes* that host Win32 services, such as the Task Scheduler and Spooler services. Many Windows 2000 server applications, such as Microsoft SQL Server and Microsoft Exchange Server, also include components that run as services.

- *User applications,* which can be one of five types: Win32, Windows 3.1, MS-DOS, POSIX, or OS/2 1.2.

- *Environment subsystems,* which expose the native operating system services to user applications through a set of callable functions, thus providing an operating system *environment,* or personality. Windows 2000 ships with three environment subsystems: Win32, POSIX, and OS/2.

In Figure 2-2, notice the "Subsystem DLLs" box below the "Service processes" and "User applications" boxes. Under Windows 2000, user applications don't call the native Windows 2000 operating system services directly; rather, they go through one or more *subsystem dynamic-link libraries* (DLLs). The role of the subsystem DLLs is to translate a documented function into the appropriate internal (and undocumented) Windows 2000 system service calls. This translation might or might not involve sending a message to the environment subsystem process that is serving the user application.

The kernel-mode components of Windows 2000 include the following:

- The Windows 2000 *executive* contains the base operating system services, such as memory management, process and thread management, security, I/O, and interprocess communication.

- The Windows 2000 *kernel* consists of low-level operating system functions, such as thread scheduling, interrupt and exception dispatching, and multiprocessor synchronization. It also provides a set of routines and basic objects that the rest of the executive uses to implement higher-level constructs.

- *Device drivers* include both hardware device drivers that translate user I/O function calls into specific hardware device I/O requests as well as file system and network drivers.

- The *hardware abstraction layer* (HAL) is a layer of code that isolates the kernel, device drivers, and the rest of the Windows 2000 executive from platform-specific hardware differences (such as differences between motherboards).

- The *windowing and graphics system* implements the graphical user interface (GUI) functions (better known as the Win32 USER and GDI functions), such as dealing with windows, user interface controls, and drawing.

Table 2-1 lists the filenames of the core Windows 2000 operating system components. (You'll need to know these filenames because we'll be referring to some system files by name.) Each of these components is covered in greater detail both later in this chapter and in the chapters that follow.

Table 2-1 Core Windows 2000 System Files

Filename	Components
Ntoskrnl.exe	Executive and kernel
Ntkrnlpa.exe	Executive and kernel with support for Physical Address Extension (PAE), which allows addressing of up to 64 GB of physical memory
Hal.dll	Hardware abstraction layer
Win32k.sys	Kernel-mode part of the Win32 subsystem
Ntdll.dll	Internal support functions and system service dispatch stubs to executive functions
Kernel32.dll, Advapi32.dll, User32.dll, Gdi32.dll	Core Win32 subsystem DLLs

Before we dig into the details of these system components, though, let's examine the differences between Windows 2000 Professional and the various editions of Windows 2000 Server.

Windows 2000 Product Packaging

There are four editions of Windows 2000: Windows 2000 Professional, Windows 2000 Server, Windows 2000 Advanced Server, and Windows 2000 Datacenter Server. These editions differ by:

- The number of processors supported

- The amount of physical memory supported

- The number of concurrent network connections supported

- Layered services that come with Server editions that don't come with the Professional edition

These differences are summarized in Table 2-2.

Table 2-2 **Differences Between Windows 2000 Professional and Server Editions**

Edition	Number of Processors Supported	Physical Memory Supported	Number of Concurrent Client Network Connections*	Additional Layered Services
Windows 2000 Professional	2	4 GB	10	
Windows 2000 Server	4	4 GB	Unlimited	Ability to be a domain controller, Active Directory service, software-based RAID, Dynamic Host Configuration Protocol (DHCP) server, Domain Name System (DNS) server, Distributed File System (DFS) server, Certificate Services, Remote install, and Terminal Services
Windows 2000 Advanced Server	8	8 GB	Unlimited	Two-node clusters
Windows 2000 Datacenter Server	32	64 GB**	Unlimited	Four-node clusters, Process Control Manager tool[†]

* The End-User License Agreement for Windows 2000 Professional (contained in \Winnt\System32\ Eula.txt) states, "You may permit a maximum of ten (10) computers or other electronic devices (each a "Device") to connect to the Workstation Computer to utilize the services of the Product solely for file and print services, internet information services, and remote access (including connection sharing and telephony services)." This limit is enforced for file and print sharing and remote access but not for Internet Information Services.

** Theoretical limit—the supported limit might be less than this due to availability of commercial hardware.

† See page 376 in Chapter 6 for more on the Process Control Manager tool.

What is *not* different between the various flavors of Windows 2000 are the core system files: the kernel image, Ntoskrnl.exe (and the PAE version, Ntkrnlpa.exe); the HAL libraries; the device drivers; and the base system utilities and DLLs. All these files are the same for all editions of Windows 2000. For example, there are no special server versions of the HAL.

However, a number of these components operate differently depending on which edition is running. Windows 2000 Server systems are optimized for system throughput as high-performance application servers, whereas Windows 2000 Professional, although it has server capabilities, is optimized for response time for interactive desktop use. For example, based on the product type, several resource allocation decisions are made differently at system boot time, such as the size and number of operating system heaps (or pools), the number of internal system worker threads, and the size of the system data cache. Also, run-time policy decisions, such as the way the memory manager trades off system and process memory demands, differ between the Windows 2000 Server editions and Windows 2000 Professional. Even some thread-scheduling details have different default behavior in the two edition families. Where there are significant operational differences in the two products, these are highlighted in the pertinent chapters throughout the rest of this book. Unless otherwise noted, everything in this book applies to both the Windows 2000 Server editions as well as Windows 2000 Professional.

If the kernel image is the same across the various product editions of Windows 2000, how does the system know which edition is booted? By querying the registry values ProductType and ProductSuite under the HKLM\ SYSTEM\CurrentControlSet\Control\ProductOptions key. ProductType is used to distinguish whether the system is a Windows 2000 Professional system or a Windows 2000 Server system (any edition). The valid values are listed in Table 2-3. The result is stored in the system global variable *MmProductType*, which can be queried from a device driver using the kernel-mode support function *MmIsThisAnNtAsSystem*, documented in the Windows 2000 DDK.

Table 2-3 ProductType Registry Values

Edition of Windows 2000	Value of ProductType
Windows 2000 Professional	WinNT
Windows 2000 Server (domain controller)	LanmanNT
Windows 2000 Server (server only)	ServerNT

A different registry value, ProductSuite, distinguishes Windows 2000 Server, Advanced Server, and Datacenter Server as well as whether Terminal Services have been installed (Server systems only). On Windows 2000 Professional systems, this value is blank.

If user programs need to determine which edition of Windows 2000 is running, they can call the Win32 *VerifyVersionInfo* function, documented in the Platform SDK. Device drivers can call the kernel-mode function *RtlGetVersion*, documented in the Windows 2000 DDK.

Checked Build

There is a special debug version of Windows 2000 Professional called the *checked build*. This version is available only with the MSDN Professional (or Universal) CD subscription. It is provided to aid device driver developers—the checked build performs more stringent error checking on kernel-mode functions called by device drivers or other system code. For example, if a driver (or some other piece of kernel-mode code) makes an invalid call to a system function that is checking parameters (such as acquiring a spinlock at the wrong interrupt level), the system will stop execution when the problem is detected rather than allow some data structure to be corrupted and the system to possibly crash at a later time.

The checked build is a recompilation of the Windows 2000 source code with the compile-time flag DEBUG set to TRUE. Much of the additional code in the checked-build binaries is a result of using the ASSERT macro, which is defined in the DDK header file Ntddk.h and documented in the DDK documentation. This macro tests a condition (such as the validity of a data structure or parameter), and if the expression evaluates to FALSE, the macro calls the kernel-mode function *RtlAssert*, which calls *DbgPrint* to pass the text of the debug message to a kernel debugger (if one is attached) to be displayed and then prompts the user for what to do (breakpoint, ignore, terminate process, or terminate thread). If the system wasn't booted with the kernel debugger (using the /DEBUG switch in Boot.ini) and no kernel debugger is currently attached, failure of an ASSERT test will crash the system.

Although Microsoft doesn't supply a checked-build version of Windows 2000 Server, Advanced Server, or Datacenter Server, you can manually copy the checked (debug) version of the kernel image onto a Windows 2000 Server system, reboot, and run with a checked kernel. (You could also do this for other

system files, but most developers who use the checked build really only need the checked version of the kernel image—not the checked versions of every device driver, utility, and DLL.)

Multiprocessor-Specific System Files

Six system files* are different on a multiprocessor system than on a uniprocessor system. (See Table 2-4.) At installation time, the appropriate file is selected and copied to the local \Winnt\System32 directory. To determine which files were copied, see the file \Winnt\Repair\Setup.log, which itemizes all the files that were copied to the local system disk and where they came from off the distribution media.

Table 2-4 Multiprocessor-Specific vs. Uniprocessor-Specific System Files

Name of File on System Disk	Name of Uniprocessor Version on CD	Name of Multiprocessor Version on CD
Ntoskrnl.exe	\I386\Ntoskrnl.exe	\I386\Ntkrnlmp.exe
Ntkrnlpa.exe	Ntkrnlpa.exe in \I386\ Driver.cab	Ntkrpamp.exe in \I386\Driver.cab
Hal.dll	Depends on system type (See the list of HALs in Table 2-5.)	Depends on system type (See the list of HALs in Table 2-5.)
Win32k.sys	\I386\UNIPROC\ Win32k.sys	Win32k.sys in \I386\Driver.cab
Ntdll.dll	\I386\UNIPROC\ Ntdll.dll	\I386\Ntdll.dll
Kernel32.dll	\I386\UNIPROC\ Kernel32.dll	\I386\Kernel32.dll

* If you look in the \I386\UNIPROC folder on a Windows 2000 CD, you'll see a file named Winsrv.dll—although this file exists in a folder named UNIPROC, implying that there is a uniprocessor version, in fact there is only one version of this image for both multiprocessor and uniprocessor systems.

EXPERIMENT: Looking at Multiprocessor-Specific Support Files

You can see the files that are different for a multiprocessor system by looking at the driver details for the Computer in Device Manager:

1. Open the System properties (either by selecting System from Control Panel or by right-clicking on the My Computer icon on your desktop and selecting Properties).

2. Click on the Hardware tab.

3. Click Device Manager.

4. Expand the Computer object.

5. Double-click on the child node underneath Computer.

6. Click on the Driver tab.

7. Click Driver Details.

You should see this dialog box for a multiprocessor system:

The reason for having uniprocessor versions of these key system files is performance—multiprocessor synchronization is inherently more complex and time consuming than the use of a single processor, so by having special uniprocessor versions of the key system files, this overhead is avoided on uniprocessor systems (which constitute the vast majority of systems running Windows 2000).

Interestingly, although the uniprocessor and multiprocessor versions of Ntoskrnl are generated using conditionally compiled source code, the uniprocessor versions of Ntdll.dll and Kernel32.dll are created by patching the x86 LOCK and UNLOCK instructions, which are used to synchronize multiple threads with no-operation (NOP) instructions (which do nothing).

The rest of the system files that comprise Windows 2000 (including all utilities, libraries, and device drivers) have the same version on both uniprocessor and multiprocessor systems (that is, they handle multiprocessor synchronization issues correctly). You should use this approach on any software you build, whether it is a Win32 application or a device driver—keep multiprocessor synchronization issues in mind when you design your software, and test the software on both uniprocessor and multiprocessor systems.

On the checked build CD, if you compare Ntoskrnl.exe and Ntkrnlmp.exe or Ntkrnlpa.exe and Ntkrpamp.exe, you'll find that they are identical—they are all multiprocessor versions of the same files. In other words, there is no debug uniprocessor version of the kernel images provided with the checked build.

EXPERIMENT: Checking Which Ntoskrnl Version You're Running

With Windows NT 4, you can tell which version of Ntoskrnl you're running by clicking on the Version tab in Windows NT Diagnostics (Winmsd.exe). In Windows 2000, there is no utility to show this information. However, an Event Log entry is written each time the system boots that does record the type of kernel image (uniprocessor vs. multiprocessor and free vs. checked), as shown in the screen shot on the following page. (From the Start menu select Programs/Administrative Tools/Event Viewer, select System Log, and double-click on an Event Log entry with an Event ID of 6009, indicating the entry was written at the system start.)

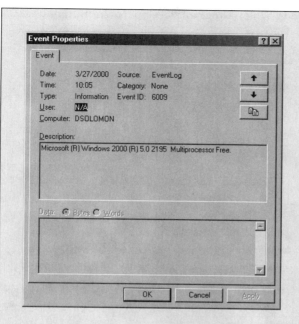

This Event Log entry doesn't indicate whether you booted the PAE version of the kernel image that supports more than 4 GB of physical memory (Ntkrnlpa.exe). However, you can tell if you booted the PAE kernel by looking at the registry value HKLM\SYSTEM\CurrentControl-Set\Control\SystemStartOptions. Also, if you boot the PAE kernel, the registry value HKLM\SYSTEM\CurrentControlSet\Control\Session Manager\Memory Management\PhysicalAddressExtension is set to 1.

You can also determine whether you installed the multiprocessor version of Ntoskrnl (or Ntkrnlpa) by examining the file properties: run Windows Explorer, right-click on Ntoskrnl.exe in your \Winnt\System32 folder, and select Properties. Then click on the Version tab, and select the Original Filename property—if you're running the multiprocessor version, you'll see the dialog box on the following page.

(continued)

EXPERIMENT: Checking Which Ntoskrnl Version You're Running *continued*

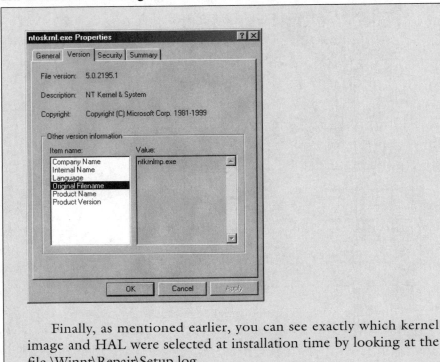

Finally, as mentioned earlier, you can see exactly which kernel image and HAL were selected at installation time by looking at the file \Winnt\Repair\Setup.log.

Key System Components

Now that we've looked at the high-level architecture of Windows 2000, let's delve deeper into the internal structure and the role each of the key operating system components plays. Figure 2-3 is a more detailed and complete diagram of the Windows 2000 system architecture and components than was shown earlier in the chapter (in Figure 2-2).

The following sections elaborate on each major element of this diagram. Chapter 3 explains the primary control mechanisms the system uses (such as the object manager, interrupts, and so forth). Chapter 4 describes the process of starting and shutting down Windows 2000, and Chapter 5 details management mechanisms such as the registry, service processes, and Windows Management Instrumentation (WMI). Then the remaining chapters explore in even more detail the internal structure and operation of key areas such as processes and threads, memory management, security, the I/O manager, storage management, the cache manager, the Windows 2000 file system (NTFS), and networking.

Figure 2-3
Windows 2000 architecture

Environment Subsystems and Subsystem DLLs

As shown in Figure 2-3, Windows 2000 has three environment subsystems: OS/2, POSIX, and Win32. As we'll explain shortly, of the three, the Win32 subsystem is special in that Windows 2000 can't run without it. (It owns the keyboard, mouse, and display, and it is required to be present even on server systems with no interactive users logged in.) In fact, the other two subsystems are configured to start on demand, whereas the Win32 subsystem must always be running.

The subsystem startup information is stored under the registry key HKLM\
SYSTEM\CurrentControlSet\Control\Session Manager\SubSystems. Figure 2-4
shows the values under this key.

Figure 2-4
Registry Editor showing Windows 2000 startup information

The Required value lists the subsystems that load when the system boots.
The value has two strings: Windows and Debug. The Windows value contains the
file specification of the Win32 subsystem, Csrss.exe, which stands for Client/Server
Run-Time Subsystem.* Debug is blank (it's used for internal testing) and there-
fore does nothing. The Optional value indicates that the OS/2 and POSIX sub-
systems will be started on demand. The registry value Kmode contains the filename
of the kernel-mode portion of the Win32 subsystem, Win32k.sys (explained later
in this chapter).

The role of an environment subsystem is to expose some subset of the base
Windows 2000 executive system services to application programs. Each subsys-
tem can provide access to different subsets of the native services in Windows 2000.
That means that some things can be done from an application built on one
subsystem that can't be done by an application built on another subsystem. For
example, a Win32 application can't use the POSIX *fork* function.

Each executable image (.exe) is bound to one and only one subsystem.
When an image is run, the process creation code examines the subsystem type
code in the image header so that it can notify the proper subsystem of the new
process. This type code is specified with the /SUBSYSTEM qualifier of the
link command in Microsoft Visual C++ and can be viewed with the Exetype
tool in the Windows 2000 resource kits.

* As a historical note, the reason the Win32 subsystem process is called Csrss.exe is that in the
original design of Windows NT, all the subsystems were going to execute as threads inside a
single systemwide environment subsystem process; when the POSIX and OS/2 subsystems were
removed and put in their own processes, the filename for the Win32 subsystem process wasn't
changed.

Function calls can't be mixed between subsystems. In other words, a POSIX application can call only services exported by the POSIX subsystem, and a Win32 application can call only services exported by the Win32 subsystem. As you'll see later, this restriction is the reason that the POSIX subsystem, which implements a very limited set of functions (only POSIX 1003.1), isn't a useful environment for porting UNIX applications.

As mentioned earlier, user applications don't call Windows 2000 system services directly. Instead, they go through one or more subsystem DLLs. These libraries export the documented interface that the programs linked to that subsystem can call. For example, the Win32 subsystem DLLs (such as Kernel32.dll, Advapi32.dll, User32.dll, and Gdi32.dll) implement the Win32 API functions. The POSIX subsystem DLL implements the POSIX 1003.1 API.

EXPERIMENT: Viewing the Image Subsystem Type

You can see the image subsystem type by using either the Exetype tool in the Windows 2000 resource kits or the Dependency Walker tool (Depends.exe) in the Windows 2000 Support Tools and Platform SDK. For example, notice the image types for two different Win32 images, Notepad.exe (the simple text editor) and Cmd.exe (the Windows 2000 command prompt):

```
C:\>exetype \winnt\system32\notepad.exe
File "\winnt\system32\notepad.exe" is of the following type:
    Windows NT
    32 bit machine
    Built for the Intel 80386 processor
    Runs under the Windows GUI subsystem

C:\>exetype \winnt\system32\cmd.exe
File "\winnt\system32\cmd.exe" is of the following type:
    Windows NT
    32 bit machine
    Built for the Intel 80386 processor
    Runs under the Windows character-based subsystem
```

In reality, there is just one Windows subsystem, not separate ones for graphical images and for character-based, or console, images. Also, Windows 2000 isn't supported on the Intel 386 processor (or the 486 for that matter)—the text output by the Exetype program hasn't been updated.

When an application calls a function in a subsystem DLL, one of three things can occur:

■ The function is entirely implemented in user mode inside the subsystem DLL. In other words, no message is sent to the environment subsystem process, and no Windows 2000 executive system services are called. The function is performed in user mode, and the results are returned to the caller. Examples of such functions include *Get-CurrentProcess* (which always returns −1, a value that is defined to refer to the current process in all process-related functions) and *GetCurrentProcessId* (the process ID doesn't change for a running process, so this ID is retrieved from a cached location, thus avoiding the need to call into the kernel).

■ The function requires one or more calls to the Windows 2000 executive. For example, the Win32 *ReadFile* and *WriteFile* functions involve calling the underlying internal (and undocumented) Windows 2000 I/O system services *NtReadFile* and *NtWriteFile*, respectively.

■ The function requires some work to be done in the environment subsystem process. (The environment subsystem processes, running in user mode, are responsible for maintaining the state of the client applications running under their control.) In this case, a client/server request is made to the environment subsystem via a message sent to the subsystem to perform some operation. The subsystem DLL then waits for a reply before returning to the caller.

Some functions can be a combination of the second and third items above, such as the Win32 *CreateProcess* and *CreateThread* functions.

Although Windows 2000 was designed to support multiple, independent environment subsystems, from a practical perspective, having each subsystem implement all the code to handle windowing and display I/O would result in a large amount of duplication of system functions that, ultimately, would have negatively affected both system size and performance. Because Win32 was the primary subsystem, the Windows 2000 designers decided to locate these basic functions there and have the other subsystems call on the Win32 subsystem to perform display I/O. Thus, the POSIX and OS/2 subsystems call services in the Win32 subsystem to perform display I/O. (In fact, if you examine the subsystem type for these images, you'll see that they are Win32 executables.)

Let's take a closer look at each of the environment subsystems.

Win32 Subsystem

The Win32 subsystem consists of the following major components:

- The environment subsystem process (Csrss.exe) contains support for:
 - ❏ Console (text) windows
 - ❏ Creating and deleting processes and threads
 - ❏ Portions of the support for 16-bit virtual DOS machine (VDM) processes
 - ❏ Other miscellaneous functions, such as *GetTempFile*, *DefineDos-Device*, *ExitWindowsEx*, and several natural language support functions

- The kernel-mode device driver (Win32k.sys) contains:
 - ❏ The window manager, which controls window displays; manages screen output; collects input from keyboard, mouse, and other devices; and passes user messages to applications.
 - ❏ The Graphics Device Interface (GDI), which is a library of functions for graphics output devices. It includes functions for line, text, and figure drawing and for graphics manipulation.

- Subsystem DLLs (such as Kernel32.dll, Advapi32.dll, User32.dll, and Gdi32.dll) translate documented Win32 API functions into the appropriate undocumented kernel-mode system service calls to Ntoskrnl.exe and Win32k.sys.

- Graphics device drivers are hardware-dependent graphics display drivers, printer drivers, and video miniport drivers.

Applications call the standard USER functions to create user interface controls, such as windows and buttons, on the display. The window manager communicates these requests to the GDI, which passes them to the graphics device drivers, where they are formatted for the display device. A display driver is paired with a video miniport driver to complete video display support.

The GDI provides a set of standard two-dimensional functions that let applications communicate with graphics devices without knowing anything about the devices. GDI functions mediate between applications and graphics devices such as display drivers and printer drivers. The GDI interprets application requests for graphic output and sends the requests to graphics display drivers. It also provides a standard interface for applications to use varying graphics output devices. This interface enables application code to be independent of the

hardware devices and their drivers. The GDI tailors its messages to the capabilities of the device, often dividing the request into manageable parts. For example, some devices can understand directions to draw an ellipse; others require the GDI to interpret the command as a series of pixels placed at certain coordinates. For more information about the graphics and video driver architecture, see the *Design Guide* section of the book *Graphics Drivers* in the Windows 2000 DDK.

Prior to Windows NT 4, the window manager and graphics services were part of the user-mode Win32 subsystem process. In Windows NT 4, the bulk of the windowing and graphics code was moved from running in the context of the Win32 subsystem process to a set of callable services running in kernel mode (in the file Win32k.sys). The primary reason for this shift was to improve overall system performance. Having a separate server process that contains the Win32 graphics subsystem required multiple thread and process context switches, which consumed considerable CPU cycles and memory resources even though the original design was highly optimized.

For example, for each thread on the client side there was a dedicated, paired server thread in the Win32 subsystem process waiting on the client thread for requests. A special interprocess communication facility called *fast LPC* was used to send messages between these threads. Unlike normal thread context switches, transitions between paired threads via fast LPC don't cause a rescheduling event in the kernel, thereby enabling the server thread to run for the remaining time slice of the client thread before having to take its turn in the kernel's preemptive thread scheduler. Moreover, shared memory buffers were used to allow fast passing of large data structures, such as bitmaps, and clients had direct but read-only access to key server data structures to minimize the need for thread/process transitions between clients and the Win32 server. Also, GDI operations were (and still are) batched. *Batching* means that a series of graphics calls by a Win32 application aren't "pushed" over to the server and drawn on the output device until a GDI batching queue is filled. You can set the size of the queue by using the Win32 *GdiSetBatchLimit* function, and you can flush the queue at any time with *GdiFlush*. Conversely, read-only properties and data structures of GDI, once they were obtained from the Win32 subsystem process, were cached on the client side for fast subsequent access.

Despite these optimizations, however, the overall system performance was still not adequate for graphics-intensive applications. The obvious solution was to eliminate the need for the additional threads and resulting context switches by moving the windowing and graphics system into kernel mode. Also, once applications have called into the window manager and the GDI, those subsystems can access other Windows 2000 executive components directly without the cost of user-mode or kernel-mode transitions. This direct access is especially important in the case of the GDI calling through video drivers, a process that involves interaction with video hardware at high frequencies and high bandwidths.

Is Windows 2000 Less Stable with Win32 USER and GDI in Kernel Mode?

Some people wondered whether moving this much code into kernel mode would substantially affect system stability. The reason the impact on system stability has been minimal is that prior to Windows NT 4 (and this is still true today), a bug (such as an access violation) in the user-mode Win32 subsystem process (Csrss.exe) resulted in a system crash. This crash occurs because the parent process of Csrss (the session manager, Smss, which is described on page 83) does a wait operation on the process handle to Csrss, and if the wait ever returns, Smss crashes the system—because the Win32 subsystem process was (and still is) a vital process to the running of the system. Because it was the process that contained the data structures that described the windows on the display, the death of that process would kill the user interface. However, even a Windows 2000 system operating as a server, with no interactive processes, can't run without this process, since server processes might be using window messaging to drive the internal state of the application. With Windows 2000, an access violation in the same code now running in kernel mode simply crashes the system more quickly, since exceptions in kernel mode result in a system crash.

There is, however, one additional theoretical danger that didn't exist prior to moving the windowing and graphics system into kernel mode. Because this body of code is now running in kernel mode, a bug (such as the use of a bad pointer) could result in corrupting kernel-mode protected data structures. Prior to Windows NT 4, such references would have caused an access violation because kernel-mode pages aren't writable from user mode. But a system crash would have then resulted, as described earlier. With the code now running in kernel mode, a bad pointer reference that caused a write operation to some kernel-mode page might not immediately cause a system crash, but if it corrupted some data structure, a crash would likely result soon after. There is a small chance, however, that such a reference could corrupt a memory buffer (rather than a data structure), possibly resulting in returning corrupt data to a user program or writing bad data to the disk.

Another area of possible impact can come from the move of the graphics drivers into kernel mode. Previously, some portions of a graphics driver ran within Csrss, and others ran in kernel mode. Now, the entire driver runs in kernel mode. Although Microsoft doesn't develop all of the graphics device drivers supported in Windows 2000, it does work

(continued)

Is Windows 2000 Less Stable with Win32 USER and GDI in Kernel Mode? *continued*

directly with hardware manufacturers to help ensure that they are able to produce reliable and efficient drivers. All drivers shipped with the system are submitted to the same rigorous testing as other executive components.

Finally, it's important to understand that this design (running the windowing and graphics subsystem in kernel mode) is not fundamentally risky. It is identical to the approaches many other device drivers use (for example, network card drivers and hard disk drivers). All these drivers have been operating in kernel mode since the inception of Windows NT with a high degree of reliability.

Some people speculated that the move of the window manager and the GDI into kernel mode would hurt the preemptive multitasking capability of Windows 2000. The theory was that with all the additional Win32 processing time spent in kernel mode, other threads would have less opportunity to be run preemptively. This view was based on a misunderstanding of the Windows 2000 architecture. It is true that in many other nominally preemptive operating systems, executing in kernel mode is never preempted by the operating system scheduler— or is preempted only at a certain limited number of predefined points of kernel reentrancy. In Windows 2000, however, threads running anywhere in the executive are preempted and scheduled alongside threads running in user mode, and all code within the executive is fully reentrant. Among other reasons, this capability is necessary to achieve a high degree of system scalability on SMP hardware.

Another line of speculation was that SMP scaling would be hurt by this change. The theory went like this: Previously, an interaction between an application and the window manager or the GDI involved two threads, one in the application and one in Csrss.exe. Therefore, on an SMP system, the two threads could run in parallel, thus improving throughput. This analysis shows a misunderstanding of how Windows NT technology worked prior to Windows NT 4. In most cases, calls from a client application to the Win32 subsystem process run synchronously; that is, the client thread entirely blocks waiting on the server thread and begins to run again only when the server thread has completed the call. Therefore, no parallelism on SMP hardware can ever be achieved. This phenomenon is easily observable with a busy graphics application using the Performance tool on an SMP system. The observer will discover that on a two-processor system each processor is approximately 50 percent loaded, and it's relatively easy to find the single Csrss thread that

is paired off with the busy application thread. Indeed, because the two threads are fairly intimate with each other and sharing state, the processors' caches must be flushed constantly to maintain coherency. This constant flushing is the reason that with Windows NT 3.51 a single-threaded graphics application typically runs slightly slower on an SMP machine than on a single processor system.

As a result, the changes in Windows NT 4 increased SMP throughput of applications that make heavy use of the window manager and the GDI, especially when more than one application thread is busy. When two application threads are busy on a two-processor Windows NT 3.51–based machine, a total of four threads (two in the application plus two in Csrss) are battling for time on the two processors. Although only two are typically ready to run at any given time, the lack of a consistent pattern in which threads run results in a loss of locality of reference and cache coherency. This loss occurs because the busy threads are likely to get shuffled from one processor to another. In the Windows NT 4 design, each of the two application threads essentially has its own processor, and the automatic thread affinity of Windows 2000 tends to run the same thread on the same processor indefinitely, thus maximizing locality of reference and minimizing the need to synchronize the private per-processor memory caches.

So in summary, moving the window manager and the GDI from user mode to kernel mode has provided improved performance without any significant decrease in system stability or reliability.

So, what remains in the user-mode process part of the Win32 subsystem? All the drawing and updating for console or text windows are handled by it, since console applications have no notion of repainting a window. It's easy to see this activity—simply open a command prompt and drag another window over it, and you'll see the Win32 subsystem process running like crazy as it repaints the console window. But other than console window support, only a few Win32 functions result in sending a message to the Win32 subsystem process anymore: process and thread creation and termination, network drive letter mapping, and creation of temporary files. In general, a running Win32 application won't be causing many, if any, context switches to the Win32 subsystem process.

POSIX Subsystem

POSIX, an acronym loosely defined as "a portable operating system interface based on UNIX," refers to a collection of international standards for UNIX-style operating system interfaces. The POSIX standards encourage vendors

implementing UNIX-style interfaces to make them compatible so that programmers can move their applications easily from one system to another.

Windows 2000 implements only one of the many POSIX standards, POSIX.1, formally known as ISO/IEC 9945-1:1990 or IEEE POSIX standard 1003.1-1990. This standard was included primarily to meet U.S. government procurement requirements set in the mid-to-late 1980s that mandated POSIX.1 compliance as specified in Federal Information Processing Standard (FIPS) 151-2, developed by the National Institute of Standards and Technology. Windows NT 3.5, 3.51, and 4 have been formally tested and certified according to FIPS 151-2.

Because POSIX.1 compliance was a mandatory goal for Windows 2000, the operating system was designed to ensure that the required base system support was present to allow for the implementation of a POSIX.1 subsystem (such as the *fork* function, which is implemented in the Windows 2000 executive, and the support for hard file links in the Windows 2000 file system). However, because POSIX.1 defines a limited set of services (such as process control, interprocess communication, simple character cell I/O, and so on), the POSIX subsystem that comes with Windows 2000 isn't a complete programming environment. And because applications can't mix calls between subsystems on Windows 2000, by default, POSIX applications are limited to the strict set of services defined in POSIX.1. This restriction means that a POSIX executable on Windows 2000 can't create a thread or a window or use remote procedure calls (RPCs) or sockets.

To address this limitation, Microsoft provides a product called Interix, which includes an enhanced POSIX subsystem environment that provides nearly 2000 UNIX functions and 300 UNIX-like tools and utilities. (See *www.microsoft .com/WINDOWS2000/guide/server/solutions/interix.asp* for more information on Microsoft Interix.) With this enhancement, it is more viable to port UNIX applications to the POSIX subsystem. However, because the programs are still linked as POSIX executables, they cannot call Win32 functions.

To port UNIX applications to Windows 2000 and allow the use of Win32 functions, you can purchase a UNIX-to-Win32 porting library, such as the one included with the MKS N*u*TCRACKER Professional product available from Mortice Kern Systems Inc. (*www.mks.com*). With this approach, a UNIX application can be recompiled and relinked as a Win32 executable and can slowly start to integrate calls to native Win32 functions.

EXPERIMENT: Watching the POSIX Subsystem Start

The POSIX subsystem is configured by default to start the first time a POSIX executable is run, so you can watch it start by running a POSIX program, such as one of the POSIX utilities that comes with the Windows 2000 resource kits. (You can find these POSIX utilities in the \Apps\POSIX folder on the resource kit CD—they are not installed as part of the resource kit tools installation.) Follow these steps to watch the POSIX subsystem start:

1. Start a command prompt.

2. Type *tlist /t*, and check that the POSIX subsystem isn't already running (that is, that there's no Psxss.exe process underneath Smss.exe).

3. Run one of the POSIX utilities available on the Windows 2000 resource kit CDs, such as \Apps\POSIX\Ls.exe.

4. You'll notice a slight pause while the POSIX subsystem starts and the *Ls* command displays the directory contents.

5. Run *tlist /t* again. This time, notice the existence of Psxss.exe as a child of Smss.exe.

6. Rerun Ls.exe a second time; you'll notice a quicker response (now that the POSIX subsystem is already started).

7. Rerun Ls.exe, but pause the output by pressing Ctrl+S; issue a *tlist /t* from another command prompt, and notice that the POSIX support image (Posix.exe) was the process created from the first command prompt and that it in turn created the Ls.exe process. You should see something similar to the following annotated output:

```
System (2)
  smss.exe (23) ——————————————— Session Manager
    csrss.exe (31) —————————————— Win32 subsystem
    .
    .
    .
    psxss.exe (187) ———————————— POSIX subsystem
explorer.exe (69) Program Manager
  CMD.EXE (93) Command Prompt - ls
    posix.exe (178) ———————————— POSIX support process
      ls.exe (97) ——————————————— POSIX application
                                   being run
```

To compile and link a POSIX application in Windows 2000 requires the POSIX headers and libraries from the Platform SDK. POSIX executables are linked against the POSIX subsystem library, Psxdll.dll. Because by default Windows 2000 is configured to start the POSIX subsystem on demand, the first time you run a POSIX application, the POSIX subsystem process (Psxss.exe) must be started. It remains running until the system reboots. (If you kill the POSIX subsystem process, you won't be able to run more POSIX applications until you reboot.) The POSIX image itself isn't run directly—instead, a special support image called Posix.exe is launched, which in turn creates a child process to run the POSIX application.

For more information about the POSIX subsystem and about porting UNIX applications to Windows 2000, do a search for POSIX and UNIX in MSDN Library.

OS/2 Subsystem

The OS/2 environment subsystem, like the built-in POSIX subsystem, is fairly limited in usefulness in that it supports only OS/2 1.2 16-bit character-based or video I/O (VIO) applications. Although Microsoft did sell a replacement OS/2 1.2 Presentation Manager subsystem for Windows NT 4, it didn't support OS/2 2.x (or later) applications (and it isn't available for Windows 2000).

Also, because Windows 2000 doesn't allow direct hardware access by user applications, OS/2 programs that contain I/O privilege segments that attempt to perform IN/OUT instructions (to access some hardware device) as well as advanced video I/O (AVIO) aren't supported. Applications that use the CLI/STI instructions are supported—but all the other OS/2 applications in the system and all the other threads in the OS/2 process issuing the CLI instructions are suspended until an STI instruction is executed. Also worth noting is the special support for calling 32-bit DLLs from OS/2 16-bit applications on Windows 2000, which can be useful in porting programs.

The 16-MB memory limitation on native OS/2 1.2 doesn't apply to Windows 2000—the OS/2 subsystem uses the 32-bit virtual address space of Windows 2000 to provide up to 512 MB of memory to OS/2 1.2 applications, as illustrated in Figure 2-5.

Figure 2-5
OS/2 subsystem virtual memory layout

The tiled area is 512 MB of virtual address space that is reserved up front and then committed or decommitted when 16-bit applications need segments. The OS/2 subsystem maintains a local descriptor table (LDT) for each process, with shared memory segments at the same LDT slot for all OS/2 processes.

As we'll discuss in detail in Chapter 6, threads are the elements of a program that execute, and as such they must be scheduled for processor time. Although Windows 2000 priority levels range from 0 through 31, the 64 OS/2 priority levels (0 through 63) are mapped to Windows 2000 dynamic priorities 1 through 15. OS/2 threads never receive Windows 2000 real-time priorities 16 through 31.

As with the POSIX subsystem, the OS/2 subsystem starts automatically the first time you activate a compatible OS/2 image. It remains running until the system is rebooted.

For more information on how Windows 2000 handles running POSIX and OS/2 applications, see the section "Flow of *CreateProcess*" beginning on page 304 in Chapter 6 of this book.

Ntdll.dll

Ntdll.dll is a special system support library primarily for the use of subsystem DLLs. It contains two types of functions:

- System service dispatch stubs to Windows 2000 executive system services

- Internal support functions used by subsystems, subsystem DLLs, and other native images

The first group of functions provides the interface to the Windows 2000 executive system services that can be called from user mode. There are more than 200 such functions, such as *NtCreateFile*, *NtSetEvent*, and so on. As noted earlier, most of the capabilities of these functions are accessible through the Win32 API. (A number are not, however, and are for Microsoft internal use only.)

For each of these functions, Ntdll contains an entry point with the same name. The code inside the function contains the architecture-specific instruction that causes a transition into kernel mode to invoke the system service dispatcher (explained in more detail in Chapter 3), which after verifying some parameters, calls the actual kernel-mode system service that contains the real code inside Ntoskrnl.exe.

Ntdll also contains many support functions, such as the image loader (functions that start with *Ldr*), the heap manager, and Win32 subsystem process communication functions (functions that start with *Csr*), as well as general run-time library routines (functions that start with *Rtl*). It also contains the user-mode asynchronous procedure call (APC) dispatcher and exception dispatcher. (APCs and exceptions are explained in Chapter 3.)

Executive

The Windows 2000 executive is the upper layer of Ntoskrnl.exe. (The kernel is the lower layer.) The executive includes the following types of functions:

- Functions that are exported and callable from user mode. These functions are called *system services* and are exported via Ntdll. Most of the services are accessible through the Win32 API or the APIs of another environment subsystem. A few services, however, aren't available through any documented subsystem function. (Examples include LPCs and various query functions such as *NtQueryInformationxxx*, specialized functions such as *NtCreatePagingFile*, and so on.)

- Functions that can be called only from kernel mode that are exported and documented in the Windows 2000 DDK or Windows 2000 Installable File System (IFS) Kit. (For information on the Windows 2000 IFS Kit, go to *www.microsoft.com/ddk/ifskit.*)

- Functions that are exported and callable from kernel mode but are not documented in the Windows 2000 DDK or IFS Kit (such as the functions called by the boot video driver, which start with *Inbv*).

- Functions that are defined as global symbols but are not exported. These would include internal support functions called within Ntoskrnl, such as those that start with *Iop* (internal I/O manager support functions) or *Mi* (internal memory management support functions).

- Functions that are internal to a module that are not defined as global symbols.

The executive contains the following major components, each of which is covered in detail in a subsequent chapter of this book:

- The *configuration manager* (explained in Chapter 5) is responsible for implementing and managing the system registry.

- The *process and thread manager* (explained in Chapter 6) creates and terminates processes and threads. The underlying support for processes and threads is implemented in the Windows 2000 kernel; the executive adds additional semantics and functions to these lower-level objects.

- The *security reference monitor* (described in Chapter 8) enforces security policies on the local computer. It guards operating system resources, performing run-time object protection and auditing.

- The *I/O manager* (explained in Chapter 9) implements device-independent I/O and is responsible for dispatching to the appropriate device drivers for further processing.

- The *Plug and Play* (PnP) *manager* (explained in Chapter 9) determines which drivers are required to support a particular device and loads those drivers. It retrieves the hardware resource requirements for each device during enumeration. Based on the resource requirements of each device, the PnP manager assigns the appropriate hardware resources such as I/O ports, IRQs, DMA channels, and memory locations. It is also responsible for sending proper event notification for device changes (addition or removal of a device) on the system.

- The *power manager* (explained in Chapter 9) coordinates power events and generates power management I/O notifications to device drivers. When the system is idle, the power manager can be configured to reduce power consumption by putting the CPU to sleep. Changes in power consumption by individual devices are handled by device drivers but are coordinated by the power manager.

- The *WDM Windows Management Instrumentation routines* (explained in Chapter 5) enable device drivers to publish performance and configuration information and receive commands from the user-mode WMI service. Consumers of WMI information can be on the local machine or remote across the network.

- The *cache manager* (explained in Chapter 11) improves the performance of file-based I/O by causing recently referenced disk data to reside in main memory for quick access (and by deferring disk writes by holding the updates in memory for a short time before sending them to the disk). As you'll see, it does this by using the memory manager's support for mapped files.

■ The *virtual memory manager* (explained in Chapter 7) implements *virtual memory,* a memory management scheme that provides a large, private address space for each process that can exceed available physical memory. The memory manager also provides the underlying support for the cache manager.

In addition, the executive contains four main groups of support functions that are used by the executive components just listed. About a third of these support functions are documented in the DDK because device drivers also use them. These are the four categories of support functions:

■ The *object manager,* which creates, manages, and deletes Windows 2000 executive objects and abstract data types that are used to represent operating system resources such as processes, threads, and the various synchronization objects. The object manager is explained in Chapter 3.

■ The *LPC facility* (explained in Chapter 3) passes messages between a client process and a server process on the same computer. LPC is a flexible, optimized version of *remote procedure call* (RPC), an industry-standard communication facility for client and server processes across a network.

■ A broad set of common *run-time library* functions, such as string processing, arithmetic operations, data type conversion, and security structure processing.

■ *Executive support routines,* such as system memory allocation (paged and nonpaged pool), interlocked memory access, as well as two special types of synchronization objects: resources and fast mutexes.

Kernel

The kernel consists of a set of functions in Ntoskrnl.exe that provide fundamental mechanisms (such as thread scheduling and synchronization services) used by the executive components, as well as low-level hardware architecture-dependent

support (such as interrupt and exception dispatching), that are different on each processor architecture. The kernel code is written primarily in C, with assembly code reserved for those tasks that require access to specialized processor instructions and registers not easily accessible from C.

Like the various executive support functions mentioned in the preceding section, a number of functions in the kernel are documented in the DDK (search for functions beginning with *Ke*) because they are needed to implement device drivers.

Kernel Objects

The kernel provides a low-level base of well-defined, predictable operating system primitives and mechanisms that allow higher-level components of the executive to do what they need to do. The kernel separates itself from the rest of the executive by implementing operating system mechanisms and avoiding policy making. It leaves nearly all policy decisions to the executive, with the exception of thread scheduling and dispatching, which the kernel implements.

Outside the kernel, the executive represents threads and other shareable resources as objects. These objects require some policy overhead, such as object handles to manipulate them, security checks to protect them, and resource quotas to be deducted when they are created. This overhead is eliminated in the kernel, which implements a set of simpler objects, called *kernel objects,* that help the kernel control central processing and support the creation of executive objects. Most executive-level objects encapsulate one or more kernel objects, incorporating their kernel-defined attributes.

One set of kernel objects, called *control objects,* establishes semantics for controlling various operating system functions. This set includes the APC object, the *deferred procedure call* (DPC) object, and several objects the I/O manager uses, such as the interrupt object.

Another set of kernel objects, known as *dispatcher objects,* incorporates synchronization capabilities that alter or affect thread scheduling. The dispatcher objects include the kernel thread, mutex (called *mutant* internally), event, kernel event pair, semaphore, timer, and waitable timer. The executive uses kernel functions to create instances of kernel objects, to manipulate them, and to construct the more complex objects it provides to user mode. Objects are explained in more detail in Chapter 3, and processes and threads are described in Chapter 6.

Hardware Support

The other major job of the kernel is to abstract or isolate the executive and device drivers from variations between the hardware architectures supported by Windows 2000. This job includes handling variations in functions such as interrupt handling, exception dispatching, and multiprocessor synchronization.

Even for these hardware-related functions, the design of the kernel attempts to maximize the amount of common code. The kernel supports a set of interfaces that are portable and semantically identical across architectures. Most of the code that implements this portable interface is also identical across architectures.

Some of these interfaces are implemented differently on different architectures, however, or some of the interfaces are partially implemented with architecture-specific code. These architecturally independent interfaces can be called on any machine, and the semantics of the interface will be the same whether or not the code varies by architecture. Some kernel interfaces (such as spinlock routines, which are described in Chapter 3) are actually implemented in the HAL (described in the next section) because their implementation can vary for systems within the same architecture family.

The kernel also contains a small amount of code with x86-specific interfaces needed to support old MS-DOS programs. These x86 interfaces aren't portable in the sense that they can't be called on a machine based on any other architecture; they won't be present. This x86-specific code, for example, supports calls to manipulate global descriptor tables (GDTs) and LDTs, hardware features of the x86.

Other examples of architecture-specific code in the kernel include the interface to provide translation buffer and CPU cache support. This support requires different code for the different architectures because of the way caches are implemented.

Another example is context switching. Although at a high level the same algorithm is used for thread selection and context switching (the context of the previous thread is saved, the context of the new thread is loaded, and the new thread is started), there are architectural differences among the implementations on different processors. Because the context is described by the processor state (registers and so on), what is saved and loaded varies depending on the architecture.

Hardware Abstraction Layer

As mentioned at the beginning of this chapter, one of the crucial elements of the Windows 2000 design is its portability across a variety of hardware platforms. The hardware abstraction layer (HAL) is a key part of making this portability possible. The HAL is a loadable kernel-mode module (Hal.dll) that provides the low-level interface to the hardware platform on which Windows 2000 is running. It hides hardware-dependent details such as I/O interfaces, interrupt controllers, and multiprocessor communication mechanisms—any functions that are both architecture-specific and machine-dependent.

So rather than access hardware directly, Windows 2000 internal components as well as user-written device drivers maintain portability by calling the HAL routines when they need platform-dependent information. For this reason, the HAL routines are documented in the Windows 2000 DDK. To find out more about the HAL and its use by device drivers, refer to the DDK.

Although several HALs are included on the Windows 2000 CD (see Table 2-5), only one is chosen at installation time and copied to the system disk with the filename Hal.dll. (Other operating systems, such as VMS, select the equivalent of the HAL at system boot time.) Therefore, you can't assume that a system disk from one x86 installation will boot on a different processor if the HAL that supports the other processor is different.

Table 2-5 List of HALs

HAL File Name	Systems Supported
Hal.dll	Standard PCs
Halacpi.dll	Advanced Configuration and Power Interface (ACPI) PCs
Halapic.dll	Advanced Programmable Interrupt Controller (APIC) PCs
Halaacpi.dll	APIC ACPI PCs
Halmps.dll	Multiprocessor PCs
Halmacpi.dll	Multiprocessor ACPI PCs
Halborg.dll	Silicon Graphics Workstation (no longer marketed)
Halsp.dll	Compaq SystemPro

EXPERIMENT: Determining Which HAL You're Running

There are two ways to determine which HAL you're running:

1. Open the file \Winnt\Repair\Setup.log, search for *Hal.dll*, and look at the filename after the equals sign. This is the name of the HAL on the distribution media extracted from Driver.cab.

2. In Device Manager (right-click on the My Computer icon on your desktop, select Properties, click on the Hardware tab, and then click Device Manager), look at the name of the "driver" under the Computer device type. For example, the following screen shot is from a system running the ACPI HAL:

Device Drivers

Although device drivers are explained in detail in Chapter 9, this section provides a brief overview of the types of drivers and explains how to list the drivers installed and loaded on your system.

Device drivers are loadable kernel-mode modules (typically ending in .sys) that interface between the I/O manager and the relevant hardware. They run in kernel mode in one of three contexts:

- In the context of the user thread that initiated an I/O function

- In the context of a kernel-mode system thread

- As a result of an interrupt (and therefore not in the context of any particular process or thread—whichever process or thread was current when the interrupt occurred)

As stated in the preceding section, device drivers in Windows 2000 don't manipulate hardware directly, but rather they call functions in the HAL to interface with the hardware. Drivers are typically written in C (sometimes C++) and therefore, with proper use of HAL routines, can be source code portable across the CPU architectures supported by Windows 2000 and binary portable within an architecture family.

There are several types of device drivers:

- *Hardware device drivers* manipulate hardware (using the HAL) to write output to or retrieve input from a physical device or network. There are many types of hardware device drivers, such as bus drivers, human interface drivers, mass storage drivers, and so on.

- *File system drivers* are Windows 2000 drivers that accept file-oriented I/O requests and translate them into I/O requests bound for a particular device.

- *File system filter drivers,* such as those that perform disk mirroring and encryption, intercept I/Os and perform some added-value processing before passing the I/O to the next layer.

- *Network redirectors* and *servers* are file system drivers that transmit file system I/O requests to a machine on the network and receive such requests, respectively.

- *Protocol drivers* implement a networking protocol such as TCP/IP, NetBEUI, and IPX/SPX.

- *Kernel streaming filter drivers* are chained together to perform signal processing on data streams, such as recording or displaying audio and video.

Because installing a device driver is the only way to add user-written kernel-mode code to the system, some programmers have written device drivers simply as a way to access internal operating system functions or data structures that are not accessible from user mode (but that are documented and supported in the DDK). For example, many of the utilities from *www.sysinternals.com* combine a Win32 GUI application and a device driver that is used to gather internal system state not accessible from the Win32 API.

Windows 2000 Device Driver Enhancements

Windows 2000 adds support for Plug and Play, Power Options, and an extension to the Windows NT driver model called the Windows Driver Model (WDM). Windows 2000 can run legacy Windows NT 4 drivers, but because these don't

support Plug and Play and Power Options, systems running these drivers will have reduced capabilities in these two areas.

From the WDM perspective, there are three kinds of drivers:

- A *bus driver* services a bus controller, adapter, bridge, or any device that has child devices. Bus drivers are required drivers, and Microsoft generally provides them; each type of bus (such as PCI, PCMCIA, and USB) on a system has one bus driver. Third parties can write bus drivers to provide support for new buses, such as VMEbus, Multibus, and Futurebus.

- A *function driver* is the main device driver and provides the operational interface for its device. It is a required driver unless the device is used raw (an implementation in which I/O is done by the bus driver and any bus filter drivers, such as SCSI PassThru). A function driver is by definition the driver that knows the most about a particular device, and it is usually the only driver that accesses device-specific registers.

- A *filter driver* is used to add functionality to a device (or existing driver) or to modify I/O requests or responses from other drivers (often used to fix hardware that provides incorrect information about its hardware resource requirements). Filter drivers are optional and can exist in any number, placed above or below a function driver and above a bus driver. Usually, system original equipment manufacturers (OEMs) or independent hardware vendors (IHVs) supply filter drivers.

In the WDM driver environment, no single driver controls all aspects of a device: a bus driver is concerned with reporting the devices on its bus to the PnP manager, while a function driver manipulates the device.

In most cases, lower-level filter drivers modify the behavior of device hardware. For example, if a device reports to its bus driver that it requires four I/O ports when it actually requires 16 I/O ports, a lower-level device-specific function filter driver could intercept the list of hardware resources reported by the bus driver to the PnP manager, and update the count of I/O ports.

Upper-level filter drivers usually provide added-value features for a device. For example, an upper-level device filter driver for a keyboard can enforce additional security checks.

Interrupt processing is explained in Chapter 3. Further details about the I/O manager, WDM, Plug and Play, and Power Options are included in Chapter 9.

69

EXPERIMENT: Viewing the Installed Device Drivers

You can list the installed drivers by running Computer Management. (From the Start menu, select Programs, Administrative Tools, and then Computer Management; or from Control Panel, open Administrative Tools and select Computer Management.) From within Computer Management, expand System Information and then Software Environment, and open Drivers. Here's an example output of the list of installed drivers:

This window displays the list of device drivers defined in the registry, their type, and their state (Running or Stopped). Device drivers and Win32 service processes are both defined in the same place: HKLM\SYSTEM\CurrentControlSet\Services. However, they are distinguished by a type code—type 1 is a kernel-mode device driver, and type 2 is a file system driver. For further details on the information stored in the registry for device drivers, see the Technical Reference to the Windows 2000 Registry help file (Regentry.chm) in the Windows 2000 resource kits under the topic HKEY_LOCAL_MACHINE\SYSTEM\CurrentControlSet\Services.

Alternatively, you list the currently loaded device drivers with the Drivers utility (Drivers.exe in the Windows 2000 resource kits) or the Pstat utility (Pstat.exe in the Platform SDK). Here is a partial output from the Drivers utility:

```
C:\>drivers
  ModuleName    Code    Data  Bss    Paged    Init        LinkDate
------------------------------------------------------------------
ntoskrnl.exe  429184   96896   0    775360   138880   Tue Dec 07 18:41:11 1999
    hal.dll    25856    6016   0     16160    10240   Tue Nov 02 20:14:22 1999
BOOTVID.DLL     5664    2464   0         0      320   Wed Nov 03 20:24:33 1999
   ACPI.sys    92096    8960   0     43488     4448   Wed Nov 10 20:06:04 1999
```

```
    WMILIB.SYS    512       0    0     1152     192  Sat Sep 25 14:36:47 1999
      pci.sys   12704    1536    0    31264    4608  Wed Oct 27 19:11:08 1999
    isapnp.sys  14368     832    0    22944    2048  Sat Oct 02 16:00:35 1999
  compbatt.sys   2496       0    0     2880    1216  Fri Oct 22 18:32:49 1999
     BATTC.SYS    800       0    0     2976     704  Sun Oct 10 19:45:37 1999
  intelide.sys   1760      32    0        0     128  Thu Oct 28 19:20:03 1999
   PCIIDEX.SYS   4544     480    0    10944    1632  Wed Oct 27 19:02:19 1999
    pcmcia.sys  32800    8864    0    23680    6240  Fri Oct 29 19:20:08 1999
    ftdisk.sys   4640      32    0    95072    3392  Mon Nov 22 14:36:23 1999
  :
  -------------------------------------------------------------------------
     Total 4363360  580320    0  3251424  432992
```

Each loaded kernel-mode component (Ntoskrnl, the HAL, as well as device drivers) is shown, along with the sizes of the sections in each image.

The Pstat utility also shows the loaded driver list, but only after it first displays the process list and the threads in each process. Pstat includes one important piece of information that the Drivers utility doesn't: the load address of the module in system space. As we'll explain later, this address is crucial to mapping running system threads to the device driver in which they exist.

Peering into Undocumented Interfaces

Just examining the names of the exported or global symbols in key system images (such as Ntoskrnl.exe, Hal.dll, or Ntdll.dll) can be enlightening—you can get an idea of the kinds of things Windows 2000 can do versus what happens to be documented and supported today. Of course, just because you know the names of these functions doesn't mean that you can or should call them—the interfaces are undocumented and are subject to change. We suggest that you look at these functions purely to gain more insight into the kinds of internal functions Windows 2000 performs, not to bypass supported interfaces.

For example, looking at the list of functions in Ntdll.dll gives you the list of all the system services that Windows 2000 provides to user-mode subsystem DLLs versus the subset that each subsystem exposes. Although many of these functions map clearly to documented and supported Win32 functions, several are not exposed via the Win32 API. (See the article "Inside the Native API" from *www.sysinternals.com*, a copy of which is on this book's companion CD.)

Conversely, it's also interesting to examine the imports of Win32 subsystem DLLs (such as Kernel32.dll or Advapi32.dll) and which functions they call in Ntdll.

Another interesting image to dump is Ntoskrnl.exe—although many of the exported routines that kernel-mode device drivers use are documented in the Windows 2000 DDK, quite a few are not. You might also find it interesting to take a look at the import table for Ntoskrnl and the HAL; this table shows the list of functions in the HAL that Ntoskrnl uses and vice versa.

Table 2-6 lists most of the commonly used function name prefixes for the executive components. Each of these major executive components also uses a variation of the prefix to denote internal functions—either the first letter of the prefix followed by an *i* (for *internal*) or the full prefix followed by a *p* (for *private*). For example, *Ki* represents internal kernel functions, and *Psp* refers to internal process support functions.

Table 2-6 **Commonly Used Prefixes**

Prefix	Component
Cc	Cache manager
Cm	Configuration manager
Ex	Executive support routines
FsRtl	File system driver run-time library
Hal	Hardware abstraction layer
Io	I/O manager
Ke	Kernel
Lpc	Local Procedure Call
Lsa	Local security authentication
Mm	Memory manager
Nt	Windows 2000 system services (most of which are exported as Win32 functions)
Ob	Object manager
Po	Power manager
Pp	PnP manager
Ps	Process support
Rtl	Run-time library
Se	Security
Wmi	Windows Management Instrumentation
Zw	Mirror entry point for system services (beginning with *Nt*) that sets previous access mode to kernel, which eliminates parameter validation, since *Nt* system services validate parameters only if previous access mode is user

EXPERIMENT: Listing Undocumented Functions

You can dump the export and import tables of an image by using the Dependency Walker tool (Depends.exe), which is contained in the Windows 2000 Support Tools and the Platform SDK. To examine an image in the Dependency Walker, select Open from the File menu to open the desired image file.

Here is a sample of output you can see by viewing the dependencies of Ntoskrnl using this tool:

Notice that Ntoskrnl is linked against the HAL, which is in turn linked against Ntoskrnl. (They both use functions in each other.) Ntoskrnl is also linked against Bootvid.dll, the boot video driver that is used to display the new GUI startup screen in Windows 2000.

For a detailed description of the information displayed by this tool, see the Dependency Walker help file (Depends.hlp).

You can decipher the names of these exported functions more easily if you understand the naming convention for Windows 2000 system routines. The general format is:

```
<Prefix><Operation><Object>
```

In this format, *Prefix* is the internal component that exports the routine, *Operation* tells what is being done to the object or resource, and *Object* identifies what is being operated on.

For example, *ExAllocatePoolWithTag* is the executive support routine to allocate from paged or nonpaged pool. *KeInitializeThread* is the routine that allocates and sets up a kernel thread object.

System Processes

The following system processes appear on every Windows 2000 system. (Two of these—Idle and System—are not full processes, as they are not running a user-mode executable.)

- Idle process (contains one thread per CPU to account for idle CPU time)

- System process (contains the majority of the kernel-mode system threads)

- Session manager (Smss.exe)

- Win32 subsystem (Csrss.exe)

- Logon process (Winlogon.exe)

- Service control manager (Services.exe) and the child service processes it creates

- Local security authentication server (Lsass.exe)

To help you understand the relationship of these processes, use the *tlist /t* command in the Windows 2000 Support Tools to display the process "tree," that is, the parent/child relationship between processes. Here is a partial annotated output from *tlist /t*:

```
System Process (0)              Idle process
System (8)                      System process (default home for system threads)
  smss.exe (144)                Session Manager
    csrss.exe (172)             Win32 subsystem process
    winlogon.exe (192)          Logon process (also contains NetDDE service)
      services.exe (220)        Service control manager
        svchost.exe (384)       Generic service host image
        spoolsv.exe (480)       Spooler service
        regsvc.exe (636)        Remote registry service
        mstask.exe (664)        Task Scheduler service
      lsass.exe (232)           Local security authentication server
```

The next sections explain the key system processes shown in this output. Although these sections briefly indicate the order of process startup, Chapter 4 contains a detailed description of the steps involved in booting and starting Windows 2000.

Idle Process

Despite the name shown, the first process listed in the preceding sample *tlist /t* output (process ID 0) is actually the System Idle process. As we'll explain in Chapter 6, processes are identified by their image name. However, this process (as well as process ID 8, named System) isn't running a real user-mode image. Hence, the names shown by the various system display utilities differ from utility to utility. Although most utilities call process ID 8 "System," not all do. Table 2-7 lists several of the names given to the Idle process (process ID 0). The Idle process is explained in detail in Chapter 6.

Table 2-7 Names for Process ID 0 in Various Utilities

Utility	Name for Process ID 0
Task Manager	System Idle Process
Process Viewer (Pviewer.exe)	Idle
Process Status (Pstat.exe)	Idle Process
Process Explode (Pview.exe)	System Process
Task List (Tlist.exe)	System Process
QuickSlice (Qslice.exe)	Systemprocess

Now let's look at system threads and the purpose of each of the system processes that are running real images.

System Process and System Threads

The System process (always process ID 8) is the home for a special kind of thread that runs only in kernel mode: a *kernel-mode system thread*. System threads have all the attributes and contexts of regular user-mode threads (such as a hardware context, priority, and so on) but are different in that they run only in kernel-mode executing code loaded in system space, whether that is in Ntoskrnl.exe

or in any other loaded device driver. In addition, system threads don't have a user process address space and hence must allocate any dynamic storage from operating system memory heaps, such as paged or nonpaged pool.

System threads are created by the *PsCreateSystemThread* function (documented in the DDK), which can be called only from kernel mode. Windows 2000 as well as various device drivers create system threads during system initialization to perform operations that require thread context, such as issuing and waiting for I/Os or other objects or polling a device. For example, the memory manager uses system threads to implement such functions as writing dirty pages to the page file or mapped files, swapping processes in and out of memory, and so forth. The kernel creates a system thread called the *balance set manager* that wakes up once per second to possibly initiate various scheduling and memory management–related events. The cache manager also uses system threads to implement both read-ahead and write-behind I/Os. The file server device driver (Srv.sys) uses system threads to respond to network I/O requests for file data on disk partitions shared to the network. Even the floppy driver has a system thread to poll the floppy device (polling is more efficient in this case because an interrupt-driven floppy driver consumes a large amount of system resources). Further information on specific system threads is included in the chapters in which the component is described.

By default, system threads are owned by the System process, but a device driver can create a system thread in any process. For example, the Win32 subsystem device driver (Win32k.sys) creates system threads in the Win32 subsystem process (Csrss.exe) so that they can easily access data in the user-mode address space of that process.

When you're troubleshooting or going through a system analysis, it's useful to be able to map the execution of individual system threads back to the driver or even to the subroutine that contains the code. For example, on a heavily loaded file server, the System process will likely be consuming considerable CPU time. But the knowledge that when the System process is running "some system thread" is running isn't enough to determine which device driver or operating system component is running.

So if the System process is running, look at the execution of the threads within that process (for example, with the Performance tool). Once you find the thread (or threads) that is running, look up in which driver the system thread began execution (which at least tells you which driver likely created the thread) or examine the call stack (or at least the current address) of the thread in question, which would indicate where the thread is currently executing.

Both of these techniques are illustrated in the following experiments.

EXPERIMENT: Identifying System Threads in the System Process

You can see that the threads inside the System process must be kernel-mode system threads because the start address for each thread is greater than the start address of system space (which by default begins at 0x80000000, unless the system was booted with the /3GB Boot.ini switch). Also, if you look at the CPU time for these threads, you'll see that those that have accumulated any CPU time have run only in kernel mode.

To find out which driver created the system thread, look up the start address of the thread (which you can display with Pviewer.exe) and look for the driver whose base address is closest to (but before) the start address of the thread. Both the Pstat utility (at the end of its output) as well as the *!drivers* kernel debugger command list the base address of each loaded device driver.

To quickly find the current address of the thread, use the *!stacks 0* command in the kernel debugger. Here is an example output from a live system (using LiveKd):

```
kd> !stacks 0
Proc.Thread  Thread  ThreadState  Blocker
                                  [System]
  8.000004  8146edb0  BLOCKED  ntoskrnl!MmZeroPageThread+0x5f
  8.00000c  8146e730  BLOCKED  ?? Kernel stack not resident ??
  8.000010  8146e4b0  BLOCKED  ntoskrnl!ExpWorkerThread+0x73
  8.000014  8146d030  BLOCKED  ?? Kernel stack not resident ??
  8.000018  8146ddb0  BLOCKED  ntoskrnl!ExpWorkerThread+0x73
  8.00001c  8146db30  BLOCKED  ntoskrnl!ExpWorkerThread+0x73
  8.000020  8146d8b0  BLOCKED  ntoskrnl!ExpWorkerThread+0x73
  8.000024  8146d630  BLOCKED  ntoskrnl!ExpWorkerThread+0x73
  8.000028  8146d3b0  BLOCKED  ntoskrnl!ExpWorkerThread+0x73
  8.00002c  8146c030  BLOCKED  ntoskrnl!ExpWorkerThread+0x73
  8.000030  8146cdb0  BLOCKED  ntoskrnl!ExpWorkerThreadBalanceManager+0x55
  8.000034  8146b470  BLOCKED  ntoskrnl!MiDereferenceSegmentThread+0x44
  8.000038  8146b1f0  BLOCKED  ntoskrnl!MiModifiedPageWriterWorker+0x31
  8.00003c  8146a030  BLOCKED  ntoskrnl!KeBalanceSetManager+0x7e
  8.000040  8146adb0  BLOCKED  ntoskrnl!KeSwapProcessOrStack+0x24
  8.000044  8146a5b0  BLOCKED  ntoskrnl!FsRtlWorkerThread+0x33
  8.000048  8146a330  BLOCKED  ntoskrnl!FsRtlWorkerThread+0x33
  8.00004c  81461030  BLOCKED  ACPI!ACPIWorker+0x46
  8.000050  8143a770  BLOCKED  ntoskrnl!MiMappedPageWriter+0x4d
```

(continued)

EXPERIMENT: Identifying System Threads in the System Process *continued*

```
8.000054   81439730   BLOCKED   dmio!voliod_loop+0x399
8.000058   81436c90   BLOCKED   NDIS!ndisWorkerThread+0x22
8.00005c   813d9170   BLOCKED   ltmdmntt!WakeupTimerThread+0x27
8.000060   813d8030   BLOCKED   ltmdmntt!WriteRegistryThread+0x1c
8.000070   8139c850   BLOCKED   raspptp!MainPassiveLevelThread+0x78
8.000074   8139c5d0   BLOCKED   raspptp!PacketWorkingThread+0xc0
8.00006c   81384030   BLOCKED   rasacd!AcdNotificationRequestThread+0xd8
8.000080   81333330   BLOCKED   rdbss!RxpWorkerThreadDispatcher+0x6f
8.000084   813330b0   BLOCKED   rdbss!RxSpinUpRequestsDispatcher+0x58
8.00008c   81321db0   BLOCKED   ?? Kernel stack not resident ??
8.00015c   81205570   BLOCKED   INO_FLTR+0x68bd
8.000160   81204570   BLOCKED   INO_FLTR+0x80e9
8.000178   811fcdb0   BLOCKED   irda!RxThread+0xfa
8.0002d0   811694f0   BLOCKED   ?? Kernel stack not resident ??
8.0002d4   81168030   BLOCKED   ?? Kernel stack not resident ??
8.000404   811002b0   BLOCKED   rdbss!RxpWorkerThreadDispatcher+0x6f
8.000430   810f4990   READY     parallel!ParallelThread+0x3e
8.00069c   80993030   READY     rdbss!RxpWorkerThreadDispatcher+0x6f
```

The first column is the process ID and thread ID (in the form "process ID.thread ID"). The second column is the current address of the thread. The third column indicates whether the thread is in a wait state, ready state, or running state. (See Chapter 6 for a description of thread states.) The last column is the top-most address on the thread's stack. The information in this last column makes it easy to see which driver each thread started in. For the threads in Ntoskrnl, the name of the function gives a further indication of what the thread is doing.

However, if the thread running is one of the system worker threads (ExpWorkerThread), you still don't really know what the thread is doing, since any device driver can submit work to a system worker thread. Therefore, the only way to trace back worker thread activity is to set a breakpoint at *ExQueueWorkItem*. When you reach the breakpoint, type *!dso work_queue_item esp+4*. This command will dump the first argument to *ExQueueWorkItem* (a work queue structure), which in turn contains the address of the worker routine to be called in the context of the worker thread. Alternatively, you can look at the caller by using the *k* command in the kernel debugger, which displays the current call stack. The current call stack will show the driver that is queuing the work to the worker thread (as opposed to the routine to be called from the worker thread).

EXPERIMENT: Mapping a System Thread to a Device Driver

In this experiment, we'll find the Raw Mouse Input thread, a system thread in the Win32 subsystem device driver (Win32k.sys) that determines which threads should be notified of mouse movements and events. To cause this system thread to run, simply move the mouse back and forth rapidly while monitoring process CPU time (using Task Manager, the Performance tool, or the Windows 2000 resource kit QuickSlice utility), and notice that the Csrss process runs for a short period.

The following steps show how to go down to the thread granularity to find out which driver contains the system thread that is running. Although this example demonstrates system thread activity in the Csrss process, the technique applies to mapping system thread activity in the System process back to the device driver that created the thread.

First, we need to set up the Performance tool to watch the activity of each system thread on the System Monitor:

1. Run the Performance tool.

2. Select System Monitor, and click the Add button (the plus sign on the toolbar).

3. Select the Thread object in the Performance Object drop-down list box.

4. Select the % Processor Time counter (or % Privileged Time—the value will be identical).

5. In the Instances box, scroll down to the thread named csrss/0. Click on this entry, and drag the mouse down until you've selected all the threads in the csrss process. (If you were monitoring threads in the System process, you would select the threads from System/0 through to the last numbered thread in the System process.)

6. Click Add.

7. Your screen at this point should look similar to the screen shot on the following page.

(continued)

EXPERIMENT: Mapping a System Thread to a Device Driver *continued*

8. Click Close.

Now change the vertical scale maximum from 100 to 10. This change will make it easier to see system thread activity because system threads usually run for very brief periods of time. To change the vertical scale, follow these steps:

9. Right-click on the graph.

10. Select Properties.

11. Click on the Graph tab.

12. Change the Vertical Scale Maximum from 100 to 10.

13. Click OK.

Now that we're monitoring the Csrss process, let's generate some activity artificially by moving the mouse around, causing threads in the Win32k.sys device driver to run. Then we'll confirm which driver created the system thread that is running when we move the mouse:

14. Move the mouse rapidly back and forth until you see one or two of the system threads running in the Performance tool's display.

15. Press Ctrl+H to turn on highlighting mode. (This highlights the currently selected counter in white.)

16. Scroll through the counters to identify a thread that was running when you moved the mouse (more than one might have run).

17. Notice the relative thread number in the Instance column on the bottom of the Performance tool's graph window (thread 7 in csrss in the following screen shot).

In this case, thread 7 in csrss ran. Now we need to find the start address of the thread by using Process Viewer in the Windows 2000 Support Tools.

18. Run Process Viewer.

19. Click on the csrss process line in the process display list box.

20. Scroll through the list of threads until you find the thread with the same relative thread number you obtained in step 17.

21. Select this thread.

If you found one of the system threads in csrss, the start address (displayed at the bottom of the Process Viewer window in the Thread Information section) should be 0xa0009cbf. (This address might be different if you're running a newer version of Windows 2000.)

22. Finally, run Pstat.exe, available from the Platform SDK or from *www.reskit.com.*

(continued)

EXPERIMENT: Mapping a System Thread to a Device Driver *continued*

At the end of the output from Pstat is a listing of each loaded device driver, including its start address in system virtual memory. Find the driver that has the closest start address *before* the start address of the thread in question. The following is an excerpt from this last section of the Pstat utility:

```
ModuleName    Load Addr   Code     Data    Paged          LinkDate
-----------------------------------------------------------------------
ntoskrnl.exe  80400000    429184   96896   775360 Tue Dec 07 18:41:11 1999
    hal.dll   80062000    25856    6016    16160 Tue Nov 02 20:14:22 1999
 BOOTVID.DLL  F7410000    5664     2464        0 Wed Nov 03 20:24:33 1999
    ACPI.sys  BFFD8000    92096    8960    43488 Wed Nov 10 20:06:04 1999
  WMILIB.SYS  F75C8000    512      0        1152 Sat Sep 25 14:36:47 1999
     pci.sys  F7000000    12704    1536    31264 Wed Oct 27 19:11:08 1999
  isapnp.sys  F7010000    14368    832     22944 Sat Oct 02 16:00:35 1999
  :
   win32k.sys A0000000    1520960  54944       0 Tue Nov 30 03:51:03 1999
   rdbss.sys  BEC8F000    27808    1952    86656 Tue Nov 30 03:52:29 1999
  mrxsmb.sys  BEBF7000    91616    21824   237568 Tue Nov 30 03:52:10 1999
  :
   ntdll.dll  77F80000    294912   12288   16384 Wed Oct 27 16:06:08 1999
-----------------------------------------------------------------------
    Total                 4375648  547040 3164960
```

The start address of the thread in question, 0xa0009cbf, is clearly part of Win32k.sys, since there is no other driver with a closer start address.

If the address falls within Ntoskrnl.exe, then the thread is executing a subroutine in the main kernel image. This information alone is not enough to determine what the thread is really doing—you need to find out the name of the function at that address. You can do that by looking it up in the list of global symbols contained in the associated symbol table file Ntoskrnl.dbg.

The easiest way to generate the list of global symbols in Ntoskrnl is to start the kernel debugger (either by connecting to a live system or by opening a crash dump file) and type the *x nt!** command in the kernel debugger with just Ntoskrnl.dbg loaded. Before typing the *x nt!** command, use the *.logopen* command to create a log file of your kernel-debugging session. That way, you can save the output in a file and then search for the addresses in question. You can also use the Visual C++ Dumpbin utility (type *dumpbin /symbols ntoskrnl.dbg*), but you then have to search for the address minus the base address of Ntoskrnl, since only the offsets are listed.

> Alternatively, as noted in the previous experiment, the kernel debugger *!stacks 0* command can be used to display the name of the driver and function at the current address for a thread (assuming you have the proper symbols loaded).

Session Manager (Smss)

The Session Manager (\Winnt\System32\Smss.exe) is the first user-mode process created in the system. The kernel-mode system thread that performs the final phase of the initialization of the executive and kernel creates the actual Smss process.

The Session Manager is responsible for a number of important steps in starting Windows 2000, such as opening additional page files, performing delayed file rename and delete operations, and creating system environment variables. It also launches the subsystem processes (normally just Csrss.exe) and the Winlogon process, which in turn creates the rest of the system processes.

Much of the configuration information in the registry that drives the initialization steps of Smss can be found under HKLM\SYSTEM\CurrentControlSet\ Control\Session Manager. You'll find it interesting to examine the kinds of data stored there. (For a description of the keys and values, see the Registry Entries help file, Regentry.chm, in the Windows 2000 resource kits.)

After performing these initialization steps, the main thread in Smss waits forever on the process handles to Csrss and Winlogon. If either of these processes terminates unexpectedly, Smss crashes the system, since Windows 2000 relies on their existence. Meanwhile, Smss waits for requests to load subsystems, new subsystems starting up, and debug events. It also acts as a switch and monitor between applications and debuggers.

Logon (Winlogon)

The Windows 2000 logon process (\Winnt\System32\Winlogon.exe) handles interactive user logons and logoffs. Winlogon is notified of a user logon request when the *secure attention sequence* (SAS) keystroke combination is entered. The default SAS on Windows 2000 is the combination Ctrl+Alt+Delete. The reason for the SAS is to protect users from password-capture programs that simulate the logon process. Once the username and password have been captured, they are sent to the local security authentication server process (described in the next section) to be validated. If they match, Winlogon extracts the value of the Userinit registry value under the registry key HKLM\SOFTWARE\Microsoft\ Windows NT\CurrentVersion\Winlogon and creates a process to run each executable image listed in that value. The default is to run a process named Userinit.exe.

EXPERIMENT: Viewing Multiple Sessions

If Terminal Services are installed, Session Manager creates a separate instance of both Csrss and Winlogon for each connected user session. The list of sessions can be displayed with the *!session* command in the kernel debugger. In the following example, there were three sessions active on the system. (The *!session* command shows only the Csrss.exe process in each session, even though there are more processes in each session.)

```
kd> !session
**** NT ACTIVE SESSION DUMP ****
PROCESS 813531e0  Cid: 00c8    Peb: 7ffdf000  SessionId: 00000000
    DirBase: 03639000  ObjectTable: 81353508  TableSize: 371.
    Image: csrss.exe

PROCESS 81180c80  Cid: 0364    Peb: 7ffdf000  SessionId: 00000001
    DirBase: 00fcc000  ObjectTable: 812c7288  TableSize: 115.
    Image: csrss.exe

PROCESS 811358e0  Cid: 0618    Peb: 7ffdf000  SessionId: 00000002
    DirBase: 040f0000  ObjectTable: 8114bcc8  TableSize: 111.
    Image: csrss.exe
```

This process performs some initialization of the user environment (such as restoring mapped drive letters, running the login script, and applying group policies) and then looks in the registry at the Shell value (under the same Winlogon key referred to previously) and creates a process to run the system-defined shell (by default, Explorer.exe). Then Userinit exits. This is the reason Explorer.exe is shown with no parent—its parent has exited, and as explained earlier, Tlist left-justifies processes whose parent isn't running. (Another way of looking at it is that Explorer is the grandchild of Winlogon.)

The identification and authentication aspects of the logon process are implemented in a replaceable DLL named GINA (Graphical Identification and Authentication). The standard Windows 2000 GINA, Msgina.dll, implements the default Windows 2000 logon interface. However, developers can provide their own GINA DLL to implement other identification and authentication mechanisms in place of the standard Windows 2000 username/password method (such as one based on a voice print). In addition, Winlogon can load additional

network provider DLLs that need to perform secondary authentication. This capability allows multiple network providers to gather identification and authentication information all at one time during normal logon.

Winlogon is active not only during user logon and logoff but also whenever it intercepts the SAS from the keyboard. For example, when you press Ctrl+Alt+Delete while logged in, the Windows Security dialog box comes up, providing the options to log off, start the Task Manager, lock the workstation, shut down the system, and so forth. Winlogon is the process that handles this interaction.

For more details on Winlogon, see Chapter 8.

Local Security Authentication Server (LSASS)

The local security authentication server process (\Winnt\System32\Lsass.exe) receives authentication requests from Winlogon and calls the appropriate authentication package (implemented as a DLL) to perform the actual verification, such as checking whether a password matches what is stored in the active directory or the SAM (the part of the registry that contains the definition of the users and groups).

Upon a successful authentication, Lsass generates an access token object that contains the user's security profile. Winlogon then uses this access token to create the initial shell process. Processes launched from the shell then by default inherit this access token.

For more details about Lsass and security authentication, see Chapter 8. For details on the callable functions that interface with Lsass (the functions that start with *Lsa*), see the documentation in the Platform SDK.

Service Control Manager (SCM)

Recall from earlier in the chapter that "services" on Windows 2000 can refer either to a server process or to a device driver. This section deals with services that are user-mode processes. Services are like UNIX "daemon processes" or VMS "detached processes" in that they can be configured to start automatically at system boot time without requiring an interactive logon. They can also be started manually (such as by running the Services administrative tool or by calling the Win32 *StartService* function). Typically, services do not interact with the logged on user, though there are special conditions when this is possible. (See Chapter 5.)

The service control manager is a special system process running the image \Winnt\System32\Services.exe that is responsible for starting, stopping, and interacting with service processes. Service programs are really just Win32 images

that call special Win32 functions to interact with the service control manager to perform such actions as registering the service's successful startup, responding to status requests, or pausing or shutting down the service. Services are defined in the registry under HKLM\SYSTEM\CurrentControlSet \Services. The resource kit Registry Entries help file (Regentry.chm) documents the subkeys and values for services.

Keep in mind that services have three names: the process name you see running on the system, the internal name in the registry, and the display name shown in the Services administrative tool. (Not all services have a display name— if a service doesn't have a display name, the internal name is shown.) With Windows 2000, services can also have a description field that can contain up to 1024 characters that further detail what the service does.

To map a service process to the services contained in that process, use the *tlist /s* command. Note that there isn't always one-to-one mapping between service process and running services, however, because some services share a process with other services. In the registry, the type code indicates whether the service runs in its own process or shares a process with other services in the image.

A number of Windows 2000 components are implemented as services, such as the spooler, Event Log, Task Scheduler, and various other networking components.

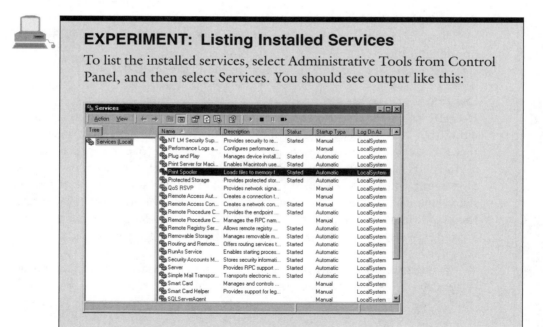

EXPERIMENT: Listing Installed Services

To list the installed services, select Administrative Tools from Control Panel, and then select Services. You should see output like this:

To see the detailed properties about a service, right-click on a service and select Properties. For example, here are the properties for the Print Spooler service (highlighted in the previous figure):

Print Spooler Properties (Local Computer)

General | Log On | Recovery | Dependencies

Service name: Spooler

Display name: Print Spooler

Description: Loads files to memory for later printing.

Path to executable:
C:\WINNT\system32\spoolsv.exe

Startup type: Automatic

Service status: Started

[Start] [Stop] [Pause] [Resume]

You can specify the start parameters that apply when you start the service from here.

Start parameters:

[OK] [Cancel] [Apply]

Notice that the Path To Executable field identifies the program that contains this service. Remember that some services share a process with other services—mapping isn't always one to one.

For more details on services, see Chapter 5.

Conclusion

In this chapter, we've taken a broad look at the overall system architecture of Windows 2000. We've examined the key components of Windows 2000 and seen how they interrelate. In the next chapter, we'll look in more detail at the core system mechanisms that these components are built on, such as the object manager and synchronization.

ntkrnlmp!Ki386CheckDelayedNpxTrap

80432255 5e pop esi 80432256 5b pop ebx 80
20800 ret 0x8 8043225b cc int 3 ntkrnlmp
95150 or [ecx+0x50],edx 8043225f 8b4158
ush ebx 80432263 56 push esi 80432264
b10 mov edx 8916 mov [esi
edx+0x4] 18 mov eax,[ea
ax,[ecx jnz ntkrnlmp
043227 60 mov ex+0x60] 8043 2
043227 02 mov [edx x 8043227e 89
0b9eb00 r [ecx+0xeb]
ax,[ecx+ cmp byte 40f jz ntkrnlmp!
0432290 80 byte ptr [eax+0x3]
dx,[eax+0x18] 80432297 8b401c mov eax,[e
eax],edx 8043229c 894204 mov [edx+0x4],e
ax,[ecx+0xe0] 804322a5 85c0 test eax,eax
tkrnlmp!KiUnwaitThread+0x50 (804322ac)
eax+0x18] 804322ac 8a5133 mov dl,[ecx+0
si,[ecx+0x44] 804322b2 80fa10 cmp dl,0x
tkrnlmp!KiUnwaitThread+0xc2 (804322ie)
x,[ecx+0x] 804322ba 8ad8 test bl,bl 8
tkrnlmp!KiUnwaitThread+0x96 (804322f2)
cx+0x1a],bl 804a000 dec ebx 804b0
s:[00000000]:ecx pop

System Mechanisms

Microsoft Windows 2000 provides several base mechanisms that kernel-mode components such as the executive, the kernel, and device drivers use. This chapter explains the following system mechanisms and describes how they are used:

- Trap dispatching, including interrupts, deferred procedure calls (DPCs), asynchronous procedure calls (APCs), exception dispatching, and system service dispatching

- The executive object manager

- Synchronization, including spinlocks, kernel dispatcher objects, and how waits are implemented

- System worker threads

- Miscellaneous mechanisms such as Windows 2000 global flags

- Local procedure calls (LPCs)

Trap Dispatching

Interrupts and exceptions are operating system conditions that divert the processor to code outside the normal flow of control. Either hardware or software can detect them. The term *trap* refers to a processor's mechanism for capturing an executing thread when an exception or an interrupt occurs and transferring control to a fixed location in the operating system. In Windows 2000, the processor transfers control to a *trap handler,* a function specific to a particular interrupt or exception. Figure 3-1 illustrates some of the conditions that activate trap handlers.

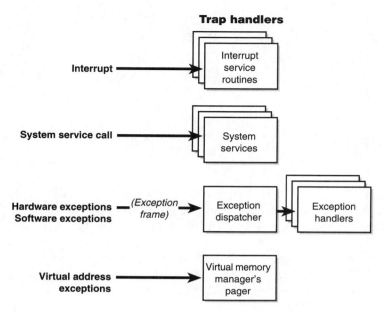

Figure 3-1
Trap dispatching

The kernel distinguishes between interrupts and exceptions in the following way. An *interrupt* is an asynchronous event (one that can occur at any time) that is unrelated to what the processor is executing. Interrupts are generated primarily by I/O devices, processor clocks, or timers, and they can be enabled (turned on) or disabled (turned off). An *exception,* in contrast, is a synchronous condition that results from the execution of a particular instruction. Running a program a second time with the same data under the same conditions can reproduce exceptions. Examples of exceptions include memory access violations, certain debugger instructions, and divide-by-zero errors. The kernel also regards system service calls as exceptions (although technically they're system traps).

Either hardware or software can generate exceptions and interrupts. For example, a bus error exception is caused by a hardware problem, whereas a divide-by-zero exception is the result of a software bug. Likewise, an I/O device can generate an interrupt, or the kernel itself can issue a software interrupt (such as an APC or DPC, described later in this chapter).

When a hardware exception or interrupt is generated, the processor records enough machine state so that it can return to that point in the control flow and continue execution as if nothing had happened. To do this, the processor creates a *trap frame* on the kernel stack of the interrupted thread into which it stores the execution state of the thread. The trap frame is usually a subset of a thread's

complete context. (Thread context is described in Chapter 6.) The kernel handles software interrupts either as part of hardware interrupt handling or synchronously when a thread invokes kernel functions related to the software interrupt.

In most cases, the kernel installs front-end trap handling functions that perform general trap handling tasks before and after transferring control to other functions that field the trap. For example, if the condition was a device interrupt, a kernel hardware interrupt trap handler transfers control to the *interrupt service routine* (ISR) that the device driver provided for the interrupting device. If the condition was caused by a call to a system service, the general system service trap handler transfers control to the specified system service function in the executive. The kernel also installs trap handlers for traps that it doesn't expect to see or doesn't handle. These trap handlers typically execute the system function *KeBugCheckEx*, which halts the computer when the kernel detects problematic or incorrect behavior that, if left unchecked, could result in data corruption. (For more information on bug checks, see the section "System Crashes" beginning on page 206 in Chapter 4.) The following sections describe interrupt, exception, and system service dispatching in greater detail.

Interrupt Dispatching

Hardware-generated interrupts typically originate from I/O devices that must notify the processor when they need service. Interrupt-driven devices allow the operating system to get the maximum use out of the processor by overlapping central processing with I/O operations. A thread starts an I/O transfer to or from a device and then can execute other useful work while the device completes the transfer. When the device is finished, it interrupts the processor for service. Pointing devices, printers, keyboards, disk drives, and network cards are generally interrupt driven.

System software can also generate interrupts. For example, the kernel can issue a software interrupt to initiate thread dispatching and to asynchronously break into the execution of a thread. The kernel can also disable interrupts so that the processor isn't interrupted, but it does so only infrequently—at critical moments while it's processing an interrupt or dispatching an exception, for example.

The kernel installs interrupt trap handlers to respond to device interrupts. Interrupt trap handlers transfer control either to an external routine (the ISR) that handles the interrupt or to an internal kernel routine that responds to the interrupt. Device drivers supply ISRs to service device interrupts, and the kernel provides interrupt handling routines for other types of interrupts.

In the following subsections, you'll find out how the hardware notifies the processor of device interrupts, the types of interrupts the kernel supports,

the way device drivers interact with the kernel (as a part of interrupt processing), and the software interrupts the kernel recognizes (plus the kernel objects that are used to implement them).

Hardware Interrupt Processing

On x86 systems, external I/O interrupts come into one of the lines on an interrupt controller. The controller in turn interrupts the processor on a single line. Once the processor is interrupted, it queries the controller to get the *interrupt request* (IRQ). The interrupt controller translates the IRQ to an interrupt number, uses this number as an index into a structure called the *interrupt dispatch table* (IDT), and transfers control to the appropriate interrupt dispatch routine. At system boot time, Windows 2000 fills in the IDT with pointers to the kernel routines that handle each interrupt and exception.

EXPERIMENT: Viewing the IDT

You can view the contents of the IDT, including information on what trap handlers Windows 2000 has assigned to interrupts (including exceptions and IRQs), using the *!idt* command implemented in the Kdex2x86.dll debugger extension library. Passing the *!idt* command a 0 flag shows device driver ISRs that are registered for hardware device interrupts.

The following example shows how you load the Kdex2x86.dll debugger extension library and what the output of the *!idt* command looks like:

```
kd> .load kdex2x86
Loaded kdex2x86 extension DLL
kd> !idt 0
    00: 80463440 (ntkrnlmp!KiTrap00)
    01: 80463590 (ntkrnlmp!KiTrap01)
    02: 0000144e
    03: 8046386c (ntkrnlmp!KiTrap03)
    04: 804639d4 (ntkrnlmp!KiTrap04)
    05: 80463b18 (ntkrnlmp!KiTrap05)
    06: 80463c78 (ntkrnlmp!KiTrap06)
    07: 804641bc (ntkrnlmp!KiTrap07)
    08: 000014a8
    09: 80464558 (ntkrnlmp!KiTrap09)
    0a: 80464660 (ntkrnlmp!KiTrap0A)
    0b: 8046478c (ntkrnlmp!KiTrap0B)
    0c: 80464a90 (ntkrnlmp!KiTrap0C)
```

```
0d: 80464c9c (ntkrnlmp!KiTrap0D)
0e: 80465708 (ntkrnlmp!KiTrap0E)
0f: 80465aac (ntkrnlmp!KiTrap0F)
10: 80465bb4 (ntkrnlmp!KiTrap10)
11: 80465cd8 (ntkrnlmp!KiTrap11)
12: 80465aac (ntkrnlmp!KiTrap0F)
  ⋮
29: 00000000
2a: 804628fe (ntkrnlmp!KiGetTickCount)
2b: 804629f0 (ntkrnlmp!KiCallbackReturn)
2c: 80462b10 (ntkrnlmp!KiSetLowWaitHighThread)
2d: 8046375c (ntkrnlmp!KiDebugService)
2e: 80462420 (ntkrnlmp!KiSystemService)
2f: 80465aac (ntkrnlmp!KiTrap0F)
30: 80461a50 (ntkrnlmp!KiStartUnexpectedRange)
  ⋮
51: 80461b9a (ntkrnlmp!KiUnexpectedInterrupt33)
52: 813dbbe4 (Vector:52,Irql:4,SyncIrql:5,Connected:TRUE, ⮑
            No:0,ShareVector:FALSE,Mode:Latched,         ⮑
            ISR:i8042prt!I8042KeyboardInterruptService(f04b10cc))
53: 80461bae (ntkrnlmp!KiUnexpectedInterrupt35)
54: 80461bb8 (ntkrnlmp!KiUnexpectedInterrupt36)
  ⋮
d0: 80462090 (ntkrnlmp!KiUnexpectedInterrupt160)
d1: 800638d4 (halmps!HalpClockInterrupt)
d2: 804620a4 (ntkrnlmp!KiUnexpectedInterrupt162)
  ⋮
```

Some of the interrupt numbers of interest in the example are in the range 0x0 to 0x10, which includes x86 exception interrupts (for example, a page fault, which is exception 0xe, is handled by *KiTrap0E*) and the range 0x2a to 0x2e, which includes the system service dispatcher and other software interrupts that the kernel uses internally as fast entry points into the kernel from environment subsystems. On the system used to provide the output for this experiment, the clock interrupt handler is at interrupt number 0xd1 and the keyboard device driver's (I8042prt.sys) keyboard ISR is at interrupt number 0x52.

Windows 2000 maps hardware IRQs to interrupt numbers into the IDT, and the system also uses the IDT to configure trap handlers for exceptions. For example, the x86 exception number for a page fault (an exception that occurs when a thread attempts to access a page of virtual memory that isn't defined or present) is 0xe. Thus, entry 0xe in the IDT points to the system's page fault

handler. Although the x86 architecture can support up to 256 IDT entries, the number of IRQs a particular machine can support is determined by the design of the interrupt controller the machine uses.

Most x86 systems rely on either the i8259A Programmable Interrupt Controller (PIC) or a variant of the i82489 Advanced Programmable Interrupt Controller (APIC); the majority of new computers include an APIC. The PIC standard originates with the original IBM PC. PICs work only with uniprocessor systems and have 15 interrupt lines. APICs work with multiprocessor systems and have 256 interrupt lines. Intel and other companies have defined the Multiprocessor Specification (MP Specification), a design standard for x86 multiprocessor systems that centers on the use of APIC. To provide compatibility with uniprocessor operating systems and boot code that starts a multiprocessor system in uniprocessor mode, APICs support a PIC compatibility mode with 15 interrupts and delivery of interrupts to only the primary processor. Figure 3-2 depicts the APIC architecture. The APIC actually consists of several components: an I/O APIC that receives interrupts from devices, local APICs that receive interrupts from the I/O APIC and that interrupt the CPU they are associated with, and an i8259A-compatible interrupt controller that translates APIC input into PIC-equivalent signals. The I/O APIC is responsible for implementing interrupt routing algorithms—which are software-selectable (the HAL makes the selection on Windows 2000)—that both balance the interrupt load across processors and attempt to take advantage of locality, delivering interrupts to the same processor that has just fielded a previous interrupt of the same type.

Figure 3-2
x86 APIC architecture

Each processor has a separate IDT so that different processors can run different ISRs, if appropriate. For example, in a multiprocessor system, each processor receives the clock interrupt, but only one processor updates the system clock in response to this interrupt. All the processors, however, use the interrupt to measure thread quantum and to initiate rescheduling when a thread's quantum ends. Similarly, some system configurations might require that a particular processor handle certain device interrupts.

EXPERIMENT: Viewing the PIC and APIC

You can view the configuration of the PIC on a uniprocessor and the APIC on a multiprocessor by using the *!pic* and *!apic* I386kd (or Kd) commands, respectively. (You can't use LiveKd for this experiment because LiveKd can't access hardware.) Here's the output of the *!pic* command on a uniprocessor. (Note that the *!pic* command doesn't work if your system is using an APIC HAL.)

```
kd> !pic
----- IRQ Number ----- 00 01 02 03 04 05 06 07 08 09 0A 0B 0C 0D 0E 0F
Physically in service:  .  .  .  .  .  .  .  .  .  .  .  .  .  .  .  .
Physically masked:      .  .  .  .  Y  .  Y  Y  .  Y  Y  Y  .  Y  .  Y
Physically requested:   Y  .  .  .  .  .  .  .  .  .  .  .  .  .  .  .
```

Here's the output of the *!apic* command on a system running with the MPS HAL. The "0:" prefix for the I386kd prompt indicates that commands are running on processor 0, so this is the I/O APIC for processor 0:

```
0: kd> !apic
Apic @ fffe0000  ID:1 (40011) LogDesc:01000000 DestFmt:ffffffff  TPR FF
TimeCnt: 03f66780clk  SpurVec:1f  FaultVec:e3  error:80
Ipi Cmd: 000008e1  Vec:E1  FixedDel  Lg:02000000      edg
Timer..: 000300fd  Vec:FD  FixedDel    Dest=Self      edg         masked
Linti0.: 0001001f  Vec:1F  FixedDel    Dest=Self      edg         masked
Linti1.: 000084ff  Vec:FF  NMI         Dest=Self      lvl
TMR: 93, a3
IRR: 41, d1, e3
ISR: d1
```

The following output is for the *!ioapic* command, which displays the configuration of the I/O APIC, the interrupt controller component connected to devices.

(continued)

EXPERIMENT: Viewing the PIC and APIC *continued*

```
0: kd> !ioapic
IoApic @ ffd02000  ID:8 (11)  Arb:0
Inti00.: 000100ff  Vec:FF  FixedDel  PhysDest:00  edg  masked
Inti01.: 00000962  Vec:62  LowestDl  Lg:03000000  edg
Inti02.: 000100ff  Vec:FF  FixedDel  PhysDest:00  edg  masked
Inti03.: 00000971  Vec:71  LowestDl  Lg:03000000  edg
Inti04.: 000100ff  Vec:FF  FixedDel  PhysDest:00  edg  masked
Inti05.: 00000961  Vec:61  LowestDl  Lg:03000000  edg
Inti06.: 00010982  Vec:82  LowestDl  Lg:02000000  edg  masked
Inti07.: 000100ff  Vec:FF  FixedDel  PhysDest:00  edg  masked
Inti08.: 000008d1  Vec:D1  FixedDel  Lg:01000000  edg
Inti09.: 000100ff  Vec:FF  FixedDel  PhysDest:00  edg  masked
Inti0A.: 000100ff  Vec:FF  FixedDel  PhysDest:00  edg  masked
Inti0B.: 000100ff  Vec:FF  FixedDel  PhysDest:00  edg  masked
Inti0C.: 00000972  Vec:72  LowestDl  Lg:03000000  edg
Inti0D.: 000100ff  Vec:FF  FixedDel  PhysDest:00  edg  masked
Inti0E.: 00000992  Vec:92  LowestDl  Lg:03000000  edg
Inti0F.: 000100ff  Vec:FF  FixedDel  PhysDest:00  edg  masked
Inti10.: 000100ff  Vec:FF  FixedDel  PhysDest:00  edg  masked
Inti11.: 000100ff  Vec:FF  FixedDel  PhysDest:00  edg  masked
Inti12.: 000100ff  Vec:FF  FixedDel  PhysDest:00  edg  masked
Inti13.: 000100ff  Vec:FF  FixedDel  PhysDest:00  edg  masked
Inti14.: 0000a9a3  Vec:A3  LowestDl  Lg:03000000  lvl
Inti15.: 0000a993  Vec:93  LowestDl  Lg:03000000  lvl
Inti16.: 000100ff  Vec:FF  FixedDel  PhysDest:00  edg  masked
Inti17.: 000100ff  Vec:FF  FixedDel  PhysDest:00  edg  masked
```

Most of the routines that handle interrupts reside in the kernel. The kernel updates the clock time, for example. However, external devices such as keyboards, pointing devices, and disk drives also generate many interrupts, and device drivers need a way to tell the kernel which routine to call when a device interrupt occurs.

Software Interrupt Request Levels (IRQLs)

Although interrupt controllers perform a level of interrupt prioritization, Windows 2000 imposes its own interrupt priority scheme known as *interrupt request levels* (IRQLs). The kernel represents IRQLs internally as a number from 0 through 31, with higher numbers representing higher-priority interrupts. Although the kernel defines the standard set of IRQLs for software in-

terrupts, the HAL maps hardware-interrupt numbers to the IRQLs. Figure 3-3 shows IRQLs defined for the x86 architecture.

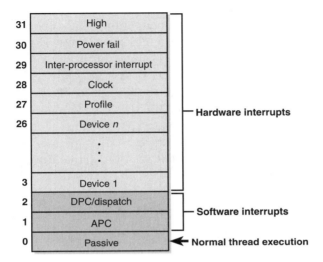

Figure 3-3
Interrupt request levels (IRQLs)

Interrupts are serviced in priority order, and a higher-priority interrupt preempts the servicing of a lower-priority interrupt. When a high-priority interrupt occurs, the processor saves the interrupted thread's state and invokes the trap dispatchers associated with the interrupt. The trap dispatcher raises the IRQL and calls the interrupt's service routine. After the service routine executes, the interrupt dispatcher lowers the processor's IRQL to where it was before the interrupt occurred and then loads the saved machine state. The interrupted thread resumes executing where it left off. When the kernel lowers the IRQL, lower-priority interrupts that were masked might materialize. If this happens, the kernel repeats the process to handle the new interrupts.

IRQL priority levels have a completely different meaning than thread-scheduling priorities (which are described in Chapter 6). A scheduling priority is an attribute of a thread, whereas an IRQL is an attribute of an interrupt source, such as a keyboard or a mouse. In addition, each processor has an IRQL setting that changes as operating system code executes.

EXPERIMENT: Viewing the IRQL

A data structure called the *processor control region* (PCR) and its extension the *processor control block* (PRCB) contain information about the state of each processor in the system, such as the current IRQL, a pointer to the hardware IDT, the currently running thread, and the next thread selected to run. The kernel and the HAL use this information to perform architecture-specific and machine-specific actions. Portions of the PCR and PRCB structures are defined publicly in the Windows 2000 Device Driver Kit (DDK) header file Ntddk.h, so examine that file if you want a complete definition of these structures.

You can view the contents of the PCR with the kernel debugger by using the *!pcr* command:

```
kd> !pcr
PCR Processor 0 @ffdff000
         NtTib.ExceptionList: f8effc68
           NtTib.StackBase: f8effdf0
          NtTib.StackLimit: f8efd000
       NtTib.SubSystemTib: 00000000
             NtTib.Version: 00000000
         NtTib.UserPointer: 00000000
             NtTib.SelfTib: 7ffde000

                   SelfPcr: ffdff000
                      Prcb: ffdff120
                      Irql: 00000000
                       IRR: 00000000
                       IDR: ffff28e8
            InterruptMode: 00000000
                       IDT: 80036400
                       GDT: 80036000
                       TSS: 802b5000

            CurrentThread: 81638020
               NextThread: 00000000
               IdleThread: 8046bdf0
```

Each processor's IRQL setting determines which interrupts that processor can receive. IRQLs are also used to synchronize access to kernel-mode data structures. (You'll find out more about synchronization later in this chapter.) As a kernel-mode thread runs, it raises or lowers the processor's IRQL either directly by calling *KeRaiseIrql* and *KeLowerIrql* or, more commonly, indirectly

via calls to functions that acquire kernel synchronization objects. As Figure 3-4 illustrates, interrupts from a source with an IRQL above the current level interrupt the processor, whereas interrupts from sources with IRQLs equal to or below the current level are *masked* until an executing thread lowers the IRQL.

Figure 3-4
Masking interrupts

Because accessing a PIC is a relatively slow operation, HALs that use a PIC implement a performance optimization, called *lazy IRQL,* that avoids PIC accesses. When the IRQL is raised, the HAL notes the new IRQL internally instead of changing the interrupt mask. If a lower-priority interrupt subsequently occurs, the HAL sets the interrupt mask to the settings appropriate for the first interrupt and postpones the lower-priority interrupt until the IRQL is lowered. Thus, if no lower-priority interrupts occur while the IRQL is raised, the HAL doesn't need to modify the PIC.

A kernel-mode thread raises and lowers the IRQL of the processor on which it's running, depending on what it's trying to do. For example, when an interrupt occurs, the trap handler (or perhaps the processor) raises the processor's IRQL to the assigned IRQL of the interrupt source. This elevation masks all interrupts at and below that IRQL (on that processor only), which ensures that the processor servicing the interrupt isn't waylaid by an interrupt at the same or a lower level. The masked interrupts are either handled by another processor

or held back until the IRQL drops. Therefore, all components of the system, including the kernel and device drivers, attempt to keep the IRQL at passive level (sometimes called low level). They do this because device drivers can respond to hardware interrupts in a timelier manner if the IRQL isn't kept unnecessarily elevated for long periods.

Because changing a processor's IRQL has such a significant effect on system operation, the change can be made only in kernel mode—user-mode threads can't change the processor's IRQL. This means that a processor's IRQL is always at passive level when it's executing user-mode code. Only when the processor is executing kernel-mode code can the IRQL be higher.

Each interrupt level has a specific purpose. For example, the kernel issues an *inter-processor interrupt* (IPI) to request that another processor perform an action, such as dispatching a particular thread for execution or updating its translation look-aside buffer cache. The system clock generates an interrupt at regular intervals, and the kernel responds by updating the clock and measuring thread execution time. If a hardware platform supports two clocks, the kernel adds another clock interrupt level to measure performance. The HAL provides a number of interrupt levels for use by interrupt-driven devices; the exact number varies with the processor and system configuration. The kernel uses software interrupts (described later in this chapter) to initiate thread scheduling and to asynchronously break into a thread's execution.

Mapping interrupts to IRQLs These IRQL levels aren't the same as the interrupt requests (IRQs) of the x86 system—the x86 architecture doesn't implement the concept of IRQLs in hardware. So how does Windows 2000 determine what IRQL to assign to an interrupt? The answer lies in the HAL. In Windows 2000, a type of device driver called a *bus driver* determines the presence of devices on its bus (PCI, USB, and so on) and what interrupts can be assigned to a device. The bus driver reports this information to the Plug and Play manager, which decides, after taking into account the acceptable interrupt assignments for all other devices, which interrupt will be assigned to each device. Then it calls the HAL function *HalpGetSystemInterruptVector*, which maps interrupts to IRQLs.

The algorithm for assignment differs for the uniprocessor and multiprocessor HALs that Windows 2000 includes. On a uniprocessor system, the HAL performs a straightforward translation: the IRQL of a given interrupt vector is calculated by subtracting the interrupt vector from 27. Thus, if a device uses interrupt level 5, its ISR executes at IRQL 22. On a multiprocessor system, the mapping isn't as simple. APICs support over 100 interrupt vectors, so there aren't enough IRQLs for a one-to-one correspondence. The multiprocessor HAL therefore assigns IRQLs to interrupt vectors in a round-robin manner,

cycling through the device IRQL (DIRQL) range. As a result, on a multiprocessor system there's no easy way for you to predict or to know what IRQL Windows 2000 assigns to APIC IRQs. You can use the *!idt* kernel debugger command (shown earlier in the chapter) to view IRQL assignments for hardware interrupts.

Predefined IRQLs Let's take a closer look at the use of the predefined IRQLs, starting from the highest level shown in Figure 3-4:

- The kernel uses *high* level only when it's halting the system in *KeBugCheckEx* and masking out all interrupts.

- *Power fail* level originated in the original Microsoft Windows NT design documents, which specified the behavior of system power failure code, but this IRQL has never been used.

- *Inter-processor interrupt* level is used to request another processor to perform an action, such as dispatching a particular thread for execution, updating the processor's translation look-aside buffer (TLB) cache, system shutdown, or system crash.

- *Clock* level is used for the system's clock, which the kernel uses to track the time of day as well as to measure and allot CPU time to threads.

- The system's real-time clock uses *profile* level when kernel profiling, a performance measurement mechanism, is enabled. When kernel profiling is active, the kernel's profiling trap handler records the address of the code that was executing when the interrupt occurred. A table of address samples is constructed over time that tools can extract and analyze. The Windows 2000 resource kits include a tool called Kernel Profiler (Kernprof.exe) that you can use to configure and view profiling-generated statistics. See the Kernel Profiler experiment for more information on using Kernprof.

- The *device* IRQLs are used to prioritize device interrupts. (See the previous section for how hardware interrupt levels are mapped to IRQLs.)

- *DPC/dispatch*-level and *APC*-level interrupts are software interrupts that the kernel and device drivers generate. (DPCs and APCs are explained in more detail later in this chapter.)

- The lowest IRQL, *passive* level, isn't really an interrupt level at all; it's the setting at which normal thread execution takes place and all interrupts are allowed to occur.

EXPERIMENT: Using Kernel Profiler to Profile Execution

You can use the Kernel Profiler tool that comes with the Windows 2000 resource kits to enable the system profiling timer, collect samples of the code that is executing when the timer fires, and display a summary showing the frequency distribution across image files and functions. Kernel Profiler is most useful in situations in which performance-critical code is running in a repeatable manner and you want to obtain a breakdown of where the system is spending time when the code executes. For the output to be useful, Kernel Profiler requires that the Windows 2000 symbols be installed on your system. Below is sample output from Kernel Profiler after collecting information for 30 seconds on a system that was relatively idle. (Notice that the majority of the samples were in *KiIdleLoop*, the idle thread loop, which is explained in Chapter 6.)

```
C:\kernprof -a -d -x -p -v -t 5 30
Symbols loaded: 80400000  ntoskrnl.exe
⋮
delaying for 30 seconds... report on values with 5 hits
end of delay
Processor 0: 30404 Total hits
30404 Total hits

PROCESSOR 0

  28708          ntoskrnl.exe --Total Hits--
      5   0  ntoskrnl.exe memmove 0x08045AEF0 0 3
      5   0  ntoskrnl.exe ExAcquireResourceExclusiveLite 0x080413A00 0 3
      6   0  ntoskrnl.exe ExReleaseResourceLite 0x080413E5E 0 3
     79   0  ntoskrnl.exe KiXMMIZeroPageNoSave 0x080430B88 0 3
      8   0  ntoskrnl.exe MiInsertPageInList 0x080442E1E 0 3
      6   0  ntoskrnl.exe MiRemovePageByColor 0x080443756 0 3
      6   0  ntoskrnl.exe ObReferenceObjectByHandle 0x08044986C 0 3
  28384   0  ntoskrnl.exe KiIdleLoop 0x08045E98C 0 3
      9   0  ntoskrnl.exe KiSystemService 0x08045F4A0 0 3
      6   0  ntoskrnl.exe ExAllocatePoolWithTag 0x080465080 0 3
      5   0  ntoskrnl.exe SepPrivilegeCheck 0x0804F7638 0 3
      5   0  ntoskrnl.exe IopParseDevice 0x0804B8F20 0 3

    563          hal.dll --Total Hits--
      5   0  hal.dll KfRaiseIrql 0x080062E90 0 2
     22   0  hal.dll KfLowerIrql 0x080062F00 0 2
```

```
    5  0  hal.dll READ_PORT_UCHAR 0x080067960 0 2
   14  0  hal.dll WRITE_PORT_UCHAR 0x0800679C8 0 2
  503  0  hal.dll HalAcpiC1Idle 0x080068334 0 2

    6            atapi.sys --Total Hits--

   15          Fastfat.sys --Total Hits--

  109            Ntfs.sys --Total Hits--
    6  0  Ntfs.SYS NtfsInitializeIrpContext 0x0F99CE432 0 2
   15  0  Ntfs.SYS NtfsCommonWrite 0x0F99CF480 0 2
    7  0  Ntfs.SYS NtfsCommonCleanup 0x0F99D6190 0 2
    7  0  Ntfs.SYS NtfsQueryDirectory 0x0F99DC430 0 2

    8           win32k.sys --Total Hits--

  229            ntdll.dll --Total Hits--
   22  0  ntdll.dll RtlIsValidHandle 0x077F9ADEE 0 2
    5  0  ntdll.dll ZwReleaseSemaphore 0x077F8872C 0 2
   14  0  ntdll.dll RtlpFreeToHeapLookaside 0x077FB0358 0 2
   17  0  ntdll.dll RtlpInterlockedPushEntrySList 0x077FB7620 0 2
    7  0  ntdll.dll RtlTimeToTimeFields 0x077FA7BFE 0 2
    8  0  ntdll.dll RtlEnterCriticalSection 0x077F87B30 0 2
    8  0  ntdll.dll wcslen 0x077FB3D6E 0 2
    8  0  ntdll.dll RtlpAllocateFromHeapLookaside 0x077FB02E4 0 2
   24  0  ntdll.dll RtlpInterlockedPopEntrySList 0x077FB75FC 0 2
   17  0  ntdll.dll RtlpFindAndCommitPages 0x077FC8DF6 0 2
   33  0  ntdll.dll RtlAllocateHeap 0x077FC6BF8 0 2
   21  0  ntdll.dll RtlFreeHeap 0x077FC7426 0 2
    5  0  ntdll.dll RtlAllocateHeap 0x077FC6BF8 0 2

  756          User Mode --Total Hits-- (NO SYMBOLS)

Context Switch Information
    Find any processor         0
    Find last processor        0
    Idle any processor         0
    Idle current processor     0
    Idle last processor        0
    Preempt any processor      0
    Preempt current processor  0
    Preempt last processor     0
    Switch to idle             0

    Total context switches    3255
```

One important restriction on code running at DPC/dispatch level or above is that it can't wait on an object if doing so would necessitate the scheduler to select another thread to execute. Another restriction is that only nonpaged memory can be accessed at IRQL DPC/dispatch level or higher. This rule is actually a side effect of the first restriction because attempting to access memory that isn't resident results in a page fault. When a page fault occurs, the memory manager initiates a disk I/O and then needs to wait for the file system driver to read the page in from disk. This wait would in turn require the scheduler to perform a context switch (perhaps to the idle thread if no user thread is waiting to run), thus violating the rule that the scheduler can't be invoked (because the IRQL is still DPC/dispatch level or higher at the time of the disk read). If either of these two restrictions is violated, the system crashes with an IRQL_NOT_LESS_OR_EQUAL crash code. (See Chapter 4 for a thorough discussion of system crashes.) Violating these restrictions is a common bug in device drivers. The Windows 2000 Driver Verifier, explained in the section "Driver Verifier" in Chapter 7 (page 413), has an option you can set to assist in finding this particular type of bug.

Interrupt objects　　The kernel provides a portable mechanism—a kernel control object called an *interrupt object*—that allows device drivers to register ISRs for their devices. An interrupt object contains all the information the kernel needs to associate a device ISR with a particular level of interrupt, including the address of the ISR, the IRQL at which the device interrupts, and the entry in the kernel's IDT with which the ISR should be associated. When an interrupt object is initialized, a few instructions of assembly language code, called the *dispatch code,* are copied from an interrupt handling template, *KiInterruptTemplate,* and stored in the object. When an interrupt occurs, this code is executed.

This interrupt-object resident code calls the real interrupt dispatcher, the kernel's *KiInterruptDispatch* routine, passing it a pointer to the interrupt object. The interrupt object contains information this second dispatcher routine needs in order to locate and properly call the ISR the device driver provides.

The interrupt object also stores the IRQL associated with the interrupt so that another routine, *KiDispatchInterrupt,* can raise the IRQL to the correct level before calling the ISR and then lower the IRQL after the ISR has returned. This two-step process is required because there's no way to pass a pointer to the interrupt object (or any other argument for that matter) on the initial dispatch since the initial dispatch is done by hardware. On a multiprocessor system, the kernel allocates and initializes an interrupt object for each CPU, enabling the local APIC on that CPU to accept the particular interrupt.

Windows 2000 and Real-Time Processing

Deadline requirements, either hard or soft, characterize real-time environments. Hard real-time systems (for example, a nuclear power plant control system) have deadlines that the system must meet to avoid catastrophic failures such as loss of equipment or life. Soft real-time systems (for example, a car's fuel-economy optimization system) have deadlines that the system can miss, but timeliness is still a desirable trait. In real-time systems, computers have sensor input devices and control output devices. The designer of a real-time computer system must know worst-case delays between the time an input device generates an interrupt and the time the device's driver can control the output device to respond. This worst-case analysis must take into account the delays the operating system introduces as well as the delays the application and device drivers impose.

Because Windows 2000 doesn't prioritize device IRQs in any controllable way and user-level applications execute only when a processor's IRQL is at passive level, Windows 2000 isn't always suitable as a real-time operating system. The system's devices and device drivers—not Windows 2000—ultimately determine the worst-case delay. This factor becomes a problem when the real-time system's designer uses off-the-shelf hardware. The designer can have difficulty determining how long every off-the-shelf device's ISR or DPC might take in the worst case. Even after testing, the designer can't guarantee that a special case in a live system won't cause the system to miss an important deadline. Furthermore, the sum of all the delays a system's DPCs and ISRs can introduce usually far exceeds the tolerance of a time-sensitive system.

Although many types of embedded systems (for example, printers and automotive computers) have real-time requirements, the special embedded version of Windows NT (currently based on Windows NT 4 but eventually to be updated for a future version of Windows 2000) doesn't have real-time characteristics. It is simply a version of Windows NT that makes it possible, using system designer technology that Microsoft licensed from VenturCom, to produce small-footprint versions of Windows NT suitable for running on devices with limited resources. For example, a device that has no networking capability would omit all the Windows NT components, including network management tools and adapter and protocol stack device drivers, related to networking.

(continued)

Windows 2000 and Real-Time Processing *continued*

> Still, there are third-party vendors that supply real-time kernels for Windows NT 4 and Windows 2000. The approach these vendors take is to embed their real-time kernel in a custom HAL and to have Windows 2000 or Windows NT 4 run as a task in the real-time operating system. The task running Windows 2000 or Windows NT serves as the user interface to the system and has a lower priority than the tasks responsible for managing the device. See VenturCom's Web site, *www.venturcom.com*, for an example of a third-party real-time kernel extension for Windows NT or Windows 2000.

Associating an ISR with a particular level of interrupt is called *connecting an interrupt object,* and dissociating an ISR from an IDT entry is called *disconnecting an interrupt object.* These operations, accomplished by calling the kernel functions *IoConnectInterrupt* and *IoDisconnectInterrupt,* allow a device driver to "turn on" an ISR when the driver is loaded into the system and to "turn off" the ISR if the driver is unloaded.

Using the interrupt object to register an ISR prevents device drivers from fiddling directly with interrupt hardware (which differs among processor architectures) and from needing to know any details about the IDT. This kernel feature aids in creating portable device drivers because it eliminates the need to code in assembly language or to reflect processor differences in device drivers.

Interrupt objects provide other benefits as well. By using the interrupt object, the kernel can synchronize the execution of the ISR with other parts of a device driver that might share data with the ISR. (See Chapter 9 for more information about how device drivers respond to interrupts.)

Furthermore, interrupt objects allow the kernel to easily call more than one ISR for any interrupt level. If multiple device drivers create interrupt objects and connect them to the same IDT entry, the interrupt dispatcher calls each routine when an interrupt occurs at the specified interrupt line. This capability allows the kernel to easily support "daisy-chain" configurations, in which several devices share the same interrupt line. The chain breaks when one of the ISRs claims ownership for the interrupt by returning a status to the interrupt dispatcher. If multiple devices sharing the same interrupt require service at the same time, devices not acknowledged by their ISRs will interrupt the system again once the interrupt dispatcher has lowered the IRQL. Chaining is permitted only if all the device drivers wanting to use the same interrupt indicate to the kernel that they can share the interrupt; if they can't, the Plug

and Play manager reorganizes their interrupt assignments to ensure that it honors the sharing requirements of each.

Software Interrupts

Although hardware generates most interrupts, the Windows 2000 kernel also generates software interrupts for a variety of tasks, including these:

- Initiating thread dispatching
- Non-time-critical interrupt processing
- Handling timer expiration
- Asynchronously executing a procedure in the context of a particular thread
- Supporting asynchronous I/O operations

These tasks are described in the following subsections.

Dispatch or deferred procedure call (DPC) interrupts

When a thread can no longer continue executing, perhaps because it has terminated or because it voluntarily enters a wait state, the kernel calls the dispatcher directly to effect an immediate context switch. Sometimes, however, the kernel detects that rescheduling should occur when it is deep within many layers of code. In this situation, the ideal solution is to request dispatching but defer its occurrence until the kernel completes its current activity. Using a DPC software interrupt is a convenient way to achieve this delay.

The kernel always raises the processor's IRQL to DPC/dispatch level or above when it needs to synchronize access to shared kernel structures. This disables additional software interrupts and thread dispatching. When the kernel detects that dispatching should occur, it requests a DPC/dispatch-level interrupt; but because the IRQL is at or above that level, the processor holds the interrupt in check. When the kernel completes its current activity, it sees that it's going to lower the IRQL below DPC/dispatch level and checks to see whether any dispatch interrupts are pending. If there are, the IRQL drops to DPC/dispatch level and the dispatch interrupts are processed. Activating the thread dispatcher by using a software interrupt is a way to defer dispatching until conditions are right. However, Windows 2000 uses software interrupts to defer other types of processing as well.

In addition to thread dispatching, the kernel also processes deferred procedure calls (DPCs) at this IRQL. A DPC is a function that performs a system task—a task that is less time-critical than the current one. The functions are called *deferred* because they might not execute immediately.

DPCs provide the operating system with the capability to generate an interrupt and execute a system function in kernel mode. The kernel uses DPCs to process timer expiration (and release threads waiting on the timers) and to reschedule the processor after a thread's quantum expires. Device drivers use DPCs to complete I/O requests. To provide timely service for hardware interrupts, Windows 2000—with the cooperation of device drivers—attempts to keep the IRQL below device IRQL levels. One way that this goal is achieved is for device driver ISRs to perform the minimal work necessary to acknowledge their device, save volatile interrupt state, and defer data transfer or other less time-critical interrupt processing activity for execution in a DPC at DPC/dispatch IRQL. (See Chapter 9 for more information on DPCs and the I/O system.)

A DPC is represented by a *DPC object,* a kernel control object that is not visible to user-mode programs but is visible to device drivers and other system code. The most important piece of information the DPC object contains is the address of the system function that the kernel will call when it processes the DPC interrupt. DPC routines that are waiting to execute are stored in kernel-managed queues, one per processor, called *DPC queues.* To request a DPC, system code calls the kernel to initialize a DPC object and then places it in a DPC queue.

By default, the kernel places DPC objects at the end of the DPC queue of the processor on which the DPC was requested (typically the processor on which the ISR executed). A device driver can override this behavior, however, by specifying a DPC priority (low, medium, or high, where medium is the default) and by targeting the DPC at a particular processor. A DPC aimed at a specific CPU is known as a *targeted DPC.* If the DPC has a low or medium priority, the kernel places the DPC object at the end of the queue; if the DPC has a high priority, the kernel inserts the DPC object at the front of the queue.

When the processor's IRQL is about to drop from an IRQL of DPC/dispatch level or higher to a lower IRQL (APC or passive level), the kernel processes DPCs. Windows 2000 ensures that the IRQL remains at DPC/dispatch level and pulls DPC objects off the current processor's queue until the queue is empty (that is, the kernel "drains" the queue), calling each DPC function in turn. Only when the queue is empty will the kernel let the IRQL drop below DPC/dispatch level and let regular thread execution continue. DPC processing is depicted in Figure 3-5.

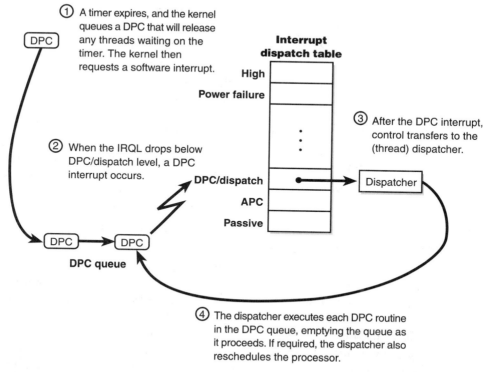

Figure 3-5
Delivering a DPC

DPC priorities can affect system behavior another way. The kernel usually initiates DPC queue draining with a DPC/dispatch-level interrupt. The kernel generates such an interrupt only if the DPC is directed at the processor the ISR is requested on and the DPC has a high or medium priority. If the DPC has a low priority, the kernel requests the interrupt only if the number of outstanding DPC requests for the processor rises above a threshold or if the number of DPCs requested on the processor within a time window is low. If a DPC is targeted at a CPU different from the one on which the ISR is running and the DPC's priority is high, the kernel immediately signals the target CPU (by sending it a dispatch IPI) to drain its DPC queue. If the priority is medium or low, the number of DPCs queued on the target processor must exceed a threshold for the kernel to trigger a DPC/dispatch interrupt. The system idle thread also drains the DPC queue for the processor it runs on. Although DPC targeting and priority levels are flexible, device drivers rarely need to change the default behavior of their DPC objects. Table 3-1 summarizes the situations that initiate DPC queue draining.

Table 3-1 DPC Interrupt Generation Rules

DPC Priority	DPC Targeted at ISR's Processor	DPC Targeted at Another Processor
Low	DPC queue length exceeds maximum DPC queue length or DPC request rate is less than minimum DPC request rate	DPC queue length exceeds maximum DPC queue length or System is idle
Medium	Always	DPC queue length exceeds maximum DPC queue length or System is idle
High	Always	Always

Because user-mode threads execute at low IRQL, the chances are good that a DPC will interrupt the execution of an ordinary user's thread. DPC routines execute without regard to what thread is running, meaning that when a DPC routine runs, it can't assume what process address space is currently mapped. DPC routines can call kernel functions, but they can't call system services, generate page faults, or create or wait on dispatcher objects (explained later in this chapter). They can, however, access nonpaged system memory addresses, since system address space is always mapped regardless of what the current process is.

DPCs are provided primarily for device drivers, but the kernel uses them too. The kernel most frequently uses a DPC to handle quantum expiration. At every tick of the system clock, an interrupt occurs at clock IRQL. The clock interrupt handler (running at clock IRQL) updates the system time and then decrements a counter that tracks how long the current thread has run. When the counter reaches 0, the thread's time quantum has expired and the kernel might need to reschedule the processor, a lower-priority task that should be done at DPC/dispatch IRQL. The clock interrupt handler queues a DPC to initiate thread dispatching and then finishes its work and lowers the processor's IRQL. Because the DPC interrupt has a lower priority than do device interrupts, any pending device interrupts that surface before the clock interrupt completes are handled before the DPC interrupt occurs.

EXPERIMENT: Monitoring Interrupt and DPC Activity

Using the Windows 2000 Performance tool, you can watch the percentage of time your system spends on handling interrupts and DPCs. The Processor object has % Interrupt Time and % DPC Time counters, including Total and per-processor instances, which means you can monitor the activity on a per-CPU or a systemwide basis. These objects also have counters to measure the number of interrupts and DPCs per second.

One situation in which you might want to look at these counters is if your system is spending an inordinate amount of time in kernel mode and you can't attribute all the kernel-mode CPU time to processes. If total kernel-mode CPU time is greater than the total kernel-mode CPU time of all processes, the remaining time has to be interrupts or DPCs because time spent at interrupt level and DPC level isn't charged to any thread's CPU time performance counter. Be aware that there are inherent inaccuracies in the way Windows 2000 accounts for CPU time, inaccuracies that relate to the granularity of the system timer. (See the section "Quantum Accounting" in Chapter 6 for an explanation of how time accounting works.)

Asynchronous procedure call (APC) interrupts Asynchronous procedure calls (APCs) provide a way for user programs and system code to execute in the context of a particular user thread (and hence a particular process address space). Because APCs are queued to execute in the context of a particular thread and run at an IRQL less than 2, they don't operate under the same restrictions as a DPC. An APC routine can acquire resources (objects), wait on object handles, incur page faults, and call system services.

APCs are described by a kernel control object, called an *APC object*. APCs waiting to execute reside in a kernel-managed *APC queue*. Unlike the DPC queue, which is systemwide, the APC queue is thread-specific—each thread has its own APC queue. When asked to queue an APC, the kernel inserts it into the queue belonging to the thread that will execute the APC routine. The kernel, in turn, requests a software interrupt at APC level, and when the thread eventually begins running, it executes the APC.

There are two kinds of APCs: kernel mode and user mode. Kernel-mode APCs don't require "permission" from a target thread to run in that thread's context, while user-mode APCs do. Kernel-mode APCs interrupt a thread and execute a procedure without the thread's intervention or consent.

The executive uses kernel-mode APCs to perform operating system work that must be completed within the address space (in the context) of a particular thread. It can use kernel-mode APCs to direct a thread to stop executing an interruptible system service, for example, or to record the results of an asynchronous I/O operation in a thread's address space. Environment subsystems use kernel-mode APCs to make a thread suspend or terminate itself or to get or set its user-mode execution context. The POSIX subsystem uses kernel-mode APCs to emulate the delivery of POSIX signals to POSIX processes.

Device drivers also use kernel-mode APCs. For example, if an I/O operation is initiated and a thread goes into a wait state, another thread in another process can be scheduled to run. When the device finishes transferring data, the I/O system must somehow get back into the context of the thread that initiated the I/O so that it can copy the results of the I/O operation to the buffer in the address space of the process containing that thread. The I/O system uses a kernel-mode APC to perform this action. (The use of APCs in the I/O system is discussed in more detail in Chapter 9.)

Several Win32 APIs, such as *ReadFileEx*, *WriteFileEx*, and *QueueUserAPC*, use user-mode APCs. For example, the *ReadFileEx* and *WriteFileEx* functions allow the caller to specify a completion routine to be called when the I/O operation finishes. The I/O completion is implemented by queueing an APC to the thread that issued the I/O. However, the callback to the completion routine doesn't necessarily take place when the APC is queued because user-mode APCs are delivered to a thread only when it's in an *alertable wait state*. A thread can enter a wait state either by waiting on an object handle and specifying that its wait is alertable (with the Win32 *WaitForMultipleObjectsEx* function) or by testing directly whether it has a pending APC (using *SleepEx*). In both cases, if a user-mode APC is pending, the kernel interrupts (alerts) the thread, transfers control to the APC routine, and resumes the thread's execution when the APC routine completes.

APC delivery can reorder the wait queues—the lists of which threads are waiting on what, and in what order they are waiting. (Wait resolution is described in the section "Executive Synchronization" later in this chapter.) If the thread

is in a wait state when an APC is delivered, after the APC routine completes, the wait is reissued or reexecuted. If the wait still isn't resolved, the thread returns to the wait state, but now it will be at the end of the list of objects it's waiting on. For example, because APCs are used to suspend a thread from execution, if the thread is waiting on any objects, its wait will be removed until the thread is resumed, after which that thread will be at the end of the list of threads waiting to access the objects it was waiting on.

Exception Dispatching

In contrast to interrupts, which can occur at any time, exceptions are conditions that result directly from the execution of the program that is running. Win32 introduced a facility known as *structured exception handling,* which allows applications to gain control when exceptions occur. The application can then fix the condition and return to the place the exception occurred, unwind the stack (thus terminating execution of the subroutine that raised the exception), or declare back to the system that the exception isn't recognized and the system should continue searching for an exception handler that might process the exception. This section assumes you're familiar with the basic concepts behind Win32 structured exception handling—if you're not, you should read the overview in the Win32 API reference documentation on the Platform SDK or chapters 23–25 in Jeffrey Richter's book *Programming Applications for Microsoft Windows* (fourth edition, Microsoft Press, 2000) before proceeding. Keep in mind that although exception handling is made accessible through language extensions (for example, the __*try* construct in Microsoft Visual C++), it is a system mechanism and hence isn't language-specific. Other examples of consumers of Windows 2000 exception handling include C++ and Java exceptions.

On the x86, all exceptions have predefined interrupt numbers that directly correspond to the entry in the IDT that points to the trap handler for a particular exception. Table 3-2 shows x86-defined exceptions and their assigned interrupt numbers. Because the first entries of the IDT are used for exceptions, hardware interrupts are assigned entries later in the table, as mentioned earlier.

Table 3-2 x86 Exceptions and Their Interrupt Numbers

Interrupt Number	Exception
0	Divide Error
1	DEBUG TRAP
2	NMI/NPX Error
3	Breakpoint
4	Overflow
5	BOUND/Print Screen
6	Invalid Opcode
7	NPX Not Available
8	Double Exception
9	NPX Segment Overrun
A	Invalid Task State Segment (TSS)
B	Segment Not Present
C	Stack Fault
D	General Protection
E	Page Fault
F	Intel Reserved
10	Floating Point
11	Alignment Check

All exceptions, except those simple enough to be resolved by the trap handler, are serviced by a kernel module called the *exception dispatcher*. The exception dispatcher's job is to find an exception handler that can "dispose of" the exception. Examples of architecture-independent exceptions that the kernel defines include memory access violations, integer divide-by-zero, integer overflow, floating-point exceptions, and debugger breakpoints. For a complete list of architecture-independent exceptions, consult the Win32 API reference documentation.

The kernel traps and handles some of these exceptions transparently to user programs. For example, encountering a breakpoint while executing a program being debugged generates an exception, which the kernel handles

by calling the debugger. The kernel handles certain other exceptions by returning an unsuccessful status code to the caller.

A few exceptions are allowed to filter back, untouched, to user mode. For example, a memory access violation or an arithmetic overflow generates an exception that the operating system doesn't handle. An environment subsystem can establish *frame-based exception handlers* to deal with these exceptions. The term *frame-based* refers to an exception handler's association with a particular procedure activation. When a procedure is invoked, a *stack frame* representing that activation of the procedure is pushed onto the stack. A stack frame can have one or more exception handlers associated with it, each of which protects a particular block of code in the source program. When an exception occurs, the kernel searches for an exception handler associated with the current stack frame. If none exists, the kernel searches for an exception handler associated with the previous stack frame, and so on, until it finds a frame-based exception handler. If no exception handler is found, the kernel calls its own default exception handlers.

When an exception occurs, whether it is explicitly raised by software or implicitly raised by hardware, a chain of events begins in the kernel. The CPU hardware transfers control to the kernel trap handler, which creates a trap frame (as it does when an interrupt occurs). The trap frame allows the system to resume where it left off if the exception is resolved. The trap handler also creates an exception record that contains the reason for the exception and other pertinent information.

If the exception occurred in kernel mode, the exception dispatcher simply calls a routine to locate a frame-based exception handler that will handle the exception. Because unhandled kernel-mode exceptions are considered fatal operating system errors, you can assume that the dispatcher always finds an exception handler.

If the exception occurred in user mode, the exception dispatcher does something more elaborate. As you'll see in Chapter 6, the Win32 subsystem has a debugger port and an exception port to receive notification of user-mode exceptions in Win32 processes. The kernel uses these in its default exception handling, as illustrated in Figure 3-6.

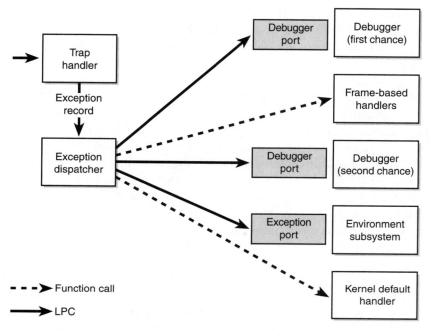

Figure 3-6
Dispatching an exception

Debugger breakpoints are common sources of exceptions. Therefore, the first action the exception dispatcher takes is to see whether the process that incurred the exception has an associated debugger process. If so, it sends the first-chance debug message (via an LPC port) to the debugger port associated with the process that incurred the exception. (The message is sent to the session manager process, which then dispatches it to the appropriate debugger process.)

If the process has no debugger process attached, or if the debugger doesn't handle the exception, the exception dispatcher switches into user mode and calls a routine to find a frame-based exception handler. If none is found, or if none handles the exception, the exception dispatcher switches back into kernel mode and calls the debugger again to allow the user to do more debugging. (This is called the second-chance notification.)

All Win32 threads have an exception handler declared at the top of the stack that processes unhandled exceptions. This exception handler is declared in the internal Win32 *start-of-process* or *start-of-thread* function. The start-of-process function runs when the first thread in a process begins execution. It calls the main entry point in the image. The start-of-thread function runs when a user creates additional threads. It calls the user-supplied thread start routine specified in the *CreateThread* call.

EXPERIMENT: Viewing the Real User Start Address for Win32 Threads

The fact that each Win32 thread begins execution in a system-supplied function (and not the user-supplied function) explains why the start address for thread 0 is the same for every Win32 process in the system (and why the start addresses for secondary threads are also the same). The start address for thread 0 in Win32 processes is the Win32 start-of-process function; the start address for any other threads would be the Win32 start-of-thread function. To see the user-supplied function address, use the Tlist utility in the Windows 2000 Support Tools. Type *tlist process-name* or *tlist process-id* to get the detailed process output that includes this information. For example, compare the thread start addresses for the Windows Explorer process as reported by Pstat (in the Platform SDK) and Tlist:

```
C:\> pstat
⋮
pid:3f8 pri: 8 Hnd:  329 Pf:  80043 Ws:   4620K explorer.exe
 tid pri Ctx Swtch StrtAddr   User Time Kernel Time  State
  7c   9     16442 77E878C1 0:00:01.241 0:00:01.251 Wait:UserRequest
 42c  11    157888 77E92C50 0:00:07.110 0:00:34.309 Wait:UserRequest
 44c   8      6357 77E92C50 0:00:00.070 0:00:00.140 Wait:UserRequest
 1cc   8      3318 77E92C50 0:00:00.030 0:00:00.070 Wait:DelayExecution
  ⋮

C:\> tlist explorer
 1016 explorer.exe        Program Manager
   CWD:     C:\
   CmdLine: Explorer.exe
   VirtualSize:    25348 KB   PeakVirtualSize:    31052 KB
   WorkingSetSize: 1804 KB    PeakWorkingSetSize: 3276 KB
   NumberOfThreads: 4
    149 Win32StartAddr:0x01009dbd LastErr:0x0000007e State:Waiting
     86 Win32StartAddr:0x77c5d4a5 LastErr:0x00000000 State:Waiting
     62 Win32StartAddr:0x00000977 LastErr:0x00000000 State:Waiting
    179 Win32StartAddr:0x0100d8d4 LastErr:0x00000002 State:Waiting
    ⋮
```

The start address of thread 0 reported by Pstat is the internal Win32 start-of-process function; the start addresses for threads 1 through 3 are the internal Win32 start-of-thread functions. Tlist, on the other hand, shows the user-supplied Win32 start address (the user function called by the internal Win32 start function).

The generic code for these internal start functions is shown here:

```
void Win32StartOfProcess(
    LPTHREAD_START_ROUTINE lpStartAddr,
    LPVOID lpvThreadParm){

    __try {

        DWORD dwThreadExitCode = lpStartAddr(lpvThreadParm);
        ExitThread(dwThreadExitCode);

    } __except(UnhandledExceptionFilter(
            GetExceptionInformation())) {

        ExitProcess(GetExceptionCode());
    }
}
```

Notice that the Win32 unhandled exception filter is called if the thread has an exception that it doesn't handle. This function looks in the registry in the HKLM\SOFTWARE\Microsoft\Windows NT\CurrentVersion\AeDebug key to determine whether to run a debugger immediately or to ask the user first.

The default "debugger" on Windows 2000 is \Winnt\System32\Drwtsn-32.exe (Dr. Watson), which isn't really a debugger but rather a postmortem tool that captures the state of the application "crash" and records it in a log file (Drwtsn32.log) and a process crash dump file (User.dmp), both found by default in the \Documents And Settings\All Users\Documents\DrWatson folder. To see (or modify) the configuration for Dr. Watson, run it interactively—it displays a window with the current settings, as shown in Figure 3-7.

The log file contains basic information such as the exception code, the name of the image that failed, a list of loaded DLLs, and a stack and instruction trace for the thread that incurred the exception. For a detailed description of the contents of the log file, run Dr. Watson and click the Help button shown in Figure 3-7.

The crash dump file contains the private pages in the process at the time of the exception. (The file doesn't include code pages from EXEs or DLLs.) This file can be opened by WinDbg, the Windows debugger that comes with the Windows 2000 debugging tools package (which is part of Windows 2000 Customer Support Diagnostics, Platform SDK, and DDK). Because the User.dmp

Figure 3-7
Dr. Watson default settings

file is overwritten each time a process crashes, unless you rename or copy the file after each process crash, you'll have only the latest one on your system.

If you install one of the Microsoft Visual Studio compilers, the Debugger value of the AeDebug registry key is changed to Msdev.exe (including the path), so that you can debug programs that incur unhandled exceptions. Another product that changes the Debugger value is Lotus Notes—it runs a Notes-specific postmortem tool named Qnc.exe.

If the debugger isn't running and no frame-based handlers are found, the kernel sends a message to the exception port associated with the thread's process. This exception port, if one exists, was registered by the environment subsystem that controls this thread. The exception port gives the environment subsystem, which presumably is listening at the port, the opportunity to translate the exception into an environment-specific signal or exception. For example, when POSIX gets a message from the kernel that one of its threads generated an exception, the POSIX subsystem sends a POSIX-style signal to the thread that caused the exception. However, if the kernel progresses this far in processing the exception and the subsystem doesn't handle the exception, the kernel executes a default exception handler that simply terminates the process whose thread caused the exception.

EXPERIMENT: Unhandled Exceptions

To see an example Dr. Watson log file, run the program \Tools\Accvio.exe from this book's companion CD. This program generates a memory access violation by attempting to write to address 0, which is always an invalid address in Win32 processes. (See Table 7-6 on page 420 in Chapter 7.)

1. Run the Registry Editor, and locate HKLM\SOFTWARE\ Microsoft\Windows NT\CurrentVersion\AeDebug.

2. If the Debugger value is "drwtsn32 -p %ld -e %ld –g", your system is set up to run Dr. Watson as the default debugger. Proceed to step 4.

3. If the value of Debugger was not set up to run Drwtsn32.exe, you can still test Dr. Watson by temporarily installing it and then restoring your previous debugger settings:

 ❑ Save the current value somewhere (for example, in a Notepad file or in the current paste buffer).

 ❑ Select Run from the taskbar Start menu, and then enter *drwtsn32 –i*. (This initializes the Debugger field to run Dr. Watson.)

4. Run the test program \Tools\Accvio.exe.

5. The Program Error message box should come up—when the log file and crash dump have been created, the button will change from Cancel to OK. (Note: This error message occurs by default only on Windows 2000 Professional installations of Dr. Watson—Windows 2000 Server by default will not show a message box, but the dump files will still be created. You also might see a different error message if Dr. Watson is not your default debugger.)

6. Click OK to dismiss the message box.

7. Run Drwtsn32.exe. (Select Run from the Start menu, and then enter *drwtsn32*.)

8. In the list of Application Errors, click on the last entry and then click the View button—the portion of the Dr. Watson log file containing the details of the access violation from Accvio.exe will be displayed. (For details on the log file format, press Help in the Dr. Watson For Windows 2000 dialog box and select Dr. Watson Log File Overview.)

9. If the original value of Debugger wasn't the default Dr. Watson settings, restore the saved value from step 1.

As another experiment, try changing the value of Debugger to another program, such as Notepad.exe (Notepad editor) or Sol.exe (Solitaire). Rerun Accvio.exe, and notice that whatever program is specified in the Debugger value is run—that is, there's no validation that the program defined in Debugger is actually a debugger. Make sure you restore your registry settings. (As noted in step 3b, to reset to the system default Dr. Watson settings, type *drwtsn32 −i* in the Run dialog box or at a command prompt.)

System Service Dispatching

As Figure 3-1 illustrated, the kernel's trap handlers dispatch interrupts, exceptions, and system service calls. In the preceding sections, you've seen how interrupt and exception handling work; in this section, you'll learn about system services. A system service dispatch is triggered as a result of executing an *int 0x2e* instruction (46 decimal) on x86 processors. Because executing the *int* instruction results in a trap, Windows 2000 fills in entry 46 in the IDT to point to the system service dispatcher. (Refer to Table 3-1.) The trap causes the executing thread to transition into kernel mode and enter the system service dispatcher. A numeric argument passed in the EAX processor register indicates the system service number being requested. The EBX register points to the list of parameters the caller passes to the system service. The following code illustrates the generic code for a system service request:

```
NtWriteFile:
  mov  eax, 0x0E ; build 2195 system service number for NtWriteFile
  mov  ebx, esp  ; point to parameters
  int  0x2E      ; execute system service trap
  ret  0x2C      ; pop parameters off stack and return to caller
```

As Figure 3-8 illustrates, the kernel uses this argument to locate the system service information in the *system service dispatch table*. This table is similar to the interrupt dispatch table described earlier in the chapter except that each entry contains a pointer to a system service rather than to an interrupt handling routine.

NOTE System service numbers can change between service packs—Microsoft occasionally adds or removes system services, and the system service numbers are generated automatically as part of a kernel compile.

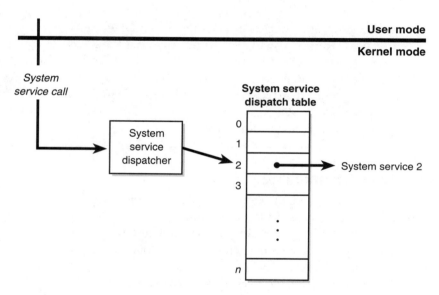

Figure 3-8
System service exceptions

The system service dispatcher, *KiSystemService*, verifies the correct minimum number of arguments, copies the caller's arguments from the thread's user-mode stack to its kernel-mode stack (so that the user can't change the arguments as the kernel is accessing them), and then executes the system service. If the arguments passed to a system service point to buffers in user space, these buffers must be probed for accessibility before kernel-mode code can copy data to or from them.

As you'll see in Chapter 6, each thread has a pointer to its system service table. Windows 2000 has two built-in system service tables, but up to four are supported. The system service dispatcher determines which table contains

the requested service by interpreting a 2-bit field in the 32-bit system service number as a table index. The low 12 bits of the system service number serve as the index into the table specified by the table index. The fields are shown in Figure 3-9.

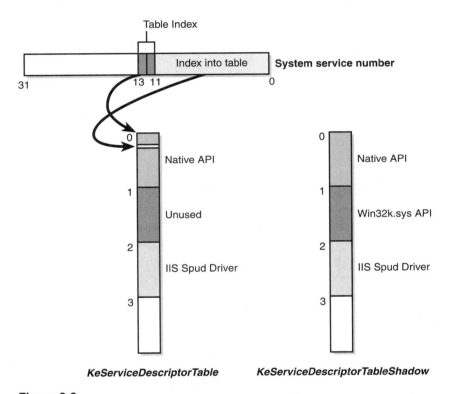

Figure 3-9
System service number to system service translation

A primary default array table, *KeServiceDescriptorTable*, defines the core executive system services implemented in Ntosrknl.exe. The other table array, *KeServiceDescriptorTableShadow*, includes the Win32 USER and GDI services implemented in the kernel-mode part of the Win32 subsystem, Win32k.sys. The first time a Win32 thread calls a Win32 USER or GDI service, the address of the thread's system service table is changed to point to a table that includes the Win32 USER and GDI services. The *KeAddSystemServiceTable* function allows Win32k.sys and other device drivers to add system service tables. If you install Internet Information Services (IIS) on Windows 2000, its support driver

(Spud.sys) upon loading defines an additional service table, leaving only one left for definition by third parties. With the exception of the Win32k.sys service table, a service table added with *KeAddSystemServiceTable* is copied into both the *KeServiceDescriptorTable* array and the *KeServiceDescriptorTableShadow* array.

The system service dispatch instructions for Windows 2000 executive services exist in the system library Ntdll.dll. Subsystem DLLs call functions in Ntdll to implement their documented functions. The exception is Win32 USER and GDI functions, in which the system service dispatch instructions are implemented directly in User32.dll and Gdi32.dll—there is no Ntdll.dll. These two cases are shown in Figure 3-10.

Figure 3-10
System service dispatching

As shown in Figure 3-10, the Win32 *WriteFile* function in Kernel32.dll calls the *NtWriteFile* function in Ntdll.dll, which in turn executes the appropriate instruction to cause a system service trap, passing the system service number

representing *NtWriteFile*. The system service dispatcher (function *KiSystemService* in Ntoskrnl.exe) then calls the real *NtWriteFile* to process the I/O request. For Win32 USER and GDI functions, the system service dispatch calls functions in the loadable kernel-mode part of the Win32 subsystem, Win32k.sys.

EXPERIMENT: Viewing System Service Activity

You can monitor system service activity by watching the System Calls/ Sec performance counter in the System object. Run the Performance tool, and in chart view, click the Add button to add a counter to the chart; select the System object, select the System Calls/Sec counter, and then click the Add button to add the counter to the chart.

Object Manager

As mentioned in Chapter 2, Windows 2000 implements an object model to provide consistent and secure access to the various internal services implemented in the executive. This section describes the Windows 2000 *object manager,* the executive component responsible for creating, deleting, protecting, and tracking objects. The object manager centralizes resource control operations that otherwise would be scattered throughout the operating system. It was designed to meet the goals listed on page 28.

EXPERIMENT: Exploring the Object Manager

Throughout this section, you'll find experiments that show you how to peer into the object manager database. These experiments use the following tools, which you should become familiar with if you aren't already:

- **Object viewer** There are two versions of this tool: the version from *www.sysinternals.com* (on this book's companion CD as \Sysint\Winobj.exe) and a different version in (the Platform SDK (in \Program Files\Microsoft Platform SDK\Bin\ Winnt\Winobj.exe). The object viewer from *www.sysinternals. com* displays more accurate information about objects (such as the reference count, the number of open handles, security descriptors, and so forth) than the object viewer in the Platform SDK does.

(continued)

EXPERIMENT: Exploring the Object Manager *continued*

- **Open handles** Two tools from *www.sysinternals.com* show open handles: a GUI tool (on this book's companion CD in \Sysint\Handleex.exe) and a command-line tool (on the companion CD in \Sysint\Nthandle.exe). The Windows 2000 resource kits include another tool that shows open handles, called Oh.exe.

- The kernel debugger *!handle* command.

The object viewer provides a way to traverse the namespace that the object manager maintains. (As we'll explain later, not all objects have names.) Try running the WinObj object manager utility from the companion CD and examining the layout, shown here:

In the Windows 2000 Resource Kit Tools Help for OH, you'll find out that if object tracking—an internal debugging feature in the executive—isn't enabled, OH will enable it by setting a Windows 2000 global flag in the registry and then rebooting your system. Neither Nthandle nor Handleex from the companion CD require object tracking. (You can enable object tracking by manually setting the flag and rebooting your system. See page 168 for more on global flags.) Because this flag uses additional memory to track object usage information, you should disable it with the Gflags utility after you've experimented with OH and then reboot your system again.

The object manager was designed to meet these goals:

- Provide a common, uniform mechanism for using system resources

- Isolate object protection to one location in the operating system so that C2 security compliance can be achieved

- Provide a mechanism to charge processes for their use of objects so that limits can be placed on the usage of system resources

- Establish an object-naming scheme that can readily incorporate existing objects, such as the devices, files, and directories of a file system, or other independent collections of objects

- Support the requirements of various operating system environments, such as the ability of a process to inherit resources from a parent process (needed by Win32 and POSIX) and the ability to create case-sensitive filenames (needed by POSIX)

- Establish uniform rules for object retention (that is, keeping an object available until all processes have finished using it)

Internally, Windows 2000 has two kinds of objects: *executive objects* and *kernel objects*. Executive objects are objects implemented by various components of the executive (such as the process manager, memory manager, I/O subsystem, and so on). Kernel objects are a more primitive set of objects implemented by the Windows 2000 kernel. These objects are not visible to user-mode code but are created and used only within the executive. Kernel objects provide fundamental capabilities, such as synchronization, on which executive objects are built. Thus, many executive objects contain (encapsulate) one or more kernel objects, as shown in Figure 3-11.

Details about the structure of kernel objects and how they are used to implement synchronization are given later in this chapter. In the remainder of this section, we'll focus on how the object manager works and on the structure of executive objects, handles, and handle tables. Here we'll just briefly describe how objects are involved in implementing Windows 2000 security access checking; we'll cover this topic thoroughly in Chapter 8.

Owned by the object manager

Name
HandleCount
ReferenceCount
Type

Owned by the kernel

Kernel object

Owned by the executive

Executive object

Figure 3-11
Executive objects that contain kernel objects

Executive Objects

Each Windows 2000 environment subsystem projects to its applications a different image of the operating system. The executive objects and object services are primitives that the environment subsystems use to construct their own versions of objects and other resources.

Executive objects are typically created either by an environment subsystem on behalf of a user application or by various components of the operating system as part of their normal operation. For example, to create a file, a Win32 application calls the Win32 *CreateFile* function, implemented in the Win32 subsystem DLL Kernel32.dll. After some validation and initialization, *CreateFile* in turn calls the native Windows 2000 service *NtCreateFile* to create an executive file object.

The set of objects an environment subsystem supplies to its applications might be larger or smaller than the set the executive provides. The Win32 subsystem uses executive objects to export its own set of objects, many of which correspond directly to executive objects. For example, the Win32 mutexes and semaphores are directly based on executive objects (which are in turn based on corresponding kernel objects). In addition, the Win32 subsystem supplies named pipes and mailslots, resources that are based on executive file objects. Some subsystems, such as POSIX, don't support objects as objects at all. The POSIX subsystem uses executive objects and services as the basis for presenting POSIX-style processes, pipes, and other resources to its applications.

Table 3-3 lists the primary objects the executive provides and briefly describes what they represent. You can find further details on executive objects in the chapters that describe the related executive components (or in the case of executive objects directly exported to Win32, in the Win32 API reference documentation).

NOTE The executive implements a total of 27 object types in Windows 2000, many of which are for use only by the executive component that defines them and not directly accessible by Win32 APIs. Examples of these objects include Driver, Device, and EventPair.

Table 3-3 **Executive Objects Exposed to Win32**

Object Type	Represents
Symbolic link	A mechanism for referring to an object name indirectly.
Process	The virtual address space and control information necessary for the execution of a set of thread objects.
Thread	An executable entity within a process.
Job	A collection of processes manageable as a single entity through the job.
Section	A region of shared memory (called a file mapping object in Win32).
File	An instance of an opened file or an I/O device.
Access token	The security profile (security ID, user rights, and so on) of a process or a thread.
Event	An object with a persistent state (signaled or not signaled) that can be used for synchronization or notification.
Semaphore	A counter that provides a resource gate by allowing some maximum number of threads to access the resources protected by the semaphore.
Mutex*	A synchronization mechanism used to serialize access to a resource.
Timer	A mechanism to notify a thread when a fixed period of time elapses.
IoCompletion	A method for threads to enqueue and dequeue notifications of the completion of I/O operations (called an I/O completion port in the Win32 API).
Key	A mechanism to refer to data in the registry. Although keys appear in the object manager namespace, they are managed by the configuration manager, in a way similar to that in which file objects are managed by file system drivers. Zero or more key values are associated with a key object; key values contain data about the key.
WindowStation	An object that contains a clipboard, a set of global atoms, and a group of desktop objects.
Desktop	An object contained within a window station. A desktop has a logical display surface and contains windows, menus, and hooks.

* Externally in the Win32 API, mutants are called *mutexes*. Internally, the kernel object that underlies mutexes is called a *mutant*.

Object Structure

As shown in Figure 3-12, each object has an object header and an object body. The object manager controls the object headers, and the owning executive components control the object bodies of the object types they create. In addition, each object header points to the list of processes that have the object open and to a special object called the *type object* that contains information common to each instance of the object.

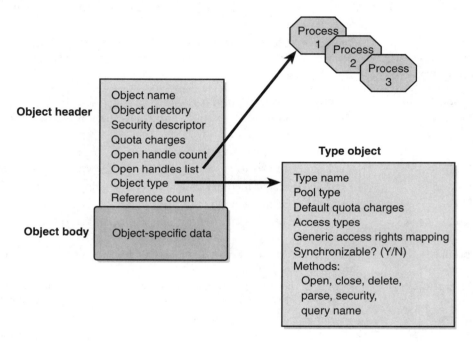

Figure 3-12
Structure of an object

Object Headers and Bodies

The object manager uses the data stored in an object's header to manage objects without regard to their type. Table 3-4 briefly describes the object header attributes.

Table 3-4 **Standard Object Header Attributes**

Attribute	Purpose
Object name	Makes an object visible to other processes for sharing
Object directory	Provides a hierarchical structure in which to store object names
Security descriptor	Determines who can use the object and what they can do with it
Quota charges	Lists the resource charges levied against a process when it opens a handle to the object
Open handle count	Counts the number of times a handle has been opened to the object
Open handles list	Points to the list of processes that have opened handles to the object
Object type	Points to a type object that contains attributes common to objects of this type
Reference count	Counts the number of times a kernel-mode component has referenced the address of the object

In addition to an object header, each object has an object body whose format and contents are unique to its object type; all objects of the same type share the same object body format. By creating an object type and supplying services for it, an executive component can control the manipulation of data in all object bodies of that type.

The object manager provides a small set of generic services that operate on the attributes stored in an object's header and can be used on objects of any type (although some generic services don't make sense for certain objects). These generic services, some of which the Win32 subsystem makes available to Win32 applications, are listed in Table 3-5.

Although these generic object services are supported for all object types, each object has its own create, open, and query services. For example, the I/O system implements a create file service for its file objects, and the process manager implements a create process service for its process objects. Although a single create object service could have been implemented, such a routine would have

Table 3-5 Generic Object Services

Service	Purpose
Close	Closes a handle to an object
Duplicate	Shares an object by duplicating a handle and giving it to another process
Query object	Gets information about an object's standard attributes
Query security	Gets an object's security descriptor
Set security	Changes the protection on an object
Wait for a single object	Synchronizes a thread's execution with one object
Wait for multiple objects	Synchronizes a thread's execution with multiple objects

been quite complicated, because the set of parameters required to initialize a file object, for example, differs markedly from that required to initialize a process object. Also, the object manager would have incurred additional processing overhead each time a thread called an object service to determine the type of object the handle referred to and to call the appropriate version of the service. For these reasons and others, the create, open, and query services are implemented separately for each object type.

Type Objects

Object headers contain data that is common to all objects but that can take on different values for each instance of an object. For example, each object has a unique name and can have a unique security descriptor. However, objects also contain some data that remains constant for all objects of a particular type. For example, you can select from a set of access rights specific to a type of object when you open a handle to objects of that type. The executive supplies terminate and suspend access (among others) for thread objects and read, write, append, and delete access (among others) for file objects. Another example of an object-type-specific attribute is synchronization, which is described shortly.

To conserve memory, the object manager stores these static, object-type-specific attributes once when creating a new object type. It uses an object of its own, a type object, to record this data. As Figure 3-13 illustrates, if the object-tracking debug flag (described on page 126) is set, a type object also links together all objects of the same type (in this case the Process type), allowing the object manager to find and enumerate them, if necessary.

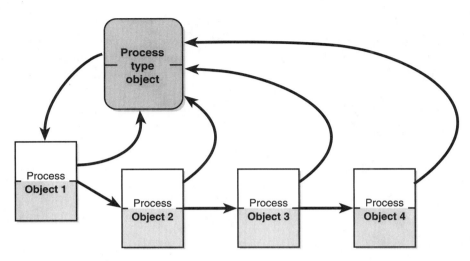

Figure 3-13
Process objects and the process type object

EXPERIMENT: Viewing the Type Objects

You can see the list of type objects declared to the object manager with
the Object Viewer utility on this book's companion CD. Just run
\Sysint\Winobj.exe, and then in the Winobj object manager open the
\ObjectTypes directory, as shown here:

Type objects can't be manipulated from user mode because the object manager supplies no services for them. However, some of the attributes they define are visible through certain native services and through Win32 API routines. The attributes stored in the type objects are described in Table 3-6.

Table 3-6 Type Object Attributes

Attribute	Purpose
Type name	The name for objects of this type ("process," "event," "port," and so on)
Pool type	Whether objects of this type should be allocated from paged or nonpaged memory
Default quota charges	Default paged and nonpaged pool values to charge to process quotas
Access types	The types of access a thread can request when opening a handle to an object of this type ("read," "write," "terminate," "suspend," and so on)
Generic access rights mapping	A mapping between the four generic access rights (read, write, execute, and all) to the type-specific access rights
Synchronization	Whether a thread can wait on objects of this type
Methods	One or more routines that the object manager calls automatically at certain points in an object's lifetime

Synchronization, one of the attributes visible to Win32 applications, refers to a thread's ability to synchronize its execution by waiting for an object to change from one state to another. A thread can synchronize with executive job, process, thread, file, event, semaphore, mutex, and timer objects. Other executive objects don't support synchronization. An object's ability to support synchronization is based on whether the object contains an embedded dispatcher object, a kernel object that is covered in the section "Executive Synchronization" later in this chapter.

Object Methods

The last attribute in Table 3-6, methods, comprises a set of internal routines that are similar to C++ constructors and destructors—that is, routines that are automatically called when an object is created or destroyed. The object manager extends this idea by calling an object method in other situations as well, such as when someone opens or closes a handle to an object or when someone attempts to change the protection on an object. Some object types specify methods, whereas others don't, depending on how the object type is to be used.

When an executive component creates a new object type, it can register one or more methods with the object manager. Thereafter, the object manager calls the methods at well-defined points in the lifetime of objects of that type, usually when an object is created, deleted, or modified in some way. The methods that the object manager supports are listed in Table 3-7.

Table 3-7 Object Methods

Method	When Method Is Called
Open	When an object handle is opened
Close	When an object handle is closed
Delete	Before the object manager deletes an object
Query name	When a thread requests the name of an object, such as a file, that exists in a secondary object domain
Parse	When the object manager is searching for an object name that exists in a secondary object domain
Security	When a process reads or changes the protection of an object, such as a file, that exists in a secondary object domain

The object manager calls the open method whenever it creates a handle to an object, which it does when an object is created or opened. However, only one object type, the Desktop, defines an open method. The Desktop object type requires an open method so that Win32k can share a piece of memory with the process that serves as a desktop-related memory pool.

135

An example of the use of a close method occurs in the I/O system. The I/O manager registers a close method for the file object type, and the object manager calls the close method each time it closes a file object handle. This close method checks whether the process that is closing the file handle owns any outstanding locks on the file and, if so, removes them. Checking for file locks isn't something the object manager itself could or should do.

The object manager calls a delete method, if one is registered, before it deletes a temporary object from memory. The memory manager, for example, registers a delete method for the section object type that frees the physical pages being used by the section. It also verifies that any internal data structures the memory manager has allocated for a section are deleted before the section object is deleted. Once again, the object manager can't do this work because it knows nothing about the internal workings of the memory manager. Delete methods for other types of objects perform similar functions.

The parse method (and similarly, the query name method) allows the object manager to relinquish control of finding an object to a secondary object manager if it finds an object that exists outside the object manager namespace. When the object manager looks up an object name, it suspends its search when it encounters an object in the path that has an associated parse method. The object manager calls the parse method, passing to it the remainder of the object name it is looking for. There are two namespaces in Windows 2000 in addition to the object manager's: the registry namespace, which the configuration manager implements, and the file system namespace, which the I/O manager implements with the aid of file system drivers. (See Chapter 5 for more information on the configuration manager and Chapter 9 for more about the I/O manager and file system drivers.)

For example, when a process opens a handle to the object named \Device\ Floppy0\docs\resume.doc, the object manager traverses its name tree until it reaches the device object named Floppy0. It sees that a parse method is associated with this object, and it calls the method, passing to it the rest of the object name it was searching for—in this case, the string \docs\resume.doc. The parse method for device objects is an I/O routine because the I/O manager defines the device object type and registers a parse method for it. The I/O manager's parse routine takes the name string and passes it to the appropriate file system, which finds the file on the disk and opens it.

The security method, which the I/O system also uses, is similar to the parse method. It is called whenever a thread tries to query or change the security information protecting a file. This information is different for files than for other

objects because security information is stored in the file itself rather than in memory. The I/O system, therefore, must be called in order to find the security information and read or change it.

Object Handles and the Process Handle Table

When a process creates or opens an object by name, it receives a *handle* that represents its access to the object. Referring to an object by its handle is faster than using its name because the object manager can skip the name lookup and find the object directly. Processes can also acquire handles to objects by inheriting handles at process creation time (if the creator specifies the inherit handle flag on the *CreateProcess* call and the handle was marked as inheritable, either at the time it was created or afterward by using the Win32 *SetHandleInformation* function) or by receiving a duplicated handle from another process. (See the Win32 *DuplicateHandle* function.)

All user-mode processes must own a handle to an object before their threads can use the object. Using handles to manipulate system resources isn't a new idea. C and Pascal (and other language) run-time libraries, for example, return handles to opened files. Handles serve as indirect pointers to system resources; this indirection keeps application programs from fiddling directly with system data structures.

> **NOTE** Executive components and device drivers can access objects directly because they are running in kernel mode and therefore have access to the object structures in system memory. However, they must declare their usage of the object by incrementing either the open handle count or the reference count so that the object won't be deallocated while it's still being used. (See the section "Object Retention" on page 143 for more details.)

Object handles provide additional benefits. First, except for what they refer to, there is no difference between a file handle, an event handle, and a process handle. This similarity provides a consistent interface to reference objects, regardless of their type. Second, the object manager has the exclusive right to create handles and to locate an object that a handle refers to. This means that the object manager can scrutinize every user-mode action that affects an object to see whether the security profile of the caller allows the operation requested on the object in question.

EXPERIMENT: Viewing Open Handles with Nthandle

As shown in the following example, the Nthandle tool (\Sysint\ Nthandle.exe, which you'll find on this book's companion CD) can display the handles open by any or all processes:

```
C:\>nthandle -a -p system

Handle V1.2
Copyright (C) 1997-2000 Mark Russinovich
Systems Internals - http://www.sysinternals.com
-----------------------------------------------------------------
System pid: 8
   4: Process
   8: Key    \REGISTRY
   c: Thread
  10: Key    HKLM\SYSTEM\ControlSet003\Control\ProductOptions
  14: Key    HKLM\SYSTEM\Setup
  18: Key    HKLM\SYSTEM\ControlSet003\Control\IDConfigDB\CurrentDockInfo
  1c: Key    HKLM\SYSTEM\ControlSet003\Hardware Profiles\Current
  20: Key    HKLM\HARDWARE\DESCRIPTION\SYSTEM\MultifunctionAdapter
```

The display above shows the first eight open handles in the System process. The process name and ID are displayed first, followed by a line for each handle. The handle value, object type, and object name are shown for each handle. Because we specified the *-a* flag, handles to objects that don't have names (handle numbers 0x4, 0xc, and 0x18) are included.

An object handle is an index into a process-specific *handle table,* pointed to by the executive process (EPROCESS) block (described in Chapter 6). The first handle index is 4, the second 8, and so on. A process's handle table contains pointers to all the objects that the process has opened a handle to. Handle tables are implemented as a three-level scheme, similar to the way that the x86 memory management unit implements virtual to physical address translation. (See Chapter 7 for details about memory management in x86 systems.) When a process is created, the object manager allocates the top level of the handle table, which contains pointers to the middle-level tables; the middle level, which contains the first array of pointers to subhandle tables; and the lowest level, which contains the first subhandle table. The arrays at each level consist of 256 entries,

allowing the initial handle table for a process to hold up to 255 handles. The reason that there are only 255 handle entries instead of 256 is that the last entry in the subhandle table is initialized with a value of −1. The −1 is an indicator to the object manager's handle allocation routine that it has come to the last entry of a subhandle table and must move to the next entry or allocate a new one if there are no free entries in the existing subhandle table. The object manager treats the low 24 bits of an object handle's value as three 8-bit fields that index into each of the three levels in the handle table. Figure 3-14 illustrates the Windows 2000 handle table architecture.

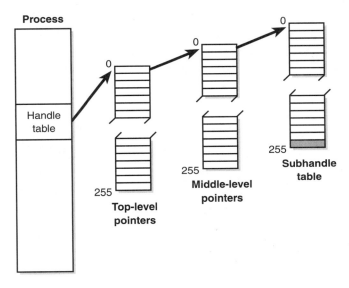

Figure 3-14
Process handle table architecture in Windows 2000

NOTE In Windows NT 4, a handle table consists of a fixed header and a variable size portion. The variable size part is an array of handle table entries, each describing one open handle. If a process opens more handles than can fit in the variable portion, the system allocates a new, larger array and copies the old array into the new one. The changes were made in Windows 2000 to improve handle table performance by avoiding copy operations and minimizing scenarios where an entire handle table must be locked.

As shown in Figure 3-15, each handle entry consists of a structure with two 32-bit members. The first 32-bit member contains both a pointer to the object header and four flags. Because object headers are always 32-bit aligned, the low-order 3 bits of this field are free for use as flags. An entry's high bit is used as a lock. When the object manager translates a handle to an object pointer, it locks the handle entry while the translation is in progress. Because all objects are located in the system address space, the high bit of the object pointer is set. (The addresses are guaranteed to be higher than 0x80000000 even on systems with the /3GB boot switch.) Thus, the object manager can keep the high bit clear when a handle table entry is unlocked and, in the process of locking the entry, set the bit and obtain the object's correct pointer value. The object manager needs to lock a process's entire handle table, using a handle table lock associated with each process, only when the process creates a new handle or closes an existing handle. The second member of a handle table entry is the granted access mask for that object. (Access masks are described in Chapter 8.)

Figure 3-15
Structure of a handle table entry

The first flag is the *inheritance designation*—that is, whether processes created by this process will get a copy of this handle in their handle tables. As already noted, handle inheritance can be specified on handle creation or later with the *SetHandleInformation* function. The second flag indicates whether the caller is allowed to close this handle. (This flag can also be specified with the Win32 *SetHandleInformation* function.) The third flag indicates whether closing the object should generate an audit message. (This flag isn't exposed to Win32—the object manager uses it internally.)

System components and device drivers often need to open handles to objects that user-mode applications shouldn't have access to. In Windows NT 4, such a handle had to be created in the System process, a process reserved for system threads and kernel-mode handles.

To reference a handle from the System process on Windows NT 4 when a kernel-mode function is executing on a user-mode thread, and therefore running in the context of a user-mode process where the handle table in effect is that of the user-mode process, the function would have to somehow switch into the System process. Drivers and the executive components accomplished this either by requesting that a system worker thread (described in the section "System Worker Threads" later in this chapter), which executes in the context of the System process, execute a function on the function's behalf to reference the appropriate handle or by switching the current thread's process context to that of the System process via the *KeAttachProcess* API function. Both options are tedious and can negatively affect performance.

Microsoft introduces a special handle table called the *kernel handle table* in Windows 2000 (referenced internally with the name *ObpKernelHandleTable*). The handles in this table are accessible only from kernel mode and in any process context. This means that a kernel-mode function can reference the handle in any process context with no performance impact. Handles from the kernel handle table are differentiated from those of the current process's handle table because the high bit of the handle is set—that is, all handles from the kernel handle table have values greater than 0x80000000.

EXPERIMENT: Viewing the Handle Table with the Kernel Debugger

The *!handle* command in the kernel debugger takes three arguments:

```
!handle <handle index> <flags> <processid>
```

The handle index identifies the handle entry in the handle table. (Zero means display all handles.) The first handle is index 4, the second 8, and so on. For example, typing *!handle 4* will show the first handle for the current process.

(continued)

EXPERIMENT: Viewing the Handle Table with the Kernel Debugger *continued*

The flags you can specify are a bitmask, where bit 0 means display only the information in the handle entry, bit 1 means display free handles (not just used handles), and bit 2 means display information about the object that the handle refers to. The following command displays full details about the handle table for process ID 0x408:

```
kd> !handle 0 7 408

processor number 0
Searching for Process with Cid == 408
PROCESS 865f0790 SessionId: 0 Cid: 0408 Peb: 7ffdf000 ParentCid: 01dc
    DirBase: 04fd3000  ObjectTable: 856ca888  TableSize: 21.
    Image: i386kd.exe

Handle Table at e2125000 with 21 Entries in use
0000: free handle
0004: Object: e20da2e0  GrantedAccess: 000f001f
Object: e20da2e0  Type: (81491b80) Section
    ObjectHeader: e20da2c8
        HandleCount: 1  PointerCount: 1

0008: Object: 80b13330  GrantedAccess: 00100003
Object: 80b13330  Type: (81495100) Event
    ObjectHeader: 80b13318
        HandleCount: 1  PointerCount: 1
```

Object Security

When you open a file, you must specify whether you intend to read or to write. If you try to write to a file that is opened for read access, you get an error. Likewise, in the executive, when a process creates an object or opens a handle to an existing object, the process must specify a set of *desired access rights*—that is, what it wants to do with the object. It can request either a set of standard access rights (such as read, write, and execute) that apply to all object types or specific access rights that vary depending on the object type. For example, the process can request delete access or append access to a file object. Similarly, it might require the ability to suspend or terminate a thread object.

When a process opens a handle to an object, the object manager calls the *security reference monitor,* the kernel-mode portion of the security system, sending it the process's set of desired access rights. The security reference monitor checks whether the object's security descriptor permits the type of access the process is requesting. If it does, the reference monitor returns a set of *granted access rights* that the process is allowed, and the object manager stores them in

the object handle it creates. How the security system determines who gets access to which objects is explored in Chapter 8.

Thereafter, whenever the process's threads use the handle, the object manager can quickly check whether the set of granted access rights stored in the handle corresponds to the usage implied by the object service the threads have called. For example, if the caller asked for read access to a section object but then calls a service to write to it, the service fails.

Object Retention

Because all user-mode processes that access an object must first open a handle to it, the object manager can easily track how many of these processes, and even which ones, are using an object. Tracking these handles represents one part in implementing *object retention*—that is, retaining temporary objects only as long as they are in use and then deleting them.

The object manager implements object retention in two phases. The first phase is called *name retention,* and it is controlled by the number of open handles to an object that exist. Every time a process opens a handle to an object, the object manager increments the open handle counter in the object's header. As processes finish using the object and close their handles to it, the object manager decrements the open handle counter. When the counter drops to 0, the object manager deletes the object's name from its global namespace. This deletion prevents new processes from opening a handle to the object.

The second phase of object retention is to stop retaining the objects themselves (that is, to delete them) when they are no longer in use. Because operating system code usually accesses objects by using pointers instead of handles, the object manager must also record how many object pointers it has dispensed to operating system processes. It increments a *reference count* for an object each time it gives out a pointer to the object; when kernel-mode components finish using the pointer, they call the object manager to decrement the object's reference count. The system also increments the reference count when it increments the handle count, and likewise decrements the reference count when the handle count decrements, because a handle is also a reference to the object that must be tracked. (For further details on object retention, see the DDK documentation on the functions *ObReferenceObjectByPointer* and *ObDereferenceObject.*)

Figure 3-16 illustrates two event objects that are in use. Process A has the first event open. Process B has both events open. In addition, the first event is being referenced by some kernel-mode structure; thus, the reference count is 3. So even if processes A and B closed their handles to the first event object, it would continue to exist because its reference count is 1. However, when process B closes its handle to the second event object, the object would be deallocated.

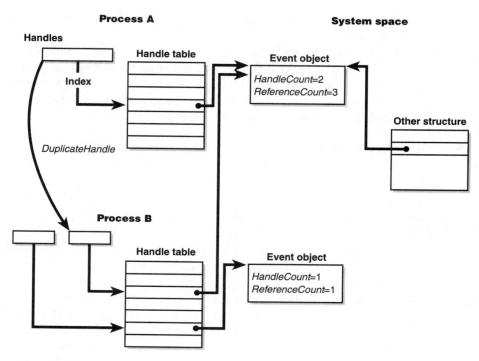

Figure 3-16
Handles and reference counts

So even after an object's open handle counter reaches 0, the object's reference count might remain positive, indicating that the operating system is still using the object. Ultimately, the reference count also drops to 0. When this happens, the object manager deletes the object from memory.

Because of the way object retention works, an application can ensure that an object and its name remain in memory simply by keeping a handle open to the object. Programmers who write applications that contain two or more cooperating processes need not be concerned that one process might delete an object before the other process has finished using it. In addition, closing an application's object handles won't cause an object to be deleted if the operating system is still using it. For example, one process might create a second process to execute a program in the background; it then immediately closes its handle to the process. Because the operating system needs the second process to run the program, it maintains a reference to its process object. Only when the background program finishes executing does the object manager decrement the second process's reference count and then delete it.

Resource Accounting

Resource accounting, like object retention, is closely related to the use of object handles. A positive open handle count indicates that some process is using that resource. It also indicates that some process is being charged for the memory the object occupies. When an object's handle count drops to 0, the process that was using the object should no longer be charged for it.

Many operating systems use a quota system to limit processes' access to system resources. However, the types of quotas imposed on processes are sometimes diverse and complicated, and the code to track the quotas is spread throughout the operating system. For example, in some operating systems, an I/O component might record and limit the number of files a process can open, whereas a memory component might impose a limit on the amount of memory a process's threads can allocate. A process component might limit users to some maximum number of new processes they can create or a maximum number of threads within a process. Each of these limits is tracked and enforced in different parts of the operating system.

In contrast, the Windows 2000 object manager provides a central facility for resource accounting. Each object header contains an attribute called *quota charges* that records how much the object manager subtracts from a process's allotted paged and/or nonpaged pool quota when a thread in the process opens a handle to the object.

Each process on Windows 2000 points to a quota structure that records the limits and current values for nonpaged pool, paged pool, and page file usage. However, all the processes in an interactive session share the same quota block (there's no documented way to create processes with their own quota blocks), and system processes, such as services, have no quota limits.

Although the system implements code to track quotas, it currently doesn't enforce them. A process's paged pool and nonpaged pool quotas default to 0 (no limit). There are registry values to override these defaults, but the limits are soft, in that the system attempts to increase process quotas automatically when they are exceeded. If opening an object will exceed the paged or nonpaged quota, the memory manager is called to see whether the quotas can be increased. The memory manager makes this decision based on the amount of memory remaining in the system pools. If it determines that the quota can't be increased, the open request to the object fails with a "quota exceeded" error. But on most systems, quotas continue to grow as needed.

EXPERIMENT: Viewing Process Quotas

You can view the paged pool, nonpaged pool, and page file current usage, peak usage, and quota (limit) for a process with the Process Explode utility, Pview.exe, available on *www.reskit.com*. (The Performance tool displays only the usage information, not the quotas.) In the following example, the process selected has a peak paged pool usage of 1062 KB, current usage of 1028 KB, and a quota of 1504 KB:

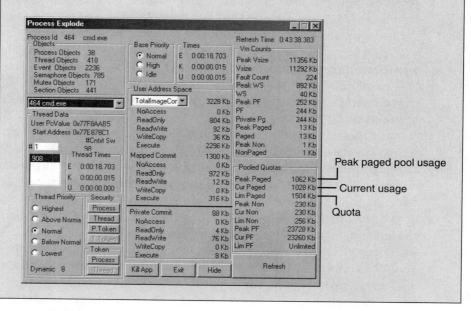

Object Names

An important consideration in creating a multitude of objects is devising a successful system for keeping track of them. The object manager requires the following information to help you do so:

- A way to distinguish one object from another
- A method for finding and retrieving a particular object

The first requirement is served by allowing names to be assigned to objects. This is an extension of what most operating systems provide—the ability to name selected resources, files, pipes, or a block of shared memory, for example. The executive, in contrast, allows any resource represented by an object to have a name. The second requirement, finding and retrieving an object, is also satisfied by object names. If the object manager stores objects by name, it can find an object by looking up its name.

Object names also satisfy a third requirement, which is to allow processes to share objects. The executive's object namespace is a global one, visible to all processes in the system. One process can create an object and place its name in the global namespace, and a second process can open a handle to the object by specifying the object's name. If an object isn't meant to be shared in this way, its creator doesn't need to give it a name.

To increase efficiency, the object manager doesn't look up an object's name each time someone uses the object. Instead, it looks up a name under only two circumstances. The first is when a process creates a named object: the object manager looks up the name to verify that it doesn't already exist before storing the new name in the global namespace. The second is when a process opens a handle to a named object: the object manager looks up the name, finds the object, and then returns an object handle to the caller; thereafter, the caller uses the handle to refer to the object. When looking up a name, the object manager allows the caller to select either a case-sensitive or a case-insensitive search, a feature that supports POSIX and other environments that use case-sensitive filenames.

Where the names of objects are stored depends on the object type. Table 3-8 lists the standard object directories found on all Windows 2000 systems and what types of objects have their names stored there. Of the directories listed, only \BaseNamedObjects and \?? are visible to user programs.

Because the base kernel objects such as mutexes, events, semaphores, waitable timers, and sections have their names stored in a single object directory, no two of these objects can have the same name, even if they are of a different type. This restriction emphasizes the need to choose names carefully so that they don't collide with other names (for example, prefix names with your company and product name).

Table 3-8 **Standard Object Directories**

Directory	Types of Object Names Stored
\??	MS-DOS device names (\DosDevices is a symbolic link to this directory.)
\BaseNamedObjects	Mutexes, events, semaphores, waitable timers, and section objects
\Callback	Callback objects
\Device	Device objects
\Driver	Driver objects
\FileSystem	File system driver objects and file system recognizer device objects
\KnownDlls	Section names and path for known DLLs (DLLs mapped by the system at startup time)
\Nls	Section names for mapped national language support tables
\ObjectTypes	Names of types of objects
\RPC Control	Port objects used by remote procedure calls (RPCs)
\Security	Names of objects specific to the security subsystem
\Windows	Win32 subsystem ports and window stations

Object names are global to a single computer (or to all processors on a multiprocessor computer), but they're not visible across a network. However, the object manager's parse method makes it possible to access named objects that exist on other computers. For example, the I/O manager, which supplies file object services, extends the functions of the object manager to remote files. When asked to open a remote file object, the object manager calls a parse method, which allows the I/O manager to intercept the request and deliver it to a network redirector, a driver that accesses files across the network. Server code on the remote Windows system calls the object manager and the I/O manager on that system to find the file object and return the information back across the network.

EXPERIMENT: Looking at the Base Named Objects

You can see the list of base objects that have names with the Object Viewer utility on this book's companion CD. (Another version of this utility is also available with the Platform SDK.) Run \Sysint\Winobj.exe, and click on \BaseNamedObjects, as shown here:

The named objects are shown on the right. The icons indicate the object type.

- Mutexes are indicated with a stop sign.
- Sections (Win32 file mapping objects) are shown as memory chips.
- Events are shown as exclamation points.
- Semaphores are indicated with an icon that resembles a traffic signal.
- Symbolic links have icons that are curved arrows.

Object directories The *object directory object* is the object manager's means for supporting this hierarchical naming structure. This object is analogous to a file system directory and contains the names of other objects, possibly even other object directories. The object directory object maintains enough information to translate these object names into pointers to the objects themselves. The object manager uses the pointers to construct the object handles that it returns to user-mode callers. Both kernel-mode code (including executive components and device drivers) and user-mode code (such as subsystems) can create object directories in which to store objects. For example, the I/O manager creates an object directory named \Device, which contains the names of objects representing I/O devices.

Symbolic links In certain file systems (on NTFS and some UNIX systems, for example), a symbolic link lets a user create a filename or a directory name that, when used, is translated by the operating system into a different file or directory name. Using a symbolic link is a simple method for allowing users to indirectly share a file or the contents of a directory, creating a cross-link between different directories in the ordinarily hierarchical directory structure.

The object manager implements an object called a *symbolic link object,* which performs a similar function for object names in its object namespace. A symbolic link can occur anywhere within an object name string. When a caller refers to a symbolic link object's name, the object manager traverses its object namespace until it reaches the symbolic link object. It looks inside the symbolic link and finds a string that it substitutes for the symbolic link name. It then restarts its name lookup.

One place in which the executive uses symbolic link objects is in translating MS-DOS-style device names into Windows 2000 internal device names. In Win32, a user refers to floppy and hard disk drives using the names A:, B:, C:, and so on. Moreover, the user can add pseudo drive names with the *subst* (substitute) command or by mapping a drive letter to a network share. Once they are created, these drive names must be visible to all processes on the system.

The Win32 subsystem makes drive letters protected, global data by placing them in the object manager namespace under the \?? object directory. (Prior to Windows NT 4, this directory was named \DosDevices; it was renamed \?? for performance reasons—that name places it first alphabetically.) When the user or an application creates a new drive letter, the Win32 subsystem adds another object under the \?? object directory.

Terminal Services Namespace

Windows NT was written with the assumption that only one user would log on to the system interactively and that the system would run only one instance of any interactive application. When you install Windows 2000 Terminal Services, these assumptions are violated, so for Windows 2000 supporting multiple interactive users required changes to the object manager.

A user logging on to the console has access to the *global* namespace, a namespace that serves as the first instance of the namespace. Users logging on remotely at terminals are given a view of the namespace known as a *local* namespace. The parts of the namespace that are localized for each remote user include \DosDevices, \Windows, and \BaseNamedObjects. Making separate copies of the same parts of the namespace is known as *instancing* the namespace. Instancing \DosDevices makes it possible for each user to have different drive letters and Win32 objects such as serial ports. The \Windows directory is where Win32k.sys creates the interactive window station, \WinSta0. A Terminal Services environment can support multiple interactive users, but each user needs an individual version of WinSta0 to preserve the illusion that he or she is accessing the predefined interactive window station in Windows 2000. Finally, applications and the system create shared objects in \BaseNamedObjects, including events, mutexes, and memory sections. If two users are running an application that creates the named object ApplicationInitialized, each user session must have a private version of the object so that the two instances of the application don't interfere with one another by accessing the same object.

The object manager implements a local namespace by creating the private versions of the three directories mentioned under a directory associated with the user's session under \Sessions\X (where X is the session identifier of the user). When a Win32 application in remote session two creates a named event, for example, the object manager transparently redirects the object's name from \BaseNamedObjects to \Sessions\2\BaseNamedObjects.

All object manager functions related to namespace management are aware of the instanced directories and participate in providing the illusion that nonconsole sessions use the same namespace as the console session. As an optimization, the process object has a field named *DeviceMap* that points to a data structure shared by other processes in the same session, which locates the \DosDevices object manager directory that belongs to the session as well as a list of drive letters that are valid for the session. The object manager uses the data structure when looking up objects in \DosDevices.

Under certain circumstances, applications that are Terminal Services–aware need to access objects in the console session even if the application is running in a remote session. The application might want to do this to synchronize with instances of itself running in other remote sessions or with the console session. For these cases, the object manager provides the special override "\Global" that an application can prefix to any object name to access the global namespace. For example, an application in session two opening an object named \Global\ApplicationInitialized is directed to \BasedNamedObjects\ApplicationInitialized instead of \Sessions\2\BaseNamedObjects\ApplicationInitialized.

EXPERIMENT: Viewing Namespace Instancing

You can see the object manager instance the namespace on a Windows 2000 Server, Advanced Server, or Datacenter Server system on which you install Terminal Services. Logon to the server using the Terminal Services client, and run the \Sysint\Winobj.exe utility from this book's companion CD.

Click on the \Sessions directory, and you'll see a subdirectory with a numeric name for each active remote session. If you open one of these directories, you'll see subdirectories named \DosDevices, \Windows, and \BaseNamedObjects, which are the local namespace subdirectories of the session. The following screen shot shows a local namespace:

Synchronization

The concept of *mutual exclusion* is a crucial one in operating systems development. It refers to the guarantee that one, and only one, thread can access a particular resource at a time. Mutual exclusion is necessary when a resource doesn't lend itself to shared access or when sharing would result in an unpredictable outcome. For example, if two threads copy a file to a printer port at the same time, their output could be interspersed. Similarly, if one thread reads a memory location while another one writes to it, the first thread will receive unpredictable data. In general, writable resources can't be shared without restrictions, whereas resources that aren't subject to modification can be shared. Figure 3-17 illustrates what happens when two threads running on different processors both write data to a circular queue.

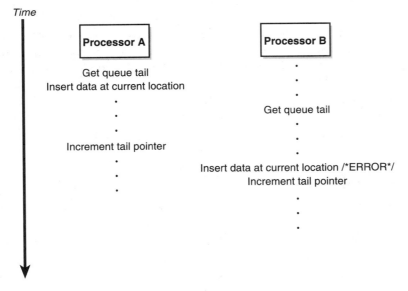

Figure 3-17
Incorrect sharing of memory

Because the second thread got the value of the queue tail pointer before the first thread had finished updating it, the second thread inserted its data into the same location that the first thread had used, overwriting data and leaving

one queue location empty. Even though this figure illustrates what could happen on a multiprocessor system, the same error could occur on a single-processor system if the operating system were to perform a context switch to the second thread before the first thread updated the queue tail pointer.

Sections of code that access a nonshareable resource are called *critical* sections. To ensure correct code, only one thread at a time can execute in a critical section. While one thread is writing to a file, updating a database, or modifying a shared variable, no other thread can be allowed to access the same resource. The pseudocode shown in Figure 3-17 is a critical section that incorrectly accesses a shared data structure without mutual exclusion.

The issue of mutual exclusion, although important for all operating systems, is especially important (and intricate) for a *tightly coupled, symmetric multiprocessing* (SMP) operating system such as Windows 2000, in which the same system code runs simultaneously on more than one processor, sharing certain data structures stored in global memory. In Windows 2000, it is the kernel's job to provide mechanisms that system code can use to prevent two threads from modifying the same structure at the same time. The kernel provides mutual-exclusion primitives that it and the rest of the executive use to synchronize their access to global data structures.

In the following sections, you'll find out how the kernel uses mutual exclusion to protect its global data structures and what mutual-exclusion and synchronization mechanisms the kernel provides to the executive that it, in turn, provides to user mode.

Kernel Synchronization

At various stages during its execution, the kernel must guarantee that one, and only one, processor at a time is executing within a critical section. Kernel critical sections are the code segments that modify a global data structure such as the kernel's dispatcher database or its DPC queue. The operating system can't function correctly unless the kernel can guarantee that threads access these data structures in a mutually exclusive manner.

The biggest area of concern is interrupts. For example, the kernel might be updating a global data structure when an interrupt occurs whose interrupt-handling routine also modifies the structure. Simple single-processor operating systems sometimes prevent such a scenario by disabling all interrupts each time they access global data, but the Windows 2000 kernel has a more sophisticated solution. Before using a global resource, the kernel temporarily masks those interrupts whose interrupt handlers also use the resource. It does so by raising

the processor's IRQL to the highest level used by any potential interrupt source that accesses the global data. For example, an interrupt at DPC/dispatch level causes the dispatcher, which uses the dispatcher database, to run. Therefore, any other part of the kernel that uses the dispatcher database raises the IRQL to DPC/dispatch level, masking DPC/dispatch-level interrupts before using the dispatcher database.

This strategy is fine for a single-processor system, but it's inadequate for a multiprocessor configuration. Raising the IRQL on one processor doesn't prevent an interrupt from occurring on another processor. The kernel also needs to guarantee mutually exclusive access across several processors.

The mechanism the kernel uses to achieve multiprocessor mutual exclusion is called a *spinlock*. A spinlock is a locking primitive associated with a global data structure, such as the DPC queue shown in Figure 3-18.

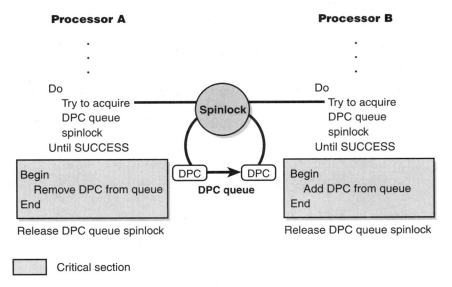

Figure 3-18
Using a spinlock

Before entering either critical section shown in the figure, the kernel must acquire the spinlock associated with the protected DPC queue. If the spinlock isn't free, the kernel keeps trying to acquire the lock until it succeeds. The spinlock gets its name from the fact that the kernel (and thus, the processor) is held in limbo, "spinning," until it gets the lock.

Spinlocks, like the data structures they protect, reside in global memory. The code to acquire and release a spinlock is written in assembly language for speed and to exploit whatever locking mechanism the underlying processor architecture provides. On many architectures, spinlocks are implemented with a hardware-supported test-and-set operation, which tests the value of a lock variable and acquires the lock in one atomic instruction. Testing and acquiring the lock in one instruction prevents a second thread from grabbing the lock between the time when the first thread tests the variable and the time when it acquires the lock.

All kernel-mode spinlocks in Windows 2000 have an associated IRQL that is always at DPC/dispatch level or higher. Thus, when a thread is trying to acquire a spinlock, all other activity at the spinlock's IRQL or lower ceases on that processor. Because thread dispatching happens at DPC/dispatch level, a thread that holds a spinlock is never preempted because the IRQL masks the dispatching mechanisms. This masking allows code executing a critical section protected by a spinlock to continue executing so that it will release the lock quickly. The kernel uses spinlocks with great care, minimizing the number of instructions it executes while it holds a spinlock.

NOTE Because the IRQL is an effective synchronization mechanism on uniprocessors, the spinlock acquisition and release functions of uniprocessor HALs don't implement spinlocks—they simply raise and lower the IRQL.

The kernel makes spinlocks available to other parts of the executive through a set of kernel functions, including *KeAcquireSpinlock* and *KeReleaseSpinlock*. Device drivers, for example, require spinlocks in order to guarantee that device registers and other global data structures are accessed by only one part of a device driver (and from only one processor) at a time. Spinlocks are not for use by user programs—user programs should use the objects described in the next section.

Kernel spinlocks carry with them restrictions for code that uses them. Because spinlocks always have an IRQL of DPC/dispatch level or higher, as explained earlier, code holding a spinlock will crash the system if it attempts to make the scheduler perform a dispatch operation or if it causes a page fault.

Windows 2000 introduces a special type of spinlock called a *queued spinlock*, which is used only by the kernel and not exported for executive components or device drivers. A queued spinlock is a form of spinlock that scales better on multiprocessors than a standard spinlock. A queued spinlock work like this: When a processor wants to acquire a queued spinlock that is currently held, it places

its identifier in a queue associated with the spinlock. When the processor that's holding the spinlock releases it, it hands the lock over to the first processor identified in the queue. In the meantime, a processor waiting for a busy spinlock checks the status not of the spinlock itself but of a per-processor flag that the processor ahead of it in the queue sets to indicate that the waiting processor's turn has arrived.

The fact that queued spinlocks result in spinning on per-processor flags rather than global spinlocks has two effects. The first is that the multiprocessor's bus isn't as heavily trafficked by interprocessor synchronization. The second is that instead of a random processor in a waiting group acquiring a spinlock, the queued spinlock enforces first-in, first-out (FIFO) ordering to the lock. FIFO ordering means more consistent performance across processors accessing the same locks.

Microsoft hasn't converted all the kernel's locks to queued spinlocks, just the half-dozen or so locks that protect the core data structures of the kernel, such as the cache manager's database, the scheduler's thread database, and the memory manager's physical memory database.

EXPERIMENT: Viewing Queued Spinlocks

You can view the state of queued spinlocks by using the *!qlock* kernel debugger command. This command is meaningful only on a multiprocessor system because uniprocessor HALs don't implement spinlocks. In the following example, the dispatcher database queued spinlock is held by processor 1, and the other queued spinlocks are not acquired. (The dispatcher database is described in Chapter 6.)

```
kd> !qlocks
Key: 0 = Owner, 1-n = Wait order, blank = not owned/waiting, C = Corrupt

                        Processor Number
    Lock Name       0  1  2  3  4  5  6  7  8  9 10 11 12 13 14 15

KE - Dispatcher        0
KE - Context Swap
MM - PFN
MM - System Space
CC - Vacb
CC - Master
```

Executive Synchronization

Executive software outside the kernel also needs to synchronize access to global data structures in a multiprocessor environment. For example, the memory manager has only one page frame database, which it accesses as a global data structure, and device drivers need to ensure that they can gain exclusive access to their devices. By calling kernel functions, the executive can create a spinlock, acquire it, and release it.

Spinlocks only partially fill the executive's needs for synchronization mechanisms, however. Because waiting on a spinlock literally stalls a processor, spinlocks can be used only under the following strictly limited circumstances:

■ The protected resource must be accessed quickly and without complicated interactions with other code.

■ The critical section code can't be paged out of memory, can't make references to pageable data, can't call external procedures (including system services), and can't generate interrupts or exceptions.

These restrictions are confining and can't be met under all circumstances. Furthermore, the executive needs to perform other types of synchronization in addition to mutual exclusion, and it must also provide synchronization mechanisms to user mode.

The kernel furnishes additional synchronization mechanisms to the executive in the form of kernel objects, known collectively as *dispatcher objects*. The user-visible synchronization objects acquire their synchronization capabilities from these kernel dispatcher objects. Each user-visible object that supports synchronization encapsulates at least one kernel dispatcher object. The executive's synchronization semantics are visible to Win32 programmers through the *WaitForSingleObject* and *WaitForMultipleObjects* functions, which the Win32 subsystem implements by calling analogous system services the object manager supplies. A thread in a Win32 application can synchronize with a Win32 process, thread, event, semaphore, mutex, waitable timer, I/O completion port, or file object.

One other type of executive synchronization object worth noting is called *executive resources*. Executive resources provide both exclusive access (like a mutex) as well as shared read access (multiple readers sharing read-only access to a structure). However, they're available only to kernel-mode code and thus aren't accessible from the Win32 API. Executive resources are not dispatcher objects but rather data structures allocated directly from nonpaged pool that

have their own specialized services to initialize, lock, release, query, and wait on them. The executive resource structure is defined in Ntddk.h, and the executive support routines are documented in the DDK reference documentation.

The remaining subsections describe the implementation details of waiting on dispatcher objects.

Waiting on Dispatcher Objects

A thread can synchronize with a dispatcher object by waiting on the object's handle. Doing so causes the kernel to suspend the thread and change its dispatcher state from running to waiting, as shown in Figure 3-19. The kernel removes the thread from the dispatcher ready queue and no longer considers it for execution.

NOTE Figure 3-19 is a process state transition diagram with focus on the ready, waiting, and running states (the states related to waiting on objects). The other states are described in Chapter 6.

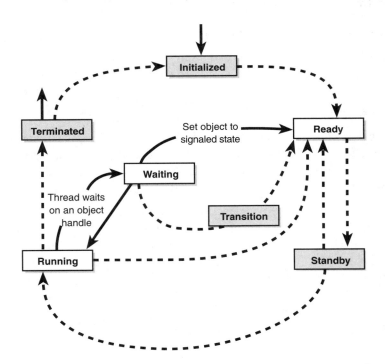

Figure 3-19
Waiting on a dispatcher object

At any given moment, a synchronization object is in one of two states: either the *signaled state* or the *nonsignaled state*. A thread can't resume its execution until the kernel changes its dispatcher state from waiting to ready. This change occurs when the dispatcher object whose handle the thread is waiting on also undergoes a state change, from the nonsignaled state to the signaled state (when a thread sets an event object, for example). To synchronize with an object, a thread calls one of the wait system services the object manager supplies, passing a handle to the object it wants to synchronize with. The thread can wait on one or several objects and can also specify that its wait should be canceled if it hasn't ended within a certain amount of time. Whenever the kernel sets an object to the signaled state, the kernel's *KiWaitTest* function checks to see whether any threads are waiting on the object. If they are, the kernel releases one or more of the threads from their waiting state so that they can continue executing.

The following example of setting an event illustrates how synchronization interacts with thread dispatching:

1. A user-mode thread waits on an event object's handle.

2. The kernel changes the thread's scheduling state from ready to waiting and then adds the thread to a list of threads waiting for the event.

3. Another thread sets the event.

4. The kernel marches down the list of threads waiting on the event. If a thread's conditions for waiting are satisfied,* the kernel changes the thread's state from waiting to ready. If it is a variable-priority thread, the kernel might also boost its execution priority.

5. Because a new thread has become ready to execute, the dispatcher reschedules. If it finds a running thread with a priority lower than that of the newly ready thread, it preempts the lower-priority thread and issues a software interrupt to initiate a context switch to the higher-priority thread.

6. If no processor can be preempted, the dispatcher places the ready thread in the dispatcher ready queue to be scheduled later.

* Some threads might be waiting for more than one object, so they continue waiting.

What Signals an Object

The signaled state is defined differently for different objects. A thread object is in the nonsignaled state during its lifetime and is set to the signaled state by the kernel when the thread terminates. Similarly, the kernel sets a process object to the signaled state when the process's last thread terminates. In contrast, the timer object, like an alarm, is set to "go off" at a certain time. When its time expires, the kernel sets the timer object to the signaled state.

When choosing a synchronization mechanism, a program must take into account the rules governing the behavior of different synchronization objects. Whether a thread's wait ends when an object is set to the signaled state varies with the type of object the thread is waiting on, as Table 3-9 illustrates.

Table 3-9 **Definitions of the Signaled State**

Object Type	Set to Signaled State When	Effect on Waiting Threads
Process	Last thread terminates	All released
Thread	Thread terminates	All released
File	I/O operation completes	All released
Event (notification type)	Thread sets the event	All released
Event (synchronization type)	Thread sets the event	One thread released; event object reset
Semaphore	Semaphore count drops by 1	One thread released
Timer (notification type)	Set time arrives or time interval expires	All released
Timer (synchronization type)	Set time arrives or time interval expires	One thread released
Mutex	Thread releases the mutex	One thread released
File	I/O completes	All threads released
Queue	Item is placed on queue	One thread released

When an object is set to the signaled state, waiting threads are generally released from their wait states immediately. Some of the kernel dispatcher objects and the system events that induce their state changes are shown in Figure 3-20.

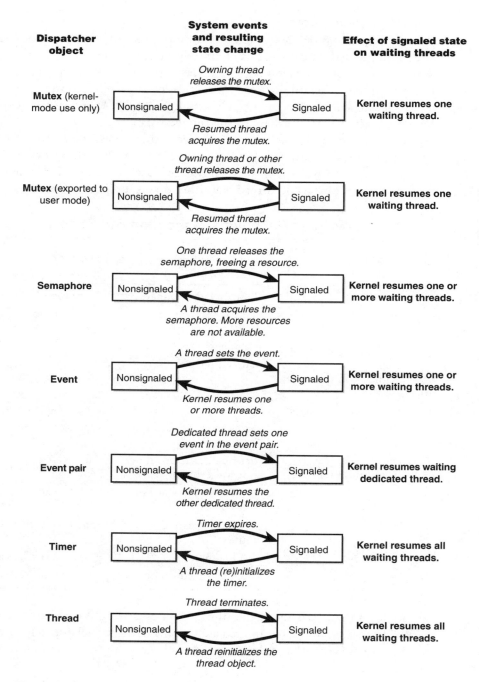

Figure 3-20
Selected kernel dispatcher objects

For example, a notification event object (called a manual reset event in the Win32 API) is used to announce the occurrence of some event. When the event object is set to the signaled state, all threads waiting on the event are released. The exception is any thread that is waiting on more than one object at a time; such a thread might be required to continue waiting until additional objects reach the signaled state.

In contrast to an event object, a mutex object has ownership associated with it. It is used to gain mutually exclusive access to a resource, and only one thread at a time can hold the mutex. When the mutex object becomes free, the kernel sets it to the signaled state and then selects one waiting thread to execute. The thread selected by the kernel acquires the mutex object, and all other threads continue waiting.

This brief discussion wasn't meant to enumerate all the reasons and applications for using the various executive objects but rather to list their basic functionality and synchronization behavior. For information on how to put these objects to use in Win32 programs, see the Win32 reference documentation on synchronization objects or Jeffrey Richter's *Programming Applications for Microsoft Windows.*

Data Structures

Two data structures are key to tracking who is waiting on what: *dispatcher headers* and *wait blocks*. Both these structures are publicly defined in the DDK include file Ntddk.h. The definitions are reproduced here for convenience:

```
typedef struct _DISPATCHER_HEADER {
    UCHAR Type;
    UCHAR Absolute;
    UCHAR Size;
    UCHAR Inserted;
    LONG SignalState;
    LIST_ENTRY WaitListHead;
} DISPATCHER_HEADER;

typedef struct _KWAIT_BLOCK {
    LIST_ENTRY WaitListEntry;
    struct _KTHREAD *RESTRICTED_POINTER Thread;
    PVOID Object;
    struct _KWAIT_BLOCK *RESTRICTED_POINTER NextWaitBlock;
    USHORT WaitKey;
    USHORT WaitType;
} KWAIT_BLOCK, *PKWAIT_BLOCK, *RESTRICTED_POINTER PRKWAIT_BLOCK;
```

The dispatcher header contains the object type, signaled state, and a list of the threads waiting on that object. The wait block represents a thread waiting on an object. Each thread that is in a wait state has a list of the wait blocks

that represent the objects the thread is waiting on. Each dispatcher object has a list of the wait blocks that represent which threads are waiting on the object. This list is kept so that when a dispatcher object is signaled, the kernel can quickly determine who is waiting on that object. The wait block has a pointer to the object being waited on, a pointer to the thread waiting on the object, and a pointer to the next wait block (if the thread is waiting on more than one object). It also records the type of wait (any or all) as well as the position of that entry in the array of handles passed by the thread on the *WaitForMultipleObjects* call (zero if the thread was waiting on only one object).

Figure 3-21 shows the relationship of dispatcher objects to wait blocks to threads. In this example, thread 1 is waiting on object B, and thread 2 is waiting on objects A and B. If object A is signaled, the kernel will see that because thread 2 is also waiting on another object, thread 2 can't be readied for execution. On the other hand, if object B is signaled, the kernel can ready thread 1 for execution right away since it isn't waiting on any other objects.

Figure 3-21
Wait data structures

EXPERIMENT: Looking at Wait Queues

Although many process viewer utilities indicate whether a thread is in a wait state (and if so, what kind of wait), you can see the list of objects a thread is waiting on only with the kernel debugger *!thread* command. For example, the following excerpt from the output of a *!process* command shows that the thread is waiting on an event object:

```
kd> !process
:
THREAD 80618030  Cid 97.7f  Teb: 7ffde000  Win32Thread: e199cea8
WAIT: (WrUserRequest) UserMode Non-Alertable
          805b4ab0  SynchronizationEvent
```

Although the kernel debugger doesn't have a command for formatting the contents of a dispatcher header, we know the layout (described on page 163), so we can interpret its contents manually:

```
kd> dd 805b4ab0
0x805B4AB0  00040001 00000000 8061809c 8061809c ..........a...a.
```

From this, we can ascertain that no other threads are waiting on this event object because the wait list head forward and backward pointers (the third and fourth 32-bit values) point to the same location (a single wait block). Dumping the wait block (at address 0x8061809c) yields the following:

```
kd> dd 8061809c
0x8061809C  805b4ab8 805b4ab8 80618030 805b4ab0 .J[..J[.0.a..J[.
0x806180AC  8061809c 00010000 00000000 00000000 ..a............
```

The first two 32-bit values point to the list head of the wait blocks in the dispatcher header. The third 32-bit value is the pointer to the thread object. The fourth value points to the dispatcher object itself. The fifth value (0x8061809c) is the pointer to the next wait block. From this, we can conclude that the thread is not waiting on any other objects, since the next wait block field points to the wait block itself.

System Worker Threads

During system initialization, Windows 2000 creates several threads in the System process, called *system worker threads,* that exist solely to perform work on behalf of other threads. In many cases, threads executing at DPC/dispatch level need to execute functions that can be performed only at a lower IRQL. For

example, a DPC routine, which executes in an arbitrary thread context (DPC execution can usurp any thread in the system) at DPC/dispatch level IRQL, might need to access paged pool or wait on a dispatcher object used to synchronize execution with an application thread. Because a DPC routine can't lower the IRQL, it must pass such processing to a thread that executes at an IRQL below DPC/dispatch level.

Some device drivers and executive components create their own threads dedicated to processing work at passive level; however, most use system worker threads instead, which avoids the unnecessary scheduling and memory overhead associated with having additional threads in the system. A device driver or an executive component requests a system worker thread's services by calling the executive functions *ExQueueWorkItem* or *IoQueueWorkItem*. These functions place a *work item* on a queue dispatcher object where the threads look for work. (Queue dispatcher objects are described in more detail in the section "I/O Completion Ports" on page 570 in Chapter 9.) Work items include a pointer to a routine and a parameter that the thread passes to the routine when it processes the work item. The routine is implemented by the device driver or executive component that requires passive-level execution.

For example, a DPC routine that must wait on a dispatcher object can initialize a work item that points to the routine in the driver that waits on the dispatcher object, and perhaps to a pointer to the object. At some stage, a system worker thread will remove the work item from its queue and execute the driver's routine. When the driver's routine finishes, the system worker thread checks to see whether there are more work items to process. If there aren't any more, the system worker thread blocks until a work item is placed on the queue. The DPC routine might or might not have finished executing when the system worker thread processes its work item. (On a uniprocessor system, a DPC routine always finishes executing before its work item is processed because thread scheduling doesn't take place when the IRQL is at DPC/dispatch level).

There are three types of system worker threads:

- *Delayed worker threads* execute at priority 12, process work items that aren't considered time-critical, and can have their stack paged out to a paging file while they wait for work items.

- *Critical worker threads* execute at priority 13, process time-critical work items, and on Windows 2000 Server installations have their stacks present in physical memory at all times.

- A single *hypercritical worker thread* executes at priority 15 and also keeps its stack in memory. The process manager uses the hypercritical work item to execute the thread "reaper" function that frees terminated threads.

The number of delayed and critical worker threads created by the executive's *ExpWorkerInitialization* function, which is called early in the boot process, depends on the amount of memory present on the system and whether the system is a server. Table 3-10 shows the default number of threads created on different system configurations. You can specify that *ExpInitializeWorker* create up to 16 additional delayed and 16 additional critical worker threads with the AdditionalDelayedWorkerThreads and AdditionalCriticalWorkerThreads values under the registry key HKLM\SYSTEM\CurrentControlSet\Control\Session Manager\Executive.

Table 3-10 Number of System Worker Threads

Worker Thread	System Memory		
	12–19 MB	*20–64 MB*	*> 64 MB*
Delayed	3	3	3
Critical	3	Professional: 3	Professional: 5
		Server: 6	Server: 10
Hypercritical	1	1	1

The executive tries to match the number of critical worker threads with changing workloads as the system executes. Once every second, the executive function *ExpWorkerThreadBalanceManager* determines whether it should create a new critical worker thread. The critical worker threads that are created by *ExpWorkerThreadBalanceManager* are called *dynamic worker threads,* and all the following conditions must be satisfied before such a thread is created:

- Work items exist in the critical work queue.

- The number of inactive critical worker threads (ones that are either blocked waiting for work items or that have blocked on dispatcher objects while executing a work routine) must be less than the number of processors on the system.

- There are fewer than 16 dynamic worker threads.

Dynamic worker threads exit after 10 minutes of inactivity. Thus, when the workload dictates, the executive can create up to 16 dynamic worker threads.

EXPERIMENT: Listing System Worker Threads

You can use the *!exqueue* kernel debugger command to see a listing of system worker threads classified by their type:

```
kd> !exqueue
Dumping ExWorkerQueue: 8046A5C0

**** Critical WorkQueue( current = 0 maximum = 1 )
THREAD 818a2d40  Cid 8.c   Teb: 00000000  Win32Thread: 00000000 WAIT
THREAD 818a2ac0  Cid 8.10  Teb: 00000000  Win32Thread: 00000000 WAIT
THREAD 818a2840  Cid 8.14  Teb: 00000000  Win32Thread: 00000000 WAIT
THREAD 818a25c0  Cid 8.18  Teb: 00000000  Win32Thread: 00000000 WAIT
THREAD 818a2340  Cid 8.1c  Teb: 00000000  Win32Thread: 00000000 WAIT

**** Delayed WorkQueue( current = 0 maximum = 1 )
THREAD 818a20c0  Cid 8.20  Teb: 00000000  Win32Thread: 00000000 WAIT
THREAD 818a1020  Cid 8.24  Teb: 00000000  Win32Thread: 00000000 WAIT
THREAD 818a1da0  Cid 8.28  Teb: 00000000  Win32Thread: 00000000 WAIT

**** HyperCritical WorkQueue( current = 0 maximum = 1 )
THREAD 818a1b20  Cid 8.2c  Teb: 00000000  Win32Thread: 00000000 WAIT
```

Windows 2000 Global Flags

Windows 2000 has a set of flags stored in a systemwide global variable named *NtGlobalFlag* that enable various internal debugging, tracing, and validation support in the operating system. The system variable *NtGlobalFlag* is initialized from the registry key HKLM\SYSTEM\CurrentControlSet\Control\Session Manager in the value GlobalFlag at system boot time. By default, this registry value is 0, so it's likely that on your systems, you're not using any global flags. In addition, each image has a set of global flags that also turn on internal tracing and validation code (though the bit layout of these flags is entirely different than the systemwide global flags). These flags aren't documented or supported for customer use, but they can be useful tools for exploring the internal operation of Windows 2000.

Fortunately, the Platform SDK and the debugging tools contain a utility named Gflags.exe that allows you to view and change the system global flags (either in the registry or in the running system) as well as image global flags. Gflags

has both a command-line and a GUI interface. To see the command-line flags, type *gflags* /?. If you run the utility without any switches, the dialog box shown in Figure 3-22 is displayed.

Figure 3-22
Setting system debugging options with Gflags

You can toggle between the settings in the registry (by clicking System Registry) and the current value of the variable in system memory (by clicking Kernel Mode). You must press the Apply button to make the changes. (You'll exit if you press the OK button.) Although you can change flag settings on a running system, most flags require a reboot to take effect, and there's no documentation on which do and which don't require rebooting. So when in doubt, reboot after changing a global flag.

The Image File Options choice requires that you fill in the filename of a valid executable image. This option is used to change a set of global flags that apply to an individual image (rather than to the whole system). In Figure 3-23, notice that the flags are different than the operating system ones shown in Figure 3-22.

Figure 3-23
Setting image global flags with Gflags

EXPERIMENT: Enabling Image Loader Tracing and Viewing *NtGlobalFlag*

To see an example of the detailed tracing information you can obtain by setting global flags, try running Gflags on a system booted with the kernel debugger that is connected to a host system running Kd or Windbg, or that is running LiveKd.

As an example, try enabling the Show Loader Snaps flag. To do this, select Kernel Mode, click the Show Loader Snaps check box, and click the Apply button. Then run an image on this machine, and in the kernel debugger you'll see volumes of output like the following:

```
LDR: PID: 0xb8 started - 'notepad'
LDR: NEW PROCESS
     Image Path: C:\WINNT\system32\notepad.exe (notepad.exe)
     Current Directory: C:\ddk\bin
     Search Path: C:\WINNT\System32;C:\WINNT\system;C:\WINNT
LDR: notepad.exe bound to comdlg32.dll
LDR: ntdll.dll used by comdlg32.dll
LDR: Snapping imports for comdlg32.dll from ntdll.dll
     ⋮
LDR: KERNEL32.dll loaded. - Calling init routine at 77f01000
```

```
LDR: RPCRT4.dll loaded. - Calling init routine at 77e1b6d5
LDR: ADVAPI32.dll loaded. - Calling init routine at 77dc1000
LDR: USER32.dll loaded. - Calling init routine at 77e78037
```

You can use the *!gflags* and *!gflag* kernel debugger commands to view the state of the *NtGlobalFlag* kernel variable. The *!gflags* command lists all the flags, indicating which ones are enabled, whereas *!gflag* reports only the flags that are enabled.

```
kd> !gflags

NT!NtGlobalFlag 0x4400

    STOP_ON_EXCEPTION            SHOW_LDR_SNAPS
    DEBUG_INITIAL_COMMAND        STOP_ON_HUNG_GUI
    HEAP_ENABLE_TAIL_CHECK       HEAP_ENABLE_FREE_CHECK
    HEAP_VALIDATE_PARAMETERS     HEAP_VALIDATE_ALL
   *POOL_ENABLE_TAGGING          HEAP_ENABLE_TAGGING
    USER_STACK_TRACE_DB          KERNEL_STACK_TRACE_DB
   *MAINTAIN_OBJECT_TYPELIST     HEAP_ENABLE_TAG_BY_DLL
    ENABLE_CSRDEBUG              ENABLE_KDEBUG_SYMBOL_LOAD
    DISABLE_PAGE_KERNEL_STACKS   HEAP_DISABLE_COALESCING
    ENABLE_CLOSE_EXCEPTIONS      ENABLE_EXCEPTION_LOGGING
    ENABLE_HANDLE_TYPE_TAGGING   HEAP_PAGE_ALLOCS
    DEBUG_INITIAL_COMMAND_EX     DISABLE_DBGPRINT

kd> !gflag
NtGlobalFlag at 8046a164
Current NtGlobalFlag contents: 0x00004400
    ptg - Enable pool tagging
    otl - Maintain a list of objects for each type
```

Local Procedure Calls (LPCs)

A local procedure call (LPC) is an interprocess communication facility for high-speed message passing. It is not directly available through the Win32 API; it is an internal mechanism available only to Windows 2000 operating system components. Here are some examples of where LPCs are used:

- Win32 applications that use remote procedure calls (RPCs), a documented API, indirectly use LPCs when they specify local-RPC, a form of RPC used to communicate between processes on the same system.

- A few Win32 APIs result in sending messages to the Win32 subsystem process.

■ Winlogon uses LPCs to communicate with the local security authentication server process, Lsass.

■ The security reference monitor (an executive component explained in Chapter 8) uses LPCs to communicate with the Lsass process.

EXPERIMENT: Viewing LPC Port Objects

You can see named LPC port objects with the Object Viewer utility included on this book's companion CD. Run \Sysint\Winobj.exe, and select the root directory. A plug icon identifies the port objects, as shown here:

To see the LPC port objects used by RPC, select the \RPC Control directory, as shown here:

You can also view LPC port objects by using the *!lpc* kernel debugger command. The command accepts parameters that direct it to show LPC ports, LPC messages, and threads that are waiting or sending LPC messages. To view the Lsass authentication port (the port that Winlogon sends logon requests to), first obtain a list of the ports on the system:

```
kd> !lpc
Usage:
    !lpc                      - Display this help
    !lpc message [MessageId]  - Display the message with a
                                given ID and all related
                                information
                                If MessageId is not
                                specified, dump all messages
    !lpc port [PortAddress]   - Display the port information
    !lpc scan PortAddress     - Search this port and any
                                connected port
    !lpc thread [ThreadAddr]  - Search the thread in rundown
                                port queues and display the
                                port info
                                If ThreadAddr is missing,
                                display all threads marked
                                as doing some lpc operations

kd> !lpc port
Scanning 206 objects
        1  Port: 0xe1360320 Connection: 0xe1360320
           Communication: 0x00000000 'SeRmCommandPort'
        1  Port: 0xe136bc20 Connection: 0xe136bc20
           Communication: 0x00000000 'SmApiPort'
        1  Port: 0xe133ba80 Connection: 0xe133ba80
           Communication: 0x00000000 'DbgSsApiPort'
        1  Port: 0xe13606e0 Connection: 0xe13606e0
           Communication: 0x00000000 'DbgUiApiPort'
        :
        1  Port: 0xe205f040 Connection: 0xe205f040
           Communication: 0x00000000 'LsaAuthenticationPort'
        :
```

Locate the port named LsaAuthenticationPort in the output and then examine it by passing its address to the *!lpc* command, as shown on the following page.

(continued)

EXPERIMENT: Viewing LPC Port Objects *continued*

```
kd> !lpc port 0xe205f040
Server connection port e205f040 Name: LsaAuthenticationPort
    Handles: 1   References: 37
    Server process  : ff7d56c0 (lsass.exe)
    Queue semaphore : ff7bfcc8
    Semaphore state 0 (0x0)
    The message queue is empty
    The LpcDataInfoChainHead queue is empty
```

Typically, LPCs are used between a server process and one or more client processes of that server. An LPC connection can be established between two user-mode processes or between a kernel-mode component and a user-mode process. For example, as noted in Chapter 2, Win32 processes send occasional messages to the Win32 subsystem by using LPCs. Also, some system processes use LPCs to communicate, such as Winlogon and Lsass. An example of a kernel-mode component using an LPC to talk to a user process is the communication between the security reference monitor and the Lsass process.

LPCs are designed to allow three methods of exchanging messages:

■ A message that is shorter than 256 bytes can be sent by calling the LPC with a buffer containing the message. This message is then copied from the address space of the sending process into system address space, and from there to the address space of the receiving process.

■ If a client and a server want to exchange more than 256 bytes of data, they can choose to use a shared section to which both are mapped. The sender places message data in the shared section and then sends a small message to the receiver with pointers to where the data is to be found in the shared section.

■ When a server wants to read or write larger amounts of data than will fit in a shared section, data can be directly read from or written to a client's address space. The LPC component supplies two functions that a server can use to accomplish this. A message sent by the first function is used to synchronize the message passing.

An LPC exports a single executive object called the *port object* to maintain the state needed for communication. Although an LPC uses a single object type, it has several kinds of ports:

- **Server connection port** A named port that is a server connection request point. Clients can connect to the server by connecting to this port.

- **Server communication port** An unnamed port a server uses to communicate with a particular client. The server has one such port per active client.

- **Client communication port** An unnamed port a particular client thread uses to communicate with a particular server.

- **Unnamed communication port** An unnamed port created for use by two threads in the same process.

LPCs are typically used as follows: A server creates a named server connection port object. A client makes a connect request to this port. If the request is granted, two new unnamed ports, a client communication port and a server communication port, are created. The client gets a handle to the client communication port, and the server gets a handle to the server communication port. The client and the server will then use these new ports for their communication.

A completed connection between a client and a server is shown in Figure 3-24.

Figure 3-24
Use of LPC ports

Conclusion

In this chapter, we've examined the key base system mechanisms on which the Windows 2000 executive is built. The next chapter details the steps involved in booting Windows 2000 and explains why Windows 2000 sometimes crashes and what you can do about it.

Startup and Shutdown

In this chapter, we'll describe the steps required to boot Microsoft Windows 2000 and the options that can affect system startup. We'll then explain what occurs on an orderly system shutdown. Finally, we'll discuss the reasons that Windows 2000 might crash and what you can do when you're dealing with a system crash. Understanding the details of the boot process will help you diagnose problems that can arise during a boot.

Boot Process

In describing the Windows 2000 boot process, we'll start with the installation of Windows 2000 and proceed through the execution of Ntldr and Ntdetect. Device drivers are a crucial part of the boot process, so we'll explain the way that they control the point in the boot process at which they load and initialize. Then we'll describe how the executive subsystems initialize and how the kernel launches the user-mode portion of Windows 2000 by starting the Session Manager process (Smss.exe), the Win32 subsystem, and the logon process (Winlogon). Along the way, we'll highlight the points at which various text appears on the screen to help you correlate the internal process with what you see when you watch Windows 2000 boot. Table 4-1 presents a summary of boot-process components with their execution modes and responsibilities.

Preboot

The Windows 2000 boot process doesn't begin when you power on your computer or press the reset button. It begins when you install Windows 2000 on your computer. At some point during the execution of the Windows 2000 Setup program, the system's primary hard disk is prepared with code that takes part in the boot process. Before we get into what this code does, let's look at how

Table 4-1 **Boot Process Components**

Component	Processor Execution	Responsibilities
Master boot record (MBR) code	16-bit real mode	Reads and loads partition boot sectors
Boot sector	16-bit real mode	Reads the root directory to load Ntldr
Ntldr	16-bit real mode and 32-bit protected mode; turns on paging	Reads Boot.ini, presents boot menu, and loads Ntoskrnl.exe, Bootvid.dll, Hal.dll, and boot-start device drivers
Ntoskrnl.exe	32-bit protected mode with paging	Initializes executive subsystems and boot and system-start device drivers, prepares the system for running native applications, and runs Smss.exe
Smss	32-bit native application	Loads Win32 subsystem, including Win32k.sys and Csrss.exe, and starts Winlogon process
Winlogon	32-bit native application	Starts the service control manager (SCM), the Local Security Subsystem (Lsass), and presents interactive logon dialog box
Service control manager (SCM)	32-bit native application	Loads and initializes auto-start device drivers and Win32 services

and where Windows 2000 places the code on a disk. Since the early days of MS-DOS, a standard has existed on x86 systems for the way physical hard disks are divided into volumes. Microsoft operating systems split hard disks into discrete areas known as *partitions* and use file systems (such as FAT and NTFS) to format each partition into a volume. A hard disk can contain up to four primary partitions. Because this apportioning scheme would limit a disk to four volumes, a special partition type, called an *extended partition*, further allocates up to four additional partitions within each primary partition. Extended partitions can contain extended partitions, which can contain extended partitions, and so on, making the number of volumes an operating system can place on a disk effectively infinite. Figure 4-1 shows an example of a hard disk layout. (You can learn

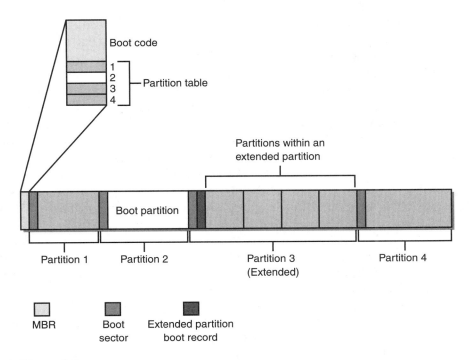

Figure 4-1
Example hard disk layout

more about Windows 2000 partitioning in Chapter 10, which covers storage management.)

Physical disks are addressed in units known as *sectors*. A hard disk sector on an IBM-compatible PC is typically 512 bytes. Utilities that prepare hard disks for the definition of logical drives, including the MS-DOS Fdisk utility or the Windows 2000 Setup program, write a sector of data called a master boot record (MBR) to the first sector on a hard disk. The MBR includes a fixed amount of space that contains executable instructions (called *boot code*) and a table (called a *partition table*) with four entries that define the locations of the primary partitions on the disk. When an IBM-compatible computer boots, the first code it executes is called the BIOS, which is encoded into the computer's ROM. The BIOS reads the MBR into memory and transfers control to the code in the MBR.

The MBRs written by Microsoft partitioning tools, such as the one integrated into Windows 2000 Setup and the Disk Management MMC snap-in, go through a similar process of reading and transferring control. First, an MBR's code scans

the primary partition table until it locates a partition containing a flag that signals the partition is bootable. When the MBR finds at least one such flag, it reads the first sector from the flagged partition into memory and transfers control to code within the partition. This type of partition is called a *boot partition,* and the first sector of such a partition is called a *boot sector.*

Operating systems generally write boot sectors to disk without a user's involvement. For example, when Windows 2000 Setup writes the MBR to a hard disk, it also writes a boot sector to the first bootable partition of the disk. You might have used the MS-DOS *sys* command to manually write MS-DOS boot sectors to disks. Windows 2000 Setup checks to see whether the boot sector it will overwrite with a Windows 2000 boot sector is a valid MS-DOS boot sector. If it is, Windows 2000 Setup copies the boot sector's contents to a file named Bootsect.dos in the root directory of the partition.

Before writing to a partition's boot sector, Windows 2000 Setup ensures that the partition is formatted with a file system that Windows 2000 supports (FAT, FAT32, or NTFS) by formatting the boot partition (and any other partition) with a file system type you specify. If partitions are already formatted, you can instruct Setup to skip this step. After Setup formats the boot partition, Setup copies the files Windows 2000 uses to the logical disk drive, including two files that are part of the boot sequence, Ntldr and Ntdetect.com.

Another of Setup's roles is to create a boot menu file, Boot.ini, in the root directory of the boot partition. This file contains options for starting the version of Windows 2000 that Setup installs and any preexisting Windows 2000 installations. If Bootsect.dos contains a valid MS-DOS boot sector, one of the entries Boot.ini creates is to boot into MS-DOS. The following output shows an example Boot.ini file from a dual-boot computer on which MS-DOS is installed before Windows 2000:

```
[boot loader]
timeout=30
default=multi(0)disk(0)rdisk(0)partition(1)\WINNT
[operating systems]
multi(0)disk(0)rdisk(0)partition(1)
\WINNT="Microsoft Windows 2000 Professional" /fastdetect
C:\="Microsoft Windows"
```

The Boot Sector and Ntldr

Setup must know the partition format before it writes a boot sector because the contents of the boot sector vary depending on the format. For example, if the boot partition is a FAT partition, Windows 2000 writes code to the boot sec-

tor that understands the FAT file system. But if the partition is in NTFS format, Windows 2000 writes NTFS-capable code. The role of the boot-sector code is to give Windows 2000 information about the structure and format of a logical disk drive and to read in the Ntldr file from the root directory of the logical disk drive. Thus, the boot-sector code contains just enough read-only file system code to accomplish this task. After the boot-sector code loads Ntldr into memory, it transfers control to Ntldr's entry point. If the boot-sector code can't find Ntldr in the logical disk drive's root directory, it displays the error message "BOOT: Couldn't find NTLDR" if the boot file system is FAT or "NTLDR is missing" if the file system is NTFS.

Ntldr begins its existence while a system is executing in an x86 operating mode called *real mode*. In real mode, no virtual-to-physical translation of memory addresses occurs, which means that programs that use the memory addresses interpret them as physical addresses and that only the first 1 MB of the computer's physical memory is accessible. Simple MS-DOS programs execute in a real mode environment. However, the first action Ntldr takes is to switch the system to *protected mode*. Still no virtual-to-physical translation occurs at this point in the boot process, but a full 32 bits of memory becomes accessible. After the system is in protected mode, Ntldr can access all of physical memory. After creating enough page tables to make memory below 16 MB accessible with paging turned on, Ntldr enables paging. Protected mode with paging enabled is the mode in which Windows 2000 executes in normal operation.

After Ntldr enables paging, it is fully operational. However, it still relies on functions supplied by the boot code to access IDE-based system and boot disks as well as the display. The boot-code functions briefly switch off paging and switch the processor back to a mode in which services provided by the BIOS can be executed. If either the boot or system drives are SCSI-based, Ntldr loads a file named Ntbootdd.sys and uses it instead of the boot-code functions for disk access. Ntldr next reads the Boot.ini file from the root directory using built-in file system code. Like the boot sector's code, Ntldr contains read-only NTFS and FAT code; unlike the boot sector's code, however, Ntldr's file system code can read subdirectories.

Ntldr clears the screen and if there is more than one boot-selection entry in Boot.ini, it presents the user with the boot-selection menu. (If there is only one entry, Ntldr bypasses the menu and proceeds to displaying the startup progress bar.) Selection entries in Boot.ini direct Ntldr to the partition on which the Windows 2000 system directory (typically \Winnt) of the selected installation resides. This partition might be the same as the boot partition, or it might be another primary partition.

If the Boot.ini entry refers to an MS-DOS installation (that is, by referring to C:\ as the system partition), Ntldr reads the contents of the Bootsect.dos file into memory, switches back to 16-bit real mode, and calls the MBR code in Bootsect.dos. This action causes the Bootsect.dos code to execute as if the MBR had read the code from disk. Code in Bootsect.dos continues an MS-DOS-specific boot, such as is used to boot Microsoft Windows 98 or Microsoft Windows 95 on a computer on which these operating systems are installed with Windows 2000.

Entries in Boot.ini can include optional arguments that Ntldr and other components involved in the boot process interpret. Table 4-2 contains a complete list of these options and their effects.

Table 4-2 Boot.ini Switches

Boot.ini Qualifier	Meaning
/3GB	Increases the size of the user process address space from 2 GB to 3 GB (and therefore reduces the size of system space from 2 GB to 1 GB). Giving virtual-memory-intensive applications such as database servers a larger address space can improve their performance. For an application to take advantage of this feature, however, two additional conditions must be met: the system must be running Windows 2000 Advanced Server or Datacenter Server and the application .exe must be flagged as a 3-GB-aware application. (See the section "Address Space Layout" in Chapter 7 for more information.)
/BASEVIDEO	Causes Windows 2000 to use the standard VGA display driver for GUI-mode operations.
/BAUDRATE=	Enables kernel-mode debugging and specifies an override for the default baud rate (19200) at which a remote kernel debugger host will connect. Example: /BAUDRATE=115200.
/BOOTLOG	Causes Windows 2000 to write a log of the boot to the file %SystemRoot%\Ntbtlog.txt.
/BREAK	Causes the hardware abstraction layer (HAL) to stop at a breakpoint at HAL initialization. The first thing the Windows 2000 kernel does when it initializes is to initialize the HAL, so this breakpoint is the earliest one possible. The HAL will wait indefinitely at the breakpoint until a kernel-debugger connection is made. If the switch is used without the /DEBUG switch, the system will Blue Screen with STOP code of 0x00000078 (PHASE0_ EXCEPTION).

Boot.ini Qualifier	Meaning
/BURNMEMORY=	Specifies an amount of memory Windows 2000 can't use (similar to the /MAXMEM switch). The value is specified in megabytes. Example: /BURNMEMORY=128 would indicate that Windows 2000 can't use 128 MB of the total physical memory on the machine.
/CLKLVL	Causes the standard x86 multiprocessor HAL (Halmps.dll) to configure itself for a level-sensitive system clock rather then an edge-triggered clock. *Level-sensitive* and *edge-triggered* are terms used to describe hardware interrupt types.
/CRASHDEBUG	Causes the kernel debugger to be loaded when the system boots, but to remain inactive unless a crash occurs. This allows the serial port that the kernel debugger would use to be available for use by the system until the system crashes (vs. /DEBUG, which causes the kernel debugger to use the serial port for the life of the system session).
/DEBUG	Enables kernel-mode debugging.
/DEBUGPORT=	Enables kernel-mode debugging and specifies an override for the default serial port (COM1) to which a remote kernel-debugger host is connected. Example: /DEBUGPORT=COM2.
/FASTDETECT	Default boot option for Windows 2000. Replaces the Windows NT 4 switch /NOSERIALMICE. The reason the qualifier exists (vs. just having NTDETECT perform this operation by default) is so that NTDETECT can support booting Windows NT 4. Windows 2000 Plug and Play device drivers perform detection of parallel and serial devices, but Windows NT 4 expects NTDETECT to perform the detection. Thus, specifying /FASTDETECT causes NTDETECT to skip parallel and serial device enumeration (actions that are not required when booting Windows 2000), whereas omitting the switch causes NTDETECT to perform this enumeration (which is required for booting Windows NT 4).
/INTAFFINITY	Directs the standard x86 multiprocessor HAL (Halmps.dll) to set interrupt affinities such that only the highest numbered processor will receive interrupts. Without the switch, the HAL defaults to its normal behavior of letting all processors receive interrupts.

(continued)

Table 4-2 *continued*

Boot.ini Qualifier	Meaning
/KERNEL= /HAL=	Enable you to override Ntldr's default filename for the kernel image (Ntoskrnl.exe) and/or the HAL (Hal.dll). These options are useful for alternating between a checked kernel environment and a free (retail) kernel environment or even to manually select a different HAL. If you want to boot a checked environment that consists solely of the checked kernel and HAL, which is typically all that is needed to test drivers, follow these steps on a system installed with the free build:

1. Copy the checked versions of the kernel images from the checked build CD to your \Winnt\System32 directory, giving the images different names than the default. For example, if you're on a uniprocessor, copy Ntoskrnl.exe to Ntoschk.exe and Ntkrnlpa.exe to Ntoschkpa.exe. If you're on a multiprocessor, copy Ntkrnlmp.exe to Ntoschk.exe and Ntkrpamp.exe to Ntoschkpa.exe. The kernel filename must be an 8.3-style short name.

2. Copy the checked version of the appropriate HAL needed for your system from \I386\Driver.cab on the checked build CD to your \Winnt\System32 directory, naming it Halchk.dll. To determine which HAL to copy, open \Winnt\Repair\Setup.log and search for Hal.dll; you'll find a line like *\WINNT\system32\ hal.dll="halacpi.dll","1d8a1"*. The name immediately to the right of the equals sign is the name of the HAL you should copy. The HAL filename must be an 8.3-style short name.

3. Make a copy of the default line in the system's Boot.ini file.

4. In the string description of the boot selection, add something that indicates that the new selection will be for a checked build environment (for example, "Windows 2000 Professional Checked").

5. Add the following to the end of the new selection's line: /KERNEL=NTOSCHK.EXE /HAL= HALCHK.DLL

Now when the selection menu appears during the boot process you can select the new entry to boot a checked environment or select the entry you were using to boot the free build.

Boot.ini Qualifier	Meaning
/MAXMEM=	Limits Windows 2000 to ignore (not use) physical memory beyond the amount indicated. The number is interpreted in megabytes. Example: /MAXMEM=32 would limit the system to using the first 32 MB of physical memory even if more were present.
/MAXPROCSPERCLUSTER=	For the standard x86 multiprocessor HAL (Halmps.dll), forces cluster-mode Advanced Programmable Interrupt Controller (APIC) addressing (not supported on systems with an 82489DX external APIC interrupt controller).
/NODEBUG	Prevents kernel-mode debugging from being initialized. Overrides the specification of any of the three debug-related switches, /DEBUG, /DEBUGPORT, and /BAUDRATE.
/NOGUIBOOT	Instructs Windows 2000 not to initialize the VGA video driver responsible for presenting bitmapped graphics during the boot process. The driver is used to display boot progress information, so disabling it will disable the ability of Windows 2000 to show this information.
/NOLOWMEM	Requires that the /PAE switch be present and that the system have more than 4 GB of physical memory. If these conditions are met, the PAE-enabled version of the Windows 2000 kernel, Ntkrnlpa.exe, won't use the first 4 GB of physical memory. Instead, it will load all applications and device drivers, and allocate all memory pools, from above that boundary. This switch is useful only to test device driver compatibility with large memory systems.
/NOPAE	Forces Ntldr to load the non-Physical Address Extension (PAE) version of the Windows 2000 kernel, even if the system is detected as supporting x86 PAEs and has more than 4 GB of physical memory.
/NOSERIALMICE=[COMx \| COMx,y,z...]	Obsolete Windows NT 4 qualifier—replaced by the absence of the /FASTDETECT switch. Disables serial mouse detection of the specified COM ports. This switch was used if you had a device other than a mouse attached to a serial port during the startup sequence. Using /NOSERIALMICE without specifying a COM port disables serial mouse detection on all COM ports. See Microsoft Knowledge Base article Q131976 for more information.
/NUMPROC=	Specifies the number of CPUs that can be used on a multiprocessor system. Example: /NUMPROC=2 on a four-way system will prevent Windows 2000 from using two of the four processors.

(continued)

185

Table 4-2 *continued*

Boot.ini Qualifier	Meaning
/ONECPU	Causes Windows 2000 to use only one CPU on a multi-processor system.
/PAE	Causes Ntldr to load Ntkrnlpa.exe, which is the version of the x86 kernel that is able to take advantage of x86 PAEs. The PAE version of the kernel presents 64-bit physical addresses to device drivers, so this switch is helpful for testing device driver support for large memory systems.
/PCILOCK	Stops Windows 2000 from dynamically assigning IO/IRQ resources to PCI devices and leaves the devices configured by the BIOS. See Microsoft Knowledge Base article Q148501 for more information.
/SAFEBOOT:	Specifies options for a safe boot. You should never have to specify this option manually, since Ntldr specifies it for you when you use the F8 menu to perform a safe boot. (A safe boot is a boot in which Windows 2000 only loads drivers and services that are specified by name or group under the Minimal or Network registry keys under HKLM\SYSTEM\CurrentControlSet\Control\SafeBoot.) Following the colon in the option you must specify one of three additional switches: MINIMAL, NETWORK, or DSREPAIR. The MINIMAL and NETWORK flags correspond to safe boot with no network and safe boot with network support, respectively. The DSREPAIR (Directory Services Repair) switch causes Windows 2000 to boot into a mode in which it restores the Active Directory directory service from a backup medium you present. An additional option you can append is (ALTERNATE-SHELL), which tells Windows 2000 to use the program specified by the HKLM\SYSTEM\CurrentControlSet\SafeBoot\AlternateShell value as the graphical shell rather than to use the default, which is Windows Explorer.
/SCSIORDINAL:	Directs Windows 2000 to the SCSI ID of the controller. (Adding a new SCSI device to a system with an on-board SCSI controller can cause the controller's SCSI ID to change.) See Microsoft Knowledge Base article Q103625 for more information.
/SOS	Causes Windows 2000 to list the device drivers marked to load at boot time and then to display the system version number (including the build number), amount of physical memory, and number of processors.

Boot.ini Qualifier	Meaning
/TIMERES=	Sets the resolution of the system timer on the standard x86 multiprocessor HAL (Halmps.dll). The argument is a number interpreted in hundreds of nanoseconds, but the rate is set to the closest resolution the HAL supports that isn't larger than the one requested. The HAL supports the following resolutions:

Hundreds of nanoseconds	Milliseconds (ms)
9766	0.98
19532	2.00
39063	3.90
78125	7.80

Boot.ini Qualifier	Meaning
	The default resolution is 7.8 ms. The system timer resolution affects the resolution of waitable timers. Example: /TIMERES=21000 would set the timer to a resolution of 2.0 ms.
/USE8254	Instructs the HAL to use the 8254 timer chip as its base timer (for systems with older BIOS's). See Microsoft Knowledge Base article Q169901 for more information.
/WIN95	Directs Ntldr to boot the Consumer Windows boot sector stored in Bootsect.w40. This switch is pertinent only on a triple-boot system that has MS-DOS, Consumer Windows, and Windows 2000 installed. See Microsoft Knowledge Base article Q157992 for more information.
/WIN95DOS	Directs Ntldr to boot the MS-DOS boot sector stored in Bootsect.dos. This switch is pertinent only on a triple-boot system that has MS-DOS, Consumer Windows, and Windows 2000 installed. See Microsoft Knowledge Base article Q157992 for more information.
/YEAR=	Instructs the Windows 2000 core time function to ignore the year that the computer's real-time clock reports and instead use the one indicated. Thus, the year used in the switch affects every piece of software on the system, including the Windows 2000 kernel. Example: /YEAR=2001. (This switch was created to assist in Y2K testing.)

If the user doesn't select an entry from the selection menu within the timeout period the Boot.ini file specifies, Ntldr chooses the default selection. Once the boot selection has been made, Ntldr loads and executes Ntdetect.com, a 16-bit real-mode program that uses a system's BIOS to query the computer for basic device and configuration information. This information includes the following:

- The time and date information stored in the system's CMOS (nonvolatile memory)

- The types of buses (for example, ISA, PCI, EISA, Micro Channel Architecture [MCA]) on the system and identifiers for devices attached to the buses

- The number, size, and type of disk drives on the system

- The types of mouse input devices connected to the system

- The number and type of parallel ports configured on the system

This information is gathered into internal data structures that will be stored under the HKLM\HARDWARE\DESCRIPTION registry key later in the boot.

Ntldr then clears the screen and displays the "Starting Windows" progress bar. This progress bar remains empty until Ntldr begins loading boot drivers. (See step 5 in the following list.) Below the progress bar is the message "For troubleshooting and advanced startup options for Windows 2000, press F8." If the user presses F8, the advanced boot menu is presented, which allows the user to select such options as booting from last known good, safe mode, debug mode, and so on.

Next, Ntldr begins loading the files from the boot partition needed to start the kernel initialization:

1. Loads the appropriate kernel and HAL images (Ntoskrnl.exe and Hal.dll by default). If Ntldr fails to load either of these files, it prints the message "Windows 2000 could not start because the following file was missing or corrupt", followed by the name of the file.

2. Reads in the SYSTEM registry hive, \Winnt\System32\Config\ System, so that it can determine which device drivers need to be loaded to accomplish the boot. (A hive is a file that contains a registry subtree. You'll find more details about the registry in Chapter 5.)

3. Scans the in-memory SYSTEM registry hive and locates all the *boot device drivers*. Boot device drivers are drivers necessary to boot the system. These drivers are indicated in the registry by a start value of

SERVICE_BOOT_START. Every device driver has a registry subkey under HKLM\SYSTEM\CurrentControlSet\Services. For example, Services has a subkey named Dmio for the Logical Disk Manager driver, which you can see in Figure 4-2. (For a detailed description of the Services registry entries, see the section "Services" on page 236 in Chapter 5.)

Figure 4-2
Logical Disk Manager driver service settings

4. Adds the file system driver that's responsible for implementing the code for the type of partition (FAT, FAT32, or NTFS) on which the installation directory resides to the list of boot drivers to load. Ntldr must load this driver at this time; if it didn't, the kernel would require the drivers to load themselves, a requirement that would introduce a circular dependency.

5. Loads the boot drivers. To indicate the progress of the loading, Ntldr updates a progress bar displayed below the text "Starting Windows". The progress bar moves for each driver loaded. (It assumes there are 80 boot device drivers—each successful load moves the progress bar by 1.25 percent.) If the /SOS switch is specified in the Boot.ini selection, Ntldr doesn't display the progress bar but instead displays the filenames of each boot driver. Keep in mind that the drivers are loaded but not initialized at this time—they initialize later in the boot sequence.

6. Prepares CPU registers for the execution of Ntoskrnl.exe.

This action is the end of Ntldr's role in the boot process. At this point, Ntldr calls the main function in Ntoskrnl.exe to perform the rest of the system initialization.

Initializing the Kernel and Executive Subsystems

When Ntldr calls Ntoskrnl, it passes a data structure that contains a copy of the line in Boot.ini that represents the selected menu option for this boot, a pointer to the memory tables Ntldr generated to describe the physical memory on the system, a pointer to the in-memory copy of the HARDWARE and SYSTEM registry hives, and a pointer to the list of boot drivers Ntldr loaded.

Ntoskrnl then begins the first of its two-phase initialization process, called *phase 0* and *phase 1*. Most executive subsystems have an initialization function that takes a parameter that identifies which phase is executing.

During phase 0, interrupts are disabled. The purpose of this phase is to build the rudimentary structures required to allow the services needed in phase 1 to be invoked. Ntoskrnl's main function calls *KiSystemStartup*, which in turn calls *HalInitializeProcessor* and *KiInitializeKernel* for each CPU. *KiInitializeKernel*, if running on the boot CPU, performs systemwide kernel initialization, such as initializing internal listheads and other data structures that all CPUs share. Each instance of *KiInitializeKernel* then calls the function responsible for orchestrating phase 0, *ExpInitializeExecutive*.

ExpInitializeExecutive starts by calling the HAL function *HalInitSystem*, which gives the HAL a chance to gain system control before Windows 2000 performs significant further initialization. One responsibility of *HalInitSystem* is to prepare the system interrupt controller of each CPU for interrupts and to configure the interval clock timer interrupt, which is used for CPU time accounting. (See the section "Quantum Accounting" on page 349 in Chapter 6 for more on CPU time accounting.)

Only on the boot processor does *ExpInitializeExecutive* perform initialization other than calling *HalInitSystem*. When *HalInitSystem* returns control, *ExpInitializeExecutive* on the boot CPU proceeds by processing the /BURNMEMORY Boot.ini switch (if the switch is present in the line from the Boot.ini file that corresponds to the menu selection the user made when choosing which installation to boot) and discarding the amount of memory the switch specifies.

Next, *ExpInitializeExecutive* calls the phase 0 initialization routines for the memory manager, object manager, security reference monitor, process manager, and Plug and Play manager. These components perform the following initialization steps:

1. The memory manager constructs page tables and internal data structures that are necessary to provide basic memory services. The memory manager also builds and reserves an area for the system file cache and creates memory areas for the paged and nonpaged pools. The other executive subsystems, the kernel, and the device drivers use these two memory pools for allocating their data structures.

2. During the object manager initialization, the objects that are necessary to construct the object manager namespace are defined so that other subsystems can insert objects into it. A handle table is created so that resource tracking can begin.

3. The security reference monitor initializes the token type object and then uses the object to create and prepare the first token for assignment to the initial process.

4. The process manager performs most of its initialization in phase 0, defining the process and thread object types and setting up lists to track active processes and threads. The process manager also creates a process object for the initial process and names it Idle. As its last step, the process manager creates the System process and creates a system thread to execute the routine *Phase1Initialization*. This thread doesn't start running right away because interrupts are still disabled.

5. The Plug and Play manager's phase 0 initialization then takes place, which involves simply initializing an executive resource used to synchronize bus resources.

When control returns to the *KiInitializeKernel* function on each processor, control proceeds to the Idle loop, which then causes the system thread created in step 4 of the previous process description to begin executing phase 1. (Secondary processors wait to begin their initialization until step 5 of phase 1, described in the following list.) Phase 1 consists of the following steps. (The steps at which the progress bar on the screen is updated are included in this list.)

1. *HalInitSystem* is called to prepare the system to accept interrupts from devices and to enable interrupts.

2. The boot video driver (\Winnt\System32\Bootvid.dll) is called, which in turn displays the Windows 2000 startup screen.

3. The power manager's initialization is called.

4. The system time is initialized (by calling *HalQueryRealTimeClock*) and then stored as the time the system booted.

5. On a multiprocessor system, the remaining processors are initialized and execution starts.

6. The progress bar is set to 5 percent.

7. The object manager creates the namespace root directory, \ObjectTypes directory, \?? directory, and the \DosDevices link to the \?? directory.

8. The executive is called to create the executive object types, including semaphore, mutex, event, and timer.

9. The kernel initializes scheduler (dispatcher) data structures and the system service dispatch table.

10. The security reference monitor creates the \Security directory in the object manager namespace and initializes auditing data structures if auditing is enabled.

11. The progress bar is set to 10 percent.

12. The memory manager is called to create the section object and the memory manager's system worker threads (explained in Chapter 7).

13. National language support (NLS) tables are mapped into system space.

14. Ntdll.dll is mapped into the system address space.

15. The cache manager initializes the file system cache data structures and creates its worker threads.

16. The configuration manager creates the \Registry key object in the object manager namespace and copies the initial registry data passed by Ntldr into the HARDWARE and SYSTEM hives.

17. Global file system driver data structures are initialized.

18. The Plug and Play manager calls the Plug and Play BIOS.

19. The progress bar is set to 20 percent.

20. The local procedure call (LPC) subsystem initializes the LPC port type object.

21. If the system was booted with boot logging (/BOOTLOG), the boot log file is initialized.

22. The progress bar is set to 25 percent.

23. The I/O manager initialization now takes place. This stage is a complex phase of system startup that accounts for 50 percent of the "progress" reported in the progress bar. The I/O manager considers each successful driver load to be another 2 percent of progress for the boot. (If there are more than 25 drivers to load, the progress bar stops at 75 percent.)

 The I/O manager first initializes various internal structures and creates the driver and device object types. It then calls the Plug and Play manager, power manager, and the HAL to begin the various stages of dynamic device enumeration and initialization. (Because this process is complex and specific to the I/O system, we'll save the details for Chapter 9.) Then the Windows Management Instrumentation (WMI) subsystem is initialized, which provides WMI support for device drivers that adhere to the Windows Driver Model (WDM). (See the section "Windows Management Instrumentation" on page 265 in Chapter 5 for more information.) Next, all the boot-start drivers are called to perform their driver-specific initialization, and the system-start device drivers are loaded and initialized. (Details on the processing of the driver load control information on the registry are also covered in Chapter 9.) Finally, the MS-DOS device names are created as symbolic links in the object manager's namespace.

24. The progress bar is set to 75 percent.

25. If booting in safe mode, this fact is recorded in the registry.

26. Unless explicitly disabled in the registry, paging of kernel-mode code (in Ntoskrnl and drivers) is enabled.

27. The progress bar is set to 80 percent.

28. The power manager is called to initialize various power management structures.

29. The progress bar is set to 85 percent.

30. The security reference monitor is called to create the Command Server Thread that communicates with Lsass. (See the section "Security System Components" on page 490 in Chapter 8 for more on how security is enforced in Windows 2000.)

31. The progress bar is set to 90 percent.

32. The last step is to create the Session Manager subsystem (Smss) process (introduced in Chapter 2). Smss is responsible for creating the user-mode environment that provides the visible interface to Windows 2000—its initialization steps are covered in the next section.

33. The progress bar is (finally) set to 100%.

As a final step before considering the executive and kernel initialization complete, the phase 1 initialization thread waits on the handle to the Session Manager process with a timeout value of 5 seconds. If the Session Manager process exits before the 5 seconds elapses, the system crashes itself with a SESSION5_INITIALIZATION_FAILED bug check code.

If the 5-second wait times out (that is, if 5 seconds elapse), the Session Manager is assumed to have started successfully, and the phase 1 initialization function calls the memory manager's zero page thread function (explained in Chapter 7). Thus, this system thread becomes the zero page thread for the remainder of the life of the system.

Smss, Csrss, and Winlogon

Smss is like any other user-mode process except for two differences: First, Windows 2000 considers Smss a trusted part of the operating system. Second, Smss is a *native* application. Because it's a trusted operating system component, Smss can perform actions few other processes can perform, such as creating security tokens. Because it's a native application, Smss doesn't use Win32 APIs—it uses only core executive APIs known collectively as the Windows 2000 native API. Smss doesn't use the Win32 APIs because the Win32 subsystem isn't executing when Smss launches. In fact, one of Smss's first tasks is to start the Win32 subsystem.

Smss then calls the configuration manager executive subsystem to finish initializing the registry, fleshing the registry out to include all its keys. The configuration manager is programmed to know where the core registry hives are stored on disk (excluding hives corresponding to user profiles) and records the paths to the hives it loads in the HKLM\SYSTEM\CurrentControlSet\Control\hivelist key.

The main thread of Smss performs the following initialization steps:

1. Creates an LPC port object (*SmApiPort*) and two threads to wait for client requests (such as to load a new subsystem or create a session).

2. Defines the symbolic links for MS-DOS device names (such as COM1 and LPT1).

3. If Terminal Services is installed, creates the \Sessions directory in the object manager's namespace (for multiple sessions).

4. Runs any programs defined in HKLM\SYSTEM\CurrentControlSet\ Control\Session Manager\BootExecute. Typically, this value contains one command to run Autochk (the boot-time version of Chkdsk).

5. Performs delayed file rename operations as directed by HKLM\ SYSTEM\CurrentControlSet\Control\Session Manager\PendingFile-RenameOperations. Pending file deletes are in PendingFileRename-Operations2.

6. Opens known DLLs.

7. Creates additional paging files.

8. Initializes the registry. The configuration manager fleshes out the registry by loading the registry hives for the HKLM\SAM, HKLM\ SECURITY, and HKLM\SOFTWARE keys. Although HKLM\ SYSTEM\CurrentControlSet\Control\hivelist locates the hive files on disk, the configuration manager is coded to look for them in \Winnt\ System32\Config.

9. Creates system environment variables.

10. Loads the kernel-mode part of the Win32 subsystem (Win23k.sys). Smss determines the location of Win32k.sys and other components it loads by looking for their paths in HKLM\SYSTEM\Current-ControlSet\Control\Session Manager. The initialization code in Win32k.sys uses the video driver to switch the screen to the resolution defined by the default profile, so this is the point at which the screen changes from the VGA mode the boot video driver uses to the default resolution chosen for the system.

11. Starts the subsystem processes, including Csrss. (As noted in Chapter 2, the POSIX and OS/2 subsystems are defined to start on demand.)

12. Starts the logon process (Winlogon). The startup steps of Winlogon are described shortly.

13. Creates LPC ports for debug event messages (*DbgSsApiPort* and *DbgUiApiPort*) and threads to listen on those ports.

After performing these initialization steps, the main thread in Smss waits forever on the process handles to Csrss and Winlogon. If either of these processes terminates unexpectedly, Smss crashes the system, since Windows 2000 relies on their existence.

Winlogon then performs its startup steps, such as creating the initial window station and desktop objects, loading GINA DLLs, and so on. It then creates the service control manager (SCM) process (\Winnt\System32\Services.exe), which loads all services and device drivers marked for auto-start, and the local security authentication subsystem (Lsass) process (\Winnt\System32\Lsass.exe). (For more details on the startup sequence for Winlogon and Lsass, see the section "Winlogon Initialization" on page 522 in Chapter 8.)

After the SCM initializes the auto-start services and drivers and a user has successfully logged on at the console, the SCM deems the boot successful. The registry last known good control set (as indicated by HKLM\SYSTEM\Select\LastKnownGood) is updated to match \CurrentControlSet. If a user chooses to boot to the last known good menu during the first steps of a boot, or if a driver returns a severe or critical error, the system uses the LastKnownGood value as the current control set. Doing so increases the chances that the system will boot successfully, because at least one previous boot using the last known good profile was successful.

That action brings us to the end of the boot process.

Safe Mode

Perhaps the most common reason Windows 2000 systems become unbootable is that a device driver crashes the machine during the boot sequence. Because software or hardware configurations can change over time, latent bugs can surface in drivers at any time. Windows 2000 offers a way for an administrator to attack the problem: booting in *safe mode*. Safe mode is a concept Windows 2000 borrows from Consumer Windows—a boot configuration that consists of the minimal set of device drivers and services. By relying on only the drivers and services that are necessary for booting, Windows 2000 avoids loading third-party and other nonessential drivers that might crash.

When Windows 2000 boots, you press the F8 key to enter a special boot menu that contains the safe-mode boot options. You typically choose from three safe-mode variations: Safe Mode, Safe Mode With Networking, and Safe Mode With Command Prompt. Standard safe mode comprises the minimum number of device drivers and services necessary to boot successfully. Networking-enabled

safe mode adds network drivers and services to the drivers and services that standard safe mode includes. Finally, safe mode with command prompt is identical to standard safe mode except that Windows 2000 runs the command prompt application (Cmd.exe) instead of Windows Explorer as the shell when the system enables GUI mode.

Windows 2000 includes a fourth safe mode—Directory Services Restore mode—which is different from the standard and networking-enabled safe modes. You use Directory Services Restore mode to boot the system into a mode that lets you restore the Active Directory directory service of a domain controller from backup media. All drivers and services load during a Directory Services Restore mode boot; therefore, you wouldn't use Directory Services Restore mode to boot unbootable systems.

Driver Loading in Safe Mode

How does Windows 2000 know which device drivers and services are part of standard and networking-enabled safe boots? The answer lies in the HKLM\SYSTEM\CurrentControlSet\Control\SafeBoot registry key. This key contains the Minimal and Network subkeys. Each subkey contains more subkeys that specify the names of device drivers or services or of groups of drivers. For example, the vga.sys subkey identifies the VGA display device driver that the startup configuration includes. The VGA display driver provides basic graphics services for any PC-compatible display adapter. The system uses this driver as the safe-mode display driver in lieu of a driver that might take advantage of an adapter's advanced hardware features but that might also prevent the system from booting. Each subkey under the SafeBoot key has a default value that describes what the subkey identifies; the vga.sys subkey's default value is Driver.

The Boot file system subkey has as its default value Driver Group. When developers design a device driver's installation script, they can specify that the device driver belong to a driver group. The driver groups that a system defines are listed in the List value of the HKLM\SYSTEM\CurrentControlSet\Control\ServiceGroupOrder key. A developer specifies a driver as a member of a group to indicate to Windows 2000 at what point during the boot process the driver should start. The ServiceGroupOrder key's primary purpose is to define the order in which driver groups load; some driver types must load either before or after other driver types. The Group value beneath a driver's configuration registry key associates the driver with a group. Driver and service configuration keys reside beneath HKLM\SYSTEM\CurrentControlSet\Services. If you look under this key, you'll find the VgaSave key for the VGA display device driver,

which you can see in the registry is a member of the Video Save group. Any file system drivers that Windows 2000 requires for access to the Windows 2000 system drive are in the Boot file system group. If the system drive is NTFS, the NTFS driver is part of this group (the value of Group under the Ntfs key is Boot file system); otherwise, the Fastfat file system driver (which supports FAT12, FAT16, and FAT32 drives in Windows 2000) is part of this group. Other file system drivers are part of the File system group, which the standard and net-working-enabled safe-mode configurations also include.

When you boot into a safe-mode configuration, the boot loader (Ntldr) passes an associated switch to the kernel (Ntoskrnl.exe) as a command-line pa-rameter, along with any switches you've specified in the Boot.ini file for the installation you're booting. If you boot into any safe mode, Ntldr passes the /SAFEBOOT: switch. Ntldr appends one or more additional strings to /SAFEBOOT:, depending on which type of safe mode you select. For stan-dard safe mode, Ntldr appends MINIMAL, and for networking-enabled safe mode, it adds NETWORK. Ntldr adds MINIMAL(ALTERNATESHELL) for safe mode with command prompt and DSREPAIR for Directory Services Re-store mode.

The Windows 2000 kernel scans boot parameters in search of the safe-mode switches early during the boot and sets the internal variable *InitSafeBootMode* to a value that reflects the switches the kernel finds. The kernel writes the *InitSafeBootMode* value to the registry value HKLM\SYSTEM\CurrentControlSet\ Control\SafeBoot\Option\OptionValue so that user-mode components, such as the SCM, can determine what boot mode the system is in. In addition, if the system is booting safe mode with command prompt, the kernel sets the HKLM\SYSTEM\CurrentControlSet\Control\SafeBoot\Option\UseAlternate-Shell value to 1. The kernel records the parameters that Ntldr passes to it in the value HKLM\SYSTEM\CurrentControlSet\Control\SystemStartOptions.

When the I/O manager kernel subsystem loads device drivers that HKLM\ SYSTEM\CurrentControlSet\Services specifies, the I/O manager executes the function *IopLoadDriver*. When the Plug and Play manager detects a new device and wants to dynamically load the device driver for the detected device, the Plug and Play manager executes the function *IopCallDriverAddDevice*. Both these functions call the function *IopSafeBootDriverLoad* before they load the driver in question. *IopSafeBootDriverLoad* checks the value of *InitSafeBootMode* and determines whether the driver should load. For example, if the system boots in standard safe mode, *IopSafeBootDriverLoad* looks for the driver's group, if the

driver has one, under the Minimal subkey. If *IopSafeBootDriverLoad* finds the driver's group listed, *IopSafeBootDriverLoad* indicates to its caller that the driver can load. Otherwise, *IopSafeBootDriverLoad* looks for the driver's name under the Minimal subkey. If the driver's name is listed as a subkey, the driver can load. If *IopSafeBootDriverLoad* can't find the driver group or driver name subkeys, the driver can't load. If the system boots in networking-enabled safe mode, *IopSafeBootDriverLoad* performs the searches on the Network subkey. If the system doesn't boot in safe mode, *IopSafeBootDriverLoad* lets all drivers load.

A loophole exists regarding the drivers that safe mode excludes from a boot: Ntldr, rather than the kernel, loads any drivers with a Start value of 0 in their registry key, which specifies loading the drivers at boot time. Because Ntldr doesn't check the SafeBoot registry key to identify which drivers to load, Ntldr loads all boot-start drivers.

Safe-Mode-Aware User Programs

When the service control manager (SCM) user-mode component (which Services.exe implements) initializes during the boot process, the SCM checks the value of HKLM\SYSTEM\CurrentControlSet\Control\SafeBoot\Option\ OptionValue to determine whether the system is performing a safe boot. If so, the SCM mirrors the actions of *IopSafeBootDriverLoad*. Although the SCM processes the services listed under HKLM\SYSTEM\CurrentControlSet\Services, it loads only those services that the appropriate safe-mode subkey specifies by name. You can find more information on the SCM initialization process in the section "Services" on page 236 in Chapter 5.

Userinit (\Winnt\System32\Userinit.exe) is another user-mode component that needs to know whether the system is booting in safe mode. Userinit, the component that initializes a user's environment when the user logs on, checks HKLM\SYSTEM\CurrentControlSet\Control\SafeBoot\Option\UseAlternate- Value. If this value is set, Userinit runs the program specified as the user's shell in the value HKLM\SYSTEM\CurrentControlSet\Control\SafeBoot\Alternate- Shell rather than executing Explorer.exe. Windows 2000 writes the program name Cmd.exe to the AlternateShell value during installation, making the Win32 command prompt the default shell for safe mode with command prompt. Even though command prompt is the shell, you can type *Explorer.exe* at the command prompt to start Windows Explorer, and you can run any other GUI program from the command prompt as well.

How does an application determine whether the system is booting in safe mode? By calling the Win32 *GetSystemMetrics(SM_CLEANBOOT)* function. Batch scripts that need to perform certain operations when the system boots in safe mode look for the SAFEBOOT_OPTION environment variable because the system defines this environment variable only when booting in safe mode.

Boot Logging in Safe Mode

When you direct the system to boot into safe mode, Ntldr hands the string specified by the /BOOTLOG option to the Windows 2000 kernel as a parameter, together with the parameter that requests safe mode. When the kernel initializes, it checks for the presence of the boot log parameter, whether or not any safe-mode parameter is present. If the kernel detects a boot log string, the kernel records the action the kernel takes on every device driver it considers for loading. For example, if *IopSafeBootDriverLoad* tells the I/O manager not to load a driver, the I/O manager calls *IopBootLog* to record that the driver wasn't loaded. Likewise, after *IopLoadDriver* successfully loads a driver that is part of the safe-mode configuration, *IopLoadDriver* calls *IopBootLog* to record that the driver loaded. You can examine boot logs to see which device drivers are part of a boot configuration.

Because the kernel wants to avoid modifying the disk until Chkdsk executes, late in the boot process, *IopBootLog* can't simply dump messages into a log file. Instead, *IopBootLog* records messages in the HKLM\SYSTEM\CurrentControlSet\BootLog registry value. As the first user-mode component to load during a boot, the Session Manager (\Winnt\System32\Smss.exe) executes Chkdsk to ensure the system drives' consistency and then completes registry initialization by executing the *NtInitializeRegistry* system call. The kernel takes this action as a cue that it can safely open a log file on the disk, which it does, invoking the function *IopCopyBootLogRegistryToFile*. This function creates the file Ntbtlog.txt in the Windows 2000 system directory (\Winnt by default) and copies the contents of the BootLog registry value to the file. *IopCopyBootLogRegistryToFile* also sets a flag for *IopBootLog* that lets *IopBootLog* know that writing directly to the log file, rather than recording messages in the registry, is now OK. The following output shows the partial contents of a sample boot log:

```
Microsoft (R) Windows 2000 (R) Version 5.0 (Build 2195)
 2 11 2000 10:53:27.500
Loaded driver \WINNT\System32\ntoskrnl.exe
Loaded driver \WINNT\System32\hal.dll
Loaded driver \WINNT\System32\BOOTVID.DLL
```

```
Loaded driver ACPI.sys
Loaded driver \WINNT\System32\DRIVERS\WMILIB.SYS
Loaded driver pci.sys
Loaded driver isapnp.sys
Loaded driver compbatt.sys
Loaded driver \WINNT\System32\DRIVERS\BATTC.SYS
Loaded driver intelide.sys
Loaded driver \WINNT\System32\DRIVERS\PCIIDEX.SYS
Loaded driver pcmcia.sys
Loaded driver ftdisk.sys
Loaded driver Diskperf.sys
Loaded driver dmload.sys
Loaded driver dmio.sys
⋮
Did not load driver Media Control Devices
Did not load driver Communications Port
Did not load driver Audio Codecs
⋮
```

Recovery Console

Safe mode is a satisfactory fallback for systems that become unbootable because a device driver crashes during the boot sequence, but in some situations a safe-mode boot won't help the system boot. For example, if a driver that prevents the system from booting is a member of a Safe group, safe-mode boots will fail. Another example of a situation in which safe mode won't help the system boot is when a third-party driver, such as a virus scanner driver, that loads at the boot prevents the system from booting. (Boot-start drivers load whether or not the system is in safe mode.) Other situations in which safe-mode boots will fail are when a system module or critical device driver file that is part of a safe-mode configuration becomes corrupt or when the system drive's master boot record (MBR) is damaged. You can get around these problems by using the Windows 2000 Recovery Console. The Recovery Console allows you to boot into a limited command-line shell from the Windows 2000 CD or boot disks to repair an installation without having to boot the installation.

When you boot a system from the Windows 2000 CD or boot disks, you eventually see a screen that gives you the choice of either installing Windows 2000 or repairing an existing installation. If you choose to repair an installation, the system prompts you to insert the Windows 2000 CD (if it isn't already loaded in the system's CD drive) and then to choose among two repair options: to start

the Recovery Console or to initiate the emergency repair process. If you press the F10 key at the Setup Welcome screen, you bypass the menu options and take a shortcut directly to the Recovery Console.

When you start the Recovery Console, it gives you a list of Windows NT and Windows 2000 installations to choose from that it compiled when it scanned the computer's hard disks. After you make a selection, the system prompts you to enter the Administrator account password to log on to the installation as the administrator. If you successfully log on, the system puts you into a command shell that is similar to an MS-DOS environment. The command set is flexible and lets you perform simple file operations (such as copy, rename, and delete), enable and disable services and drivers, and even repair MBRs and boot records. However, the Recovery Console won't let you access directories other than root directories, the system directory of the installation you logged on to, or directories on removable drives such as CDs and 3.5-inch floppy disks. This prohibition provides a certain level of security for data that an administrator might not usually be able to access.

The Recovery Console uses the native Windows 2000 system call interface to perform file I/O to support commands such as Cd, Rename, and Move. The Enable and Disable commands, which let you change the startup modes of device drivers and services, work differently. For example, when you tell the Recovery Console that you want to disable a device driver, it reaches into the installation's Services key and manipulates the Start value of the specified driver's key, changing the value to SERVICE_DISABLED. The next time the installation boots, that device driver won't load. (The Recovery Console also loads the SYSTEM hive [\Winnt\System32\Config\System] for the installation you log on to. This hive contains the information stored in the HKLM\SYSTEM\CurrentControl-Set\Services registry key.)

When you boot from the Windows 2000 CD or the boot disks, by the time the system gives you the choice to install or repair Windows 2000, the CD has booted a copy of the Windows 2000 kernel, including all necessary supporting device drivers (for example, NTFS or FAT drivers, SCSI drivers, a video driver). On x86 systems, the Txtsetup.sif file in the I386 directory of the Windows 2000 CD guides the boot from the CD; the file contains directives that identify which files need to load and where the files are located on the CD. Just as when you boot Windows 2000 from a hard disk, the first user-mode program the kernel executes is Session Manager (Smss.exe), located in the I386\System32 folder. The

Session Manager that Windows 2000 Setup uses differs from the standard-installation Session Manager. The former component presents you with the menus that let you install or repair Windows 2000 and the menu that asks you what type of repair you want to perform. If you're installing Windows 2000, Session Manager is the component that guides you through choosing a partition to install to and copies files to the hard disk.

When you run the Recovery Console, Session Manager loads and starts two device drivers that implement the Recovery Console: Spcmdcon.sys and Setupdd.sys. Spcmdcon.sys presents an interactive command prompt and performs high-level command processing. Setupdd.sys is a support driver that gives Spcmdcon.sys a set of functions that let Spcmdcon.sys manage disk partitions, load registry hives, and display and manage video output. Setupdd.sys also communicates with disk drivers to manage disk partitions and uses basic video support built into the Windows 2000 kernel to display messages on the screen.

When you choose an installation to log on to and the Recovery Console accepts your password, the Recovery Console must validate your logon attempt, even though the installation's Windows 2000 security subsystem isn't up and running. Thus, the Recovery Console alone must determine whether your password matches the system's Administrator account. The Recovery Console's first step in this process is to use Setupdd.sys to load the installation's Security Accounts Manager (SAM) registry hive, which stores password information, from the hard disk. The SAM hive resides in \Winnt\System32\Config\Sam. After loading the hive, the Recovery Console locates the system key in the installation's registry and uses the system key to decrypt the in-memory copy of the SAM. SAM hive encryption is a feature introduced in Windows NT 4 Service Pack 3 that adds protection against MS-DOS-based password snoopers who try to read passwords directly out of a hive file.

Next, the Recovery Console (Spcmdcon.sys) locates the Administrator account password in the SAM, and in the final authentication step, the Recovery Console uses the RC4 hash algorithm—the same algorithm that the Windows 2000 logon process uses—to hash the password entered and compares the hash against the hashed password that the SAM stores. If the Recovery Console finds a match, the system considers you logged on. If the Recovery Console doesn't find a match, the system denies you access to the Recovery Console.

Shutdown

If someone is logged on and a process initiates a shutdown by calling the Win32 *ExitWindowsEx* function, a message is sent to Csrss instructing it to perform the shutdown. Csrss in turn impersonates the caller and sends a Windows message to a hidden window owned by Winlogon telling it to perform a system shutdown. Winlogon then impersonates the currently logged on user (who might or might not have the same security context as the user who initiated the system shutdown) and calls *ExitWindowsEx* with some special internal flags. Again, this call causes a message to be sent to Csrss requesting a system shutdown.

This time, Csrss sees that the request is from Winlogon and loops through all the processes in the logon session of the interactive user (again, not the user who requested a shutdown). For each process that owns a top-level window, Csrss sends the WM_QUERYENDSESSION message to each thread in the process that has a Windows message loop. If the thread returns TRUE, the system shutdown can proceed. Csrss then sends the WM_ENDSESSION Windows message to the thread to request it to exit. Csrss waits the number of seconds defined in HKCU\Control Panel\Desktop\HungAppTimeout for the thread to exit. (The default is 5000 milliseconds.)

If the thread doesn't exit before the timeout, Csrss displays the hung-program dialog box shown in Figure 4-3. (You can disable this dialog box by changing the registry value HKCU\Control Panel\Desktop\AutoEndTasks to 1). This dialog box indicates that a program isn't shutting down in a timely manner and gives the user a choice of either killing the process or aborting the shutdown. (There is no timeout on this dialog box, which means that a shutdown request could wait forever at this point.)

Figure 4-3
Hung program dialog box

If the thread does exit before the timeout, Csrss continues sending the WM_QUERYENDSESSION/WM_ENDSESSION message pairs to the other threads in the process that own windows. Once all the threads that own windows in the process have exited, Csrss terminates the process and goes on to the next process in the interactive session.

If Csrss finds a console application, it invokes the console control handler by sending the CTRL_LOGOFF_EVENT event. (Only service processes receive the CTRL_SHUTDOWN_EVENT event on shutdown.) If the handler returns FALSE, Csrss kills the process. If the handler returns TRUE or doesn't respond by the number of seconds defined by HKCU\Control Panel\Desktop\WaitToKillAppTimeout (the default is 20000 milliseconds), Csrss displays the hung-program dialog box shown in Figure 4-3.

Next, Winlogon calls *ExitWindowsEx* to have Csrss terminate any COM processes that are part of the interactive user's session.

At this point, all the processes in the interactive user's session have been terminated. Winlogon calls *ExitWindowsEx* again, but this time in the system process context, which again sends a message to Csrss, which looks at all the processes belonging to the system context and performs and sends the WM_QUERYENDSESSION/WM_ENDSESSION messages to GUI threads (as before). Instead of sending CTRL_LOGOFF_EVENT, however, it sends CTRL_SHUTDOWN_EVENT to console applications that have registered control handlers. Note that the SCM is a console program that does register a control handler. When it receives the shutdown request, it in turn sends the service shutdown control message to all services that registered for shutdown notification. For more details on service shutdown (such as the shutdown timeout Csrss uses for the SCM), see the "Services" section on page 236 in Chapter 5.

Although Csrss performs the same timeouts as when it was terminating the user processes, it doesn't display any dialog boxes and doesn't kill any processes. (The registry values for the system process timeouts are taken from the default user profile.) These timeouts simply allow system processes a chance to clean up and exit before the system shuts down. Therefore, many system processes are in fact still running when the system shuts down, such as Smss, Winlogon, the SCM, and Lsass.

Once Csrss has finished its pass notifying system processes that the system is shutting down, Winlogon finishes the shutdown process by calling the executive subsystem function *NtShutdownSystem*. This function calls the function

NtSetSystemPowerState to orchestrate the shutdown of drivers and the rest of the executive subsystems (Plug and Play manager, power manager, executive, I/O manager, configuration manager, and memory manager).

For example, *NtSetSystemPowerState* calls the I/O manager to send shutdown I/O packets to all device drivers that have requested shutdown notification. This action gives device drivers a chance to perform any special processing their device might require before Windows 2000 exits. The configuration manager flushes any modified registry data to disk, and the memory manager writes all modified pages containing file data back to their respective files. If the option to clear the paging file at shutdown is enabled, the memory manager clears the paging file at this time. The I/O manager is called a second time to inform the file system drivers that the system is shutting down. System shutdown ends in the power manager. The action the power manager takes depends on whether the user specified a shutdown, a reboot, or a power down.

System Crashes

Almost every Windows NT or Windows 2000 user has heard of, if not experienced, the infamous "blue screen of death." This ominous term refers to the blue screen that is displayed when Windows 2000 crashes, or stops executing, because of a catastrophic fault or an internal condition that prevents the system from continuing to run.

In this section, we'll cover the basic problems that cause Windows 2000 to crash, describe the information presented on the blue screen, and explain the various configuration options available to create a *crash dump*, a record of system memory at the time of a crash that can help you figure out which component caused the crash. This section is *not* intended to provide detailed troubleshooting information on how to analyze a Windows 2000 system crash.

Why Does Windows 2000 Crash?

Windows 2000 crashes (stops execution and displays the blue screen) for the following reasons:

- A device driver or an operating system function running in kernel mode incurs an unhandled exception, such as a memory access violation (whether attempting to write to a read-only page or attempting to read an address that isn't currently mapped).

■ A call to a kernel support routine results in a reschedule, such as waiting on an unsignaled dispatcher object, when the interrupt request level (IRQL) is DPC/dispatch level or higher. (See Chapter 3 for details on IRQLs.)

■ A page fault on memory backed by data in a paging file or a memory mapped file occurs at an IRQL of DPC/dispatch level or above (which would require the memory manager to have to wait for an I/O operation to occur—as just stated, waits can't occur at DPC/dispatch level or higher because that would require a reschedule).

■ A device driver or operating system function explicitly crashes the system (by calling the system function *KeBugCheckEx*) because it detects an internal condition that indicates either a corruption or some other situation that indicates the system can't continue execution without risking data corruption.

■ A hardware error, such as a machine check or a Non-Maskable Interrupt (NMI), occurs.

When a kernel-mode device driver or subsystem causes an illegal exception, Windows 2000 faces a difficult dilemma. It has detected that a part of the operating system with the ability to access any hardware device and any valid memory has done something it wasn't supposed to do.

But why does that mean Windows 2000 has to crash? Couldn't it just ignore the exception and let the device driver or subsystem continue as if nothing had happened? The possibility exists that the error was isolated and that the component will somehow recover. But what's more likely is that the detected exception resulted from deeper problems—for example, from a general corruption of memory or from a hardware device that's not functioning properly. Permitting the system to continue operating would probably result in more exceptions, and data stored on disk or other peripherals could become corrupt—a risk that's too high to take.

The Blue Screen

Regardless of the reason for a system crash, the function that actually performs the crash is *KeBugCheckEx* (documented in the Windows 2000 DDK). This function takes a s*top code* (sometimes called a *bug check code*), and four parameters that are interpreted on a per-stop code basis. After *KeBugCheckEx* masks out all

interrupts on all processors of the system, it switches the display into blue-screen mode (80-columns-by-50-lines text mode), paints a blue background, and then displays the stop code, followed by some text suggesting what the user can do. (It's possible that system data structures have been so seriously corrupted that the blue screen isn't displayed.) Figure 4-4 shows a sample blue screen.

Figure 4-4
Example blue screen

The first line lists the stop code and the four additional parameters passed to *KeBugCheckEx*. The text line below the stop code provides the text equivalent of the stop code's numeric identifier. According to the example in Figure 4-4, the stop code 0x0000000A is an IRQL_NOT_LESS_OR_EQUAL crash. When a parameter contains an address of a piece of operating system or device driver code (as in Figure 4-4), Windows 2000 displays the base address of the module the address falls in, the date stamp, and the file name of the device driver. This information alone might help you pinpoint the faulty component.

Although there are more than a hundred unique stop codes, most are rarely, if ever, seen on production systems. Instead, just a few common stop codes represent the majority of Windows 2000 system crashes. Also, the meaning of the four additional parameters depends on the stop code (and not all stop codes have extended parameter information). Nevertheless, looking up the stop code and the meaning of the parameters (if applicable) might at least assist you in diagnosing the component that is failing (or the hardware device that is causing the crash). You can find stop code information in the following places:

- The section "Bug Checks (Blue Screens)" in the Debugging help file (Ddkdbg.chm), which is shipped in three places: the Windows 2000 debugging tools (Customer Support Diagnostics), the Platform SDK, and the Windows 2000 DDK.

- The subsection "Windows 2000 Stop Messages" in the Troubleshooting chapter in the Windows 2000 Server Operations Guide (part of the Windows 2000 Server Resource Kit). This section includes details such as the meaning of the stop code parameters for the common stop codes.

■ You can also search Microsoft's online Knowledge Base (*support. microsoft.com*) for the stop code and the name of the suspect hardware or application. You might find information about a workaround, an update, or a service pack that fixes the problem you're having. Knowledge Base article Q103059 lists the majority of the stop codes and provides details on the meaning of the parameters. (This article applies to Windows NT, but the information holds true for Windows 2000.)

■ The Bugcodes.h file in the Windows 2000 DDK contains a complete list of the 150 or so stop codes with some additional details on the reasons for some of them.

You often begin seeing blue screens after you install a new software product or piece of hardware. If you've just added a driver, rebooted, and gotten a blue screen early in system initialization, you can reset the machine, press the F8 key when instructed, and then select Last Known Good Configuration. Enabling last known good causes Windows 2000 to revert to a copy of the registry's device driver registration key (HKLM\SYSTEM\CurrentControlSet\Services) from the last successful boot (before you installed the driver). From the perspective of last known good, a successful boot is one in which all services and drivers have finished loading and at least one logon has succeeded.

If you keep getting blue screens, an obvious approach is to uninstall the components you added just before the first blue screen appeared. If some time has passed since you added something new or you added several things at about the same time, you need to note the names of the device drivers referenced in any of the parameters. If you recognize any of the names as being related to something you just added (such as Scsiport.sys if you put on a new SCSI drive), you've possibly found your culprit.

Many device drivers have cryptic names, but one approach you can take to figure out which application or hardware device is associated with a name is to find out the name of the service in the registry associated with a device driver by searching for the name of the device driver under the HKLM\SYSTEM\ CurrentControlSet\Services key. This branch of the registry is where Windows 2000 stores registration information for every device driver in the system. If you find a match, look for values named DisplayName and Description. Some drivers fill in these values to describe the device driver's purpose. For example, you might find the string "Virus Scanner" in the DisplayName value, which can implicate the antivirus software you have running. The list of drivers can be displayed in the

Computer Management tool (from the Start menu, select Programs/Administrative Tools/Computer Management). In Computer Management, expand System Tools, System Information, and Software Environment, and then select Drivers.

More often than not, however, the stop code and the four associated parameters aren't enough information to troubleshoot a system crash. For example, you might need to examine the kernel-mode call stack to pinpoint the driver or system component that triggered the crash. Also, because the default behavior on Windows 2000 systems is to automatically reboot after a system crash, it's unlikely that you would have time to record the information displayed on the blue screen. That is why, by default, Windows 2000 attempts to record information about the system crash to the disk for later analysis, which takes us to our final topic, crash dump files.

Crash Dump Files

By default, all Windows 2000 systems are configured to attempt to record information about the state of the system when the system crashes. You can see these settings by opening the System tool in Control Panel, then in the System Properties dialog box, click the Advanced tab and then click the Startup And Recovery button. The default settings for a Windows 2000 Professional system are shown in Figure 4-5.

Figure 4-5
Crash dump settings

Three levels of information can be recorded on a system crash:

■ **Complete memory dump** A complete memory dump contains all of physical memory at the time of the crash. This type of dump requires that a page file be at least the size of physical memory. Because it can require an inordinately large page file on large memory systems, this type of dump file is the least common setting. Windows NT 4 supported only this type of crash dump file.

■ **Kernel memory dump** A kernel memory dump (the default on Windows 2000 Server systems) contains only the kernel-mode read/write pages present in physical memory at the time of the crash. This type of dump doesn't contain pages belonging to user processes. Because only kernel-mode code can directly cause Windows 2000 to crash, however, it's unlikely that user process pages are necessary to debug a crash. There is no way to predict the size of a kernel memory dump because its size depends on the amount of kernel-mode memory allocated by the operating system and drivers present on the machine. As an example, on a test system running Windows 2000 on a 128-MB laptop, a kernel memory dump took up 35 MB.

■ **Small memory dump** A small memory dump (the default on Windows 2000 Professional), which is 64 KB in size, contains the stop code and parameters, the list of loaded device drivers, the data structures that describe the current process and thread (called the EPROCESS and ETHREAD—described in Chapter 6), and the kernel stack for the thread that caused the crash.

When Windows 2000 is configured to write crash dump information, it writes the information to the paging file because trying to create a new file on the disk would depend on more of the system data structures being intact. (If there is more than one paging file, the first or primary page file is used.) After the system reboots, the logon process (Winlogon.exe) creates a child process (Savedump.exe) to copy the crash dump information out of the page file and into a new file. Small memory dumps are by default created in the directory \Winnt\Minidump and are given unique file names consisting of the string "Mini" plus the date plus a sequence number (for example, Mini031000-01.dmp). Kernel memory and complete memory dumps are copied to a file named \Winnt\Memory.dmp, which means that only the latest dump file is retained on the disk.

As mentioned earlier, there's no guarantee that the crash dump information will be recorded since the data structures used to access the paging file might themselves be corrupted, thus preventing the system from being able to write anything to disk. If the system isn't able to record the crash dump, you can try booting the crashing system with the kernel debugger so that you can gain control from a host debugger when the system crashes. In that way, you can use the interactive kernel debugger to look at the kernel stack or examine other operating system structures to try and determine the reason for the crash. For more information on how to set up the kernel debugger, see the Windows 2000 Debugging help file (Ddkdbg.chm) mentioned earlier.

Once you have a crash dump file (whether it's a small memory dump, a kernel memory dump, or a complete memory dump), how can you retrieve the stop code or perform further analysis? The simplest tool to use is Dumpchk (available in the Windows 2000 Support Tools, the Platform SDK, the Windows 2000 DDK, and the debugging tools). By default, Dumpchk opens a dump file and displays the basic information about a crash, such as the operating system version, stop code, and parameters. If you call it with the "-e" option, it displays more details, such as the list of loaded device drivers, the current process and thread, and the kernel stack. (This option requires the symbol file for Ntoskrnl.exe to match the version of Windows 2000 that crashed. See the section "Symbols for Kernel Debugging" on page 23 in Chapter 1 for more information on symbol files).

Finally, an advanced tool called the Kernel Memory Space Analyzer (Kanalyze.exe) might also be useful in debugging a crash dump. This tool is part of the debugging tools package, the Windows 2000 DDK, and the Platform SDK and is documented in a separate Microsoft Word document called OEM Tool Help. (You can find this file at \Program Files\Debuggers\bin\kanalyze\user-docs.doc if you have the Windows 2000 debugging tools installed. You can also find it in the Platform SDK and the DDK directory trees.)

Unfortunately, you can't run a magical program to identify the exact cause of blue screens or to make them go away. Even with extensive knowledge of Windows 2000 internals and device drivers, analyzing a blue screen or a crash dump can be very difficult. However, being able to retrieve the stop code and parameters can at least point you in the right direction.

EXPERIMENT: Forcing a Crash and Retrieving the Stop Code

To generate a crash dump for the purposes of experimenting with the dump analysis tools referred to in this section, you can force Windows 2000 to crash by either running the \Sysint\Bsod.exe tool on this book's companion CD (this program loads a device driver that calls *KeBugCheckEx*) or by enabling the support added in Windows 2000 to force the system to crash by holding the right Ctrl key down and pressing Scroll Lock twice. To enable this feature, add a DWORD value named CrashOnCtrlScroll with a value of 1 to the registry key HKLM\SYSTEM\CurrentControlSet\Services\i8042prt\Parameters. You must reboot the system for this change to take effect.

Once you've created a crash dump file, try using Dumpchk to display the basic crash dump information. Then try the Dumpchk -e option to display the extended information. Finally, try opening the crash dump file with the interactive kernel debugger (Kd, I386kd.exe, or Windbg.exe) and using some of the built-in kernel debugger extensions, such as *!process*, *!thread*, and *!drivers*.

For instructions on how to use these tools, see the Debugging help file (Ddkdbg.chm).

Conclusion

In this chapter, we've examined the detailed steps involved in starting and shutting down Windows 2000 (both normally and in error cases). In the next chapter, we'll look at three important mechanisms involved in the management infrastructure of Windows 2000: the registry, services, and Windows Management Instrumentation (WMI).

ntkrnlmp!Ki386CheckDelayedNpx

80432255 5e pop esi 80432256 5b pop ebx 8
20800 ret 0x8 8043225b cc int 3 ntkrnlmp
095150 or [ecx+0x50],edx 8043225f 8b4
push ebx 80432263 56 push esi 80432264 8
3b10 mov ed 8916 mov [esi
[edx+0x4] mov eax,[ea
eax,[ecx jnz ntkrnlmp
8043227 0x60] 8043
8043227 60 mov x60] 8043
80432276 mov [edx 8043227f 39
80b9eb00 or [ecx+0xeb],dx
eax,[ecx jz ntkrnlmp!
80432290 80 byte ptr [eax+0x3]
edx,[eax+0x18] 80432297 8b401c mov eax,[e
eax],edx 8043229c 894204 mov [edx+0x4],
eax,[ecx+0xe0] 804322a5 85c0 test eax,
ntkrnlmp!KiUnwaitThread+0x50 (804322
eax+0x18] 804322ac 8a5133 mov dl,[ecx+0x
i,[ecx+0x44] 804322b2 80fa10 cmp dl,0x
krnlmp!KiUnwaitThread

Management Mechanisms

This chapter describes three fundamental mechanisms in Microsoft Windows 2000 that are critical to the management and configuration of the system:

- The registry
- Services
- Windows Management Instrumentation

The Registry

The registry plays a key role in the configuration and control of Windows 2000 systems. It is the repository for both systemwide and per-user settings. Although most people think of the registry as static data stored on the hard disk, as you'll see in this section, the registry is also a window into various in-memory structures maintained by the Windows 2000 executive and kernel. This section isn't meant to be a complete reference to the contents of the Windows 2000 registry. That kind of in-depth information is documented in the *Technical Reference to the Windows 2000 Registry* help file in the Windows 2000 resource kits (Regentry.chm).

We'll start by providing you with an overview of the registry structure, a discussion of the data types it supports, and a brief tour of the key information Windows 2000 maintains in the registry. Then we'll look inside the internals of the *configuration manager,* the executive component responsible for implementing the registry database. Among the topics we'll cover are the internal on-disk structure of the registry, how Windows 2000 retrieves configuration information when an application requests it, and what measures are employed to protect this critical system database.

Registry Data Types

The registry is a database whose structure is similar to that of a logical disk drive. The registry contains *keys,* which are similar to a disk's directories, and *values,* which are comparable to files on a disk. A key is a container that can consist of other keys (*subkeys*) or values. Values, on the other hand, store data. Top-level keys are *root keys.* Throughout this section, we'll use the words *subkey* and *key* interchangeably. (Only root keys are not subkeys.)

Both keys and values borrow their naming convention from the file system. Thus, you can uniquely identify a value with the name mark, which is stored in a key called trade, with the name trade\mark. One exception to this naming scheme is each key's unnamed value. The two Registry Editor utilities, Regedit and Regedt32, display these values differently: Regedit displays the unnamed value as (Default); Regedt32 uses <No Name>.

Values store different kinds of data and can be one of the 11 types listed in Table 5-1. The majority of registry values are REG_DWORD, REG_BINARY, or REG_SZ. Values of type REG_DWORD can store numbers or Booleans (on/off values); REG_BINARY values can store numbers larger than 32 bits or raw data such as encrypted passwords; REG_SZ values store strings (Unicode, of course) that can represent elements such as names, filenames, paths, and types.

Table 5-1 Registry Value Types

Value Type	Description
REG_NONE	No value type
REG_SZ	Fixed-length Unicode NULL-terminated string
REG_EXPAND_SZ	Variable-length Unicode NULL-terminated string that can have embedded environment variables
REG_BINARY	Arbitrary-length binary data
REG_DWORD	32-bit number
REG_DWORD_LITTLE_ENDIAN	32-bit number, low byte first. This is equivalent to REG_DWORD.
REG_DWORD_BIG_ENDIAN	32-bit number, high byte first
REG_LINK	Unicode symbolic link
REG_MULTI_SZ	Array of Unicode NULL-terminated strings
REG_RESOURCE_LIST	Hardware resource description
REG_FULL_RESOURCE_DESCRIPTOR	Hardware resource description
REG_RESOURCE_REQUIREMENTS_LIST	Resource requirements

The REG_LINK type is particularly interesting because it lets a value transparently point to another key or value. When you traverse the registry through a link, the path searching continues at the target of the link. For example, if \Root1\Link has a REG_LINK value of \Root2\RegKey, and RegKey contains the value RegValue, two paths identify RegValue: \Root1\Link\RegValue and \Root2\RegKey\RegValue. As explained in the next section, Windows 2000 prominently uses registry links: three of the six registry root keys are links to subkeys within the three nonlink root keys. Links aren't saved; they must be dynamically created after each reboot.

Registry Logical Structure

You can chart the organization of the registry via the data stored within it. There are six root keys (you can't add new root keys or delete existing ones) that store information as follows:

- **HKEY_CURRENT_USER** Stores data associated with the currently logged-on user

- **HKEY_USER** Stores information about all the accounts on the machine

- **HKEY_CLASSES_ROOT** Stores file association and Component Object Model (COM) object registration information

- **HKEY_LOCAL_MACHINE** Stores system-related information

- **HKEY_PERFORMANCE_DATA** Stores performance information

- **HKEY_CURRENT_CONFIG** Stores some information about the current hardware profile

Why do root-key names begin with an H? Because the root-key names represent Win32 handles (H) to keys (KEY). As mentioned in Chapter 1, HKLM is an abbreviation used for HKEY_LOCAL_MACHINE. Table 5-2 lists all the root keys and their abbreviations. The following sections explain in detail the contents and purpose of each of these six root keys. Again, see the *Technical Reference to the Windows 2000 Registry* help file (Regentry.chm) in the Windows 2000 resource kits for details on the contents of these keys.

Table 5-2 Registry Root Keys

Root Key	Abbreviation	Description	Link
HKEY_CURRENT_USER	HKCU	Points to the user profile of the currently logged-on user	Subkey under HKEY_USERS corresponding to currently logged-on user
HKEY_USERS	HKU	Contains subkeys for all loaded user profiles	Not a link
HKEY_CLASSES_ROOT	HKCR	Contains file association and COM registration information	HKLM\ SOFTWARE\ Classes
HKEY_LOCAL_MACHINE	HKLM	Placeholder— contains other keys	Not a link
HKEY_CURRENT_CONFIG	HKCC	Current hardware profile	HKLM\ SYSTEM\ CurrentControlSet\ Hardware Profiles\ Current
HKEY_PERFORMANCE_DATA	HKPD	Performance counters	Not a link

HKEY_CURRENT_USER

The HKCU root key contains data regarding the preferences and software configuration of the locally logged-on user. It points to the currently logged-on user's user profile, located on the hard disk at \Documents and Settings\ <username>\Ntuser.dat. (See the section "Registry Internals" later in this chapter to find out how root keys are mapped to files on the hard disk.) Whenever a user profile is loaded (such as at logon time or when a service process runs under the context of a specific username), HKCU is created as a link to the user's key under HKEY_USERS. Table 5-3 lists some of the subkeys under HKCU.

Table 5-3 HKEY_CURRENT_USER Subkeys

Subkey	Description
AppEvents	Sound/event associations
Console	Command window settings (for example, width, height, and colors)
Control Panel	Screen saver, desktop scheme, keyboard, and mouse settings as well as accessibility and regional settings
Environment	Environment variable definitions
Keyboard Layout	Keyboard layout setting (for example, U.S. or U.K.)
Network	Network drive mappings and settings
Printers	Printer connection settings
Software	User-specific software preferences
UNICODE Program Groups	User-specific start menu group definitions
Windows 3.1 Migration Status	File status data for systems that upgrade from Windows 3.x to Windows 2000

HKEY_USERS

HKU contains a subkey for each loaded user profile and user class registration database on the system. It also contains a subkey named HKU\.DEFAULT that is linked to the default workstation profile (used by processes running under the local system account, described in more detail in the section "Services" later in this chapter).

HKEY_CLASSES_ROOT

HKCR consists of two types of information: file extension associations and COM class registrations. A key exists for every registered filename extension. Most keys contain a REG_SZ value that points to another key in HKCR containing the association information for the class of files that extension represents. For example, HKCR\.xls would point to information on Microsoft Excel files in a key such as HKCU\Excel.Sheet.8. Other keys contain configuration details for COM objects registered on the system.

The data under HKEY_CLASSES_ROOT comes from two sources:

- The per-user class registration data in HKCU\SOFTWARE\Classes (mapped to the file on hard disk \Documents and Settings\ <username>\Local Settings\Application Data\Microsoft\Windows\ Usrclass.dat)

- Systemwide class registration data in HKLM\SOFTWARE\Classes

The addition of per-user class registration data is new to Windows 2000. This change was made to separate per-user registration data from systemwide state so that roaming profiles can contain these customizations. It also closes a security hole: in Microsoft Windows NT 4, a nonprivileged user could change or delete keys in HKEY_CLASSES_ROOT, thus affecting the operation of applications on the system. In Windows 2000, nonprivileged users and applications can read systemwide data but can modify only their private data.

HKEY_LOCAL_MACHINE

HKLM is the root key that contains all the systemwide configuration subkeys: HARDWARE, SAM, SECURITY, SOFTWARE, and SYSTEM.

The HKLM\HARDWARE subkey maintains descriptions of the system's hardware and all hardware device-to-driver mappings. The Device Manager tool (available by running System from Control Panel, clicking the Hardware tab, and then clicking Device Manager) lets you view registry hardware information that it obtains by simply reading values out of the HARDWARE key.

HKLM\SAM holds local account and group information, such as user passwords, group definitions, and domain associations. Windows 2000 Server systems that are operating as domain controllers store domain accounts and groups in Active Directory, a database that stores domainwide settings and information. (Active Directory isn't described in this book.) By default, the security descriptor on the SAM key is configured such that even the administrator account doesn't have access. You can change the security descriptor to allow read access to administrators if you want to peer inside, but that glimpse won't be very revealing because the data is undocumented and the passwords are encrypted with one-way mapping—that is, you can't determine a password from its encrypted form.

HKLM\SECURITY stores systemwide security policies and user-rights assignments. HKLM\SAM is linked into the SECURITY subkey under HKLM\ SECURITY\SAM. By default, you can't view the contents of HKLM\SECURITY

or HKLM\SAM\SAM because the security settings of those keys allow access only by the system account. (System accounts are discussed in greater detail later in this chapter.)

HKLM\SOFTWARE is where Windows 2000 stores systemwide configuration information not needed to boot the system. Also, third-party applications store their systemwide settings here, such as paths to application files and directories, and licensing and expiration date information.

HKLM\SYSTEM contains the systemwide configuration information needed to boot the system, such as which device drivers to load and which services to start. Because this information is critical to starting the system, Windows 2000 also maintains a copy of part of this information, called the *last known good control set,* under this key. The maintenance of a copy allows an administrator to select a previously working control set in the case that configuration changes made to the current control set prevent the system from booting. For details on when Window 2000 declares the current control set "good," see the section "Accepting the Boot and Last Known Good" on page 256.

HKEY_CURRENT_CONFIG

HKEY_CURRENT_CONFIG is just a link to the current hardware profile, stored under HKLM\SYSTEM\CurrentControlSet\Hardware Profiles\Current. Hardware profiles allow the administrator to configure variations to the base system driver settings. Although the underlying profile might change from boot to boot, applications can always reference the currently active profile through this key.

EXPERIMENT: Viewing the SAM and SECURITY Keys

Although the SAM and SECURITY keys are protected with security settings that permit access only by the system account, you can use a trick that will enable you to explore their contents from a Registry Editor without changing their security. The *at* command launches applications at a time you specify and starts them in the system account. Therefore, if you specify Regedit.exe as the application and tell *at* to start Regedit interactively, you'll have an instance of Regedit that is able to look inside the SAM and SECURITY keys.

HKEY_PERFORMANCE_DATA

The registry is the mechanism to access performance counter values on Windows 2000, whether those are from operating system components or server applications. One of the side benefits of providing access to the performance counters via the registry is that remote performance monitoring works "for free" because the registry is easily accessible remotely through the normal registry APIs.

You can access the registry performance counter information directly by opening a special key named HKEY_PERFORMANCE_DATA and querying values beneath it. You won't find this key by looking in the Registry Editor; this key is available only programmatically through the Win32 registry functions, such as *RegQueryValueEx*. Performance information isn't actually stored in the registry; the registry functions use this key to locate the information from performance data providers.

You can also access performance counter information by using the Performance Data Helper (PDH) functions available through the Performance Data Helper API (Pdh.dll). Figure 5-1 shows the components involved in accessing performance counter information.

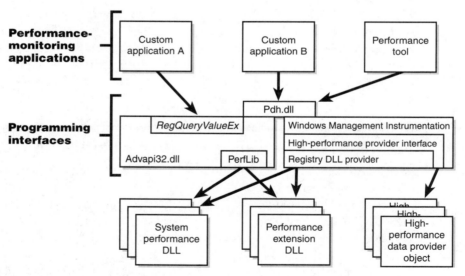

Figure 5-1
Registry performance counter architecture

EXPERIMENT: Watching Registry Activity

The Registry Monitor utility (\Sysint\Regmon.exe on the companion CD) lets you monitor registry activity as it occurs. For each registry access, Regmon shows you the process that performed the access and the time, type, and result of the access. This information is useful for understanding the way that applications and the system rely on the registry, seeing where applications and the system store configuration settings and troubleshooting problems related to applications having missing registry keys or values. The following screen shot shows Regmon displaying some of the registry accesses Microsoft Management Console (MMC) performs as it launches the Computer Management snap-in. (Regmon also includes a column showing the access time, but we've omitted that column from this screen shot to save space.)

Regmon relies on *system-call hooking*, a technique whereby a kernel-mode driver replaces the entries for registry-related functions in the system service dispatch table. Whenever an application executes a Win32 registry call, such as *RegCreateKey*, a corresponding system service (in this case, *NtCreateKey*) is invoked, which results in the execution of Regmon's hook routine.

Registry Internals

In this section, you'll find out how the configuration manager—the executive subsystem that implements the registry—organizes the registry's on-disk files. We'll examine how the configuration manager manages the registry as applications and other operating system components read and change registry keys and values. We'll also discuss the mechanisms by which the configuration manager tries to ensure that the registry is always in a recoverable state, even if the system crashes while the registry is being modified.

Hives

On disk, the registry isn't simply one large file but rather a set of discrete files called *hives*. Each hive contains a registry tree, which has a key that serves as the root or starting point of the tree. Subkeys and their values reside beneath the root. You might think that the root keys displayed by the Registry Editor tools correlate to the root keys in the hives, but such is not the case. Table 5-4 lists registry hives and their on-disk filenames. The pathnames of all hives except for user profiles are coded into the configuration manager. As the configuration manager loads hives, including system profiles, it notes each hive's path in the values under the HKLM\SYSTEM\CurrentControlSet\Control\hivelist subkey, removing the path if the hive is unloaded. (User profiles are unloaded when not referenced.) It creates the root keys, linking these hives together to build the registry structure you're familiar with and that the Registry Editor displays.

Table 5-4 On-Disk Files Corresponding to Paths in the Registry

Hive Registry Path	Hive File Path
HKEY_LOCAL_MACHINE\SYSTEM	\Winnt\System32\Config\System
HKEY_LOCAL_MACHINE\SAM	\Winnt\System32\Config\Sam
HKEY_LOCAL_MACHINE\SECURITY	\Winnt\System32\Config\Security
HKEY_LOCAL_MACHINE\SOFTWARE	\Winnt\System32\Config\Software
HKEY_LOCAL_MACHINE\HARDWARE	Volatile hive
HKEY_LOCAL_MACHINE\SYSTEM\Clone	Volatile hive
HKEY_USERS\<security ID of username>	\Documents and Settings\ <username>\Ntuser.dat
HKEY_USERS\<security ID of username>_Classes	\Documents and Settings\ <username>\Local Settings\ Application Data\Microsoft\ Windows\Usrclass.dat
HKEY_USERS\.DEFAULT	\Winnt\System32\Config\Default

You'll notice that some of the hives listed in Table 5-4 are volatile and don't have associated files. The system creates and manages these hives entirely in memory; the hives are therefore temporary. The system creates volatile hives every time it boots. An example of a volatile hive is the HKLM\HARDWARE hive, which stores information about physical devices and the devices' assigned resources. Resource assignment and hardware detection occur every time the system boots, so not storing this data on disk is logical.

EXPERIMENT: Looking at Hive Handles

The configuration manager opens hives by using the kernel handle table (described in Chapter 3) so that it can access hives from any process context. Using the kernel handle table is an efficient alternative to approaches that involve using drivers or executive components to access from the system process only handles that must be protected from user processes. You can use the HandleEx utility, available on the companion CD in \Sysint\Handleex.exe, to see the hive handles. Because the object manager reports kernel handle table handles as being opened in the System Idle process, select System Idle Process in the top pane to see the hive handles, as shown here. (Be sure View Handles is selected in the View menu.)

A special type of key known as a *symbolic link* makes it possible for the configuration manager to link hives to organize the registry. A symbolic link is a key that redirects the configuration manager to another key. Thus, the key HKLM\SAM is a symbolic link to the key at the root of the SAM hive.

Hive Structure

The configuration manager logically divides a hive into allocation units called *blocks* in much the same way that a file system divides a disk into clusters. By definition, the registry block size is 4096 bytes (4 KB). When new data expands a hive, the hive always expands in block-granular increments. The first block of a hive is the *base block*. The base block includes global information about the hive, including a signature—*regf*—that identifies the file as a hive, updated sequence numbers, a time stamp that shows the last time a write operation was initiated on the hive, the hive format version number, a checksum, and the hive file's internal filename (for example, \Device\HarddiskVolume1\WINNT\ CONFIG\SAM). We'll clarify the significance of the updated sequence numbers and time stamp when we describe how data is written to a hive file. The hive format version number specifies the data format within the hive. Hive formats changed from Windows NT 3.51 to Windows NT 4, so if you try to load a Windows NT 4 or Windows 2000 hive on earlier versions of Windows NT, you'll fail.

Windows 2000 organizes the registry data that a hive stores in containers called *cells*. A cell can hold a key, a value, a security descriptor, a list of subkeys, or a list of key values. A field at the beginning of a cell's data describes the data's type. Table 5-5 describes each cell data type in detail. A cell's header is a field that specifies the cell's size. When a cell joins a hive and the hive must expand to contain the cell, the system creates an allocation unit called a *bin*. A bin is the size of the new cell rounded up to the next block boundary. The system considers any space between the end of the cell and the end of the bin free space that it can allocate to other cells. Bins also have headers that contain a signature, *hbin*, and a field that records the offset into the hive file of the bin and the bin's size.

Table 5-5 Cell Data Types

Data Type	Description
Key cell	A cell that contains a registry key, also called a key node. A key cell contains a signature (kn for a key, kl for a symbolic link), the time stamp of the most recent update to the key, the cell index of the key's parent key cell, the cell index of the subkey-list cell that identifies the key's subkeys, a cell index for the key's security descriptor cell, a cell index for a string key that specifies the class name of the key, and the name of the key (for example, CurrentControlSet).
Value cell	A cell that contains information about a key's value. This cell includes a signature (kv), the value's type (for example, REG_DWORD or REG_BINARY), and the value's name (for example, Boot-Execute). A value cell also contains the cell index of the cell that contains the value's data.
Subkey-list cell	A cell composed of a list of cell indexes for key cells that are all subkeys of a common parent key.
Value-list cell	A cell composed of a list of cell indexes for value cells that are all values of a common parent key.
Security-descriptor cell	A cell that contains a security descriptor. Security-descriptor cells include a signature (ks) at the head of the cell and a reference count that records the number of key nodes that share the security descriptor. Multiple key cells can share security-descriptor cells.

By using bins, instead of cells, to track active parts of the registry, Windows 2000 minimizes some management chores. For example, the system usually allocates and deallocates bins less frequently than it does cells, which lets the configuration manager manage memory more efficiently. When the configuration manager reads a registry hive into memory, it can choose to read only bins that contain cells (that is, active bins) and to ignore empty bins. When the system adds and deletes cells in a hive, the hive can contain empty bins interspersed with active bins. This situation is similar to disk fragmentation, which occurs when the system creates and deletes files on the disk. When a bin becomes empty, the configuration manager joins to the empty bin any adjacent empty bins to form as large a contiguous empty bin as possible. The configuration manager also joins adjacent deleted cells to form larger free cells. (The configuration

manager never tries to compact a registry hive—you can compact the registry by backing it up and restoring it using the Win32 *RegSaveKey* and *RegReplaceKey* functions, which are used by the Windows Backup utility.)

The links that create the structure of a hive are called *cell indexes*. A cell index is the offset of a cell into the hive file. Thus, a cell index is like a pointer from one cell to another cell that the configuration manager interprets relative to the start of a hive. For example, as you saw in Table 5-5, a cell that describes a key contains a field specifying the cell index of its parent key; a cell index for a subkey specifies the cell that describes the subkeys that are subordinate to the specified subkey. A subkey-list cell contains a list of cell indexes that refer to the subkey's key cells. Therefore, if you want to locate, for example, the key cell of subkey A, whose parent is key B, you must first locate the cell containing key B's subkey list using the subkey-list cell index in key B's cell. Then you locate each of key B's subkey cells by using the list of cell indexes in the subkey-list cell. For each subkey cell, you check to see whether the subkey's name, which a key cell stores, matches the one you want to locate, in this case, subkey A.

The distinction between cells, bins, and blocks can be confusing, so let's look at an example of a simple registry hive layout to help clarify the differences. The sample registry hive file in Figure 5-2 contains a base block and two bins. The first bin is empty, and the second bin contains several cells. Logically, the hive has only two keys: the root key Root, and a subkey of Root, Sub Key. Root has two values, *Val 1* and *Val 2*. A subkey-list cell locates the root key's subkey, and a value-list cell locates the root key's values. The free spaces in the second bin are empty cells. The figure doesn't show the security cells for the two keys, which would be present in a hive.

Figure 5-2
Internal structure of a registry hive

Figure 5-3 shows an example of the Disk Probe utility (Dskprobe.exe) examining the first bin in a SYSTEM hive. Notice the bin's signature, *hbin*, at the top right side of the image. Look beneath the bin signature and you'll see the signature *nk*. This signature is the signature of a key cell (*kn*). The signature displays backward because of the way x86 computers store data. The cell is the SYSTEM hive's root cell, which the configuration manager has named internally $$$PROTO.HIV, as specified by the name that follows the *nk* signature.

Figure 5-3
Binary contents of first bin in the SYSTEM hive

To optimize searches for both values and subkeys, the configuration manager sorts subkey-list cells alphabetically. The configuration manager can then perform a binary search when it looks for a subkey within a list of subkeys. The configuration manager examines the subkey in the middle of the list, and if the name of the subkey the configuration manager is looking for is alphabetically before the name of the middle subkey, the configuration manager knows that the subkey is in the first half of the subkey list; otherwise, the subkey is in the second half of the subkey list. This splitting process continues until the configuration manager locates the subkey or finds no match. Value-list cells aren't sorted, however, so new values are always added to the end of the list.

Cell Maps

The configuration manager doesn't access a hive's image on disk every time a registry access occurs. Instead, Windows 2000 keeps a version of every hive in the kernel's address space. When a hive initializes, the configuration manager determines the size of the hive file, allocates enough memory from the kernel's paged pool to store it, and reads the hive file into memory. (For more information on paged pool, see Chapter 7.) Because all loaded registry hives are read into paged pool, that registry data is typically the largest consumer of paged pool. (To check paged pool allocation, use the Poolmon utility, described in the experiment "Monitoring Pool Usage" on page 406 in Chapter 7.)

If hives never grew, the configuration manager could perform all its registry management on the in-memory version of a hive as if the hive were a file. Given a cell index, the configuration manager could calculate the location in memory of a cell simply by adding the cell index, which is a hive file offset, to the base of the in-memory hive image. Early in the system boot, this process is exactly what Ntldr does with the SYSTEM hive: Ntldr reads the entire SYSTEM hive into memory as a read-only hive and adds the cell indexes to the base of the in-memory hive image to locate cells. Unfortunately, hives grow as they take on new keys and values, which means the system must allocate paged pool memory to store the new bins that contain added keys and values. Thus, the paged pool that keeps the registry data in memory isn't necessarily contiguous.

EXPERIMENT: Viewing Hive Paged Pool Usage

There are no administrative-level tools that show you the amount of paged pool that registry hives, including user profiles, are consuming. However, the *!regpool* kernel debugger command shows you not only how many pages of paged pool each loaded hive consumes but also how many of the pages store volatile and nonvolatile data. The command prints the total hive memory usage at the end of the output. (The command shows only the last 32 characters of a hive's name.)

```
kd> !regpool

dumping hive at e20d66a8 (a\Microsoft\Windows\UsrClass.dat)
   Stable Length = 1000
   1/1 pages present
   Volatile Length = 0

dumping hive at e215ee88 (ettings\Administrator\ntuser.dat)
   Stable Length = f2000
```

```
   242/242 pages present
   Volatile Length = 2000
   2/2 pages present

dumping hive at e13fa188 (\SystemRoot\System32\Config\SAM)
   Stable Length = 5000
   5/5 pages present
   Volatile Length = 0

dumping hive at e142fe68 (stemRoot\System32\Config\DEFAULT)
   Stable Length = 24000
   36/36 pages present
   Volatile Length = 0

dumping hive at e13fbb48 (temRoot\System32\Config\SOFTWARE)
   Stable Length = b40000
   1856/2880 pages present
   Volatile Length = 1000
   1/1 pages present

dumping hive at e13fa948 (temRoot\System32\Config\SECURITY)
   Stable Length = b000
   11/11 pages present
   Volatile Length = 1000
   1/1 pages present

dumping hive at e128c008 (NONAME)
   Stable Length = d000
   10/13 pages present
   Volatile Length = 4000
   4/4 pages present

dumping hive at e1008528 (SYSTEM)
   Stable Length = 274000
   628/628 pages present
   Volatile Length = 36000
   54/54 pages present

dumping hive at e10088e8 (NONAME)
   Stable Length = 1000
   1/1 pages present
   Volatile Length = 0
Total pages present = 2852 / 3879
```

To deal with noncontiguous memory buffers storing hive data in memory, the configuration manager adopts a strategy similar to what the Windows 2000 memory manager uses to map virtual memory addresses to physical memory addresses. The configuration manager employs a two-level scheme, which Figure 5-4 illustrates, that takes as input a cell index (that is, a hive file offset) and returns as output both the address in memory of the block the cell index resides in and the address in memory of the bin the cell resides in. Remember that a bin can contain one or more blocks and that hives grow in bins, so Windows 2000 always represents a bin with a contiguous memory buffer. Therefore, all blocks within a bin occur within the same portion of a paged pool.

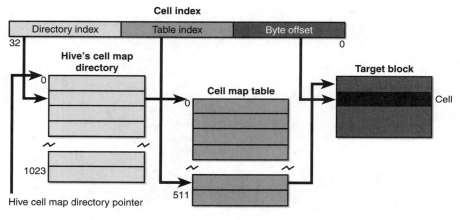

Figure 5-4
Structure of a cell index

To implement the mapping, the configuration manager divides a cell index logically into fields, in the same way that the memory manager divides a virtual address into fields. Windows 2000 interprets a cell index's first field as an index into a hive's cell map directory. The cell map directory contains 1024 entries, each of which refers to a cell map table that contains 512 map entries. An entry in this cell map table is specified by the second field in the cell index. That entry locates the bin and block memory addresses of the cell. In the final step of the translation process, the configuration manager interprets the last field of the cell index as an offset into the identified block to precisely locate a cell in memory. When a hive initializes, the configuration manager dynamically creates the mapping tables, designating a map entry for each block in the hive, and adds and deletes tables from the cell directory as the changing size of the hive requires.

The Registry Namespace and Operation

The configuration manager defines a *key object* object type to integrate the registry's namespace with the kernel's general namespace. The configuration manager inserts a key object named *Registry* into the root of the Windows 2000 namespace, which serves as the entry point to the registry. Regedit shows key names in the form HKEY_LOCAL_MACHINE\SYSTEM\CurrentControlSet, but the Win32 subsystem translates such names into their object namespace form (for example, \Registry\Machine\System\CurrentControlSet). When the Windows 2000 object manager parses this name, it encounters the key object by the name of Registry first and hands the rest of the name to the configuration manager. The configuration manager takes over the name parsing, looking through its internal hive tree to find the desired key or value. Before we describe the flow of control for a typical registry operation, we need to discuss key objects and *key control blocks*. Whenever an application opens or creates a registry key, the object manager gives a handle with which to reference the key to the application. The handle corresponds to a key object that the configuration manager allocates with the help of the object manager. By using the object manager's object support, the configuration manager takes advantage of the security and reference-counting functionality that the object manager provides.

For each open registry key, the configuration manager also allocates a key control block. A key control block stores the full pathname of the key, includes the cell index of the key node that the control block refers to, and contains a flag that notes whether the configuration manager needs to delete the key cell that the key control block refers to when the last handle for the key closes. Windows 2000 places all key control blocks into an alphabetized binary tree to enable quick searches for existing key control blocks by name. A key object points to its corresponding key control block, so if two applications open the same registry key, each will receive a key object, and both key objects will point to a common key control block.

When an application opens an existing registry key, the flow of control starts with the application specifying the name of the key in a registry API that invokes the object manager's name-parsing routine. The object manager, upon encountering the configuration manager's registry key object in the namespace, hands the pathname to the configuration manager. The configuration manager uses the in-memory hive data structures to search through keys and subkeys to find the specified key. If the configuration manager finds the key cell, the configuration manager searches the key control block tree to determine whether the key is open (by the same or another application). The search routine is optimized to always start from the closest ancestor with a key control block already opened.

For example, if an application opens \Registry\Machine\Key1\Subkey2, and \Registry\Machine is already opened, the parse routine uses the registry control block of \Registry\Machine as a starting point. If the key is open, the configuration manager increments the existing key control block's reference count. If the key isn't open, the configuration manager allocates a new key control block and inserts it into the tree. Then the configuration manager allocates a key object, points the key object at the key control block, and returns control to the object manager, which returns a handle to the application.

When an application creates a new registry key, the configuration manager first finds the key cell for the new key's parent. The configuration manager then searches the list of free cells for the hive in which the new key will reside to determine whether cells exist that are large enough to hold the new key cell. If there aren't, the configuration manager allocates a new bin and uses it for the cell, placing any space at the end of the bin on the free cell list. The new key cell fills with pertinent information—including the key's name—and the configuration manager adds the key cell to the subkey list of the parent key's subkey-list cell. Finally, the system stores the cell index of the parent cell in the new subkey's key cell.

The configuration manager uses a key control block's reference count to determine when to delete the key control block. When all the handles that refer to a key in a key control block close, the reference count becomes 0, which denotes that the key control block is no longer necessary. If an application that calls an API to delete the key sets the delete flag, the configuration manager can delete the associated key from the key's hive because it knows that no application is keeping the key open.

Stable Storage

To make sure that a nonvolatile registry hive (one with an on-disk file) is always in a recoverable state, the configuration manager uses *log hives*. Each nonvolatile hive has an associated log hive, which is a hidden file with the same base name as the hive and a *.log* extension. For example, if you look in your \Winnt\ System32\Config directory (and you have the Show Hidden Files And Folders folder option selected), you'll see System.log, Sam.log, and other .log files. When a hive initializes, the configuration manager allocates a bit array in which each bit represents a 512-byte portion, or *sector,* of the hive. This array is called the *dirty sector array* because an *on* bit in the array means that the system has modified the corresponding sector in the hive in memory and must write the sector back to the hive file. (An *off* bit means that the corresponding sector is up to date with the in-memory hive's contents.)

When the creation of a new key or value or the modification of an existing key or value takes place, the configuration manager notes the sectors of the hive that change in the hive's dirty sector array. Then the configuration manager schedules a lazy write operation, or a *hive sync*. The hive lazy writer system thread wakes up 5 seconds after the request to synchronize the hive and writes dirty hive sectors for all hives from memory to the hive files on disk. Thus, the system flushes, at the same time, all the registry modifications that take place between the time a hive sync is requested and the time the hive sync occurs. When a hive sync takes place, the next hive sync will occur no sooner than 5 seconds later.

If the lazy writer simply wrote all a hive's dirty sectors to the hive file and the system crashed in midoperation, the hive file would be in an inconsistent (corrupted) and unrecoverable state. To prevent such an occurrence, the lazy writer first dumps the hive's dirty sector array and all the dirty sectors to the hive's log file, increasing the log file's size if necessary. The lazy writer then updates a sequence number in the hive's base block and writes the dirty sectors to the hive. When the lazy writer is finished, it updates a second sequence number in the base block. Thus, if the system crashes during the write operations to the hive, at the next reboot the configuration manager will notice that the two sequence numbers in the hive's base block don't match. The configuration manager can update the hive with the dirty sectors in the hive's log file to roll the hive forward. The hive is then up to date and consistent.

To further protect the integrity of the crucial SYSTEM hive, the configuration manager maintains a mirror of the SYSTEM hive on disk. If you look at the nonhidden files in your \Winnt\System32\Config directory, you'll see three files with the base name *System:* System, System.alt, and System.sav. System.alt is the *alternate hive*. Whenever a hive sync flushes dirty sectors to the SYSTEM hive, the hive sync also updates the System.alt hive. If the configuration manager detects that the SYSTEM hive is corrupt when the system boots, the configuration manager attempts to load the hive's alternate. If that hive is usable, it then uses that alternate to update the original SYSTEM hive.

System.sav is a copy of the SYSTEM hive that exists when Windows 2000 finishes installing. This copy can be used, usually only in extreme circumstances, to restore the computer's configuration to its initial state.

Registry Optimizations

The configuration manager makes a few noteworthy performance optimizations. First, virtually every registry key has a security descriptor that protects access to the key. Storing a unique security-descriptor copy for every key in a hive would be highly inefficient, however, because the same security settings often apply to

entire subtrees of the registry. When the system applies security to a key, the configuration manager first checks the security descriptors associated with the key's parent key and then checks all the parent's subkeys. If any of those security descriptors match the security descriptor the system is applying to the key, the configuration manager simply shares the existing descriptors with the key, employing a reference count to track how many keys share the same descriptor.

The configuration manager also optimizes the way it stores key and value names in a hive. Although the registry is fully Unicode-capable and specifies all names using the Unicode convention, if a name contains only ASCII characters, the configuration manager stores the name in ASCII form in the hive. When the configuration manager reads the name (such as when performing name lookups), it converts the name into Unicode form in memory. Storing the name in ASCII form can significantly reduce the size of a hive.

To minimize memory usage, key control blocks don't store full key registry pathnames. Instead, they reference only a key's name. For example, a key control block that refers to \Registry\System\Control would refer to the name *Control* rather than to the full path. A further memory optimization is that the configuration manager uses key name control blocks to store key names, and all key control blocks for keys with the same name share the same key name control block. To optimize performance, the configuration manager stores the key control block names in a hash table for quick lookups.

To provide fast access to key control blocks, the configuration manager stores frequently accessed key control blocks in the cache table, which is configured as a hash table. When the configuration manager needs to look up a key control block, it first checks the cache table. Finally, the configuration manager has another cache, the delayed close table, that stores key control blocks that applications close, so that an application can quickly reopen a key it has recently closed. The configuration manager removes the oldest key control blocks from the delayed close table as it adds the most recently closed blocks to the table.

Services

Almost every operating system has a mechanism to start processes at system startup time that provide services not tied to an interactive user. In Windows 2000, such processes are called *services,* or *Win32 services,* because they rely on the Win32 API to interact with the system. Services are similar to UNIX daemon processes and often implement the server side of client/server applications. An example of a Win32 service might be a Web server since it must be running regardless

of whether anyone is logged on to the computer and it must start running when the system starts so that an administrator doesn't have to remember, or even be present, to start it.

Win32 services consist of three components: a service application, a service control program (SCP), and the service control manager (SCM). First, we'll describe service applications, service accounts, and the operations of the SCM. Then we'll explain how auto-start services are started during the system boot. We'll also cover the steps the SCM takes when a service fails during its startup and the way the SCM shuts down services.

Service Applications

Service applications, such as Web servers, consist of at least one executable that runs as a Win32 service. A user wanting to start, stop, or configure a service uses an SCP. Although Windows 2000 supplies built-in SCPs that provide general start, stop, pause, and continue functionality, some service applications include their own SCP that allows administrators to specify configuration settings particular to the service they manage.

Service applications are simply Win32 executables (GUI or console) with additional code to receive commands from the SCM as well as to communicate the application's status back to the SCM. Because most services don't have a user interface, they are built as console programs.

When you install an application that includes a service, the application's setup program must register the service with the system. To register the service, the setup program calls the Win32 *CreateService* function, a services-related function implemented in Advapi32.dll (\Winnt\System32\Advapi32.dll). Advapi32, the "Advanced API" DLL, implements all the client-side SCM APIs.

When a setup program registers a service by calling *CreateService*, a message is sent to the SCM on the machine where the service will reside. The SCM then creates a registry key for the service under HKLM\SYSTEM\CurrentControlSet\Services. The Services key is the nonvolatile representation of the SCM's database. The individual keys for each service define the path of the executable image that contains the service as well as parameters and configuration options.

After creating a service, an installation or management application can start the service via the *StartService* function. Because some service-based applications also must initialize during the boot process to function, it's not unusual for a setup program to register a service as an auto-start service, ask the user to reboot the system to complete an installation, and let the SCM start the service as the system boots.

When a program calls *CreateService*, it must specify a number of parameters describing the service's characteristics. The characteristics include the service's type (whether it's a service that runs in its own process rather than a service that shares a process with other services), the location of the service's executable image file, an optional display name, an optional account name and password used to start the service in a particular account's security context, a start type that indicates whether the service starts automatically when the system boots or manually under the direction of an SCP, an error code that indicates how the system should react if the service detects an error when starting, and, if the service starts automatically, optional information that specifies when the service starts relative to other services.

The SCM stores each characteristic as a value in the service's registry key. Figure 5-5 shows an example of a service registry key.

Figure 5-5
Example of a service registry key

Table 5-6 lists all the service characteristics. (Not every characteristic applies to every type of service.) If a service needs to store configuration information that is private to the service, the convention is to create a subkey named Parameters under its service key and then store the configuration information in values under that subkey. The service then can retrieve the values by using standard registry functions.

Table 5-6 Service and Driver Registry Parameters

Value Name	Value Setting	Value Setting Description
Start	SERVICE_BOOT_START (0)	Ntldr or Osloader preloads the driver so that it is in memory during the boot. These drivers are initialized just prior to SERVICE_SYSTEM_START drivers.
	SERVICE_SYSTEM_START (1)	The driver loads and initializes after SERVICE_BOOT_START drivers have initialized.
	SERVICE_AUTO_START (2)	The SCM starts the driver or service.
	SERVICE_DEMAND_START (3)	The SCM must start the driver or service on demand.
	SERVICE_DISABLED (4)	The driver or service doesn't load or initialize.
ErrorControl	SERVICE_ERROR_IGNORE (0)	The I/O manager ignores errors the driver returns. No warning is logged or displayed.
	SERVICE_ERROR_NORMAL (1)	If the driver reports an error, a warning displays.
	SERVICE_ERROR_SEVERE (2)	If the driver returns an error and last known good isn't being used, reboot into last known good; otherwise, continue the boot.
	SERVICE_ERROR_CRITICAL (3)	If the driver returns an error and last known good isn't being used, reboot into last known good; otherwise, stop the boot with a blue screen crash.

(continued)

Table 5-6 *continued*

Value Name	Value Setting	Value Setting Description
Type	SERVICE_KERNEL_DRIVER (1)	Device driver.
	SERVICE_FILE_SYSTEM_DRIVER (2)	Kernel-mode file system driver.
	SERVICE_RECOGNIZER_DRIVER (8)	File system recognizer driver.
	SERVICE_WIN32_OWN_PROCESS (16)	The service runs in a process that hosts only one service.
	SERVICE_WIN32_SHARE_PROCESS (32)	The service runs in a process that hosts multiple services.
	SERVICE_INTERACTIVE_PROCESS (256)	The service is allowed to display windows on the console and receive user input.
Group	Group name	The driver or service initializes when its group is initialized.
Tag	Tag number	The specified location in a group initialization order. This parameter doesn't apply to services.
ImagePath	Path to service or driver executable file	If ImagePath isn't specified, the I/O manager looks for drivers in \Winnt\System32\Drivers and the SCM looks for services in \Winnt\System32.
DependOnGroup	Group name	The driver or service won't load unless a driver or service from the specified group loads.
DependOnService	Service name	The service won't load until after the specified service loads. This parameter doesn't apply to device drivers.

Value Name	Value Setting	Value Setting Description
ObjectName	Usually LocalSystem but can be an account name, such as .\Administrator	Specifies the account in which the service will run. If ObjectName isn't specified, LocalSystem is the account used. This parameter doesn't apply to device drivers.
DisplayName	Name of service	The service application shows services by this name. If no name is specified, the name of the service's registry key becomes its name.
Description	Description of service	Up to 1024-byte description of the service.
FailureActions	Description of actions the SCM should take when service process exits unexpectedly	Failure actions include restarting the service process, rebooting the system, and running a specified program. This value doesn't apply to drivers.
FailureCommand	Program command line	The SCM reads this value only if FailureActions specifies that a program should execute upon service failure. This value doesn't apply to drivers.
Security	Security descriptor	This value contains the security descriptor that defines who has what access to the service.

Notice that Type values include three that apply to device drivers: device driver, file system driver, and file system recognizer. These are used by Windows 2000 device drivers, which also store their parameters as registry data in the Services registry key. The SCM is responsible for starting drivers with a Start value of SERVICE_AUTO_START, so it's natural for the SCM database to include drivers. Services use the other types, SERVICE_WIN32_OWN_PROCESS

and SERVICE_WIN32_SHARE_PROCESS, which are mutually exclusive. An executable that hosts more than one service specifies the SERVICE_WIN32_SHARE_PROCESS type. An advantage to having a process run more than one service is that the system resources that would otherwise be required to run them in distinct processes are saved. A potential disadvantage is that if one of the services of a collection running in the same process causes an error that terminates the process, all the services of that process terminate.

When the SCM starts a service process, the process immediately invokes the *StartServiceCtrlDispatcher* function. *StartServiceCtrlDispatcher* accepts a list of entry points into services, one entry point for each service in the process. Each entry point is identified by the name of the service the entry point corresponds to. After making a named pipe communications connection to the SCM, *StartServiceCtrlDispatcher* sits in a loop waiting for commands to come through the pipe from the SCM. The SCM sends a service-start command each time it starts a service the process owns. For each start command it receives, the *StartServiceCtrlDispatcher* function creates a thread, called a service thread, to invoke the starting service's entry point and implement the command loop for the service. *StartServiceCtrlDispatcher* waits indefinitely for commands from the SCM and returns control to the process's main function only when all the process's service threads have terminated, allowing the service process to clean up resources before exiting.

A service entry point's first action is to call the *RegisterServiceCtrlHandler* function. This function receives and stores a table of functions that the service implements to handle various commands it receives from the SCM. *RegisterServiceCtrlHandler* doesn't communicate with the SCM, but it stores the table in local process memory for the *StartServiceCtrlDispatcher* function. The service entry point continues initializing the service, which can include allocating memory, creating communications end points, and reading private configuration data from the registry. A convention most services follow is to store their parameters under a subkey of their service registry key, named Parameters. While the entry point is initializing the service, it might periodically send status messages to the SCM indicating how the service's startup is progressing. After the entry point finishes initialization, a service thread usually sits in a loop waiting for requests from client applications. For example, a Web server would initialize a TCP listen socket and wait for inbound HTTP connection requests.

A service process's main thread, which executes in the *StartServiceCtrlDispatcher* function, receives SCM commands directed at services in the process and uses the service's table of handler functions (stored by *RegisterServiceCtrlHandler*) to locate and invoke the service function responsible for responding to a command. SCM commands include stop, pause, resume, interrogate, and shutdown, or application-defined commands. Figure 5-6 shows the

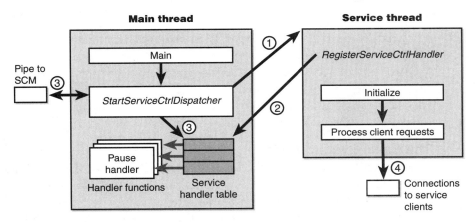

Figure 5-6
Inside a service process

1. *StartServiceCtrlDispatcher* launches service thread.
2. Service thread registers service handlers.
3. *StartServiceCtrlDispatcher* calls handlers in response to SCM commands.
4. Service thread processes client requests.

internal organization of a service process. Pictured are the two threads that make up a process hosting one service: the main thread and the service thread.

SrvAny Tool

If you have a program that you want to run as a service, you need to modify the startup code to conform to the requirements for services outlined in this section. If you don't have the source code, you can use the SrvAny tool in the Windows 2000 resource kits. SrvAny enables you to run any application as a service. It reads the path of the service file that it must load from the Parameters subkey of the service's registry key. When SrvAny starts, it notifies the SCM that it is hosting a particular service, and when it receives a start command, it launches the service executable as a child process. The child process receives a copy of the SrvAny process's access token and a reference to the same window station, so the executable runs within the same security account and with the same interactivity setting as you specified when configuring the SrvAny process. SrvAny services don't have the share-process Type value, so each application you install as a service with SrvAny runs in a separate process with a different instance of the SrvAny host program.

Service Accounts

The security context of a service is an important consideration for service developers as well as for system administrators because it dictates what resources the process can access. Unless a service installation program or administrator specifies otherwise, services run in the security context of the *local system account* (displayed sometimes as SYSTEM and other times as LocalSystem). The following two subsections describe the special characteristics of this account.

The Local System Account

The local system account is the same account in which all the Windows 2000 user-mode operating system components run, including the Session Manager (\Winnt\System32\Smss.exe), the Win32 subsystem process (Csrss.exe), the local security authority subsystem (\Winnt\System32\Lsass.exe), and the Winlogon process (\Winnt\System32\Winlogon.exe).

From a security perspective, the local system account is extremely powerful—more powerful than any local or domain account when it comes to security ability on a local system. This account has the following characteristics:

- It is a member of the local administrators group.

- It has the right to enable virtually every privilege (even privileges not normally granted to the local administrator account, such as creating security tokens).

- Most files and registry keys grant full access to the local system account. (Even if they don't grant full access, a process running under the local system account can exercise the take-ownership privilege to gain access.)

- Processes running under the local system account run with the default user profile (HKU\.DEFAULT). Therefore, they can't access configuration information stored in the user profiles of other accounts.

- When a system is a member of a Windows 2000 domain, the local system account includes the machine security identifier (SID) for the computer on which a service process is running. Therefore, a service running in the local system account will be automatically authenticated on other machines in the same forest by using its computer account. (A forest is a grouping of domains.)

■ Unless the machine account is specifically granted access to resources (such as network shares, named pipes, and so on), a process can access network resources that allow null sessions—that is, connections that require no credentials. You can specify the shares and pipes on a particular computer that permit null sessions in the NullSessionPipes and NullSessionShares registry values under HKLM\SYSTEM\Current-ControlSet\Services\lanmanserver\parameters.

Running Services in Alternate Accounts

Because of the restrictions just outlined, some services need to run with the security credentials of a user account. You can configure a service to run in an alternate account when the service is created or by specifying an account and password that the service should run under with the Windows 2000 Services MMC snap-in. In the Services snap-in, right-click on a service and select Properties, click the Log On tab, and select the This Account option, as shown in Figure 5-7.

Figure 5-7
Service account settings

Interactive Services

Another restriction for services running under the local system account is that they can't (without using a special flag on the *MessageBox* function, discussed in a moment) display dialog boxes or windows on the interactive user's desktop. This limitation isn't the direct result of running under the local system account but rather a consequence of the way the service controller assigns service processes to window stations.

The Win32 subsystem associates every Win32 process with a *window station*. A window station contains desktops and desktops contain windows. Only one window station can be visible on a console and receive user mouse and keyboard input. In a Terminal Services environment, one window station per session is visible, but services all run as part of the console session. Win32 names the visible window station WinSta0, and all interactive processes access WinSta0.

Unless otherwise directed, the SCM associates services with a nonvisible window station named Service-0x0-3e7$ that all noninteractive services share. The number in the name, *3e7*, represents the logon session identifier Lsass assigns to the logon session the SCM uses for noninteractive services running in the local system account.

Services configured to run under a user account (that is, not the local system account) are run in a different nonvisible window station named with the Lsass logon identifier assigned for the service's logon session. Figure 5-8 shows an example display from \Sysint\Winobj (which you'll find on this book's

Figure 5-8
List of window stations

companion CD) viewing the object manager directory in which Win32 places window station objects. Visible are the interactive window station (WinSta0), the noninteractive system service window station (Service-0x0-3e7$), and a noninteractive window station assigned to a service process logged on as a user (Service-0x0-6368f$).

Regardless of whether services are running in a user account or in the local system account, services that aren't running on the visible window station can't receive input from a user or display windows on the console. In fact, if a service were to pop up a normal dialog box on the window station, the service would appear hung because no user would be able to see the dialog box, which of course would prevent the user from providing keyboard or mouse input to dismiss it and allow the service to continue executing. (The one exception is if the special flag MB_SERVICE_NOTIFICATION or MB_DEFAULT_DESKTOP_ONLY is set on the *MessageBox* call—if MB_SERVICE_NOTIFICATION is specified, the message box will always be displayed on the interactive window station, even if the service wasn't configured with permission to interact with the user; if MB_DEFAULT_DESKTOP_ONLY is specified, the message box is displayed on the default desktop of the interactive window station.)

Although rare, some services can have a valid reason to interact with the user via dialog boxes or windows. An example of a built-in Windows 2000 service that has this requirement is the Windows Installer—the interactive user needs to see messages relating to on-demand software installation. To configure a service with the right to interact with the user, the SERVICE_INTERACTIVE_PROCESS modifier must be present in the service's registry key's Type parameter. (Note that services configured to run under a user account can't be marked as interactive.) When the SCM starts a service marked as interactive, it launches the service's process in the local system account's security context but connects the service with WinSta0 instead of the noninteractive service window station. This connection to WinSta0 allows the service to display dialog boxes and windows on the console and allows those windows to respond to user input.

The Service Control Manager

The SCM's executable file is \Winnt\System32\Services.exe, and like most service processes, it runs as a Win32 console program. The Winlogon process starts the SCM early during the system boot. (Refer to Chapter 4 for details on the boot process.) The SCM's startup function, *SvcCtrlMain*, orchestrates the launching of services that are configured for automatic startup. *SvcCtrlMain* executes shortly after the screen switches to a blank desktop but generally before Winlogon has loaded the graphical identification and authentication interface (GINA) that presents a logon dialog box.

SvcCtrlMain first creates a synchronization event named SvcCtrlEvent_ A3752DX that it initializes as nonsignaled. Only after the SCM completes steps necessary to prepare it to receive commands from SCPs does the SCM set the event to a signaled state. The function that an SCP uses to establish a dialog with the SCM is *OpenSCManager*. *OpenSCManager* prevents an SCP from trying to contact the SCM before the SCM has initialized by waiting for SvcCtrl-Event_A3752DX to become signaled.

Next, *SvcCtrlMain* gets down to business and calls *ScCreateServiceDB*, the function that builds the SCM's internal service database. *ScCreateServiceDB* reads and stores the contents of HKLM\SYSTEM\CurrentControlSet\Control\ServiceGroupOrder\List, a REG_MULTI_SZ value that lists the names and order of the defined service groups. A service's registry key contains an optional Group value if that service or device driver needs to control its startup ordering with respect to services from other groups. For example, the Windows 2000 networking stack is built from the bottom up, so networking services must specify Group values that place them later in the startup sequence than networking device drivers. SCM internally creates a group list that preserves the ordering of the groups it reads from the registry. Groups include (but are not limited to) NDIS, TDI, Primary Disk, Keyboard Port, and Keyboard Class. Add-on and third-party applications can even define their own groups and add them to the list. Microsoft Transaction Server, for example, adds a group named MS Transactions.

ScCreateServiceDB then scans the contents of HKLM\SYSTEM\Current-ControlSet\Services, creating an entry in the service database for each key it encounters. A database entry includes all the service-related parameters defined for a service as well as fields that track the service's status. The SCM adds entries for device drivers as well as for services because the SCM starts services and drivers marked as auto-start and detects startup failures for drivers marked boot-start and system-start. The I/O manager loads drivers marked boot-start and system-start before any user-mode processes execute, and therefore any drivers having these start types load before the SCM starts.

ScCreateServiceDB reads a service's Group value to determine its membership in a group and associates this value with the group's entry in the group list created earlier. The function also reads and records in the database the service's group and service dependencies by querying its DependOnGroup and DependOnService registry values. Figure 5-9 shows how the SCM organizes the service entry and group order lists. Notice that the service list is alphabetically sorted. The reason this list is sorted alphabetically is that the SCM creates the list from the Services registry key, and Windows 2000 stores registry keys alphabetically.

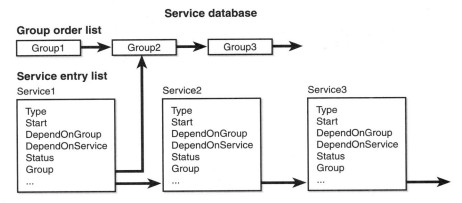

Figure 5-9
Organization of a service database

During service startup, the SCM might need to call on Lsass (for example, to log on a service in a user account), so the SCM waits for Lsass to signal the LSA_RPC_SERVER_ACTIVE synchronization event, which it does when it finishes initializing. Winlogon also starts the Lsass process, so the initialization of Lsass is concurrent with that of the SCM, and the order in which Lsass and the SCM complete initialization can vary. Then *SvcCtrlMain* calls *ScGetBootAnd-SystemDriverState* to scan the service database looking for boot-start and system-start device driver entries. *ScGetBootAndSystemDriverState* determines whether or not a driver successfully started by looking up its name in the object manager namespace directory named \Driver. When a device driver successfully loads, the I/O manager inserts the driver's object in the namespace under this directory, so if its name isn't present, it hasn't loaded. Figure 5-10 shows Winobj displaying the contents of the Driver directory. If a driver isn't loaded, the SCM looks for its name in the list of drivers returned by the *PnP_DeviceList* function. *PnP_DeviceList* supplies the drivers included in the system's current hardware profile. *SvcCtrlMain* notes the names of drivers that haven't started and that are part of the current profile in a list named ScFailedDrivers.

Before starting the auto-start services, the SCM performs a few more steps. It creates its remote procedure call (RPC) named pipe, which is named \Pipe\Ntsvcs, and then launches a thread to listen on the pipe for incoming messages from SCPs. It then signals its initialization-complete event, SvcCtrl-Event_A3752DX. Registering a console application shutdown event handler and registering with the Win32 subsystem process via *RegisterServiceProcess* prepares the SCM for system shutdown.

Figure 5-10
List of driver objects

Network Drive Letters

In addition to its role as an interface to services, the SCM has another totally unrelated responsibility: it notifies GUI applications in a system whenever the system creates or deletes a network drive-letter connection. The SCM waits for the LAN Manager workstation service to signal a named event, ScNetDrvMsg, which the workstation service signals whenever an application assigns a drive letter to a remote network share or deletes a remote-share drive-letter assignment. When the workstation service signals the event, the SCM calls the *GetDriveType* Win32 function to query the list of connected network drive letters. If the list changes across the event signal, the SCM sends a Windows broadcast message of type WM_DEVICECHANGE. The SCM uses either DBT_DEVICEREMOVECOMPELTE or DBT_DEVICEARRIVAL as the message's subtype. This message is primarily intended for Windows Explorer so that it can update any open My Computer windows to show the presence or absence of a network drive letter.

Service Startup

SvcCtrlMain invokes the SCM function *ScAutoStartServices* to start all services that have a Start value designating auto-start. *ScAutoStartServices* also starts auto-start device drivers. To avoid confusion, you should assume that the term *services* means *services and drivers* unless indicated otherwise. The algorithm in *ScAutoStartServices* for starting services in the correct order proceeds in phases, whereby a phase corresponds to a group and phases proceed in the sequence defined by the group ordering stored in the HKLM\SYSTEM\CurrentControl-Set\Control\ServiceGroupOrder\List registry value. The List value, shown in Figure 5-11, includes the names of groups in the order that the SCM should start them. Thus, assigning a service to a group has no effect other than to fine-tune its startup with respect to other services belonging to different groups.

Figure 5-11
ServiceGroupOrder registry key

When a phase starts, *ScAutoStartServices* marks all the service entries belonging to the phase's group for startup. Then *ScAutoStartServices* loops through the marked services seeing whether it can start each one. Part of the check it makes consists of determining whether the service has a dependency on another group, as specified by the existence of the DependOnGroup value in the service's registry key. If a dependency exists, the group on which the service is dependent must have already initialized, and at least one service of that group must have successfully started. If the service depends on a group that starts later than the service's group in the group startup sequence, the SCM notes a "circular dependency" error for the service. If *ScAutoStartServices* is considering a Win32

service and not a device driver, it next checks to see whether the service depends on one or more other services, and if so, if those services have already started. Service dependencies are indicated with the DependOnService registry value in a service's registry key. If a service depends on other services that belong to groups that come later in the ServiceGroupOrder\List, the SCM also generates a "circular dependency" error and doesn't start the service. If the service depends on any services from the same group that haven't yet started, the service is skipped.

When the dependencies of a service have been satisfied, *ScAutoStartServices* makes a final check to see whether the service is part of the current boot configuration before starting the service. When the system is booted in safe mode, the SCM ensures that the service is either identified by name or by group in the appropriate safe boot registry key. There are two safe boot keys, Minimal and Network, under HKLM\SYSTEM\CurrentControlSet\Control\SafeBoot, and the one that the SCM checks depends on what safe mode the user booted. If the user chose Safe Mode or Safe Mode With Command Prompt at the special boot menu (which you can access by pressing F8 when prompted in the boot process), the SCM references the Minimal key; if the user chose Safe Mode With Networking, the SCM refers to Network. The existence of a string value named Option under the SafeBoot key indicates not only that the system booted in safe mode but also the type of safe mode the user selected. For more information about safe boots, see the section "Safe Mode" on page 196 in Chapter 4.

Once the SCM decides to start a service, it calls *ScStartService*, which takes different steps for services than for device drivers. When *ScStartService* starts a Win32 service, it first determines the name of the file that runs the service's process by reading the ImagePath value from the service's registry key. It then examines the service's Type value, and if that value is SERVICE_WIN32_SHARE_PROCESS (0x20), the SCM ensures that the process the service runs in, if already started, is logged on using the same account as specified for the service being started. A service's ObjectName registry value stores the user account in which the service should run. A service with no ObjectName or an ObjectName of LocalSystem runs in the local system account.

The SCM verifies that the service's process hasn't already been started in a different account by checking to see whether the service's ImagePath value has an entry in an internal SCM database called the *image database*. If the image database doesn't have an entry for the ImagePath value, the SCM creates one. When the SCM creates a new entry, it stores the logon account name used for the service and the data from the service's ImagePath value. The SCM requires services to have an ImagePath value. If a service doesn't have an ImagePath value,

the SCM reports an error stating that it couldn't find the service's path and isn't able to start the service. If the SCM locates an existing image database entry with matching ImagePath data, the SCM ensures that the user account information for the service it's starting is the same as the information stored in the database entry—a process can be logged on as only one account, so the SCM reports an error when a service specifies a different account name than another service that has already started in the same process.

The SCM calls *ScLogonAndStartImage* to log on a service if the service's configuration specifies and to start the service's process. The SCM logs on services that don't run in the system account by calling the Lsass function *LsaLogonUser*. *LsaLogonUser* normally requires a password, but the SCM indicates to Lsass that the password is stored as a service's Lsass "secret" under the key HKLM\SECURITY\Policy\Secrets in the registry. (Keep in mind that the contents of the SECURITY aren't typically visible because its default security settings permit access only from the system account.) When the SCM calls *LsaLogonUser*, it specifies a service logon as the logon type, so Lsass looks up the password in the Secrets subkey that has a name in the form _SC_<service name>. The SCM directs Lsass to store a logon password as a secret when an SCP configures a service's logon information. When a logon is successful, *LsaLogonUser* returns a handle to an access token to the caller. Windows 2000 uses access tokens to represent a user's security context, and the SCM later associates the access token with the process that implements the service.

After a successful logon, the SCM loads the account's profile information, if it's not already loaded, by calling the UserEnv DLL's (\Winnt\System32\Userenv.dll) *LoadUserProfile* function. The value HKLM\SOFTWARE\Microsoft\Windows NT\CurrentVersion\ProfileList\<user profile key>\ProfileImagePath contains the location on disk of a registry hive that *LoadUserProfile* loads into the registry, making the information in the hive the HKEY_CURRENT_USER key for the service.

An interactive service must open the WinSta0 window station, but before *ScLogonAndStartImage* allows an interactive service to access WinSta0 it checks to see whether the value HKLM\SYSTEM\CurrentControlSet\Control\Windows\NoInteractiveServices is set. Administrators set this value to prevent services marked as interactive from displaying windows on the console. This option is desirable in unattended server environments in which no user is present to respond to popups from interactive services.

As its next step, *ScLogonAndStartImage* proceeds to launch the service's process, if the process hasn't already been started (for another service, for example). The SCM starts the process in a suspended state with the *CreateProcessAsUser*

Win32 function. The SCM next creates a named pipe through which it communicates with the service process, and it assigns the pipe the name \Pipe\Net\ NetControlPipeX, where *X* is a number that increments each time the SCM creates a pipe. The SCM resumes the service process via the *ResumeThread* function and waits for the service to connect to its SCM pipe. If it exists, the registry value HKLM\SYSTEM\CurrentControlSet\Control\ServicesPipeTimeout determines the length of time that the SCM waits for a service to call *StartServiceCtrl-Dispatcher* and connect before it gives up, terminates the process, and concludes that the service failed to start. If ServicesPipeTimeout doesn't exist, the SCM uses a default timeout of 30 seconds. The SCM uses the same timeout value for all its service communications.

When a service connects to the SCM through the pipe, the SCM sends the service a start command. If the service fails to respond positively to the start command within the timeout period, the SCM gives up and moves on to start the next service. When a service doesn't respond to a start request, the SCM doesn't terminate the process, as it does when a service doesn't call *StartServiceCtrlDispatcher* within the timeout; instead, it notes an error in the system Event Log that indicates the service failed to start in a timely manner.

If the service the SCM starts with a call to *ScStartService* has a Type registry value of SERVICE_KERNEL_DRIVER or SERVICE_FILE_SYSTEM_ DRIVER, the service is really a device driver, and so *ScStartService* calls *ScLoadDeviceDriver* to load the driver. *ScLoadDeviceDriver* enables the load driver security privilege for the SCM process and then invokes the kernel service *NtLoadDriver*, passing in the data in the ImagePath value of the driver's registry key. Unlike services, drivers don't need to specify an ImagePath value, and if the value is absent, the SCM builds an image path by appending the driver's name to the string \Winnt\System32\Drivers\.

ScAutoStartServices continues looping through the services belonging to a group until all the services have either started or generated dependency errors. This looping is the SCM's way of automatically ordering services within a group according to their DependOnService dependencies. The SCM will start the services that other services depend on in earlier loops, skipping the dependent services until subsequent loops. Note that the SCM ignores Tag values for Win32 services, which you might come across in subkeys under the HKLM\ SYSTEM\CurrentControlSet\Services key; the I/O manager honors Tag values to order device driver startup for boot and system-start drivers.

Once the SCM completes phases for all the groups listed in the Service-GroupOrder\List value, it performs a phase for services belonging to groups not listed in the value and a final phase for services without a group.

Startup Errors

If a driver or a service reports an error in response to the SCM's startup command, the ErrorControl value of the service's registry key determines how the SCM reacts. If the ErrorControl value is SERVICE_ERROR_IGNORE (0) or the ErrorControl value isn't specified, the SCM simply ignores the error and continues processing service startups. If the ErrorControl value is SERVICE_ERROR_ NORMAL (1), the SCM writes an event to the system Event Log that says, "The <service name> service failed to start due to the following error:" The SCM includes the textual representation of the Win32 error code that the service returned to the SCM as the reason for the startup failure in the Event Log record. Figure 5-12 shows the Event Log entry that reports a service startup error.

Figure 5-12
Service startup failure Event Log entry

If a service with an ErrorControl value of SERVICE_ERROR_SEVERE (2) or SERVICE_ERROR_CRITICAL (3) reports a startup error, the SCM logs a record to the Event Log and then calls the internal function *ScRevert-ToLastKnownGood*. This function switches the system's registry configuration to a version, named last known good, with which the system last booted successfully. Then it restarts the system using the *NtShutdownSystem* system service,

which is implemented in the executive. If the system is already booting with the last known good configuration, the system just reboots.

Accepting the Boot and Last Known Good

Besides starting services, the system charges the SCM with determining when the system's registry configuration, HKLM\SYSTEM\CurrentControlSet, should be saved as the last known good control set. The CurrentControlSet key contains the Services key as a subkey, so CurrentControlSet includes the registry representation of the SCM database. It also contains the Control key, which stores many kernel-mode and user-mode subsystem configuration settings. By default, a successful boot consists of a successful startup of auto-start services and a successful user logon. A boot fails if the system halts because a device driver crashes the system during the boot or if an auto-start service with an ErrorControl value of SERVICE_ERROR_SEVERE or SERVICE_ERROR_CRITICAL reports a startup error.

The SCM obviously knows when it has completed a successful startup of the auto-start services, but Winlogon (\Winnt\System32\Winlogon.exe) must notify it when there is a successful logon. Winlogon invokes the *NotifyBootConfigStatus* function when a user logs on, and *NotifyBootConfigStatus* sends a message to the SCM. Following the successful start of the auto-start services or the receipt of the message from *NotifyBootConfigStatus* (whichever comes last), the SCM calls the system function *NtInitializeRegistry* to save the current registry startup configuration.

Third-party software developers can supersede Winlogon's definition of a successful logon with their own definition. For example, a system running Microsoft SQL Server might not consider a boot successful until after SQL Server is able to accept and process transactions. Developers impose their definition of a successful boot by writing a boot-verification program and installing the program by pointing to its location on disk with the value stored in the registry key HKLM\SYSTEM\CurrentControlSet\Control\BootVerificationProgram. In addition, a boot-verification program's installation must disable Winlogon's call to *NotifyBootConfigStatus* by setting HKLM\SOFTWARE\Microsoft\ Windows NT\CurrentVersion\Winlogon\ReportBootOk to 0. When a boot-verification program is installed, the SCM launches it after finishing auto-start services and waits for the program's call to *NotifyBootConfigStatus* before saving the last known good control set.

Windows 2000 maintains several copies of CurrentControlSet, and Current-ControlSet is really a symbolic registry link that points to one of the copies. The control sets have names in the form HKLM\SYSTEM\ControlSet*nnn*, where

nnn is a number such as 001 or 002. The HKLM\SYSTEM\Select key contains values that identify the role of each control set. For example, if CurrentControlSet points to ControlSet001, the Current value under Select has a value of 1. The LastKnownGood value under Select contains the number of the last known good control set, which is the control set last used to boot successfully. Another value that might be on your system under the Select key is Failed, which points to the last control set for which the boot was deemed unsuccessful and aborted in favor of an attempt at booting with the last known good control set. Figure 5-13 displays a system's control sets and Select values.

Figure 5-13
Control set selection key

NtInitializeRegistry takes the contents of the last known good control set and synchronizes it with that of the CurrentControlSet key's tree. If this was the system's first successful boot, the last known good won't exist and the system will create a new control set for it. If the last known good tree exists, the system simply updates it with differences between it and CurrentControlSet.

Last known good is helpful in situations in which a change to Current-ControlSet, such as the modification of a system performance-tuning value under HKLM\SYSTEM\Control or the addition of a service or device driver, causes the subsequent boot to fail. Users can press F8 early in the boot process to bring up a menu that lets them direct the boot to use the last known good control set, rolling the system's registry configuration back to the way it was the last time the system booted successfully.

Service Failures

A service can have optional FailureActions and FailureCommand values in its registry key that the SCM records during the service's startup. The SCM registers with the system so that the system signals the SCM when a service process exits. When a service process terminates unexpectedly, the SCM determines which services ran in the process and takes the recovery steps specified by their failure-related registry values.

Actions that a service can configure for the SCM include restarting the service, running a program, and rebooting the computer. Furthermore, a service can specify the failure actions that take place the first time the service process fails, the second time, and subsequent times, and can indicate a delay period that the SCM waits before restarting the service if the service asks to be restarted. The service failure action of the IIS Admin Service results in the SCM running the IISReset application, which performs cleanup work and then restarts the service. You can easily manage the recovery actions for a service with the Recovery tab of the service's Properties dialog box in the Services MMC snap-in, as shown in Figure 5-14.

Figure 5-14
Service recovery options

Service Shutdown

When Winlogon calls the Win32 *ExitWindowsEx* function, *ExitWindowsEx* sends a message to Csrss, the Win32 subsystem process, to invoke Csrss's shutdown routine. Csrss loops through the active processes and notifies them that the system is shutting down. For every system process except the SCM, Csrss waits up to the number of seconds specified by HKU\\.DEFAULT\Control Panel\ Desktop\WaitToKillAppTimeout (which defaults to 20 seconds) for the process to exit before moving on to the next process. When Csrss encounters the SCM process, it also notifies it that the system is shutting down but employs a timeout specific to the SCM. Csrss recognizes the SCM using the process ID Csrss saved when the SCM registered with Csrss using the *RegisterServicesProcess* function during system initialization. The SCM's timeout differs from that of other processes because Csrss knows that the SCM communicates with services that need to perform cleanup when they shutdown, and so an administrator might need to tune only the SCM's timeout. The SCM's timeout value resides in the HKLM\ SYSTEM\CurrentControlSet\Control\WaitToKillServiceTimeout registry value, and it defaults to 20 seconds.

The SCM's shutdown handler is responsible for sending shutdown notifications to all the services that requested shutdown notification when they initialized with the SCM. The SCM function *ScShutdownAllServices* loops through the SCM services database searching for services desiring shutdown notification and sends each one a shutdown command. For each service to which it sends a shutdown command, the SCM records the value of the service's *wait hint,* a value that a service also specifies when it registers with the SCM. The SCM keeps track of the largest wait hint it receives. After sending the shutdown messages, the SCM waits either until one of the services it notified of shutdown exits or until the time specified by the largest wait hint passes.

If the wait hint expires without a service exiting, the SCM determines whether one or more of the services it was waiting on to exit have sent a message to the SCM telling the SCM that the service is progressing in its shutdown process. If at least one service made progress, the SCM waits again for the duration of the wait hint. The SCM continues executing this wait loop until either all the services have exited or none of the services upon which it's waiting has notified it of progress within the wait hint timeout period.

While the SCM is busy telling services to shut down and waiting for them to exit, Csrss waits for the SCM to exit. If Csrss's wait ends without the SCM having exited (the WaitToKillServiceTimeout time expires), Csrss simply moves

on, continuing the shutdown process. Thus, services that fail to shut down in a timely manner are simply left running, along with the SCM, as the system shuts down. Unfortunately, there's no way for administrators to know whether they should raise the WaitToKillServiceTimeout value on systems where services aren't getting a chance to shut down completely before the system shuts down.

Shared Service Processes

Running every service in its own process instead of having services share a process whenever possible wastes system resources. However, sharing processes means that if any of the services in the process has a bug that causes the process to exit, all the services in that process terminate.

Of the Windows 2000 built-in services, some run in their own process and some share a process with other services. For example, the SCM process hosts the Event Log service, the file server service (LanmanServer), and the LAN Manager name resolution service. The services that SCM hosts in Windows 2000 are listed in Table 5-7. (Not all these services are active on every system.)

Table 5-7 Windows 2000 Services That Run in the SCM

Service	Service Description
Alerter	Notifies selected users and computers of administrative alerts.
AppMgmt	Provides software installation services such as Assign, Publish, and Remove.
Browser	Maintains an up-to-date list of computers on your network and supplies the list to programs that request it.
Dhcp	Manages network configuration by registering and updating IP addresses and Domain Name System (DNS) names.
Dmserver	Logical Disk Manager Watchdog Service
Dnscache	Resolves and caches DNS names.
Eventlog	Logs event messages that applications and Windows issue. Event Log reports contain information that can be useful in diagnosing problems. Reports are viewed in Event Viewer.

Service	Service Description
LanmanServer	Provides remote procedure call (RPC) support and file, print, and named pipe sharing.
LanmanWorkstation	Provides network connections and communications.
LmHosts	Enables support for NetBIOS over TCP/IP (NetBT) service and for NetBIOS name resolution.
Messenger	Sends and receives messages that administrators or the Alerter service transmit.
PlugPlay	Manages device installation and configuration and notifies programs of device changes.
ProtectedStorage	Provides protected storage for sensitive data, such as private keys, to prevent access by unauthorized services, processes, or users.
Seclogon	Enables starting processes under alternate credentials.
TrkSvr	Stores information so that files moved between volumes can be tracked for each volume in the domain.
TrkWks	Sends notifications of files moving between NTFS volumes in a network domain.
W32Time	Sets the computer clock.
Wmi	Provides systems management information to and from drivers.

The security-related services, such as the Security Accounts Manager (SamSs) service, the Net Logon (Netlogon) service, and the IPSec Policy Agent (Policy-Agent) service, share the Lsass process.

There is also a "generic" process named Service Host (SvcHost - \Winnt\ System32\Svchost.exe) to contain multiple services. Multiple instances of SvcHost can be running in different processes. Services that run in SvcHost processes include Telephony (TapiSrv), Remote Procedure Call (RpcSs), and Remote Access Connection Manager (RasMan). Windows 2000 implements services that run in SvcHost as DLLs and includes an ImagePath definition of the form "%SystemRoot%\System32\svchost.exe -k netsvcs" in the service's registry key. The service's registry key must also have a registry value named ServiceDll under a Parameters subkey that points to the service's DLL file.

All services that share a common SvcHost process specify the same parameter ("-k netsvcs" in the example in the preceding paragraph) so that they have a single entry in the SCM's image database. When the SCM encounters the first service that has a SvcHost ImagePath with a particular parameter during service startup, it creates a new image database entry and launches a SvcHost process with the parameter. The new SvcHost process takes the parameter and looks for a value having the same name as the parameter under HKLM\ SOFTWARE\Microsoft\Windows NT\CurrentVersion\Svchost. SvcHost reads the contents of the value, interpreting it as a list of service names, and notifies the SCM that it's hosting those services when SvcHost registers with the SCM. Figure 5-15 presents an example Svchost registry key that shows that a SvcHost process started with the "-k netsvcs" parameter is prepared to host a number of different network-related services.

Figure 5-15
Svchost registry key

When the SCM encounters a SvcHost service during service startup with an ImagePath matching an entry it already has in the image database, it doesn't launch a second process but instead just sends a start command for the service to the SvcHost it already started for that ImagePath value. The existing SvcHost process reads the ServiceDll parameter in the service's registry key and loads the DLL into its process to start the service.

EXPERIMENT: Viewing Services Running Inside Processes

The Tlist utility, in the Windows 2000 Support Tools, accepts the */s* command-line option. With this option specified, Tlist displays a list of the services, if any, that are executing within processes, as shown in the following example output. A process that has "Svcs:" instead of "Title:" following its name is a service process, and the names listed are those of services hosted by that process.

```
C:\>tlist /s
    0 System Process
    8 System
  144 smss.exe
  172 csrss.exe      Title:
  192 winlogon.exe   Title: NetDDE Agent
  220 services.exe   Svcs:  Browser,Dhcp,dmserver,Dnscache,
                            Eventlog,lanmanserver,lanmanworkstation,
                            LmHosts,Messenger,PlugPlay,ProtectedStorage,
                            seclogon,TrkWks,Wmi
  232 lsass.exe      Svcs:  PolicyAgent,SamSs
  392 svchost.exe    Svcs:  RpcSs
  428 spoolsv.exe    Svcs:  Spooler
  456 ati2plab.exe   Svcs:  Ati HotKey Poller
  472 svchost.exe    Svcs:  EventSystem,Netman,NtmsSvc,RasMan,SENS,TapiSrv
  508 regsvc.exe     Svcs:  RemoteRegistry
  544 WinMgmt.exe    Svcs:  WinMgmt
  836 Explorer.Exe   Title: Program Manager
  712 RealPlay.exe   Title:
  748 Atiptaxx.exe   Title: ATI Tray Icon Application
  724 DESKTOPS.EXE   Title: MultiDesk
  824 Explorer.Exe   Title: Program Manager
  900 Explorer.Exe   Title: Program Manager
  564 cmd.exe        Title: Command Prompt - tlist /s
  752 ntvdm.exe
  668 calc.exe       Title: Calculator
  848 calc.exe       Title: Calculator
  308 calc.exe       Title: Calculator
  660 tlist.exe
```

Service Control Programs

Service control programs are standard Win32 applications that use the SCM functions *CreateService*, *OpenService*, *StartService*, *ControlService*, *QueryServiceStatus*, and *DeleteService*. To use the SCM functions, an SCP must first open a communications channel to the SCM by calling the *OpenSCManager* function. At the time of the open call, the SCP must specify what types of actions it wants to perform. For example, if an SCP simply wants to enumerate and display the services present in the SCM's database, it requests enumerate-service access in its call to *OpenSCManager*. During its initialization, the SCM creates an internal object that represents the SCM database and uses the Windows 2000 security functions to protect the object with a security descriptor that specifies what accounts can open the object with what access permissions. For example, the security descriptor indicates that the Everyone group (of which every account is a member) can open the SCM object with enumerate-service access. However, only administrators can open the object with the access required to create or delete a service.

As it does for the SCM database, the SCM implements security for services themselves. When an SCP creates a service by using the *CreateService* function, it specifies a security descriptor that the SCM associates internally with the service's entry in the service database. The SCM stores the security descriptor in the service's registry key as the Security value, and it reads that value when it scans the registry's Services key during initialization so that the security settings persist across reboots. In the same way that an SCP must specify what types of access it wants to the SCM database in its call to *OpenSCManager*, an SCP must tell the SCM what access it wants to a service in a call to *OpenService*. Accesses that an SCP can request include the ability to query a service's status and to configure, stop, and start a service.

The SCP you're probably most familiar with is the Services MMC snap-in that's included in Windows 2000, which resides in \Winnt\System32\ Filemgr.dll. The Windows 2000 resource kits include a command-line SCP named Sc.exe (Service Controller tool) and a GUI SCP named Srvinstw.exe (Service Creation Wizard).

SCPs sometimes layer service policy on top of what the SCM implements. A good example is the timeout that the Services MMC snap-in implements when a service is started manually. The snap-in presents a progress bar that represents the progress of a service's startup. Whereas the SCM waits indefinitely for a service to respond to a start command, the Services snap-in waits only 2 minutes before the progress bar reaches 100 percent and the snap-in announces that the service didn't start in a timely manner. Services indirectly interact with SCPs by setting their configuration status to reflect their progress as they respond to

SCM commands such as the start command. SCPs query the status with the *QueryServiceStatus* function. They can tell when a service actively updates the status versus when a service appears to be hung, and the SCM can take appropriate actions in notifying a user about what the service is doing.

Windows Management Instrumentation

Windows NT has always had integrated performance and system-event monitoring tools. Applications and the system typically use the Event Manager to report errors and diagnostic messages. The Event Viewer utility lets administrators view event output from either the local computer or another computer on the network. Similarly, the performance counter mechanism lets applications and operating system components report performance-related statistics to performance-monitoring applications such as the Performance Monitor.

Although the Windows NT 4 event-monitoring and performance-monitoring features met their design goals, they had limitations. For example, the programming interfaces differ from one another, and this variation increases the complexity of applications that use both event and performance monitoring to collect data. The level of granularity the performance counter mechanism provides can be poor, especially across a network, because it retrieves all the performance counters defined on the system and not just the object you're interested in. It's an all-or-nothing proposition: no way exists for an application to query the performance information of only specific components. Perhaps the biggest drawback to the monitoring facilities in Windows NT 4 is that they have little or no extensibility and that neither event logging nor performance data collection provides the two-way interaction necessary in a management API. Applications must provide data in predefined formats. The Performance API provides no way for an application to receive notification of performance-related events, and applications that request notification of Event Manager events can't restrict notification to specific event types or sources. Finally, clients of either collection facility can't communicate with event-data or performance-data providers through the Event Manager or Performance API.

To address these limitations as well as to provide management capabilities for other types of data sources, Windows 2000 has a new management mechanism, Windows Management Instrumentation (WMI). WMI is an implementation of Web-Based Enterprise Management (WBEM), a standard that the Distributed Management Task Force (DMTF—an industry consortium) defines. The WBEM standard encompasses the design of an extensible enterprise data-collection and data-management facility that has the flexibility and extensibility required to manage local and remote systems that comprise arbitrary components.

WMI support was added to Windows NT 4 in Service Pack 4. It is also supported in Windows 95 OSR2 and Windows 98. Although most of this section applies to all the Windows platforms that support WMI, implementation details are specific to Windows 2000.

WMI Architecture

WMI consists of four main components, as shown in Figure 5-16: management applications, WMI infrastructure, providers, and managed objects. Management applications are Windows applications that access and display or process data that the applications obtain about managed objects. A simple example of a management application is a Performance tool replacement that relies on WMI rather than the Performance API to obtain performance information. A more complex example is an enterprise-management tool that lets administrators perform automated inventories of the software and hardware configuration of every computer in their enterprise.

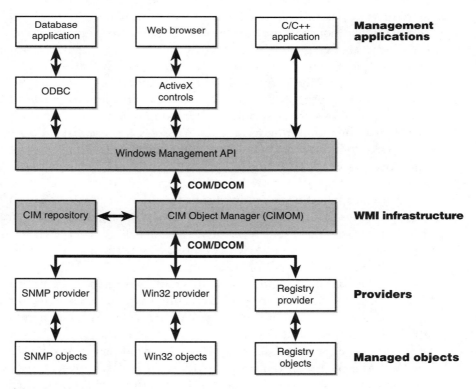

Figure 5-16
WMI architecture

Developers typically must target management applications to collect data from and manage specific objects. An object might represent one component, such as a network adapter device, or a collection of components, such as a computer. (The computer object might contain the network adapter object.) Providers need to define and export the representation of the objects that management applications are interested in. For example, the vendor of a network adapter might want to add adapter-specific properties to the network adapter WMI support that Windows 2000 includes, querying and setting the adapter's state and behavior as the management applications direct. In some cases (for example, for device drivers), Microsoft supplies a provider that has its own API to help developers leverage the provider's implementation for their own managed objects with minimal coding effort.

The WMI infrastructure, the heart of which is the Common Information Model (CIM) Object Manager (CIMOM), is the glue that binds management applications and providers. (CIM is described later in this chapter.) The infrastructure also serves as the object-class store and, in many cases, as the storage manager for persistent object properties. WMI implements the store, or repository, as an on-disk database named the CIMOM Object Repository. As part of its infrastructure, WMI supports several APIs through which management applications access object data and providers supply data and class definitions.

Win32 programs use the WMI COM API, the primary management API, to directly interact with WMI. Other APIs layer on top of the COM API and include an Open Database Connectivity (ODBC) adapter for the Microsoft Access database application. A database developer uses the WMI ODBC adapter to embed references to object data in the developer's database. Then the developer can easily generate reports with database queries that contain WMI-based data. WMI ActiveX controls support another layered API. Web developers use the ActiveX controls to construct Web-based interfaces to WMI data. Another management API is the WMI scripting API, for use in script-based applications and Microsoft Visual Basic programs. WMI scripting support exists for all Microsoft programming language technologies.

As they are for management applications, WMI COM interfaces constitute the primary API for providers. However, unlike management applications, which are COM clients, providers are COM or Distributed COM (DCOM) servers (that is, the providers implement COM objects that WMI interacts with). Possible embodiments of a WMI provider include DLLs that load into WMI's manager process and stand-alone Win32 applications or Win32 services. Microsoft includes a number of built-in providers that present data from well-known sources, such as the Performance API, the registry, the Event Manager, Active Directory, SNMP, and Windows Driver Model (WDM) device drivers. The WMI SDK lets developers develop third-party WMI providers.

Providers

At the core of WBEM is the DMTF-designed CIM specification. The CIM specifies how management systems represent, from a systems management perspective, anything from a computer to an application or device on a computer. Provider developers use the CIM to represent the components that make up the parts of an application for which the developers want to enable management. Developers use the Managed Object Format (MOF) language to implement a CIM representation.

In addition to defining classes that represent objects, a provider must interface WMI to the objects. WMI classifies providers according to the interface features the providers supply. Table 5-8 lists WMI provider classifications. Note that a provider can implement one or more features; therefore, a provider can be, for example, both a class and an event provider. To clarify the feature definitions in Table 5-8, let's look at a provider that implements several of those features. The Event Log provider defines several objects, including an Event Log Computer, an Event Log Record, and an Event Log File. The Event Log provider is a Class provider because it defines these objects by using classes and must give the class definitions to WMI. This provider is an Instance provider as well because it can define multiple instances for several of its classes. One class for which the Event Log provider defines multiple instances is the Event Log File class; the Event Log provider defines an instance of this class for each of the system's event logs (that is, System Event Log, Application Event Log, and Security Event Log).

Table 5-8 Provider Classifications

Classification	Description
Class	Can supply, modify, delete, and enumerate a provider-specific class. Can also support query processing. Active Directory is a rare example of a service that is class provider.
Instance	Can supply, modify, delete, and enumerate instances of system and provider-specific classes. An instance represents a managed object. Can also support query processing.
Property	Can supply and modify individual object property values.
Method	Supplies methods for a provider-specific class.
Event	Generates event notifications.
Event consumer	Maps a physical consumer to a logical consumer to support event notification.

The Event Log provider defines the instance data and lets management applications enumerate the records. To let management applications use WMI to back up and restore the Event Log files, the Event Log provider implements backup and restore methods for Event Log File objects. Doing so makes the Event Log provider a Method provider. Finally, a management application can register to receive notification whenever a new record writes to one of the Event Logs. Thus, the Event Log provider serves as an Event provider when it uses WMI event notification to tell WMI that Event Log records have arrived.

The Common Information Model and the Managed Object Format Language

The CIM follows in the steps of object-oriented languages such as C++ and Java, in which a modeler designs representations as classes. Working with classes lets developers use the powerful modeling techniques of inheritance and composition. Subclasses can inherit the attributes of a parent class, and they can add their own characteristics and override the characteristics they inherit from the parent class. A class that inherits properties from another class *derives* from that class. Classes also *compose*: a developer can build a class that includes other classes.

The DMTF provides multiple classes as part of the WBEM standard. These classes are CIM's basic language and represent objects that apply to all areas of management. The classes are part of the CIM *core model*. An example of a core class is CIM_ManagedSystemElement. This class contains a few basic properties that identify physical components such as hardware devices, and logical components such as processes and files. The properties include a caption, description, installation date, and status. Thus, the CIM_LogicalElement and CIM_PhysicalElement classes inherit the attributes of the CIM_Managed-SystemElement class. These two classes are also part of the CIM core model. The WBEM standard calls these classes *abstract* classes because they exist solely as classes that other classes inherit (that is, no object instances of an abstract class exist). You can therefore think of abstract classes as templates that define properties for use in other classes.

A second category of classes represents objects that are specific to management areas but independent of a particular implementation. These classes constitute the *common model* and are considered an extension of the core model. An example of a common-model class is the CIM_FileSystem class, which inherits the attributes of CIM_LogicalElement. Because virtually every operating system, including Windows 2000, Linux, and other varieties of UNIX, rely on file-system-based structured storage, the CIM_FileSystem class is an appropriate constituent of the common model.

The final class category comprises technology-specific additions to the common model. Windows 2000 defines a large set of these classes to represent objects specific to the Win32 environment. Because all operating systems store data in files, the CIM common model includes the CIM_LogicalFile class. The CIM_DataFile class inherits the CIM_LogicalFile class, and Win32 adds the Win32_PageFile and Win32_ShortcutFile file classes for those Win32 file types.

The Event Log provider makes extensive use of inheritance. Figure 5-17 shows a view of the WMI CIM Studio, a class browser that ships with the WMI SDK. (Microsoft supplies the WMI SDK with MSDN software and the Platform SDK.) You can see where the Event Log provider relies on inheritance in the provider's Win32_NTEventlogFile class, which derives from CIM_DataFile. Event Log files are data files that have additional Event Log–specific attributes such as a log file name (LogfileName) and a count of the number of records that the file contains (NumberOfRecords). The tree that the class browser shows reveals that Win32_NTEventlogFile is based on several levels of inheritance, in which CIM_DataFile derives from CIM_LogicalFile, which derives from CIM_LogicalElement, and CIM_LogicalElement derives from CIM_Managed-SystemElement.

Figure 5-17
WMI CIM Studio

As stated earlier, WMI provider developers write their classes in the MOF language. The following output shows the definition of the Event Log provider's Win32_NTEventlogFile, which is selected in Figure 5-17. Notice the correlation between the properties that the right panel in Figure 5-17 lists and those properties' definitions in the MOF file below. CIM Studio uses yellow arrows to tag those properties that a class inherits. Thus, you don't see those properties specified in Win32_NTEventlogFile's definition.

```
[dynamic,provider("MS_NT_EVENTLOG_PROVIDER"),Locale(1033),
UUID("{8502C57B-5FBB-11D2-AAC1-006008C78BC7}")]
class Win32_NTEventlogFile : CIM_DataFile
{
  [read] string LogfileName;
  [read,write] uint32 MaxFileSize;
  [read] uint32 NumberOfRecords;
  [read,volatile,ValueMap{"0", "1..365", "4294967295"}]
    string OverWritePolicy;
  [read,write,Units("Days"),Range("0-365 | 4294967295")]
    uint32 OverwriteOutDated;
  [read] string Sources[];
  [implemented,Privileges{"SeSecurityPrivilege", "SeBackupPrivilege"}]
    uint32 ClearEventlog([in] string ArchiveFileName);
  [implemented,Privileges{"SeSecurityPrivilege", "SeBackupPrivilege"}]
    uint32 BackupEventlog([in] string ArchiveFileName);
};
```

One term worth reviewing is *dynamic,* which is a descriptive designator for the Win32_NTEventlogFile class that the MOF file in the preceding output shows. *Dynamic* means that the WMI infrastructure asks the WMI provider for the values of properties associated with an object of that class whenever a management application queries the object's properties. A *static* class is one in the WMI repository; the WMI infrastructure refers to the repository to obtain the values instead of asking a provider for the values. Because updating the repository is a relatively expensive operation, dynamic providers are more efficient for objects that have properties that change frequently.

After constructing classes in MOF, WMI developers can supply the class definitions to WMI in several ways. WDM provider developers compile an MOF file into a binary MOF (BMF) file—a more compact binary representation than an MOF file—and give the BMF files to the WDM infrastructure. Another way

is for the provider to compile the MOF and use WMI COM APIs to give the definitions to the WMI infrastructure. Finally, a provider can use the MOF Compiler (Mofcomp.exe) tool to give the WMI infrastructure a classes-compiled representation directly.

The WMI Namespace

Classes define the properties of objects, and objects are class instances on a system. WMI uses a namespace that contains several subnamespaces that WMI arranges hierarchically to organize objects. A management application must connect to a namespace before the application can access objects within the namespace.

WMI names the namespace root directory *root*. All WMI installations have four predefined namespaces that reside beneath root: CIMV2, Default, Security, and WMI. Some of these namespaces have other namespaces within them. For example, CIMV2 includes the Applications and ms_409 namespaces as subnamespaces. Providers sometimes define their own namespaces; you can see the WMI namespace (which the Windows device driver WMI provider defines) beneath root on Windows 2000.

Unlike a file system namespace, which comprises a hierarchy of directories and files, a WMI namespace is only one level deep. Instead of using names as a file system does, WMI uses object properties that it defines as *keys* to identify the objects. Management applications specify class names with key names to locate specific objects within a namespace. Thus, each instance of a class must be uniquely identifiable by its key values. For example, the Event Log provider uses the Win32_NTLogEvent class to represent records in an Event Log. This class has two keys: Logfile, a string; and RecordNumber, an unsigned integer. A management application that queries WMI for instances of Event Log records obtains them from the provider key pairs that identify records. The application refers to a record using the syntax that you see in this example object pathname:

```
\\PICKLES\CIMV2:Win32_NTLogEvent.Logfile="Application",
                                  RecordNumber="1"
```

The first component in the name (\\PICKLES) identifies the computer on which the object is located, and the second component (\CIMV2) is the namespace in which the object resides. The class name follows the colon, and key names and their associated values follow the period. A comma separates the key values.

WMI provides interfaces that let applications enumerate all the objects in a particular class or to make queries that return instances of a class that match a query criteria.

Class Association

Many object types are related to one another in some way. For example, a computer object has a processor, software, an operating system, active processes, and so on. WMI lets providers construct an *association class* to represent a logical connection between two different classes. Association classes associate one class with another, so the classes have only two properties: a class name and the *Ref* modifier. The following output shows an association in which the Event Log provider's MOF file associates the Win32_NTLogEvent class with the Win32_ComputerSystem class. Given an object, a management application can query associated objects. In this way, a provider defines a hierarchy of objects.

```
[dynamic,provider("MS_NT_EVENTLOG_PROVIDER"),
 EnumPrivileges{"SeSecurityPrivilege"},Locale(1033),
 UUID("{8502C57F-5FBB-11D2-AAC1-006008C78BC7}"),
 Association : ToInstance]
class Win32_NTLogEventComputer
{
  [key,read] Win32_ComputerSystem Ref Computer;
  [key,read] Win32_NTLogEvent Ref Record;
};

Instance of __Win32Provider as $EventProv
{
  Name = "MS_NT_EVENTLOG_EVENT_PROVIDER";
  ClsId = "{F55C5B4C-517D-11d1-AB57-00C04FD9159E}";
};
```

Figure 5-18 shows the WMI Object Browser (another development tool that the WMI SDK includes) displaying the root of the CIMV2 namespace. Win32 system components typically place their objects within the CIMV2 namespace. The Object Browser first locates the Win32_ComputerSystem object instance DSOLOMON, which is the object that represents the computer. Then, the Object Browser obtains the objects associated with Win32_ComputerSystem

Figure 5-18
WMI Object Browser

and displays them beneath DSOLOMON. The Object Browser user interface displays association objects with a double-arrow folder icon. The associated class type's objects display beneath the folder.

You can see in the Object Browser that the Event Log provider's association class Win32_NTLogEventComputer is beneath DSOLOMON and that numerous instances of the Win32_NTLogEvent class exist. Refer to the preceding output to verify that the MOF file defines the Win32_NTLogEvent-Computer class to associate the Win32_ComputerSystem class with the Win32_NTLogEvent class. Selecting an instance of Win32_NTLogEvent in the Object Browser reveals that class's properties under the Properties tab in the right-hand pane. Microsoft intended the Object Browser to help WMI developers examine their objects, but a management application would perform the same operations and display properties or collected information more intelligibly.

WMI Implementation

The WMI infrastructure implements primarily in the \Winnt\System32\Wbem\ Winmgmt.exe file. This file runs as a Win32 service that the Windows 2000 SCM starts the first time a management application or WMI provider tries to access WMI APIs. Most WMI components reside by default in \Winnt\System32 and \Winnt\System32\Wbem, including Win32 MOF files, built-in provider DLLs, and management application WMI DLLs. Look in the \Winnt\System32\Wbem directory, and you'll find Ntevt.mof, the Event Log provider MOF file. You'll also find Ntevt.dll, the Event Log provider's DLL, which Winmgmt.exe loads.

Directories beneath \Winnt\System32\Wbem store the repository, log files, and third-party MOF files. WMI implements the repository—named the CIMOM repository—as the file \Winnt\System32\Wbem\Repository\Cim.rep. Winmgmt honors numerous registry settings related to the repository (including various internal performance parameters such as CIMOM backup locations and intervals) that the repository's HKLM\SOFTWARE\Microsoft\WBEM\CIMOM registry key stores.

Device drivers use special interfaces to provide data to and accept commands—called the WMI System Control commands—from WMI. These interfaces are part of the WDM, which is explained in Chapter 9. Because the interfaces are cross-platform, they fall under the \root\WMI namespace.

WMI Security

WMI implements security at the namespace level. If a management application successfully connects to a namespace, the application can view and access the properties of all the objects in that namespace. An administrator can use the WMI Control application to control which users can access a namespace. To start the WMI Control application, from the Start menu, select Programs, Administrative Tools, Computer Management. Next, open the Services And Applications branch. Right-click WMI Control and select Properties to launch the WMI Control Properties dialog box, which Figure 5-19 shows. To configure security for namespaces, click the Security tab, select the namespace, and click Security. The other tabs in the WMI Control Properties dialog box let you modify the performance and backup settings that the registry stores.

Figure 5-19
WMI security properties

Conclusion

So far, we've examined the overall structure of Windows 2000 and the core system mechanisms that get the system going, keep it running, and eventually shut it down. With this foundation laid, we're ready to explore the individual executive components in more detail, starting with processes and threads.

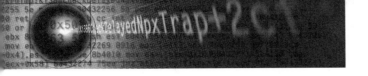

CHAPTER SIX

Processes, Threads, and Jobs

In this chapter, we'll explain the data structures and algorithms that deal with processes, threads, and jobs in Microsoft Windows 2000. The first section focuses on the internal structures that make up a process. The second section outlines the steps involved in creating a process (and its initial thread). The internals of threads and thread scheduling are then described. The chapter concludes with a description of the job object.

Where relevant performance counters or kernel variables exist, they are mentioned. Although this book isn't a Win32 programming book, the pertinent process, thread, and job Win32 functions are listed so that you can pursue additional information on their use.

Because processes and threads touch so many components in Windows 2000, a number of terms and data structures (such as working sets, objects and handles, system memory heaps, and so on) are referred to in this chapter but are explained in detail elsewhere in the book. To fully understand this chapter, you need to be familiar with the terms and concepts explained in chapters 1 and 2, such as the difference between a process and a thread, the Windows 2000 virtual address space layout, and the difference between user mode and kernel mode.

Process Internals

This section describes the key Windows 2000 process data structures. Also listed are key kernel variables, performance counters, and functions and tools that relate to processes.

Data Structures

Each Windows 2000 process is represented by an executive process (EPROCESS) block. Besides containing many attributes relating to a process, an EPROCESS block contains and points to a number of other related data structures. For example, each process has one or more threads represented by executive thread

(ETHREAD) blocks. (Thread data structures are explained in the section "Thread Internals" later in this chapter.) The EPROCESS block and its related data structures exist in system space, with the exception of the process environment block (PEB), which exists in the process address space (because it contains information that is modified by user-mode code).

In addition to the EPROCESS block, the Win32 subsystem process (Csrss) maintains a parallel structure for each Windows 2000 process that executes a Win32 program. Also, the kernel-mode part of the Win32 subsystem (Win32k.sys) has a per-process data structure that is created the first time a thread calls a Win32 USER or GDI function that is implemented in kernel mode.

Figure 6-1 is a simplified diagram of the process and thread data structures. Each data structure shown in the figure is described in detail in this chapter.

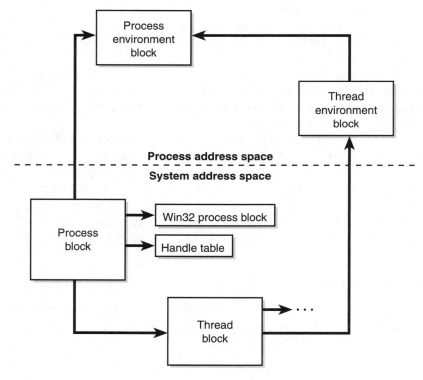

Figure 6-1
Data structures associated with processes and threads

First let's focus on the process block. (We'll get to the thread block in the section "Thread Internals" later in the chapter.) Figure 6-2 shows the key fields in an EPROCESS block.

Figure 6-2
Structure of an executive process block

EXPERIMENT: Displaying the Format of an EPROCESS Block

For a list of most of the fields that make up an EPROCESS block and their offsets in hexadecimal, type *!processfields* in the kernel debugger. (See Chapter 1 for more information on the kernel debugger.) The output looks like this:

```
kd> !processfields
 EPROCESS structure offsets:
    Pcb:                        0x0
    ExitStatus:                 0x6c
    LockEvent:                  0x70
    LockCount:                  0x80
    CreateTime:                 0x88
    ExitTime:                   0x90
    LockOwner:                  0x98
    UniqueProcessId:            0x9c
    ActiveProcessLinks:         0xa0
    QuotaPeakPoolUsage[0]:      0xa8
    QuotaPoolUsage[0]:          0xb0
    PagefileUsage:              0xb8
    CommitCharge:               0xbc
    PeakPagefileUsage:          0xc0
    PeakVirtualSize:            0xc4
    VirtualSize:                0xc8
    Vm:                         0xd0
    DebugPort:                  0x120
    ExceptionPort:              0x124
    ObjectTable:                0x128
    Token:                      0x12c
    WorkingSetLock:             0x130
    WorkingSetPage:             0x150
    ProcessOutswapEnabled:      0x154
    ProcessOutswapped:          0x155
    AddressSpaceInitialized:    0x156
    AddressSpaceDeleted:        0x157
    AddressCreationLock:        0x158
    ForkInProgress:             0x17c
    VmOperation:                0x180
    VmOperationEvent:           0x184
```

```
           PageDirectoryPte:                  0x1f0
           LastFaultCount:                    0x18c
           VadRoot:                           0x194
           VadHint:                           0x198
           CloneRoot:                         0x19c
           NumberOfPrivatePages:              0x1a0
           NumberOfLockedPages:               0x1a4
           ForkWasSuccessful:                 0x182
           ExitProcessCalled:                 0x1aa
           CreateProcessReported:             0x1ab
           SectionHandle:                     0x1ac
           Peb:                               0x1b0
           SectionBaseAddress:                0x1b4
           QuotaBlock:                        0x1b8
           LastThreadExitStatus:              0x1bc
           WorkingSetWatch:                   0x1c0
           InheritedFromUniqueProcessId:      0x1c8
           GrantedAccess:                     0x1cc
           DefaultHardErrorProcessing         0x1d0
           LdtInformation:                    0x1d4
           VadFreeHint:                       0x1d8
           VdmObjects:                        0x1dc
           DeviceMap:                         0x1e0
           ImageFileName[0]:                  0x1fc
           VmTrimFaultValue:                  0x20c
           Win32Process:                      0x214
           Win32WindowStation:                0x1c4
```

The *!processfields* command shows the format of a process block, not its contents. (The *!process* command actually dumps the contents of a process block. An annotated example of the output from this command is included later in this chapter on page 303.) Although some of the field names are self-explanatory, the output doesn't give the data type of the fields, nor does it show the format of the structures that are included within or pointed to by the EPROCESS block, such as the kernel process block (Pcb), quota block (QuotaBlock), and so on. By examining the offsets, however, you can at least tell the length of a field. (*Hint*: Fields that are 4 bytes long and refer to some other structure are likely pointers.)

(continued)

EXPERIMENT: Displaying the Format of an EPROCESS Block *continued*

You can also use the *!strct* command (in the secondary kernel debugger extension library Kdex2x86.dll) to display the format of a process block. This command displays every field and its data type (whereas the *!processfields* command displays only some of the fields and doesn't display data type information). A portion of the output follows:

```
kd> !kdex2x86.strct eprocess
Loaded kdex2x86 extension DLL
struct    _EPROCESS (sizeof=648)
+000 struct    _KPROCESS Pcb
+000     struct    _DISPATCHER_HEADER Header
+000         byte      Type
+001         byte      Absolute
+002         byte      Size
+003         byte      Inserted
+004         int32     SignalState
+008         struct    _LIST_ENTRY WaitListHead
+008             struct    _LIST_ENTRY *Flink
+00c             struct    _LIST_ENTRY *Blink
+010     struct    _LIST_ENTRY ProfileListHead
+010         struct    _LIST_ENTRY *Flink
+014         struct    _LIST_ENTRY *Blink
+018     uint32    DirectoryTableBase[2]
+020     struct    _KGDTENTRY LdtDescriptor
+020         uint16    LimitLow
+022         uint16    BaseLow
+024         union     __unnamed9 HighWord
+024             struct    __unnamed10 Bytes
+024                 byte      BaseMid
+025                 byte      Flags1
+026                 byte      Flags2
+027                 byte      BaseHi
+024             struct    __unnamed11 Bits
+024                 bits0-7 BaseMid
+024                 bits8-12 Type
+024                 bits13-14 Dpl
+024                 bits15-15 Pres
+024                 bits16-19 LimitHi
+024                 bits20-20 Sys
+024                 bits21-21 Reserved_0
+024                 bits22-22 Default_Big
+024                 bits23-23 Granularity
+024                 bits24-31 BaseHi
+028     struct    _KIDTENTRY Int21Descriptor
```

```
+028       uint16    Offset
+02a       uint16    Selector
+02c       uint16    Access
+02e       uint16    ExtendedOffset
+030    uint16    IopmOffset
+032    byte      Iopl
+033    byte      VdmFlag
+034    uint32    ActiveProcessors
+038    uint32    KernelTime
+03c    uint32    UserTime
+040    struct    _LIST_ENTRY ReadyListHead
+040       struct    _LIST_ENTRY *Flink
+044       struct    _LIST_ENTRY *Blink
+048    struct    _LIST_ENTRY SwapListEntry
+048       struct    _LIST_ENTRY *Flink
+04c       struct    _LIST_ENTRY *Blink
+050    struct    _LIST_ENTRY ThreadListHead
+050       struct    _LIST_ENTRY *Flink
+054       struct    _LIST_ENTRY *Blink
+058    uint32    ProcessLock
+05c    uint32    Affinity
+060    uint16    StackCount
+062    char      BasePriority
+063    char      ThreadQuantum
+064    byte      AutoAlignment
+065    byte      State
+066    byte      ThreadSeed
+067    byte      DisableBoost
+068    byte      PowerState
+069    byte      DisableQuantum
+06a    byte      Spare[2]
+06c int32     ExitStatus
+070 struct    _KEVENT LockEvent
+070    struct    _DISPATCHER_HEADER Header
+070       byte      Type
+071       byte      Absolute
+072       byte      Size
+073       byte      Inserted
+074       int32     SignalState
+078       struct    _LIST_ENTRY WaitListHead
+078          struct    _LIST_ENTRY *Flink
+07c          struct    _LIST_ENTRY *Blink
+080 uint32    LockCount
+088 union     _LARGE_INTEGER CreateTime
+088    uint32    LowPart
```

(continued)

EXPERIMENT: Displaying the Format of an EPROCESS Block *continued*

```
+08c    int32    HighPart
+088    struct   __unnamed3 u
+088        uint32  LowPart
+08c        int32   HighPart
+088    int64    QuadPart
+090 union     _LARGE_INTEGER ExitTime
+090    uint32   LowPart
+094    int32    HighPart
+090    struct   __unnamed3 u
+090        uint32  LowPart
+094        int32   HighPart
+090    int64    QuadPart
+098 struct    _KTHREAD *LockOwner
+09c void     *UniqueProcessId
+0a0 struct    _LIST_ENTRY ActiveProcessLinks
+0a0    struct   _LIST_ENTRY *Flink
+0a4    struct   _LIST_ENTRY *Blink
+0a8 uint32    QuotaPeakPoolUsage[2]
+0b0 uint32    QuotaPoolUsage[2]
+0b8 uint32    PagefileUsage
+0bc uint32    CommitCharge
+0c0 uint32    PeakPagefileUsage
+0c4 uint32    PeakVirtualSize
+0c8 uint32    VirtualSize
+0d0 struct    _MMSUPPORT Vm
+0d0    union     _LARGE_INTEGER LastTrimTime
+0d0        uint32  LowPart
+0d4        int32   HighPart
+0d0        struct   __unnamed3 u
+0d0            uint32  LowPart
+0d4            int32   HighPart
+0d0        int64    QuadPart
+0d8    uint32   LastTrimFaultCount
+0dc    uint32   PageFaultCount
+0e0    uint32   PeakWorkingSetSize
+0e4    uint32   WorkingSetSize
+0e8    uint32   MinimumWorkingSetSize
+0ec    uint32   MaximumWorkingSetSize
+0f0    *VmWorkingSetList
+0f4    struct    _LIST_ENTRY WorkingSetExpansionLinks
+0f4        struct  _LIST_ENTRY *Flink
+0f8        struct  _LIST_ENTRY *Blink
+0fc    byte     AllowWorkingSetAdjustment
+0fd    byte     AddressSpaceBeingDeleted
+0fe    byte     ForegroundSwitchCount
```

```
+0ff   byte      MemoryPriority
+100   union     __unnamed13 u
+100      uint32    LongFlags
+100      struct    _MMSUPPORT_FLAGS Flags
+100         bits0-0 SessionSpace
+100         bits1-1 BeingTrimmed
+100         bits2-2 ProcessInSession
+100         bits3-3 SessionLeader
+100         bits4-4 TrimHard
+100         bits5-5 WorkingSetHard
+100         bits6-6 WriteWatch
+100         bits7-31 Filler
+104   uint32    Claim
+108   uint32    NextEstimationSlot
+10c   uint32    NextAgingSlot
+110   uint32    EstimatedAvailable
+114   uint32    GrowthSinceLastEstimate
+118 struct   _LIST_ENTRY SessionProcessLinks
+118      struct    _LIST_ENTRY *Flink
+11c      struct    _LIST_ENTRY *Blink
+120 void    *DebugPort
+124 void    *ExceptionPort
+128 struct   _HANDLE_TABLE *ObjectTable
+12c void    *Token
+130 struct   _FAST_MUTEX WorkingSetLock
+130      int32    Count
+134      struct    _KTHREAD *Owner
+138      uint32    Contention
+13c      struct    _KEVENT Event
+13c         struct    _DISPATCHER_HEADER Header
+13c            byte      Type
+13d            byte      Absolute
+13e            byte      Size
+13f            byte      Inserted
+140            int32     SignalState
+144            struct    _LIST_ENTRY WaitListHead
+144               struct    _LIST_ENTRY *Flink
+148               struct    _LIST_ENTRY *Blink
+14c      uint32    OldIrql
+150 uint32    WorkingSetPage
+154 byte    ProcessOutswapEnabled
+155 byte    ProcessOutswapped
+156 byte    AddressSpaceInitialized
+157 byte    AddressSpaceDeleted
+158 struct    _FAST_MUTEX AddressCreationLock
```

(continued)

EXPERIMENT: Displaying the Format of an EPROCESS Block *continued*

```
+158    int32     Count
+15c    struct    _KTHREAD *Owner
+160    uint32    Contention
+164    struct    _KEVENT Event
+164        struct    _DISPATCHER_HEADER Header
+164            byte      Type
+165            byte      Absolute
+166            byte      Size
+167            byte      Inserted
+168            int32     SignalState
+16c            struct    _LIST_ENTRY WaitListHead
+16c                struct    _LIST_ENTRY *Flink
+170                struct    _LIST_ENTRY *Blink
+174    uint32    OldIrql
+178 uint32    HyperSpaceLock
+17c struct    _ETHREAD *ForkInProgress
+180 uint16    VmOperation
+182 byte      ForkWasSuccessful
+183 byte      MmAgressiveWsTrimMask
+184 struct    _KEVENT *VmOperationEvent
+188 void      *PaeTop
+18c uint32    LastFaultCount
+190 uint32    ModifiedPageCount
+194 void      *VadRoot
+198 void      *VadHint
+19c void      *CloneRoot
+1a0 uint32    NumberOfPrivatePages
+1a4 uint32    NumberOfLockedPages
+1a8 uint16    NextPageColor
+1aa byte      ExitProcessCalled
+1ab byte      CreateProcessReported
+1ac void      *SectionHandle
+1b0 struct    _PEB *Peb
+1b4 void      *SectionBaseAddress
+1b8 struct    _EPROCESS_QUOTA_BLOCK *QuotaBlock
+1bc int32     LastThreadExitStatus
+1c0 struct    _PAGEFAULT_HISTORY *WorkingSetWatch
+1c4 void      *Win32WindowStation
+1c8 void      *InheritedFromUniqueProcessId
+1cc uint32    GrantedAccess
+1d0 uint32    DefaultHardErrorProcessing
+1d4 void      *LdtInformation
+1d8 void      *VadFreeHint
+1dc void      *VdmObjects
+1e0 void      *DeviceMap
```

```
+1e4 uint32    SessionId
+1e8 struct    _LIST_ENTRY PhysicalVadList
+1e8    struct    _LIST_ENTRY *Flink
+1ec    struct    _LIST_ENTRY *Blink
+1f0 struct    _HARDWARE_PTE_X86 PageDirectoryPte
+1f0    bits0-0 Valid
+1f0    bits1-1 Write
+1f0    bits2-2 Owner
+1f0    bits3-3 WriteThrough
+1f0    bits4-4 CacheDisable
+1f0    bits5-5 Accessed
+1f0    bits6-6 Dirty
+1f0    bits7-7 LargePage
+1f0    bits8-8 Global
+1f0    bits9-9 CopyOnWrite
+1f0    bits10-10 Prototype
+1f0    bits11-11 reserved
+1f0    bits12-31 PageFrameNumber
+1f0 uint64    Filler
+1f8 uint32    PaePageDirectoryPage
+1fc byte      ImageFileName[16]
+20c uint32    VmTrimFaultValue
+210 byte      SetTimerResolution
+211 byte      PriorityClass
+212 byte      SubSystemMinorVersion
+213 byte      SubSystemMajorVersion
+212 uint16    SubSystemVersion
+214 void      *Win32Process
+218 struct    _EJOB *Job
+21c uint32    JobStatus
+220 struct    _LIST_ENTRY JobLinks
+220    struct    _LIST_ENTRY *Flink
+224    struct    _LIST_ENTRY *Blink
+228 void      *LockedPagesList
+22c void      *SecurityPort
+230 struct    _WOW64_PROCESS *Wow64Process
+238 union     _LARGE_INTEGER ReadOperationCount
+238    uint32    LowPart
+23c    int32     HighPart
+238    struct    __unnamed3 u
+238       uint32    LowPart
+23c       int32     HighPart
+238    int64     QuadPart
+240 union     _LARGE_INTEGER WriteOperationCount
+240    uint32    LowPart
```

(continued)

EXPERIMENT: Displaying the Format of an EPROCESS Block *continued*

```
+244    int32    HighPart
+240    struct   __unnamed3 u
+240        uint32   LowPart
+244        int32    HighPart
+240    int64    QuadPart
+248 union    _LARGE_INTEGER OtherOperationCount
+248    uint32   LowPart
+24c    int32    HighPart
+248    struct   __unnamed3 u
+248        uint32   LowPart
+24c        int32    HighPart
+248    int64    QuadPart
+250 union    _LARGE_INTEGER ReadTransferCount
+250    uint32   LowPart
+254    int32    HighPart
+250    struct   __unnamed3 u
+250        uint32   LowPart
+254        int32    HighPart
+250    int64    QuadPart
+258 union    _LARGE_INTEGER WriteTransferCount
+258    uint32   LowPart
+25c    int32    HighPart
+258    struct   __unnamed3 u
+258        uint32   LowPart
+25c        int32    HighPart
+258    int64    QuadPart
+260 union    _LARGE_INTEGER OtherTransferCount
+260    uint32   LowPart
+264    int32    HighPart
+260    struct   __unnamed3 u
+260        uint32   LowPart
+264        int32    HighPart
+260    int64    QuadPart
+268 uint32   CommitChargeLimit
+26c uint32   CommitChargePeak
+270 struct   _LIST_ENTRY ThreadListHead
+270    struct   _LIST_ENTRY *Flink
+274    struct   _LIST_ENTRY *Blink
+278 struct   _RTL_BITMAP *VadPhysicalPagesBitMap
+27c uint32   VadPhysicalPages
+280 uint32   AweLock
```

Table 6-1 explains some of the fields in the preceding experiment in more detail and includes references to other places in the book where you can find more information about them. As we've said before and will no doubt say again, processes and threads are such an integral part of Windows 2000 that it's impossible

to talk about them without referring to many other parts of the system. To keep the length of this chapter manageable, however, we've covered those related subjects (such as memory management, security, objects, and handles) elsewhere.

Table 6-1 Contents of the EPROCESS Block

Element	Purpose	Additional Reference
Kernel process (KPROCESS) block	Common dispatcher object header, pointer to the process page directory, list of kernel thread (KTHREAD) blocks belonging to the process, default base priority, quantum, affinity mask, and total kernel and user time for the threads in the process.	Thread scheduling (page 337)
Process identification	Unique process ID, creating process ID, name of image being run, window station process is running on.	
Quota block	Limits on nonpaged pool, paged pool, and page file usage plus current and peak process nonpaged and paged pool usage. (*Note*: Several processes can share this structure: all the system processes point to the single systemwide default quota block; all the processes in the interactive session share a single quota block Winlogon sets up.	
Virtual address descriptors (VADs)	Series of data structures that describes the status of the portions of the address space that exist in the process.	Memory management (Chapter 7)
Working set information	Pointer to working set list (MMWSL structure); current, peak, minimum, and maximum working set size; last trim time; page fault count; memory priority; outswap flags; page fault history.	Memory management (Chapter 7)
Virtual memory information	Current and peak virtual size, page file usage, hardware page table entry for process page directory.	Memory management (Chapter 7)
Exception local procedure call (LPC) port	Interprocess communication channel to which the process manager sends a message when one of the process's threads causes an exception.	Local procedure calls (Chapter 3, page 171)

(continued)

Table 6-1 *continued*

Element	Purpose	Additional Reference
Debugging LPC port	Interprocess communication channel to which the process manager sends a message when one of the process's threads causes a debug event.	Local procedure calls (Chapter 3, page 171)
Access token (ACCESS_TOKEN)	Executive object describing the security profile of this process.	Security (Chapter 8)
Handle table	Address of per-process handle table.	Object handles (Chapter 3, page 137)
Device map	Address of object directory to resolve device name references in (supports multiple users).	Object manager (Chapter 3)
Process environment block (PEB)	Image information (base address, version numbers, module list), process heap information, and thread-local storage utilization. (*Note*: The pointers to the process heaps start at the first byte after the PEB.)	Page 312
Win32 subsystem process block (W32PROCESS)	Process details needed by the kernel-mode component of the Win32 subsystem.	

The kernel process (KPROCESS) block, which is part of the EPROCESS block, and the process environment block (PEB), which is pointed to by the EPROCESS block, contain additional details about the process object. The KPROCESS block (which is sometimes called the PCB, or process control block) is illustrated in Figure 6-3. It contains the basic information that the Windows 2000 kernel needs to schedule threads. (Page directories are covered in Chapter 7, and kernel thread blocks are described in more detail later in this chapter.)

The PEB, which lives in the user process address space, contains information needed by the image loader, the heap manager, and other Win32 system DLLs that need to be writable from user mode. (The EPROCESS and KPROCESS blocks are accessible only from kernel mode.) The PEB is always mapped at address 0x7FFDF000. The basic structure of the PEB is illustrated in Figure 6-4 and is explained in more detail later in this chapter.

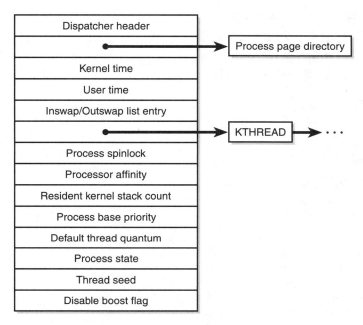

Figure 6-3
Structure of the kernel process block

Figure 6-4
Fields of the process environment block

EXPERIMENT: Examining the PEB

You can dump the PEB structure with the *!peb* command in the kernel debugger. The following example, which uses LiveKd, shows the PEB for the LiveKd process:

```
kd> !peb
PEB at 7FFDF000
    InheritedAddressSpace:      No
    ReadImageFileExecOptions:  No
    BeingDebugged:              No
    ImageBaseAddress:             00400000
    Ldr.Initialized: Yes
    Ldr.InInitializationOrderModuleList: 131f40 . 134b98
    Ldr.InLoadOrderModuleList: 131ec0 . 134b88
    Ldr.InMemoryOrderModuleList: 131ec8 . 134b90
        00400000 C:\nt\livekd.exe
        77F80000 C:\WINNT\System32\ntdll.dll
        77920000 C:\WINNT\system32\IMAGEHLP.dll
        78000000 C:\WINNT\system32\MSVCRT.DLL
        77E80000 C:\WINNT\system32\KERNEL32.dll
        77E10000 C:\WINNT\system32\USER32.dll
        77F40000 C:\WINNT\system32\GDI32.DLL
        77DB0000 C:\WINNT\system32\ADVAPI32.dll
        77D40000 C:\WINNT\system32\RPCRT4.DLL
        72A00000 C:\WINNT\system32\DBGHELP.dll
    SubSystemData:     0
    ProcessHeap:       130000
    ProcessParameters: 20000
        WindowTitle:   '\nt\livekd'
        ImageFile:     'C:\nt\livekd.exe'
        CommandLine:   '\nt\livekd'
        DllPath:       'C:\nt;.;C:\WINNT\System32;
                        C:\WINNT\system;C:\WINNT;
                        C:\WINNT\system32;C:\WINNT;
                        C:\WINNT\system32\WBEM;
                        C:\Program Files\Support Tools\;
                        C:\Program Files\Resource Kit\'
        Environment:   0x10000
```

Kernel Variables

A few of the key kernel global variables that relate to processes are listed in Table 6-2. These variables are referred to later in the chapter, when the steps in creating a process are described.

Table 6-2 Process-Related Kernel Variables

Variable	Type	Description
PsActiveProcessHead	Queue header	List head of process blocks
PsIdleProcess	EPROCESS	Idle process block
PsInitialSystemProcess	Pointer to EPROCESS	Pointer to the process block of the initial system process (process ID 2) that contains the system threads
PspCreateProcessNotifyRoutine	Array of pointers	Array of pointers to routines to be called on process creation and deletion (maximum of eight)
PspCreateProcessNotifyRoutineCount	DWORD	Count of registered process notification routines
PspLoadImageNotifyRoutine	Array of pointers	Array of pointers to routines to be called on image load
PspLoadImageNotifyRoutineCount	DWORD	Count of registered image-load notification routines
PspCidTable	Pointer to HANDLE_TABLE	Handle table for process and thread client IDs

Performance Counters

Windows 2000 maintains a number of counters with which you can track the processes running on your system; you can retrieve these counters programmatically or view them with the Performance tool. Table 6-3 lists the performance counters relevant to processes (except for memory management and I/O–related counters, which are described in chapters 7 and 9, respectively).

Table 6-3 Process-Related Performance Counters

Object: Counter	Function
Process: % Privileged Time	Describes the percentage of time that the threads in the process have run in kernel mode during a specified interval.
Process: % Processor Time	Describes the percentage of CPU time that the threads in the process have used during a specified interval. This count is the sum of % Privileged Time and % User Time.
Process: % User Time	Describes the percentage of time that the threads in the process have run in user mode during a specified interval.
Process: Elapsed Time	Describes the total elapsed time in seconds since this process was created.
Process: ID Process	Returns the process ID. This ID applies only while the process exists because process IDs are reused.
Process: Creating Process ID	Returns the process ID of the creating process. This value isn't updated if the creating process exits.
Process: Thread Count	Returns the number of threads in the process.
Process: Handle Count	Returns the number of handles open in the process.

Relevant Functions

For reference purposes, some of the Win32 functions that apply to processes are described in Table 6-4. For further information, consult the Win32 API documentation in the MSDN Library.

Table 6-4 Process-Related Functions

Function	Description
CreateProcess	Creates a new process and thread using the caller's security identification
CreateProcessAsUser	Creates a new process and thread with the specified alternate security token
CreateProcessWithLogonW	Creates a new process and thread with the specified alternate security token, allowing the user profile to be loaded

Function	Description
OpenProcess	Returns a handle to the specified process object
ExitProcess	Ends a process and notifies all attached DLLs
TerminateProcess	Ends a process without notifying the DLLs
FlushInstructionCache	Empties the specified process's instruction cache
GetProcessTimes	Obtains a process's timing information, describing how much time the process has spent in user and kernel mode
GetExitCodeProcess	Returns the exit code for a process, indicating how and why the process shut down
GetCommandLine	Returns a pointer to the command-line string passed to the current process
GetCurrentProcessId	Returns the ID of the current process
GetProcessVersion	Returns the major and minor versions of the Windows version on which the specified process expects to run
GetStartupInfo	Returns the contents of the START-UPINFO structure specified during *CreateProcess*
GetEnvironmentStrings	Returns the address of the environment block
GetEnvironmentVariable	Returns a specific environment variable
Get/SetProcessShutdownParameters	Defines the shutdown priority and number of retries for the current process
GetGuiResources	Returns a count of USER and GDI handles

Relevant Tools

A number of tools for viewing (and modifying) processes and process information are available. These tools are included within Windows 2000 itself and within the Windows 2000 Support Tools, Windows 2000 debugging tools,

Windows 2000 resource kits, the Platform SDK, and the DDK. The trouble is, you can't get all the information you need with one single tool. However, most information is available from more than one tool, but the data is sometimes identified by different names (and sometimes assigned different values) in each of the tools. To help you determine which tool to use to get the basic process information you need, consult Table 6-5. This table isn't a comprehensive list of all the information available about a process—for example, you'll find out what tools you can use to gather memory management information in Chapter 7— but if you need the basics, you'll find them here.

Table 6-5 Process-Related Tools

Object	Taskman	Perfmon	Pview	Pviewer	Qslice	Pmon	Pstat	Pulist	Tlist	KD !process
Process ID	✓	✓	✓	✓	✓		✓	✓	✓	✓
Image Name	✓		✓	✓	✓	✓	✓	✓	✓	✓
Total CPU Time	✓	✓				✓				✓
% CPU Time	✓	✓		✓	✓	✓				
Handle Count	✓	✓								
Thread Count	✓	✓	✓	✓	✓	✓	✓			
View Priority Class	✓		✓	✓						
% User Time		✓			✓					
% Privileged Time		✓			✓					
Total User Time			✓				✓			✓
Total Privileged Time			✓				✓			✓
Quota Limits			✓							
Elapsed Time	✓	✓								✓
Creating Process									✓	
Current Directory									✓	
Command Line	✓								✓	
Security ID								✓		

The following experiments illustrate the various views of process information you can obtain with some of these tools.

EXPERIMENT: Viewing Process Information with Task Manager

The built-in Windows 2000 Task Manager provides a quick list of the processes running on the system. You can start Task Manager in one of three ways: (1) press Ctrl+Shift+Esc, (2) right-click on the taskbar and select Task Manager, or (3) press Ctrl+Alt+Delete and click the Task Manager button. Once Task Manager has started, click the Processes tab to see the list of running processes. Notice that processes are identified by the name of the image of which they are an instance. Unlike some objects in Windows 2000, processes can't be given global names. To display additional details, choose Select Columns from the View menu and select additional columns to be added, as shown here:

Select Columns

Select the columns that will appear on the Process page of the Task Manager.

☑ Image Name	☐ Page Faults Delta
☑ PID (Process Identifier)	☑ Virtual Memory Size
☑ CPU Usage	☐ Paged Pool
☑ CPU Time	☐ Non-paged Pool
☑ Memory Usage	☑ Base Priority
☐ Memory Usage Delta	☑ Handle Count
☐ Peak Memory Usage	☑ Thread Count
☐ Page Faults	☐ GDI Objects
☐ USER Objects	☐ I/O Writes
☐ I/O Reads	☐ I/O Write Bytes
☐ I/O Read Bytes	☐ I/O Other
	☐ I/O Other Bytes

OK Cancel

Although what you see in the Task Manager Processes tab is clearly a list of processes, what the Applications tab displays isn't as obvious. The Applications tab lists the top-level visible windows on all the desktops in the interactive window station. (By default, there are two desktop objects—you can create more by using the Win32 *CreateDesktop* function.) The Status column indicates whether or not the thread that owns the window is in a Windows message wait state. "Running" means the thread is waiting for windowing input; "Not Responding" means the thread isn't waiting for windowing input (for example, the thread might be running or waiting for I/O or some Win32 synchronization object).

(continued)

EXPERIMENT: **Viewing Process Information with Task Manager** *continued*

From the Applications tab, you can match a task to the process that owns the thread that owns the task window by right-clicking on the task name and choosing Go To Process.

EXPERIMENT: Viewing the Process Tree

One unique attribute about a process that most tools don't display is the parent or creator process ID. You can retrieve this value with the Performance tool (or programmatically) by querying the Creating Process ID. The Windows 2000 Support Tools command *tlist /t* uses the information in the attribute to display a *process tree* that shows the relationship of a process to its parent. Here's an example of output from *tlist /t*:

```
C:\>tlist /t
System Process (0)
System (2)
  smss.exe (21)
    csrss.exe (24)
```

```
    winlogon.exe (35)
      services.exe (41)
        spoolss.exe (69)
        llssrv.exe (94)
        LOCATOR.EXE (96)
        RpcSs.exe (112)
        inetinfo.exe (128)
      lsass.exe (44)
    nddeagnt.exe (119)
explorer.exe (123) Program Manager
  OSA.EXE (121)
  WINWORD.EXE (117) Microsoft Word - msch02(s).doc
  cmd.exe (72) Command Prompt - tlist /t
    tlist.EXE (100)
```

Tlist indents each process to show its parent/child relationship. Processes whose parents aren't alive are left-justified, because even if a grandparent process exists, there's no way to find that relationship. Windows 2000 maintains only the creator process ID, not a link back to the creator of the creator, and so forth.

To demonstrate the fact that Windows 2000 doesn't keep track of more than just the parent process ID, follow these steps:

1. Open a Command Prompt window.

2. Type *start cmd* (which runs a second Command Prompt).

3. Bring up Task Manager.

4. Switch to the second Command Prompt.

5. Type *mspaint* (which runs Microsoft Paint).

6. Click the intermediate (second) Command Prompt window.

7. Type *exit*. (Notice that Paint remains.)

8. Switch to Task Manager.

9. Click the Applications tab.

10. Right-click on the Command Prompt task, and select Go To Process.

11. Click on the Cmd.exe process highlighted in gray.

12. Right-click on this process, and select End Process Tree.

13. Click Yes in the Task Manager Warning message box.

(continued)

EXPERIMENT: Viewing the Process Tree *continued*

The first Command Prompt window will disappear, but you should still see the Paintbrush window because it was the grandchild of the Command Prompt process you terminated; and because the intermediate process (the parent of Paintbrush) was terminated, there was no link between the parent and the grandchild.

EXPERIMENT: Viewing Thread Activity with QuickSlice

QuickSlice gives a quick, dynamic view of the proportions of system and kernel time that each process currently running on your system is using. On line, the red part of the bar shows the amount of CPU time spent in kernel mode, and the blue part shows the user-mode time. (Although reproduced in the window below in black and white, the bars in the online display are always red and blue.) The total of all bars shown in the QuickSlice window should add up to 100 percent of CPU time. To run QuickSlice, click the Start button, choose Run, and enter *Qslice.exe* (assuming the Windows 2000 resource kit is in your path). For example, try running a graphics-intensive application such as Paint (Mspaint.exe). Open QuickSlice and Paint side by side, and draw squiggles in the Paint window. When you do so, you'll see Mspaint.exe running in the QuickSlice window, as shown here:

For additional information about the threads in a process, you can also double-click on a process (on either the process name or the col-

ored bar). Here you can see the threads within the process and the relative CPU time each thread uses (not across the system):

EXPERIMENT: Viewing Process Details with Process Viewer

The Process Viewer (Pviewer.exe) that comes with the Windows 2000 Support Tools permits you to view information about the running processes and threads as well as to kill processes and change process priority classes. You can use this tool to view processes both on the local computer and across the network on remote machines running Windows 2000. This tool is also available in the Platform SDK (where it's called Pview.exe.) The Process Viewer is well documented in the Windows 2000 Support Tools help file, but here's a quick overview of the options available to you. The basic display of the Process Viewer looks like this:

(continued)

EXPERIMENT: Viewing Process Details with Process Viewer *continued*

Here's what the various options do:

- The Computer text box displays the name of the computer whose processes are currently displayed. Click the Connect button to browse for another computer.

- The Memory Detail button shows memory management details about the selected process, such as the amount of memory committed to the process, the size of the working set, and so forth.

- The Kill Process button kills the selected process. Be *very* careful which process you kill, since the process will have no chance to perform any cleanup.

- The Refresh button refreshes the display—the Process Viewer doesn't update the information unless you request it.

- The Processor Time columns in the Process and Thread(s) list boxes show the total processor time the process or thread has used since it was created.

- The Priority collection of radio buttons regulates the selected process's priority class (the Real-time priority class isn't shown), and the Thread Priority collection displays the relative thread priorities of the threads within a process.

- At the bottom of the window, the number of context switches and the thread's dynamic priority, start address, and current PC are displayed.

To see the other displays of process and thread information, try running Tlist.exe (Support Tools), Pstat.exe (Platform SDK or *www. reskit.com*), Pmon.exe (Support Tools), or Pulist.exe (resource kit).

EXPERIMENT: Using the Kernel Debugger *!process* Command

The *!process* command for the kernel debugger (described in Chapter 1) displays a subset of the information in an EPROCESS block. This output is arranged in two parts for each process. First you see

the information about the process, as shown here. (Not all the fields in the output are labeled—only the parts germane to this experiment.)

| EPROCESS address | Process ID | Address of process environment block | Process ID of parent process |

```
PROCESS ff704020  Cid: 0075    Peb: 7ffdf000  ParentCid: 005d
    DirBase: 0063c000  ObjectTable: ff7063c8  TableSize: 70.
    Image: Explorer.exe
    VadRoot ff70d6e8 Clone 0 Private 229. Modified 236. Locked 0.
    FF7041DC MutantState Signalled OwningThread 0
    Token                              e1462030
    ElapsedTime                        0:01:19.0874
    UserTime                           0:00:00.0991
    KernelTime                         0:00:02.0613
    QuotaPoolUsage[PagedPool]          18317
    QuotaPoolUsage[NonPagedPool]       3824
    Working Set Sizes (now,min,max)    (727, 20, 45) (2908KB, 80KB, 180KB)
    PeakWorkingSetSize                 757
    VirtualSize                        29 Mb
    PeakVirtualSize                    31 Mb
    PageFaultCount                     1396
    MemoryPriority                     FOREGROUND
    BasePriority                       8
    CommitCharge                       250
```

Time the process has been running, broken out into user time and kernel time

After the basic process output comes a list of the threads in the process. That output is explained in the experiment "Using the Kernel Debugger *!thread* Command" on page 332. Other commands that display process information include *!handle*, which dumps the process handle table (described in more detail in the section "Object Handles and the Process Handle Table" in Chapter 3 on page 137). Process and thread security structures are described in Chapter 8.

Another command that dumps an EPROCESS block is the *!strct* command. See the experiment "Displaying the Format of an EPROCESS Block" beginning on page 280 for more information on this command.

Flow of *CreateProcess*

So far in this chapter, you've seen the structures that are part of a process and the API functions with which you (and the operating system) can manipulate processes. You've also found out how you can use tools to view how processes interact with your system. But how did those processes come into being, and how do they exit once they've fulfilled their purpose? In the following sections, you'll discover how a Win32 process comes to life.

A Win32 process is created when an application calls one of the process creation functions, such as *CreateProcess*, *CreateProcessAsUser*, or *CreateProcessWithLogonW*. Creating a Win32 process consists of several stages carried out in three parts of the operating system: the Win32 client-side library Kernel32.dll, the Windows 2000 executive, and the Win32 subsystem process (Csrss). Because of the multiple environment subsystem architecture of Windows 2000, creating a Windows 2000 executive process object (which other subsystems can use) is separated from the work involved in creating a Win32 process. So, although the following description of the flow of the Win32 *CreateProcess* function is complicated, keep in mind that part of the work is specific to the semantics added by the Win32 subsystem as opposed to the core work needed to create a Windows 2000 executive process object.

The following list summarizes the main stages of creating a process with the Win32 *CreateProcess* function. The operations performed in each stage are described in detail in the subsequent sections.

1. Open the image file (.exe) to be executed inside the process.

2. Create the Windows 2000 executive process object.

3. Create the initial thread (stack, context, and Windows 2000 executive thread object).

4. Notify the Win32 subsystem of the new process so that it can set up for the new process and thread.

5. Start execution of the initial thread (unless the CREATE_SUSPENDED flag was specified).

6. In the context of the new process and thread, complete the initialization of the address space (such as load required DLLs) and begin execution of the program.

Figure 6-5 shows an overview of the stages Windows 2000 follows to create a process.

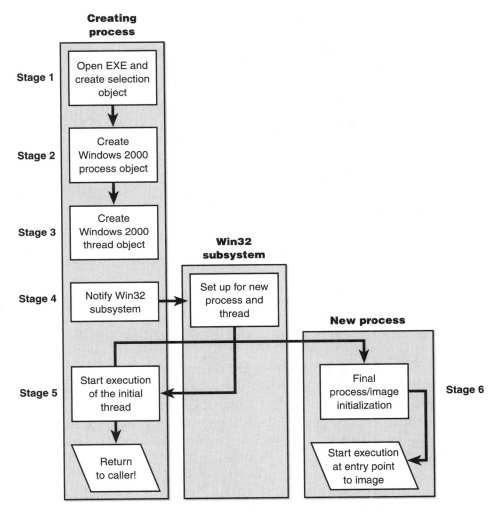

Figure 6-5
The main stages of process creation

Before describing these stages in more detail, we should mention a few notes that pertain to all the stages.

■ In *CreateProcess*, the priority class for the new process is specified as independent bits in the *CreationFlags* parameter. Thus, you can specify more than one priority class for a single *CreateProcess* call. Windows 2000 resolves the question of which priority class to assign to the process by choosing the lowest-priority class set.

■ If no priority class is specified for the new process, the priority class defaults to Normal unless the priority class of the process that created it is Idle or Below Normal, in which case the priority class of the new process will have the same priority as the creating class.

■ If a Real-time priority class is specified for the new process and the process's caller doesn't have the Increase Scheduling Priority privilege, the High priority class is used instead. In other words, *CreateProcess* doesn't fail just because the caller has insufficient privileges to create the process in the Real-time priority class; the new process just won't have as high a priority as Real-time.

■ All windows are associated with desktops, the graphical representation of a workspace. If no desktop is specified in *CreateProcess*, the process is associated with the caller's current desktop.

Enough background. The steps of *CreateProcess* are described in detail in the following sections.

NOTE Many steps of *CreateProcess* are related to the setup of the process virtual address space and hence refer to many memory management terms and structures, which are defined in Chapter 7.

Stage 1: Opening the Image to Be Executed

As illustrated in Figure 6-6, the first stage in *CreateProcess* is to find the appropriate Win32 image that will run the executable file specified by the caller and to create a section object to later map it into the address space of the new process. If no image name is specified, the first token of the command line (defined to be the first part of the command-line string ending with a space or tab that is a valid file specification) is used as the image filename.

If the executable file specified is a Win32 .exe, it is used directly. If it's not a Win32 .exe (for example, if it's an MS-DOS, a Win16, a POSIX, or an OS/2 application), *CreateProcess* goes through a series of steps to find a Win32 *support image* to run it. This process is necessary because non-Win32 applications aren't run directly—Windows 2000 instead uses one of a few special support images that in turn are responsible for actually running the non-Win32 program. For example, if you attempt to run a POSIX application, *CreateProcess* identifies it as such and changes the image to be run on the Win32 executable file Posix.exe. If you attempt to run an MS-DOS or a Win16 executable, the image to be run

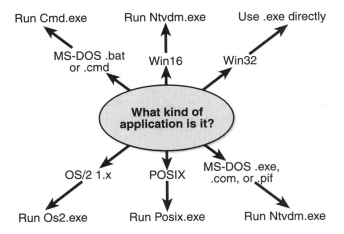

Figure 6-6
Choosing a Win32 image to activate

becomes the Win32 executable Ntvdm.exe. In short, you can't directly create a process that is *not* a Win32 process. If Windows 2000 can't find a way to resolve the activated image as a Win32 process (as shown in Table 6-6), *CreateProcess* fails.

Table 6-6 Decision Tree for Stage 1 of *CreateProcess*

If the image is a/an	This image will run	And this will happen
POSIX executable file	Posix.exe	*CreateProcess* restarts Stage 1
OS/2 1.x image	Os2.exe	*CreateProcess* restarts Stage 1
MS-DOS application with an .exe, a .com, or a .pif extension	Ntvdm.exe	*CreateProcess* restarts Stage 1
Win16 application	Ntvdm.exe	*CreateProcess* restarts Stage 1
Command procedure MS-DOS application with a .bat or a .cmd extension	Cmd.exe	*CreateProcess* restarts Stage 1

Specifically, the decision tree that *CreateProcess* goes through to run an image is as follows:

- If the image is an OS/2 1.x application, the image to be run changes to Os2.exe and *CreateProcess* restarts at Stage 1.

- If the image is an MS-DOS application with an .exe, a .com, or a .pif extension, a message is sent to the Win32 subsystem to check whether an MS-DOS support process (Ntvdm.exe, specified in the registry value HKLM\SYSTEM\CurrentControlSet\Control\WOW\ cmdline) has already been created for this session. If a support process has been created, it is used to run the MS-DOS application (the Win32 subsystem sends the message to the VDM [Virtual DOS Machine] process to run the new image) and *CreateProcess* returns. If a support process hasn't been created, the image to be run changes to Ntvdm.exe and *CreateProcess* restarts at Stage 1.

- If the file to run has a .bat or a .cmd extension, the image to be run becomes Cmd.exe, the Windows 2000 command prompt, and *CreateProcess* restarts at Stage 1. (The name of the batch file is passed as the first parameter to Cmd.exe.)

- If the image is a Win16 (Windows 3.1) executable, *CreateProcess* must decide whether a new VDM process must be created to run it or whether it should use the default systemwide shared VDM process (which might not yet have been created). The *CreateProcess* flags CREATE_SEPARATE_WOW_VDM and CREATE_SHARED_ WOW_VDM control this decision. If these flags aren't specified, the registry value HKLM\SYSTEM\CurrentControlSet\Control\WOW\ DefaultSeparateVDM dictates the default behavior. If the application is to be run in a separate VDM, the image to be run changes to the value of HKLM\SYSTEM\CurrentControlSet\Control\WOW\ wowcmdline and *CreateProcess* restarts at Stage 1. Otherwise, the Win32 subsystem sends a message to see whether the systemwide VDM process exists and can be used. (If the VDM process is running on a different desktop or isn't running under the same security as the caller, it can't be used and a new VDM process must be created.) If a systemwide VDM process can be used, the Win32 subsystem sends a message to it to run the new image and *CreateProcess* returns. If the VDM process hasn't yet been created (or if it exists but can't be used), the image to be run changes to the VDM support image and *CreateProcess* restarts at Stage 1.

At this point, *CreateProcess* has successfully opened a valid Windows 2000 executable file and created a section object for it. The object isn't mapped into memory yet, but it is open. Just because a section object has been successfully created doesn't mean that the file is a valid Win32 image, however; it could be a DLL or a POSIX executable. If the file is a POSIX executable, the image to be run changes to Posix.exe and *CreateProcess* restarts from the beginning of Stage 1. If the file is a DLL, *CreateProcess* fails.

Now that *CreateProcess* has found a valid Win32 executable, it looks in the registry under HKLM\SOFTWARE\Microsoft\Windows NT\CurrentVersion\ Image File Execution Options to see whether a subkey with the filename and extension of the executable image (but without the directory and path information—for example, Image.exe) exists there. If it does, *CreateProcess* looks for a value named Debugger for that key. If the value isn't null, the image to be run becomes the string in that value and *CreateProcess* restarts at Stage 1.

TIP You can take advantage of this *CreateProcess* behavior and debug the startup code of Windows 2000 service processes before they start rather than attach the debugger after starting the service, which doesn't allow you to debug the startup code. If you're feeling mischievous, you can also exploit this behavior to confuse people by causing another file to be run rather than the one they specified.

Stage 2: Creating the Windows 2000 Executive Process Object

At this point, *CreateProcess* has opened a valid Win32 executable file and created a section object to map it into the new process address space. Next it creates a Windows 2000 executive process object to run the image by calling the internal system function *NtCreateProcess*. Creating the executive process object (which is done by the creating thread) involves the following substages:

A. Setting up the EPROCESS block

B. Creating the initial process address space

C. Creating the kernel process block

D. Concluding the setup of the process address space

E. Setting up the PEB

F. Completing the setup of the executive process object

NOTE The only time there won't be a parent process is during system initialization. After that point, a parent process is always required in order to provide a security context for the new process.

Stage 2A: Setting Up the EPROCESS Block

This substage involves five steps:

1. Allocate and initialize the Windows 2000 EPROCESS block.

2. Set the new process's quota block to the address of its parent process's quota block, and increment the reference count for the parent's quota block.

3. Store the parent process's process ID and session ID (if applicable) in the *InheritedFromUniqueProcessId* field in the new process object.

4. Set the new process's exit status to STATUS_PENDING.

5. Create the process's primary access token (a duplicate of its parent's primary token). New processes inherit the security profile of their parent. If the *CreateProcessAsUser* function is being used to specify a different access token for the new process, the token is then changed appropriately.

Stage 2B: Creating the Initial Process Address Space

The initial process address space consists of three pages:

- Page directory
- Hyperspace page
- Working set list

To create these three pages, the following steps are taken:

1. Page table entries are created in the appropriate page tables to map the three initial pages.

2. To account for these new pages, the value 3 is deducted from the kernel variable *MmTotalCommittedPages* and added to *MmProcessCommit*.

3. The systemwide default process minimum working set size (*PsMinimumWorkingSet*) is deducted from *MmResidentAvailablePages*.

4. The page table pages for the nonpaged portion of system space and the system cache are mapped into the process.

5. The process minimum and maximum working set size are set to the values of *PsMinimumWorkingSet* and *PsMaximumWorkingSet*, respectively.

Stage 2C: Creating the Kernel Process Block

The next stage of *CreateProcess* is the initialization of the KPROCESS block, which contains a pointer to a list of kernel threads. (The kernel has no knowledge of handles, so it bypasses the object table.) The kernel process block also points to the process's page table directory (used to keep track of the process's virtual address space), the total time the process's threads have executed, the process's default base-scheduling priority (which starts as Normal, or 8, unless the parent process was set to Idle or Below Normal, in which case the setting is inherited), the default processor affinity for the threads in the process, and the initial value of the process default quantum, which is taken from the value of *PspForegroundQuantum[0]*, the first entry in the systemwide quantum array.

> **NOTE** The default initial quantum differs between Windows 2000 Professional and Windows 2000 Server. For more information on thread quantums, turn to their discussion in the section "Thread Scheduling" on page 337.

Stage 2D: Concluding the Setup of the Process Address Space

Setting up the address space for a new process is somewhat complicated, so let's look at what's involved one step at a time. To get the most out of this section, you should have some familiarity with the internals of the Windows 2000 memory manager, which are described in Chapter 7.

1. The virtual memory manager sets the value of the process's last trim time to the current time. The working set manager (which runs in the context of the balance set manager system thread) uses this value to determine when to initiate working set trimming.

2. The page frame number (PFN) database for the page directory as well as the page directory entry, which maps hyperspace, are initialized.

3. The memory manager initializes the process's working set list—page faults can now be taken.

4. The major and minor version numbers are copied from the executable file to the EPROCESS block.

5. The section (created when the image file was opened) is now mapped into the new process's address space, and the process section base address is set to the base address of the image.

6. Ntdll.dll is mapped into the process.

7. The systemwide national language support (NLS) tables are mapped into the process's address space.

NOTE POSIX processes clone the address space of their parents, so they don't have to go through these steps to create a new address space. In the case of POSIX applications, the new process's section base address is set to that of its parent process and the parent's PEB is cloned for the new process.

8. If the parent process was contained in a job, the new process is added to the job. (Jobs are described at the end of this chapter.)

9. *CreateProcess* inserts the new process block at the end of the Windows 2000 list of active processes (*PsActiveProcessHead*).

Stage 2E: Setting Up the PEB

CreateProcess allocates a page for the PEB and initializes a number of fields, which are described in Table 6-7.

Table 6-7 Initial Values of the Fields of the PEB

Field	Initial Value
ImageBaseAddress	Base address of section
NumberOfProcessors	*KeNumberProcessors* kernel variable
NtGlobalFlag	*NtGlobalFlag* kernel variable
CriticalSectionTimeout	*MmCriticalSectionTimeout* kernel variable
HeapSegmentReserve	*MmHeapSegmentReserve* kernel variable
HeapSegmentCommit	*MmHeapSegmentCommit* kernel variable
HeapDeCommitTotalFreeThreshold	*MmHeapDeCommitTotalFreeThreshold* kernel variable
HeapDeCommitFreeBlockThreshold	*MmHeapDeCommitFreeBlockThreshold* kernel variable
NumberOfHeaps	0
MaximumNumberOfHeaps	(Size of a page – size of a PEB) / 4
ProcessHeaps	First byte after PEB
OSMajorVersion	*NtMajorVersion* kernel variable
OSMinorVersion	*NtMinorVersion* kernel variable
OSBuildNumber	*NtBuildNumber* kernel variable & 0x3FFF
OSPlatformId	2

If the image file specifies explicit Win32 version values, this information replaces the initial values shown in Table 6-7. The mapping from image version information fields to PEB fields is described in Table 6-8.

Table 6-8 Win32 Replacements for Initial PEB Values

Field Name	Value Taken from Image Header
OSMajorVersion	OptionalHeader.Win32VersionValue & 0xFF
OSMinorVersion	(OptionalHeader.Win32VersionValue >> 8) & 0xFF
OSBuildNumber	(OptionalHeader.Win32VersionValue >> 16) & 0x3FFF
OSPlatformId	(OptionalHeader.Win32VersionValue >> 30) ^ 0x2

Stage 2F: Completing the Setup of the Executive Process Object

Before the handle to the new process can be returned, a few final setup steps must be completed:

1. The process handle table is initialized; if the inherit handles flag is set for the parent process, any inheritable handles are copied from the parent's object handle table into the new process. (For more information about object handle tables, see Chapter 3.)

2. If you're running Windows 2000 Professional and the image header specifies IMAGE_FILE_AGGRESIVE_WS_TRIM, the PS_WS_TRIM_FROM_EXE_HEADER flag is set in the process block. This causes the working set manager to aggressively steal pages from the process. If you're running Windows 2000 Professional on a small-memory x86 system, the PS_WS_TRIM_BACKGROUND_ONLY_APP flag is set in the process block, which limits the aggressive trimming to processes that aren't associated with the foreground window. These working set flags are not set for processes created on systems running Windows 2000 Server.

3. If the image header characteristics IMAGE_FILE_UP_SYSTEM_ONLY flag is set (indicating that the image can run only on a uniprocessor system), a single CPU is chosen for all the threads in this new process to run on. This choosing process is done by simply cycling through the available processors—each time this type of image is run, the next processor is used. In this way, these types of images are spread out across the processors evenly.

4. If the image specifies an explicit processor affinity mask (for example, a field in the configuration header), this value is copied to the PEB and later set as the default process affinity mask.

5. If the parent process had an Event Log section in its PEB, the Event Log is copied to the new process and a handle is duplicated to the section for the new process.

6. If systemwide auditing of processes is enabled (which is accomplished through the Group Policy snap-in), the process's creation is written to the Audit Log.

7. The process's creation time is set, the handle to the new process is returned to the caller (*CreateProcess* in Kernel32.dll), and execution returns to the original caller of *CreateProcess*.

Stage 3: Creating the Initial Thread and Its Stack and Context

At this point, the Windows 2000 executive process object is completely set up. It still has no thread, however, so it can't do anything yet. Before the thread can be created, it needs a stack and a context in which to run, so these are set up now. The stack size for the initial thread is taken from the image—there's no way to specify another size.

Now the initial thread can be created, which is done by calling *NtCreate-Thread*. (For a detailed description of how a thread is created, see the section "Flow of *CreateThread*" on page 333.) The thread parameter (which can't be specified in *CreateProcess* but can be specified in *CreateThread*) is the address of the PEB. This parameter will be used by the initialization code that runs in the context of this new thread (as described in Stage 6). However, the thread won't do anything yet—it is created in a suspended state and isn't resumed until the process is completely initialized (as described in Stage 5).

Stage 4: Notifying the Win32 Subsystem About the New Process

After all the necessary executive process and thread objects have been created, Kernel32.dll sends a message to the Win32 subsystem so that it can set up for the new process and thread. The message includes the following information:

- Process and thread handles
- Entries in the creation flags
- ID of the process's creator
- Flag indicating whether the process belongs to a Win32 application (so that Csrss can determine whether or not to show the startup cursor)

The Win32 subsystem performs the following steps when it receives this message:

1. *CreateProcess* duplicates a handle for the process and thread. In this step, the usage count of the process and the thread is incremented from 1 (set at creation time) to 2.

2. If a process priority class isn't specified, *CreateProcess* sets it according to the algorithm described on page 306.

3. The Csrss process block is allocated.

4. The new process's exception port is set to be the general function port for the Win32 subsystem so that the Win32 subsystem will receive a message when an exception occurs in the process. (For further information on exception handling, see Chapter 3.)

5. If the process is being debugged (that is, if it is attached to a debugger process), the process debug port is set to the Win32 subsystem's general function port. This setting ensures that Windows 2000 will send debug events that occur in the new process (such as thread creation and deletion, exceptions, and so on) as messages to the Win32 subsystem so that it can then dispatch the events to the process that is acting as the new process's debugger.

6. The Csrss thread block is allocated and initialized.

7. *CreateProcess* inserts the thread in the list of threads for the process.

8. The count of processes in this session is incremented.

9. The process shutdown level is set to x280 (the default process shutdown level—see *SetProcessShutdownParameters* in the MSDN Library documentation for more information).

10. The new process block is inserted into the list of Win32 subsystem-wide processes.

11. The per-process data structure used by the kernel-mode part of the Win32 subsystem (W32PROCESS structure) is allocated and initialized.

12. The application start cursor is displayed. This cursor is the familiar arrow with an hourglass attached—the way that Windows 2000 says to the user, "I'm starting something, but you can use the cursor in the meantime." If the process doesn't make a GUI call after 2 seconds, the cursor reverts to the standard pointer. If the process does make a GUI call in the allotted time, *CreateProcess* waits 5 seconds for the application to show a window. After that time, *CreateProcess* will reset the cursor again.

Stage 5: Starting Execution of the Initial Thread

At this point, the process environment has been determined, resources for its threads to use have been allocated, the process has a thread, and the Win32 subsystem knows about the new process. Unless the caller specified the CREATE_SUSPENDED flag, the initial thread is now resumed so that it can start running and perform the remainder of the process initialization work that occurs in the context of the new process (Stage 6).

Stage 6: Performing Process Initialization in the Context of the New Process

KiInitializeContextThread, which is called by *KeInitializeThread*, builds the initial context of the thread and the thread's kernel stack. The new thread begins life running the kernel-mode thread startup routine *KiThreadStartup*. (For a more detailed description of the thread startup steps leading to this, see the section "Flow of *CreateThread*" on page 333.) The *KiThreadStartup* routine performs the following steps:

1. Lowers the IRQL level from DPC/dispatch level to APC (asynchronous procedure call) level.

2. Enables working set expansion.

3. Queues a user-mode APC to the new thread to execute the user-mode thread startup routine *LdrInitializeThunk* inside Ntdll.dll.

4. Lowers the IRQL level to 0, causing the APC to fire and *LdrInitializeThunk* to be called. The *LdrInitializeThunk* routine initializes the loader, heap manager, NLS tables, thread-local storage (TLS) array, and critical section structures. It then loads any required DLLs and calls the DLL entry points with the DLL_PROCESS_ATTACH function code.

5. If the process being created is a debuggee, all threads in the process are suspended. (Threads might have been created during step 3.) A create process message is then sent to the process's debug port (the Win32 subsystem function port because this is a Win32 process) so that the subsystem can deliver the process startup debug event (CREATE_PROCESS_DEBUG_INFO) to the appropriate debugger process. *KiThreadStartup* then waits for the Win32 subsystem to get the reply from the debugger (via the *ContinueDebugEvent* function). When the Win32 subsystem replies, all the threads are resumed.

6. Finally, the image begins execution in user mode. This is done by creating a trap frame that specifies the previous mode as user and the address to return to as the main entry point of the image. Thus, when the trap that caused the thread to start execution in kernel mode is dismissed, the program begins running in user mode at the right place.

Thread Internals

Now that we've dissected processes, let's turn our attention to the structure of a thread. Unless explicitly stated otherwise, you can assume that anything in this section applies to both normal user-mode threads and kernel-mode system threads (described in Chapter 3).

Data Structures

At the operating system level, a Windows 2000 thread is represented by an executive thread (ETHREAD) block, which is illustrated in Figure 6-7. The ETHREAD block and the structures it points to exist in the system address space, with the exception of the thread environment block (TEB), which exists in the process address space. In addition, the Win32 subsystem process (Csrss) maintains a parallel structure for each thread created in a Win32 process. Also, for threads that have called a Win32 subsystem USER or GDI function, the kernel-mode portion of the Win32 subsystem (Win32k.sys) maintains a per-thread data structure (called the W32THREAD structure) that the ETHREAD block points to.

Figure 6-7
Structure of the executive thread block

Fibers vs. Threads

Fibers allow an application to schedule its own "threads" of execution rather than rely on the priority-based scheduling mechanism built into Windows 2000. Fibers are often called "lightweight" threads, and in terms of scheduling, they're invisible to the kernel because they're implemented in user mode in Kernel32.dll. To use fibers, a call is first made to the Win32 *ConvertThreadToFiber* function. This function converts the thread to a running fiber. Afterward, the newly converted fiber can create additional fibers with the *CreateFiber* function. (Each fiber can have its own set of fibers.) Unlike a thread, however, a fiber doesn't begin execution until it's manually selected through a call to the *SwitchToFiber* function. The new fiber runs until it exits or until it calls *SwitchToFiber*, again selecting another fiber to run. For more information, see the Platform SDK documentation on fiber functions.

Most of the fields illustrated in Figure 6-7 are self-explanatory. The first field is the kernel thread (KTHREAD) block. Following that are the thread identification information, the process identification information (including

a pointer to the owning process so that its environment information can be accessed), security information in the form of a pointer to the access token and impersonation information, and finally, fields relating to LPC messages and pending I/O requests. As you can see in Table 6-9, some of these key fields are covered in more detail elsewhere in this book.

Table 6-9 Key Contents of the Executive Thread Block

Element	Description	Additional Reference
KTHREAD block	See Table 6-10	Page 320
Thread time information	Thread create and exit time	
Process identification	Process ID and pointer to EPROCESS block of the process that the thread belongs to	
Start address	Address of thread start routine	
Impersonation information	Access token and impersonation level (if the thread is impersonating a client)	Security (Chapter 8)
LPC information	Message ID that the thread is waiting for and address of message	Local procedure calls (Chapter 3, page 171)
I/O information	List of pending I/O request packets (IRPs)	I/O system (Chapter 9)

For more details on the internal structure of an ETHREAD block, you can use the kernel debugger *!threadfields* or *!kdex2x86.strct ethread* command to display the offsets in hexadecimal for almost every field in the structure. Although many of the field names are self-explanatory, the output doesn't give the data type of the fields, nor does it show the format of the structures that are included within or pointed to by the ETHREAD block.

Let's take a closer look at two of the key thread data structures referred to above: the KTHREAD block and the TEB. The KTHREAD block contains the information that the Windows 2000 kernel needs to access to perform thread scheduling and synchronization on behalf of running threads. Its layout is illustrated in Figure 6-8.

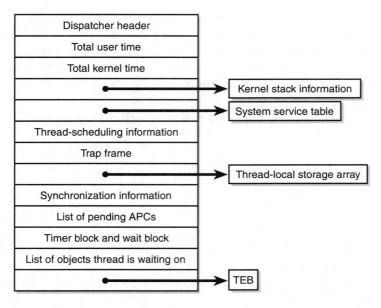

Figure 6-8
Structure of the kernel thread block

The key fields of the KTHREAD block are described briefly in Table 6-10.

Table 6-10 Key Contents of the KTHREAD Block

Element	Description	Additional Reference
Dispatcher header	Because the thread is an object that can be waited on, it starts with a standard kernel dispatcher object header.	Dispatcher objects (Chapter 3, page 158)
Execution time	Total user and kernel CPU time.	
Pointer to kernel stack information	Base and upper address of the kernel stack.	Memory management (Chapter 7)
Pointer to system service table	Each thread starts out with this field pointing to the main system service table (*KeServiceDescriptorTable*). When a thread first calls a Win32 GUI service, its system service table is changed to one that includes the GDI and USER services in Win32k.sys.	System service dispatching (Chapter 3, page 121)
Scheduling information	Base and current priority, quantum, affinity mask, ideal processor, scheduling state, freeze count, and suspend count.	Thread scheduling (page 337)

Element	Description	Additional Reference
Wait blocks	The thread block contains four built-in wait blocks so that wait blocks don't have to be allocated and initialized each time the thread waits on something. (One wait block is dedicated to timers.)	Synchronization (Chapter 3, page 134)
Wait information	List of objects the thread is waiting on, wait reason, and time at which the thread entered the wait state.	Synchronization (page 134)
Mutant list	List of mutant objects the thread owns.	Synchronization (page 134)
APC queues	List of pending user-mode and kernel-mode APCs, and alertable flag.	APC queues (Chapter 3, page 111)
Timer block	Built-in timer block (also a corresponding wait block).	
Queue list	Pointer to queue object that the thread is associated with.	Synchronization (page 134)
Pointer to TEB	Thread ID, TLS information, PEB pointer, and GDI and OpenGL information.	

EXPERIMENT: Displaying ETHREAD and KTHREAD Structures

Although you can use the kernel debugger command *!threadfields* to see information similar to that in the output of *!processfields* shown in the experiment on page 280, you'll get more detailed output of the fields in ETHREAD and KTHREAD blocks if you use *!ethread*. The *!ethread* command is one of the commands provided in Kdex2x86.dll, the secondary kernel debugger extension DLL. To use these extension commands, you must first load this DLL as shown in the following output listing. The *!ethread* command takes the address of an ETHREAD block and displays both the KTHREAD and the ETHREAD blocks that follow. In the following example, we used *!process* to dump a process and find the address of the ETHREAD blocks for the threads in the process. The output looks like this:

```
kd> .load kdex2x86
kd> !process 2c8 2
Searching for Process with Cid == 2c8
```

(continued)

EXPERIMENT: Displaying ETHREAD and KTHREAD Structures *continued*

```
PROCESS 810bad70  SessionId: 0  Cid: 02c8  Peb: 7ffdf000 ParentCid: 0430
    DirBase: 04e4c000  ObjectTable: 81114628  TableSize:  42.
    Image: notepad.exe

        THREAD 810a4310  Cid 2c8.5a4  Teb: 7ffde000
            Win32Thread: e267f908 WAIT:
    (WrUserRequest) UserMode Non-Alertable
            842f75b0  SynchronizationEvent

        THREAD 8112f710  Cid 2c8.5bc  Teb: 7ffdd000
            Win32Thread: 00000000 WAIT:
    (WrLpcReceive) UserMode Non-Alertable
            8109a0a8  Semaphore Limit 0x7fffffff

kd> !ethread 8112f710
struct   _ETHREAD (sizeof=584)
+000 struct   _KTHREAD Tcb
+000    struct   _DISPATCHER_HEADER Header
+000       byte     Type =              06
+001       byte     Absolute =          00
+002       byte     Size =              6c
+003       byte     Inserted =          00
+004       int32    SignalState =       00000000
+008       struct   _LIST_ENTRY WaitListHead
+008          struct   _LIST_ENTRY *Flink =    8112F718
+00c          struct   _LIST_ENTRY *Blink =    8112F718
+010    struct   _LIST_ENTRY MutantListHead
+010       struct   _LIST_ENTRY *Flink =    8112F720
+014       struct   _LIST_ENTRY *Blink =    8112F720
+018    void     *InitialStack =     BDEBD000
+01c    void     *StackLimit =       BDEBA000
+020    void     *Teb =              7FFDD000
+024    void     *TlsArray =         00000000
+028    void     *KernelStack =      BDEBCC48
+02c    byte     DebugActive =       00
+02d    byte     State =             05
+02e    byte     Alerted[2] =        00 00
+030    byte     Iopl =              00
+031    byte     NpxState =          0a
+032    char     Saturation =        00
+033    char     Priority =          08
+034    struct   _KAPC_STATE ApcState
+034       struct   _LIST_ENTRY ApcListHead[2]
+034             ApcListHead[0]
```

```
+034                   struct   _LIST_ENTRY *Flink =           8112F744
+038                   struct   _LIST_ENTRY *Blink =           8112F744
+03c           ApcListHead[1]
+03c                   struct   _LIST_ENTRY *Flink =           8112F74C
+040                   struct   _LIST_ENTRY *Blink =           8112F74C
+044     struct   _KPROCESS *Process =           810BAD70
+048     byte     KernelApcInProgress =          00
+049     byte     KernelApcPending =             00
+04a     byte     UserApcPending =               00
+04c     uint32   ContextSwitches =              00000003
+050     int32    WaitStatus =                   00000000
+054     byte     WaitIrql =                     00
+055     char     WaitMode =                     01
+056     byte     WaitNext =                     00
+057     byte     WaitReason =                   10
+058     struct   _KWAIT_BLOCK *WaitBlockList =  8112F77C
+05c     struct   _LIST_ENTRY WaitListEntry
+05c         struct   _LIST_ENTRY *Flink =       84F478AC
+060         struct   _LIST_ENTRY *Blink =       8114458C
+064     uint32   WaitTime =                     00064800
+068     char     BasePriority =                 08
+069     byte     DecrementCount =               00
+06a     char     PriorityDecrement =            00
+06b     char     Quantum =                      05
+06c     struct   _KWAIT_BLOCK WaitBlock[4]
+06c           WaitBlock[0]
+06c             struct   _LIST_ENTRY WaitListEntry
+06c               struct   _LIST_ENTRY *Flink =         8109A0B0
+070               struct   _LIST_ENTRY *Blink =         8109A0B0
+074           struct   _KTHREAD *Thread =   8112F710
+078           void     *Object =            8109A0A8
+07c           struct   _KWAIT_BLOCK *NextWaitBlock =    8112F77C
+080           uint16   WaitKey =            0000
+082           uint16   WaitType =           0001
   :
    (three more wait blocks)
   :
+0cc     void     *LegoData =                    00000000
+0d0     uint32   KernelApcDisable =             00000000
+0d4     uint32   UserAffinity =                 00000001
+0d8     byte     SystemAffinityActive =         00
+0d9     byte     PowerState =                   00
+0da     byte     NpxIrql =                      00
+0db     byte     Pad[1] =                       00
+0dc     void     *ServiceTable =                8046AB80
+0e0     struct   _KQUEUE *Queue =               00000000
+0e4     uint32   ApcQueueLock =                 00000000
```

(continued)

EXPERIMENT: Displaying ETHREAD and KTHREAD Structures *continued*

```
+0e8    struct   _KTIMER Timer
+0e8      struct   _DISPATCHER_HEADER Header
+0e8        byte     Type =                   08
+0e9        byte     Absolute =               00
+0ea        byte     Size =                   0a
+0eb        byte     Inserted =               00
+0ec        int32    SignalState =            00000001
+0f0        struct   _LIST_ENTRY WaitListHead
+0f0          struct   _LIST_ENTRY *Flink =   8112F800
+0f4          struct   _LIST_ENTRY *Blink =   8112F800
+0f8      union    _ULARGE_INTEGER DueTime
+0f8        uint32   LowPart =                9925c310
+0fc        uint32   HighPart =               00000009
+0f8        struct   __unnamed12 u
+0f8          uint32   LowPart =              9925c310
+0fc          uint32   HighPart =             00000009
+0f8        uint64   QuadPart =               000000099925c310
+100      struct   _LIST_ENTRY TimerListEntry
+100        struct   _LIST_ENTRY *Flink =     81BDBEB0
+104        struct   _LIST_ENTRY *Blink =     8046FD70
+108      struct   _KDPC *Dpc =               00000000
+10c      int32    Period =                   00000000
+110    struct   _LIST_ENTRY QueueListEntry
+110      struct   _LIST_ENTRY *Flink =       00000000
+114      struct   _LIST_ENTRY *Blink =       00000000
+118    uint32   Affinity =                   00000001
+11c    byte     Preempted =                  00
+11d    byte     ProcessReadyQueue =          00
+11e    byte     KernelStackResident =        00
+11f    byte     NextProcessor =              00
+120    void     *CallbackStack =             00000000
+124    void     *Win32Thread =               00000000
+128    struct   _KTRAP_FRAME *TrapFrame =    BDEBCD64
+12c    struct   _KAPC_STATE *ApcStatePointer[2] =     8112F744
                                                       8112F850
+134    char     PreviousMode =               01
+135    byte     EnableStackSwap =            01
+136    byte     LargeStack =                 00
+137    byte     ResourceIndex =              00
+138    uint32   KernelTime =                 00000000
+13c    uint32   UserTime =                   00000000
+140    struct   _KAPC_STATE SavedApcState
+140      struct   _LIST_ENTRY ApcListHead[2]
+140              ApcListHead[0]
+140                struct   _LIST_ENTRY *Flink =       00000000
+144                struct   _LIST_ENTRY *Blink =       00000000
+148              ApcListHead[1]
```

```
+148                   struct   _LIST_ENTRY *Flink =            00000000
+14c                   struct   _LIST_ENTRY *Blink =            00000000
+150    struct   _KPROCESS *Process =           00000000
+154    byte     KernelApcInProgress =          00
+155    byte     KernelApcPending =             00
+156    byte     UserApcPending =               00
+158  byte     Alertable =               00
+159  byte     ApcStateIndex =           00
+15a  byte     ApcQueueable =            01
+15b  byte     AutoAlignment =           00
+15c  void     *StackBase =              BDEBD000
+160  struct   _KAPC SuspendApc
+160     int16    Type =                 0012
+162     int16    Size =                 0030
+164     uint32   Spare0 =               00000000
+168     struct   _KTHREAD *Thread =     8112F710
+16c     struct   _LIST_ENTRY ApcListEntry
+16c        struct   _LIST_ENTRY *Flink =     8112F744
+170        struct   _LIST_ENTRY *Blink =     8112F744
+174     function *KernelRoutine =       80430B27
+178     function *RundownRoutine =      00000000
+17c     function *NormalRoutine =       80430E2B
+180     void     *NormalContext =       00000000
+184     void     *SystemArgument1 =     00000000
+188     void     *SystemArgument2 =     00000000
+18c     char     ApcStateIndex =        00
+18d     char     ApcMode =              00
+18e     byte     Inserted =             00
+190  struct   _KSEMAPHORE SuspendSemaphore
+190     struct   _DISPATCHER_HEADER Header
+190        byte     Type =              05
+191        byte     Absolute =          00
+192        byte     Size =              05
+193        byte     Inserted =          00
+194        int32    SignalState =       00000000
+198        struct   _LIST_ENTRY WaitListHead
+198           struct   _LIST_ENTRY *Flink =   8112F8A8

+19c           struct   _LIST_ENTRY *Blink =   8112F8A8
+1a0     int32    Limit =                00000002
+1a4  struct   _LIST_ENTRY ThreadListEntry
+1a4     struct   _LIST_ENTRY *Flink =   810BADC0
+1a8     struct   _LIST_ENTRY *Blink =   810A44B4
+1ac  char     FreezeCount =             00
+1ad  char     SuspendCount =            00
+1ae  byte     IdealProcessor =          00
+1af  byte     DisableBoost =            00
```

(continued)

EXPERIMENT: Displaying ETHREAD and KTHREAD Structures *continued*

```
+1b0 union    _LARGE_INTEGER CreateTime
+1b0    uint32   LowPart =                      ade71268
+1b4    int32    HighPart =                     0dfd0747
+1b0    struct   __unnamed3 u
+1b0       uint32   LowPart =                   ade71268
+1b4       int32    HighPart =                  0dfd0747
+1b0       int64    QuadPart =                  0dfd0747ade71268
+1b0 bits0-1 NestedFaultCount =                0
+1b0 bits2-2 ApcNeeded =                       0
+1b8 union    _LARGE_INTEGER ExitTime
+1b8    uint32   LowPart =                      8112f8c8
+1bc    int32    HighPart =                     8112f8c8
+1b8    struct   __unnamed3 u
+1b8       uint32   LowPart =                   8112f8c8
+1bc       int32    HighPart =                  8112f8c8
+1b8       int64    QuadPart =                  8112f8c88112f8c8
+1b8 struct   _LIST_ENTRY LpcReplyChain
+1b8    struct   _LIST_ENTRY *Flink =           8112F8C8
+1bc    struct   _LIST_ENTRY *Blink =           8112F8C8
+1c0 int32    ExitStatus =                      00000000
+1c0 void     *OfsChain =                       00000000
+1c4 struct   _LIST_ENTRY PostBlockList
+1c4    struct   _LIST_ENTRY *Flink =           8112F8D4
+1c8    struct   _LIST_ENTRY *Blink =           8112F8D4
+1cc struct   _LIST_ENTRY TerminationPortList
+1cc    struct   _LIST_ENTRY *Flink =           E252C508
+1d0    struct   _LIST_ENTRY *Blink =           E252C508
+1d4 uint32   ActiveTimerListLock =             00000000
+1d8 struct   _LIST_ENTRY ActiveTimerListHead
+1d8    struct   _LIST_ENTRY *Flink =           8112F8E8
+1dc    struct   _LIST_ENTRY *Blink =           8112F8E8
+1e0 struct   _CLIENT_ID Cid
+1e0    void     *UniqueProcess =               000002C8
+1e4    void     *UniqueThread =                000005BC
+1e8 struct   _KSEMAPHORE LpcReplySemaphore
+1e8    struct   _DISPATCHER_HEADER Header
+1e8       byte     Type =                      05
+1e9       byte     Absolute =                  00
+1ea       byte     Size =                      05
+1eb       byte     Inserted =                  00
+1ec       int32    SignalState =               00000000
+1f0       struct   _LIST_ENTRY WaitListHead
+1f0          struct   _LIST_ENTRY *Flink =     8112F900
+1f4          struct   _LIST_ENTRY *Blink =     8112F900
+1f8    int32    Limit =                        00000001
```

```
+1fc void     *LpcReplyMessage =              00000000
+200 uint32   LpcReplyMessageId =             00000000
+204 uint32   PerformanceCountLow =           00000000
+208 struct _PS_IMPERSONATION_INFORMATION *ImpersonationInfo = 00000000
+20c struct   _LIST_ENTRY IrpList
+20c    struct   _LIST_ENTRY *Flink =         8112F91C
+210    struct   _LIST_ENTRY *Blink =         8112F91C
+214 uint32   TopLevelIrp =                   00000000
+218 struct   _DEVICE_OBJECT *DeviceToVerify =  00000000
+21c uint32   ReadClusterSize =               00000007
+220 byte     ForwardClusterOnly =            00
+221 byte     DisablePageFaultClustering =    00
+222 byte     DeadThread =                    00
+223 byte     HideFromDebugger =              00
+224 uint32   HasTerminated =                 00000000
+228 uint32   GrantedAccess =                 001f03ff
+22c struct   _EPROCESS *ThreadsProcess =     810BAD70
+230 void     *StartAddress =                 77E92C50
+234 void     *Win32StartAddress =            77D4B759
+234 uint32   LpcReceivedMessageId =          77d4b759
+238 byte     LpcExitThreadCalled =           00
+239 byte     HardErrorsAreDisabled =         00
+23a byte     LpcReceivedMsgIdValid =         00
+23b byte     ActiveImpersonationInfo =       00
+23c int32    PerformanceCountHigh =          00000000
+240 struct   _LIST_ENTRY ThreadListEntry
+240    struct   _LIST_ENTRY *Flink =         810BAFE0
+244    struct   _LIST_ENTRY *Blink =         810A4550
```

The TEB, illustrated in Figure 6-9, is the only data structure explained in this section that exists in the process address space (as opposed to the system space).

The TEB stores context information for the image loader and various Win32 DLLs. Because these components run in user mode, they need a data structure writable from user mode. That's why this structure exists in the process address space instead of in the system space, where it would be writable only from kernel mode. You can find the address of the TEB with the kernel debugger *!thread* command.

Exception list
Stack base
Stack limit
● → Subsystem thread information block (TIB)
● → Fiber information
Thread ID
Active RPC handle
● → PEB
LastError value
Count of owned critical sections
Current locale
User32 client information
GDI32 information
OpenGL information
TLS array
● → Winsock data

Figure 6-9
Fields of the thread environment block

EXPERIMENT: Examining the TEB

You can dump the TEB structure with the *!teb* command in the kernel debugger. The output looks like this:

```
kd> !teb
TEB at 7FFDE000
    ExceptionList:      12ffb0
    Stack Base:         130000
    Stack Limit:        12d000
    SubSystemTib:       0
    FiberData:          1e00
    ArbitraryUser:      0
    Self:               7ffde000
    EnvironmentPtr:     0
    ClientId:           490.458
    Real ClientId:      490.458
    RpcHandle:          0
    Tls Storage:        0
```

```
PEB Address:        7ffdf000
LastErrorValue:     0
LastStatusValue:    0
Count Owned Locks:0
HardErrorsMode:     0
```

Kernel Variables

As with processes, a number of Windows 2000 kernel variables control how threads run. Table 6-11 shows the kernel-mode kernel variables that relate to threads.

Table 6-11 Thread-Related Kernel Variables

Variable	Type	Description
PspCreateThreadNotifyRoutine	Array of pointers	Array of pointers to routines to be called on during thread creation and deletion (maximum of eight).
PspCreateThreadNotifyRoutineCount	DWORD	Count of registered thread-notification routines.
PspCreateProcessNotifyRoutine	Array of pointers	Array of pointers to routines to be called on during process creation and deletion (maximum of eight).
PspCreate ProcessNotifyRoutineCount	DWORD	Count of registered process-notification routines.
PspCidTable	Handle table	Handle table that stores process and thread objects. Using a thread's or process's handle value as its thread or process ID guarantees uniqueness.

Performance Counters

Most of the key information in the thread data structures is exported as performance counters, which are listed in Table 6-12. You can extract much information about the internals of a thread just by using the Performance tool in Windows 2000.

Table 6-12 Thread-Related Performance Counters

Object: Counter	Function
Process: Priority Base	Returns the current base priority of the process. This is the starting priority for threads created within this process.
Thread: % Privileged Time	Describes the percentage of time that the thread has run in kernel mode during a specified interval.

Table 6-12 *continued*

Object: Counter	Function
Thread: % Processor Time	Describes the percentage of CPU time that the thread has used during a specified interval. This count is the sum of % Privileged Time and % User Time.
Thread: % User Time	Describes the percentage of time that the thread has run in user mode during a specified interval.
Thread: Context Switches/Sec	Returns the number of context switches per second that the system is executing. The higher this number, the more threads of an equal priority are attempting to execute.
Thread: Elapsed Time	Returns the amount of CPU time (in seconds) that the thread has consumed.
Thread: ID Process	Returns the process ID of the thread's process. This ID is valid only during the process's lifetime because process IDs are reused.
Thread: ID Thread	Returns the thread's thread ID. This ID is valid only during the thread's lifetime because thread IDs are reused.
Thread: Priority Base	Returns the thread's current base priority. This number might be different from the thread's starting base priority.
Thread: Priority Current	Returns the thread's current dynamic priority.
Thread: Start Address	Returns the thread's starting virtual address (*Note*: This address will be the same for most threads.)
Thread: Thread State	Returns a value from 0 through 7 relating to the current state of the thread.
Thread: Thread Wait Reason	Returns a value from 0 through 19 relating to the reason why the thread is in a wait state.

Relevant Functions

Table 6-13 shows the Win32 functions for creating and manipulating threads. This table doesn't include functions that have to do with thread scheduling and priorities—those are included in the section "Thread Scheduling" later in this chapter.

Table 6-13 Win32 Thread Functions

Function	Description
CreateThread	Creates a new thread
CreateRemoteThread	Creates a thread in another process
ExitThread	Ends execution of a thread normally
TerminateThread	Terminates a thread
GetExitCodeThread	Gets another thread's exit code
GetThreadTimes	Returns another thread's timing information

Function	Description
Get/SetThreadContext	Returns or changes a thread's CPU registers
GetThreadSelectorEntry	Returns another thread's descriptor table entry (applies only to x86 systems)

Relevant Tools

Besides the Performance tool, several other tools expose various elements of the state of Windows 2000 threads. (The tools that show thread-scheduling information are listed in the section "Thread Scheduling" on page 337.) These tools are itemized in Table 6-14.

> **NOTE** To display thread details with Tlist, you must type *tlist xxx*, where *xxx* is a process image name or window title. (Wildcards are supported.)

Table 6-14 Thread-Related Tools and Their Functions

Object	Perfmon	Pview	Pviewer	Pstat	Qslice	Tlist	KD !thread
Thread ID	✓	✓		✓		✓	✓
Actual start address	✓	✓	✓	✓			✓
Win32 start address						✓	✓
Current address	✓	✓	✓				✓
Number of context switches	✓	✓	✓	✓			
Total user time		✓		✓			✓
Total privileged time		✓		✓			✓
Elapsed time	✓	✓					✓
Thread state	✓			✓		✓	✓
Reason for wait state	✓			✓		✓	✓
Last error						✓	
Security descriptor			✓				
Access token			✓				
Percentage of CPU time	✓				✓		
Percentage of user time	✓		✓		✓		
Percentage of privileged time	✓		✓		✓		
Address of TEB							✓
Address of ETHREAD							✓
Objects waiting on							✓

EXPERIMENT: Using the Kernel Debugger *!thread* Command

The kernel debugger *!thread* command dumps a subset of the information in the thread data structures. Some key elements of the information the kernel debugger displays can't be displayed by any Windows 2000 utility: internal structure addresses; priority details; stack information; the pending I/O request list; and, for threads in a wait state, the list of objects the thread is waiting on. (Refer to Table 6-14.)

To display thread information, use either the *!process* command (which displays all the thread blocks after displaying the process block) or the *!thread* command to dump a specific thread. The output of the thread information, along with some annotations of key fields, is shown here:

EXPERIMENT: Viewing Thread Information

The following output is the detailed display of a process produced by using the Tlist utility in the Windows 2000 Support Tools. Notice that the thread list shows the Win32 start address. (All the other utilities that show the thread start address show the actual start address, not the Win32 start address.)

```
C:\> tlist winword
  155 WINWORD.EXE         Document1 - Microsoft Word
    CWD:      C:\book\
    CmdLine: "C:\Program Files\Microsoft Office\Office\WINWORD.EXE"
    VirtualSize:     64448 KB    PeakVirtualSize:    106748 KB
    WorkingSetSize: 1104 KB     PeakWorkingSetSize:  6776 KB
    NumberOfThreads: 2
     156 Win32StartAddr:0x5032cfdb LastErr:0x00000000 State:Waiting
     167 Win32StartAddr:0x00022982 LastErr:0x00000000 State:Waiting
                   0x50000000  WINWORD.EXE
     5.0.2163.1 shp  0x77f60000  ntdll.dll
     5.0.2191.1 shp  0x77f00000  KERNEL32.dll
      :
          list of DLLs loaded in process
```

Flow of *CreateThread*

A thread's life cycle starts when a program creates a new thread. The request filters down to the Windows 2000 executive, where the process manager allocates space for a thread object and calls the kernel to initialize the kernel thread block. The steps in the following list are taken inside the Win32 *CreateThread* function in Kernel32.dll to create a Win32 thread. The work that occurs inside the Windows 2000 executive are substeps of step 3, and the work that occurs in the context of the new thread are substeps of step 7. Because process creation includes creating a thread, some of the information here is repeated from the earlier description of the flow of *CreateProcess*.

1. *CreateThread* creates a user-mode stack for the thread in the process's address space.

2. *CreateThread* initializes the thread's hardware context (CPU architecture–specific). (For further information on the thread context block, see the Win32 API reference documentation on the CONTEXT structure.)

3. *NtCreateThread* is called to create the executive thread object in the suspended state. The following steps execute in kernel mode inside the Windows 2000 executive and kernel:

 a. The thread count in the process object is incremented.

 b. An executive thread block (ETHREAD) is created and initialized.

 c. A thread ID is generated for the new thread.

 d. The thread's kernel stack is allocated from the nonpaged pool.

 e. The TEB is set up in the user-mode address space of the process.

 f. The thread start address (*KiThreadStartup*) is stored on the kernel stack. (The kernel stack address is stored in the KTHREAD.) The user's specified Win32 start address is stored in the ETHREAD block.

 g. *KeInitializeThread* is called to set up the KTHREAD block. The thread's initial and current base priorities are set to the process's base priority, and its affinity and quantum are set to that of the process. This function also sets the initial thread ideal processor based on the process thread seed (a random number set during execution of *CreateProcess*). The seed is then incremented so that each thread in the process will have a different ideal processor, assuming the system has more than one. *KeInitializeThread* next sets the thread's state to Initialized and initializes the machine-dependent hardware context for the thread, including the context, trap, and exception frames. The thread's context is set up so that the thread will start in kernel mode in *SwapContext*, the context switch code. *SwapContext* loads the thread's context from the thread's kernel stack, which results in the thread starting its execution in the systemwide startup routine *KiThreadStartup* (described in step 6a), the function that was stored in the stack by step 3f.

 h. Any registered systemwide thread creation notification routines are called.

 i. The thread's access token is set to point to the process access token, and an access check is made to determine whether the caller has the right to create the thread. This check will always succeed if you're creating a thread in the local process but might fail if you're using *CreateRemoteThread* to create a thread in another process and the process creating the thread doesn't have the debug privilege enabled.

4. *CreateThread* notifies the Win32 subsystem about the new thread, and the subsystem does some setup work for the new thread.

5. The thread handle and the thread ID (generated during step 3) are returned to the caller.

6. Unless the caller created the thread with the CREATE_SUSPENDED flag set, the thread is now resumed so that it can be scheduled for execution. When the thread starts running, it executes the following additional steps (in the context of the new thread) before calling the actual user's specified start address. (A flowchart of this final part of thread creation is shown in Figure 6-10.)

 a. *KiThreadStartup* lowers the thread's IRQL level from DPC/dispatch level to APC level and then calls the system initial thread routine, *PspUserThreadStartup*. The user-specified thread start address is passed as a parameter to this routine.

 b. The system initial thread routine enables working set expansion and then queues a user-mode APC to run the image loader initialization routine (*LdrInitializeThunk* in Ntdll.dll). The IRQL is lowered to 0, thus causing the pending APC to fire.

 c. The loader initialization routine then performs a number of additional thread-specific initialization steps, such as calling loaded DLLs to notify them of the new thread. (The detailed steps of the initialization of the Win32 subsystem DLLs, such as USER32, KERNEL32, and GDI32, are beyond the scope of this book.)

 d. If the process has a debugger attached, the thread startup routine suspends all other active threads in the process and notifies the Win32 subsystem so that it can deliver the thread startup debug event (CREATE_THREAD_DEBUG_INFO) to the appropriate debugger process. The startup routine then waits for the Win32 subsystem to get the reply from the debugger (via the *Continue-DebugEvent* function). When the Win32 subsystem receives a reply from the debugger, it in turn replies to the thread startup routine and all the threads are resumed.

 e. Finally, the main thread begins execution in user mode at the entry point to the image being run. Execution begins when the trap that started the thread execution, using a trap frame (built earlier when the kernel thread block was being initialized) that specifies previous mode as user and the PC as the start address of the thread, is dismissed.

Figure 6-10
In-context thread initialization

Thread Scheduling

This section describes the Windows 2000 scheduling policies and algorithms. The first subsection provides a condensed description of how scheduling works on Windows 2000 and a definition of key terms. Then Windows 2000 priority levels are described from both the Win32 API and the Windows 2000 kernel points of view. After a review of the relevant Win32 functions and Windows 2000 utilities and tools that relate to scheduling, the detailed data structures and algorithms that comprise the Windows 2000 scheduling system are presented.

Overview of Windows 2000 Scheduling

Windows 2000 implements a priority-driven, preemptive scheduling system—the highest-priority runnable (*ready*) thread always runs, with the caveat that the thread chosen to run might be limited by the processors on which the thread is allowed to run, a phenomenon called *processor affinity*. By default, threads can run on any available processor, but you can alter processor affinity by using one of the Win32 scheduling functions.

EXPERIMENT: Viewing Ready Threads

You can view the list of ready threads with the kernel debugger *!ready* command. This command displays the thread or list of threads that are ready to run at each priority level. In the following example, two threads are ready to run at priority 10 and six at priority 8. Because this output was generated using LiveKd on a uniprocessor system, the current thread will always be the kernel debugger (Kd or I386kd).

```
kd> !ready 1
Ready Threads at priority 10
  THREAD 810de030  Cid 490.4a8  Teb: 7ffd9000  Win32Thread: e297e008 READY
  THREAD 81110030  Cid 490.48c  Teb: 7ffde000  Win32Thread: e29425a8 READY
Ready Threads at priority 8
  THREAD 811fe790  Cid 23c.274  Teb: 7ffdb000  Win32Thread: e258cda8 READY
  THREAD 810bec70  Cid 23c.50c  Teb: 7ffd9000  Win32Thread: e2ccf748 READY
  THREAD 8003a950  Cid 23c.550  Teb: 7ffda000  Win32Thread: e29a7ae8 READY
  THREAD 85ac2db0  Cid 23c.5e4  Teb: 7ffd8000  Win32Thread: e297a9e8 READY
  THREAD 827318d0  Cid 514.560  Teb: 7ffd9000  Win32Thread: 00000000 READY
  THREAD 8117adb0  Cid 2d4.338  Teb: 7ffaf000  Win32Thread: 00000000 READY
```

When a thread is selected to run, it runs for an amount of time called a *quantum*. A quantum is the length of time a thread is allowed to run before Windows 2000 interrupts the thread to find out whether another thread at the same priority level or higher is waiting to run or whether the thread's priority needs to be reduced. Quantum values can vary from thread to thread (and differ between Windows 2000 Professional and Windows 2000 Server). (Quantums are described in more detail on page 349.) A thread might not get to complete its quantum, however. Because Windows 2000 implements a preemptive scheduler, if another thread with a higher priority becomes ready to run, the currently running thread might be preempted before finishing its time slice. In fact, a thread can be selected to run next and be preempted before even beginning its quantum!

The Windows 2000 scheduling code is implemented in the kernel. There's no single "scheduler" module or routine, however—the code is spread throughout the kernel in which scheduling-related events occur. The routines that perform these duties are collectively called the kernel's *dispatcher*. Thread dispatching occurs at DPC/dispatch level and is triggered by any of the following events:

- A thread becomes ready to execute—for example, a thread has been newly created or has just been released from the wait state.

- A thread leaves the running state because its time quantum ends, it terminates, or it enters a wait state.

- A thread's priority changes, either because of a system service call or because Windows 2000 itself changes the priority value.

- The processor affinity of a running thread changes.

At each of these junctions, Windows 2000 must determine which thread should run next. When Windows 2000 selects a new thread to run, it performs a *context switch* to it. A context switch is the procedure of saving the volatile machine state associated with a running thread, loading another thread's volatile state, and starting the new thread's execution.

As already noted, Windows 2000 schedules at the thread granularity. This approach makes sense when you consider that processes don't run but only provide resources and a context in which their threads run. Because scheduling decisions are made strictly on a thread basis, no consideration is given to what process the thread belongs to. For example, if process *A* has 10 runnable threads and process *B* has 2 runnable threads, and all 12 threads are at the same priority, each thread would receive one-twelfth of the CPU time—Windows 2000 wouldn't give 50 percent of the CPU to process *A* and 50 percent to process *B*.

To understand the thread-scheduling algorithms, you must first understand the priority levels that Windows 2000 uses.

EXPERIMENT: Thread-Scheduling State Changes

You can watch thread-scheduling state changes with the Performance tool in Windows 2000. This utility can be useful when you're debugging a multithreaded application if you're unsure about the state of the threads running in the process. To watch thread-scheduling stage changes using the Performance tool, follow these steps:

1. Run the Microsoft Notepad utility (Notepad.exe).

2. Start the Performance tool by selecting Programs from the Start menu and then selecting Administrative Tools/ Performance.

3. Select chart view if you're in some other view.

4. Right-click on the graph, and choose Properties.

5. Click the Graph tab, and change the chart vertical scale maximum to 7. (As you'll see from the explanation text for the performance counter, thread states are numbers from 0 through 7.) Click OK.

6. Click the Add button on the toolbar to bring up the Add Counters dialog box.

7. Select the Thread performance object, and then select the Thread State counter. Click the Explain button to see the definition of the values:

8. In the Instances box, scroll down until you see the Notepad process (notepad/0); select it, and click the Add button.

9. Scroll back up in the Instances box to the Mmc process (the Microsoft Management Console process running the System Monitor ActiveX control), select all the threads (mmc/0, mmc/1, and so on), and add them to the chart by clicking the Add button. Before you click Add, you should see something like the following dialog box.

(continued)

EXPERIMENT: Thread-Scheduling State Changes *continued*

10. Now close the Add Counters dialog box by clicking Close.

11. You should see the state of the Notepad thread (the very top line in the following figure) as a 5, which, as shown in the explanation text you saw under step 5, represents the waiting state (because the thread is waiting for GUI input):

12. Notice that one thread in the Mmc process (running the Performance tool snap-in) is in the running state (number 2). This is the thread that's querying the thread states, so it's always displayed in the running state.

13. You'll never see Notepad in the running state (unless you're on a multiprocessor system) because Mmc is always in the running state when it gathers the state of the threads you're monitoring.

Priority Levels

As illustrated in Figure 6-11, internally, Windows 2000 uses 32 priority levels, ranging from 0 through 31. These values divide up as follows:

- Sixteen real-time levels (16–31)

- Fifteen variable levels (1–15)

- One system level (0), reserved for the zero page thread

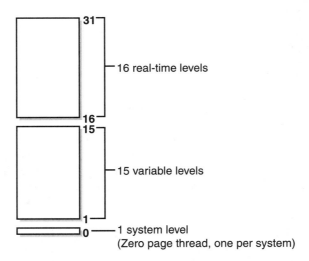

Figure 6-11
Thread priority levels

Thread priority levels are assigned from two different perspectives: those of the Win32 API and those of the Windows 2000 kernel. The Win32 API first

organizes processes by the priority class to which they are assigned at creation (Real-time, High, Above Normal, Normal, Below Normal, and Idle) and then by the relative priority of the individual threads within those processes (Time-critical, Highest, Above-normal, Normal, Below-normal, Lowest, and Idle).

In the Win32 API, each thread has a priority based on a combination of its process priority class and its relative thread priority. The mapping from Win32 priority to internal Windows 2000 numeric priority is shown in Figure 6-12.

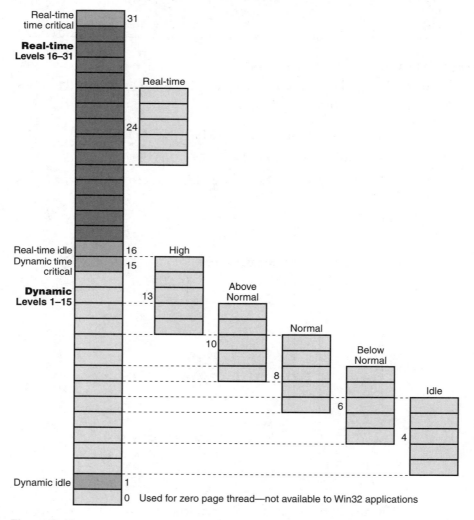

Figure 6-12
Kernel priorities in Win32 vs. Windows 2000

The priorities shown in Figure 6-12 are thread base priorities. Threads start out inheriting the process base priority, which can be changed with Task Manager (as described in the section "Relevant Tools" on the following page) or with the Win32 *SetPriorityClass* function.

Normally, the process base priority (and hence the starting-thread base priority) will default to the value at the middle of each process priority range (24, 13, 10, 8, 6, or 4). However, some Windows 2000 system processes (such as the Session Manager, service controller, and local security authentication server) have a base process priority slightly higher than the default for the Normal class (8). This higher default value ensures that the threads in these processes will all start at a higher priority than the default value of 8. A system process uses internal Windows 2000 functions to set its process base priority to a numeric value other than its default starting Win32 base priority.

Whereas a process has only a single priority value (base priority), each thread has two priority values: current and base. The current priority for threads in the dynamic range (1 through 15) might be, and often is, higher than the base priority. Windows 2000 never adjusts the priority of threads in the real-time range (16 through 31), so they always have the same base and current priority.

Win32 Scheduling APIs

The Win32 API functions that relate to thread scheduling are listed in Table 6-15. (For more information, see the Win32 API reference documentation.)

Table 6-15 **Scheduling-Related APIs and Their Functions**

API	Function
Suspend/ResumeThread	Suspends or resumes a paused thread from execution.
Get/SetPriorityClass	Returns or sets a process's priority class (base priority).
Get/SetThreadPriority	Returns or sets a thread's priority (relative to its process base priority).
Get/SetProcessAffinityMask	Returns or sets a process's affinity mask.
SetThreadAffinityMask	Sets a thread's affinity mask (must be a subset of the process's affinity mask) for a particular set of processors, restricting it to running on those processors.
Get/SetThreadPriorityBoost	Returns or sets the ability for Windows 2000 to boost the priority of a thread temporarily (applies only to threads in the dynamic range).

(continued)

Table 6-15 *continued*

API	Function
SetThreadIdealProcessor	Establishes a preferred processor for a particular thread but doesn't restrict the thread to that processor.
Get/SetProcessPriorityBoost	Returns or sets the default priority boost control state of the current process. (This function is used to set the thread priority boost control state when a thread is created.)
SwitchToThread	Yields execution for one or more quantums.
Sleep	Puts the current thread into a wait state for a specified time interval (figured in milliseconds [msec]). A zero value relinquishes the rest of the thread's quantum.
SleepEx	Causes the current thread to go into a wait state until either an I/O completion callback is completed, an APC is queued to the thread, or the specified time interval ends.

Relevant Tools

You can view (and change) the base-process priority class with Task Manager, Pview, or Pviewer. You can view the numeric base-process priority value with the Performance tool or Pstat. You can view thread priorities with the Performance tool, Pview, Pviewer, and Pstat. There is no general utility to change relative thread priority levels, however. Table 6-16 lists the tools related to thread scheduling.

Table 6-16 Tools Related to Thread Scheduling

Object	Taskman	Perfmon	Pviewer	Pview	Pstat	KD !thread
Process priority class	✓		✓	✓		
Process base priority		✓			✓	
Thread base priority		✓				
Thread current priority		✓	✓	✓	✓	✓

The only way to specify a starting priority class for a process is with the *start* command in the Windows 2000 command prompt.

EXPERIMENT: Examining and Specifying Process and Thread Priorities

Try the following experiment:

1. From the command prompt, type *start/realtime notepad*. Notepad should open.

2. Run the Process Viewer utility in the Support Tools (Pviewer.exe), and select Notepad.exe from the list of processes, as shown here. Notice that the dynamic priority of the thread in Notepad is 24. This matches the real-time value shown in Figure 6-12.

3. Task Manager can show you similar information. Press Ctrl+Shift+Esc to start Task Manager, and go to the Processes tab. Right-click on the Notepad.exe process, and select the Set Priority option. You can see that Notepad's process priority class is Realtime, as shown in the following dialog box.

(continued)

345

EXPERIMENT: Examining and Specifying Process and Thread Priorities *continued*

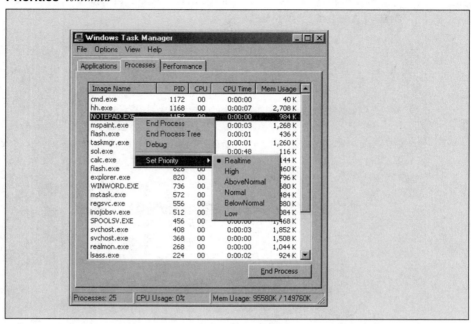

Real-Time Priorities

You can raise or lower thread priorities within the dynamic range in any application; however, you must have the *increase scheduling priority* privilege to enter the real-time range. (If you attempt to move a process into the Real-time priority class and don't have the privilege, the operation doesn't fail—the High class is used.)

Be aware that many important Windows 2000 kernel-mode system threads run in the real-time priority range, so if your process spends excessive time running in this range, it might be blocking critical system functions in the memory manager, cache manager, local and network file systems, and even other device drivers. It won't block hardware interrupts because they have a higher priority than any thread, but it might block system threads from running.

There is one behavioral difference for threads in the real-time range (mentioned in the section "Preemption" on page 356): their thread quantum is reset if they are preempted.

NOTE Although Windows 2000 has a set of priorities called *real-time*, they are not real-time in the common definition of the term in that Windows 2000 doesn't provide true real-time operating system facilities, such as guaranteed interrupt latency or a way for threads to obtain a guaranteed execution time. For more information, see the sidebar "Windows 2000 and Real-Time Processing" on page 105 in Chapter 3 as well as the MSDN Library article "Real-Time Systems and Microsoft Windows NT."

Interrupt Levels vs. Priority Levels

As illustrated in Figure 6-13, all threads run at IRQL 0 or 1. (For a description of how Windows 2000 uses interrupt levels, see page 000 in Chapter 3.) User-mode threads run at IRQL 0; only kernel-mode APCs execute at IRQL 1, since they interrupt the execution of a thread. (For more information on APCs, see page 111 in Chapter 3.) Also, threads running in kernel mode can raise IRQL. Because of this, no user-mode thread, regardless of its priority, blocks hardware interrupts (although high-priority real-time threads can block the execution of important system threads).

Figure 6-13
Interrupt priorities vs. thread priorities

Thread-scheduling decisions are made at DPC/dispatch level. Thus, while the kernel is deciding which thread should run next, no thread can be running and possibly changing scheduling-related information (such as priorities). On a multiprocessor system, access to the thread-scheduling data structures is synchronized by acquiring the Dispatcher spinlock (*KiDispatcherLock*).

Thread States

Before you can comprehend the thread-scheduling algorithms and data structures, you need to understand the various execution states that a thread can be in. Figure 6-14 illustrates the state transitions for a Windows 2000 thread. More details on what happens at each transition are included later in this section.

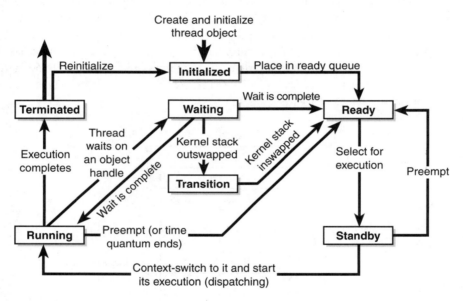

Figure 6-14
Thread states

The thread states are as follows:

- **Ready** When looking for a thread to execute, the dispatcher considers only the pool of threads in the ready state. These threads are simply waiting to execute.

■ **Standby** A thread in the standby state has been selected to run next on a particular processor. When the correct conditions exist, the dispatcher performs a context switch to this thread. Only one thread can be in the standby state for each processor on the system.

■ **Running** Once the dispatcher performs a context switch to a thread, the thread enters the running state and executes. The thread's execution continues until the kernel preempts it to run a higher priority thread, its quantum ends, it terminates, or it voluntarily enters the wait state.

■ **Waiting** A thread can enter the wait state in several ways: a thread can voluntarily wait on an object to synchronize its execution, the operating system (the I/O system, for example) can wait on the thread's behalf, or an environment subsystem can direct the thread to suspend itself. When the thread's wait ends, depending on the priority, the thread either begins running immediately or is moved back to the ready state.

■ **Transition** A thread enters the transition state if it is ready for execution but its kernel stack is paged out of memory. For example, the thread's kernel stack might be paged out of memory. Once its kernel stack is brought back into memory, the thread enters the ready state.

■ **Terminated** When a thread finishes executing, it enters the terminated state. Once terminated, a thread object might or might not be deleted. (The object manager sets policy regarding when to delete the object.) If the executive has a pointer to the thread object, it can reinitialize the thread object and use it again.

■ **Initialized** Used internally while a thread is being created.

Quantum

As mentioned earlier in the chapter, a quantum is the amount of time a thread gets to run before Windows 2000 checks whether another thread at the same priority should get to run. If a thread completes its quantum and there are no other threads at its priority, Windows 2000 reschedules the thread to run for another quantum.

Each thread has a quantum value that represents how long the thread can run until its quantum expires. This value isn't a time length but rather an integer value, which we'll call *quantum units*.

Quantum Accounting

By default, threads start with a quantum value of 6 on Windows 2000 Professional and 36 on Windows 2000 Server. (We'll explain how you can change these values later.) The rationale for the longer default value on Windows 2000 Server is to minimize context switching. By having a longer quantum, server applications that wake up as the result of a client request have a better chance of completing the request and going back into a wait state before their quantum ends.

Each time the clock interrupts, the clock-interrupt routine deducts a fixed value (3) from the thread quantum. If there is no remaining thread quantum, the quantum end processing is triggered and another thread might be selected to run. On Windows 2000 Professional, because 3 is deducted each time the clock interrupt fires, by default a thread runs for 2 clock intervals; on Windows 2000 Server, by default a thread runs for 12 clock intervals.

Even if the system were at DPC/dispatch level or above (for example, if a DPC or an interrupt service routine was executing) when the clock interrupt occurred, the current thread would still have its quantum decremented, even if it hadn't been running for a full clock interval. If this was not done and device interrupts or DPCs occurred right before the clock interval timer interrupts, threads might not ever get their quantum reduced.

The length of the clock interval varies according to the hardware platform. The frequency of the clock interrupts is up to the HAL, not the kernel. For example, the clock interval for most x86 uniprocessors is 10 milliseconds, and for most x86 multiprocessors, 15 milliseconds.

EXPERIMENT: Determining the Clock Interval Frequency

The Win32 *GetSystemTimeAdjustment* function returns the clock interval. To determine the clock interval, run the Clockres program from *www.sysinternals.com* (\Sysint\Clockres on the companion CD). Here's the output from a uniprocessor x86 system:

```
C:\>clockres

ClockRes - View the system clock resolution
By Mark Russinovich
SysInternals - www.sysinternals.com

The system clock interval is 10 ms
```

The reason quantum is expressed in terms of a multiple of 3 quantum units per clock tick rather than as single units is to allow for partial quantum decay on wait completion. When a thread that has a base priority less than 14 executes a wait function (such as *WaitForSingleObject* or *WaitForMultipleObjects*), its quantum is reduced by 1 quantum unit. (Threads running at priority 14 or higher have their quantums reset after a wait.)

This partial decay addresses the case in which a thread enters a wait state before the clock interval timer fires. If this adjustment were not made, it would be possible for threads never to have their quantums reduced. For example, if a thread ran, entered a wait state, ran again, and entered another wait state but was never the currently running thread when the clock interval timer fired, it would never have its quantum charged for the time it was running.

Controlling the Quantum

The registry value HKLM\SYSTEM\CurrentControlSet\Control\Priority-Control\Win32PrioritySeparation allows you to specify the relative length of thread quantums (short or long) and whether or not threads in the foreground process should have their quantums boosted (and if so, the amount of the boost). This value consists of 6 bits divided into the three 2-bit fields shown in Figure 6-15.

4	2	0
Short vs. Long	Variable vs. Fixed	Foreground Quantum Boost

Figure 6-15
Fields of the Win32PrioritySeparation registry value

- **Short vs. Long** 1 specifies long, and 2 specifies short. 0 or 3 indicates that the default will be used (short for Windows 2000 Professional, long for Windows 2000 Server).

- **Variable vs. Fixed** 1 means to vary the quantum for the foreground process, and 2 means that quantum values don't change for foreground processes. 0 or 3 means that the default will be used (variable for Windows 2000 Professional, fixed for Windows 2000 Server).

■ **Foreground Quantum Boost** This field, which must have a value of 0, 1, or 2 (3 is invalid and treated as 2) is an index into a three-entry quantum table used to obtain the quantum for the threads in the foreground process. The quantum for threads in background processes is taken from the first entry in this quantum table. The field's value is stored in the kernel variable PsPrioritySeparation.

The foreground process is the process that owns the thread that owns the window that's in focus. When the foreground window changes to one owned by a thread in a process higher than the Idle priority class, the Win32 subsystem changes the quantum values for all the threads in that process by using the lower-order 2 bits of the Win32PrioritySeparation registry value as an index into a three-element array named *PspForegroundQuantum*. This array contains values determined by the other two bit fields in the Win32PrioritySeparation registry value. Table 6-17 shows the possible settings for *PspForegroundQuantum*.

Table 6-17 Quantum Values

	Short			Long		
Variable	6	12	18	12	24	36
Fixed	18	18	18	36	36	36

The reason that Windows 2000 boosts the quantum of foreground threads and not the priority is best illustrated with the following example, which shows the potential problems resulting from an approach based on foreground priority boosting. Suppose you start a long-running spreadsheet recalculation and then switch to a CPU-intensive application (such as a graphics-intensive game). The spreadsheet process running in the background will get little CPU time if the game process, which is in the foreground, has its priority boosted. Increasing the quantum of the game process doesn't prevent the spreadsheet calculation from running but instead favors the game process. If you do want to run an interactive application at a higher priority than all other interactive processes, you can always change the priority class to Above Normal or High using Task Manager (or start the application from the command prompt with the command *start /abovenormal* or *start /high*).

When you're setting the quantum length by modifying the Win32Priority-Separation registry value directly, you can select any combination. When you're using the Performance Options dialog box, you can choose from only two combinations. To see this dialog box (shown in Figure 6-16), open the System utility in Control Panel (or right-click on My Computer and select Properties), click the Advanced tab, and then click the Performance Options button.

Figure 6-16
Adjusting the quantum settings

The Applications option under Optimize Performance For designates the use of short, variable quantums—the default for Windows 2000 Professional. The Background Services option designates the use of long, fixed quantums—the default for Windows 2000 Server. If you install Terminal Services on Windows 2000 Advanced Server or Windows 2000 Datacenter Server and configure the server as an application server, this setting is changed to optimize for applications.

Scheduling Data Structures

To make thread-scheduling decisions, the kernel maintains a set of data structures known collectively as the *dispatcher database*, which is illustrated in Figure 6-17. The dispatcher database keeps track of which threads are waiting to execute and which processes are executing which threads. The most important structure in the dispatcher database is the *dispatcher ready queue* (located at *KiDispatcherReadyListHead*). This queue is really a series of queues, one queue for each scheduling priority. The queues contain threads that are in the ready state, waiting to be scheduled for execution.

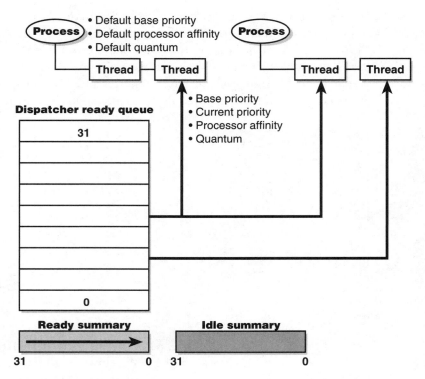

Figure 6-17
Dispatcher database

To speed up the selection of which thread to run or preempt, Windows 2000 maintains a 32-bit bitmask called the *ready summary* (*KiReadySummary*). Each bit set indicates one or more threads in the ready queue for that priority level. (Bit 0 represents priority 0, and so on.) Windows 2000 maintains another bitmask, the *idle summary* (*KiIdleSummary*), in which each set bit represents an idle processor.

As noted earlier, thread dispatching takes place at DPC/dispatch level. In addition to preventing other threads from running, being at DPC/dispatch level synchronizes access to the dispatcher database. On a multiprocessor system, however, changes to the dispatcher database require the additional step of acquiring the kernel dispatcher spinlock (*KiDispatcherLock*). Table 6-18 shows the kernel-mode kernel variables that are related to thread scheduling.

Table 6-18 Thread-Scheduling Kernel Variables

Variable	Type	Description
KiDispatcherLock	Spinlock	Dispatcher spinlock
KeNumberProcessors	Byte	Number of processors active in system
KeActiveProcessors	Bitmask (32 bits)	Bitmask of active processors in system
KiIdleSummary	Bitmask (32 bits)	Bitmask of idle processors
KiReadySummary	Bitmask (32 bits)	Bitmask of priority levels that have one or more ready threads
KiDispatcherReadyListHead	Array of 32 list entries	List heads for the 32 ready queues

Scheduling Scenarios

Windows 2000 bases the question of "Who gets the CPU?" on thread priority; but how does this approach work in practice? The following sections illustrate just how priority-driven preemptive multitasking works on the thread level. Note that there are differences in the way Windows 2000 handles scheduling decisions on a multiprocessor system vs. on a uniprocessor system. These differences are explained in the section "Thread Scheduling on Symmetric Multiprocessing Systems" later in this chapter.

Voluntary Switch

First a thread might voluntarily relinquish use of the processor by entering a wait state on some object (such as an event, a mutex, a semaphore, an I/O completion port, a process, a thread, a window message, and so on) by calling one of the many Win32 wait functions (such as *WaitForSingleObject* or *WaitForMultiple-Objects*). Waiting on objects is described in more detail in Chapter 3.

Voluntary switching is roughly equivalent to a thread ordering an item that isn't ready to go at a fast-food counter. Rather than hold up the queue of the other diners, the thread will step aside and let the next thread place its order (execute its routine) while the first thread's hamburger is being prepared. When the hamburger is ready, the first thread goes to the end of the ready queue of the priority level. However, as you'll see later in the chapter, most wait operations result in a temporary priority boost so that the thread can pick up its hamburger right away and start eating.

Figure 6-18 illustrates a thread entering a wait state and Windows 2000 selecting a new thread to run.

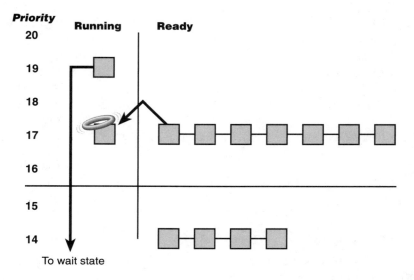

Figure 6-18
Voluntary switching

In Figure 6-18, the top block (thread) is voluntarily relinquishing the processor so that the next thread in the ready queue can run (as represented by the halo it has when in the Running column). Although it might appear from this figure that the relinquishing thread's priority is being reduced, it's not—it's just being moved to the wait queue of the objects the thread is waiting on. What about any remaining quantum for the thread? The quantum value isn't reset when a thread enters a wait state—in fact, as explained earlier, when the wait is satisfied, the thread's quantum value is decremented by 1 quantum unit, equivalent to one-third of a clock interval (except for threads running at priority 14 or higher—they have their quantum reset after a wait).

Preemption

In this scheduling scenario, a lower-priority thread is preempted when a higher-priority thread becomes ready to run. This situation might occur for a couple of reasons.

- A higher-priority thread's wait completes. (The event that the other thread was waiting on has occurred.)

- A thread priority is increased or decreased.

In either of these cases, Windows 2000 must determine whether the currently running thread should still continue to run or whether it should be preempted to allow a higher-priority thread to run.

NOTE Threads running in user mode can preempt threads running in kernel mode—the mode in which the thread is running doesn't matter. The thread priority is the determining factor.

When a thread is preempted, it is put at the head of the ready queue for the priority it was running at. Threads running in the real-time priority range have their quantum reset to a full time slice while threads running in the dynamic priority range finish their quantum when they get to run again. Figure 6-19 illustrates this situation.

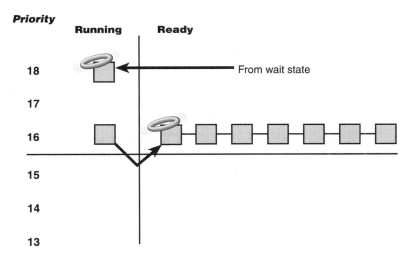

Figure 6-19
Preemptive thread scheduling

In Figure 6-19, a thread with priority 18 emerges from a wait state and repossesses the CPU, causing the thread that had been running (at priority 16) to be bumped to the head of the ready queue. Notice that the bumped thread isn't going to the end of the queue but to the beginning; when the preempting thread has finished running, the bumped thread can complete its quantum. In this example, the threads are in the real-time range; as explained in the note on page 361, in the section "Priority Boosts," no dynamic priority boosts are allowed for threads in the real-time range.

If voluntary switching is roughly equivalent to a thread letting another thread place its lunch order while the first thread waits for its meal, preemption is roughly equivalent to a thread being bumped from its place in line because the president of the United States has just walked in and ordered a hamburger. The preempted thread doesn't get bumped to the back of the line but is simply moved aside while the president gets his lunch. As soon as the president leaves, the first thread can resume ordering its meal.

Quantum End

When the running thread exhausts its CPU quantum, Windows 2000 must determine whether the thread's priority should be decremented and then whether another thread should be scheduled on the processor.

If the thread priority is reduced, Windows 2000 looks for a more appropriate thread to schedule. (For example, a more appropriate thread would be a thread in a ready queue with a higher priority than the new priority for the currently running thread.) If the thread priority isn't reduced and there are other threads in the ready queue at the same priority level, Windows 2000 selects the next thread in the ready queue at that same priority level and moves the previously running thread to the tail of that queue (giving it a new quantum value and changing its state from running to ready). This case is illustrated in Figure 6-20. If no other thread of the same priority is ready to run, the thread gets to run for another quantum.

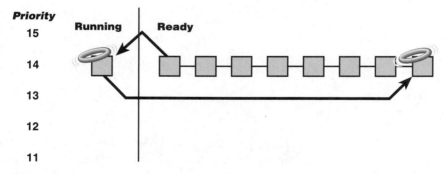

Figure 6-20
Quantum end thread scheduling

Termination

When a thread finishes running (either because it returned from its main routine, called *ExitThread*, or was killed with *TerminateThread*), it moves from the running state to the terminated state. If there are no handles open on the thread object, the thread is removed from the process thread list and the associated data structures are deallocated and released.

Context Switching

A thread's context and the procedure for context switching vary depending on the processor's architecture. A typical context switch requires saving and reloading the following data:

- Program counter
- Processor status register
- Other register contents
- User and kernel stack pointers
- A pointer to the address space in which the thread runs (the process's page table directory)

The kernel saves this information from the old thread by pushing it onto the current (old thread's) kernel-mode stack, updating the stack pointer, and saving the stack pointer in the old thread's KTHREAD block. The kernel stack pointer is then set to the new thread's kernel stack, and the new thread's context is loaded. If the new thread is in a different process, it loads the address of its page table directory into a special processor register so that its address space is available. (See the description of address translation in Chapter 7.) If a kernel APC that needs to be delivered is pending, an interrupt at IRQL 1 is requested. Otherwise, control passes to the new thread's restored program counter and the thread resumes execution.

Idle Thread

When no runnable thread exists on a CPU, Windows 2000 dispatches the per-CPU idle thread. Each CPU is allotted one idle thread because on a multiprocessor system one CPU can be executing a thread while other CPUs might have

no threads to execute. Windows 2000 reports the priority of the idle thread as 0. In reality, however, such threads don't have a priority level because they run only when there are no threads to run. (Remember, only one thread per Windows 2000 system is actually running at priority 0—the zero page thread.) In fact, the idle loop runs at DPC/dispatch level, polling for work to do: deferred procedure calls (DPCs) to deliver or threads to dispatch to. Although some details of the flow vary between architectures, the basic flow of control of the idle thread is as follows:

1. Enables and disables interrupts (allowing any pending interrupts to be delivered).

2. Checks whether any DPCs (described in Chapter 3) are pending on the processor. If DPCs are pending, clears the pending software interrupt and delivers them.

3. Checks whether a thread has been selected to run next on the processor, and if so, dispatches that thread.

4. Calls the HAL processor idle routine (in case any power management functions need to be performed).

Various Windows 2000 process viewer utilities report the idle process using different names. Task Manager calls it "System Idle Process," Process Viewer reports it as "Idle," Pstat calls it "Idle Process," Process Explode and Tlist call it "System Process," and Qslice calls it "SystemProcess."

Priority Boosts

In five cases, Windows 2000 can boost (increase) the current priority value of threads:

- On completion of I/O operations
- After waiting on executive events or semaphores
- After threads in the foreground process complete a wait operation
- When GUI threads wake up because of windowing activity
- When a thread that's ready to run hasn't been running for some time (CPU starvation)

The intent of these adjustments is to improve overall system throughput and responsiveness as well as resolve potentially unfair scheduling scenarios. Like any scheduling algorithms, however, these adjustments aren't perfect, and they might not benefit all applications.

> **NOTE** Windows 2000 never boosts the priority of threads in the real-time range (16 through 31). Therefore, scheduling is always predictable with respect to other threads in the real-time range. Windows 2000 assumes that if you're using the real-time thread priorities, you know what you're doing.

Priority Boosting After I/O Completion

Windows 2000 gives temporary priority boosts upon completion of certain I/O operations so that threads that were waiting on an I/O will have more of a chance to run right away and process whatever was being waited on. Recall that 1 quantum unit is deducted from the thread's remaining quantum when it wakes up so that I/O bound threads aren't unfairly favored. Although you'll find recommended boost values in the DDK header files (search for "#define IO" in Wdm.h or Ntddk.h—these values are listed in Table 6-19), the actual value for the boost is up to the device driver. It is the device driver that specifies the boost when it completes an I/O request on its call to the kernel function *IoCompleteRequest*. In Table 6-19, notice that I/O requests to devices that warrant better responsiveness have higher boost values.

Table 6-19 Recommended Boost Values

Device	Boost
Disk, CD-ROM, parallel, video	1
Network, mailslot, named pipe, serial	2
Keyboard, mouse	6
Sound	8

The boost is always applied to a thread's base priority, not its current priority. As illustrated in Figure 6-21, after the boost is applied, the thread gets to run for one quantum at the elevated priority level. After the thread has completed its quantum, it decays one priority level and then runs another quantum. This

cycle continues until the thread's priority level has decayed back to its base priority. A thread with a higher priority can still preempt the boosted thread, but the interrupted thread gets to finish its time slice at the boosted priority level before it decays to the next lower priority.

Figure 6-21
Priority boosting and decay

As noted earlier, these boosts apply only to threads in the dynamic priority range (0 through 15). No matter how large the boost is, the thread will never be boosted beyond level 15 into the real-time priority range. In other words, a priority 14 thread that receives a boost of 5 will go up to priority 15. A priority 15 thread that receives a boost will remain at priority 15.

Boosts After Waiting for Events and Semaphores

When a thread that was waiting on an executive event or a semaphore object has its wait satisfied (because of a call to the function *SetEvent*, *PulseEvent*, or *ReleaseSemaphore*), it receives a boost of 1. (See the value for EVENT_INCREMENT and SEMAPHORE_INCREMENT in the DDK header files.) Threads that wait for events and semaphores warrant a boost for the same reason that threads that wait on I/O operations do—threads that block on events are requesting CPU cycles less frequently than CPU-bound threads. This adjustment helps balance the scales.

This boost operates the same as the boost that occurs after I/O completion as described in the previous section: the boost is always applied to the base priority (not the current priority), the priority will never be boosted over 15, and the thread gets to run at the elevated priority for its remaining quantum (as described earlier, quantums are reduced by 1 when threads exit a wait) before decaying one priority level at a time until it reaches its original base priority.

Priority Boosts for Foreground Threads After Waits

Whenever a thread in the foreground process completes a wait operation on a kernel object, the kernel function *KiUnwaitThread* boosts its current (not base) priority by the current value of *PsPrioritySeparation*. (The windowing system is responsible for determining which process is considered to be in the foreground.) As described in the section on quantum controls, *PsPrioritySeparation* reflects the quantum-table index used to select quantums for the threads of foreground applications.

The reason for this boost is to improve the responsiveness of interactive applications—by giving the foreground application a small boost when it completes a wait, it has a better chance of running right away, especially when other processes at the same base priority might be running in the background.

Unlike other types of boosting, this boost applies to both Windows 2000 Professional and Windows 2000 Server, and you *can't* disable this boost, even if you've disabled priority boosting using the Win32 *SetThreadPriorityBoost* function.

EXPERIMENT: Watching Foreground Priority Boosts and Decays

Using the CPU Stress tool (in the resource kit and the Platform SDK), you can watch priority boosts in action. Take the following steps:

1. Open the System utility in Control Panel (or right-click on My Computer and select Properties), click the Advanced tab, and click the Performance Options button. Select the Applications option. This causes *PsPrioritySeparation* to get a value of 2.

2. Run Cpustres.exe.

3. Run the Windows NT 4 Performance Monitor (Perfmon4.exe in the Windows 2000 resource kits). This older version of the Performance tool is needed for this experiment because it can query performance counter values at a frequency faster than the Windows 2000 Performance tool (which has a maximum interval of once per second).

4. Click the Add Counter toolbar button (or press Ctrl+I) to bring up the Add To Chart dialog box.

(continued)

EXPERIMENT: Watching Foreground Priority Boosts and Decays *continued*

5. Select the Thread object, and then select the Priority Current counter.

6. In the Instance box, scroll down the list until you see the cpustres process. Select the second thread (thread 1). (The first thread is the GUI thread.) You should see something like this:

7. Click the Add button, and then click the Done button.

8. Select Chart from the Options menu. Change the Vertical Maximum to 16 and the Interval to 0.010 as follows, and click OK:

9. Now bring the Cpustres process to the foreground. You should see the priority of the Cpustres thread being boosted by 2 and then decaying back to the base priority as follows:

10. The reason Cpustres receives a boost of 2 periodically is because the thread you're monitoring is sleeping about 75 percent of the time and then waking up—the boost is applied when the thread wakes up. To see the thread get boosted more frequently, increase the Activity level from Low to Medium to Busy. If you set the Activity level to Maximum, you won't see any boosts because Maximum in Cpustres puts the thread into an infinite loop. Therefore, the thread doesn't invoke any wait functions and hence doesn't receive any boosts.

11. When you've finished, exit Performance Monitor and CPU Stress.

Priority Boosts After GUI Threads Wake Up

Threads that own windows receive an additional boost of 2 when they wake up because of windowing activity, such as the arrival of window messages. The windowing system (Win32k.sys) applies this boost when it calls *KeSetEvent* to set an event used to wake up a GUI thread. The reason for this boost is similar to the previous one—to favor interactive applications.

EXPERIMENT: Watching Priority Boosts on GUI Threads

You can also see the windowing system apply its boost of 2 for GUI threads that wake up to process window messages by monitoring the current priority of a GUI application and moving the mouse across the window. Just follow these steps:

1. Open the System utility in Control Panel (or right-click on My Computer and select Properties), click the Advanced tab, and click the Performance Options button. Ensure that the Applications option is selected. This causes *PsPriority-Separation* to get a value of 2.

2. Run Notepad from the Start menu by selecting Programs/Accessories/Notepad.

3. Run the Windows NT 4 Performance Monitor (Perfmon4.exe in the Windows 2000 resource kits). This older version of the Performance tool is needed for this experiment because it can query performance counter values at a faster frequency. (The Windows 2000 Performance tool has a maximum interval of once per second.)

4. Click the Add Counter toolbar button (or press Ctrl+I) to bring up the Add To Chart dialog box.

5. Select the Thread object, and then select the Priority Current counter.

6. In the Instance box, scroll down the list until you see Notepad thread 0. Click it, click the Add button, and then click the Done button.

7. As in the previous experiment, select Chart from the Options menu. Change the Vertical Maximum to 16 and the Interval to 0.010, and click OK.

8. You should see the priority of thread 0 in Notepad at 8, 9, or 10. Because Notepad entered a wait state shortly after it received the boost of 2 that threads in the foreground process receive, it might not yet have decayed from 10 to 9 and then to 8.

9. With Performance Monitor in the foreground, move the mouse across the Notepad window. (Make both windows visible on the desktop.) You'll see that the priority sometimes remains at 10 and sometimes at 9, for the reasons just explained. (The reason you won't likely catch Notepad at 8 is that it runs so little after receiving the GUI thread boost of 2 that it never experiences more than one priority level decay before waking up again because of additional windowing activity and receiving the boost of 2 again.)

10. Now bring Notepad to the foreground. You should see the priority rise to 12 and remain there (or drop to 11, because it might experience the normal priority decay that occurs for boosted threads on quantum end) because the thread is receiving two boosts: the boost of 2 applied to GUI threads when they wake up to process windowing input and an additional boost of 2 because Notepad is in the foreground.

11. If you then move the mouse over Notepad (while it's still in the foreground), you might see the priority drop to 11 (or maybe even 10) as it experiences the priority decay that normally occurs on boosted threads as they complete quantums. However, the boost of 2 applied because it's the foreground process remains as long as Notepad remains in the foreground.

12. When you've finished, exit Performance Monitor and Notepad.

Priority Boosts for CPU Starvation

Imagine the following situation: you've got a priority 7 thread that's running, preventing a priority 4 thread from ever receiving CPU time; however, a priority 11 thread is waiting on some resource that the priority 4 thread has locked. But because the priority 7 thread in the middle is eating up all the CPU time, the priority 4 thread will never run long enough to finish whatever it's doing and release the resource blocking the priority 11 thread. What does Windows 2000 do to address this situation? Once per second, the *balance set manager* (a system thread that exists primarily to perform memory management functions and is described in more detail in Chapter 7) scans the ready queues for any threads that have been in the ready state (that is, haven't run) for longer than 300 clock ticks (approximately 3 to 4 seconds, depending on the clock interval). If it finds

such a thread, the balance set manager boosts the thread's priority to 15 and gives it double the normal quantum. Once the 2 quantums are up, the thread's priority decays immediately to its original base priority. If the thread wasn't finished and a higher priority thread is ready to run, the decayed thread will return to the ready queue, where it again becomes eligible for another boost if it remains there for another 300 clock ticks.

The balance set manager doesn't actually scan all ready threads every time it runs. To minimize the CPU time it uses, it scans only 16 ready threads; if there are more threads at that priority level, it remembers where it left off and picks up again on the next pass. Also, it will boost only 10 threads per pass—if it finds 10 threads meriting this particular boost (which would indicate an unusually busy system), it stops the scan at that point and picks up again on the next pass.

Will this algorithm always solve the priority inversion issue? No—it's not perfect by any means. But over time, CPU-starved threads should get enough CPU time to finish whatever processing they were doing and reenter a wait state.

Thread Scheduling on Symmetric Multiprocessing Systems

If scheduling access to system processors is based on thread priority, what happens if you're using more than one processor? While Windows 2000 attempts to schedule the highest priority runnable threads on all available CPUs, several factors influence the choice of which CPU a thread will run on such that Windows 2000 is only guaranteed to be running the (single) highest priority thread. Before we describe the algorithms, we need to define a few terms.

Affinity

Each thread has an *affinity mask* that specifies the processors on which the thread is allowed to run. The thread affinity mask is inherited from the process affinity mask. By default, all processes (and therefore all threads) begin with an affinity mask that is equal to the set of active processors on the system—in other words, all threads can run on all processors.

Two things can alter that:

- A call made by the application to the *SetProcessAffinityMask* or *SetThreadAffinityMask* function

- An imagewide affinity mask specified in the image header (For more information on the detailed format of Windows 2000 images, see the article "Portable Executable and Common Object File Format Specification" in the MSDN Library.)

EXPERIMENT: Watching Priority Boosts for CPU Starvation

Using the CPU Stress tool (in the resource kit and the Platform SDK), you can watch priority boosts in action. In this experiment, we'll see CPU usage change when a thread's priority is boosted. Take the following steps:

1. Run Cpustres.exe. Change the activity level of the active thread (by default Thread 1) from Low to Maximum. Change the thread priority from Normal to Below Normal. The screen should look like this:

2. Run the Windows NT 4 Performance Monitor (Perfmon4.exe in the Windows 2000 resource kits). Again, you need the older version for this experiment because it can query performance counter values at a frequency faster than once per second.

3. Click the Add Counter toolbar button (or press Ctrl+I) to bring up the Add To Chart dialog box.

4. Select the Thread object, and then select the % Processor Time counter.

(continued)

EXPERIMENT: Watching Priority Boosts for CPU Starvation *continued*

5. In the Instance box, scroll down the list until you see the cpustres process. Select the second thread (thread 1). (The first thread is the GUI thread.) You should see something like this:

6. Click the Add button, and then click the Done button.

7. Raise the priority of Performance Monitor to real-time by running Task Manager, clicking on the Processes tab, and selecting the Perfmon4.exe process. Right-click on the process, select Set Priority, and then select Realtime. (If you receive a Task Manager Warning message box warning you of system instability, click the Yes button.)

8. Run another copy of CPU Stress. In this copy, change the activity level of Thread 1 from Low to Maximum. The screen should look like the one on page 371.

9. Now switch back to Performance Monitor. You should see CPU activity every 4 or so seconds because the thread is boosted to priority 15.

When you've finished, exit Performance Monitor and the two copies of CPU Stress.

Ideal and Last Processor

Each thread has two CPU numbers stored in the kernel thread block:

■ *Ideal processor,* or the preferred processor that this thread should run on

■ *Last processor,* or the processor on which the thread last ran

The ideal processor is chosen randomly when a thread is created, based on a seed in the process block. The seed is incremented each time a thread is created so that the ideal processor for each new thread in the process will rotate through the available processors on the system. Windows 2000 doesn't change the ideal processor once the thread is created; however, an application can change the ideal processor value for a thread by using the *SetThreadIdeal-Processor* function.

Choosing a Processor for a Ready Thread

When a thread becomes ready to run, Windows 2000 first tries to schedule the thread to run on an idle processor. If there is a choice of idle processors, preference is given first to the thread's ideal processor, then to the thread's last processor, and then to the currently executing processor (that is, the CPU on which the scheduling code is running). If none of these CPUs are idle, Windows 2000 picks the first available idle processor by scanning the idle processor mask from highest to lowest CPU number.

If all processors are currently busy and a thread becomes ready, Windows 2000 looks to see whether it can preempt a thread in the running or standby state on one of the CPUs. Which CPU is examined? The first choice is the thread's ideal processor, and the second choice is the thread's last processor. If neither of those CPUs are in the thread's affinity mask, Windows 2000 selects the highest processor in the active processor mask that the thread can run on.

If the processor selected already has a thread selected to run next (waiting in the standby state to be scheduled) and that thread's priority is less than the priority of the thread being readied for execution, the new thread preempts that first thread out of the standby state and becomes the next thread for that CPU. If there is already a thread running on that CPU, Windows 2000 checks whether the priority of the currently running thread is less than the thread being readied for execution. If so, the currently running thread is marked to be preempted and Windows 2000 queues an interprocessor interrupt to kick off the currently running thread in favor of this new thread.

> **NOTE** Windows 2000 doesn't look at the priority of the current and next threads on all the CPUs—just on the one CPU selected as described above. If no thread can be preempted on that one CPU, the new thread is put in the ready queue for its priority level, where it awaits its turn to get scheduled.

Selecting a Thread to Run on a Specific CPU

In several cases (such as when a thread lowers its priority, changes its affinity, or delays or yields execution), Windows 2000 must find a new thread to run on the CPU that the currently executing thread is running on. On a single processor system, Windows 2000 simply picks the first thread in the ready queue, starting with the highest-priority ready queue with at least one thread and working its way down. On a multiprocessor system, however, Windows 2000

doesn't simply pick the first thread in the ready queue. Instead, it looks for a thread that meets one of the following conditions:

- Ran last on the specified processor

- Has its ideal processor set to the specified processor

- Has been ready to run for longer than 2 quantums

- Has a priority greater than or equal to 24

Threads that don't have the specified processor in their hard affinity mask are skipped, obviously. If Windows 2000 doesn't find any threads that meet one of these conditions, it picks the thread at the head of the ready queue it began searching from.

Why does it matter which processor a thread was last running on? As usual, the answer is speed—giving preference to the last processor a thread executed on maximizes the chances that thread data remains in the secondary cache of the processor in question.

When the Highest-Priority Ready Threads Are Not Running

As just explained, on a multiprocessor system, Windows 2000 doesn't always select the highest-priority thread to run on a given CPU. Thus, a thread with a higher priority than the currently running thread on a given CPU can become ready but might not immediately preempt the current thread.

Another situation in which the highest-priority thread might not preempt the current thread is when a thread's affinity mask is set as a subset of the available CPUs. In that case, the processors to which the thread has affinity are currently running higher-priority threads and the thread must wait for one of those processors—even if another processor is free or running lower-priority threads that it could otherwise preempt. Windows 2000 won't move a running thread that could run on a different processor from one CPU to a second processor to permit a thread with an affinity for the first processor to run on the first processor.

For example, consider this scenario: CPU 0 is running a priority 8 thread that can run on any processor, and CPU 1 is running a priority 4 thread that can run on any processor. A priority 6 thread that can run on only CPU 0 becomes ready. What happens? Windows 2000 won't move the priority 8 thread from CPU 0 to CPU 1 (preempting the priority 4 thread) so that the priority 6 thread can run; the priority 6 thread has to wait.

Job Objects

A *job* object is a nameable, securable, shareable kernel object that allows control of one or more processes as a group. A job object's basic function is to allow groups of processes to be managed and manipulated as a unit. A process can be a member of only one job object. By default, its association with the job object can't be broken and all processes created by the process and its descendents are associated with the same job object as well. The job object also records basic accounting information for all processes associated with the job and for all processes that were associated with the job but have since terminated. Table 6-20 lists the Win32 functions to create and manipulate job objects.

Table 6-20 Win32 API Functions for Jobs

Function	Description
CreateJobObject	Creates a job object (with an optional name)
OpenJobObject	Opens an existing job object by name
AssignProcessToJobObject	Adds a process to a job
TerminateJobObject	Terminates all processes in a job
SetInformationJobObject	Sets limits
QueryInformationJobObject	Retrieves information about the job, such as CPU time, page fault count, number of processes, list of process IDs, quotas or limits, and security limits

The following are some of the CPU-related and memory-related limits you can specify for a job:

- **Maximum number of active processes** Limits the number of concurrently executing processes in the job.

- **Jobwide user-mode CPU time limit** Limits the maximum amount of user-mode CPU time that the processes in the job can consume (including processes that have run and exited). Once this limit is reached, by default all the processes in the job will be terminated with an error code and no new processes can be created in the job (unless the limit is reset). The job object is signaled, so any threads waiting on the job will be released. You can change this default behavior with a call to *EndOfJobTimeAction*.

- **Per-process user-mode CPU time limit** Allows each process in the job to accumulate only a fixed maximum amount of user-mode CPU time. When the maximum is reached, the process terminates (with no chance to clean up).

- **Job scheduling class** Sets the length of the time slice (or quantum) for threads in processes in the job. This setting applies only on systems running with long, fixed quantums (the default for Windows 2000 Server). The value of the job-scheduling class determines the quantum as shown here:

Scheduling Class	Quantum Units
0	6
1	12
2	18
3	24
4	30
5	36
6	42
7	48
8	54
9	Infinite if real-time; 60 otherwise

- **Job processor affinity** Sets the processor affinity mask for each process in the job. (Individual threads can alter their affinity to any subset of the job affinity, but processes can't alter their process affinity setting.)

- **Job process priority class** Sets the priority class for each process in the job. Threads can't increase their priority relative to the class (as they normally can). Attempts to increase thread priority are ignored. (No error is returned on calls to *SetThreadPriority*, but the increase doesn't occur.)

- **Default working set minimum and maximum** Defines the specified working set minimum and maximum for each process in the job. (This setting isn't jobwide—each process has its own working set with the same minimum and maximum values.)

■ **Process and job committed virtual memory limit** Defines the maximum amount of storage that can be committed by either a single process or the entire job.

Jobs can also be set to queue an entry to an I/O completion port object, which other threads might be waiting on with the Win32 *GetQueuedCompletion-Status* function.

You can also place security limits on processes in a job. You can set a job such that each process runs under the same jobwide access token. You can then create a job to restrict processes from impersonating or creating processes that have access tokens that contain the local administrator's group. In addition, you can apply security filters such that when threads in processes contained in a job impersonate client threads, certain privileges and security IDs (SIDs) can be eliminated from the impersonation token.

Finally, you can also place user interface limits on processes in a job. Such limits include being able to restrict processes from opening handles to windows owned by threads outside the job, reading and/or writing to the clipboard, and changing the many user interface system parameters via the Win32 *SystemParametersInfo* function.

Windows 2000 Datacenter Server has a tool called the Process Control Manager that allows an administrator to define job objects, the various quotas and limits that can be specified for a job, and which processes, if run, should be added to the job. A service component monitors process activity and adds the specified processes to the jobs.

EXPERIMENT: Viewing the Job Object

You can view named job objects with the Performance tool. (See the Job Object and Job Object Details performance objects.) To view unnamed job objects, you must use the kernel debugger *!job* command. Follow these steps to create and view an unnamed job object:

1. From the command prompt, use the *runas* command to create a process running the command prompt (Cmd.exe). For example, type *runas /user:<domain>\< username> cmd*. You'll be prompted for your password. Enter your password, and a command prompt window will appear. The service behind the *runas* command creates an unnamed job to contain all processes (so that it can terminate these processes at logoff time).

2. From the kernel debugger (such as LiveKd), display the process list with *!process* and find the recently created process running Cmd.exe. Then display the process block by using *!process <process ID>*, find the address of the job object, and finally display the job object with the *!job* command.

Here's some partial debugger output from the command sequence described in step 2:

```
kd> !process 0 8
**** NT ACTIVE PROCESS DUMP ****
    :
PROCESS 84eab6d0  SessionId: 0  Cid: 0478  Peb: 7ffdf000 ParentCid: 0240
    DirBase: 03834000  ObjectTable: 8097ef88  TableSize:  42.
    Image: livekd.exe

PROCESS 857e0d70  SessionId: 0  Cid: 0550  Peb: 7ffdf000 ParentCid: 00dc
    DirBase: 05337000  ObjectTable: 82273ac8  TableSize:  22.
    Image: cmd.exe

PROCESS 83390710  SessionId: 0  Cid: 0100  Peb: 7ffdf000 ParentCid: 0478
    DirBase: 05b3b000  ObjectTable: 81bb7e08  TableSize:  34.
    Image: i386kd.exe

kd> !process 550
Searching for Process with Cid == 550
PROCESS 857e0d70  SessionId: 0  Cid: 0550  Peb: 7ffdf000 ParentCid: 00dc
    DirBase: 05337000  ObjectTable: 82273ac8  TableSize:  22.
    Image: cmd.exe
    :
    Job                             85870970
    :
kd> !job 85870970 7
Job at 85870970
  TotalPageFaultCount       0
  TotalProcesses            1
  ActiveProcesses           1
  TotalTerminatedProcesses 0
  LimitFlags                0
  MinimumWorkingSetSize     0
  MaximumWorkingSetSize     0
  ActiveProcessLimit        0
  PriorityClass             0
  UIRestrictionsClass       0
```

(continued)

EXPERIMENT: Viewing the Job Object *continued*

```
    SecurityLimitFlags      0
    Token                   0
    Processes assigned to this job:
     PROCESS 857e0d70 SessionId: 0 Cid: 0550 Peb: 7ffdf000 ParentCid: 00dc
         DirBase: 05337000  ObjectTable: 82273ac8  TableSize: 22.
         Image: cmd.exe
```

Conclusion

In this chapter, we've examined the structure of processes and threads, seen how they are created and destroyed, and looked at how Windows 2000 decides which threads should run and for how long.

Many references in this chapter are to topics related to memory management. Because threads run inside processes and processes in large part define an address space, the next logical topic is how Windows 2000 performs virtual and physical memory management—the subjects of Chapter 7.

Memory Management

In this chapter, you'll learn how Microsoft Windows 2000 implements virtual memory and how it manages the subset of virtual memory kept in physical memory. These jobs involve two primary tasks:

- Translating, or mapping, a process's virtual address space into physical memory so that when a thread running in the context of that process reads or writes to the virtual address space, the correct physical address is referenced. (The subset of a process's virtual address space that is physically resident is called the *working set*. Working sets are described in more detail later in this chapter.)

- Paging some of the contents of memory to disk when it becomes overcommitted—that is, when running threads or system code try to use more physical memory than is currently available—and bringing the contents back into physical memory when needed.

As you saw in Chapter 2 (Table 2-2 on page 39), Windows 2000 Professional and Server systems support up to 4 GB of physical memory, Windows 2000 Advanced Server supports up to 8 GB, and Windows 2000 Datacenter Server up to 64 GB. (Actual supported maximum memory for Windows 2000 Datacenter Server depends on available hardware. Windows 2000 Datacenter Server wasn't released at the time we wrote this book, so we were unable to verify whether the hardware currently available will support the operating system maximum of 64 GB.)

Because Windows 2000 is a 32-bit operating system, user processes have a flat 4-GB 32-bit virtual address space. How a 32-bit process can allocate and use large amounts of physical memory is explained in the section "Address Windowing Extensions" later in this chapter.

NOTE Microsoft has publicly announced plans to provide a true 64-bit version of Windows that will support the Intel Itanium processor family. A new 64-bit API, called Win64, will support true 64-bit addresses. The reason for supporting this platform is the same reason Microsoft moved from a 16-bit to a 32-bit address space—ever increasing requirements for storing and processing huge amounts of data in memory. The 64-bit version of Windows alleviates the address space limitations of Windows 2000 by providing a large, flat 64-bit virtual address space for processes. For more on 64-bit Windows, see the section "Getting Ready for 64-bit Windows" in the Platform SDK or the information on Microsoft's Web site at *www.microsoft.com/windows2000/guide/platform/strategic/64bit.asp.*

In addition to providing virtual memory management, the memory manager provides a core set of services on which the various Windows 2000 environment subsystems are built. These services include memory mapped files (internally called *section objects*), copy-on-write memory, and support for applications using large, sparse address spaces. In this chapter, we'll summarize these basic services and review pertinent concepts such as reserved versus committed memory and shared memory. We'll also describe the internal structure and components that make up the memory manager, including key data structures and algorithms.

Memory Manager Components

The memory manager is part of the Windows 2000 executive and therefore exists in the file Ntoskrnl.exe. No parts of the memory manager exist in the HAL. The memory manager consists of the following components:

- A set of executive system services for allocating, deallocating, and managing virtual memory, most of which are exposed through the Win32 API or kernel-mode device driver interfaces

- A translation-not-valid and access fault trap handler for resolving hardware-detected memory management exceptions and making virtual pages resident on behalf of a process

■ Several key components that run in the context of six different kernel-mode system threads:

❏ The *working set manager* (priority 16), which the balance set manager (a system thread the kernel creates) calls once per second as well as when free memory falls below a certain threshold, drives the overall memory management policies, such as working set trimming, aging, and modified page writing.

❏ The *process/stack swapper* (priority 23) performs both process and kernel thread stack inswapping and outswapping. The balance set manager and the thread-scheduling code in the kernel awaken this thread when an inswap or outswap operation needs to take place.

❏ The *modified page writer* (priority 17) writes dirty pages on the modified list back to the appropriate paging files. This thread is awakened when the size of the modified list needs to be reduced. (See the section "Modified Page Writer" on page 472 to find out how you can change this default value.)

❏ The *mapped page writer* (priority 17) writes dirty pages in mapped files to disk. It is awakened when the size of the modified list needs to be reduced or if pages for mapped files have been on the modified list for more than 5 minutes. This second modified page writer thread is necessary because it can generate page faults that result in requests for free pages. If there were no free pages and there was only one modified page writer thread, the system could dead-lock waiting for free pages.

❏ The *dereference segment thread* (priority 18) is responsible for system cache and page file growth and shrinkage. (For example, if there is no virtual address space for paged pool growth, this thread reduces the size of the system cache.)

❏ The *zero page thread* (priority 0) zeros out pages on the free list so that a cache of zero pages is available to satisfy future demand-zero page faults.

Each of these components is covered in more detail later in the chapter.

Like all other components of the Windows 2000 executive, the memory manager is fully reentrant and supports simultaneous execution on multiprocessor systems—that is, it allows two threads to acquire resources in such a way that they don't corrupt each other's data. To accomplish the goal of being fully reentrant, the memory manager uses several different internal synchronization mechanisms to control access to its own internal data structures, such as spinlocks and executive resources. (Synchronization objects are discussed in Chapter 3.)

Systemwide resources to which the memory manager must synchronize access include the page frame number (PFN) database (controlled by a spinlock), section objects and the system working set (controlled by executive resources), and page file creation (controlled by a mutex), as well as other internal structures. Per-process memory management data structures are synchronized using two per-process mutexes: the working set lock (held while changes are being made to the working set list) and the address space lock (held whenever the address space is being changed).

Configuring the Memory Manager

Like most of Windows 2000, the memory manager attempts to automatically provide optimal system performance for varying workloads on systems of varying sizes and types. You can use registry values under the key HKLM\SYSTEM\CurrentControlSet\Control\Session Manager\Memory Management to override these default performance calculations. Some of these values are listed in Table 7-1. For more details, see the Windows 2000 resource kit Technical Reference to the Registry help file.

Table 7-1 Registry Values That Affect the Memory Manager

Registry Value	Description
ClearPageFileAtShutdown	Specifies whether inactive pages in the paging file are filled with zeros when the system is shut down. This is a security feature.
DisablePagingExecutive	Specifies whether user-mode and kernel-mode drivers and kernel-mode system code can be paged to disk when not in use. If the value of this entry is 0 (the default), drivers and the kernel must remain in physical memory. If the value is 1, they can be paged to disk as needed.
IoPageLockLimit	Specifies the limit of the number of bytes that can be locked in a user process for I/O operations. When this value is 0, the system uses the default (512 KB). The maximum value is approximately the equivalent of physical memory minus 7 MB. This registry key isn't used in Windows 2000 Datacenter Server and is no longer used in Windows 2000 starting with Windows 2000 Service Pack 1.

Registry Value	Description
LargePageMinimum	Indicates the minimum number of megabytes necessary to map Ntoskrnl and HAL using large (4-MB) pages. (This value isn't documented and isn't present by default; you must add it manually.)
LargeSystemCache	Affects whether the file system cache or the working sets of processes are given priority when it comes to memory trade-offs. Also affects the size of the file system cache. (On Windows 2000 Server systems, you can adjust this value indirectly by setting the properties of the file server service—see page 666 in Chapter 11 for details.)
NonPagedPoolQuota	Indicates the maximum nonpaged pool that can be allocated by any process (in megabytes). If the value of this entry is 0, the system calculates the value.
NonPagedPoolSize	Indicates the initial size of nonpaged pool in bytes. When this value is 0, the system calculates the value.
PagedPoolQuota	Indicates the maximum paged pool (in megabytes) that any process can allocate. If the value of this entry is 0, the system calculates the value.
PagedPoolSize	Indicates the maximum size of paged pool in bytes. When the value of this entry is 0, the system calculates the value. A value of −1 indicates that the largest possible size is selected, which means allowing a larger paged pool in favor of system page table entries (PTEs).
SystemPages	Indicates the number of system page table entries reserved for mapping I/O buffers, device drivers, kernel thread stacks, or pages for programmed I/O into the system address space. If the value is 0, the system calculates the value. If the value is −1, the maximum number of system PTEs will be reserved. (This value might be needed to support, for example, a device that requires a large number of system PTEs, such as a video card with 512 MB of video memory that has to be mapped all at one time.)

Most of the interesting "knobs" or controls that affect memory manager policy are kernel variables that contain various thresholds and limits computed at system boot time on the basis of memory size and product type (Windows 2000 Professional being optimized for desktop interactive use and Windows 2000 Server systems for running server applications). Examples of these knobs include the sizing of system memory (paged pool, nonpaged pool, system cache, number of system page table entries), page read cluster size, counters that trigger working set trimming, and thresholds for the modified page writer. To find some of

these, search for global variables in Ntoskrnl.exe that have names beginning with *Mm* that contain the word "maximum" or "minimum."

WARNING Although you'll find references to many of these knobs, you shouldn't change them. Windows 2000 has been tested to operate properly with the current possible permutations of these values that can be computed. Changing the value of these kernel variables on a running system can result in unpredictable system behavior, including system hangs or even crashes.

The current memory sizes that determine whether Windows 2000 considers a system to have a small, medium, or large amount of memory are listed in Table 7-2. The memory manager uses this value in many of its boot-time calculations.

Table 7-2 Values That Determine System Memory Size

System Memory Size	Physical Memory
Small	<19 MB
Medium	20–32 MB
Large	>32 MB if Windows 2000 Professional
	>64 MB if Windows 2000 Server

Determining the System Memory Size

Because device drivers (as well as other Windows 2000 kernel-mode components) might make resource allocation and run-time policy decisions based on memory size values, the following kernel-mode routines have been provided (and are documented in the DDK):

Function	Description
MmQuery-SystemSize	Returns whether the machine has a small, medium, or large amount of available memory.
MmIsThisAn-NtAsSystem	Returns TRUE for Windows 2000 Server, Windows 2000 Advanced Server, and Windows 2000 Datacenter Server, and FALSE for Windows 2000 Professional. (This routine's name was based on the original product name of the server of the server edition of Microsoft Windows NT, Windows NT Advanced Server.)

Examining Memory Usage

The Memory and Process performance counter objects provide access to most of the details about system and process memory utilization. Throughout the chapter, we'll include references to specific performance counters that contain information related to the component being described.

Besides the Performance tool, a number of tools in the Windows 2000 Support Tools and Windows 2000 resource kits display different subsets of memory usage information. We've included relevant examples and experiments throughout the chapter. One word of caution, however—different utilities use varying and sometimes inconsistent or confusing names when displaying memory information. The following experiment illustrates this point. (We'll explain the terms used in this example in subsequent sections.)

EXPERIMENT: Viewing System Memory Information

The Performance tab in the Windows 2000 Task Manager, shown in the following screen shot, displays basic system memory information. This information is a subset of the detailed memory information available through the performance counters.

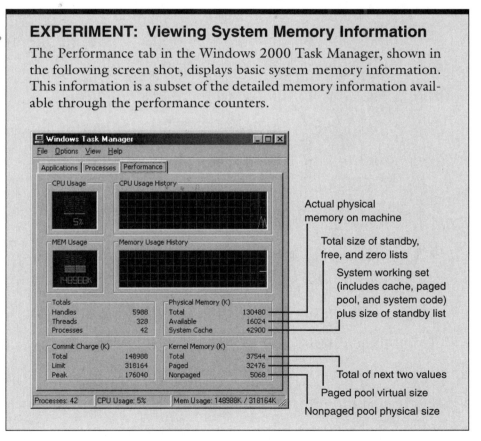

(continued)

385

EXPERIMENT: Viewing System Memory Information *continued*

Both Pmon.exe (in the Windows 2000 Support Tools) and Pstat.exe (in the Platform SDK) display system and process memory information. The annotations in the following output from Pstat explain the information reported. (For an explanation of the commit total and limit, see Table 7-8 on page 421.)

```
Memory:  64692K Avail:   3676K TotalWs: 62836K InRam Kernel: 3788K P: 9604K
Commit: 111848K/  85808K Limit: 182400K Peak: 113732K    Pool N: 2344K P:14448K
```

```
User Time      Kernel Time    Ws   Faults  Commit Pri Hnd Thd Pid Name
                            20032   194378                       File Cache
0:00:00.000    8:03:55.734    16        1       0   0   0   2   0 Idle Process
0:00:00.000    0:01:24.421    32     1601      36   8 140  27   2 System
0:00:00.140    0:00:00.468   200     2008     164  11  35   6  20 smss.exe
0:00:00.640    0:00:02.843   716     8625    1588  13 245   9  30 csrss.exe
```

To see the specific usage of paged and nonpaged pool, use the Poolmon utility, described in the experiment on page 406.

Finally, the *!vm* command in the kernel debugger shows the basic memory management information available through the memory-related performance counters. This command can be useful if you're looking at a crash dump or hung system. Here's an example of its output:

```
kd> !vm

*** Virtual Memory Usage ***
        Physical Memory:    32620   (  130480 Kb)
        Page File: \??\C:\pagefile.sys
          Current:    204800Kb Free Space:     101052Kb
          Minimum:    204800Kb Maximum:        204800Kb
        Available Pages:     3604   (   14416 Kb)
        ResAvail Pages:     24004   (   96016 Kb)
```

```
Modified Pages:        768  (    3072 Kb)
NonPagedPool Usage:   1436  (    5744 Kb)
NonPagedPool Max:    12940  (   51760 Kb)
PagedPool 0 Usage:    6817  (   27268 Kb)
PagedPool 1 Usage:     982  (    3928 Kb)
PagedPool 2 Usage:     984  (    3936 Kb)
PagedPool Usage:      8783  (   35132 Kb)
PagedPool Maximum:   26624  (  106496 Kb)
Shared Commit:        1361  (    5444 Kb)
Special Pool:            0  (       0 Kb)
Free System PTEs:   189291  (  757164 Kb)
Shared Process:       3165  (   12660 Kb)
PagedPool Commit:     8783  (   35132 Kb)
Driver Commit:        1098  (    4392 Kb)
Committed pages:     45113  (  180452 Kb)
Commit limit:        79556  (  318224 Kb)

Total Private:       30536  (  122144 Kb)
    IEXPLORE.EXE      3028  (   12112 Kb)
    svchost.exe       2128  (    8512 Kb)
    WINWORD.EXE       1971  (    7884 Kb)
    POWERPNT.EXE      1905  (    7620 Kb)
    Acrobat.exe       1761  (    7044 Kb)
    winlogon.exe      1361  (    5444 Kb)
    explorer.exe      1300  (    5200 Kb)
    livekd.exe        1015  (    4060 Kb)
    hh.exe             960  (    3840 Kb)
    :
```

EXPERIMENT: Accounting for Physical Memory Use

By combining information available from performance counters with output from kernel debugger commands, you can come close to accounting for physical memory usage on a machine running Windows 2000. To examine the memory usage information available through performance counters, run the Performance tool and add the counters to view the following information. (You'll see the results more easily if you change the vertical scale maximum on the graph to 1000.)

(continued)

EXPERIMENT: Accounting for Physical Memory Use *continued*

■ **Total process working set size** To view this information, select the Process performance object and the Working Set counter for the _Total process instance. This number will be larger than the actual total process memory utilization because shared pages are counted in each process working set. To get a more accurate picture of process memory utilization, subtract free memory (available bytes), operating system memory used (nonpaged pool, resident paged pool, and resident operating system and driver code), and the size of the modified list from the total physical memory on the machine. What you're left with is the memory being used by processes. Comparing this value against the total process working set size as reported by the Performance tool gives you some indication of the amount of sharing occurring between processes. Although examining process physical memory usage is interesting, of more concern is the private committed virtual memory usage by processes, because memory leaks show up as an increasing private virtual size, not an increasing working set size. (At some point, the memory manager will stop the process from growing in physical size, though it can continue to grow in its virtual size until the commit limit—the maximum amount of private committed virtual memory available on the system—is reached. For more information, see the section "Page Files" on page 450.)

■ **Total system working set size** To view this information, select the Memory processor object and the Cache Bytes counter. As explained in the section "System Working Set," the total system working set size includes more than just the cache size—it includes resident paged pool and resident operating system and driver code.

■ **Size of nonpaged pool** View this information by adding the Memory: Pool Nonpaged Bytes counter.

■ **Size of the free, zero, and standby lists** View the sizes of these lists by adding the Memory: Available Bytes counter. (Use the *!memusage* kernel debugger command to get the size of each of the lists separately.)

Your graph or report now contains a representation of all of physical memory except for two components that you can't obtain from a performance counter:

- Nonpaged operating system and driver code
- The modified and modified-no-write paging lists

Although you can easily obtain the size of both the modified and modified-no-write lists by using the kernel debugger *!memusage* command, there's no easy way to get the size of the nonpaged operating system and driver code. You can, however, get the amount of physical memory being used by nonpaged and paged operating system and device driver code by using the kernel debugger *!drivers 1* command and the total of the Resident column. This column represents the number of pages that physically reside in each loaded kernel-mode module.

Services the Memory Manager Provides

The memory manager provides a set of system services to allocate and free virtual memory, share memory between processes, map files into memory, flush virtual pages to disk, retrieve information about a range of virtual pages, change the protection of virtual pages, and lock the virtual pages into memory.

Like other Windows 2000 executive services, the memory management services allow their caller to supply a process handle, indicating the particular process whose virtual memory is to be manipulated. The caller can thus manipulate either its own memory or (with the proper permissions) the memory of another process. For example, if a process creates a child process, by default it has the right to manipulate the child process's virtual memory. Thereafter, the parent process can allocate, deallocate, read, and write memory on behalf of the child process by calling virtual memory services and passing a handle to the child process as an argument. This feature is used by subsystems to manage the memory of their client processes, and it is also key for implementing debuggers because debuggers must be able to read and write to the memory of the process being debugged.

Most of these services are exposed through the Win32 API. The Win32 API has three groups of functions for managing memory in applications: page granularity virtual memory functions (*Virtualxxx*), memory-mapped file functions (*CreateFileMapping, MapViewOfFile*), and heap functions (*Heapxxx* and the older interfaces *Localxxx* and *Globalxxx*). (We'll describe the heap manager later in this section.)

The memory manager also provides a number of services, such as allocating and deallocating physical memory and locking pages in physical memory for direct memory access (DMA) transfers, to other kernel-mode components inside the executive as well as to device drivers. These functions begin with the prefix *Mm*. In addition, though not strictly part of the memory manager, executive support routines that begin with *Ex* are used to allocate and deallocate from the system heaps (paged and nonpaged pool) as well as to manipulate look-aside lists. We'll touch on these topics later in this chapter, in the section "System Memory Pools" on page 403.

Although we'll be referring to Win32 functions and kernel-mode memory management and memory allocation routines provided for device drivers, we won't cover the interface and programming details but rather the internal operations of these functions. Refer to the Win32 API and Device Driver Kit (DDK) documentation on MSDN for a complete description of the available functions and their interfaces.

Reserving and Committing Pages

Pages in a process address space are free, reserved, or committed. Applications can first *reserve* address space and then *commit* pages in that address space. Or they can reserve and commit in the same function call. These services are exposed through the Win32 *VirtualAlloc* and *VirtualAllocEx* functions.

Reserved address space is simply a way for a thread to reserve a range of virtual addresses for future use. Attempting to access reserved memory results in an access violation because the page isn't mapped to any storage that can resolve the reference.

Committed pages are pages that, when accessed, ultimately translate to valid pages in physical memory. Committed pages are either private and not shareable or mapped to a view of a section (which might or might not be mapped by other processes). Sections are described in the next section as well as in "Section Objects" on page 478.

If the pages are private to the process and have never been accessed before, they are created at the time of first access as zero-initialized pages (or *demand*

zero). Private committed pages can later be automatically written to the paging file by the operating system if memory demands dictate. Committed pages that are private are inaccessible to any other process unless they're accessed using cross-process memory functions, such as *ReadProcessMemory* or *WriteProcessMemory*. If committed pages are mapped to a portion of a mapped file, they might need to be brought in from disk when accessed unless they've already been read earlier, either by the process accessing the page or by another process that had the same file mapped and had accessed the page.

Pages are written to disk through normal modified page writing as pages are moved from the process working set to the modified list and ultimately to disk. (Working sets and the modified list are explained later in this chapter.) Mapped file pages can also be written back to disk as a result of an explicit call to *FlushViewOfFile*.

You can decommit pages and/or release address space with the *VirtualFree* or *VirtualFreeEx* functions. The difference between decommittal and release is similar to the difference between reservation and committal—decommitted memory is still reserved, but released memory is neither committed nor reserved. (It's free.)

Using the two-step process of reserving and committing memory can reduce memory usage by deferring committing pages until needed. Reserving memory is a relatively fast and inexpensive operation under Windows 2000 because it doesn't consume any committed pages (a precious system resource) or process page file quota (a limit on the number of committed pages a process can consume—not necessarily page file space). All that needs to be updated or constructed is the relatively small internal data structures that represent the state of the process address space. (We'll explain these data structures, called *virtual address descriptors,* or VADs, later in the chapter.)

Reserving and then committing memory is useful for applications that need a potentially large contiguous memory buffer; rather than committing pages for the entire region, the address space can be reserved and then committed later when needed. A utilization of this technique in the operating system is the user-mode stack for each thread. When a thread is created, a stack is reserved. (1 MB is the default; you can override this size with the *CreateThread* function call or on an imagewide basis by using the /STACK linker flag.) By default, the initial page in the stack is committed and the next page is marked as a guard page, which isn't committed, that traps references beyond the end of the committed portion of the stack and expands it.

Locking Memory

Pages can be locked in memory in two ways:

- Device drivers can call the kernel-mode functions *MmProbeAndLock-Pages*, *MmLockPagableCodeSection*, *MmLockPagableDataSection*, or *MmLockPagableSectionByHandle*. Pages locked using this mechanism remain in memory until explicitly unlocked. Although no quota is imposed on the number of pages a driver can lock in memory, a driver can't lock more pages than the resident available page count will allow. Also, each page does use a system page table entry (PTE), which is a limited resource. (PTEs are described later in the chapter.)

- Win32 applications can call the *VirtualLock* function to lock pages in their process working set. Note that such pages are not immune from paging—if all the threads in the process are in a wait state, the memory manager is free to remove such pages from the working set (which, for modified pages, ultimately would result in writing the pages to disk) if memory demands dictate. In such cases, locking pages in your working set can actually degrade performance because when a thread wakes up to run, the memory manager must first read in all the locked pages before the thread can begin execution. Therefore, in general, it's better to let the memory manager decide which pages remain in physical memory. The number of pages a process can lock can't exceed its minimum working set size minus eight pages.

Allocation Granularity

Windows 2000 aligns each region of reserved process address space to begin on an integral boundary defined by the value of the system *allocation granularity*, which can be retrieved from the Win32 *GetSystemInfo* function. Currently, this value is 64 KB. This size was chosen so that if support were added for future processors with large page sizes (for example, up to 64 KB), the risk of requiring changes to applications that made assumptions about allocation alignment would be reduced. (Windows 2000 kernel-mode code isn't subject to the same restrictions; it can reserve memory on a single-page granularity.)

Finally, when a region of address space is reserved, Windows 2000 ensures that the size of the region is a multiple of the system page size, whatever that might be. For example, because x86 systems use 4-KB pages, if you tried to reserve a region of memory 18 KB in size, the actual amount reserved on an x86 system would be 20 KB.

Shared Memory and Mapped Files

As is true with most modern operating systems, Windows 2000 provides a mechanism to share memory among processes and the operating system. *Shared memory* can be defined as memory that is visible to more than one process or that is present in more than one process virtual address space. For example, if two processes use the same DLL, it would make sense to load the referenced code pages for that DLL into physical memory only once and share those pages between all processes that map the DLL, as illustrated in Figure 7-1.

Figure 7-1
Sharing memory between processes

Each process would still maintain its private memory areas in which to store private data, but the program instructions and unmodified data pages could be shared without harm. As we'll explain later, this kind of sharing happens automatically because the code pages in executable images are mapped as execute-only and writable pages are mapped copy-on-write. (See the section "Copy-on-Write" on page 398 for more information.)

The underlying primitives in the memory manager used to implement shared memory are called *section objects*, which are called *file mapping objects* in the Win32 API. The internal structure and implementation of section objects are described later in this chapter (beginning on page 478).

This fundamental primitive in the memory manager is used to map virtual addresses, whether in main memory, in the page file, or in some other file that an application wants to access as if it were in memory. A section can be opened by one process or by many; in other words, section objects don't necessarily equate to shared memory.

A section object can be connected to an open file on disk (called a mapped file) or to committed memory (to provide shared memory). Sections mapped to committed memory are called *page file backed sections* because the pages can be written to the paging file if memory demands dictate. (Because Windows 2000 can run with no paging file, page file backed sections might in fact be "backed" only by physical memory). As with private committed pages, shared committed pages are always zero-filled when they are first accessed.

To create a section object, call the Win32 *CreateFileMapping* function, specifying the file handle to map it to (or INVALID_HANDLE_VALUE for a page file backed section), and optionally a name and security descriptor. If the section has a name, other processes can open it with *OpenFileMapping*. Or you can grant access to section objects through handle inheritance (by specifying that the handle be inheritable when opening or creating the handle) or handle duplication (by using *DuplicateHandle*). Device drivers can also manipulate section objects with the *ZwOpenSection*, *ZwMapViewOfSection*, and *ZwUnmapViewOfSection* functions.

A section object can refer to files that are much larger than can fit in the address space of a process. (If the paging file backs a section object, sufficient space must exist in the paging file to contain it.) To access a very large section object, a process can map only the portion of the section object that it requires (called a *view* of the section) by calling the *MapViewOfFile* function and then specifying the range to map. Mapping views permits processes to conserve address space because only the views of the section object needed at the time must be mapped into memory.

Win32 applications can use mapped files to conveniently perform I/O to files by simply making them appear in their address space. User applications aren't the only consumers of section objects: the image loader uses section objects to map executable images, DLLs, and device drivers into memory, and the cache manager uses them to access data in cached files. (For information on how the cache manager integrates with the memory manager, see Chapter 11.)

How shared memory sections are implemented both in terms of address translation and the internal data structures is explained later in this chapter.

Protecting Memory

As explained in Chapter 1, Windows 2000 provides memory protection so that no user process can inadvertently or deliberately corrupt the address space of another process or the operating system itself. Windows 2000 provides this protection in four primary ways.

First, all systemwide data structures and memory pools used by kernel-mode system components can be accessed only while in kernel mode—user-mode threads can't access these pages. If they attempt to do so, the hardware generates a fault, which in turn the memory manager reports to the thread as an access violation.

> **NOTE** In contrast, Microsoft Windows 95, Microsoft Windows 98, and Microsoft Windows Millennium Edition have some pages in system address space that are writable from user mode, thus allowing an errant application to corrupt key system data structures and crash the system.

Second, each process has a separate, private address space, protected from being accessed by any thread belonging to another process. The only exceptions are if the process is sharing pages with other processes or if another process has virtual memory read or write access to the process object and thus can use the *ReadProcessMemory* or *WriteProcessMemory* functions. Each time a thread references an address, the virtual memory hardware, in concert with the memory manager, intervenes and translates the virtual address into a physical one. By controlling how virtual addresses are translated, Windows 2000 can ensure that threads running in one process don't inappropriately access a page belonging to another process.

Third, in addition to the implicit protection virtual-to-physical address translation offers, all processors supported by Windows 2000 provide some form of hardware-controlled memory protection (such as read/write, read-only, and so on); the exact details of such protection vary according to the processor. For example, code pages in the address space of a process are marked read-only and

are thus protected from modification by user threads. Code pages for loaded device drivers are similarly marked read-only.

> **NOTE** By default, system-code write protection doesn't apply to Ntoskrnl.exe or Hal.dll on systems with 128 MB or more of physical memory. On such systems, Windows 2000 maps the first 512 MB of system address space with large (4-MB) pages to increase the efficiency of the translation look-aside buffer (explained later in this chapter). Because image sections are mapped at a granularity of 4 KB, the use of 4-MB pages means that a code section of an image might reside on the same page as a data section. Thus, marking such a page read-only would prevent the data on that page from being modifiable. You can override this value by adding the DWORD registry value HKLM\ SYSTEM\CurrentControlSet\Control\SessionManager\Memory Management\LargePageMinimum as the number of megabytes required on the system to map Ntoskrnl and the HAL with large pages.

Table 7-3 lists the memory protection options defined in the Win32 API. (See the *VirtualProtect*, *VirtualProtectEx*, *VirtualQuery*, and *VirtualQueryEx* functions.)

Table 7-3 Memory Protection Options Defined in the Win32 API

Attribute	Description
PAGE_NOACCESS	Any attempt to read from, write to, or execute code in this region causes an access violation.
PAGE_READONLY	Any attempt to write to or execute code in memory causes an access violation, but reads are permitted.
PAGE_READWRITE	The page is readable and writable—no action will cause an access violation.
PAGE_EXECUTE*	Any attempt to read from or write to code in memory in this region causes an access violation, but execution is permitted.
PAGE_EXECUTE_READ*	Any attempt to write to code in memory in this region causes an access violation, but executes and reads are permitted.
PAGE_EXECUTE_READWRITE*	The page is readable, writable, and executable—no action will cause an access violation.

Attribute	Description
PAGE_WRITECOPY	Any attempt to write to memory in this region causes the system to give the process a private copy of the page. Attempts to execute code in memory in this region cause an access violation.
PAGE_EXECUTE_WRITECOPY	Any attempt to write to memory in this region causes the system to give the process a private copy of the page.
PAGE_GUARD	Any attempt to read from or write to a guard page raises an EXCEPTION_ GUARD_PAGE exception and turns off the guard page status. Guard pages thus act as a one-shot alarm. Note that this flag can be specified with any of the page protections listed in this table except PAGE_NOACCESS.

* The x86 architecture doesn't implement execute-only access (that is, code can be executed in any readable page), so Windows 2000 doesn't support this option in any practical sense (though IA-64 does). Windows 2000 treats PAGE_EXECUTE_READ as PAGE_ READONLY and PAGE_EXECUTE_READWRITE as PAGE_READWRITE.

And finally, shared memory section objects have standard Windows 2000 access-control lists (ACLs) that are checked when processes attempt to open them, thus limiting access of shared memory to those processes with the proper rights. Security also comes into play when a thread creates a section to contain a mapped file. To create the section, the thread must have at least read access to the underlying file object or the operation will fail.

Once a thread has successfully opened a handle to a section, its actions are still subject to the memory manager and the hardware-based page protections described earlier. A thread can change the page-level protection on virtual pages in a section if the change doesn't violate the permissions in the ACL for that section object. For example, the memory manager allows a thread to change the pages of a read-only section to have copy-on-write access but not to have read/ write access. The copy-on-write access is permitted because it has no effect on other processes sharing the data.

These four primary memory protection mechanisms are part of the reason that Windows 2000 is a robust, reliable operating system that is impervious to and resilient to application errors.

Copy-on-Write

Copy-on-write page protection is an optimization the memory manager uses to conserve physical memory. When a process maps a copy-on-write view of a section object that contains read/write pages, instead of making a process private copy at the time the view is mapped (as the Compaq OpenVMS operating system does), the memory manager defers making a copy of the pages until the page is written to. All modern UNIX systems use this technique as well. For example, as shown in Figure 7-2, two processes are sharing three pages, each marked copy-on-write, but neither of the two processes has attempted to modify any data on the pages.

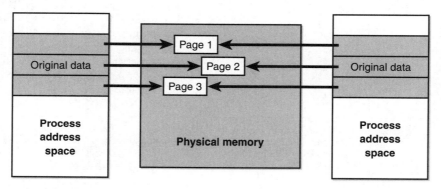

Figure 7-2
The "before" of copy-on-write

If a thread in either process writes to a page, a memory management fault is generated. The memory manager sees that the write is to a copy-on-write page, so instead of reporting the fault as an access violation, it allocates a new read/write page in physical memory, copies the contents of the original page to the new page, updates the corresponding page-mapping information (explained later in this chapter) in this process to point to the new location, and dismisses the exception, thus causing the instruction that generated the fault to be reexecuted. This time, the write operation succeeds, but as shown in Figure 7-3, the newly copied page is now private to the process that did the writing and isn't visible to the other processes still sharing the copy-on-write page. Each new process that writes to that same shared page will also get its own private copy.

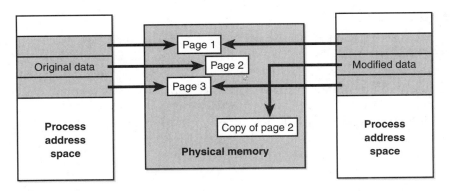

Figure 7-3
The "after" of copy-on-write

One application of copy-on-write is to implement breakpoint support in debuggers. For example, by default, code pages start out as execute-only. If a programmer sets a breakpoint while debugging a program, however, the debugger must add a breakpoint instruction to the code. It does this by first changing the protection on the page to PAGE_EXECUTE_READWRITE and then changing the instruction stream. Because the code page is part of a mapped section, the memory manager creates a private copy for the process with the breakpoint set, while other processes continue using the unmodified code page.

Copy-on-write is one example of an evaluation technique known as *lazy evaluation* that the memory manager uses as often as possible. Lazy-evaluation algorithms avoid performing an expensive operation until absolutely required—if the operation is never required, no time is wasted on it.

The POSIX subsystem takes advantage of copy-on-write to implement the *fork* function. Typically, when a UNIX application calls the *fork* function to create another process, the first thing that the new process does is call the *exec* function to reinitialize the address space with an executable program. Instead of copying the entire address space on *fork*, the new process shares the pages in the parent process by marking them copy-on-write. If the child writes to the data, a process private copy is made. If not, the two processes continue sharing and no copying takes place. One way or the other, the memory manager copies only the pages the process tries to write to rather than the entire address space.

To examine the rate of copy-on-write faults, see the performance counter Memory: Write Copies/Sec.

Heap Functions

A *heap* is a region of one or more pages of reserved address space that can be subdivided and allocated in smaller chunks by the *heap manager*. The heap manager is a set of functions that can be used to allocate and deallocate variable amounts of memory (not necessarily on a page-size granularity as is done in the *VirtualAlloc* function). The heap manager functions exist in two places: Ntdll.dll and Ntoskrnl.exe. The subsystem APIs (such as the Win32 heap APIs) call the functions in Ntdll, and various executive components and device drivers call the functions in Ntoskrnl.

Every process starts out with a default process heap, usually 1 MB in size (unless specified otherwise in the image file by using the /HEAP linker flag). This size is just the initial reserve, however—it will expand automatically as needed. (You can also specify the initial committed size in the image file.) Win32 applications as well as several Win32 functions that might need to allocate temporary memory blocks use this process default heap. Processes can also create additional private heaps with the *HeapCreate* function. When a process no longer needs a private heap, it can recover the virtual address space by calling *HeapDestroy*. Only a private heap created with *HeapCreate*—not the default heap—can be destroyed during the life of a process.

To allocate memory from the default heap, a thread must obtain a handle to it by calling *GetProcessHeap*. (This function returns the address of the data structure that describes the heap, but callers should never rely on that.) A thread can then use the heap handle in calls to *HeapAlloc* and *HeapFree* to allocate and free memory blocks from that heap. The heap manager also provides an option for each heap to serialize allocations and deallocations so that multiple threads can call heap functions simultaneously without corrupting heap data structures. The default process heap is set to have this serialization by default (though you can override this on a call-by-call basis). For additional private heaps, a flag passed to *HeapCreate* is used to specify whether serialization should be performed.

The heap manager supports a number of internal validation checks that, although not currently documented, you can enable on a systemwide or a per-image basis by using the Global Flags (Gflags.exe) utility in the Windows 2000 Support Tools, Platform SDK, and DDK. Many of the flags are self-explanatory in terms of what they cause the heap manager to do. In general, enabling these flags will cause invalid use or corruption of the heap—to generate error notifications to an application either through the use of exceptions or through returned error codes. (See Chapter 3 for information about exceptions.)

For more information on the heap functions, see the Win32 API reference documentation on MSDN.

Address Windowing Extensions

Although Windows 2000 systems can support up to 64 GB of physical memory (as shown in Table 2-2 on page 39), each 32-bit user process has only a 2-GB or 3-GB virtual address space (depending on whether the /3GB boot switch is enabled). To allow a 32-bit process to allocate and access more physical memory than can be represented in its limited address space, Windows 2000 provides a set of functions called *Address Windowing Extensions* (AWE). For example, on a Windows 2000 Advanced Server system with 8 GB of physical memory, a database server application could use AWE to allocate and use nearly 8 GB of memory as a database cache.

Allocating and using memory via the AWE functions is done in three steps:

1. Allocating the physical memory to be used

2. Creating a region of virtual address space to act as a window to map views of the physical memory

3. Mapping views of the physical memory into the window

To allocate physical memory, an application calls the Win32 function *AllocateUserPhysicalPages*. (This function requires the Lock Pages in Memory user right.) The application then uses the Win32 *VirtualAlloc* function with the MEM_PHYSICAL flag to create a window in the private portion of the process's address space that is mapped to some or all of the physical memory previously allocated. The AWE-allocated memory can then be used with nearly all the Win32 APIs. (For example, the Microsoft DirectX functions can't use AWE memory.)

If an application creates a 256-MB window in its address space and allocates 4 GB of physical memory (on a system with more than 4 GB of physical memory), the application can use the *MapUserPhysicalPages* or *MapUserPhysicalPagesScatter* Win32 functions to access any portion of the physical memory by mapping the memory into the 256-MB window. The size of the application's virtual address space window determines the amount of physical memory that the application can access with a given mapping. Figure 7-4 shows an AWE window in a server application address space mapped to a portion of physical memory previously allocated by *AllocateUserPhysicalPages*.

Figure 7-4
Using AWE to map physical memory

The AWE functions exist on all editions of Windows 2000 and are usable regardless of how much physical memory a system has. However, AWE is most useful on systems with more than 2 GB of physical memory because it's the only way for a 32-bit process to directly use more than 2 GB of memory.

Finally, there are some restrictions on memory allocated and mapped by the AWE functions:

- Pages can't be shared between processes.
- The same physical page can't be mapped to more than one virtual address in the same process.
- Page protection is limited to read/write.

For a description of the page table data structures used to map memory on systems with more than 4 GB of physical memory, see the section "Physical Address Extension" on page 442.

System Memory Pools

At system initialization, the memory manager creates two types of dynamically sized memory pools that the kernel-mode components use to allocate system memory:

- **Nonpaged pool** Consists of ranges of system virtual addresses that are guaranteed to reside in physical memory at all times and thus can be accessed at any time (from any IRQL level and from any process context) without incurring a page fault. One of the reasons nonpaged pool is required is due to the rule described in Chapter 2: page faults can't be satisfied at DPC/dispatch level or above.

- **Paged pool** A region of virtual memory in system space that can be paged in and out of the system. Device drivers that don't need to access the memory from DPC/dispatch level or above can use paged pool. It is accessible from any process context.

Both memory pools are located in the system part of the address space and are mapped in the virtual address space of every process. (In Table 7-10 on page 427, you'll find out where in the system memory they start.) The executive provides routines to allocate and deallocate from these pools; for information on these routines, see the functions that start with *ExAllocatePool* in the Windows 2000 DDK documentation.

There are two types of nonpaged pools: one for general use and a small one (four pages) reserved for emergency use when nonpaged pool is full and the caller can't tolerate allocation failures. (This latter pool type should no longer be used; device drivers should be written to properly handle low memory conditions. Driver Verifier, discussed later in this chapter, makes it easier to test such conditions.) Uniprocessor systems have three paged pools; multiprocessor systems have five. Having more than one paged pool reduces the frequency of system code blocking on simultaneous calls to pool routines. Both nonpaged and paged pool start at an initial size based on the amount of physical memory on the system and then grow, if necessary, up to a maximum size computed at system boot time. You can override the initial size of these pools by changing the values NonPagedPoolSize and PagedPoolSize in the registry key HKLM\SYSTEM\CurrentControlSet\Control\Session Manager\Memory Management from 0 (which causes the system to compute the size) to the size desired in bytes. You can't, however, go beyond the maximum pool sizes listed in Table 7-4.

Table 7-4 Maximum Pool Sizes

Pool Type	Maximum Size
Nonpaged	256 MB (128 MB if booted /3GB)
Paged	491.875 MB

The computed sizes are stored in four kernel variables, three of which are exposed as performance counters. These variables and counters, as well as the two registry keys that can alter the sizes, are listed in Table 7-5.

Table 7-5 System Pool Size Variables and Performance Counters

Kernel Variable	Performance Counter	Registry Key to Override	Description
MmSizeOfNonPaged-PoolInBytes	Memory: Pool Nonpaged Bytes	Not applicable	Current size of nonpaged pool
MmMaximumNon-PagedPoolInBytes	Not available	HKLM\SYSTEM\CurrentControlSet\Control\Session Manager\Memory Management\NonPagedPoolSize	Maximum size of nonpaged pool
Not available	Memory: Pool Paged Bytes	Not applicable	Current virtual size of paged pool
MmPagedPoolPage (number of pages)	Memory: Pool Paged Resident Bytes	Not applicable	Current physical (resident) size of paged pool
MmSizeOfPagedPool-InBytes	Not available	HKLM\SYSTEM\CurrentControlSet\Control\Session Manager\Memory Management\PagedPoolSize	Maximum (virtual) size of paged pool

EXPERIMENT: Determining the Maximum Pool Sizes

Because paged and nonpaged pool represent a critical system resource, it is important to know when you're nearing the maximum size computed for your system so that you can determine whether you need to override the default maximum with the appropriate registry values. The pool-size performance counters report only the current size, however, not the maximum size. So you don't know when you're reaching the limit until you've exhausted pool.

With LiveKd, you can easily view the maximum sizes by examining the values of the kernel variables listed in Table 7-5. Here's an example:

```
kd> dd mmmaximumnonpagedpoolinbytes l1
8047f620  0328c000
kd> ? 328c000
Evaluate expression: 53002240 = 0328c000
kd> dd mmsizeofpagedpoolinbytes l1
80470a98  06800000
kd> ? 6800000
Evaluate expression: 109051904 = 06800000
```

From this example, you can see that the maximum size of nonpaged pool is 53,002,240 bytes (approximately 50 MB) and the maximum size of paged pool is 109,051,904 bytes (104 MB). On the test system we used for this example, current nonpaged pool usage was 5.5 MB and paged pool usage was 34 MB, so both pools were far from full. (To quickly see these numbers, run Task Manager, click the Performance tab, and view the Kernel Memory section.)

EXPERIMENT: Monitoring Pool Usage

The Memory performance counter object has separate counters for the size of nonpaged pool and paged pool (both virtual and physical). In addition, the Poolmon utility (in the Windows 2000 Support Tools) allows you to monitor the detailed usage of nonpaged and paged pool. To do so, you must have the internal Enable Pool Tagging option enabled. (Pool tagging is always turned on in the checked build, so you need to enable it only on a retail system.) To enable pool tagging, run the Gflags utility in the Windows 2000 Support Tools, Platform SDK, or DDK, and select Enable Pool Tagging, as shown here:

Then click Apply, and reboot the system. After the system reboots, run Poolmon; you should see a display like this one:

The highlighted lines represent changes to the display. (You can disable the highlighting feature by typing *l* while running Poolmon. Type *l* again to reenable highlighting.) Type *?* while Poolmon is running to bring up its help screen. You can configure which pools you want to monitor (paged, nonpaged, or both) and the sort order. Also, the command-line options are shown, which allow you to monitor specific structures (or everything but one structure type). For example, the command *poolmon -iCM* will monitor only structures of type CM (the configuration manager, which manages the registry). The columns have the following meanings:

Column	Explanation
Tag	Four-byte tag given to the pool allocation
Type	Pool type (paged or nonpaged pool)
Allocs	Count of all allocations (The number in parentheses shows the difference in the Allocs column since the last update.)
Frees	Count of all Frees (The number in parentheses shows the difference in the Frees column since the last update.)
Diff	Allocs minus Frees
Bytes	Total bytes consumed by this structure type (The number in parentheses shows the difference in the Bytes column since the last update.)
Per Alloc	Size in bytes of a single instance of this structure type

In this example, CM structures are taking up the most space in paged pool, and MmSt structures (a memory management–related structure used for mapped files) are taking up the most space in nonpaged pool.

You can also view pool usage with the kernel debugger *!poolused* and *!xpool* commands. (*!xpool* is in the secondary kernel debugger extension DLL, Kdex2x86.dll.) The command *!poolused 2* shows nonpaged pool usage sorted by structure tag using the most amount of pool. The command *!poolused 4* lists paged pool usage, again sorted by structure tag using the most amount of pool. The following example shows the partial output from these two commands:

```
kd>   .load kdex2x86
kd>   !poolused 2
   Sorting by NonPaged Pool Consumed
```

(continued)

EXPERIMENT: **Monitoring Pool Usage** *continued*

```
    Pool Used:
              NonPaged              Paged
    Tag    Allocs      Used     Allocs      Used
    File     1702    326784          0         0
    Thre      376    240640          0         0
    Vad      3167    202688          0         0
    Ntf0        3    196608        967     51264
    Even     2869    187264          0         0
    Npfs      335    154080        221     41504
    Devi      249    148480          0         0
    WDMA      333    146176        319     49984
    Pool        3    134368          0         0
    Irp       305    134272          0         0
    AmlH        2    131072          0         0
    ⋮
kd> !poolused 4
    Sorting by Paged Pool Consumed

    Pool Used:
              NonPaged              Paged
    Tag    Allocs      Used     Allocs      Used
    CM         11       704       5146  22311904
    Gh 5        0         0        727   2523648
    MmSt        0         0        968   1975872
    Ntff       10      2240        790    682560
    Gla1        1       128        383    600544
    Ttfd        0         0        265    545440
    Gla5        1       128       1099    457184
    NtFB        0         0          2    376832
    LXMK        0         0        948    319680
    Gla:        1       128        444    298368
    Obtb       52      6656         68    278528
    NtfF        0         0        250    248000
    Gcac        0         0         54    243424
    Mmpp        0         0         55    225280
    Grgb        0         0          5    163840
    ⋮
```

The *!xpool –map* command displays a map of the status of each page in nonpaged pool (*!xpool –map 1* displays paged pool) as well as total pool usage. The following are partial examples using this command:

```
kd> !xpool -map

Status Map of Pool Area Pages
==============================
 'O': one page in use                                ('P': paged out)
 '<': start page of contiguous pages in use          ('{': paged out)
 '>': last page of contiguous pages in use           ('}': paged out)
 '=': intermediate page of contiguous pages in use ('-': paged out)
 '.': one page not used

Non-Paged Pool Area Summary
----------------------------
Maximum Number of Pages  = 12940 pages
Number of Pages In Use   =  1459 pages (11.3%)

           +00000   +08000   +10000   +18000   +20000   +28000   +30000   +38000
81093000: ....000000000000 0000000000000000 0000000000000000
          00000000<=>00000
810d3000: 0000000000000000 0000000000000000 0000000000000000
          <=>0000000000000
81113000: 0000000000000000 0000000000000000 0000000000000000
          0000000000000000
81153000: 0000000000000000 0000000000000000 0000000000000000
          0000000000000<=>
81193000: 0000000000000000 0000000000000000 0000000000000000
          0000000000000000
811d3000: 0000000000<=>000 0000<>0000000000 0000000000000000
          0000000000000000
81213000: 000000000000<=== ><============= ================>
          <==========><===
81253000: =============== ================ ================
          =====><=========
81293000: =============== ================ ================
          ================
812d3000: ==><===========> 0000000000000000 0000000000000000
          0000000000000<==
81313000: =============== ====><======>0<> 000000<>000<=>00
          00<======>0<====
81353000: ==>0000000000000 <============== ==><==>000<><===
          ===>0<=>00000000
81393000: 0<===>00000000<= ========>0000000 0000000000000000
          000000000<=><===
```

(continued)

EXPERIMENT: Monitoring Pool Usage *continued*

```
813d3000: ====>00<>00000<= =====><=>0000000 000000000000<===
          ==========><===
81413000: ==========>0000 00000<========== ====>00000000000
          0000000000<=====
81453000: =========>000000 0000<=>00000000< ==============>0
          0000<==========>
81493000: 0000000000000000 <======>
fcd6c000: ................ ................ ................
          ................
fcdac000: ................ ................ ................
          ................
fcdec000: ................ ................ ................
          ................
  ⋮

kd> !xpool -map 1

Status Map of Pool Area Pages
==============================
  'O': one page in use                            ('P': paged out)
  '<': start page of contiguous pages in use      ('{': paged out)
  '>': last page of contiguous pages in use       ('}': paged out)
  '=': intermediate page of contiguous pages in use ('-': paged out)
  '.': one page not used

Paged Pool Area Summary
-----------------------
Maximum Number of Pages  = 26624 pages
Number of Pages In Use   =  8685 pages (32.6%)
        +00000  +08000  +10000  +18000  +20000  +28000  +30000  +38000
e1000000: 00000<>00<><>P00 00000000PPPPPPP0 PPPPPPPPPPPPP0P0
          0PPPPPPPPPPPP000
e1040000: 00PP0PPPPPPP0000 00000P000PPPPPPP P000000000000000
          P0{}P0PP0P0PPPPP
e1080000: 0PPP00PPPPPPPP00 {>PPPPPP0PPPPPPP PPPPPPPPPPPPPP00
          0P{}PPPPPPPPPPPP
e10c0000: PPPPPPPPPPPPPPPP PPPPPPPPPPPPPPPP PPPPPPPP00PPPPP
          00000000P0000000
```

```
e1100000:  P000000000000{>0 0000000000000000 000000000000P000
           0000000000000000
e1140000:  00PP000000000000 0PP000000<>00PP0 0000PPPPPP0PPPPP
           PPPPPPPPP0PP0PPP
e1180000:  PPPPPPPPP00PPPP PPPPPPPPPPPPPPPP PPPP0PPPPPPPPPPP
           PPPPPPPPPPPPP0P{
e11c0000:  >0PP0PPPPPPPPPP POPPPPPPPPPPP{}P PPPPPPPPPPPPPPPP
           PPPPPPPPPPPPP{}P
e1200000:  PPPPPPPPPPPPPPPP PPPPPP0PPP0PP0PP PPPPPPPPPPPPPPPP
           PPPPPPPPPPPPPPPP
e1240000:  PPPP0PPPPPPP00PP PPPPPPPPP{}PPPPP PPPPPPPPPP0P0PPP
           0P00PPPPPPPPPP0P
e1280000:  PPPPPP0PPPPP00PP P0P0PPPPPPPPP<>0 PPP0P0{>PPPP0P00
           P0PP{}P0PP0PPPPP
e12c0000:  PPP00P000P0PPPPP PPPP000PPPPPPPPP PPPPPP00PP0PPP00
           P00P000000P0PP00
⋮
```

Look-Aside Lists

Windows 2000 also provides a fast memory allocation mechanism called *look-aside lists*. The basic difference between pools and look-aside lists is that while general pool allocations can vary in size, a look-aside list contains only fixed-sized blocks. Although the general pools are more flexible in terms of what they can supply, look-aside lists are faster because they don't use any spinlocks and also because the system doesn't have to search for free memory that fits a varying size allocation.

Executive components and device drivers can create look-aside lists that match the size of frequently allocated data structures using the *ExInitialize-NPagedLookasideList* and *ExInitializePagedLookasideList* functions (documented in the DDK). To minimize the overhead of multiprocessor synchronization, several executive subsystems (such as the I/O manager, cache manager, and object manager) create separate look-aside lists for each processor for their frequently accessed data structures. The executive also creates a general per-processor paged and nonpaged look-aside list for small allocations (256 bytes or less).

If a look-aside list is empty (as it is when it's first created), the system must allocate from paged or nonpaged pool. But if it contains a freed structure, the allocation can be satisfied very quickly. (The list grows as structures are returned

to it.) The pool allocation routines automatically tune the number of freed buffers that look-aside lists store according to how often a device driver or executive subsystem allocates from the list—the more frequent the allocations, the more buffers are stored on a list. Look-aside lists are automatically reduced in size if they aren't being allocated from. (This check happens once per second when the balance set manager system thread wakes up and calls the function *KiAdjustLookasideDepth*.)

EXPERIMENT: Viewing the System Look-Aside Lists

You can display the contents and sizes of the various system look-aside lists with the kernel debugger *!lookaside* command. The following excerpt is from the output of this command:

```
kd> !lookaside

Lookaside "nt!IopSmallIrpLookasideList" @ 804758a0 "Irps"
    Type      =    0000 NonPagedPool
    Current Depth =        3  Max Depth  =        4
    Size      =        148  Max Alloc  =      592
    AllocateMisses =       32  FreeMisses =        9
    TotalAllocates =       52  TotalFrees =       32
    Hit Rate  =        38%  Hit Rate   =      71%
Lookaside "nt!IopLargeIrpLookasideList" @ 804756a0 "Irpl"
    Type      =    0000 NonPagedPool
    Current Depth =        4  Max Depth  =        4
    Size      =        436  Max Alloc  =     1744
    AllocateMisses =     2623  FreeMisses =     2443
    TotalAllocates =     7039  TotalFrees =     6863
    Hit Rate  =        62%  Hit Rate   =      64%

Lookaside "nt!IopMdlLookasideList" @ 80475740 "Mdl "
    Type      =    0000 NonPagedPool
    Current Depth =        3  Max Depth  =        4
    Size      =        120  Max Alloc  =      480
    AllocateMisses =     7017  FreeMisses =     1824
    TotalAllocates =    10901  TotalFrees =     5711
    Hit Rate  =        35%  Hit Rate   =      68%
  :
Total NonPaged currently allocated for above lists = 4200
Total NonPaged potential for above lists      = 6144
Total Paged currently allocated for above lists   = 5136
Total Paged potential for above lists         = 12032
```

Driver Verifier

Driver Verifier is a mechanism that can be used to help find and isolate commonly found bugs in device driver or other kernel-mode system code. Microsoft uses Driver Verifier to check all device drivers that vendors submit for Hardware Compatibility List (HCL) testing. Doing so ensures that the drivers on the HCL are compatible with Windows 2000 and free from common driver errors.

Driver Verifier consists of support in several system components: the memory manager, I/O manager, HAL, and Win32k.sys all have driver verification options that can be enabled. This section describes the memory management–related verification options Driver Verifier provides.

Driver Verifier Configuration and Initialization

To configure Driver Verifier and view statistics about its operation, run the Driver Verifier Manager (\Winnt\System32\Verifier.exe). As shown in Figure 7-5, when you run Driver Verifier, it displays several tabbed pages. You use the Settings tab to specify which device drivers you want to verify (there's an option to Verify All Drivers) and what types of verification you want performed.

Figure 7-5
The Driver Verifier Manager

The settings are stored in the registry under HKLM\SYSTEM\Current-ControlSet\Control\Session Manager\Memory Management. The value Verify-DriverLevel contains a bitmask that represents the verification types enabled. The VerifyDrivers value contains the names of the drivers to validate. (These

413

values won't exist in the registry until you select drivers to verify in the Driver Verifier Manager.) If you choose to verify all drivers, VerifyDrivers is set to an asterisk (*) character. After you've entered or changed Driver Verifier settings, you might need to reboot the system for verification to occur.

Early in the boot process, the memory manager reads the Driver Verifier registry values to determine which drivers to verify and which Driver Verifier options you enabled. Subsequently, if you've selected at least one driver for verification, the kernel checks the name of every device driver it loads into memory against the list of drivers you've selected for verification. For every device driver that appears in both places, the kernel invokes the *MiApplyDriverVerifier* function, which replaces the driver's references to any of approximately 40 kernel functions with references to Driver Verifier–equivalent versions of those functions. For example, *ExAllocatePool* is replaced with a call to *VerifierAllocatePool*. The windowing system driver also makes similar changes to use Driver Verifier–equivalent functions.

Now that we've reviewed how to set up Driver Verifier, let's examine the four memory-related verification options that can be applied to device drivers: Special Pool, Pool Tracking, Force IRQL Checking, and Low Resources Simulation.

Special Pool The Special Pool option causes the pool allocation routines to bracket pool allocations with an invalid page so that references before or after the allocation will result in a kernel-mode access violation, thus crashing the system with the finger pointed at the buggy driver. Special pool also causes some additional validation checks to be performed when a driver allocates or frees memory.

When special pool is enabled, the pool allocation routines allocate a region of kernel memory for Driver Verifier to use. Driver Verifier redirects memory allocation requests that drivers under verification make to the special pool area rather than to the standard kernel-mode memory pools. When a device driver allocates memory from special pool, Driver Verifier rounds up the allocation to an even-page boundary. Because Driver Verifier brackets the allocated page with invalid pages, if a device driver attempts to read or write past the end of the buffer, the driver will access an invalid page and the memory manager will raise a kernel-mode access violation.

Figure 7-6 shows an example of the special pool buffer that Driver Verifier allocates to a device driver when Driver Verifier checks for overrun errors.

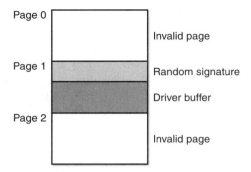

Figure 7-6
Layout of special pool allocations

By default, Driver Verifier performs *overrun* detection. It does this by placing the buffer that the device driver uses at the end of the allocated page and fills the beginning of the page with a random pattern. Although the Driver Verifier Manager doesn't let you specify underrun detection, you can set this type of detection manually by adding the DWORD registry value HKLM\SYSTEM\CurrentControlSet\Control\Session Manager\MemoryManagement\PoolTagOverruns and setting it to 1 (or by running the Gflags utility and selecting the Verify Start option instead of the default option Verify End). When Windows 2000 enforces underrun detection, Driver Verifier allocates the driver's buffer at the beginning of the page rather than at the end.

The overrun-detection configuration includes some measure of underrun detection as well. When the driver frees its buffer to return the memory to Driver Verifier, Driver Verifier ensures that the pattern preceding the buffer hasn't changed. If the pattern is modified, the device driver has underrun the buffer and written to memory outside the buffer.

Special pool allocations also check to ensure that the processor IRQL at the time of an allocation and deallocation is legal. This check catches an error that some device drivers make: allocating pageable memory from an IRQL at DPC/dispatch level or above.

You can also configure special pool manually by adding the DWORD registry value HKLM\SYSTEMCurrentControlSet\Control\Session Manager\Memory Management\PoolTag, which represents the allocation tag the system uses for special pool. Thus, even if Driver Verifier isn't configured to verify a

particular device driver, if the tag the driver associates with the memory it allocates matches what is specified in the PoolTag registry value, the pool allocation routines will allocate the memory from special pool. If you set the value of PoolTag to 0x0000002a or the wildcard (*), all memory that drivers allocate is from special pool, provided there's enough virtual and physical memory. (The drivers will revert to allocating from regular pool if there aren't enough free pages—bounding exists, but each allocation uses two pages).

Pool Tracking When device drivers allocate memory, they can specify an optional four-letter tag in their allocation requests. When you disable pool tracking, Windows 2000 ignores the tag. When you enable pool tracking, however, the pool allocation routines associate the tag with memory the driver allocates. Using Poolmon (part of the Windows 2000 Support Tools), a developer can view how much memory Windows 2000 assigned to each tag. Monitoring driver memory usage lets a developer detect memory leaks, an error that occurs when a driver fails to deallocate memory it no longer requires. Driver Verifier also shows general pool statistics on the Driver Verifier Manager's Pool Tracking tab. You can also use the *!verifier* kernel debugger command. This command shows more information than Driver Verifier and is useful to driver writers.

If pool tracking is enabled, the memory manager checks at driver unload time whether the driver freed all the memory allocations it made. If it didn't, it crashes the system, indicating the buggy driver.

Force IRQL Checking One of the most common device driver bugs occurs when a driver accesses pageable data or code when the processor on which the device driver is executing is at an elevated IRQL. As explained in Chapter 3, the memory manager can't service a page fault when the IRQL is DPC/dispatch level or above. The system often doesn't detect instances of a device driver accessing pageable data when the processor is executing at a high IRQL level because the pageable data being accessed happens to be physically resident at the time. At other times, however, the data might be paged out, which results in a system crash with the stop code IRQL_NOT_LESS_OR_EQUAL (that is, the IRQL wasn't less than or equal to the level required for the operation attempted—in this case, accessing pageable memory).

Although testing device drivers for this kind of bug is usually difficult, Driver Verifier makes it easy. If you select the Force IRQL Checking option, Driver Verifier forces all kernel-mode pageable code and data out of the system working set whenever a device driver under verification raises the IRQL. The internal function that does this is *MmTrimAllSystemPagableMemory*. With this

setting enabled, whenever a device driver under verification accesses pageable memory when the IRQL is elevated, the system instantly detects the violation and the resulting system crash identifies the faulty driver.

Low Resources Simulation Enabling Low Resources Simulation causes Driver Verifier to randomly fail memory allocations that verified device drivers perform. In the past, developers wrote many device drivers under the assumption that kernel memory would always be available and that if memory ran out, the device driver didn't have to worry about it because the system would crash anyway. However, because low-memory conditions can occur temporarily, it's important that device drivers properly handle allocation failures that indicate kernel memory is exhausted.

Beginning 7 minutes after the system boots—which is enough time to get past the critical initialization period in which a low-memory condition might prevent a device driver from loading—Driver Verifier starts randomly failing allocation calls for device drivers it is verifying. If a driver doesn't correctly handle allocation failures, this will likely show up as a system crash.

Driver Verifier is a valuable addition to the arsenal of verification and debugging tools available to device driver writers. Many device drivers that first ran with Driver Verifier had bugs that Driver Verifier was able to expose. Thus, Driver Verifier has resulted in an overall improvement in the quality of all kernel-mode code running on Windows 2000.

Address Space Layout

By default, each user process on the 32-bit version of Windows 2000 can have up to a 2 GB private address space; the operating system takes the remaining 2 GB. Windows 2000 Advanced Server and Windows 2000 Datacenter Server support a boot-time option that allows 3-GB user address spaces. These two possible address space layouts are shown in Figure 7-7.

The 3-GB address space option (enabled by the /3GB flag in Boot.ini) gives processes a 3-GB address space (leaving 1 GB for system space). This feature was added as a short-term solution to accommodate the need for applications such as database servers to keep more data in memory than could be done with a 2-GB address space. The AWE functions described earlier in this chapter provide a much better solution to the need for accessing more data than can fit in the limited 2-GB (or 3-GB) process address space.

Figure 7-7
x86 virtual address space layouts

For a process to access the full 3-GB address space, the image file must have the IMAGE_FILE_LARGE_ADDRESS_AWARE flag set in the image header. Otherwise, Windows 2000 reserves the third gigabyte so that the application won't see virtual addresses greater than 0x7FFFFFFF. You set this flag by specifying the linker flag /LARGEADDRESSAWARE when building the executable. This flag has no effect when running the application on a system with a 2-GB user address space. (If you boot Windows 2000 Professional or Windows 2000 Server with the /3GB switch, system space is reduced to 1 GB, but user processes are still limited to 2 GB, even if the large-address-space aware flag is set on an image that is run.)

Virtual Address Space in Consumer Windows

The virtual address space for Windows 95, Windows 98, and Windows Millennium Edition is organized a bit differently from that of Windows 2000. It also provides a 4-GB virtual 32-bit address space, allocating a 2-GB private address space to each process; but it divides the remaining 2 GB between system space (1 GB) and a single shared user space for all shared memory sections (1 GB), as shown here:

The 1-GB shared region is writable from user mode, so any Win32 process can write to shared memory sections or mapped files, even if they don't have that section object (file mapping object in Win32 terms) open. Windows 2000, on the other hand, places shared memory sections inside the private process address space, thus avoiding this security hole. Also, because all MS-DOS and Win16 applications are in this same shared 1-GB region, Win32 processes can corrupt the address space of Win16 and MS-DOS applications in Consumer Windows.

User Address Space Layout

Table 7-6 details the layout of the 2-GB Windows 2000 user process address space.

Table 7-6 Windows 2000 User Process Address Space Layout

Range	Size	Function
0x0 through 0xFFFF	64 KB	No-access region to aid programmers in avoiding incorrect pointer references; attempts to access an address within this range will cause an access violation. (Note that this range of addresses could be used— this is just a convention to assist in finding bugs.)
0x10000 through 0x7FFEFFFF	2 GB minus at least 192 KB	The private process address space.
0x7FFDE000 through 0x7FFDEFFF	4 KB	Thread environment block (TEB) for first thread. (See Chapter 6.) Additional TEBs are created at the page prior to this page (starting at address 0x7FFDD000 and working backward).
0x7FFDF000 through 0x7FFDFFFF	4 KB	Process environment block (PEB). (See Chapter 6.)
0x7FFE0000 through 0x7FFE0FFF	4 KB	Shared user data page. This read-only page is mapped to a page in system space that contains information such as system time, clock tick count, and version number. This page exists so that this data is directly readable from user mode without requiring a kernel-mode transition.
0x7FFE1000 through 0x7FFEFFFF	60 KB	No-access region (remainder of 64-KB region following shared user data page).
0x7FFF0000 through 0x7FFFFFFF	64 KB	No-access region that prevents threads from passing buffers that straddle the user/ system space boundary. *MmUserProbeAddress* contains the start of this page.

The system variables shown in Table 7-7 define the range of the user address space.

Table 7-7 Windows 2000 User Address Space System Variables

System Variable	Description	x86 2-GB User Space	x86 3-GB User Space
MmHighestUserAddress	Highest user address (The highest usable address is actually less because of TEBs and PEBs.)	0x7FFEFFFF	0xBFFEFFFF
MmUserProbeAddress	Highest user address +1 (used in probing accessibility of user buffers)	0x7FFF0000	0xBFFF0000

The performance counters listed in Table 7-8 provide information about total system virtual memory utilization.

Table 7-8 Windows 2000 Virtual Memory Use Performance Counters

Performance Counter	System Variable	Description
Memory: Committed Bytes	*MmTotalCommittedPages*	The amount of committed private address space (of which some can be in physical memory and some in the paging files)
Memory: Commit Limit	*MmTotalCommitLimit*	The amount (in bytes) of memory that can be committed without increasing the size of the paging file (Page files are extensible.)
Memory: % Committed Bytes In Use	*MmTotalCommittedPages / MmTotalCommitLimit*	Ratio of committed bytes to commit limit

You can obtain the address space utilization of a single process via the process performance counters in Table 7-9.

Table 7-9 **Windows 2000 Address Space Use for Single Process's Performance Counters**

Performance Counter	Description
Process: Virtual Bytes	Total size of the process address space (including shared as well as private pages)
Process: Private Bytes	Size of the private (nonshared) committed address space (same as Process: Page File Bytes)
Process: Page File Bytes	Size of the private (nonshared) committed address space (same as Process: Private Bytes)
Process: Page File Bytes Peak	Peak of Process: Page File Bytes

There is also a performance object named Process Address Space that the Performance tool doesn't display. There are 32 counters associated with this object that identify the address space usage of the selected process. For each of the four types of process address space (Image, Mapped, Reserved, and Unassigned), eight separate counters exist (No Access, Read Only, Read/Write, Write Copy, Executable, Exec Read Only, Exec Read/Write, and Exec Write Copy). In addition, there are counters for the total process address space reserved and free. For even more details about user address space layouts, you can query the Image performance object to report per-image (for example, DLLs) memory utilization.

EXPERIMENT: Viewing Process Memory Utilization

Try examining the various process memory performance counters listed in Tables 7-8 and 7-9 with the Performance tool. You can also use several other utilities to examine process physical and virtual memory usage.

For example, start Task Manager (press Ctrl+Shift+Esc), and click the Processes tab. Then from the View menu, choose Select Columns. Select Memory Usage and Virtual Memory Size, and then click OK. You should see a display like this:

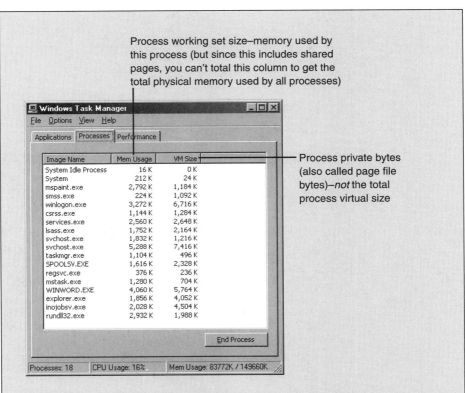

Process working set size–memory used by this process (but since this includes shared pages, you can't total this column to get the total physical memory used by all processes)

Process private bytes (also called page file bytes)–*not* the total process virtual size

Keep in mind that the VM Size column is *not* the process virtual memory size but rather the process private virtual size (the same as the Process: Private Bytes performance counter described in Table 7-9).

Also, as you'll discover in the section on working sets, the Mem Usage column counts shared pages in each process's memory usage total.

The Process Viewer utility (Pviewer.exe in the Windows 2000 Support Tools; Pview.exe in the Platform SDK) can display per-process address space details. (The source of this utility is one of the Win32 sample programs on MSDN.) From the Start menu, select Programs/ Windows 2000 Support Tools/Tools/Process Viewer, select a process, and click the Memory Detail button. You should see something like the following screen shot. Try clicking on the User Address Space For list box—you can select the address space used by the image alone or by loaded DLLs.

(continued)

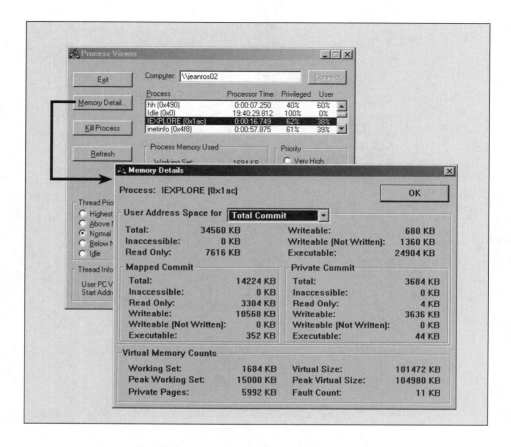

System Address Space Layout

This section describes the detailed layout and contents of system space. Figure 7-8 shows the overall structure on x86 systems with a 2-GB system space. (The details of x86 systems with a 1-GB system space are included later in this section.)

Figure 7-8
x86 system space layout (not proportional)

The x86 architecture has the following components in system space:

- **System code** Contains the operating system image, HAL, and device drivers used to boot the system.

- **System mapped views** Used to map Win32k.sys, the loadable kernel-mode part of the Win32 subsystem, as well as kernel-mode graphics drivers it uses. (See Chapter 2 for more information on Win32k.sys.)

■ **Session space** Used to map information specific to a user session. (Windows 2000 supports multiple user sessions when Terminal Services is installed.) The session working set list describes the parts of session space that are resident and in use.

■ **Process page tables and page directory** Structures that describe the mapping of virtual addresses.

■ **Hyperspace** A special region used to map the process working set list and to temporarily map other physical pages for such operations as zeroing a page on the free list (when the zero list is empty and a zero page is needed), invalidating page table entries in other page tables (such as when a page is removed from the standby list), and on process creation to set up a new process's address space.

■ **System working set list** The working set list data structures that describe the system working set.*

■ **System cache** Virtual address space used to map files open in the system cache. (See Chapter 11 for detailed information about the cache manager.)

■ **Paged pool** Pageable system memory heap.

■ **System page table entries (PTEs)** Pool of system PTEs used to map system pages such as I/O space, kernel stacks, and memory descriptor lists. You can see how many system PTEs are available by examining the value of the Memory: Free System Page Table Entries counter in the Performance tool.

■ **Nonpaged pool** Nonpageable system memory heap, usually existing in two parts—one in the lower end of system space and one in the upper end.

■ **Crash dump information** Reserved to record information about the state of a system crash.

■ **HAL usage** System memory reserved for HAL-specific structures.

* Internally, the system working set is called the *system cache working set*. This term is misleading, however, because it includes not only the system cache but also the paged pool, pageable system code and data, and pageable driver code and data.

The rest of this section consists of two tables that list the detailed structure of system space. Table 7-10 lists the kernel variables that contain start and end addresses of various system space regions. Some of these regions are fixed; some are computed at system boot time on the basis of memory size and whether the system is running Windows 2000 Professional or Windows 2000 Server. Table 7-11 lists the structure of system space on x86 systems. Keep in mind that these tables reflect non-PAE systems. Systems running the PAE-enabled kernel image have a slightly different system address space layout.

Table 7-10 System Variables That Describe System Space Regions

System Variable	Description	x86 2-GB System Space (non-PAE)	x86 1-GB System Space (non-PAE)
MmSystemRangeStart	Start address of system space	0x80000000	0xC0000000
MmSystemCache-WorkingSetList	System working set list	0xC0C00000	0xC0C00000
MmSystemCacheStart	Start of system cache	0xC1000000	0xC1000000
MmSystemCacheEnd	End of system cache	Calculated	Calculated
MiSystemCacheStart-Extra	Start of system cache or system PTE extension	0xA4000000	0
MiSystemCacheEnd-Extra	End of system cache or PTE extension	0xC0000000	0
MmPagedPoolStart	Start of paged pool	0xE1000000	0xE1000000
MmPagedPoolEnd	End of paged pool	Calculated (maximum size is 482 MB)	Calculated (maximum size is 160 MB)
MmNonPagedSystem-Start	Start of system PTEs	Calculated (lowest value is 0xEB000000)	Calculated
MmNonPagedPoolStart	Start of nonpaged pool	Calculated	Calculated
MmNonPagedPool-ExpansionStart	Start of nonpaged pool expansion	Calculated	Calculated
MmNonPagedPoolEnd	End of nonpaged pool	0xFFBE0000	0xFFBE0000

Table 7-11 x86 System Space (non-PAE)

Range	Size	Function
0x80000000 through 0x9FFFFFFF	512 MB	System code used to boot the system (Ntoskrnl.exe and Hal.dll) and the initial part of nonpaged pool. On x86 systems with a 2-GB system space and 128 MB or more of RAM, the first 512 MB are mapped using x86 large page PDEs.
0xA0000000 through 0xA2FFFFFF	48 MB	System mapped views if Terminal Services not installed; otherwise, session space. (See Table 7-12.)
0xA3000000 through 0xA3FFFFFF	16 MB	System mapped views for systems running Terminal Services.
0xA4000000 through 0xBFFFFFFF	448 MB	Additional system PTEs (used for kernel stacks, mapping I/O space, and so on) or additional system cache (for systems with large system cache enabled).
0xC0000000 through 0xC03FFFFF	4 MB	Process page tables (page directory is at 0xC0300000 and is 4 KB in size). This is per-process data mapped in system space.
0xC0400000 through 0xC07FFFFF	4 MB	Working set list and hyperspace. This is per-process data mapped in system space.
0xC0800000 through 0xC0BFFFFF	4 MB	Unused.
0xC0C00000 through 0xC0FFFFFF	4 MB	System working set list.
0xC1000000 through 0xE0FFFFFF	512 MB (maximum)	System cache (size calculated at boot time).
0xE1000000 through 0xEAFFFFFF*	160 MB (maximum)	Paged pool (size calculated at boot time).
0xEB000000 through 0xFFBDFFFF	331.875 MB (339,840 KB)	System PTEs and nonpaged pool (size calculated at boot time). If the registry PagedPoolSize value is set to −1, system PTEs move from the 0xEB000000 range to the 0xA4000000 range, which lets paged pool grow to use this area of the address space.
0xFFBE0000 through 0xFFFFFFFF	4.125 MB (4224 KB)	Crash dump structures and private HAL data structures.

* Because paged pool is limited by the start address of the region containing nonpaged pool and the system PTEs, it can go beyond address 0xEB000000 only if those addresses aren't used.

Session Space

A *session* consists of the processes and other system objects (such as the window station, desktops, and windows) that represent a single user's workstation logon session. Each session has a session-specific paged pool area used by the kernel-mode portion of the Win32 subsystem (Win32k.sys) to allocate session-private GUI data structures. In addition, each session has its own copy of the Win32 subsystem process (Csrss.exe) and logon process (Winlogon.exe). The session manager process (Smss.exe) is responsible for creating new sessions, which includes loading a session-private copy of Win32k.sys, creating the session-private object manager namespace, and creating the session-specific instances of the Csrss and Winlogon processes.

To virtualize sessions, all sessionwide data structures are mapped into a region of system space called *session space* that begins at address 0xA0000000 and extends through address 0xA2FFFFFF. When a process is created, this range of addresses is mapped to the pages appropriate to the session that the process belongs to. Table 7-12 lists the layout of session space on systems with Terminal Services installed.

Table 7-12 Session Space Layout

Range	Size	Function
0xA0000000 through 0xA07FFFFF	8 MB	Win32k.sys and rebased Windows NT 4 print drivers
0xA0800000 through 0xA0BFFFFF	4 MB	MM_SESSION_SPACE structure and session working set lists
0xA0C00000 through 0xA1FFFFFF	20 MB	Mapped views for this session
0xA2000000 through 0xA2FFFFFF	16 MB	Paged pool for this session

Address Translation

Now that you've seen how Windows 2000 structures the 32-bit virtual address space, let's look at how it maps these address spaces to real physical pages. We'll describe what happens when such a translation doesn't resolve to a physical

memory address (paging) and explain how Windows 2000 manages physical memory via working sets and the page frame database.

User applications reference 32-bit virtual addresses. Using data structures the memory manager creates and maintains, the CPU translates virtual addresses into physical addresses. For example, Figure 7-9 shows three consecutive virtual pages mapped to three physically discontiguous pages.

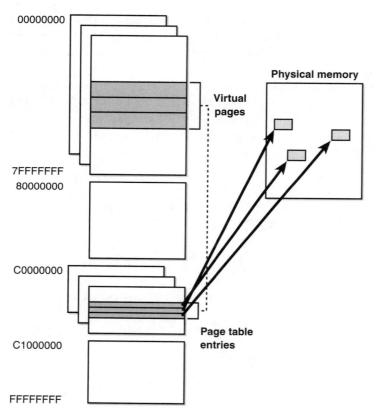

Figure 7-9
Mapping virtual addresses to physical memory

The dashed line connecting the virtual pages to the PTEs in Figure 7-9 represents the indirect relationship between virtual pages and physical memory. Virtual addresses aren't mapped directly to physical ones. Instead, as you'll discover in this section, each virtual address is associated with a system-space

structure called a *page table entry* (PTE), which contains the physical address to which the virtual one is mapped.

> **N O T E** Kernel-mode code (such as device drivers) can reference physical memory addresses by mapping them to virtual addresses. For more information, see the memory descriptor list (MDL) support routines described in the DDK documentation.

Throughout the remainder of this section, we'll explain the details of how Windows 2000 accomplishes this mapping.

Translating a Virtual Address

By default, Windows 2000 on an x86 system uses a two-level page table structure to translate virtual to physical addresses. (Systems running the PAE kernel use a three-level page table—this section assumes non-PAE systems.) A 32-bit virtual address is interpreted as three separate components—the page directory index, the page table index, and the byte index—that are used as indexes into the structures that describe page mappings, as illustrated in Figure 7-10. The page size and the PTE width dictate the width of the page directory and page table index fields. For example, on x86 systems, the byte index is 12 bits because pages are 4096 bytes ($2^{12} = 4096$).

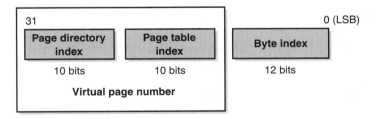

Figure 7-10
Components of a 32-bit virtual address on x86 systems

The *page directory index* is used to locate the page table in which the virtual address's PTE is located. The *page table index* is used to locate the PTE, which, as mentioned earlier, contains the physical address to which a virtual page maps. The *byte index* finds the proper address within that physical page. Figure 7-11 shows the relationship of these three values and how they are used to map a virtual address into a physical address.

Figure 7-11
Translating a valid virtual address (x86-specific)

The following basic steps are involved in translating a virtual address:

1. The memory management hardware locates the page directory for the current process. On each process context switch, the hardware is told the address of a new process page directory, typically by the operating system setting a special CPU register.

2. The page directory index is used as an index into the page directory to locate the page directory entry (PDE) that describes the location of the page table needed to map the virtual address. The PDE contains the page frame number (PFN) of the page table (if it is resident—page tables can be paged out).

3. The page table index is used as an index into the page table to locate the PTE that describes the physical location of the virtual page in question.

4. The PTE is used to locate the page. If the page is valid, it contains the PFN of the page in physical memory that contains the virtual page. If the PTE indicates that the page isn't valid, the memory management fault handler locates the page and tries to make it valid. (See the section on page fault handling on page 443.) If the page can't be made valid (for example, because of a protection fault), the fault handler generates an access violation or a bug check.

5. When the PTE is pointed to a valid page, the byte index is used to locate the address of the desired data within the physical page.

Now that you have the overall picture, let's look at the detailed structure of page directories, page tables, and PTEs.

Page Directories

Each process has a single *page directory*, a page the memory manager creates to map the location of all page tables for that process. The physical address of the process page directory is stored in the kernel process (KPROCESS) block but is also mapped virtually at address 0xC0300000 on x86 systems (0xC06000000 on systems running the PAE kernel image). All code running in kernel mode references virtual addresses, not physical ones. (For more detailed information about KPROCESS and other process data structures, refer to Chapter 6.)

The CPU knows the location of the page directory page because a special register (CR3 on x86 systems) inside the CPU that is loaded by the operating system contains the physical address of the page directory. Each time a context switch occurs to a thread that is in a different process than that of the currently executing thread, this register is loaded from the KPROCESS block of the target process being switched to by the context-switch routine in the kernel. Context switches between threads in the same process don't result in reloading the physical address of the page directory because all threads within the same process share the same process address space.

The page directory is composed of *page directory entries* (PDEs), each of which is 4 bytes long (8 bytes on systems running the PAE kernel image) and describes the state and location of all the possible page tables for that process. (As described later in the chapter, page tables are created on demand, so the page directory for most processes points only to a small set of page tables.) The format of a PDE isn't repeated here because it's mostly the same as a hardware PTE (shown on page 437).

433

On x86 systems, 1024 page tables (2048 on PAE systems) are required to describe the full 4-GB virtual address space. The process page directory that maps these page tables contains 1024 PDEs. Therefore, the page directory index needs to be 10 bits wide ($2^{10} = 1024$).

EXPERIMENT: Examining the Page Directory and PDEs

You can see the physical address of the currently running process's page directory by examining the DirBase field in the *!process* kernel debugger output:

```
                            Physical address of PDE

kd> !process
PROCESS 80145880  │Cid:  0000    Peb:  00000000  ParentCid:  0000
    DirBase:  00030000  ObjectTable:  80695668  TableSize:  126.
    Image:  Idle
    VadRoot 0 Clone 0 Private 0. Modified 0. Locked 0.
    80145A3C MutantState Locked OwningThread 0
    Process Lock Owned by Thread 0
              .
              .
              .
```

You can see the page directory's virtual address by examining the kernel debugger output for the PTE of a particular virtual address, as shown here:

```
                            Virtual address of PDE
                                 Contents of PDE

kd> !pte 50001
00050001  -  PDE at C0300000        PTE at C0000140
             contains 00700067──    contains 00E63047
           pfn 00700  --DA--UW      pfn 00E63  --D---UWV
              │            │
       PFN of page    State and
       table page     protection of
                      page table
                      page
```

The PTE part of the kernel debugger output is defined in the section "Page Table Entries" on page 436.

Process and System Page Tables

Before referencing a byte within a page with the byte offset, the CPU first needs to be able to find the page that contains the desired byte of data. To find this page, the operating system constructs another page of memory that contains the mapping information needed to find the desired page containing the data. This page of mapping information is called a *page table*. Because Windows 2000 provides a private address space for each process, each process has its own set of process page tables to map that private address space because the mappings will be different for each process.

The page tables that describe system space are shared among all processes, however. When a process is created, system space PDEs are initialized to point to the existing system page tables. But as shown in Figure 7-12, not all processes have the same view of system space. For example, if paged pool expansion requires the allocation of a new system page table, the memory manager doesn't go back and update all the process page directories to point to the new system page table. Instead, it updates the process page directories when the processes reference the new virtual address.

Thus, a process can take a page fault when referencing paged pool that is in fact physically resident because its process page directory doesn't yet point to the new system page table that describes the new area of pool. Page faults don't occur when accessing nonpaged pool, even though it too can be expanded, because Windows 2000 builds enough system page tables to describe the maximum size during system initialization.

System PTEs aren't an infinite resource—Windows 2000 calculates how many system PTEs to allocate based on the memory size. You can see how many system PTEs are available by examining the value of the Memory: Free System Page Table Entries counter in the Performance tool. You can also override the calculation made at boot time by setting the registry value HKLM\SYSTEM\CurrentControlSet\Control\Session Manager\Memory Management\SystemPages to the number of PTEs you want. However, the maximum that Windows 2000 will allocate is 128,000 on x86 systems.

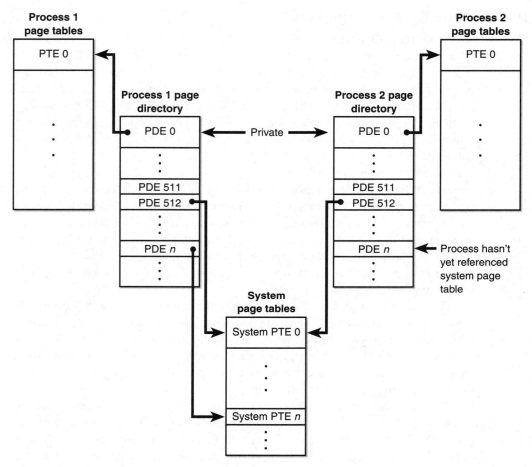

Figure 7-12
System and process-private page tables

Page Table Entries

As mentioned earlier, page tables are composed of an array of page table entries (PTEs). You can use the *!pte* command in the kernel debugger to examine PTEs. (See the experiment "Translating Addresses" on page 440.) Valid PTEs (the kind we'll be discussing here; we'll cover invalid PTEs in a later section) have two main fields: the page frame number (PFN) of the physical page containing the data or of the physical address of a page in memory, and some flags that describe the state and protection of the page, as shown in Figure 7-13.

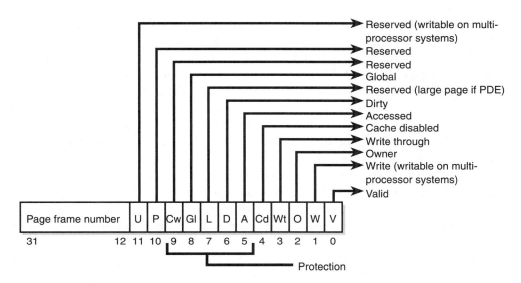

Figure 7-13
Valid x86 hardware PTEs

As you'll see later, the bits labeled Reserved in Figure 7-13 are used only when the PTE isn't valid (the bits are interpreted by software). Table 7-13 briefly describes the hardware-defined bits in a valid PTE.

Table 7-13 PTE Status and Protection Bits

Name of Bit	Meaning
Accessed	Page has been read.
Cache disabled	Disables caching for that page.
Dirty	Page has been written to.
Global	Translation applies to all processes. (For example, a translation buffer flush won't affect this PTE.)
Large page	Indicates that the PDE maps a 4-MB page (used to map Ntoskrnl and HAL, initial nonpaged pool, etc.) on systems with 128 MB or more of memory.
Owner	Indicates whether user-mode code can access the page or whether the page is limited to kernel-mode access.
Valid	Indicates whether the translation maps to a page in physical memory.
Write through	Disables caching of writes to this page so that changes are immediately flushed to disk.
Write	On uniprocessor systems, indicates whether the page is read/write or read-only; on multiprocessor systems, indicates whether the page is writable. (The Write bit is stored in a reserved bit in the PTE.)

On x86 systems, a hardware PTE contains a Dirty bit and an Accessed bit. The Accessed bit is clear if a physical page represented by the PTE hasn't been read or written; the processor sets this bit when the page is first read or written. The processor sets the Dirty bit only when a page is first written. In addition to those two bits, the x86 architecture has a Write bit that provides page protection—when this bit is clear, the page is read-only; when it is set, the page is read/write. If a thread attempts to write to a page with the Write bit clear, a memory management exception occurs and the memory manager's access fault handler (described in the next section) must determine whether the thread can write to the page (for example, if the page was really marked copy-on-write) or whether an access violation should be generated.

Hardware PTEs on multiprocessor x86 systems have an additional Write bit implemented in software that is intended to avoid stalls when flushing the PTE cache (called the translation look-aside buffer) across processors. This bit indicates that a page has been written to by a thread running on some processor.

On the x86 hardware platform, PTEs are always 4 bytes (32 bits) in size (8 bytes for systems running with PAE enabled), so each page table contains 1024 PTEs (512 on PAE systems) (4096 bytes per page at 4 bytes per PTE) and therefore can map 1024 pages (512 pages PAE), for a total of 4 MB (2 MB PAE) of data pages.

The virtual address's page table index field indicates which PTE within the page table maps the data page in question. On x86 systems, the page table index is 10 bits wide (9 on PAE), allowing you to reference up to 1024 PTEs (512 on PAE). However, because Windows 2000 provides a 4-GB private virtual address space, more than one page table is needed to map the entire address space. To calculate the number of page tables required to map the entire 4-GB process virtual address space, divide 4 GB by the virtual memory mapped by a single page table. Recall that each page table on an x86 system maps 4 MB (2 MB on PAE) of data pages. Thus, 1024 page tables (4 GB/4 MB)—or 2048 page tables, 4 GB/2 MB for PAE—are required to map the full 4-GB address space.

Byte Within Page

Once the memory manager has found the physical page in question, it must find the requested data within that page. This is where the byte index field comes in. The byte index field tells the CPU which byte of data in the page you want to reference. On x86 systems, the byte index is 12 bits wide, allowing you to reference up to 4096 bytes of data (the size of a page).

Translation Look-Aside Buffer

As we've learned so far, each address translation requires two lookups: one to find the right page table in the page directory and one to find the right entry *in* the page table. Because doing two additional memory lookups for every reference to a virtual address would result in unacceptable system performance, most CPUs cache address translations so that repeated accesses to the same addresses don't have to be retranslated. The x86 processor provides such a cache in the form of an array of associative memory called the *translation look-aside buffer*, or TLB. Associative memory, such as the TLB, is a vector whose cells can be read simultaneously and compared to a target value. In the case of the TLB, the vector contains the virtual-to-physical page mappings of the most recently used pages, as shown in Figure 7-14, and the type of page protection applied to each page. Each entry in the TLB is like a cache entry, whose tag holds portions of the virtual address and whose data portion holds a physical page number, protection field, valid bit, and usually a dirty bit indicating the condition of the page to which the cached PTE corresponds. If a PTE's global bit is set (used for system space pages that are globally visible to all processes), the TLB entry isn't invalidated on process context switches.

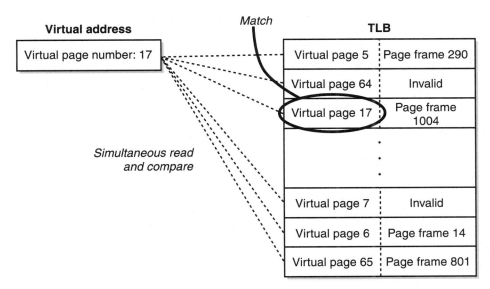

Figure 7-14
Accessing the translation look-aside buffer

Virtual addresses that are used frequently are likely to have entries in the TLB, which provides extremely fast virtual-to-physical address translation and, therefore, fast memory access. If a virtual address isn't in the TLB, it might still be in memory, but multiple memory accesses are needed to find it, which makes the access time slightly slower. If a virtual page has been paged out of memory or if the memory manager changes the PTE, the memory manager must explicitly invalidate the TLB entry. If a process accesses it again, a page fault occurs and the memory manager brings the page back into memory and re-creates an entry for it in the TLB.

To maximize the amount of common code, the memory manager treats all PTEs the same whenever possible, whether they are maintained by hardware or by software. For example, the memory manager calls a kernel routine when a PTE changes from invalid to valid. The job of this routine is to load this new PTE into the TLB in whatever hardware-specific manner the architecture requires. On x86 systems, the code is a NOP because the processor loads the TLB without any intervention from the software.

EXPERIMENT: Translating Addresses

To clarify how address translation works, let's go through a real example of translating a virtual address on an x86 non-PAE system, using the available tools in the kernel debugger to examine page directories, page tables, and PTEs. In this example, we'll use a process that has virtual address 0x50001 currently mapped to a valid physical address. In later examples, you'll see how to follow address translation for invalid addresses with the kernel debugger.

First let's convert 0x50001 to binary and break it into the three fields that are used to translate an address. In binary, 0x50001 is 101.0000.0000.0000.0001. Breaking into the component fields yields the following:

To start the translation process, the CPU needs the physical address of the process page directory, stored in the CR3 register while a thread

in that process is running. You can display this address either by examining the CR3 register itself or by dumping the KPROCESS block for the process in question using the *!process* command, as shown here:

```
kd> !process
PROCESS 81555020  Cid:  0099    Peb:  7ffdf000  ParentCid:  0094
   DirBase:  012f0000  ObjectTable:  80695ba8  TableSize:   46.
   Image: IEXPLORE.EXE
     .
     .
     .                          ─── Physical address of page directory
kd> r cr3
Cr3: 012F0000 ──────
```

In this case, the page directory is stored at physical address 0x12F0000. As shown in the preceding illustration, the page directory index field in this example is 0. Therefore, the PDE is at physical address 0x12F0000.

The kernel debugger *!pte* command displays the PDE and PTE that describe a virtual address, as shown here:

In the first column, the kernel debugger displays the PDE and in the second column the PTE. Notice that the PDE address is shown as a virtual address, not a physical address—as noted earlier, the process page directory starts at virtual address 0xC0300000 on x86 systems. Because we're looking at the first PDE in the page directory, the PDE address is the same as the page directory address.

(continued)

EXPERIMENT: Translating Addresses *continued*

> The PTE is at virtual address 0xC0000140. You can compute this address by multiplying the page table index (0x50 in this example) by the size of a PTE: 0x50 multiplied by 4 equals 0x140. Because the memory manager maps page tables starting at 0xC0000000, adding 140 yields the virtual address shown in the kernel debugger output: 0xC0000140. The page table page is at PFN 0x700, and the data page is at PFN 0xe63.
>
> The PTE flags are displayed to the right of the PFN number. For example, the PTE that describes the page being referenced has flags of D---UWV. *D* here stands for dirty (the page has been modified), *U* for user-mode page (as opposed to a kernel-mode page), *W* for writable page (rather than read-only), and *V* for valid. (The PTE represents a valid page in physical memory.)

Physical Address Extension

All of the Intel x86 family processors since the Pentium Pro include a memory-mapping mode called *Physical Address Extension* (PAE). With the proper chipset, the PAE mode allows access to up to 64 GB of physical memory. When the x86 executes in PAE mode, the memory management unit (MMU) divides virtual addresses into four fields, as shown in Figure 7-15.

The MMU still implements page directories and page tables, but a third level, the page directory pointer table, exists above them. PAE mode can address more memory than the standard translation mode not because of the extra level of translation but because PDEs and PTEs are 64-bits wide rather than 32-bits. The system represents physical addresses internally with 24 bits, which gives the x86 the ability to support a maximum of 2^{24+12} bytes, or 64 GB, of memory.

As explained in Chapter 2, there is a special version of the core kernel image (Ntoskrnl.exe) with support for PAE called Ntkrnlpa.exe. (The multiprocessor version is called Ntkrpamp.exe.) To select this PAE-enabled kernel, you must boot with the /PAE switch in Boot.ini.

This special version of the kernel image is installed on all Windows 2000 systems, even Windows 2000 Professional systems with small memory. The reason for this is to facilitate testing. Because the PAE kernel presents 64-bit addresses to device drivers and other system code, booting /PAE even on a small memory system allows a device driver developer to test parts of their drivers with large addresses. The other relevant Boot.ini switch is /NOLOWMEM,

Figure 7-15
Page mappings with PAE

which discards memory below 4 GB and relocates device drivers above this range, thus guaranteeing that these drivers will be presented with physical addresses greater than 32 bits.

Only Windows 2000 Advanced Server and Windows 2000 Datacenter Server are required to support more than 4 GB of physical memory. (See Table 2-2 on page 39.) Using the AWE Win32 functions (described on page 401), 32-bit user processes can allocate and control large amounts of physical memory on these systems.

Page Fault Handling

Earlier, you saw how address translations are resolved when the PTE is valid. When the PTE valid bit is clear, this indicates that the desired page is for some reason not (currently) accessible to the process. This section describes the types of invalid PTEs and how references to them are resolved.

A reference to an invalid page is called a *page fault*. The kernel trap handler (introduced in Chapter 3 on page 89) dispatches this kind of fault to the memory manager fault handler (*MmAccessFault*) to resolve. This routine runs in the context of the thread that incurred the fault and is responsible for attempting to resolve the fault (if possible) or raise an appropriate exception. These faults can be caused by a variety of conditions, as listed in Table 7-14.

Table 7-14 Reasons for Access Faults

Reason for Fault	Result
Accessing a page that isn't resident in memory but is on disk in a page file or a mapped file	Allocate a physical page and read the desired page from disk and into the working set
Accessing a page that is on the standby or modified list	Transition the page to the process or system working set
Accessing a page that isn't committed (for example, reserved address space or address space that isn't allocated)	Access violation
Accessing a page from user mode that can be accessed only in kernel mode	Access violation
Writing to a page that is read-only	Access violation
Accessing a demand-zero page	Add a zero-filled page to the process working set
Writing to a guard page	Guard-page violation (if a reference to a user-mode stack, perform automatic stack expansion)
Writing to a copy-on-write page	Make process-private (or session-private) copy of page and replace original in process, session, or system working set
Referencing a page in system space that is valid but not in the process page directory (for example, if paged pool expanded after the process page directory was created)	Copy page directory entry from master system page directory structure and dismiss exception
On a multiprocessor system, writing to a page that is valid but hasn't yet been written to	Set dirty bit in PTE

The following section describes the four basic kinds of invalid PTEs that are processed by the access fault handler. Following that is an explanation of

a special case of invalid PTEs, prototype PTEs, which are used to implement shareable pages.

Invalid PTEs

The following list details the four kinds of invalid PTEs and their structure. Some of the flags are the same as those for a hardware PTE as described in Table 7-13 on page 437.

- **Page file** The desired page resides within a paging file. An in-page operation is initiated, as illustrated here:

- **Demand zero** The desired page must be satisfied with a page of zeros. The pager looks at the zero page list. If the list is empty, the pager takes a page from the free list and zeros it. If that list is empty, it takes a page from the standby list and zeros it. The PTE format is the same as the page file PTE shown in the previous entry, but the page file number and offset are zeros.

- **Transition** The desired page is in memory on either the standby, modified, or modified-no-write list. The page is removed from the list and added to the working set, as shown here:

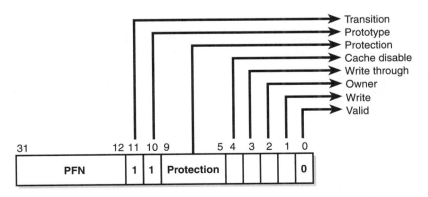

■ **Unknown** The PTE is zero, or the page table doesn't yet exist. In both cases, this flag means that you should examine the virtual address descriptors (VADs) to determine whether this virtual address has been committed. If so, page tables are built to represent the newly committed address space. (See the discussion of VADs on page 452.)

Prototype PTEs

If a page can be shared between two processes, the memory manager relies on a software structure called *prototype page table entries* (prototype PTEs) to map these potentially shared pages. An array of prototype PTEs is created when a section object is first created. These prototype PTEs are part of the *segment* structure, described at the end of this chapter.

When a process first references a page mapped to a view of a section object (recall that the VADs are created only when the view is mapped), the memory manager uses the information in the prototype PTE to fill in the real PTE used for address translation in the process page table. When a shared page is made valid, both the process PTE and the prototype PTE point to the physical page containing the data. To track the number of process PTEs that reference a valid shared page, a counter in the PFN database entry (described on page 465) is incremented. Thus, the memory manager can determine when a shared page is no longer referenced by any page table and thus can be made invalid and moved to a transition list or written out to disk.

When a shareable page is invalidated, the PTE in the process page table is filled in with a special PTE that points to the prototype PTE entry that describes the page, as shown in Figure 7-16.

Figure 7-16
Structure of an invalid PTE that points to the prototype PTE

Thus, when the page is later accessed, the memory manager can locate the prototype PTE using the information encoded in this PTE, which in turn describes the page being referenced. A shared page can be in one of six different states as described by the prototype PTE entry:

■ **Active/valid** The page is in physical memory as a result of another process that accessed it.

■ **Transition** The desired page is in memory on the standby or modified list.

■ **Modified-no-write** The desired page is in memory and on the modified-no-write list. (See Table 7-22 on page 466.)

■ **Demand zero** The desired page should be satisfied with a page of zeros.

■ **Page file** The desired page resides within a page file.

■ **Mapped file** The desired page resides within a mapped file.

Although the format of these prototype PTE entries is the same as that of the real PTE entries described earlier, these prototype PTEs aren't used for address translation—they are a layer between the page table and the page frame number database and never appear directly in page tables.

By having all the accessors of a potentially shared page point to a prototype PTE to resolve faults, the memory manager can manage shared pages without needing to update the page tables of each process sharing the page. For example, a shared code or data page might be paged out to disk at some point. When the memory manager retrieves the page from disk, it needs only to update the prototype PTE to point to the page's new physical location—the PTEs in each of the processes sharing the page remain the same (with the valid bit clear and still pointing to the prototype PTE). Later, as processes reference the page, the real PTE will get updated.

Figure 7-17 illustrates two virtual pages in a mapped view. One is valid, and the other is invalid. As shown, the first page is valid and is pointed to by the process PTE and the prototype PTE. The second page is in the paging file—the prototype PTE contains its exact location. The process PTE (and any other processes with that page mapped) points to this prototype PTE.

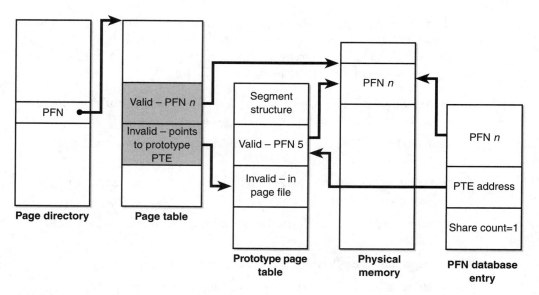

Figure 7-17
Prototype page table entries

In-Paging I/O

In-paging I/O occurs when a read operation must be issued to a file (paging or mapped) to satisfy a page fault. Also, because page tables are pageable, the processing of a page fault can incur additional page faults when the system is loading the page table page that contains the PTE or the prototype PTE that describes the original page being referenced.

The in-page I/O operation is synchronous—that is, the thread waits on an event until the I/O completes—and isn't interruptible by asynchronous procedure call (APC) delivery. The pager uses a special modifier in the I/O request function to indicate paging I/O. Upon completion of paging I/O, the I/O system triggers an event, which wakes up the pager and allows it to continue in-page processing.

While the paging I/O operation is in progress, the faulting thread doesn't own any critical memory management synchronization objects. Other threads within the process are allowed to issue virtual memory functions and handle page faults while the paging I/O takes place. But a number of interesting conditions that the pager must recognize when the I/O completes are exposed.

- Another thread in the same process or a different process could have faulted the same page (called a *collided page fault* and described in the next section).

- The page could have been deleted (and remapped) from the virtual address space.

- The protection on the page could have changed.

- The fault could have been for a prototype PTE, and the page that maps the prototype PTE could be out of the working set.

The pager handles these conditions by saving enough state on the thread's kernel stack before the paging I/O request such that when the request is complete, it can detect these conditions and, if necessary, dismiss the page fault without making the page valid. When the faulting instruction is reissued, the pager is again invoked and the PTE is reevaluated in its new state.

Collided Page Faults

The case when another thread or process faults a page that is currently being in-paged is known as a *collided page fault*. The pager detects and handles collided page faults optimally because they are common occurrences in multithreaded systems. If another thread or process faults the same page, the pager detects the collided page fault, noticing that the page is in transition and that a read is in progress. (This information is in the PFN database entry.) In this case, the pager issues a wait operation on an event specified in the PFN database entry. This event was initialized by the thread that first issued the I/O needed to resolve the fault.

When the I/O operation completes, all threads waiting on the event have their wait satisfied. The first thread to acquire the PFN database lock is responsible for performing the in-page completion operations. These operations consist of checking I/O status to ensure the I/O operation completed successfully, clearing the read-in-progress bit in the PFN database, and updating the PTE.

When subsequent threads acquire the PFN database lock to complete the collided page fault, the pager recognizes that the initial updating has been performed as the read-in-progress bit is clear and checks the in-page error flag in the PFN database element to ensure that the in-page I/O completed successfully. If the in-page error flag is set, the PTE isn't updated and an in-page error exception is raised in the faulting thread.

Page Files

Page files are used to store modified pages that are still in use by some process but have had to be written to disk (because of modified page writing). Page file space isn't reserved until pages are written out to disk, not when they are committed. However, the system commit limit is charged for private pages as they are created. Thus, the Process: Page File Bytes performance counter is actually the total process private committed memory, of which none, some, or all may be in the paging file. (In fact, it's the same as the Process: Private Bytes performance counter.)

The memory manager keeps track of private committed memory usage on a global basis, termed *commitment,* and on a per-process basis as *page file quota.* (Again, this memory usage doesn't represent page file usage—it represents private committed memory usage.) Commitment and page file quota are charged whenever virtual addresses that require new private physical pages are committed. Once the global commit limit has been reached (physical memory and the page files are full), allocating virtual memory will fail until processes free committed memory (for example, when a process exits).

Windows 2000 supports up to 16 paging files. When the system boots, the session manager process (described in Chapter 2) reads the list of page files to open by examining the registry value HKLM\SYSTEM\CurrentControlSet\Control\Session Manager\Memory Management\PagingFiles. If no paging files are specified, a default 20-MB page file is created on the boot partition. (Embedded versions, such as Windows NT 4 Embedded, have no page file by default.) Once open, the page files can't be deleted while the system is running because the System process (also described in Chapter 2) maintains an open handle to each page file.

EXPERIMENT: Viewing System Page Files

To view the list of page files, look in the registry at HKLM\SYSTEM\CurrentControlSet\Control\Session Manager\Memory Management\PagingFiles. Don't attempt to add or remove page files by changing the registry setting. To add or remove page files, use the System utility in Control Panel. Click the Performance Options button on the Advanced tab, and then click the Change button.

To add a new page file, Control Panel uses the (internal only) *NtCreate-PagingFile* system service defined in Ntdll.dll. Page files are always created as noncompressed files, even if the directory they are in is compressed. To keep new page files from being deleted, a handle is duplicated into the System process so that when the creating process closes the handle to the new page file, another process can still open the page file.

The performance counters listed in Table 7-15 allow you to examine private committed memory usage on a systemwide or per-page-file basis. There's no way to determine how much of a process's private committed memory is resident verses paged out to paging files.

Table 7-15 Committed Memory and Page File Performance Counters

Performance Counter	Description
Memory: Committed Bytes	Number of bytes of virtual (not reserved) memory that has been committed. This number doesn't necessarily represent page file usage because it includes private committed pages in physical memory that have never been paged out. Rather, it represents the amount of page file space that would be used if the process was completely made nonresident.
Memory: Commit Limit	Number of bytes of virtual memory that can be committed without having to extend the paging files; if the paging files can be extended, this limit is soft.
Paging File: % Usage	Percentage of the paging file committed.
Paging File: % Usage Peak	Highest percentage of the paging file committed.

EXPERIMENT: Viewing Page File Usage with Task Manager

You can also view committed memory usage with Task Manager by clicking its Performance tab. You'll see the following counters related to page files:

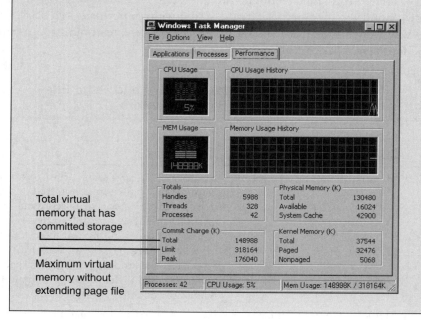

Total virtual memory that has committed storage

Maximum virtual memory without extending page file

Virtual Address Descriptors

The memory manager uses a demand-paging algorithm to know when to load pages into memory, waiting until a thread references an address and incurs a page fault before retrieving the page from disk. Like copy-on-write, demand paging is a form of *lazy evaluation*—waiting to perform a task until it is required.

The memory manager uses lazy evaluation not only to bring pages into memory but also to construct the page tables required to describe new pages. For example, when a thread commits a large region of virtual memory with *VirtualAlloc*, the memory manager could immediately construct the page tables required to access the entire range of allocated memory. But what if some of that range is never accessed? Creating page tables for the entire range would be a wasted effort. Instead, the memory manager waits to create a page table

until a thread incurs a page fault, and then it creates a page table for that page. This method significantly improves performance for processes that reserve and/ or commit a lot of memory but access it sparsely.

With the lazy-evaluation algorithm, allocating even large blocks of memory is a fast operation. This performance gain isn't without its trade-offs, however: when a thread allocates memory, the memory manager must respond with a range of addresses for the thread to use. Because the memory manager doesn't build page tables until the thread actually accesses the memory, it can't look to determine which virtual addresses are free. To solve this problem, the memory manager maintains another set of data structures to keep track of which virtual addresses have been reserved in the process's address space and which have not. These data structures are known as *virtual address descriptors* (VADs). For each process, the memory manager maintains a set of VADs that describes the status of the process's address space. VADs are structured as a self-balancing binary tree to make lookups efficient. A diagram of a VAD tree is shown in Figure 7-18.

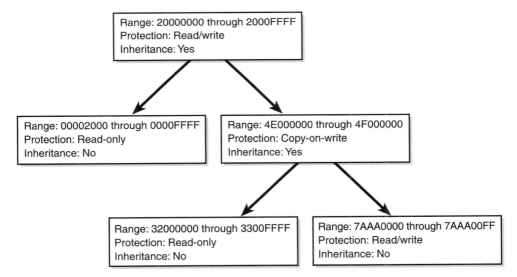

Figure 7-18
Virtual address descriptors

When a process reserves address space or maps a view of a section, the memory manager creates a VAD to store any information supplied by the allocation request, such as the range of addresses being reserved, whether the range will be shared or private, whether a child process can inherit the contents of the range, and the page protection applied to pages in the range.

When a thread first accesses an address, the memory manager must create a PTE for the page containing the address. To do so, it finds the VAD whose address range contains the accessed address and uses the information it finds to fill in the PTE. If the address falls outside the range covered by the VAD or in a range of addresses that are reserved but not committed, the memory manager knows that the thread didn't allocate the memory before attempting to use it and therefore generates an access violation.

EXPERIMENT: Viewing Virtual Address Descriptors

You can use the kernel debugger's *!vad* command to view the VADs for a given process. First find the address of the root of the VAD tree with the *!process* command. Then specify that address to the *!vad* command, as shown in the following example of the VAD tree for a process running Notepad.exe:

```
kd> !process 2a0 1
Searching for Process with Cid == 2a0
PROCESS 8614d030 SessionId: 0 Cid: 02a0 Peb: 7ffdf000 ParentCid: 0554
    DirBase: 00d93000  ObjectTable: 81bc47c8  TableSize:  41.
    Image: notepad.exe
    VadRoot 8118d868 Clone 0 Private 252. Modified 0. Locked 0.
    :

kd> !vad 8118d868
VAD       level      start     end     commit
84df4148 ( 2)          10      10         1 Private     READWRITE
850cdbe8 ( 3)          20      20         1 Private     READWRITE
810b0ee8 ( 1)          30      6f         7 Private     READWRITE
8109d308 ( 3)          70     16f        32 Private     READWRITE
810e9a28 ( 2)         170     17f         0 Mapped      READWRITE
84aedfc8 ( 3)         180     195         0 Mapped      READONLY
8118d868 ( 0)         1a0     1ce         0 Mapped      READONLY
81190a08 ( 4)         1d0     210         0 Mapped      READONLY
85c7b928 ( 3)         220     223         0 Mapped      READONLY
86253a08 ( 4)         230     2f7         0 Mapped      EXECUTE_READ
810aab48 ( 2)         300     342         0 Mapped      READONLY
80db5448 ( 5)         350     64f         0 Mapped      EXECUTE_READ
:

Total VADs:    49  average level:    6  maximum depth: 13
```

Working Sets

In the last several sections, we've concentrated on the virtual view of a Windows 2000 process—page tables, PTEs, and VADs. In the remainder of this chapter, we'll explain how Windows 2000 keeps a subset of virtual addresses in physical memory.

As you'll recall, the term used to describe a subset of virtual pages resident in physical memory is called a *working set*. There are two kinds of working sets— process working sets and the system working set.

> **NOTE** The kernel extensions to support Terminal Services for Windows 2000 (which supports multiple independent interactive user sessions on a single Windows 2000 server system) add a third type of working set: the session working set. A session consists of a set of processes as well as a session working set for kernel-mode session-specific data structures allocated by the kernel-mode part of the Win32 subsystem (Win32k.sys), the session working set's code and data, session paged pool, session mapped views, and other session-space device drivers.

Before examining the details of each type of working set, let's look at the overall policy for deciding which pages are brought into physical memory and how long they remain. After that, we'll explore the two types of working sets.

Paging Policies

Virtual memory systems generally define three policies that dictate how (or when) paging is performed: a fetch policy, a placement policy, and a replacement policy.

A *fetch policy* determines when the pager brings a page from disk into memory. One type of fetch policy attempts to load the pages a process will need before it asks for them. Other fetch policies, called *demand-paging policies,* load a page into physical memory only when a page fault occurs. In a demand-paging system, a process incurs many page faults when its threads first begin executing because the threads reference the initial set of pages they need to get going. Once this set of pages is loaded into memory, the paging activity of the process decreases.

> **NOTE** To optimize the startup time of an image, a tool named the Working Set Tuner has been provided in the Platform SDK. This utility reorders the pages in an executable image, placing them in the order in which they are referenced during image startup and thus decreasing load time.

The Windows 2000 memory manager uses a demand-paging algorithm with clustering to load pages into memory. When a thread receives a page fault, the memory manager loads into memory the faulted page plus a small number of pages following it. This strategy attempts to minimize the number of paging I/Os a thread will incur. Because programs, especially large ones, tend to execute in small regions of their address space at any given time, loading clusters of virtual pages reduces the number of disk reads. The values that determine the default page read cluster sizes depend on physical memory size and are listed in Table 7-16. Notice that the values differ for pages in executable images versus other pages.

Table 7-16 Page Fault Read Clustering Values

Memory Size*	Cluster Size for Code Pages in Images	Cluster Size for Data Pages in Images	Cluster Size for All Other Pages
< 12 MB	3	2	5
12–19 MB	3	2	5
> 19 MB	8	4	8

* Note that the minimum memory size supported by Windows 2000 is 32 MB. However, future embedded versions might support systems with less memory.

When a thread receives a page fault, the memory manager must also determine where in physical memory to put the virtual page. The set of rules it uses to determine the best position is called a *placement policy*. Windows 2000 considers the size of CPU memory caches when choosing page frames to minimize unnecessary thrashing of the cache.

If physical memory is full when a page fault occurs, a *replacement policy* is used to determine which virtual page must be removed from memory to make room for the new page. Common replacement policies include *least recently used* (LRU) and *first in, first out* (FIFO). The LRU algorithm requires the virtual memory system to track when a page in memory is used. When a new page frame is required, the page that hasn't been used for the greatest amount of time is paged to disk and its frame is freed to satisfy the page fault. The FIFO algorithm is somewhat simpler; it removes the page that has been in physical memory for the greatest amount of time, regardless of how often it's been used.

Replacement policies can be further characterized as either global or local. A global replacement policy allows a page fault to be satisfied by any page frame, whether or not that frame is owned by another process. For example, a global replacement policy using the FIFO algorithm would locate the page that has been in memory the longest and would free it to satisfy a page fault; a local replacement policy would limit its search for the oldest page to the set of pages already owned by the process that incurred the page fault. Global replacement policies make processes vulnerable to the behavior of other processes—an ill-behaved application can undermine the entire operating system by inducing excessive paging activity in all processes.

On multiprocessor systems, Windows 2000 implements a variation of a local FIFO replacement policy. On uniprocessor systems, it implements something closer to a least recently used policy (LRU) (known as the *clock algorithm,* as implemented in most versions of UNIX). It allocates a number of page frames (dynamically adjusted) to each process, called the *process working set* (or in the case of pageable system code and data, to the *system working set*). When a process working set reaches its limit and/or a working set needs to be trimmed because of demands for physical memory from other processes, the memory manager removes pages from the working set until it has determined there are enough free pages. How working sets are managed is described in the next section.

Working Set Management

Every process starts with the same default working set minimum and maximum. These values, which are listed in Table 7-17, are calculated at system initialization time and are based strictly on the size of physical memory. (For an explanation of small, medium, and large memory systems, see page 384.)

Table 7-17 Default Minimum and Maximum Working Set Sizes

Memory Size	Default Minimum Working Set Size (in Pages)	Default Maximum Working Set Size (in Pages)
Small	20	45
Medium	30	145
Large	50	345

You can change these default values on a per-process basis with the Win32 *SetProcessWorkingSetSize* function, though you must have the "increase scheduling priority" user right to do this. The maximum working set size can't exceed the systemwide maximum calculated at system initialization time and stored in the kernel variable *MmMaximumWorkingSetSize*. This value is set to be the number of available pages (the size of the zero, free, and standby list) at the time the computation is made minus 512 pages. However, this computed value has a fixed limit of 1984 MB or 3008 MB on a system running with a 3-GB user space.

When a page fault occurs, the process's working set limits and the amount of free memory on the system are examined. If conditions permit, the memory manager allows a process to grow to its working set maximum (or beyond— the maximum can be exceeded if enough free pages are available). However, if memory is tight, Windows 2000 replaces rather than adds pages in a working set when a fault occurs.

Although Windows 2000 attempts to keep memory available by writing modified pages to disk, when modified pages are being generated at a very high rate, more memory is required in order to meet memory demands. Therefore, when physical memory runs low (*MmAvailablePages* is less than *MmMinimumFreePages*), the *working set manager*, a routine that runs in the context of the balance set manager system thread (described in the next section), is called to initiate automatic working set trimming to increase the amount of free memory available in the system. (With the Win32 *SetProcessWorkingSetSize* function mentioned earlier, you can also initiate working set trimming of your own process, for example, after your application is initialized.)

The working set manager examines available memory and decides which, if any, working sets need to be trimmed. If there is ample memory, the working set manager calculates how many pages could be removed from working sets if needed. If trimming is needed, it looks at working sets that are above their minimum setting. It also dynamically adjusts the rate at which it examines working sets as well as arranges the list of processes that are candidates to be trimmed into an optimal order. For example, larger processes that have been idle longer are considered before smaller processes that are running more often; the process running the foreground application is considered last; and so on.

Some of the kernel variables that affect working set expansion and trimming are listed in Table 7-18. The values of these variables are fixed or system set and can't be adjusted by registry values.

Table 7-18 **Working Set–Related System Control Variables**

Variable	Value	Description
MmWorkingSetSize-Increment	6	The number of pages to add to a working set if there are sufficient available pages and the working set is below its maximum.
MmWorkingSetSize-Expansion	20	The number of pages by which to expand the maximum working set if it is at its maximum and there are sufficient available pages.
MmWsExpandThreshold	90	The number of pages that must be available to expand the working set above its maximum.
MmPagesAboveWs-Minimum	Dynamic	The number of pages that would be removed from working sets if every working set was at its minimum.
MmPagesAboveWs-Threshold	37	If memory is getting short and *MmPagesAboveWs-Minimum* is above this value, trim working sets.
MmWsAdjustThreshold	45	The number of pages required to be freed by working set reduction before working set reduction is attempted
MmWsTrimReduction-Goal	29	The total number of pages to reduce by working set trimming.

When it finds processes using more than their minimums, the working set manager looks for pages to remove from their working sets, making the pages available for other uses. If the amount of free memory is still too low, the working set manager continues removing pages from processes' working sets until it achieves a minimum number of free pages on the system.

If a process has incurred more than a few page faults since the last time it was trimmed, it becomes exempt from trimming, the theory being that if the working set manager makes a mistake and trims pages that were being used, it won't trim any more out until the next periodic trim cycle (6 seconds later).

The algorithm to determine which pages to remove from a working set is different on a single-processor system than on a multiprocessor system. On a single-processor system, the working set manager tries to remove pages that haven't been accessed recently. It does this by checking the accessed bit in the hardware PTE to see whether the page has been accessed. If the bit is clear, the page is *aged*, that is, a count is incremented indicating that the page hasn't been referenced since the last working set trim scan. Later, the age of pages is used to locate candidate pages to remove from the working set.

If the hardware PTE accessed bit is set, the working set manager clears it and goes on to examine the next page in the working set. In this way, if the accessed bit is clear the next time the working set manager examines the page, it knows that the page hasn't been accessed since the last time it was examined. This scan for pages to remove continues through the working set list until either the number of desired pages has been removed or the scan has returned to the starting point. (The next time the working set is trimmed, the scan picks up where it left off last.)

On a multiprocessor system, the working set manager doesn't check the access bit; clearing it would require invalidating TLB entries on other processors, which would result in unnecessary TLB cache misses by threads in the same process that might be running on other processors. Thus, on a multiprocessor system, pages are removed from the working set without regard to the state of the accessed bit.

EXPERIMENT: Viewing Process Working Set Sizes

You can use the Performance tool to examine process working set sizes by looking at the following performance counters:

Counter	Description
Process: Working Set	Current size of the selected process's working set in bytes
Process: Working Set Peak	Peak size of the selected process's working set in bytes
Process: Page Faults/Sec	Number of page faults for the process that occur each second

Several other process viewer utilities (such as Task Manager, Pview, and Pviewer) also display the process working set size.

You can also get the total of all the process working sets by selecting the _Total process in the instance box in the Performance tool. This process isn't real—it's simply a total of the process-specific counters for all processes currently running on the system. The total you see is misleading, however, because the size of each individual process working set includes pages being shared by other processes. Thus, if two or more processes share a page, the page is counted in each process's working set.

EXPERIMENT: Viewing the Working Set List

You can view the individual entries in the working set by using the kernel debugger *!wsle* command. The following example shows a partial output of the working set list of LiveKd. (This command was run on the LiveKd process.)

```
kd> !wsle 7

Working Set @ c0502000
      Quota:      9f  FirstFree:  40  FirstDynamic:      3
      LastEntry  1fe  NextSlot:    3  LastInitialized  257
      NonDirect   5c  HashTable:   0  HashTableSize:     0

Virtual Address  Age  Locked  ReferenceCount
c0300203          0      1        1
c0301203          0      1        1
c0502203          0      1        1
c01df201          0      0        1
c01ff201          0      0        1
c0005201          0      0        1
c0001201          0      0        1
c0002201          0      0        1
c0000201          0      0        1
c0006201          0      0        1
77e87119          0      0        1
00402319          0      0        1
77e01201          0      0        1
7ffdf201          0      0        1
00130201          0      0        1
77e9e119          0      0        1
78033201          0      0        1
00230221          0      0        1
00131201          0      0        1
77d50119          0      0        1
00132201          0      0        1
c01e0201          0      0        1
00411309          0      0        1
0040d201          0      0        1
77edf201          0      0        1
77ee0201          0      0        1
77fcd201          0      0        1
0040e201          0      0        1
7ffc1009          0      0        1
00401319          0      0        1
```

(continued)

EXPERIMENT: Viewing the Working Set List *continued*

Notice that some entries in the working set list are page table pages (the ones with addresses greater than 0xC0000000), some are from system DLLs (the ones in the 0x7nnnnnnn range), and some are from the code of LiveKd.exe itself (those in the 0x004nnnnn range).

Balance Set Manager and Swapper

Working set expansion and trimming take place in the context of a system thread called the *balance set manager* (routine *KeBalanceSetManager*). The balance set manager is created during system initialization. Although the balance set manager is technically part of the kernel, it calls the memory manager's working set manager to perform working set analysis and adjustment.

The balance set manager waits on two different event objects: an event that is signaled when a periodic timer set to fire once per second expires and an internal working set manager event that the memory manager signals at various points when it determines that working sets need to be adjusted. For example, if the system is experiencing a high page fault rate or the free list is too small, the memory manager wakes up the balance set manager so that it will call the working set manager to begin trimming working sets. When memory is more plentiful, the working set manager will permit faulting processes to gradually increase the size of their working sets by faulting pages back into memory, but the working sets will grow only as needed.

When the balance set manager wakes up as the result of its 1-second timer expiring, it takes the following four steps:

1. Every fourth time the balance set manager wakes up because its 1-second timer has expired, it signals an event that wakes up another system thread called the swapper (routine *KeSwapProcessOrStack*).

2. The balance set manager then checks the look-aside lists and adjusts their depths if necessary (to improve access time and to reduce pool usage and pool fragmentation).

3. It looks for threads that might warrant having their priority boosted because they are CPU starved. (See the section "Priority Boosts for CPU Starvation" in Chapter 6 on page 367.)

4. It calls the memory manager's working set manager. (The working set manager has its own internal counters that regulate when to perform working set trimming and how aggressively to trim.)

The swapper is also awakened by the scheduling code in the kernel if a thread that needs to run has its kernel stack swapped out or if the process has been swapped out. The swapper looks for threads that have been in a wait state for a specified amount of time (3 seconds on small memory systems, 7 seconds on medium or large memory systems). If it finds one, it puts the thread's kernel stack in transition (moving the pages to the modified or standby lists) so as to reclaim its physical memory, operating on the principle that, if a thread's been waiting that long, it's going to be waiting even longer. When the last thread in a process has its kernel stack removed from memory, the process is marked to be entirely outswapped. That's why, for example, processes that have been idle for a long time (such as Winlogon is after you log on) can have a zero working set size.

System Working Set

Just as processes have working sets, the pageable code and data in the operating system are managed by a single *system working set*. Five different kinds of pages can reside in the system working set:

- System cache pages
- Paged pool
- Pageable code and data in Ntoskrnl.exe
- Pageable code and data in device drivers
- System mapped views (sections mapped at 0xA0000000, such as Win32k.sys)

You can examine the size of the system working set or the size of the five components that contribute to it with the performance counters or system variables shown in Table 7-19. Keep in mind that the performance counter values are in bytes whereas the system variables are measured in terms of pages.

You can also examine the paging activity in the system working set by examining the Memory: Cache Faults/Sec performance counter, which describes page faults that occur in the system working set (both hard and soft).

Table 7-19 System Working Set Performance Counters

Performance Counter (in Bytes)	System Variable (in Pages)	Description
Memory: Cache Bytes*	*MmSystemCacheWs.WorkingSetSize*	Total size of system working set (including the cache, paged pool, pageable Ntoskrnl and driver code, and system mapped views); this is *not* the size of the system cache alone, even though the name implies that it is.
Memory: Cache Bytes Peak	*MmSystemCacheWs.Peak*	Peak system working set size.
Memory: System Cache Resident Bytes	*MmSystemCachePage*	Physical memory consumed by the system cache.
Memory: System Code Resident Bytes	*MmSystemCodePage*	Physical memory consumed by pageable code in Ntoskrnl.exe.
Memory: System Driver Resident Bytes	*MmSystemDriverPage*	Physical memory consumed by pageable device driver code.
Memory: Pool Paged Resident Bytes	*MmPagedPoolPage*	Physical memory consumed by paged pool.

* Internally, this working set is called the system *cache* working set, even though the system cache is just one of five different components in it. Thus, several utilities think they are displaying the size of the file cache when they are displaying the total size of the system working set.

The system variable that contains the value for this counter is *MmSystemCacheWs.PageFaultCount*.

The minimum and maximum system working set size is computed at system initialization time based on the amount of physical memory on the machine and whether the system is running Windows 2000 Professional or Windows 2000 Server. The initial values, which are listed in Table 7-20, are chosen based on system memory size.

Table 7-20 Minimum and Maximum Size of System Working Set

Memory Size	System Working Set Minimum (in Pages)	System Working Set Maximum (in Pages)
Small	388	500
Medium	688	1150
Large	1188	2050

These numbers are further altered if the registry value HKLM\
SYSTEM\CurrentControlSet\Control\Session Manager\Memory Management\
LargeSystemCache is set to 1 (the default on Windows 2000 Server systems)
and the number of available pages (*MmAvailablePages*, as described in Table 7-25
on page 478) is greater than 350 plus 6 MB (a total of 1886 pages on x86 sys-
tems). In this case, the system working set maximum is set to available pages
minus 4 MB. If this value is greater than the maximum working set size sup-
ported by Windows 2000 (1984 MB for normal x86 systems or 3008 MB on
a system running with a 3-GB user space), the system working set maximum is
reduced to that maximum value minus 5 pages.

Windows 2000 then checks to see whether the new system working set
maximum is greater than the virtual size of the system cache—if it is, the working
set maximum is reduced to the virtual size of the system cache. In other words,
the system working set could potentially expand to use all the virtual memory
reserved for the system cache. (See Chapter 11 for more information about the
virtual size of the system cache.)

Finally, a check is made to determine whether the difference between the
system working set minimum and maximum is less than 500 pages. If it is, the
working set minimum is reduced to the working set maximum minus 500 pages.

The final calculated working set minimum and maximum are then stored
in the system variables shown in Table 7-21. (These variables aren't available
through any performance counter.)

**Table 7-21 System Variables That Store Working Set Minimums
or Maximums**

Variable	Type	Description
MmSystemCacheWsMinimum or *MmSystemCacheWs.MinimumWorkingSetSize*	ULONG	Minimum working set size
MmSystemCacheWsMaximum or *MmSystemCacheWs.MaximumWorkingSetSize*	ULONG	Maximum working set size

Page Frame Number Database

Whereas working sets describe the resident pages owned by a process or the
system, the *page frame number (PFN) database* describes the state of each page
in physical memory. Pages are in one of eight states, as shown in Table 7-22.

Table 7-22 **Page States**

Status	Description
Active (also called Valid)	The page is part of a working set (either a process working set or the system working set) or it's not in any working set (e.g. nonpaged kernel page), and a valid PTE points to it.
Transition	A temporary state for a page that isn't owned by a working set and isn't on any paging list. A page is in this state when an I/O to the page is in progress. The PTE is encoded so that collided page faults can be recognized and handled properly.
Standby	The page previously belonged to a working set but was removed. The page wasn't modified since it was last written to disk. The PTE still refers to the physical page but is marked invalid and in transition.
Modified	The page previously belonged to a working set but was removed. However, the page was modified while it was in use and its current contents haven't yet been written to disk. The PTE still refers to the physical page but is marked invalid and in transition. It must be written to disk before the physical page can be reused.
Modified no-write	Same as a modified page, except that it has been marked so that the memory manager's modified page writer won't write it to disk. The cache manager marks pages as modified no-write at the request of file system drivers. For example, NTFS uses this state for pages containing file system metadata so that it can first ensure that transaction log entries are flushed to disk before the pages they are protecting are written to disk. (NTFS transaction logging is explained in Chapter 12.)
Free	The page is free but has unspecified dirty data in it. (These pages can't be given as a user page to a user process without being initialized with zeros, for security reasons.)
Zeroed	The page is free and has been initialized with zeros by the zero page thread.
Bad	The page has generated parity or other hardware errors and can't be used.

The PFN database consists of an array of structures that represent each physical page of memory on the system. The PFN database and its relationship to page tables are shown in Figure 7-19. As this figure shows, valid PTEs point to entries in the PFN database, and the PFN database entries (for nonprototype PFNs) point back to the page table that is using them. For prototype PFNs, they point back to the prototype PTE.

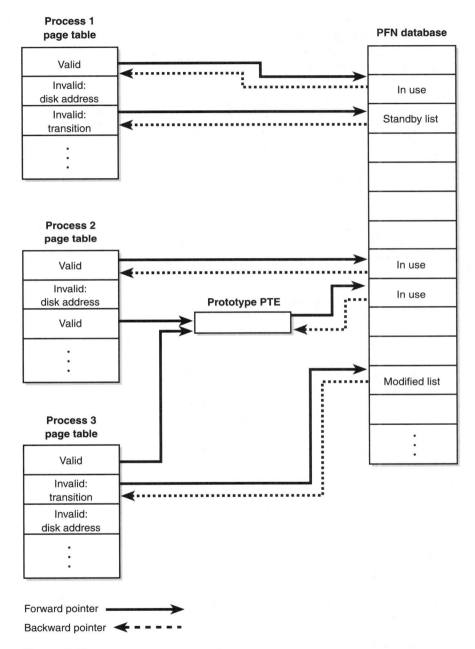

Figure 7-19
Page tables and the page frame number database

Of the page states listed in Table 7-22, six are organized into linked lists so that the memory manager can quickly locate pages of a specific type. (Active/valid pages and transition pages aren't in any systemwide page list.) Figure 7-20 shows an example of how these entries are linked together.

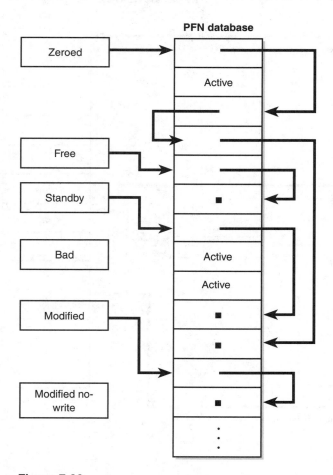

Figure 7-20
Page lists in the PFN database

In the next section, you'll find out how these linked lists are used to satisfy page faults and how pages move to and from the various lists.

EXPERIMENT: Viewing the PFN Database

Using the kernel debugger *!memusage* command, you can dump the size of the various paging lists. The following is the output from this command:

```
kd> !memusage
 loading PFN database
loading (99% complete)
          Zeroed:       8 (    32 kb)
            Free:       0 (     0 kb)
         Standby:    2809 ( 11236 kb)
        Modified:     756 (  3024 kb)
 ModifiedNoWrite:       1 (     4 kb)
    Active/Valid:   29150 (116600 kb)
      Transition:      10 (    40 kb)
         Unknown:       0 (     0 kb)
           TOTAL:   32734 (130936 kb)
 Building kernel map
 :
```

Page List Dynamics

Figure 7-21 shows a state diagram for page frame transitions. For simplicity, the modified-no-write list isn't shown.

Page frames move between the paging lists in the following ways:

- When the memory manager needs a zero-initialized page to service a demand-zero page fault (a reference to a page that is defined to be all zeros or to a user-mode committed private page that has never been accessed), it first attempts to get one from the zero page list; if the list is empty, it gets one from the free page list and zeros the page. If the free list is empty, it goes to the standby list and zeros that page.

 One reason zero-initialized pages are required is to meet C2 security requirements. C2 specifies that user-mode processes must be given initialized page frames to prevent them from reading a previous

469

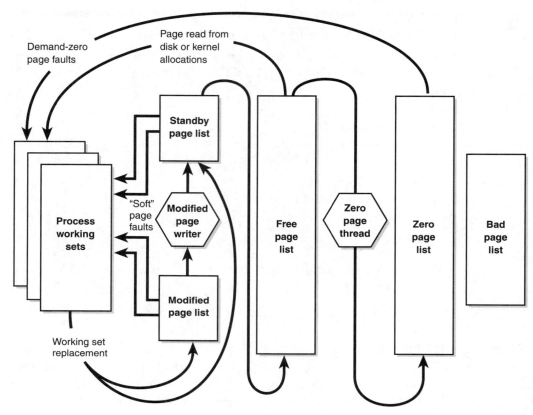

Figure 7-21
State diagram for page frames

process's memory contents. Therefore, the memory manager gives user-mode processes zeroed page frames unless the page is being read in from a mapped file. If that's the case, the memory manager prefers to use nonzeroed page frames, initializing them with the data off the disk.

The zero page list is populated from the free list by a system thread called the *zero page thread* (thread 0 in the System process). The zero page thread waits on an event object to signal it to go to work. When the free list has eight or more pages, this event is signaled. However, the zero page thread will run only if no other threads are running, because the zero page thread runs at priority 0 and the lowest priority that a user thread can be set to is 1.

■ When the memory manager doesn't require a zero-initialized page, it goes first to the free list; if that's empty, it goes to the zeroed list. If the zeroed list is empty, it goes to the standby list. Before the memory manager can use a page frame from the standby list, it must first backtrack and remove the reference from the invalid PTE (or prototype PTE) that still points to the page frame. Because entries in the PFN database contain pointers back to the previous user's page table (or to a prototype PTE for shared pages), the memory manager can quickly find the PTE and make the appropriate change.

■ When a process has to give up a page out of its working set (either because it referenced a new page and its working set was full or the memory manager trimmed its working set), the page goes to the standby list if the page was clean (not modified) or to the modified list if the page was modified while it was resident. When a process exits, all the private pages go to the free list. Also, when the last reference to a page file backed section is closed, these pages also go to the free list.

EXPERIMENT: Viewing Page Fault Behavior

With the Pfmon tool in the Windows 2000 resource kit, you can watch page fault behavior as it occurs. A *soft fault* refers to a page fault satisfied from one of the transition lists. *Hard faults* refer to a disk-read. The following example is a portion of output you'll see if you start Notepad with Pfmon and then exit. Be sure to notice the summary of page fault activity at the end.

```
C:\> pfmon notepad
SOFT: KiUserApcDispatcher : KiUserApcDispatcher
SOFT: LdrInitializeThunk : LdrInitializeThunk
SOFT: 0x77f61016 :  : 0x77f61016
SOFT: 0x77f6105b :  : fltused+0xe00
HARD: 0x77f6105b :  : fltused+0xe00
SOFT: LdrQueryImageFileExecutionOptions :
                        LdrQueryImageFileExecutionOptions
SOFT: RtlAppendUnicodeToString : RtlAppendUnicodeToString
SOFT: RtlInitUnicodeString : RtlInitUnicodeString
```

(continued)

471

EXPERIMENT: Viewing Page Fault Behavior *continued*

```
  ⋮
  notepad Caused   8 faults had   9 Soft  5 Hard faulted VA's
    ntdll Caused  94 faults had  42 Soft  8 Hard faulted VA's
 comdlg32 Caused   3 faults had   0 Soft  3 Hard faulted VA's
  shlwapi Caused   2 faults had   2 Soft  2 Hard faulted VA's
    gdi32 Caused  18 faults had  10 Soft  2 Hard faulted VA's
 kernel32 Caused  48 faults had  36 Soft  3 Hard faulted VA's
   user32 Caused  38 faults had  26 Soft  6 Hard faulted VA's
 advapi32 Caused   7 faults had   6 Soft  3 Hard faulted VA's
   rpcrt4 Caused   6 faults had   4 Soft  2 Hard faulted VA's
 comctl32 Caused   6 faults had   5 Soft  2 Hard faulted VA's
  shell32 Caused   6 faults had   5 Soft  2 Hard faulted VA's
          Caused  10 faults had   9 Soft  5 Hard faulted VA's
 winspool Caused   4 faults had   2 Soft  2 Hard faulted VA's

PFMON: Total Faults 250
       (KM 74 UM 250 Soft 204, Hard 46, Code 121, Data 129)
```

When the modified list gets too big, or if the size of the zeroed and standby lists falls below a minimum threshold (as indicated by the kernel variable *Mm-MinimumFreePages*, which is computed at system boot time), a system thread called the *modified page writer* is awakened to write pages back to disk and move the pages to the standby list.

Modified Page Writer

The modified page writer is responsible for limiting the size of the modified page list by writing pages back to disk when the list becomes too big. It consists of two system threads: one to write out modified pages (*MiModifiedPageWriter*) to the paging file and a second one to write modified pages to mapped files (*MiMappedPageWriter*). Two threads are required to avoid creating a deadlock, which would occur if the writing of mapped file pages caused a page fault that in turn required a free page when no free pages were available (thus requiring the modified page writer to create more free pages). By having the modified page writer perform mapped file paging I/Os from a second system thread, that thread can wait without blocking regular page file I/O.

Both threads run at priority 17 and, after initialization, wait on separate event objects to trigger their operation. The modified page writer event is triggered for one of two reasons:

■ When the number of modified pages exceeds the maximum value computed at system initialization (*MmModifiedPageMaximum*)

■ When the number of available pages (*MmAvailablePages*) goes below *MmMinimumFreePages*

Table 7-23 shows the number of pages that trigger the waking of the modified page writer to reduce the size of the modified list and how many pages it leaves on the list. As with other memory management variables, this value is computed at system boot time and depends on the amount of physical memory.

Table 7-23 Modified Page Writer Values

Memory Size	Modified Page Threshold	Retain Modified Pages
< 12 MB	100	40
12–19 MB	150	80
19–33 MB	300	150
>33 MB (special case)	400	800

The modified page writer waits on an additional event (*MiMappedPages-TooOldEvent*) that is set after a predetermined number of seconds (*MmModified-PageLifeInSeconds*) to indicate that mapped pages (not modified pages) should be written to disk. By default, this value is 300 seconds (5 minutes). (You can override this value by adding the DWORD registry value HKLM\SYSTEM\CurrentControlSet\Control\Session Manager\Memory Management\ModifiedPageLife). The reason for this additional event is to reduce data loss in the case of a system crash or power failure by eventually writing out modified mapped pages even if the modified list hasn't reached the thresholds listed in Table 7-23.

When invoked, the mapped page writer attempts to write as many pages as possible to disk with a single I/O request. It accomplishes this by examining the original PTE field of the PFN database elements for pages on the modified page list to locate pages in contiguous locations on the disk. Once a list is created, the pages are removed from the modified list, an I/O request is issued, and at successful completion of the I/O request, the pages are placed at the tail of the standby list.

Pages that are in the process of being written can be referenced by another thread. When this happens, the reference count and the share count in the PFN entry that represents the physical page are incremented to indicate that another process is using the page. When the I/O operation completes, the modified page writer notices that the share count is no longer 0 and doesn't place the page on the standby list.

PFN Data Structures

Although PFN database entries are of fixed length, they can be in several different states, depending on the state of the page. Thus, individual fields have different meanings depending on the state. The states of a PFN entry are shown in Figure 7-22.

| Working set index |
| PTE address |
| Share count |
| Flags | Type | Reference count |
| Original PTE contents |
| PFN of PTE |

PFN for a page in a working set

| Forward link |
| PTE address |
| Backward link |
| Flags | Type | Reference count |
| Original PTE contents |
| PFN of PTE |

PFN for a page on the standby or the modified list

| Forward link |
| PTE address |
| Color chain PFN number |
| Flags | Type | Reference count |
| Original PTE contents |
| PFN of PTE |

PFN for a page on the zero or free list

| Event address |
| PTE address |
| Share count |
| Flags | Type | Reference count |
| Original PTE contents |
| PFN of PTE |

PFN for a page with an I/O in progess

Figure 7-22
States of PFN database entries

Several fields are the same for several of the PFN types, but others are specific to a given type of PFN. The following fields appear in more than one PFN type:

- **PTE address** Virtual address of the PTE that points to this page.

- **Reference count** The number of references to this page. The reference count is incremented when a page is first added to a working set and/or when the page is locked in memory for I/O (for example, by a device driver). The reference count is decremented when the share count becomes 0 or when pages are unlocked from memory. When the share count becomes 0, the page is no longer owned by a working set. Then, depending on the reference count, the PFN database entry that describes the page is updated to add the page to the free, standby, or modified list.

- **Type** The type of page represented by this PFN (active/valid, transition, standby, modified, modified-no-write, free, zeroed, bad, and transition).

- **Flags** The information contained in the flags field is shown in Table 7-24.

- **Original PTE contents** All PFN database entries contain the original contents of the PTE that pointed to the page (which could be a prototype PTE). Saving the contents of the PTE allows it to be restored when the physical page is no longer resident.

- **PFN of PTE** Physical page number of the page table page containing the PTE that points to this page.

Table 7-24 Flags Within PFN Database Entries

Flag	Meaning
Modified state	Indicates whether the page was modified. (If the page is modified, its contents must be saved to disk before removing it from memory.)
Prototype PTE	Indicates that the PTE referenced by the PFN entry is a prototype PTE. (For example, this page is sharable.)
Parity error	Indicates that the physical page contains parity or error correction control errors.

(continued)

Table 7-24 *continued*

Flag	Meaning
Read in progress	Indicates that an in-page operation is in progress for the page. The first DWORD contains the address of the event object that will be signaled when the I/O is complete; also used to indicate the first PFN for nonpaged pool allocations.
Write in progress	Indicates that a page write operation is in progress. The first DWORD contains the address of the event object that will be signaled when the I/O is complete; also used to indicate the last PFN for nonpaged pool allocations.
Start of nonpaged pool	For nonpaged pool pages, indicates that this is the first PFN for a given nonpaged pool allocation.
End of nonpaged pool	For nonpaged pool pages, indicates that this is the last PFN for a given nonpaged pool allocation.
In-page error	Indicates that an I/O error occurred during the in-page operation on this page. (In this case, the first field in the PFN contains the error code.)

The remaining fields are specific to the type of PFN. For example, the first PFN in Figure 7-22 represents a page that is active and part of a working set. The share count field represents the number of PTEs that refer to this page. (Pages marked read-only, copy-on-write, or shared read/write can be shared by multiple processes.) For page table pages, this field is the number of valid PTEs in the page table. As long as the share count is greater than 0, the page isn't eligible for removal from memory.

The working set index field is an index into the process working set list (or the system or session working set list, or zero if not in any working set) where the virtual address that maps this physical page resides. If the page is a private page, the working set index field refers directly to the entry in the working set list because the page is mapped only at a single virtual address. In the case of a shared page, the working set index is a hint that is guaranteed to be correct only for the first process that made the page valid. (Other processes will try to use the same index where possible.) The process that initially sets this field is guaranteed to refer to the proper index and doesn't need to add a working set

list hash entry referenced by the virtual address into its working set hash tree. This guarantee reduces the size of the working set hash tree and makes searches faster for these particular direct entries.

The second PFN in Figure 7-22 is for a page on either the standby or the modified list. In this case, the forward and backward link fields link the elements of the list together within the list. This linking allows pages to be easily manipulated to satisfy page faults. When a page is on one of the lists, the share count is by definition 0 (because no working set is using the page) and therefore can be overlaid with the backward link. However, the reference count might not be 0 because an I/O could be in progress for this page (for example, when the page is being written to disk).

The third PFN in Figure 7-22 is for a page on the free or zeroed list. Besides being linked together within the two lists, these PFN database entries use an additional field to link physical pages by "color," their location in the processor CPU memory cache. Windows 2000 attempts to minimize unnecessary thrashing of CPU memory caches by using different physical pages in the CPU cache. It achieves this optimization by avoiding using the same cache entry for two different pages wherever possible. For systems with direct mapped caches, optimally using the hardware's capabilities can result in a significant performance advantage.

The fourth PFN in Figure 7-22 is for a page that has an I/O in progress (for example, a page read). While the I/O is in progress, the first field points to an event object that will be signaled when the I/O completes. If an in-page error occurs, this field contains the Windows 2000 error status code representing the I/O error. This PFN type is used to resolve collided page faults.

EXPERIMENT: Viewing PFN Entries

You can examine individual PFN entries with the kernel debugger *!pfn* command. You first need to supply the PFN as an argument. (For example, *!pfn 0* shows the first entry, *!pfn 1* shows the second, and so on.) In the following example, the PTE for virtual address 0x50000 is displayed, followed by the PFN that contains the page directory and then the actual page:

```
kd> !pte 50000
00050000  - PDE at C0300000      PTE at C0000140
          contains 00700067      contains 00DAA047
          pfn 00700 --DA--UWV    pfn 00DAA --D---UWV
```

(continued)

EXPERIMENT: Viewing PFN Entries *continued*

```
kd> !pfn 700
  PFN 00000700 at address 827CD800
  flink   00000004 blink / share count 00000010 pteaddress C0300000
  reference count 0001                              color 0
  restore pte 00000080  containing page     00030 Active    M
  Modified

kd> !pfn daa
  PFN 00000DAA at address 827D77F0
  flink   00000077 blink / share count 00000001 pteaddress C0000140
  reference count 0001                              color 0
  restore pte 00000080  containing page     00700 Active    M
  Modified
```

In addition to the PFN database, the system variables in Table 7-25 describe the overall state of physical memory.

Table 7-25 System Variables That Describe Physical Memory

Variable	Description
MmNumberOfPhysicalPages	Total number of physical pages available on the system
MmAvailablePages	Total number of available pages on the system—the sum of the pages on the zeroed, free, and standby lists
MmResidentAvailablePages	Total number of physical pages that would be available if every process were at its minimum working set size

Section Objects

As you'll remember from the section on shared memory earlier in the chapter, the *section object,* which the Win32 subsystem calls a *file mapping object,* represents a block of memory that two or more processes can share. A section object can be mapped to the paging file or to another file on disk.

The executive uses sections to load executable images into memory, and the cache manager uses them to access data in a cached file. (See Chapter 11 for more information on how the cache manager uses section objects.) You can also use section objects to map a file into a process address space. The file can then be accessed as a large array by mapping different views of the section object and reading or writing to memory rather than to the file (an activity called *mapped file I/O*). When the program accesses an invalid page (one not in physical memory), a page fault occurs and the memory manager automatically brings the page into memory from the mapped file. If the application modifies the page, the memory manager writes the changes back to the file during its normal paging operations (or the application can flush a view by using the Win32 *FlushViewOfFile* function).

Section objects, like other objects, are allocated and deallocated by the object manager. The object manager creates and initializes an object header, which it uses to manage the objects; the memory manager defines the body of the section object. The memory manager also implements services that user-mode threads can call to retrieve and change the attributes stored in the body of section objects. The structure of a section object is shown in Figure 7-23.

Object type	**Section**
Object body attributes	Maximum size Page protection Paging file/Mapped file Based/Not based
Services	Create section Open section Extend section Map/Unmap view Query section

Figure 7-23
A section object

Table 7-26 summarizes the unique attributes stored in section objects.

Table 7-26 Section Object Body Attributes

Attribute	Purpose
Maximum size	The largest size to which the section can grow in bytes; if mapping a file, the maximum size is the size of the file.
Page protection	Page-based memory protection assigned to all pages in the section when it is created.
Paging file/Mapped file	Indicates whether the section is created empty (backed by the paging file—as explained earlier, page file backed sections use page-file resources only when the pages need to be written out to disk) or loaded with a file (backed by the mapped file).
Based/Not based	Indicates whether a section is a based section, which must appear at the same virtual address for all processes sharing it, or a nonbased section, which can appear at different virtual addresses for different processes.

EXPERIMENT: Viewing Section Objects

With the Object Viewer (\Sysint\Winobj from the book's companion CD or Winobj.exe in the Platform SDK), you can see the list of sections that have global names. As explained in Chapter 3, these names are stored in the object manager directory \BaseNamedObjects.

With the Windows 2000 resource kit OH (Open Handles) tool, you can list the open handles to section objects. The following command displays all open handles to objects of type *section*, whether or not they have names. (A section must have a name only if other processes need to open it by name.)

```
c:\> oh -t section -a
00000008 System        Section  0070
0000008C smss.exe       Section  0004
000000A4 csrss.exe      Section  0004
```

```
000000A4 csrss.exe    Section  0024
000000A4 csrss.exe    Section  0038
000000A4 csrss.exe    Section  0040  \NLS\NlsSectionUnicode
000000A4 csrss.exe    Section  0044  \NLS\NlsSectionLocale
000000A4 csrss.exe    Section  0048  \NLS\NlsSectionCType
000000A4 csrss.exe    Section  004c  \NLS\NlsSectionSortkey
000000A4 csrss.exe    Section  0050  \NLS\NlsSectionSortTbls
000000A0 winlogon.exe Section  0004
000000A0 winlogon.exe Section  0034
000000A0 winlogon.exe Section  0168  \BaseNamedObjects\mmGlobalPnpInfo
⋮
```

You can also use HandleEx (\Sysint\Handleex on the companion CD) to view mapped files. Select View DLLs from the View menu. Files marked with an asterisk in the MM column are mapped files (rather than DLLs and other files the image loader loads as modules). Here's an example:

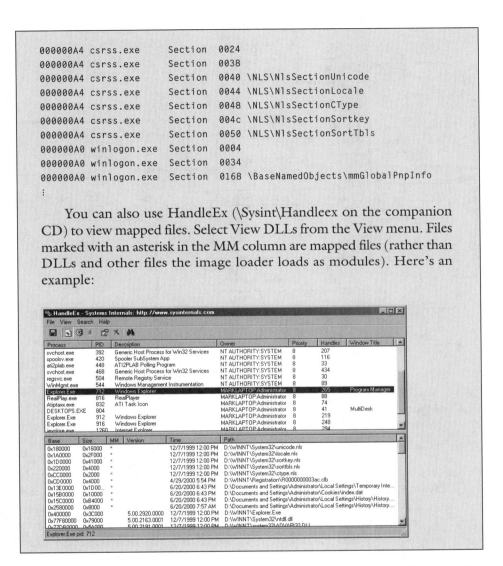

The data structures maintained by the memory manager that describe mapped sections are shown in Figure 7-24. These structures ensure that data read from mapped files is consistent, regardless of the type of access (open file, mapped file, and so on).

481

Figure 7-24
Internal section structures

For each open file (represented by a file object), there is a single *section object pointers* structure. (This structure is also discussed in Chapter 11.) This structure is the key to maintaining data consistency for all types of file access as well as to providing caching for files. The section object pointers structure points to one or two *control areas*. One control area is used to map the file when it is accessed as a data file, and one is used to map the file when it is run as an executable image.

A control area in turn points to *subsection* structures that describe the mapping information for each section of the file (read-only, read-write, copy-on-write, and so on). The control area also points to a *segment* structure allo-

cated in paged pool, which in turn points to the prototype PTEs used to map to the actual pages mapped by the section object. As described earlier in the chapter, process page tables point to these prototype PTEs, which in turn map the pages being referenced.

Although Windows 2000 ensures that any process that accesses (reads or writes) a file will always see the same, consistent data, there is one case in which two copies of pages of a file can reside in physical memory (but even in this case, all accessors get the latest copy and data consistency is maintained). This duplication can happen when an image file has been accessed as a data file (having been read or written) and then run as an executable image (for example, when an image is linked and then run—the linker had the file open for data access, and then when the image was run, the image loader mapped it as an executable). Internally, the following actions occur:

1. When the image file is created, a data control area is created to represent the data pages in the image file being read or written.

2. When the image is run and the section object is created to map the image as an executable, the memory manager finds that the section object pointers for the image file point to a data control area and flushes the section. This step is necessary to ensure that any modified pages have been written to disk before accessing the image through the image control area.

3. The memory manager then creates a control area for the image file.

4. As the image begins execution, its (read-only) pages are faulted in from the image file.

Because the pages mapped by the data control area might still be resident (on the standby list), this is the one case in which two copies of the same data are in two different pages in memory. However, this duplication doesn't result in a data consistency issue because, as mentioned, the data control area has already been flushed to disk, so the pages read from the image are up to date.

EXPERIMENT: Viewing Control Areas

To find the address of the control area structures for a file, you must first get the address of the file object in question. You can obtain this address through the kernel debugger by dumping the process handle table with the *!handle* command and noting the object address of a file object. Although the kernel debugger *!file* command displays the basic information in a file object, it doesn't display the pointer to the section object pointers structure. However, because file objects are defined in the public DDK header file Ntddk.h, you can look up the offset (0x14 in Windows 2000). So, simply examine the pointer at offset 0x14 into the file object, and you'll have the section object pointers structure. That structure is also defined in Ntddk.h. It consists of three 32-bit pointers: a pointer to the data control area, a pointer to the shared cache map (explained in Chapter 11), and a pointer to the image control area. From the section object pointers structure, you can obtain the address of a control area for the file (if one exists) and feed that address into the *!ca* command.

Another technique is to display the list of all control areas with the *!memusage* command. The following excerpt is from the output of this command:

```
kd> !memusage
 loading PFN database
loading (99% complete)
             Zeroed:      9 (     36 kb)
               Free:      0 (      0 kb)
            Standby:   2103 (   8412 kb)
           Modified:    300 (   1200 kb)
    ModifiedNoWrite:      1 (      4 kb)
       Active/Valid:  30318 ( 121272 kb)
         Transition:      3 (     12 kb)
            Unknown:      0 (      0 kb)
              TOTAL:  32734 ( 130936 kb)
  Building kernel map
  Finished building kernel map
  Usage Summary (in Kb):
Control Valid Standby Dirty Shared Locked PageTables  name
8119b608  3000   528     0     0      0        0 mapped_file( WINWORD.EXE )
849e7c68    96     0     0     0      0        0    No Name for File
8109c388    24     0     0     0      0        0 mapped_file( DEVDTG.PKG )
81402488   236     0     0     0      0        0    No Name for File
```

```
80fba0a8   268    0    0    0    0    0  mapped_file( kernel32.pdb )
810ab168  1504  380    0    0    0    0  mapped_file( OUTLLIB.DLL )
81126a08     0  276    0    0    0    0  mapped_file( H )
81112d28   656    0    0    0    0    0   No Name for File
  ⋮
```

The Control column points to the control area structure that de-scribes the mapped file. You can display control areas, segments, and subsections with the kernel debugger *!ca* command. For example, to dump the control area for the mapped file Winword.exe in this example, type the *!ca* command followed by the Control number, as shown here:

```
kd> !ca 8119b608

ControlArea @8119b608
  Segment:      e2c28000  Flink          0  Blink:            0
  Section Ref         1  Pfn Ref      372  Mapped Views:     1
  User Ref            2  Subsections    6  Flush Count:      0
  File Object 8213fb98  ModWriteCount   0  System Views:     0
  WaitForDel          0  Paged Usage  3000  NonPaged Usage  100
  Flags (90000a0) Image File HadUserReference Accessed

   File: \Program Files\Microsoft Office\Office\WINWORD.EXE

Segment @ e2c28000:
   Base address         0  Total Ptes      86a  NonExtendPtes:      86a
   Image commit        d7  ControlArea 8119b608  SizeOfSegment: 86a000
   Image Base           0  Committed         0  PTE Template:  919b6c38
   Based Addr    30000000  ProtoPtes   e2c28038  Image Info:    e2c2a1e4

Subsection 1. @ 8119b640
   ControlArea: 8119b608  Starting Sector 0 Number Of Sectors 8
   Base Pte     e2c28038  Ptes In subsect       1 Unused Ptes         0
   Flags              15  Sector Offset         0 Protection          1
    ReadOnly CopyOnWrite

Subsection 2. @ 8119b660
   ControlArea: 8119b608  Starting Sector 10 Number Of Sectors 3c00
   Base Pte     e2c2803c  Ptes In subsect     780 Unused Ptes         0
   Flags              35  Sector Offset         0 Protection          3
    ReadOnly CopyOnWrite

Subsection 3. @ 8119b680
   ControlArea: 8119b608  Starting Sector 3C10 Number Of Sectors 5d8
```

(continued)

485

EXPERIMENT: Viewing Control Areas *continued*

```
        Base Pte    e2c29e3c  Ptes In subsect        c1 Unused Ptes        0
        Flags             55  Sector Offset           0 Protection         5
        ReadOnly CopyOnWrite

   Subsection 4. @ 8119b6a0
        ControlArea: 8119b608  Starting Sector 41E8 Number Of Sectors a8
        Base Pte    e2c2a140  Ptes In subsect        15 Unused Ptes        0
        Flags             55  Sector Offset           0 Protection         5
        ReadOnly CopyOnWrite

   Subsection 5. @ 8119b6c0
        ControlArea: 8119b608  Starting Sector 0 Number Of Sectors 0
        Base Pte    e2c2a194  Ptes In subsect         1 Unused Ptes        0
        Flags             55  Sector Offset           0 Protection         5
        ReadOnly CopyOnWrite

   Subsection 6. @ 8119b6e0
        ControlArea: 8119b608  Starting Sector 4290 Number Of Sectors 90
        Base Pte    e2c2a198  Ptes In subsect        12 Unused Ptes        0
        Flags             15  Sector Offset           0 Protection         1
        ReadOnly CopyOnWrite
```

Conclusion

In this chapter, we've examined how the Windows 2000 memory manager implements virtual memory management. As with most 32-bit operating systems, each process is given access to a private 32-bit address space, protecting one process's memory from another's but allowing processes to share memory efficiently and securely. Advanced capabilities, such as the inclusion of mapped files and the ability to sparsely allocate memory, are also available. The Win32 environment subsystem makes most of the memory manager's capabilities available to applications through the Win32 API.

The memory manager's implementation relies on lazy-evaluation techniques whenever possible to avoid performing time-consuming and unnecessary operations unless they are required. It is also self-tuning, adapting to both large multiprocessor servers as well as uniprocessor desktop workstations.

One aspect of the memory manager that we didn't describe in this chapter is its tight integration with the cache manager, which we'll cover in Chapter 11. But before we get to that, let's take a closer look at the Windows 2000 security mechanisms.

Security

Preventing unauthorized access to sensitive data is essential in any environment in which multiple users have access to the same physical or network resources. An operating system, as well as individual users, must be able to protect files, memory, and configuration settings from unwanted viewing and modification. Operating system security includes obvious mechanisms such as accounts, passwords, and file protection. It also includes less obvious mechanisms such as protecting the operating system from corruption, preventing less privileged users from performing actions (rebooting the computer, for example), and not allowing user programs to adversely affect the programs of other users or the operating system.

In this chapter, we explain how every aspect of the design and implementation of Microsoft Windows 2000 was influenced in some way by the stringent requirements of providing robust security.

Security Ratings

The National Computer Security Center (NCSC, at *www.radium.ncsc.mil*) was established in 1981 as part of the U.S. Department of Defense's (DoD) National Security Agency (NSA) to help the government, corporations, and home users protect proprietary and personal data stored in computer systems. As part of this goal, the NCSC created a range of security ratings, listed in Table 8-1, that are used to indicate the degree of protection commercial operating systems, network components, and trusted applications offer. These security ratings, which are assigned based on the DoD's Trusted Computer System Evaluation Criteria (TCSEC), were defined in 1983 and are commonly referred to as "the Orange Book."

Table 8-1 TCSEC Rating Levels

Rating	Description
A1	Verified Design
B3	Security Domains
B2	Structured Protection
B1	Labeled Security Protection
C2	Controlled Access Protection
C1	Discretionary Access Protection (obsolete)
D	Minimal Protection

The TCSEC standard consists of "levels of trust" ratings, where higher levels build on lower levels by adding more rigorous protection and validation requirements. No operating system meets the A1, or "Verified Design," rating. Although a few operating systems have earned one of the B-level ratings, C2 is considered sufficient and the highest rating practical for a general-purpose operating system.

In July 1995, Microsoft Windows NT 3.5 (Workstation and Server) with Service Pack 3 was the first version of Windows NT to earn the C2 rating. In March 1999, Windows NT 4 with Service Pack 3 achieved an E3 rating from the U.K. government's Information Technology Security (ITSEC) organization, a rating equivalent to a U.S. C2 rating. In November 1999, Windows NT 4 with Service Pack 6a earned a C2 rating in both stand-alone and networked configurations.

The rating process takes several years, so although Windows 2000 has been submitted to international security certification organizations, it will probably be some time before its evaluations are complete. However, the fundamental security architecture of Windows 2000 is, if anything, a more robust evolution of that in Windows NT 4, just as Windows NT 4 evolved the Windows NT 3.5 implementation. Windows 2000 will almost certainly achieve the same ratings that Windows NT 4 has.

What's involved in earning a C2 security rating? The following are the key requirements:

- A *secure logon facility,* which requires that users can be uniquely identified and that they must be granted access to the computer only after they have been authenticated in some way.

- *Discretionary access control,* which allows the owner of a resource to determine who can access the resource and what they can do with it. The owner grants rights that permit various kinds of access to a user or to a group of users.

- *Security auditing,* which affords the ability to detect and record security-related events or any attempts to create, access, or delete system resources. Logon identifiers record the identities of all users, making it easy to trace anyone who performs an unauthorized action.

- *Object reuse protection,* which prevents users from seeing data that another user has deleted or from accessing memory that another user previously used and then released. For example, in some operating systems, it's possible to create a new file of a certain length and then examine the contents of the file to see data that happens to have occupied the location on the disk where the file is allocated. This data might be sensitive information that was stored in another user's file but that has been deleted. Object reuse protection prevents this potential security hole by initializing all objects, including files and memory, before they are allocated to a user.

Windows NT also meets two requirements of B-level security:

- *Trusted path functionality,* which prevents Trojan horse programs from being able to intercept users' names and passwords as they try to log on. The trusted path functionality in Windows NT comes in the form of its Ctrl+Alt+Delete logon-attention sequence. This sequence of keystrokes, which is also known as the secure attention sequence (SAS), always pops up a logon dialog box, so would-be Trojan horses can easily be recognized: a Trojan horse presenting a fake logon dialog box will be bypassed when the SAS is entered.

- *Trusted facility management,* which requires support for separate account roles for administrative functions. For example, separate accounts are provided for administration (Administrators), user accounts charged with backing up the computer, and standard users.

Windows 2000 meets all of these requirements through its security subsystem and related components.

> ## The Common Criteria
>
> In January 1996, the United States, United Kingdom, Germany, France, Canada, and the Netherlands released the jointly developed Common Criteria for Information Technology Security Evaluation (CCITSE) specification. CCITSE, usually referred to as the Common Criteria (CC), is becoming the recognized multinational standard for product security evaluation.
>
> The CC is more flexible than the TCSEC trust ratings and has a structure closer to the ITSEC than to the TCSEC. The CC includes the concept of a *Protection Profile* (PP) to collect security requirements into easily specified and compared sets, and the concept of a Security Target (ST) that contains a set of security requirements that can be made by reference to a PP.
>
> Windows 2000 will be rated using the CC rather than the TCSEC because the U.S. government no longer evaluates products against the TCSEC. You can find out more about the CC at *www.radium.ncsc.mil/ tpep/library/ccitse.*

Security System Components

Here are some of the components and databases that implement Windows 2000 security:

- **Security reference monitor (SRM)** A component in the Windows 2000 executive (\Winnt\System32\Ntoskrnl.exe) that is responsible for performing security access checks on objects, manipulating privileges (user rights), and generating any resulting security audit messages.

- **Local security authority subsystem (Lsass)** A user-mode process running the image \Winnt\System32\Lsass.exe that is responsible for the local system security policy (such as which users are allowed to log on to the machine, password policies, privileges granted to users and groups, and the system security auditing settings), user authentication, and sending security audit messages to the Event Log. The local security authority service (Lsasrv—\Winnt\System32\Lsasrv.dll), a library that Lsass loads, implements most of this functionality.

- **Lsass policy database** A database that contains the local system security policy settings. This database is stored in the registry under HKLM\SECURITY. It includes such information as what domains

are entrusted to authenticate logon attempts, who has permission to access the system and how (interactive, network, and service logons), who is assigned which privileges, and what kind of security auditing is to be performed. The Lsass policy database also stores "secrets" that include logon information used for cached domain logons and Win32 service user-account logons. (See Chapter 5 for more information on Win32 services.)

- **Security Accounts Manager (SAM) service** A set of subroutines responsible for managing the database that contains the usernames and groups defined on the local machine. The SAM service, which is implemented as \Winnt\System32\Samsrv.dll, runs in the Lsass process.

- **SAM database** A database that contains the defined local users and groups, along with their passwords and other attributes. This database is stored in the registry under HKLM\SAM.

- **Active Directory** A directory service that contains a database that stores information about objects in a domain. A *domain* is a collection of computers and their associated security groups that are managed as a single entity. Active Directory stores information about the objects in the domain, including users, groups, and computers. Password information and privileges for domain users and groups are stored in Active Directory, which is replicated across the computers that are designated as *domain controllers* of the domain. The Active Directory server, implemented as \Winnt\System32\Ntdsa.dll, runs in the Lsass process.

- **Authentication packages** DLLs that run in the context of the Lsass process and that implement Windows 2000 authentication policy. An authentication DLL is responsible for checking whether a given username and password match, and if so, returning to the Lsass information detailing the user's security identity.

- **Logon process (Winlogon)** A user-mode process running \Winnt\System32\Winlogon.exe that is responsible for responding to the SAS and for managing interactive logon sessions. Winlogon creates a user's shell (user-interface) process when the user logs on, for example.

- **Graphical Identification and Authentication (GINA)** A user-mode DLL that runs in the Winlogon process and that Winlogon uses to obtain a user's name and password or smart card PIN. The standard GINA is \Winnt\System32\Msgina.dll.

- **Net Logon service (Netlogon)** A Win32 service (\Winnt\ System32\Netlogon.dll) that runs inside Lsass and responds to Microsoft LAN Manager 2 Windows NT (pre-Windows 2000) network logon requests. Authentication is handled as local logons are, by sending them to Lsass for verification. Netlogon also has a locator service built into it for locating domain controllers.

- **Kernel Security Device Driver (KSecDD)** A kernel-mode library of functions that implement the local procedure call (LPC) interfaces that other kernel-mode security components, including the Encrypting File System (EFS), use to communicate with Lsass in user mode. KSecDD is located in \Winnt\System32\Drivers\Ksecdd.sys.

Figure 8-1 shows the relationships among some of these components and the databases they manage.

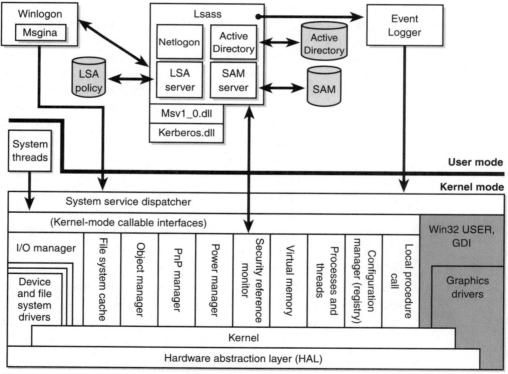

Figure 8-1
Windows 2000 security components

The SRM, which runs in kernel mode, and Lsass, which runs in user mode, communicate using the LPC facility described in Chapter 3. During system initialization, the SRM creates a port, named SeRmCommandPort, to which Lsass connects. When the Lsass process starts, it creates an LPC port named SeLsaCommandPort. The SRM connects to this port, resulting in the creation of private communication ports. The SRM creates a shared memory section for messages longer than 256 bytes, passing a handle in the connect call. Once the SRM and Lsass connect to each other during system initialization, they no longer listen on their respective connect ports. Therefore, a later user process has no way to connect successfully to either of these ports for malicious purposes—the connect request will never complete.

Figure 8-2 shows the communication paths as they exist after system initialization.

Figure 8-2
Communication between the SRM and Lsass

Protecting Objects

Object protection and access accounting is the essence of discretionary access control and auditing. The objects that can be protected on Windows 2000 include files, devices, mailslots, pipes (named and anonymous), jobs, processes, threads, events, mutexes, semaphores, shared memory sections, I/O completion ports, LPC ports, waitable timers, access tokens, window stations, desktops, network shares, services, registry keys, and printers.

Because system resources that are exported to user mode (and hence require security validation) are implemented as objects in kernel mode, the Windows 2000 object manager plays a key role in enforcing object security. (For more information on the object manager, see Chapter 3.) To control who can manipulate an object, the security system must first be sure of each user's identity. This need to guarantee the user's identity is the reason that Windows 2000 requires authenticated logon before accessing any system resources. When a process requests a handle to an object, the object manager and the security system use the caller's security identification to determine whether the caller should be assigned a handle that grants the process access to the object it desires.

As we'll discuss later in this chapter, a thread can assume a different security context than that of its process. This mechanism is called *impersonation*, and when a thread is impersonating, security validation mechanisms use the thread's security context instead of that of the thread's process. When a thread isn't impersonating, security validation falls back on using the security context of the thread's owning process. It's important to keep in mind that all the threads in a process share the same handle table, so when a thread opens an object—even if it's impersonating—all the threads of the process have access to the object.

Access Checks

The Windows 2000 security model requires that a thread specify up front, at the time that it opens an object, what types of actions it wants to perform on the object. The system performs access checks based on a thread's desired access, and if the access is granted, a handle is assigned to the thread's process with which the thread (or other threads in the process) can perform further operations on the object. As explained in Chapter 3, the object manager records the access permissions granted for a handle in the process's handle table.

One event that causes the object manager to perform security access validation is when a process opens an existing object using a name. When an object is opened by name, the object manager performs a lookup of the specified

object in the object manager namespace. If the object isn't located in a secondary namespace, such as the configuration manager's registry namespace or a file system driver's file system namespace, the object manager calls the internal function *ObpCreateHandle* once it locates the object. As its name implies, *ObpCreateHandle* creates an entry in the process's handle table that becomes associated with the object. However, *ObpCreateHandle* calls the executive function *ExCreateHandle* to create the handle only if another object manager function, *ObpIncrementHandleCount*, indicates that the thread has permission to access the object. Another object manager function, *ObCheckObjectAccess*, actually carries out the security access check and returns the results to *ObpIncrementHandleCount*.

ObpIncrementHandleCount passes *ObCheckObjectAccess* the security credentials of the thread opening the object, the types of access to the object that the thread is requesting (read, write, delete, and so forth), and a pointer to the object. *ObCheckObjectAccess* first locks the object's security and the security context of the thread. The object security lock prevents another thread in the system from changing the object's security while the access check is in progress. The lock on the thread's security context prevents another thread of that process or a different process from altering the security identity of the thread while security validation is in progress. *ObCheckObjectAccess* then calls the object's security method to obtain the security settings of the object. (See Chapter 3 for a description of object methods.) The call to the security method might invoke a function in a different executive component. However, many executive objects rely on the system's default security management support.

When an executive component defining an object doesn't want to override the SRM's default security policy, it marks the object type as having default security. Whenever the SRM calls an object's security method, it first checks to see whether the object has default security. An object with default security stores its security information in its header, and its security method is *SeDefaultObjectMethod*. An object that doesn't rely on default security must manage its own security information and supply a specific security method. Objects that rely on default security include mutexes, events, and semaphores. A file object is an example of an object that overrides default security. The I/O manager, which defines the file object type, has the file system driver on which a file resides manage (or choose not to implement) the security for its files. Thus, when the system queries the security on a file object that represents a file on an

NTFS volume, the I/O manager file object security method retrieves the file's security using the NTFS file system driver. Note, however, that *ObCheckObject-Access* isn't executed when files are opened because they reside in secondary namespaces; the system invokes a file object's security method only when a thread explicitly queries or sets the security on a file (with the Win32 *SetFileSecurity* or *GetFileSecurity* functions, for example).

After obtaining an object's security information, *ObCheckObjectAccess* invokes the SRM function *SeAccessCheck*. *SeAccessCheck* is one of the functions at the heart of the Windows 2000 security model. Among the input parameters *SeAccessCheck* accepts are the object's security information, the security identity of the thread as captured by *ObCheckObjectAccess*, and the access that the thread is requesting. *SeAccessCheck* returns True or False, depending on whether the thread is granted the access it requested to the object.

Another event that causes the object manager to execute access validation is when a process references an object using an existing handle. Such references often occur indirectly, as when a process calls on a Win32 API to manipulate an object and passes an object handle. For example, a thread opening a file can request access to the object that permits it to read from the file. If the thread has permission to access the object in this way, as dictated by its security context and the security settings of the file, the object manager creates a handle—representing the file—in the handle table of the thread's process. The accesses the process is granted through the handle are stored with the handle by the object manager.

Subsequently, the thread can attempt to write to the file using the *WriteFile* Win32 function, passing the file's handle as a parameter. The system service *NtWriteFile*, which *WriteFile* calls via Ntdll.dll, uses the object manager function *ObReferenceObjectByHandle* to obtain a pointer to the file object from the handle. *ObReferenceObjectByHandle* accepts the access that the caller wants from the object as a parameter. After finding the handle entry in the process's handle table, *ObReferenceObjectByHandle* compares the access being requested with the access granted at the time the file was opened. In this case, *ObReference-ObjectByHandle* will indicate that the write operation should fail because the caller didn't obtain write access when the file was opened.

The Windows 2000 security functions also enable Win32 applications to define their own private objects and to call on the services of the SRM to enforce the Windows 2000 security model on those objects. Many kernel-mode functions

that the object manager and other executive components use to protect their own objects are exported as Win32 user-mode APIs. The user-mode equivalent of *SeAccessCheck* is *AccessCheck*, for example. Win32 applications can therefore leverage the flexibility of the security model and transparently integrate with the authentication and administrative interfaces that are present in Windows 2000.

The essence of the SRM's security model is an equation that takes three inputs: the security identity of a thread, the access that the thread wants to an object, and the security settings of the object. The output is either "yes" or "no" and indicates whether or not the security model grants the thread the access it desires. The following sections describe the inputs in more detail and then document the model's access validation algorithm.

Security Identifiers

Instead of using names (which might or might not be unique) to identify entities that perform actions in a system, Windows 2000 uses *security identifiers* (SIDs). Users have SIDs, and so do local and domain groups, local computers, domains, and domain members. A SID is a variable-length numeric value that consists of a SID structure revision number, a 48-bit identifier authority value, and a variable number of 32-bit subauthority or *relative identifier* (RID) values. The authority value identifies the agent that issued the SID, and this agent is typically a Windows 2000 local system or a domain. Subauthority values identify trustees relative to the issuing authority, and RIDs are simply a way for Windows 2000 to create unique SIDs based on a common-base SID. Because SIDS are long and Windows 2000 takes care to generate truly random values within each SID, it is virtually impossible for Windows 2000 to issue the same SID twice on machines or domains anywhere in the world.

When displayed textually, each SID carries an *S* prefix, and its various components are separated with hyphens:

S-1-5-21-1463437245-1224812800-863842198-1128

In this SID, the revision number is 1, the identifier authority value is 5 (the Windows 2000 security authority), and four subauthority values plus one RID (1128) make up the remainder of the SID. This SID is a domain SID, but a local computer on the domain would have a SID with the same revision number, identifier authority value, and number of subauthority values.

EXPERIMENT: Using GetSID to View Account SIDs

You can easily see the SID representation for any account you're using by running the GetSID utility, located in the Windows 2000 resource kits. It has the following interface:

```
C:\>getsid
Usage: getsid \\server1 account \\server2 account
```

GetSID's intended use is as a tool for detecting inconsistencies in the account databases of two domain controllers. It accepts the names of two users, each relative to a server, and retrieves the SIDs of each user from the server specified for them. It then compares the SIDs and indicates whether or not they match, at the same time displaying their textual representations. Despite the fact that GetSID requires you to specify two account names, you can still use it to obtain the SID of a single account simply by specifying the same account and server for both names. Here's an example of obtaining a single SID:

```
C:\>getsid \\w2kpro administrator \\w2kpro administrator
The SID for account W2KPRO\administrator matches account
  W2KPRO\administrator
The SID for account W2KPRO\administrator is
S-1-5-21-1123561945-484763869-1957994488-500
The SID for account W2KPRO\administrator is
S-1-5-21-1123561945-484763869-1957994488-500
```

When you install Windows 2000, the Windows 2000 Setup program issues the computer a SID. Windows 2000 assigns SIDs to local accounts on the computer. Each local-account SID is based on the source computer's SID and has a RID at the end. RIDs for user accounts and groups start at 1000 and increase in increments of 1 for each new user or group. Similarly, Windows 2000 issues a SID to each newly created Windows 2000 domain. Windows 2000 issues to new domain accounts SIDS that are based on the domain SID and have an appended RID (again starting at 1000 and increasing in increments of 1 for each new user or group). A RID of 1028 indicates that the SID is the 29th SID the domain issued.

Windows 2000 issues SIDS that consist of a computer or domain SID with a predefined RID to many predefined accounts and groups. For example, the RID for the administrator account is 500, and the RID for the guest account is 501. A computer's local administrator account, for example, has the computer SID as its base with the RID of 500 appended to it:

S-1-5-21-13124455-12541255-61235125-500

Windows 2000 also defines a number of built-in local and domain SIDs to represent groups. For example, a SID that identifies any and every account is the Everyone, or World, SID: S-1-1-0. Another example of a group that a SID can represent is the network group, which is the group that represents users who can log on to a machine from the network. The network-group SID is S-1-5-2. Table 8-2, reproduced here from the Platform SDK documentation, shows some of the basic well-known SIDs, their numeric values, and their use.

Table 8-2 Well-Known SIDs

SID	Group	Use
S-1-1-0	Everyone	A group that includes all users.
S-1-2-0	Local	Users who log on to terminals locally (physically) connected to the system.
S-1-3-0	Creator Owner ID	A security identifier to be replaced by the security identifier of the user who created a new object. This SID is used in inheritable access-control entries (ACEs).
S-1-3-1	Creator Group ID	Identifies a security identifier to be replaced by the primary-group SID of the user who created a new object. Use this SID in inheritable ACEs.

Tokens

The SRM uses an object called a *token* (or *access token*) to identify the security context of a process or thread. A security context consists of information that describes the privileges, accounts, and groups associated with the process or thread. During the logon process (described at the end of this chapter), Winlogon creates an initial token to represent the user logging on and attaches the token to the user's logon shell process. All programs the user executes inherit a copy of the initial token. You can also generate a token by using the Win32 *LogonUser* function. You can then use this token to create a process that runs within the security context of the user logged on by the *LogonUser* function by passing the token to the Win32 *CreateProcessAsUser* function. Tokens vary in size because different user accounts have different sets of privileges and associated group accounts. However, all tokens contain the same information, shown in Figure 8-3.

Token source
Impersonation type
Token ID
Authentication ID
Modified ID
Expiration time
Defaul primary group
Default DACL
User account SID
Group 1 SID

Group *n* SID
Restricted SID 1

Restricted SID n
Privilege 1

Privilege *n*

Figure 8-3
Access tokens

The security mechanisms in Windows 2000 use two token components to determine what a token's thread or process can do. One component comprises the token's user account SID and group SID fields. The SRM uses SIDs to determine whether a process or thread can obtain requested access to a securable object, such as an NTFS file.

The group SIDs in a token signify which groups a user's account is a member of. A server application can disable specific groups to restrict a token's credentials when the server application is performing actions a client requests. Disabling a group produces nearly the same effect as if the group wasn't present in the token. (Disabled SIDs are used as part of security access checks, described later in the chapter.)

The second component in a token that determines what the token's thread or process can do is the privilege array. A token's privilege array is a list of rights associated with the token. An example privilege is the right for the process or

thread associated with the token to shut down the computer. There are about two-dozen token privileges, and a few of the most commonly used are shown in Table 8-3.

Table 8-3 Some Common Privileges

Privilege Name	Privilege Usage
SeBackup	Bypasses security checks during backups
SeDebug	Required to debug a process
SeShutdown	Required to shut down a local system
SeTakeOwnership	Required to take ownership of an object without being granted discretionary access

A token's default primary group field and default discretionary access-control list (DACL) field are security attributes that Windows 2000 applies to objects that a process or thread creates when it uses the token. By including security information in tokens, Windows 2000 makes it convenient for a process or thread to create objects with standard security attributes because the process or thread doesn't need to request discrete security information for every object it creates.

Each token's type distinguishes a primary token (a token that identifies the security context of a process) from an impersonation token (a token threads use to temporarily adopt a different security context, usually of another user). Impersonation tokens carry an impersonation level that signifies what type of impersonation is active in the token. We'll describe impersonation in more detail shortly.

The remainder of the fields in a token serve informational purposes. The token source field contains a short textual description of the entity that created the token. Programs that want to know where a token originated use the token source to distinguish among sources such as the Windows 2000 Session Manager, a network file server, or the remote procedure call (RPC) server. The token identifier is a locally unique identifier (LUID) that the SRM assigns to the token when it creates the token. The Windows 2000 executive maintains the executive LUID, a counter it uses to assign a unique numeric identifier to each token.

The token authentication ID is another kind of LUID. A token's creator assigns the token's authentication ID. Lsass is typically the only token creator on a system, and Lsass obtains the LUID from the executive LUID. Lsass then copies the authentication ID for all tokens descended from an initial logon token. A program can obtain a token's authentication ID to see whether the token belongs to the same logon session as other tokens the program has examined.

The executive LUID refreshes the modified ID every time a token's characteristics are modified. An application can test the modified ID to discover changes in a security context since the context's last use.

Tokens contain an expiration time field that has been present but unused in Windows NT technology since Windows NT 3.1. A future version of Windows 2000 might allow for tokens that are valid for a period of time before expiring. Consider a user for which the systems administrator sets an account expiration time. Currently, if the user logs on and remains logged on past the account expiration, the system will let the user continue to access resources. The only way to prevent the user from accessing resources is to forcibly log the user off the machine. If Windows 2000 supported token expiration, the system could prevent the user from opening resources past the token expiration time.

EXPERIMENT: Viewing Access Tokens with the Kernel Debugger

The kernel debugger *!tokenfields* command displays the format of an internal token object. Although this structure differs from the user-mode token structure returned by Win32 API security functions, the fields are similar. For further information on tokens, see the description in the Platform SDK documentation.

The following output is from the kernel debugger's *!tokenfields* command:

```
kd> !tokenfields
!tokenfields
 TOKEN structure offsets:
    TokenSource:          0x0
    AuthenticationId:     0x18
    ExpirationTime:       0x28
    ModifiedId:           0x30
    UserAndGroupCount:    0x3c
    PrivilegeCount:       0x44
    VariableLength:       0x48
    DynamicCharged:       0x4c
    DynamicAvailable:     0x50
    DefaultOwnerIndex:    0x54
    DefaultDacl:          0x6c
    TokenType:            0x70
    ImpersonationLevel:   0x74
    TokenFlags:           0x78
    TokenInUse:           0x79
```

```
        ProxyData:              0x7c
        AuditData:              0x80
        VariablePart:           0x84
```

You can examine the token for a process with the *!token* command. You'll find the address of the token in the output of the *!process* command, as shown here:

```
kd> !process 380 1
!process 380 1
Searching for Process with Cid == 380
PROCESS ff8027a0 SessionId: 0  Cid: 0380  Peb: 7ffdf000  ParentCid: 0124
   DirBase: 06433000  ObjectTable: ff7e0b68  TableSize:  23.
   Image: cmd.exe
   VadRoot 84c30568 Clone 0 Private 77. Modified 0. Locked 0.
   DeviceMap 818a3368
   Token                                e22bc730
   ElapsedTime                          14:22:56.0536
   UserTime                             0:00:00.0040
   KernelTime                           0:00:00.0100
   QuotaPoolUsage[PagedPool]            13628
   QuotaPoolUsage[NonPagedPool]         1616
   Working Set Sizes (now,min,max)  (261, 50, 345)(1044KB, 200KB, 1380KB)
   PeakWorkingSetSize                   262
   VirtualSize                          11 Mb
   PeakVirtualSize                      11 Mb
   PageFaultCount                       313
   MemoryPriority                       FOREGROUND
   BasePriority                         8
   CommitCharge                         86

kd> !token e22bc730
!token e22bc730
TOKEN e22bc730  Flags: 9  Source User32  b"  AuthentId (0, ae6d)
    Type:                    Primary (IN USE)
    Token ID:                1803a
    ParentToken ID:          0
    Modified ID:             (0, 12bf5)
    TokenFlags:              0x9
    SidCount:                9
    Sids:                    e22bc880
    RestrictedSidCount:      0
    RestrictedSids:          0
    PrivilegeCount:          17
    Privileges:              e22bc7b4
```

Impersonation

Impersonation is a powerful feature Windows 2000 uses frequently in its security model. Windows 2000 also uses impersonation in its client/server programming model. For example, a server application can export resources such as files, printers, or databases. Clients wanting to access a resource send a request to the server. When the server receives the request, it must ensure that the client has permission to perform the desired operations on the resource. For example, if a user on a remote machine tries to delete a file on an NTFS share, the server exporting the share must determine whether the user is allowed to delete the file. The obvious process to determine whether a user has permission is for the server to query the user's account and group SIDs, and scan the security attributes on the file. This process is tedious to program, prone to errors, and wouldn't permit new security features to be supported transparently. Thus, Windows 2000 provides impersonation services to simplify the server's job.

Impersonation lets a server notify the SRM that the server is temporarily adopting the security profile of a client making a resource request. The server can then access resources on behalf of the client, and the SRM carries out the access validations. Usually, a server has access to more resources than a client does and loses some of its security credentials during impersonation. However, the reverse can be true: the server can gain security credentials during impersonation.

A server impersonates a client only within the thread that makes the impersonation request. Thread-control data structures contain an optional entry for an impersonation token. However, a thread's primary token, which represents the thread's real security credentials, is always accessible in the process's control structure.

Windows 2000 makes impersonation available through several mechanisms. If a server communicates with a client through a named pipe, the server can use the *ImpersonateNamedPipeClient* Win32 API function to tell the SRM that it wants to impersonate the user on the other end of the pipe. If the server is communicating with the client through Dynamic Data Exchange (DDE) or an RPC, it can make similar impersonation requests using *DdeImpersonateClient* and *RpcImpersonateClient*. A thread can create an impersonation token that's simply a copy of its process token with the *ImpersonateSelf* function. The thread can then alter its impersonation token, to disable SIDs or privileges, for example. Finally, a Security Support Provider Interface (SSPI) package can impersonate its clients with *ImpersonateSecurityContext*. SSPIs implement a network security model such as LAN Manager 2 or Kerberos.

After the server thread finishes its task, it reverts to its primary security profile. These forms of impersonation are convenient for carrying out specific actions at the request of a client. The disadvantage to these forms of impersonation is that they can't execute an entire program in the context of a client. In addition, an impersonation token can't access files or printers on network shares unless the file or printer share supports null sessions. (A null session is one that results from an anonymous logon.)

If an entire application must execute in a client's security context or must access network resources, the client must be logged on to the system. The *LogonUser* Win32 API function enables this action. *LogonUser* takes an account name, a password, a domain or computer name, a logon type (such as interactive, batch, or service), and a logon provider as input, and it returns a primary token. A server thread can adopt the token as an impersonation token, or the server can start a program that has the client's credentials as its primary token. From a security standpoint, the process that *LogonUser* creates to run the program in an interactive logon session looks like a program a user starts by logging on to the machine interactively.

A second way Windows 2000 provides for impersonation of a client's security context that is similar to the use of *LogonUser* is by taking a client's access token, duplicating it, and using it as the primary token that is passed to the *CreateProcessAsUser* command. The disadvantage to using the *LogonUser* and *CreateProcessAsUser* approaches is that a server must obtain the user's account name and password. If the server transmits this information across the network, the server must encrypt it securely so that a malicious user snooping network traffic can't capture it.

To prevent the misuse of impersonation, Windows 2000 doesn't let servers perform impersonation without a client's consent. A client process can limit the level of impersonation that a server process can perform by specifying a *security quality of service* (SQOS) when connecting to the server. A process can specify SECURITY_ANONYMOUS, SECURITY_IDENTIFICATION, SECURITY_IMPERSONATION, and SECURITY_DELEGATION as flags for the Win32 *CreateFile* function. Each level lets a server perform different types of operations with respect to the client's security context:

- *SecurityAnonymous* is the most restrictive level of impersonation—the server can't impersonate or identify the client.

- *SecurityIdentification* level lets the server obtain the identity (the SIDs) of the client and the client's privileges, but the server can't impersonate the client.

- *SecurityImpersonation* level lets the server identify and impersonate the client on the local system.

- *SecurityDelegation* is the most permissive level of impersonation. It lets the server impersonate the client on local and remote systems. Windows NT 4 and earlier don't fully support SecurityDelegation level impersonation.

If the client doesn't set an impersonation level, Windows 2000 chooses the SecurityImpersonation level by default. The *CreateFile* function also accepts SECURITY_EFFECTIVE_ONLY and SECURITY_CONTEXT_TRACKING as modifiers for the impersonation setting:

- SECURITY_EFFECTIVE_ONLY prevents a server from accessing a client's privileges or groups while the server is impersonating.

- SECURITY_CONTEXT_TRACKING specifies that any change a client makes to its security context is reflected in a server that is impersonating it. If this option isn't specified, the server adopts the context of the client at the time of the impersonation and doesn't receive any changes. This option is honored only when the client and server processes are on the same system.

Restricted Tokens

Windows 2000 introduces a new type of token called a *restricted token*. A restricted token is created from a primary or impersonation token using the *Create-RestrictedToken* function. The restricted token is a copy of the token it's derived from, with the following possible modifications:

- Privileges can be removed from the token's privilege array.

- SIDs in the token can be marked as *deny-only*.

- SIDS in the token can be marked as *restricted*.

The behavior of deny-only and restricted SIDs is covered shortly. Restricted tokens are useful when an application wants to impersonate a client at a reduced security level, primarily for safety reasons when running untrusted code. For example, the restricted token can have the reboot-system privilege removed from it to prevent code executed in the restricted token's security context from rebooting the system.

Security Descriptors and Access Control

Tokens, which identify a user's credentials, are only part of the object security equation. Another part of the equation is the security information associated with an object, which specifies who can perform what actions on the object. The data structure for this information is called a *security descriptor*. A security descriptor consists of the following attributes:

- **Revision number** The version of the SRM security model used to create the descriptor.

- **Flags** Optional modifiers that define the behavior or characteristics of the descriptor. An example is the SE_DACL_PROTECTED flag, which prevents the descriptor from inheriting a security setting from another object.

- **Owner SID** The owner's security ID.

- **Group SID** The security ID of the primary group for the object (used only by POSIX).

- **Discretionary access-control list (DACL)** Specifies who has what access to the object.

- **System access-control list (SACL)** Specifies which operations by which users should be logged in the security audit log.

An *access-control list* (ACL) is made up of a header and zero or more *access-control entry* (ACE) structures. There are two types of ACLs: DACLs and SACLs. In a DACL, each ACE contains a SID and an access mask (and a set of flags, explained shortly). Four types of ACEs can appear in a DACL: access allowed, access denied, allowed-object, and denied-object. As you would expect, the access-allowed ACE grants access to a user, and the access-denied ACE denies the access rights specified in the access mask.

The difference between allowed-object and access allowed, and between denied-object and access denied, is that the object types are used only within Active Directory. ACEs of these types have a GUID (globally unique identifier) field that indicates that the ACE applies only to particular objects or subobjects (those that have GUID identifiers). In addition, another optional GUID indicates what type of child object will inherit the ACE when a child is created within an Active Directory container that has the ACE applied to it. (A GUID is a 128-bit identifier guaranteed to be universally unique.)

The accumulation of access rights granted by individual ACEs forms the set of access rights granted by an ACL. If no DACL is present (a null DACL) in a security descriptor, everyone has full access to the object. If the DACL is empty (has 0 ACEs), no user has access to the object.

The ACEs used in DACLs also have a set of flags that control and specify characteristics of the ACE related to inheritance. Some object namespaces have *container objects* and *leaf objects* (or just *objects*). A container can hold other container objects and leaf objects, which are its *child objects*. Examples of containers are directories in the file system namespace and keys in the registry namespace. Certain flags in an ACE control how the ACE propagates to child objects of the container associated with the ACE. Table 8-4, reproduced in part from the Platform SDK, lists the inheritance rules for ACE flags.

Table 8-4 Inheritance Rules for ACE Flags

Flag	Inheritance Rule
CONTAINER_INHERIT_ACE	Child objects that are containers, such as directories, inherit the ACE as an effective ACE. The inherited ACE is inheritable unless the NO_PROPAGATE_INHERIT_ACE bit flag is also set.
INHERIT_ONLY_ACE	Indicates an inherit-only ACE that doesn't control access to the object it's attached to.
INHERITED_ACE	Indicates that the ACE was inherited. The system sets this bit when it propagates an inheritable ACE to a child object.
NO_PROPAGATE_INHERIT_ACE	If the ACE is inherited by a child object, the system clears the OBJECT_INHERIT_ACE and CONTAINER_INHERIT_ACE flags in the inherited ACE. This action prevents the ACE from being inherited by subsequent generations of objects.
OBJECT_INHERIT_ACE	Noncontainer child objects inherit the ACE as an effective ACE. For child objects that are containers, the ACE is inherited as an inherit-only ACE unless the NO_PROPAGATE_INHERIT_ACE bit flag is also set.

A SACL contains two types of ACEs, *system audit* ACEs and *system audit-object* ACEs. These ACEs specify which operations performed on the object by specific users or groups should be audited. Audit information is stored in the system Audit Log. Both successful and unsuccessful attempts can be audited. Like their DACL object-specific ACE cousins, system audit-object ACEs specify a GUID indicating the types of objects or subobjects that the ACE applies to and an optional GUID that controls propagation of the ACE to particular child object types. If a SACL is null, no auditing takes place on the object. (Security auditing is described later in this chapter.) The inheritance flags that apply to DACL ACEs also apply to system audit and system audit-object ACEs.

Figure 8-4 is a simplified picture of a file object and its DACL.

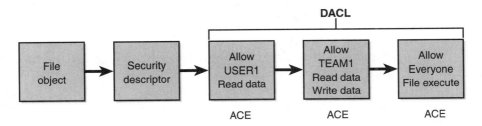

Figure 8-4
Discretionary access-control list (DACL)

As shown in Figure 8-4, the first ACE allows USER1 to read the file. The second ACE allows members of the group TEAM1 to have read and write access to the file, and the third ACE grants all other users (Everyone) execute access.

ACL Assignment

To determine which DACL to assign to a new object, the security system uses the first applicable rule of the following four assignment rules:

1. If a caller explicitly provides a security descriptor when creating the object, the security system applies it to the object. If the object has a name and resides in a container object (for example, a named event object in the \BaseNamedSecurity object manager namespace directory), the system merges any inheritable ACEs (ACEs that might propagate from the object's container) into the DACL unless the security descriptor has the SE_DACL_PROTECTED flag set, which prevents inheritance.

509

2. If a caller doesn't supply a security descriptor and the object has a name, the security system looks at the security descriptor in the container in which the new object name is stored. Some of the object directory's ACEs might be marked as inheritable, meaning that they should be applied to new objects created in the object directory. If any of these inheritable ACEs are present, the security system forms them into an ACL, which it attaches to the new object. (Separate flags indicate ACEs that should be inherited only by container objects rather than by objects that aren't containers.)

3. If no security descriptor is specified and the object doesn't inherit any ACEs, the security system retrieves the default DACL from the caller's access token and applies it to the new object. Several subsystems on Windows 2000 have hard-coded DACLs that they assign on object creation (for example, services, LSA, and SAM objects).

4. If there is no specified descriptor, no inherited ACEs, and no default DACL, the system creates the object with no DACL, which allows everyone (all users and groups) full access to the object. This rule is the same as the third rule when a token contains a null default DACL.

The rules the system uses when assigning a SACL to a new object are similar to those used for DACL assignment, with a couple exceptions. The first is that inherited system audit ACEs don't propagate to objects with security descriptors marked with the SE_SACL_PROTECTED flag (similar to the SE_DACL_PROTECTED flag, which protects DACLs). Second, if there are no specified security audit ACEs and there is no inherited SACL, no SACL is applied to the object. This behavior is different than that used to apply default DACLs because tokens don't have a default SACL.

When a new security descriptor containing inheritable ACEs is applied to a container, the system automatically propagates the inheritable ACEs to the security descriptors of child objects. (Note that a security descriptor's DACL doesn't accept inherited DACL ACES if its SE_DACL_PROTECTED flag is enabled, and its SACL doesn't inherit SACL ACES if the descriptor has the SE_SACL_PROTECTED flag set.) The order with which inheritable ACEs are merged with an existing child object's security descriptor is such that any ACEs that were explicitly applied to the ACL are kept ahead of ACEs that the object inherits. The system uses the following rules for propagating inheritable ACEs:

■ If a child object with no DACL inherits an ACE, the result is a child object with a DACL containing only the inherited ACE.

- If a child object with an empty DACL inherits an ACE, the result is a child object with a DACL containing only the inherited ACE.

- For objects in Active Directory only, if an inheritable ACE is removed from a parent object, automatic inheritance removes any copies of the ACE inherited by child objects.

- For objects in Active Directory only, if automatic inheritance results in the removal of all ACEs from a child object's DACL, the child object has an empty DACL rather than no DACL.

As you'll soon discover, the order of ACEs in an ACL is an important aspect of the Windows 2000 security model.

NOTE Because inheritance isn't supported for file system directories and registry keys, Windows Explorer and Regedt32 manually propagate security settings that you specify to apply to a directory and its contents or to an entire registry subkey.

Determining Access

Two algorithms are used for determining access to an object:

- One to determine the maximum access allowed to the object, a form of which is exported to user mode with the Win32 *GetEffective-RightsFromAcl* function.

- One to determine whether a specific desired access is allowed, which can be done with the Win32 *AccessCheck* function or the *AccessCheck-ByType* function.

The first algorithm examines the entries in the DACL as follows:

1. If the object has no DACL (a null DACL), the object has no protection and the security system grants all access.

2. If the caller has the take-ownership privilege, the security system grants write-owner access before examining the DACL. (Take-ownership privilege and write-owner access are explained in a moment.)

3. If the caller is the owner of the object, the read-control and write-DACL access rights are granted.

4. For each access-denied ACE that contains a SID that matches one in the caller's access token, the ACE's access mask is removed from the granted-access mask.

5. For each access-allowed ACE that contains a SID that matches one in the caller's access token, the ACE's access mask is added to the granted-access mask being computed, unless that access has already been denied.

When all the entries in the DACL have been examined, the computed granted-access mask is returned to the caller as the maximum allowed access to the object. This mask represents the total set of access types that the caller will be able to successfully request when opening the object.

The preceding description applies only to the kernel-mode form of the algorithm. The Win32 version implemented by *GetEffectiveRightsFromAcl* differs in that it doesn't perform step 2, and it considers a single user or group SID rather than an access token.

The second algorithm is used to determine whether a specific access request can be granted, based on the caller's access token. Each open function in the Win32 API that deals with securable objects has a parameter that specifies the desired access mask, which is the last component of the security equation. To determine whether the caller has access, the following steps are performed:

1. If the object has no DACL (a null DACL), the object has no protection and the security system grants the desired access.

2. If the caller has the take-ownership privilege, the security system grants write-owner access and then examines the DACL. However, if write-owner access was the only access requested by a caller with take-ownership privilege, the security system grants that access and never examines the DACL.

3. If the caller is the owner of the object, the read-control and write-DACL access rights are granted. If these rights were the only access rights that caller requested, access is granted without examining the DACL.

4. Each ACE in the DACL is examined from first to last. An ACE is processed if one of the following conditions is satisfied:

 a. The SID in the ACE matches an *enabled* SID (SIDs can be enabled or disabled) in the caller's access token (whether that be the primary SID or a group SID).

 b. The ACE is an access-allowed ACE and the SID in the ACE matches a SID in the caller's token that isn't of type deny-only.

c. It is the second pass through the descriptor for restricted-SID checks, and the SID in the ACE matches a restricted SID in the caller's access token.

If it is an access-allowed ACE, the rights in the access mask in the ACE that were requested are granted; if all the requested access rights have been granted, the access check succeeds. If it is an access-denied ACE and any of the requested access rights are in the denied-access rights, access is denied to the object.

5. If the end of the DACL is reached and some of the requested access rights still haven't been granted, access is denied.

6. If all accesses are granted but the caller's access token has at least one restricted SID, the system rescans the DACL's ACEs looking for ACEs with access-mask matches for the accesses the user is requesting and a match of the ACE's SID with any of the caller's restricted SIDs. Only if both scans of the DACL grant the requested access rights is the user granted access to the object.

The behavior of both access-validation algorithms depends on the relative ordering of allow and deny ACEs. Consider an object with only two ACEs where one ACE specifies that a certain user is allowed full access to an object and the other ACE denies the user access. If the allow ACE precedes the deny ACE, the user can obtain full access to the object, but if the order is reversed, the user can not gain any access to the object.

Older Win32 functions, such as *AddAccessAllowedAce*, add ACEs to the end of a DACL, which usually isn't the desired behavior, so most Win32 applications prior to Windows 2000 were forced to construct DACLs manually, with deny ACEs placed at the front of the list. New Windows 2000 functions such as *SetSecurityInfo* and *SetNamedSecurityInfo* apply ACEs in the preferred order of deny ACEs preceding allow ACEs. Note that the security editor dialog boxes with which you edit permissions on NTFS files and registry keys, for example, construct security descriptors by placing all the deny ACEs at the front of the list. *SetSecurityInfo* and *SetNamedSecurityInfo* also apply ACE inheritance rules to the security descriptor on which they are applied.

Figure 8-5 shows an example access validation demonstrating the importance of ACE ordering. In the example, access is denied a user wanting to open a file even though an ACE in the object's DACL grants the access (by virtue of the user's membership in the Writers group) because the ACE denying the user access precedes the ACE granting access.

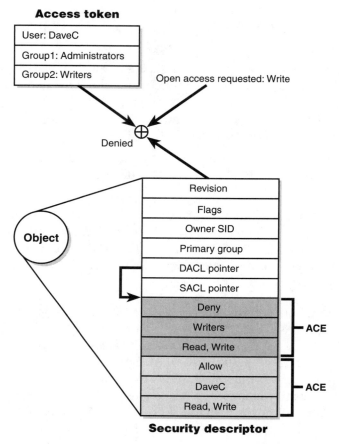

Figure 8-5
Access validation example

As we stated earlier, because it wouldn't be efficient for the security system to process the DACL every time a process uses a handle, the SRM makes this access check only when a handle is opened, not each time the handle is used. Thus, once a process successfully opens a handle, the security system can't revoke the access rights that have been granted, even if the object's DACL changes. Also keep in mind that because kernel-mode code uses pointers rather than handles to access objects, the access check isn't performed when the operating system uses objects. In other words, the Windows 2000 executive "trusts" itself in a security sense.

The fact that an object's owner is always granted write-DACL access to an object means that users can never be prevented from accessing the objects they own. If, for some reason, an object had an empty DACL (no access), the owner would still be able to open the object with write-DACL access and then apply a new DACL with the desired access permissions.

The take-ownership privilege is a similarly powerful tool for accounts, such as the Administrator account, to which it is assigned. Any object on the system is accessible using this privilege. Consider an object that is owned by another user and that explicitly denies the Administrator account all access to the object. With the take-ownership privilege, an administrator can open the object with write-owner permission and change the owner to Administrator. Then the administrator can close and reopen the object with write-DACL access and change the DACL to give the Administrator account full access to the object.

Security Auditing

The object manager can generate audit events as a result of an access check, and Win32 functions available to user applications can generate them directly. Kernel-mode code is always allowed to generate an audit event. Two privileges, SeSecurityPrivilege and SeAuditPrivilege, relate to auditing. A process must have the SeSecurityPrivilege privilege to manage the security Event Log and to view or set an object's SACL. Processes that call audit system services, however, must have the SeAuditPrivilege privilege to successfully generate an audit record.

The audit policy of the local system controls the decision to audit a particular type of security event. The audit policy, also called the local security policy, is one part of the security policy Lsass maintains on the local system. Lsass sends messages to the SRM to inform it of the auditing policy at system initialization time and when the policy changes. Lsass is responsible for receiving audit records generated based on the audit events from the SRM, editing the records, and sending them to the Event Logger. Lsass (instead of the SRM) sends these records because it adds pertinent details, such as the information needed to more completely identify the process that is being audited.

The SRM sends audit records via its LPC connection to Lsass. The Event Logger then writes the audit record to the security Event Log. In addition to audit records the SRM passes, both Lsass and the SAM generate audit records that Lsass sends directly to the Event Logger. Figure 8-6 depicts this overall flow.

Figure 8-6
Flow of security audit records

Audit records are put on a queue to be sent to the LSA as they are received—they are not submitted in batches. The audit records are moved from the SRM to the security subsystem in one of two ways. If the audit record is small (less than the maximum LPC message size), it is sent as an LPC message. The audit records are copied from the address space of the SRM to the address space of the Lsass process. If the audit record is large, the SRM uses shared memory to make the message available to Lsass and simply passes a pointer in an LPC message.

Figure 8-7 brings together the concepts covered so far in this chapter by illustrating the basic process and thread security structures. In the figure, notice that the process object and the thread objects have ACLs, as do the access-token objects themselves. Also in this figure, thread 2 and thread 3 each has an impersonation token, whereas thread 1 defaults to the process access token.

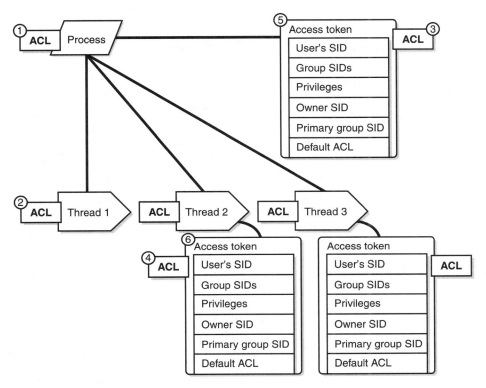

Figure 8-7
Process and thread security structures

EXPERIMENT: Viewing Process and Thread Security Information

You can view process and thread security descriptors and access tokens with the Process Explode utility (Pview.exe). (This tool is part of the Windows NT 4 resource kits, but it isn't included with the Windows 2000 resource kit tools. You can, however, download it from *www.reskit.com*.) The numbering of the six buttons in the Security and Token sections of the Process Explode utility matches up with the process and thread security structures shown in Figure 8-7.

(continued)

EXPERIMENT: Viewing Process and Thread Security Information *continued*

In this example, buttons 4 (ACL for thread token) and 6 (thread access token) are grayed out (disabled) because the currently selected thread (number 1700) has no thread-specific access token.

Try looking at the process ACL for a process in your interactive session—you should see your user ID and SYSTEM in the ACL with full control permissions.

To see process security in action, try the following:

1. Create a local username named "test". To add a user, start Computer Management. (In Control Panel, open Administrative Tools and then click on Computer Management; or select Run from the Start menu and enter *compmgmt.msc*.) Expand Local Users And Groups (under System Tools), right-click on Users, and select New User. Enter the username *test* (no password), clear the User Must Change Password At Next Logon flag, and press Create. (*Note*: Your domain or local group policies might require that you enter a password.)

2. Open a Windows 2000 Command Prompt window. (From the Start menu, select Programs/Accessories/Command Prompt.)

3. Type *runas /user:test cmd* to create a command prompt running under the test username you just added. (*Note*: You might need to prefix *test* with the machine name or domain name, as in *runas /user:machine\test cmd*.)

4. From this command prompt, run Pulist from the Windows 2000 resource kit. Notice that you can't see the security ID of the processes on the system other than the one running Cmd.exe and Pulist.exe under the security context of the test username. The reason you can't see this security ID is that the test username isn't in the ACL on the process access token on any of the other processes—therefore, you have no permission to see who these processes are.

5. Now switch back to the command prompt started in step 2 (running under whatever account you were logged on to for this experiment), and run Pulist again. You should see the security IDs of all the processes in your interactive session (and the system processes if your account is a member of the local Administrators group). However, you shouldn't be able to see the security ID of the process running Cmd.exe under the test username (created in step 3) for the same reason that from the test username you can't see the processes not running under test.

6. Now run Process Explode again, select a process in your interactive session (such as Explorer.exe), and change the ACL on the process and the process access token to allow the user test to have read access. Modify the process by pressing the Process button to bring up the Process Permissions dialog box. Press Add to add an entry to the process ACL. When the list of groups is displayed, press the Show Users button, scroll down the Names list, select the test username, press Add, and then press OK. You should now see the test username in the ACL. Press OK to make the change on the Explorer process. Follow the same steps again for the process access token, this time pressing the P.Token button instead of the Process button.

(continued)

EXPERIMENT: Viewing Process and Thread Security Information *continued*

7. Now go back to the process running Cmd as user test, and run Pulist again. This time, you should be able to see the security ID of the process Explorer.exe because you've granted read access to that process's access token.

The following steps don't work on Windows 2000 server systems that have Terminal Services installed. The reason they don't work in this context is explained after step 10.

8. As a final test, start Task Manager, click on the Applications tab, right-click on "cmd (running as test)", and select Go To Process. This takes you to the Processes tab with the cmd.exe process highlighted. Click on this process, and then press the End Process button. (Press Yes in the warning message box that appears.) You should get an access denied error because you're not in the process ACL for that process.

9. As an added exercise, rerun Pview.exe from the command prompt running under test and alter the process access for the Cmd.exe process running under test to grant full access to the username you're currently running under. (Press the Process button in PView, press Add, and then add your username to the ACL, remembering to select full control access.)

10. Retry step 8—this time, you should be able to terminate the command prompt running under the test username because you granted yourself full access to that process.

The reason that steps 8 through 10 don't work on a system with Terminal Services installed is because the steps rely on the fact that, on systems without Terminal Services, Task Manager uses the *Terminate-Process* function to end processes. However, when you direct Task Manager to end a process on a system running in a Terminal Services environment, Task Manager calls on Termsrv.exe, the terminal services service, to perform the process termination. Because Termsrv.exe is a service process running in the System account, it has the debug privilege, which it uses to open a process it's terminating without regard to the process's token or process security settings.

Logon

Interactive logon (as opposed to network logon) occurs through the interaction of the logon process (Winlogon), Lsass, one or more authentication packages, and the SAM or Active Directory. *Authentication packages* are DLLs that perform authentication checks. Kerberos is the Windows 2000 authentication package for interactive logon to a domain, and MSV1_0 is the Windows 2000 authentication package for interactive logon to a local computer, for domain logons to trusted pre-Windows 2000 domains, and for when no domain controller is accessible.

Winlogon is a trusted process responsible for managing security-related user interactions. It coordinates logon, starts the user's shell at logon, handles logoff, and manages various other operations relevant to security, including entering passwords at logon, changing passwords, and locking and unlocking the workstation. The Winlogon process must ensure that operations relevant to security aren't visible to any other active processes. For example, Winlogon guarantees that an untrusted process can't get control of the desktop during one of these operations and thus gain access to the password.

Winlogon relies on a Graphical Identification and Authentication (GINA) DLL to obtain a user's account name and password. The default GINA is Msgina (\Winnt\System32\Msgina.dll). Msgina presents the standard Windows 2000 logon dialog box. Allowing for other GINAs to replace Msgina enables Windows 2000 to use different user identification mechanisms. For example, a third party might supply a GINA that uses a thumbprint recognition device to identify users and extract their passwords from an encrypted database.

Winlogon is the only process that intercepts logon requests from the keyboard. After obtaining a username and password from the GINA, Winlogon calls Lsass to authenticate the user attempting to log on. If the user is authenticated, the logon process activates a logon shell on behalf of that user. The interaction between the components involved in logon is illustrated in Figure 8-8.

In addition to supporting alternate GINAs, Winlogon can load additional network provider DLLs that need to perform secondary authentication. This capability allows multiple network providers to gather identification and authentication information all at one time during normal logon. A user logging on to a Windows 2000 system might simultaneously be authenticated on a UNIX server. That user would then be able to access resources of the UNIX server from the Windows 2000 machine without requiring additional authentication. Such a capability is known as one form of *single sign-on*.

Figure 8-8
Components involved in logon

Winlogon Initialization

During system initialization, before any user applications are active, Winlogon performs the following steps to ensure that it controls the workstation once the system is ready for user interaction:

1. Creates and opens the interactive window station, \Windows\WinSta0, to represent the keyboard, mouse, and monitor. Winlogon creates a security descriptor for the station that has one and only one ACE containing only the Winlogon SID. This unique security descriptor ensures that no other process can access the workstation unless explicitly allowed by Winlogon.

2. Creates and opens three desktops: an application desktop (\Windows\ WinSta0\Default), a Winlogon desktop (\Windows\WinSta0\ Winlogon), and a screen saver desktop (\Windows\WinSta0\Screen-Saver). The security on the Winlogon desktop is created so that only Winlogon can access that desktop. The other two desktops allow both Winlogon and users to access them. This arrangement means

that any time the Winlogon desktop is active, no other process has access to any active code or data associated with the desktop. Windows 2000 uses this feature to protect the secure operations that involve passwords and locking and unlocking the desktop.

Before anyone logs on to a computer, the visible desktop is Winlogon's. After a logon, typing Ctrl+Alt+Delete switches the desktop from Default to Winlogon. (This explains why all the windows on your interactive desktop seem to disappear when you press Ctrl+Alt+Delete and then return when you dismiss the Windows Security dialog box.) Thus, the SAS always brings up a secure desktop controlled by Winlogon.

3. Establishes an LPC connection with Lsass's LsaAuthenticationPort. This connection will be used for exchanging information during logon, logoff, and password operations and is made by calling *LsaRegisterLogonProcess*.

Winlogon then performs the following Windows operations to set up the window environment:

4. Initializes and registers a window class data structure that associates a Winlogon procedure with the window it subsequently creates.

5. Registers the SAS associating it with the window just created, guaranteeing that Winlogon's window procedure is called whenever the user enters the SAS. This measure prevents Trojan horse programs from gaining control of the screen when the SAS is entered.

6. Registers the window so that the procedure associated with this window gets called if a user logs off or if the screen saver times out. The Win32 subsystem checks to verify that the process requesting notification is the Winlogon process.

Once the Winlogon desktop is created during initialization, it becomes the active desktop. When the Winlogon desktop is active, it is always locked. Winlogon unlocks its desktop only to switch to the application desktop or the screen saver desktop. (Only the Winlogon process can lock or unlock a desktop.)

User Logon Steps

Logon begins when a user presses the SAS (Ctrl+Alt+Delete). After the SAS is pressed, Winlogon calls the GINA to obtain a username and password. Winlogon also creates a unique local group for this user that it assigns to this instance of

the desktop (keyboard, screen, and mouse). Winlogon passes this group to Lsass as part of the *LsaLogonUser* call. If the user is successfully logged on, this group will be included in the logon process token—a step that protects access to the desktop. For example, another user logging on to the same account but on a different system will be unable to write to the first user's desktop because this second user won't be in the first user's group.

When the username and password have been entered, Winlogon calls each of the registered authentication packages in turn. Authentication packages are listed in the registry under HKLM\SYSTEM\CurrentControlSet\Control\Lsa. Winlogon retrieves a handle to a package by calling the Lsass function *LsaLookup-AuthenticationPackage*. Winlogon passes package logon information via *LsaLogon-User*. Once a package authenticates a user, Winlogon continues the logon process for that user. If none of the authentication packages indicates a successful logon, the logon process is aborted.

Windows 2000 uses two standard authentication packages: Kerberos and MSV1_0. The default authentication package on a stand-alone Windows 2000 system is MSV1_0 (\Winnt\System32\Msv1_0.dll), an authentication package that implements LAN Manager 2 protocol. Lsass also uses MSV1_0 on domain-member computers to authenticate pre-Windows 2000 domains and computers that can't locate a domain controller for authentication. (Laptop computers that are disconnected from the network fall into this latter category.) The Kerberos authentication package, \Winnt\System32\Kerberos.dll, is used on computers that are members of Windows 2000 domains. The Windows 2000 Kerberos package, with the cooperation of Kerberos services running on a domain controller, supports version 5, revision 6, of the Kerberos protocol. This protocol is based on Internet RFC 1510. (Visit the Internet Engineering Task Force [IETF] Web site, *www.ietf.org*, for detailed information on the Kerberos standard.)

The MSV1_0 authentication package takes the username and a hashed version of the password and sends a request to the local SAM to retrieve the account information, which includes the password, the groups to which the user belongs, and any account restrictions. MSV1_0 first checks the account restrictions, such as hours or type of accesses allowed. If the user can't log on because of the restrictions in the SAM database, the logon call fails and MSV1_0 returns a failure status to the LSA.

MSV1_0 then compares the hashed password and username to that stored by the SAM. In the case of a cached domain logon, MSV1_0 accesses the cached information by using Lsass functions that store and retrieve "secrets" from the LSA database (the SECURITY hive of the registry). If the information matches, MSV1_0 generates an LUID for the logon session and creates the logon session

by calling Lsass, associating this unique identifier with the session and passing the information needed to ultimately create an access token for the user. (Recall that an access token includes the user's SID; group SIDs; and user profile information, such as home directory.)

If MSV1_0 needs to authenticate using a remote system, as when a user logs on to a trusted pre-Windows 2000 domain, MSV1_0 uses the Net Logon service to communicate with an instance of Netlogon on the remote system. Netlogon on the remote system interacts with the MSV1_0 authentication package on that system, passing back authentication results to the system on which the logon is being performed.

The basic control flow for Kerberos authentication is the same as the flow for MSV1_0. However, in most cases, domain logons are performed from member workstations or servers (rather than on a domain controller), so the authentication package must communicate across the network as part of the authentication process. The package does so by communicating via the Kerberos TCP/IP port (port 88) with the Kerberos service on a domain controller. The Kerberos service (\Winnt\System32\Kdcsvc.dll), which implements the Kerberos authentication protocol, runs in the Lsass process on domain controllers.

After validating hashed username and password information with Active Directory's user account objects (using the Active Directory server - \Winnt\ System32\Ntdsa.dll), Kdcsvc returns domain credentials to Lsass, which returns the result of the authentication and the user's domain logon credentials (if the logon was successful) across the network to the system where the logon is taking place.

> **NOTE** This description of Kerberos authentication is highly simplified, but it highlights the roles of the various components involved. Although the Kerberos authentication protocol plays a key role in distributed domain security in Windows 2000, its details are outside the scope of this book.

After a logon has been authenticated, Lsass looks in the local policy database for the user's allowed access—interactive, network, or service process. If the requested logon doesn't match the allowed access, the logon attempt will be terminated. Lsass deletes the newly created logon session by cleaning up any of its data structures and then returns failure to Winlogon, which in turn displays an appropriate message to the user. If the requested access is allowed, Lsass adds any additional security IDs (such as Everyone, Interactive, and the like). It then checks its policy database for any granted privileges for all the IDs for this user and adds these privileges to the user's access token.

When Lsass has accumulated all the necessary information, it calls the executive to create the access token. The executive creates a primary access token for an interactive or a service logon and an impersonation token for a network logon. After the access token is successfully created, Lsass duplicates the token, creating a handle that can be passed to Winlogon, and closes its own handle. If necessary, the logon operation is audited. At this point, Lsass returns success to Winlogon along with a handle to the access token, the LUID for the logon session, and the profile information, if any, that the authentication package returned.

Winlogon then looks in the registry at the value HKLM\SOFTWARE\ Microsoft\Windows NT\Current Version\Winlogon\Userinit and creates a process to run whatever the value of that string is. (This value can be several .exes separated by commas.) The default value is Userinit.exe, which loads the user profile and then creates a process to run whatever the value is of HKLM\ SOFTWARE\Microsoft\Windows NT\Current Version\Winlogon\Shell, which defaults to Explorer.exe. Userinit then exits (which is why Explorer.exe shows up as having no parent when examined with commands such as *tlist /t*).

Conclusion

Windows 2000 provides an extensive array of security functions that meet the key requirements of both government agencies and commercial installations. In this chapter, we've taken a brief tour of the internal components that are the basis of these security features.

In the next chapter, we'll look at the last major executive component considered in this book: the I/O system.

I/O System

The Microsoft Windows 2000 I/O system consists of several executive components that together manage hardware devices and provide interfaces to hardware devices for applications and the system. In this chapter, we'll first list the design goals of the I/O system, which have influenced its implementation. We'll then cover the components that make up the I/O system, including the I/O manager, Plug and Play (PnP) manager, and power manager. Then we'll examine the structure and components of the I/O system and the various types of device drivers. We'll look at the key data structures that describe devices, device drivers, and I/O requests, after which we'll describe the way device detection and driver installation works. Finally, we'll go over the steps necessary to complete I/O requests as they move through the system.

Design Goals

The design goals for the Windows 2000 I/O system include the following:

- Make I/O processing fast on both single and multiprocessor systems.

- Protect shareable resources by using the standard Windows 2000 security mechanisms (described in Chapter 8).

- Meet the requirements for I/O services dictated by the Microsoft Win32, OS/2, and POSIX subsystems.

- Provide services to make device driver development as easy as possible and allow drivers to be written in a high-level language.

- Allow device drivers to be added or removed from the system dynamically, based on user direction or automatic configuration as the result of the addition or removal of a hardware device from the system.

■ Allow for the addition of drivers that transparently modify the behavior of other drivers or devices, without requiring any changes to the driver whose behavior or device is modified.

■ Provide support for multiple installable file systems, including FAT, the CD-ROM file system (CDFS), the Universal Disk Format (UDF) file system, and the Windows 2000 file system (NTFS). (See Chapter 12 for more specific information on file system types and architecture.)

■ Allow the system and individual hardware devices to enter and leave low-power states to prolong battery life and conserve energy.

In subsequent sections, we'll look at how the I/O system components are implemented to meet these goals.

I/O System Components

The Windows 2000 I/O system consists of several executive components as well as device drivers, which are shown in Figure 9-1.

■ The I/O manager connects applications and system components to virtual, logical, and physical devices, and defines the infrastructure that supports device drivers.

■ A device driver typically provides an I/O interface for a particular type of device. Device drivers receive commands routed to them by the I/O manager that are directed at devices they manage, and they inform the I/O manager when those commands complete. Device drivers often use the I/O manager to forward I/O commands to other device drivers that share in the implementation of a device's interface or control.

■ The PnP manager works closely with the I/O manager and a type of device driver called a *bus driver* to guide the allocation of hardware resources as well as to detect and respond to the arrival and removal of hardware devices. The PnP manager and bus drivers are responsible for loading a device's driver when the device is detected. When a device is added to a system that doesn't have an appropriate device driver, the executive Plug and Play component calls on the device installation services of a user-mode PnP manager.

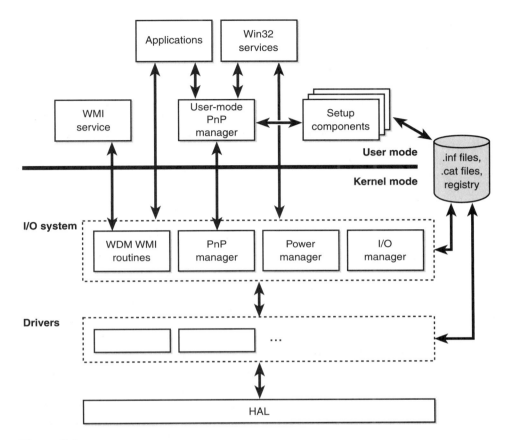

Figure 9-1
I/O system components

- The power manager also works closely with the I/O manager to guide the system, as well as individual device drivers, through power-state transitions.

- Windows Management Instrumentation (WMI) support routines, called the Windows Driver Model (WDM) WMI provider, allow device drivers to indirectly act as providers, using the WDM WMI provider as an intermediary to communicate with the WMI service in user mode. (For more information on WMI, see the section "Windows Management Instrumentation" on page 265 in Chapter 5.)

■ The registry serves as a database that stores a description of basic hardware devices attached to the system as well as driver initialization and configuration settings.

■ INF files, which are designated by the .inf extension, are driver installation files. INF files are the link between a particular hardware device and the driver that assumes primary control of the device. They are made up of scriptlike instructions describing the device they correspond to, the source and target locations of driver files, required driver-installation registry modifications, and driver dependency information. Digital signatures that Windows 2000 uses to verify that a driver file has passed testing by the Microsoft Windows Hardware Quality Lab (WHQL) are stored in .cat files.

■ The hardware abstraction layer (HAL) insulates drivers from the specifics of the processor and interrupt controller by providing APIs that hide differences between platforms. In essence, the HAL is the bus driver for all the devices on the computer's motherboard that aren't controlled by other drivers.

Most I/O operations don't involve all the components just described. A typical I/O request starts with an application executing an I/O-related function (for example, reading data from a device) that is processed by the I/O manager, one or more device drivers, and the HAL.

In Windows 2000, threads perform I/O on virtual files. The operating system abstracts all I/O requests as operations on a virtual file, hiding the fact that the target of an I/O operation might not be a file-structured device. This abstraction generalizes an application's interface to devices. A virtual file refers to any source or destination for I/O that is treated as if it were a file (such as files, directories, pipes, and mailslots). All data that is read or written is regarded as a simple stream of bytes directed to these virtual files. User-mode applications (whether Win32, POSIX, or OS/2) call documented functions, which in turn call internal I/O system functions to read from a file, write to a file, and perform other operations. The I/O manager dynamically directs these virtual file requests to the appropriate device driver. Figure 9-2 illustrates the basic structure of a typical I/O request flow.

Figure 9-2
The flow of a typical I/O request

In the following sections, we'll be looking at these components more closely, examining the I/O manager in more detail, covering the various types of device drivers and the key I/O system data structures. Then we'll cover the operation and roles of the PnP manager and the power manager.

The I/O Manager

The *I/O manager* defines the orderly framework, or model, within which I/O requests are delivered to device drivers. The I/O system is *packet driven*. Most I/O requests are represented by an *I/O request packet* (IRP), which travels from one I/O system component to another. (As you'll discover on page 588, fast I/O is the exception; it doesn't use IRPs.) The design allows an individual application thread to manage multiple I/O requests concurrently. An IRP is a

data structure that contains information completely describing an I/O request. (You'll find more information about IRPs in the section "I/O Request Packets" on page 562.)

The I/O manager creates an IRP that represents an I/O operation, passing a pointer to the IRP to the correct driver and disposing of the packet when the I/O operation is complete. In contrast, a driver receives an IRP, performs the operation the IRP specifies, and passes the IRP back to the I/O manager, either for completion or to be passed on to another driver for further processing.

In addition to creating and disposing of IRPs, the I/O manager supplies code that is common to different drivers and that the drivers call to carry out their I/O processing. By consolidating common tasks in the I/O manager, individual drivers become simpler and more compact. For example, the I/O manager provides a function that allows one driver to call other drivers. It also manages buffers for I/O requests, provides timeout support for drivers, and records which installable file systems are loaded into the operating system. There are close to a hundred different routines in the I/O manager that can be called by device drivers.

The I/O manager also provides flexible I/O services that allow environment subsystems, such as Win32 and POSIX, to implement their respective I/O functions. These services include sophisticated services for asynchronous I/O that allow developers to build scalable high-performance server applications.

The uniform, modular interface that drivers present allows the I/O manager to call any driver without requiring any special knowledge of its structure or internal details. As we stated earlier, the operating system treats all I/O requests as if they were directed at a file; the driver converts the requests from requests made to a virtual file to hardware-specific requests. Drivers can also call each other (using the I/O manager) to achieve layered, independent processing of an I/O request.

Besides the normal open, close, read, and write functions, the Windows 2000 I/O system provides several advanced features, such as asynchronous, direct, buffered, and scatter/gather I/O, which are described in the "Types of I/O" section later in this chapter.

Device Drivers

To integrate with the I/O manager and other I/O system components, a device driver must conform to implementation guidelines specific to the type of device it manages and the role it plays in managing the device. In this sec-

tion, we'll look at the types of device drivers Windows 2000 supports as well as the internal structure of a device driver.

Types of Device Drivers

Windows 2000 supports a wide range of different device driver types and programming environments. Even within a type of device driver, programming environments can differ, depending on the specific type of device for which a driver is intended. In this chapter, the focus is on kernel-mode device drivers. There are many different types of kernel-mode drivers, which can be divided into the following broad categories:

- *File system drivers* accept I/O requests to files and satisfy the requests by issuing their own, more explicit requests to mass storage or network device drivers.

- *Windows 2000 drivers* are device drivers that integrate with the Windows 2000 power manager and PnP manager, when required. They include drivers for mass storage devices, protocol stacks, and network adapters.

- *Legacy drivers* are device drivers written for Microsoft Windows NT but that run unchanged on Windows 2000. They are differentiated from other Windows 2000 drivers in that they don't support power management or work with the Windows 2000 PnP manager. If the driver controls a hardware device, that driver might limit the power management and Plug and Play capabilities of the system.

- Win32 subsystem *display drivers* translate device-independent graphics requests into device-specific requests. The device-specific requests are then paired with a kernel-mode video miniport driver to complete video display support. A display driver is responsible for implementing drawing operations, either by writing directly to the frame buffer or by communicating with the graphics accelerator chip on the controller. The miniport driver is responsible for global changes to the state of the display controller, such as mode setting (screen resolution, refresh rate, pixel depth, and so on) as well as cursor (pointer) positioning and loading the color lookup table.

■ *WDM drivers* are device drivers that adhere to the Windows Driver Model (WDM). WDM includes support for Windows 2000 power management, Plug and Play, and WMI. WDM is implemented on Windows 2000, Windows 98, and Windows Millennium Edition, so WDM drivers are source-compatible between these operating systems and in many cases are also binary compatible. There are three types of WDM drivers:

❑ *Bus drivers* manage a logical or physical bus. Example buses include PCMCIA, PCI, USB, IEEE 1394, and ISA. A bus driver is responsible for detecting and informing the PnP manager of devices attached to the bus it controls as well as managing the power setting of the bus.

❑ *Function drivers* manage a particular type of device. Bus drivers present devices to function drivers via the PnP manager. The function driver is the driver that exports the operational interface of the device to the operating system. In general, it's the driver with the most knowledge about the operation of the device.

❑ *Filter drivers* logically layer above or below function drivers, augmenting or changing the behavior of a device or another driver. For example, a keyboard capture utility could be implemented with a keyboard filter driver that layers above the keyboard function driver.

In WDM, no one driver is responsible for controlling all aspects of a particular device. The bus driver is responsible for detecting bus membership changes (device addition or removal), assisting the PnP manager in enumerating the devices on the bus, accessing bus-specific configuration registers, and in some cases, controlling power to devices on the bus. The function driver is generally the only driver that accesses the device's hardware.

NOTE The role of the HAL in Windows 2000 differs from the role it had in Windows NT. Prior to Windows 2000, third-party hardware vendors that wanted to add support for hardware buses not natively supported had to implement a custom HAL. Windows 2000 allows third parties to implement a bus driver to provide support for hardware buses not natively supported.

In addition to the above device driver types, Windows 2000 also supports several types of user-mode drivers:

- *Virtual device drivers* (VDDs) are used to emulate 16-bit MS-DOS applications. They trap what an MS-DOS application thinks are references to I/O ports and translates them into native Win32 I/O functions, which are then passed to the actual device driver. Because Windows 2000 is a fully protected operating system, user-mode MS-DOS applications can't access hardware directly and thus must go through a real kernel-mode device driver.

- Win32 subsystem *printer drivers* translate device-independent graphics requests to printer-specific commands. These commands are then typically forwarded to a kernel-mode port driver such as the parallel port driver (Parport.sys) or the universal serial bus (USB) printer port driver (Usbprint.sys).

Support for an individual piece of hardware is often divided among several drivers, each providing a part of the functionality required to make the device work properly. In addition to WDM bus drivers, function drivers, and filter drivers, hardware support might be split between the following components:

- *Class drivers* implement the I/O processing for a particular class of devices, such as disk, tape, or CD-ROM.

- *Port drivers* implement the processing of an I/O request specific to a type of I/O port, such as SCSI, and are also implemented as kernel-mode libraries of functions rather than actual device drivers.

- *Miniport drivers* map a generic I/O request to a type of port into an adapter type, such as a specific SCSI adapter. Miniport drivers are actual device drivers that import the functions supplied by a port driver.

An example will help demonstrate how these device drivers work. A file system driver accepts a request to write data to a certain location within a particular file. It translates the request into a request to write a certain number of bytes to the disk at a particular "logical" location. It then passes this request (via the I/O manager) to a simple disk driver. The disk driver, in turn, translates the request into a physical location (cylinder/track/sector) on the disk and manipulates the disk heads to write the data. This layering is illustrated in Figure 9-3.

This figure illustrates the division of labor between two layered drivers. The I/O manager receives a write request that is relative to the beginning of a particular file. The I/O manager passes the request to the file system driver, which translates the write operation from a file-relative operation to a starting location (a sector boundary on the disk) and a number of bytes to read. The file system driver calls the I/O manager to pass the request to the disk driver, which translates the request to a physical disk location and transfers the data.

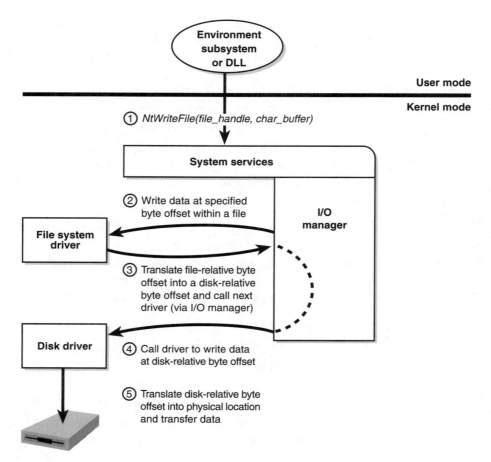

Figure 9-3
Layering of a file system driver and a disk driver

Because all drivers—both device drivers and file system drivers—present the same framework to the operating system, another driver can easily be inserted into the hierarchy without altering the existing drivers or the I/O system. For example, several disks can be made to seem like a very large single disk by adding a driver. Such a driver exists in Windows 2000 to provide fault tolerant disk support. (Whereas the driver is present on all versions of Windows 2000, fault tolerant disk support is available only on Windows 2000 Server versions.) This logical, volume manager driver is located between the file system and the disk drivers, as shown in Figure 9-4.

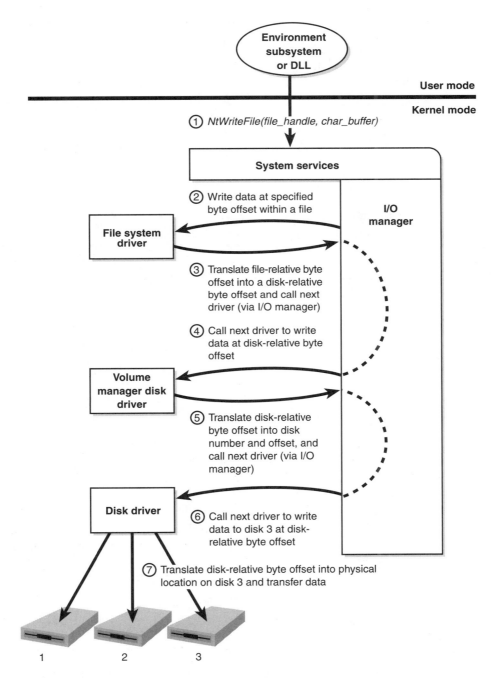

Figure 9-4
Adding a layered driver

EXPERIMENT: Viewing the Loaded Driver List

You can see a list of registered drivers by going to the Drivers section of the Computer Management Microsoft Management Console (MMC) snap-in or by right-clicking the My Computer icon on the desktop and selecting Manage from the context menu. (The Computer Management snap-in is in the Programs/Administrative Tools folder of the Start menu.) You can view the Drivers section within Computer Management by expanding System Tools, System Information, Software Environment and selecting Drivers, as shown here:

You can also obtain a list of loaded kernel-mode drivers with the Drivers utility in the Windows 2000 resource kits or the Pstat utility (ships in the Platform SDK and is available for download from the Windows 2000 Resource Kits Web site at *www.microsoft.com/windows-2000/library/resources/reskit.*) Pstat lists the drivers at the end of its display. (It first lists all the processes and threads in the system.) The only difference in the output of the two utilities is that Pstat shows the load address of the driver in system address space. The following output is a partial display of the driver information from Pstat:

```
C:\>pstat
    :
  ModuleName  Load Addr   Code    Data   Paged     LinkDate
---------------------------------------------------------------------
ntoskrnl.exe  80400000  429184   96896  775360 Tue Dec 07 18:41:11 1999
     hal.dll  80062000   25856    6016   16160 Tue Nov 02 20:14:22 1999
```

```
   BOOTVID.DLL EE010000    5664    2464       0 Wed Nov 03 20:24:33 1999
      ACPI.sys BFFD8000   92096    8960   43488 Wed Nov 10 20:06:04 1999
    WMILIB.SYS EE1C8000     512       0    1152 Sat Sep 25 14:36:47 1999
       pci.sys EDC00000   12704    1536   31264 Wed Oct 27 19:11:08 1999
    isapnp.sys EDC10000   14368     832   22944 Sat Oct 02 16:00:35 1999
  compbatt.sys EE014000    2496       0    2880 Fri Oct 22 18:32:49 1999
     BATTC.SYS EE100000     800       0    2976 Sun Oct 10 19:45:37 1999
  intelide.sys EE1C9000    1760      32       0 Thu Oct 28 19:20:03 1999
   PCIIDEX.SYS EDE80000    4544     480   10944 Wed Oct 27 19:02:19 1999
    pcmcia.sys BFFBD000   32800    8864   23680 Fri Oct 29 19:20:08 1999
    ftdisk.sys BFFA0000    4640      32   95072 Mon Nov 22 14:36:23 1999
  Diskperf.sys EE102000    1728      32    2016 Thu Sep 30 20:30:40 1999
      dmio.sys BFF7E000  104672   15168       0 Tue Nov 30 14:47:49 1999
  ⋮
```

If you're looking at a crash dump (or live system) with the kernel debugger, you can get a similar display with the kernel debugger *!drivers* command.

Structure of a Driver

The I/O system drives the execution of device drivers. Device drivers consist of a set of routines that are called to process the various stages of an I/O request. Figure 9-5 illustrates the key driver-function routines, which are described on the following page.

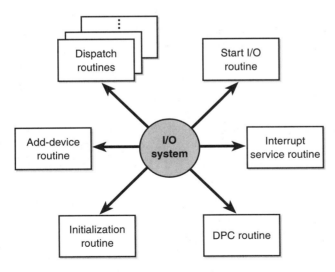

Figure 9-5
Primary device driver routines

■ **An initialization routine** The I/O manager executes a driver's initialization routine, which is typically named *DriverEntry*, when it loads the driver into the operating system. The routine fills in system data structures to register the rest of the driver's routines with the I/O manager and performs any global driver initialization that's necessary.

■ **An add-device routine** A driver that supports Plug and Play implements an add-device routine. The PnP manager sends a driver notification via this routine whenever a device for which the driver is responsible is detected. In this routine, a driver typically allocates a device object (described later in this chapter) to represent the device.

■ **A set of dispatch routines** Dispatch routines are the main functions that a device driver provides. Some examples are open, close, read, and write and any other capabilities the device, file system, or network supports. When called on to perform an I/O operation, the I/O manager generates an IRP and calls a driver through one of the driver's dispatch routines.

■ **A start I/O routine** The driver can use a start I/O routine to initiate a data transfer to or from a device. This routine is defined only in drivers that rely on the I/O manager for IRP serialization. The I/O manager serializes IRPs for a driver by ensuring that the driver processes only one IRP at a time. Most drivers process multiple IRPs concurrently, but serialization makes sense for some drivers, such as a keyboard driver.

■ **An interrupt service routine (ISR)** When a device interrupts, the kernel's interrupt dispatcher transfers control to this routine. In the Windows 2000 I/O model, ISRs run at device interrupt request level (DIRQL), so they perform as little work as possible to avoid blocking lower-level interrupts unnecessarily. (See Chapter 3 for more information on IRQLs.) An ISR queues a deferred procedure call (DPC), which runs at a lower IRQL (DPC/dispatch level), to execute the remainder of interrupt processing. (Only drivers for interrupt-driven devices have ISRs; a file system driver, for example, doesn't have one.)

■ **An interrupt-servicing DPC routine** A DPC routine performs most of the work involved in handling a device interrupt after the ISR executes. The DPC routine executes at a lower IRQL (DPC/dispatch level) than that of the ISR, which runs at device level, to avoid blocking other interrupts unnecessarily. A DPC routine initiates I/O completion and starts the next queued I/O operation on a device.

Although the following routines aren't shown in Figure 9-5, they're found in many types of device drivers:

- **One or more I/O completion routines** A layered driver might have I/O completion routines that will notify it when a lower-level driver finishes processing an IRP. For example, the I/O manager calls a file system driver's I/O completion routine after a device driver finishes transferring data to or from a file. The completion routine notifies the file system driver about the operation's success, failure, or cancellation, and it allows the file system driver to perform cleanup operations.

- **A cancel I/O routine** If an I/O operation can be canceled, a driver can define one or more cancel I/O routines. When the driver receives an IRP for an I/O request that can be canceled, it assigns a cancel routine to the IRP. If a thread that issues an I/O request exits before the request is completed or cancels the operation (with the *CancelIo* Win32 function, for example), the I/O manager executes the IRP's cancel routine if one is assigned to it. A cancel routine is responsible for performing whatever steps are necessary to release any resources acquired during the processing that has already taken place for the IRP as well as completing the IRP with a canceled status.

- **An unload routine** An unload routine releases any system resources a driver is using so that the I/O manager can remove them from memory. Any resources acquired in the initialization routine are usually released in the unload routine. A driver can be loaded and unloaded while the system is running.

- **A system shutdown notification routine** This routine allows driver cleanup on system shutdown.

- **Error-logging routines** When unexpected errors occur (for example, when a disk block goes bad), a driver's error-logging routines note the occurrence and notify the I/O manager. The I/O manager writes this information to an error log file.

The Plug and Play (PnP) Manager

The PnP manager is the primary component involved in supporting the ability of Windows 2000 to recognize and adapt to changing hardware configurations. A user doesn't need to understand the intricacies of hardware or manual configuration in order to install and remove devices. For example, it's the PnP

manager that enables a running Windows 2000 laptop that is placed on a docking station to automatically detect additional devices located in the docking station and make them available to the user.

Plug and Play support requires cooperation at the hardware, device driver, and operating system levels. Industry standards for the enumeration and identification of devices attached to buses are the foundation of Windows 2000 Plug and Play support. For example, the USB standard defines the way that devices on a USB bus identify themselves. With this foundation in place, Windows 2000 Plug and Play support provides the following capabilities:

- The PnP manager automatically recognizes installed devices, a process that includes enumerating devices attached to the system during a boot and detecting the addition and removal of devices as the system executes.

- Hardware resource allocation is a role the PnP manager fills by gathering the hardware resource requirements (interrupts, I/O memory, I/O registers, or bus-specific resources) of the devices attached to a system and, in a process called *resource arbitration,* optimally assigning resources so that each device meets the requirements necessary for its operation. Because hardware devices can be added to the system after boot-time resource assignment, the PnP manager must also be able to reassign resources to accommodate the needs of dynamically added devices.

- Loading appropriate drivers is another responsibility of the PnP manager. The PnP manager determines, based on the identification of a device, whether a driver capable of managing the device is installed on the system, and if one is, instructs the I/O manager to load it. If a suitable driver isn't installed, the kernel-mode PnP manager communicates with the user-mode PnP manager to install the device, possibly requesting the user's assistance in locating a suitable set of drivers.

- The PnP manager also implements application and driver mechanisms for the detection of hardware configuration changes. Applications or drivers sometimes require a specific hardware device to function, so Windows 2000 includes a means for them to request notification of the presence, addition, or removal of devices.

Level of Plug and Play Support

Windows 2000 aims to provide full support for Plug and Play, but the level of support possible depends on the attached devices and installed drivers. If a single device or driver doesn't support Plug and Play, the extent of Plug and Play support for the system can be compromised. In addition, a driver that doesn't support Plug and Play might prevent other devices from being usable by the system. Table 9-1 shows the outcome of various combinations of devices and drivers that can and can't support Plug and Play.

Table 9-1 Device and Driver Plug and Play Capability

	Type of Driver	
Type of Device	Plug and Play	Non–Plug and Play
Plug and Play	Full Plug and Play	No Plug and Play
Non–Plug and Play	Possible partial Plug and Play	No Plug and Play

A device that isn't Plug and Play compatible is one that doesn't support automatic detection, such as a legacy ISA sound card. Because the operating system doesn't know where the hardware physically lies, certain operations, such as laptop undocking, sleep, and hibernation, are disallowed. However, if a Plug and Play driver is manually installed for the device, the driver can at least implement PnP manager–directed resource assignment for the device.

Drivers that aren't Plug and Play compatible include legacy drivers, such as those that ran on Windows NT 4. Although these drivers continue to function on Windows 2000, the PnP manager can't reconfigure the resources assigned to such devices in the event that resource reallocation is necessary to accommodate the needs of a dynamically added device. For example, a device might be able to use I/O memory ranges A and B, and during the boot the PnP manager assigns it range A. If a device that can use only A is attached to the system later, the PnP manager can't direct the first device's driver to reconfigure itself to use range B. This prevents the second device from obtaining required resources, which results in the device being unavailable for use by the system. Legacy drivers also impair a machine's ability to sleep or hibernate. (See the section "The Power Manager" on page 546 for more details.)

Driver Support for Plug and Play

To support Plug and Play, a driver must implement a Plug and Play dispatch routine as well as an add-device routine. Bus drivers must support different types of Plug and Play requests than function or filter drivers do, however. For example, when the PnP manager is guiding device enumeration during the system boot (described in detail later in this chapter), it asks bus drivers for a description of the devices that they find on their respective buses. The description includes data that uniquely identifies each device as well as the resource requirements of the devices. The PnP manager takes this information and loads any function or filter drivers that have been installed for the detected devices. It then calls the add-device routine of each driver for every installed device the drivers are responsible for.

Function and filter drivers prepare to begin managing their devices in their add-device routines, but they don't actually communicate with the device hardware. Instead, they wait for the PnP manager to send a *start-device* command for the device to their Plug and Play dispatch routine. The *start-device* command includes the resource assignment that the PnP manager determined during resource arbitration. When a driver receives a *start-device* command, it can configure its device to use the specified resources.

After a device has started, the PnP manager can send the driver additional Plug and Play commands, including ones related to a device's removal from the system or to resource reassignment. For example, when the user invokes the remove/eject device utility, shown in Figure 9-6 (accessible by right-clicking on the PC card icon in the taskbar and selecting Unplug Or Eject Hardware), to tell Windows 2000 to eject a PCMCIA card, the PnP manager sends a *query-remove* notification to any applications that have registered for Plug and Play notifications for the device. Applications typically register for notification on their handles, which they close during a query-remove notification. If no applications veto the query-remove request, the PnP manager sends a *query-remove* command to the driver that owns the device being ejected. At that point, the driver has a chance to deny the removal or to ensure that any pending I/O operations involving the device have completed and to begin rejecting further I/O requests aimed at the device. If the driver agrees to the remove request and no open handles to the device remain, the PnP manager next sends a *remove* command to the driver to request that the driver discontinue accessing the device and release any resources the driver has allocated on behalf of the device.

Figure 9-6
PC card remove/eject utility

When the PnP manager needs to reassign a device's resources, it first asks the driver whether it can temporarily suspend further activity on the device by sending the driver a *query-stop* command. The driver either agrees to the request, if doing so wouldn't cause data loss or corruption, or denies the request. As with a *query-remove* command, if the driver agrees to the request, the driver completes pending I/O operations and won't initiate further I/O requests for the device that can't be aborted and subsequently restarted. The driver typically queues new I/O requests so that the resource reshuffling is transparent to applications currently accessing the device. The PnP manager then sends the driver a *stop* command. At that point, the PnP manager can direct the driver to assign different resources to the device and once again send the driver a *start-device* command for the device.

The various Plug and Play commands essentially guide a device through an assortment of operational states, forming a well-defined state-transition table, which is shown in simplified form in Figure 9-7. (Several possible transitions and Plug and Play commands have been omitted for clarity. Also, the state diagram depicted is that implemented by function drivers. Bus drivers implement a more complex state diagram.) A state shown in the figure that we haven't discussed is the one that results from the PnP manager's *surprise-remove* command. This

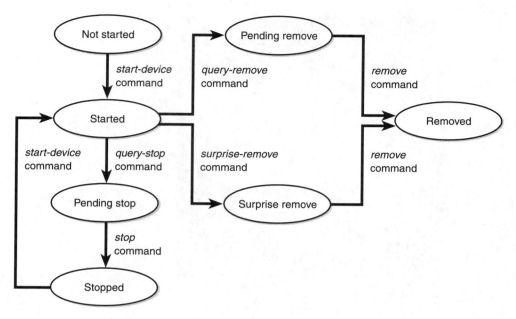

Figure 9-7
Device Plug and Play state transitions

command results when either a user removes a device without warning, as when the user ejects a PCMCIA card without using the remove/eject utility, or the device fails. The *surprise-remove* command tells the driver to immediately cease all interaction with the device because the device is no longer attached to the system and to cancel any pending I/O requests.

The Power Manager

Just as Windows 2000 Plug and Play features require support from a system's hardware, its power-management capabilities require hardware that complies with the Advanced Configuration and Power Interface (ACPI) specification (available at *www.teleport.com/~acpi/spec.htm*). As a result of this requirement, the computer's BIOS (Basic Input Output System), the code that runs when the computer turns on, must also conform to the ACPI standard. Most x86 computers manufactured since the end of 1998 are ACPI compliant.

NOTE Some computers, especially ones more than few years old, don't comply with the ACPI standard. Instead, they often conform to the older Advanced Power Management (APM) standard, which mandates fewer power-management capabilities than ACPI. Windows 2000 provides limited power management for APM systems, but we won't go into the details of that topic here. In this book, we focus on the behavior of Windows 2000 on ACPI computers.

The ACPI standard defines various power levels for a system and for devices. The six system power states are described in Table 9-2. They are referred to as S0 (*fully on* or *working*) through S5 (*fully off*). Each state has the following characteristics:

- **Power consumption** The amount of power the computer consumes
- **Software resumption** The software state from which the computer resumes when moving to a "more on" state
- **Hardware latency** The length of time it takes to return the computer to the fully on state

Table 9-2 System Power-State Definitions

State	Power Consumption	Software Resumption	Hardware Latency
S0 (fully on)	Maximum	Not applicable	None
S1 (sleeping)	Less than S0, more than S2	System resumes where it left off (returns to S0)	Less than 2 seconds
S2 (sleeping)	Less than S1, more than S3	System resumes where it left off (returns to S0)	2 or more seconds
S3 (sleeping)	Less than S2; processor is off	System resumes where it left off (returns to S0)	Same as S2
S4 (hibernating)	Trickle current to power button and wake circuitry	System restarts from saved hibernate file and resumes where it left off prior to hibernation (returns to S0)	Long and undefined
S5 (fully off)	Trickle current to power button	System boot	Long and undefined

States S1 through S4 are sleeping states, in which the computer appears to be off because of reduced power consumption. However, the computer retains enough information, either in memory or on disk, to move to S0. For states S1 through S3, enough power is required to preserve the contents of the computer's memory so that when the transition is made to S0 (when the user or a device wakes up the computer), the power manager continues executing where it left off before the suspend. When the system moves to S4, the power manager saves the compressed contents of memory to a hibernation file named Hiberfile.sys, which is large enough to hold the uncompressed contents of memory, in the root directory of the boot volume. (Compression is used to minimize disk I/O and to improve hibernation and resume-from-hibernation performance.) After it finishes saving memory, the power manager shuts off the computer. When a user subsequently turns on the computer, a normal boot process occurs except that Ntldr checks for and detects a valid memory image stored in the hibernation file. If the hibernation file contains saved system state, Ntldr reads the contents of the file into memory, and then resumes execution at the point in memory that is recorded in the hibernation file.

The computer never directly transitions between states S1 and S4; instead, it must move to state S0 first. As illustrated in Figure 9-8, when the system is moving from any of states S1 through S5 to state S0, it's said to be *waking*, and when it's transitioning from state S0 to any of states S1 through S5, it's said to be *sleeping*.

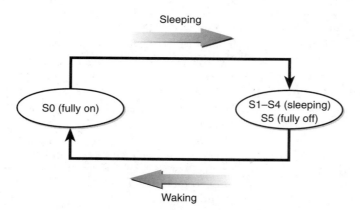

Figure 9-8
System power-state transitions

Although the system can be in one of six power states, ACPI defines devices as being in one of four power states, D0 through D3. State D0 is *fully on*, and state D3 is *fully off*. The ACPI standard leaves it to individual drivers and devices to define the meanings of states D1 and D2, except that state D1 must consume an amount of power less than or equal to that consumed in state D0, and when the device is in state D2, it must consume power less than or equal to that consumed in D1. Microsoft, in conjunction with the major hardware OEMs, has defined a series of power management reference specifications (available on Microsoft's Web site at *www.microsoft.com/hwdev/specs/pmref*) that specify the device power states that are required for all devices in a particular class (for the major device classes: display, network, SCSI, and so on). For some devices, there's no intermediate power state between fully on and fully off, which results in these states being undefined.

Power Manager Operation

Power management policy in Windows 2000 is split between the power manager and the individual device drivers. The power manager is the owner of the system power policy. This ownership means that the power manager decides which system power state is appropriate at any given point, and when a sleep, hibernation, or shutdown is required, the power manager instructs the power-capable devices in the system to perform appropriate system power-state transitions. The power manager decides when a system power-state transition is necessary by considering a number of factors:

- System activity level
- System battery level
- Shutdown, hibernate, or sleep requests from applications
- User actions, such as pressing the power button
- Control Panel power settings

When the PnP manager performs device enumeration, part of the information it receives about a device is its power-management capabilities. A driver reports whether or not its devices support device states D1 and D2 and, optionally, the latencies, or times required, to move from states D1 through D3 to D0. To help the power manager determine when to make system power-state transitions, bus drivers also return a table that implements a mapping between each of the system power states (S0 through S5) and the device power states that a device supports. The table lists the lowest possible device power state for each system state and directly reflects the state of various power planes when the

machine sleeps or hibernates. For example, a bus that supports all four device power states might return the mapping table shown in Table 9-3. Most device drivers turn their devices completely off (D3) when leaving S0 to minimize power consumption when the machine isn't in use. Some devices, however, such as network adapter cards, support the ability to wake up the system from a sleeping state. This ability, along with the lowest device power state in which the capability is present, is also reported during device enumeration.

Table 9-3 Example System-to-Device Power Mappings

System Power State	Device Power State
S0 (fully on)	D0 (fully on)
S1 (sleeping)	D2
S2 (sleeping)	D2
S3 (sleeping)	D2
S4 (hibernating)	D3 (fully off)
S5 (fully off)	D3 (fully off)

Driver Power Operation

When the power manager decides to make a transition between system power states, it sends power commands to a driver's power dispatch routine. More than one driver can be responsible for managing a device, but only one of the drivers is designated as the device power-policy owner. This driver determines, based on the system state, a device's power state. For example, if the system transitions between state S0 and S1, a driver might decide to move a device's power state from D0 to D1. Instead of directly informing the other drivers that share the management of the device of its decision, the device power-policy owner asks the power manager, via the *PoRequestPowerIrp* function, to tell the other drivers by issuing a device power command to their power dispatch routines. This behavior allows the power manager to control the number of power commands that are active on a system at any given time. For example, some devices in the system might require a significant amount of current to power up. The power manager ensures that such devices aren't powered up simultaneously.

Many power commands have corresponding query commands. For example, when the system is moving to a sleep state, the power manager will first ask the devices on the system if the transition is acceptable. A device that is busy performing time-critical operations or interacting with device hardware might reject the command, which results in the system maintaining its current system power-state setting.

EXPERIMENT: Viewing the System Power Capabilities and Policy

You can view a computer's system power capabilities by using the *!pocaps* kernel debugger command. Here's the output of the command when run on an ACPI-compliant laptop running Windows 2000 Professional:

```
kd> !pocaps
PopCapabilities @ 0x8046adc0
  Misc Supported Features:  PwrButton SlpButton Lid S1 S3 S4 S5
                            HiberFile FullWake
  Processor Features:       Thermal Throttle (MinThrottle = 03, Scale = 08)
  Disk Features:            SpinDown
  Battery Features:         BatteriesPresent
    Battery 0 - Capacity: 00000000  Granularity: 00000000
    Battery 1 - Capacity: 00000000  Granularity: 00000000
    Battery 2 - Capacity: 00000000  Granularity: 00000000
  Wake Caps
    Ac OnLine Wake:         Sx
    Soft Lid Wake:          Sx
    RTC Wake:               S3
    Min Device Wake:        Sx
    Default Wake:           Sx
```

The Misc Supported Features line reports that, in addition to S0 (fully on), the system supports system power states S1, S3, S4, and S5 (it doesn't implement S2) and has a valid hibernation file to which it can save system memory when it hibernates (state S4).

The Power Options Properties dialog box, shown on the following page (available by selecting Power Options in Control Panel), lets you configure various aspects of the system's power policy. The exact properties you can configure depends on the system's power capabilities, which we just examined.

Windows 2000 Professional on an ACPI-compliant laptop (such as the system on which we captured the following screen shot) generally provides the most power-management features. On such systems, you can set the idle detection timeouts that control when the system turns off the monitor, spins down hard disks, goes to standby mode (moves to system power state S1), and hibernates (moves the system to power state S4). In addition, the Advanced tab in Power Options lets you specify the power-related behavior of the system when you press the power or sleep buttons or close a laptop's lid.

(continued)

EXPERIMENT: Viewing the System Power Capabilities and Policy *continued*

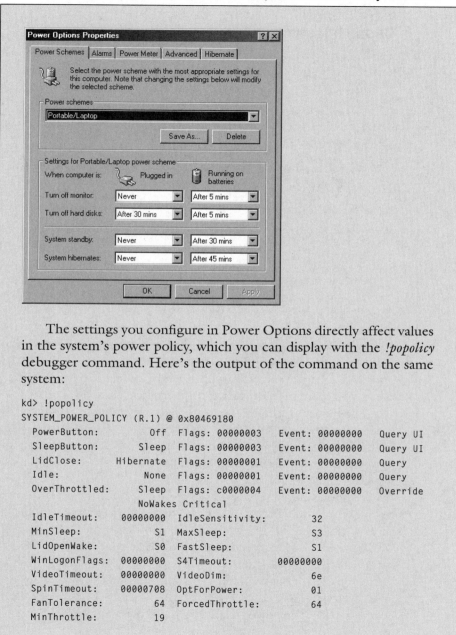

The settings you configure in Power Options directly affect values in the system's power policy, which you can display with the *!popolicy* debugger command. Here's the output of the command on the same system:

```
kd> !popolicy
SYSTEM_POWER_POLICY (R.1) @ 0x80469180
    PowerButton:        Off   Flags: 00000003   Event: 00000000   Query UI
    SleepButton:        Sleep Flags: 00000003   Event: 00000000   Query UI
    LidClose:           Hibernate Flags: 00000001  Event: 00000000  Query
    Idle:               None  Flags: 00000001   Event: 00000000   Query
    OverThrottled:      Sleep Flags: c0000004   Event: 00000000   Override
                        NoWakes Critical
    IdleTimeout:        00000000  IdleSensitivity:        32
    MinSleep:                 S1  MaxSleep:               S3
    LidOpenWake:              S0  FastSleep:              S1
    WinLogonFlags:      00000000  S4Timeout:        00000000
    VideoTimeout:       00000000  VideoDim:               6e
    SpinTimeout:        00000708  OptForPower:            01
    FanTolerance:             64  ForcedThrottle:         64
    MinThrottle:              19
```

The first lines of the display correspond to the button behaviors specified on the Advanced tab of Power Options, and on this system the power button is interpreted as an off switch, the sleep button moves the system to a sleep state, and the closing of the laptop lid causes the system to hibernate.

The timeout values shown at the end of the output are expressed in seconds and displayed in hexadecimal notation. The values reported here directly correspond to the settings you can see configured in the Power Options screen shot. (The laptop is plugged in.) For example, the video timeout is 0, meaning the monitor never turns off, and the hard disk spin-down timeout is 0x708, which corresponds to 1800 seconds, or 30 minutes.

Driver Control of Device Power

Besides responding to power manager commands related to system power-state transitions, a driver can unilaterally control the device power state of its devices. In some cases, a driver might want to reduce the power consumption of a device it controls when the device is left inactive for a period of time. A driver can either detect an idle device itself or use facilities provided by the power manager. If the device uses the power manager, it registers the device with the power manager by calling the *PoRegisterDeviceForIdleDetection* function. This function informs the power manager of the timeout values to use to detect a device as idle and of the device power state that the power manager should apply when it detects the device as being idle. The driver specifies two timeouts: one to use when the user has configured the computer to conserve energy and the other to use when the user has configured the computer for optimum performance. After calling *PoRegisterDeviceForIdleDetection*, the driver must inform the power manager, by calling the *PoSetDeviceBusy* function, whenever the device is active.

I/O Data Structures

Four primary data structures are associated with I/O requests: file objects, driver objects, device objects, and I/O request packets (IRPs). Each of these structures is defined in the DDK header file Ntddk.h as well as in the DDK documentation. You can display each of them with the kernel debugger by using the *!file*, *!drvobj*, *!devobj*, and *!irp* commands.

File Objects

File objects are the kernel-mode constructs for handles to files or devices. File objects clearly fit the criteria for objects in Windows 2000: they are system resources that two or more user-mode processes can share, they can have names, they are protected by object-based security, and they support synchronization. Although most shared resources in Windows 2000 are memory-based resources, most of those that the I/O system manages are located on physical devices or represent actual physical devices. Despite this difference, shared resources in the I/O system, like those in other components of the Windows 2000 executive, are manipulated as objects. (See Chapter 3 for a description of the object manager and Chapter 8 for information on object security.)

File objects provide a memory-based representation of resources that conform to an I/O-centric interface, in which they can be read from or written to. Table 9-4 lists some of the file object's attributes. For specific field declarations and sizes, see the structure definition for FILE_OBJECT in Ntddk.h.

Table 9-4 File Object Attributes

Attribute	Purpose
Filename	Identifies the physical file that the file object refers to
Current byte offset	Identifies the current location in the file (valid only for synchronous I/O)
Share modes	Indicate whether other callers can open the file for read, write, or delete operations while the current caller is using it
Open mode flags	Indicate whether I/O will be synchronous or asynchronous, cached or noncached, sequential or random, and so on
Pointer to device object	Indicates the type of device the file resides on
Pointer to the volume parameter block (VPB)	Indicates the volume, or partition, that the file resides on
Pointer to section object pointers	Indicates a root structure that describes a mapped file
Pointer to private cache map	Identifies which parts of the file are cached by the cache manager and where they reside in the cache

When a caller opens a file or a simple device, the I/O manager returns a handle to a file object. Figure 9-9 illustrates what occurs when a file is opened.

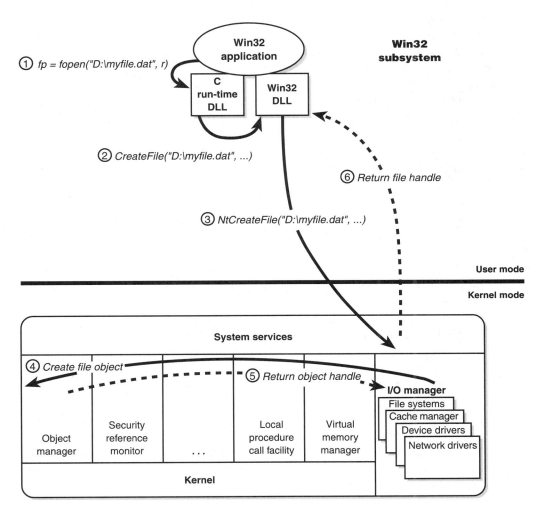

Figure 9-9
Opening a file object

In this example, (1) a C program calls the run-time library function *fopen*, which in turn (2) calls the Win32 *CreateFile* function. The Win32 subsystem DLL (in this case, Kernel32.dll) then (3) calls the native *NtCreateFile* function in Ntdll.dll. The routine in Ntdll.dll contains the appropriate instruction to cause a transition into kernel mode to the system service dispatcher, which then (4) calls the real *NtCreateFile* routine in Ntoskrnl.exe. (See Chapter 3 for more information about system service dispatching.)

Like other executive objects, file objects are protected by a security descriptor that contains an access-control list (ACL). The I/O manager consults the security subsystem to determine whether the file's ACL allows the process to access the file in the way its thread is requesting. If it does, (5,6) the object manager grants the access and associates the granted access rights with the file handle that it returns. If this thread or another thread in the process needs to perform additional operations not specified in the original request, the thread must open another handle, which prompts another security check. (See Chapter 8 for more information about object protection.)

Because a file object is a memory-based representation of a shareable resource and not the resource itself, it's different from other executive objects. A file object contains only data that is unique to an object handle, whereas the file itself contains the data or text to be shared. Each time a thread opens a file handle, a new file object is created with a new set of handle-specific attributes. For example, the current byte offset attribute refers to the location in the file at which the next read or write operation using that handle will occur. Each handle to a file has a private byte offset even though the underlying file is shared. A file object is also unique to a process, except when a process duplicates a file handle to another process (by using the Win32 *DuplicateHandle* function) or when a child process inherits a file handle from a parent process. In these situations, the two processes have separate handles that refer to the same file object.

Although a file handle might be unique to a process, the underlying physical resource is not. Therefore, as with any shared resource, threads must synchronize their access to shareable files, file directories, and devices. If a thread is writing to a file, for example, it should specify exclusive write access when opening the file handle to prevent other threads from writing to the file at the same time. Alternatively, by using the Win32 *LockFile* function, the thread could lock a portion of the file while writing to it.

Driver Objects and Device Objects

When a thread opens a handle to a file object, the I/O manager must determine from the file object's name which driver (or drivers) it should call to process the request. Furthermore, the I/O manager must be able to locate this information the next time a thread uses the same file handle. The following system objects fill this need:

- A *driver object* represents an individual driver in the system. The I/O manager obtains the address of each of the driver's dispatch routines (entry points) from the driver object.

■ A *device object* represents a physical or logical device on the system and describes its characteristics, such as the alignment it requires for buffers and the location of its device queue to hold incoming IRPs.

The I/O manager creates a driver object when a driver is loaded into the system, and it then calls the driver's initialization routine (for example, *Driver-Entry*), which fills in the object attributes with the driver's entry points.

After loading, a driver can create device objects to represent devices, or even an interface to the driver, at any time by calling *IoCreateDevice*. However, most Windows 2000 and WDM drivers create devices with their add-device routine when the PnP manager informs them of the presence of a device for them to manage. Legacy drivers, on the other hand, usually create device objects when the I/O manager invokes their initialization routine. The I/O manager unloads a driver when its last device object has been deleted and no references to the device remain.

When a driver creates a device object, the driver can optionally assign the device a name. A name places the device object in the object manager namespace, and a driver can either explicitly define a name or let the I/O manager auto-generate one. (The object manager namespace is described in Chapter 3.) By convention, device objects are placed in the \Device directory in the namespace, which is inaccessible by applications using the Win32 API.

NOTE Some drivers place device objects in directories other than \Device. For example, the Windows 2000 Logical Disk Manager volume manager creates device objects that represent disk partitions in the \Device\HarddiskDmVolumes directory. See Chapter 10 for a description of storage architecture, including the way storage drivers use device objects.

If a driver needs to make it possible for applications to open the device object, it must create a symbolic link in the \?? directory to the device object's name in the \Device directory. Legacy drivers and non-hardware-oriented drivers (such as file system drivers) typically create a symbolic link with a well-known name (for example, \Device\Hardware2). Because well-known names don't work well in an environment in which hardware appears and disappears dynamically, Plug and Play drivers expose one or more interfaces by calling the *IoRegisterDeviceInterface* function, specifying a GUID (globally unique identifier) that represents the type of functionality exposed. GUIDs are 128-bit values that you can generate by using a tool included with the DDK and the Platform SDK, called Guidgen. Given the range of values that 128 bits represents, it's statistically almost certain that each GUID Guidgen creates will be forever and globally unique.

IoRegisterDeviceInterface determines the symbolic link that is associated with a device instance; however, a driver must call *IoSetDeviceInterfaceState* to enable the interface to the device before the I/O manager actually creates the link. Drivers usually do this when the PnP manager starts the device by sending the driver a *start-device* command.

An application wanting to open a device object represented with a GUID can call Plug and Play setup functions in user space, such as *SetupDiEnum-DeviceInterfaces*, to enumerate the interfaces present for a particular GUID and to obtain the names of the symbolic links it can use to open the device objects. For each device reported by *SetupDiEnumDeviceInterfaces*, an application executes *SetupDiGetDeviceInterfaceDetail* to obtain additional information about the device, such as its autogenerated name. After obtaining a device's name from *SetupDiGetDeviceInterfaceDetail*, the application can execute the Win32 function *CreateFile* to open the device and obtain a handle.

EXPERIMENT: Looking at the \Device Directory

You can use the Winobj tool, included as \Sysint\Winobj.exe on the companion CD, or the *!object* kernel debugger command to view the device names under \Device in the object manager namespace. The following screen shot shows an I/O manager–assigned symbolic link that points to a device object in \Device with an autogenerated name:

When you run the *!object* kernel debugger command and specify the \Device directory, you should see output similar to the following:

```
kd> !object \device
Object: 81a8e170  Type: (81ab6120) Directory
    ObjectHeader: 81a8e158
    HandleCount: 0  PointerCount: 198
    Directory Object: 81a914d0  Name: Device
    9 symbolic links snapped through this directory
    HashBucket[ 00 ]: 81a6de10 Device 'KsecDD'
                      819c43f0 Device 'Beep'
                      81a6d6d0 Device 'Ndis'
                      81a61030 Device '00000019'
                      81aa7830 Device '003018'
                      81aa7a30 Device '002918'
    HashBucket[ 01 ]: 817c3c70 Device '00000026'
                      819c3d90 Device 'Netbios'
    HashBucket[ 02 ]: 818d1850 Device 'KSENUM#00000001'
                      81966890 Device 'Ip'
    HashBucket[ 03 ]: 818c5b70 Device 'KSENUM#00000002'
                      81a31038 Device 'Video0'
                      81a4fc70 Device 'KeyboardClass0'
    HashBucket[ 04 ]: 819d4410 Device 'NDProxy'
                      819c0040 Device 'Video1'
    HashBucket[ 05 ]: 817e7650 Device 'PcCard0-0'
                      819c70d0 Device 'Eawdmfd'
                      81a2aa50 Device
                      '{13199AF4-86FA-48C2-8074-468CA06AFB6C}'
                      819c0ce0 Device 'Video2'
                      81a52040 Device 'Serial0'
                      81a6cbb0 Device 'PointerClass0'
                      81a215f0 Device '0000000a'
    HashBucket[ 06 ]: 817cb8c0 Device 'Serial1'
                      81900570 Device 'DebugMessageDevice'
                      81a277d0 Device 'USBPDO-0'
                      81a5e030 Device 'CompositeBattery'
    ⋮
```

When you execute *!object* and specify an object manager directory object, the kernel debugger dumps the contents of the directory according to the way the object manager organizes it internally. For fast lookups, a directory stores objects in a hash table based on a hash of the object names, so the output shows the objects stored in each bucket of the directory's hash table.

When a file is opened, the filename includes the name of the device object on which the file resides. For example, the name \Device\Floppy0\Myfile.dat refers to the file Myfile.dat on floppy disk drive A. The substring \Device\ Floppy0 is the name of the internal Windows 2000 device object representing that floppy disk drive. When opening Myfile.dat, the I/O manager creates a file object and stores a pointer to the Floppy0 device object in the file object and then returns a file handle to the caller. Thereafter, when the caller uses the file handle, the I/O manager can find the Floppy0 device object directly. Keep in mind that internal Windows 2000 device names can't be used in Win32 applications—instead, the device name must appear in a special directory in the object manager's namespace, \?? (named \DosDevices prior to Windows NT 4). This directory contains symbolic links to the real, internal Windows 2000 device names. Device drivers are responsible for creating links in this directory so that their devices will be accessible to Win32 applications. You can examine or even change these links programmatically with the Win32 *QueryDosDevice* and *DefineDosDevice* functions.

EXPERIMENT: Viewing Win32 Device Name to Windows 2000 Device Name Mappings

You can examine the symbolic links that define the Win32 device namespace with the Winobj utility included on the companion CD (\Sysint\Winobj.exe). Run Winobj, and click on the \?? directory, as shown here:

Notice the symbolic links on the right. Try double-clicking on the device C:. You should see something like this:

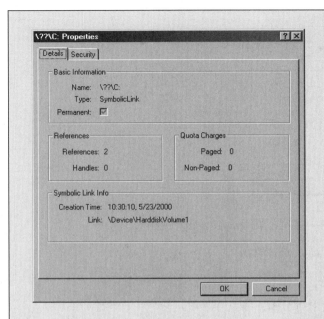

C: is a symbolic link to the internal device named \Device\ HarddiskVolume1, or the first volume on the first hard drive in the system. The COM1 entry in Winobj is a symbolic link to \Device\ Serial0, and so forth. Try creating your own links with the *subst* command at a command prompt.

As Figure 9-10 illustrates, a device object points back to its driver object, which is how the I/O manager knows which driver routine to call when it receives an I/O request. It uses the device object to find the driver object representing the driver that services the device. It then indexes into the driver object by using the function code supplied in the original request; each function code corresponds to a driver entry point. (The function codes shown in Figure 9-10 are described in the section "IRP Stack Locations" later in this chapter.)

A driver object often has multiple device objects associated with it. The list of device objects represents the physical and logical devices that the driver controls. For example, each partition of a hard disk has a separate device object that contains partition-specific information. However, the same hard disk driver is used to access all partitions. When a driver is unloaded from the system, the I/O manager uses the queue of device objects to determine which devices will be affected by the removal of the driver.

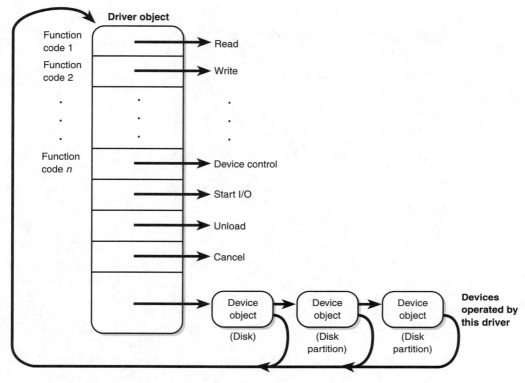

Figure 9-10
The driver object

Using objects to record information about drivers means that the I/O manager doesn't need to know details about individual drivers. The I/O manager merely follows a pointer to locate a driver, thereby providing a layer of portability and allowing new drivers to be loaded easily. Representing devices and drivers with different objects also makes it easy for the I/O system to assign drivers to control additional or different devices if the system configuration changes.

I/O Request Packets

The I/O request packet (IRP) is where the I/O system stores information it needs to process an I/O request. When a thread calls an I/O service, the I/O manager constructs an IRP to represent the operation as it progresses through the I/O system. If possible, the I/O manager allocates IRPs from one of two per-processor IRP nonpaged look-aside lists: the small-IRP look-aside list stores

IRPs with one stack location (IRP stack locations are described shortly), and the large-IRP look-aside list contains IRPs with eight stack locations. If an IRP requires more than eight stack locations, the I/O manager allocates IRPs from nonpaged pool. After allocating and initializing an IRP, the I/O manager stores a pointer to the caller's file object in the IRP.

EXPERIMENT: Displaying Driver and Device Objects

You can display driver and device objects with the kernel debugger *!drvobj* and *!devobj* commands, respectively. In the following example, the driver object for the keyboard class driver is examined, and its lone device object viewed.

```
kd> !drvobj kbdclass
Driver object (81869cb0) is for:
 \Driver\Kbdclass
Driver Extension List: (id , addr)

Device Object list:
81869310

kd> !devobj 81869310
Device object (81869310) is for:
 KeyboardClass0 \Driver\Kbdclass DriverObject 81869cb0
Current Irp a57a0e90 RefCount 0 Type 0000000b Flags 00002044
DevExt 818693c8 DevObjExt 818694b8
ExtensionFlags (0000000000)
AttachedDevice (Upper) 818691e0 \Driver\Ctrl2cap
AttachedTo (Lower) 81869500 \Driver\i8042prt
Device queue is busy -- Queue empty.
```

Notice that the *!devobj* command also shows you the addresses and names of any device objects that the object you're viewing is layered over (the *AttachedTo* line) as well as the device objects layered on top of the object specified (the *AttachedDevice* line).

Figure 9-11 shows an example I/O request that demonstrates the relationship between an IRP and the file, device, and driver objects described in the preceding sections. Although this example shows an I/O request to a single-layered device driver, most I/O operations aren't this direct; they involve one or more layered drivers. (This case will be shown later in this section.)

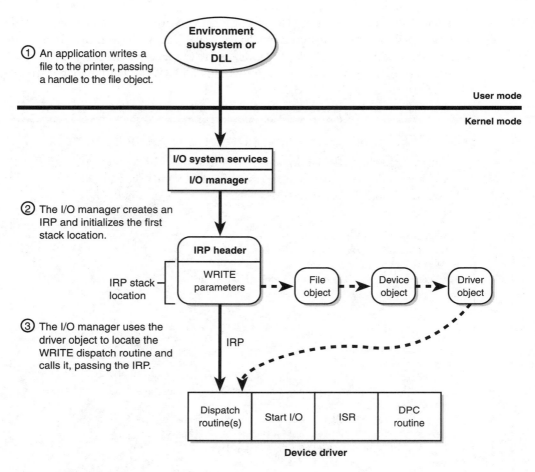

Figure 9-11
Data structures involved in a single-layered driver I/O request

IRP Stack Locations

An IRP consists of two parts: a fixed header (often referred to as the IRP's *body*) and one or more stack locations. The fixed portion contains information such as the type and size of the request, whether the request is synchronous or asynchronous, a pointer to a buffer for buffered I/O, and state information that changes as the request progresses. An IRP stack location contains a function code (consisting of a major code and a minor code), function-specific parameters, and a pointer to the caller's file object. The *major function code* identifies which of a driver's dispatch routines the I/O manager invokes when passing an IRP to

a driver. An optional *minor function code* sometimes serves as a modifier of the major function code. Power and Plug and Play commands always have minor function codes.

Most drivers specify dispatch routines to handle only a subset of possible major function codes, including create (open), read, write, device I/O control, power, Plug and Play, System (for WMI commands), and close. (See the following experiment for a complete listing of major function codes.) File system drivers are an example of a driver type that often fills in most or all of its dispatch entry points with functions. The I/O manager sets any dispatch entry points that a driver doesn't fill to point to its own *IopInvalidDeviceRequest*, which returns an error code to the caller indicating that the function specified for the device is invalid.

EXPERIMENT: Looking at Driver Dispatch Routines

You can obtain a listing of the functions a driver has defined for its dispatch routines by entering a *2* after the driver object's name (or address) in the *!drvobj* kernel debugger command:

```
kd> !drvobj kbdclass 2
Driver object (81869cb0) is for:
 \Driver\Kbdclass
Dispatch routines:
[00] IRP_MJ_CREATE                        edf0866e
     kbdclass!KeyboardClassCreate
[01] IRP_MJ_CREATE_NAMED_PIPE             80425354
     ntoskrnl!IopInvalidDeviceRequest
[02] IRP_MJ_CLOSE                         edf088ec
     kbdclass!KeyboardClassClose
[03] IRP_MJ_READ                          edf08b1c
      kbdclass!KeyboardClassRead
[04] IRP_MJ_WRITE                         80425354
     ntoskrnl!IopInvalidDeviceRequest
[05] IRP_MJ_QUERY_INFORMATION             80425354
     ntoskrnl!IopInvalidDeviceRequest
[06] IRP_MJ_SET_INFORMATION               80425354
     ntoskrnl!IopInvalidDeviceRequest
[07] IRP_MJ_QUERY_EA                      80425354
     ntoskrnl!IopInvalidDeviceRequest
[08] IRP_MJ_SET_EA                        80425354
     ntoskrnl!IopInvalidDeviceRequest
[09] IRP_MJ_FLUSH_BUFFERS                 edf085d4
     kbdclass!KeyboardClassFlush
```

(continued)

565

EXPERIMENT: Looking at Driver Dispatch Routines *continued*

```
[0a]  IRP_MJ_QUERY_VOLUME_INFORMATION       80425354
          ntoskrnl!IopInvalidDeviceRequest
[0b]  IRP_MJ_SET_VOLUME_INFORMATION         80425354
          ntoskrnl!IopInvalidDeviceRequest
[0c]  IRP_MJ_DIRECTORY_CONTROL              80425354
          ntoskrnl!IopInvalidDeviceRequest
[0d]  IRP_MJ_FILE_SYSTEM_CONTROL            80425354
          ntoskrnl!IopInvalidDeviceRequest
[0e]  IRP_MJ_DEVICE_CONTROL                 edf0a8ec
          kbdclass!KeyboardClassDeviceControl
[0f]  IRP_MJ_INTERNAL_DEVICE_CONTROL        edf0a380
          kbdclass!KeyboardClassPassThrough
[10]  IRP_MJ_SHUTDOWN                       80425354
          ntoskrnl!IopInvalidDeviceRequest
[11]  IRP_MJ_LOCK_CONTROL                   80425354
          ntoskrnl!IopInvalidDeviceRequest
[12]  IRP_MJ_CLEANUP                        edf084b6
          kbdclass!KeyboardClassCleanup
[13]  IRP_MJ_CREATE_MAILSLOT               80425354
          ntoskrnl!IopInvalidDeviceRequest
[14]  IRP_MJ_QUERY_SECURITY                 80425354
          ntoskrnl!IopInvalidDeviceRequest
[15]  IRP_MJ_SET_SECURITY                   80425354
          ntoskrnl!IopInvalidDeviceRequest
[16]  IRP_MJ_POWER                          edf0b5e2
          kbdclass!KeyboardClassPower
[17]  IRP_MJ_SYSTEM_CONTROL                 edf0bbfe
          kbdclass!KeyboardClassSystemControl
[18]  IRP_MJ_DEVICE_CHANGE                  80425354
          ntoskrnl!IopInvalidDeviceRequest
[19]  IRP_MJ_QUERY_QUOTA                    80425354
          ntoskrnl!IopInvalidDeviceRequest
[1a]  IRP_MJ_SET_QUOTA                      80425354
          ntoskrnl!IopInvalidDeviceRequest
[1b]  IRP_MJ_PNP                            edf09168
          kbdclass!KeyboardPnP
```

While active, each IRP is usually stored in an IRP list associated with the thread that requested the I/O. This arrangement allows the I/O system to find and cancel any outstanding IRPs if a thread terminates or is terminated with outstanding I/O requests.

IRP Buffer Management

When an application or a device driver indirectly creates an IRP by using the *NtReadFile*, *NtWriteFile*, or *NtDeviceIoControlFile* system services (the Win32 API functions corresponding to these services are *ReadFile*, *WriteFile*, and *DeviceIoControl*), the I/O manager determines whether it needs to participate in the management of the caller's input or output buffers. The I/O manager performs three types of buffer management:

- **Buffered I/O** The I/O manager allocates a buffer in nonpaged pool of equal size to the caller's buffer. For write operations, the I/O manager copies the caller's buffer data into the allocated buffer when creating the IRP. For read operations, the I/O manager copies data from the allocated buffer to the user's buffer when the IRP completes and then frees the allocated buffer.

- **Direct I/O** When the I/O manager creates the IRP, it locks the user's buffer into memory (makes it nonpaged). When the I/O manager has finished using the IRP, it unlocks the buffer. The I/O manager stores a description of the memory in the form of a *memory descriptor list* (MDL). An MDL specifies the physical memory occupied by a buffer. (See the Windows 2000 DDK for more information on MDLs.) Devices that perform directory memory access (DMA) require only physical descriptions of buffers, so an MDL is sufficient for the operation of such devices. (Devices that support DMA transfer data directly between the device and the computer's memory, without using the CPU.) If a driver must access the contents of a buffer, however, it can map the buffer into the system's address space.

- **Neither I/O** The I/O manager doesn't perform any buffer management. Instead, buffer management is left to the discretion of the device driver, which can choose to manually perform the steps the I/O manager performs with the other buffer management types.

For each type of buffer management, the I/O manager places applicable references in the IRP to the locations of the input and output buffers. The type of buffer management the I/O manager performs depends on the type of buffer management a driver requests for each type of operation. A driver registers the type of buffer management it desires for read and write operations in the device object that represents the device. Device I/O control operations (those performed by *NtDeviceIoControlFile*) are specified with driver-defined I/O control codes, and a control code includes a description of the buffer management the I/O manager should use when issuing IRPs that contain that code.

Drivers commonly use buffered I/O when callers transfer requests smaller than one page (4 KB) and use direct I/O for larger requests. A page is approximately the buffer size at which the trade-off between the copy operation of buffered I/O matches the overhead of the memory lock performed by direct I/O. File system drivers commonly use neither I/O because no buffer management overhead is incurred when data can be copied from the file system cache into the caller's original buffer. The reason that most drivers don't use neither I/O is that a pointer to a caller's buffer is valid only while a thread of the caller's process is executing. If a driver must transfer data from or to a device in an ISR or a DPC routine, it must ensure that the caller's data is accessible from any process context, which means that the buffer must have a system virtual address.

EXPERIMENT: Examining IRPs and the Thread IRP Queue

You can examine the pending IRPs for a thread with the *!thread* kernel debugger command. One thread that almost always has a pending IRP is the Win32 environment subsystem's keyboard-input thread. To find this thread, execute the *!stacks* kernel debugger command and locate the thread in Csrss that is listed as having started in the Win32k *RawInputThread* function:

```
kd> !stacks
Proc.Thread   Thread    ThreadState   Blocker
                                      [System]
    8.000004  fe504a60  BLOCKED       ntoskrnl!MmZeroPageThread+0x5f
    8.00000c  fe503ce0  BLOCKED       ntoskrnl!ExpWorkerThread+0x73
    8.000010  fe503a60  BLOCKED       ntoskrnl!ExpWorkerThread+0x73
    8.000014  fe5037e0  BLOCKED       ntoskrnl!ExpWorkerThread+0x73
    8.000018  fe503560  BLOCKED       ntoskrnl!ExpWorkerThread+0x73
    8.00001c  fe5032e0  BLOCKED       ntoskrnl!ExpWorkerThread+0x73
    8.000020  fe502020  BLOCKED       ntoskrnl!ExpWorkerThread+0x73
    8.000024  fe502da0  BLOCKED       ntoskrnl!ExpWorkerThread+0x73
  ⋮
                                      [csrss.exe]
   c0.0000c4  ff2d5020  BLOCKED       ?? Kernel stack not resident ??
   c0.0000c8  ff2d5d80  BLOCKED       ?? Kernel stack not resident ??
   c0.0000cc  ff2d4820  BLOCKED       ntdll+0xaaa7
   c0.0000d0  ff2d4460  BLOCKED       ?? Kernel stack not resident ??
   c0.0000d4  ff2d4120  BLOCKED       ?? Kernel stack not resident ??
   c0.0000dc  ff2cfda0  BLOCKED       ntdll+0xaaa7
   c0.00007c  ff2cbc40  BLOCKED       win32k!RawInputThread+0x3c2
   c0.0000e0  ff2cb480  BLOCKED       win32k!xxxMsgWaitForMultipleObjects+0x92
  ⋮
```

Then perform the *!thread* command on the thread's address (the second column):

```
kd> !thread ff2cbc40
THREAD ff2cbc40  Cid c0.7c  Teb: 00000000  Win32Thread: a20836e8
WAIT: (WrUserRequest) KernelMode Alertable
    ff2cc1a0  SynchronizationEvent
    ff2cbb28  SynchronizationEvent
    ff2cbae8  NotificationTimer
    ff2cbb68  SynchronizationEvent
IRP List:
    fee25388: (0006,0100) Flags: 00000970  Mdl: 00000000
Not impersonating
Owning Process ff2d9020
WaitTime (seconds)     15420441
Context Switch Count   328592
UserTime               0:00:00.0000
KernelTime             0:00:00.0721
Start Address win32k!RawInputThread (0xa000c0b0)
Stack Init f20d0000 Current f20cfaf0 Base f20d0000 Limit f20cd000 Call 0
Priority 19 BasePriority 13 PriorityDecrement 0 DecrementCount 0

ChildEBP RetAddr  Args to Child
f20cfb08 8042d33d 80400b46 00000001 00000000 ntoskrnl!KiSwapThread+0xc5
f20cfb3c a000c3f3 00000004 ff2cbc08 00000001
 ntoskrnl!KeWaitForMultipleObjects+0x266
f20cfda8 804524f6 00000002 00000000 00000000 win32k!RawInputThread+0x3c2
f20cfddc 80465b62 a000c0b0 f1caf7d0 00000000
 ntoskrnl!PspSystemThreadStartup+0x69
00000000 00000000 00000000 00000000 00000000 ntoskrnl!KiThreadStartup+0x16
```

The sample output shows that the thread's IRP list contains one pending IRP. If you use the *!irp* command on this IRP, you're likely to see something like this:

```
kd> !irp fee25388
Irp is active with 4 stacks 4 is current (= 0xfee25440)
 No Mdl System buffer = ff0acc48 Thread ff2cbc40:  Irp stack trace.
    cmd  flg cl Device   File     Completion-Context
 [ 0, 0]   0  0 00000000 00000000 00000000-00000000

           Args: 00000000 00000000 00000000 00000000
 [ 0, 0]   0  0 00000000 00000000 00000000-00000000

           Args: 00000000 00000000 00000000 00000000
 [ 0, 0]   0  0 00000000 00000000 00000000-00000000
```

(continued)

EXPERIMENT: Examining IRPs and the Thread IRP Queue *continued*

```
              Args: 00000000 00000000 00000000 00000000
>[  4, 0]    0 e1 ff43b390 ff2cb928 00000000-00000000
             \Driver\Kbdclass
              Args: 00000078 00000000 00000000 00000000
```

This output shows that the IRP has four stack locations and that the keyboard class driver, which is waiting for keyboard input before it completes the IRP, currently owns it.

Another IRP-related debugger command, *!irpfind*, lets you see all the pending IRPs on the system:

```
kd> !irpfind
Scanning large pool allocation table for Tag: Irp?

Searching NonPaged pool (fe314000 : fe52c000) for Tag: Irp?

  Irp    [ Thread ] irpStack: (Mj,Mn)  DevObj  [Driver]
fe4f0568 [00000000] irpStack: ( 0, 0)  ff453790 [ \Driver\Cdrom]
fe4f22e8 [fe5028a0] irpStack: ( e, 0)  fe4f13b0 [ \Driver\Ftdisk]
fe4f3b28 [fe5028a0] irpStack: ( e, 0)  fe4f33f0 [ \Driver\Ftdisk]
fe4fdf68 [ff2ae8c0] irpStack: ( e, 0)  ff3f45f0 [ \Driver\NetBT]
  0xff2c9780
fe50b6a8 [00000000] Irp is complete (CurrentLocation 3 > StackCount 2)
fe50d648 [00000000] irpStack: ( f, 0)  ff4526f0 [ \Driver\openhci]
fe513e68 [fe5028a0] irpStack: ( e, 0)  fe4f3690 [ \Driver\Ftdisk]
fe515e68 [fe5028a0] irpStack: ( e, 0)  fe4f2570 [ \Driver\Ftdisk]

Searching NonPaged pool (fe52c000 : ffb7f000) for Tag: Irp?

fefa4848 [ff1124e0] irpStack: ( e, 9)  ff2b3490 [ \Driver\AFD]
fefcc2e8 [ff0ecda0] irpStack: ( 3, 0)  ff3f3e70 [ \FileSystem\Npfs]
⋮
```

I/O Completion Ports

Writing a high-performance server application requires implementing an efficient threading model. Having either too few or too many server threads to process client requests can lead to performance problems. For example, if a server creates a single thread to handle all requests, clients can become starved because the server will be tied up processing one request at a time. A single thread could simultaneously process multiple requests, switching from one to another as

I/O operations are started, but this architecture introduces significant complexity and can't take advantage of multiprocessor systems. At the other extreme, a server could create a big pool of threads so that virtually every client request is processed by a dedicated thread. This scenario usually leads to thread-thrashing, in which lots of threads wake up, perform some CPU processing, block while waiting for I/O, and then, after request processing is completed, block again waiting for a new request. If nothing else, having too many threads results in excessive context switching, caused by the scheduler having to divide processor time among multiple active threads.

The goal of a server is to incur as few context switches as possible by having its threads avoid unnecessary blocking, while at the same time maximizing parallelism by using multiple threads. The ideal is for there to be a thread actively servicing a client request on every processor and for those threads not to block when they complete a request if additional requests are waiting. For this optimal process to work correctly, however, the application must have a way to activate another thread when a thread processing a client request blocks on I/O (such as when it reads from a file as part of the processing).

The *IoCompletion* Object

Applications use the *IoCompletion* executive object, which is exported to Win32 as a *completion port*, as the focal point for the completion of I/O associated with multiple file handles. Once a file is associated with a completion port, any asynchronous I/O operations that complete on the file result in a completion packet being queued to the completion port. A thread can wait for any outstanding I/Os to complete on multiple files simply by waiting for a completion packet to be queued to the completion port. The Win32 API provides similar functionality with the *WaitForMultipleObjects* API function, but the advantage that completion ports have is that *concurrency*, or the number of threads that an application has actively servicing client requests, is controlled with the aid of the system.

When an application creates a completion port, it specifies a concurrency value. This value indicates the maximum number of threads associated with the port that should be running at any given time. As stated earlier, the ideal is to have one thread active at any given time for every processor in the system. Windows 2000 uses the concurrency value associated with a port to control how many threads an application has active. If the number of active threads associated with a port equals the concurrency value, a thread that is waiting on the completion port won't be allowed to run. Instead, it is expected that one of the

active threads will finish processing its current request and check to see whether another packet is waiting at the port. If one is, the thread simply grabs the packet and goes off to process it. When this happens, there is no context switch, and the CPUs are utilized nearly to their full capacity.

Using Completion Ports

Figure 9-12 shows a high-level illustration of completion port operation. A completion port is created with a call to the Win32 API function *Create-IoCompletionPort*. Threads that block on a completion port become associated with the port and are awakened in last in, first out (LIFO) order so that the thread that blocked most recently is the one that is given the next packet. Threads that block for long periods of time can have their stacks swapped out to disk, so if there are more threads associated with a port than there is work to process, the in-memory footprints of threads blocked the longest are minimized.

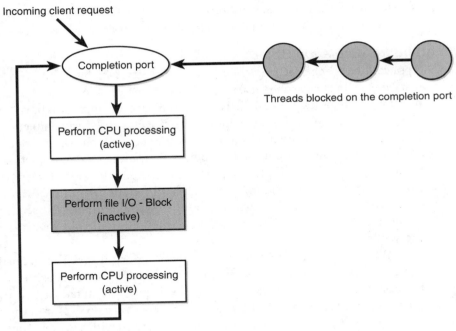

Figure 9-12
I/O completion port operation

A server application will usually receive client requests via network endpoints that are represented as file handles. Examples include Windows Sockets 2 (Winsock2) sockets or named pipes. As the server creates its communications endpoints, it associates them with a completion port and its threads wait for incoming requests by calling *GetQueuedCompletionStatus* on the port. When a thread is given a packet from the completion port, it will go off and start processing the request, becoming an active thread. A thread will block many times during its processing, such as when it needs to read or write data to a file on disk or when it synchronizes with other threads. Windows 2000 detects this activity and recognizes that the completion port has one less active thread. Therefore, when a thread becomes inactive because it blocks, a thread waiting on the completion port will be awakened if there is a packet in the queue.

Microsoft's guidelines are to set the concurrency value roughly equal to the number of processors in a system. Keep in mind that it's possible for the number of active threads for a completion port to exceed the concurrency limit. Consider a case in which the limit is specified as 1. A client request comes in, and a thread is dispatched to process the request, becoming active. A second request arrives, but a second thread waiting on the port isn't allowed to proceed because the concurrency limit has been reached. Then the first thread blocks waiting for a file I/O, so it becomes inactive. The second thread is then released, and while it's still active, the first thread's file I/O is completed, making it active again. At that point—and until one of the threads blocks—the concurrency value is 2, which is higher than the limit of 1. Most of the time, the active count will remain at or just above the concurrency limit.

The completion port API also makes it possible for a server application to queue privately defined completion packets to a completion port by using the *PostQueuedCompletionStatus* function. A server typically uses this function to inform its threads of external events, such as the need to shut down gracefully.

Driver Loading, Initialization, and Installation

Driver loading and initialization on Windows 2000 consists of two types of loading: explicit loading and enumeration-based loading. Explicit loading is guided by the HKLM\SYSTEM\CurrentControlSet\Services branch of the registry, as described in the section "Service Applications" on page 237 in Chapter 5. Enumeration-based loading results when the PnP manager dynamically loads drivers for the devices that a bus driver reports during bus enumeration.

The Start Value

In Chapter 5, we explained that every driver and Win32 service has a registry key under the Services branch of the current control set. The key includes values that specify the type of the image (for example, Win32 service, driver, and file system), the path to the driver or service's image file, and values that control the driver or service's load ordering. There are two main differences between explicit device driver loading and Win32 service loading:

- Only device drivers can specify Start values of boot-start (0) or system-start (1).

- Device drivers can use the Group and Tag values to control the order of loading within a phase of the boot, but unlike services, they can't specify DependOnGroup or DependOnService values.

Chapter 4 describes the phases of the boot process and explains that a driver Start value of 0 means that the operating system loader loads the driver. A Start value of 1 means that the I/O manager loads the driver after the executive subsystems have finished initializing. The I/O manager calls driver initialization routines in the order that the drivers load within a boot phase. Like Win32 services, drivers use the Group value in their registry key to specify which group they belong to; the registry value HKLM\SYSTEM\CurrentControlSet\Control\ServiceGroupOrder\List determines the order that groups are loaded within a boot phase.

A driver can further refine its load order by including a Tag value to control its order within a group. The I/O manager sorts the drivers within each group according to the Tag values defined in the drivers' registry keys. Drivers without a tag go to the end of the list in their group. You might assume that the I/O manager initializes drivers with lower-number tags before it initializes drivers with higher-number tags, but such isn't necessarily the case. The registry key HKLM\SYSTEM\CurrentControlSet\Control\GroupOrderList defines tag precedence within a group; with this key, Microsoft and device driver developers can take liberties with redefining the integer number system.

Here are the guidelines by which drivers set their Start value:

- Legacy drivers set their Start value to reflect the boot phase they want to load in.

- Drivers, including legacy and Windows 2000 drivers, that must be loaded by the boot loader during the system boot specify a Start value of boot-start (0). Examples include system bus drivers and the boot file system driver.

■ A driver that isn't required for booting the system and that detects a device that a system bus driver can't enumerate specifies a Start value of system-start (1). An example is the serial port driver, which informs the PnP manager of the presence of standard PC serial ports that were detected by Setup and recorded in the registry.

■ A Windows 2000 driver that doesn't have to support Plug and Play or a legacy driver that doesn't have to be present when the system boots specifies a Start value of auto-start (2). An example is the Multiple Universal Naming Convention (UNC) Provider (MUP) driver, which provides support for UNC-based path names to remote resources (for example, (\\REMOTECOMPUTERNAME\SHARE).

■ Plug and Play drivers that aren't required to boot the system specify a Start value of demand-start (3). Examples include network adapter drivers.

The only purpose that the Start values for Plug and Play drivers and drivers for enumerable devices have is to ensure that the operating system loader loads the driver—if the driver is required for the system to boot successfully. Beyond that, the PnP manager's device enumeration process, described next, determines the load order for Plug and Play drivers.

Device Enumeration

The PnP manager begins device enumeration with a virtual bus driver called Root, which represents the entire computer system and that acts as the bus driver for legacy drivers and for the HAL. The HAL acts as a bus driver that enumerates devices directly attached to the motherboard as well as system components such as batteries. Instead of actually enumerating, the HAL relies on the hardware description the Setup process recorded in the registry to detect the primary bus (a PCI bus in most cases) and devices such as batteries and fans.

The primary bus driver enumerates the devices on its bus, possibly finding other buses, for which the PnP manager initializes drivers. Those drivers in turn can detect other devices, including other subsidiary buses. This recursive process of enumeration, driver loading (if the driver isn't already loaded), and further enumeration proceeds until all the devices on the system have been detected and configured.

As the bus drivers report detected devices to the PnP manager, the PnP manager creates an internal tree called the *device tree* that represents the relationships between devices. Nodes in the tree are called *devnodes,* and a devnode contains information about the device objects that represent the device as well

as other Plug and Play–related information stored in the devnode by the PnP manager. Figure 9-13 shows an example of a simplified device tree. This system is ACPI-compliant, so an ACPI-compliant HAL serves as the primary bus enumerator. A PCI bus serves as the system's primary bus, which USB, ISA, and SCSI buses are connected to.

Figure 9-13
Example device tree

The Device Manager utility, which is accessible from the Computer Management snap-in in the Programs/Administrative Tools folder of the Start menu (and also from the Hardware tab of the System utility in Control Panel), shows a simple list of devices present on a system in its default configuration. You can also select the Devices By Connection option from the Device Manager's View menu to see the devices as they relate to the device tree. Figure 9-14 shows an example of the Device Manager's Devices By Connection view.

Figure 9-14
Device Manager showing the device tree

Taking device enumeration into account, the load and initialization order of drivers is as follows:

1. The I/O manager invokes the driver entry routine of each boot-start driver. If a boot driver has child devices, the I/O manager enumerates those devices, reporting their presence to the PnP manager. The child devices are configured and started if their drivers are boot-start drivers. If a device has a driver that isn't a boot-start driver, the PnP manager creates a devnode for the device but doesn't start it or load its driver.

2. After the boot-start drivers are initialized, the PnP manager walks the device tree, loading the drivers for devnodes that weren't loaded in step 1 and starting their devices. As each device starts, the PnP manager enumerates its child devices, if it has any, starting those devices' drivers and performing enumeration of their children as required. The PnP manager loads the drivers for detected devices in this step *regardless of the driver's Start value.* (The one exception is if the Start value is set to disabled.) At the end of this step, all Plug and Play devices have their drivers loaded and are started, except devices that aren't enumerable and the children of those devices.

3. The PnP manager loads any drivers with a Start value of system-start that aren't yet loaded. Those drivers detect and report their nonenumerable devices. The PnP manager loads drivers for those devices until all enumerated devices are configured and started.

4. The Service Control Manager loads drivers marked as auto-start.

The device tree serves to guide both the PnP manager and the power manager as they issue Plug and Play and power IRPs to devices. In general, IRPs flow from the top of a devnode to the bottom, and in some cases a driver in one devnode creates new IRPs to send to other devnodes, always moving toward the root. The flow of Plug and Play and power IRPs is further described later in this chapter.

EXPERIMENT: Dumping the Device Tree

A more detailed way to view the device tree than using Device Manager is to use the *!devnode* kernel debugger command. Specifying *0 1* as command options dumps the internal device tree devnode structures, indenting entries to show their hierarchical relationships, as shown here:

```
kd> !devnode 0 1
Dumping IopRootDeviceNode (= 0x818a78e8)
DevNode 0x818a78e8 for PDO 0x818a79e0
  Parent 0000000000   Sibling 0000000000   Child 0x818a74c8
  InstancePath is "HTREE\ROOT\0"
  Flags (0x00040459)  DNF_MADEUP, DNF_PROCESSED,
                      DNF_ENUMERATED, DNF_ADDED,
                      DNF_NO_RESOURCE_REQUIRED, DNF_STARTED
  DisableableDepends = 10 (from children)
  DevNode 0x818a74c8 for PDO 0x818a75d0
    Parent 0x818a78e8  Sibling 0x818a7248  Child 0x81883228
    InstancePath is "Root\ACPI_HAL\0000"
    Flags (0x000405dd)  DNF_MADEUP, DNF_HAL_NODE,
                        DNF_PROCESSED, DNF_ENUMERATED,
                        DNF_ADDED, DNF_HAS_BOOT_CONFIG,
                        DNF_BOOT_CONFIG_RESERVED, DNF_NO_RESOURCE_REQUIRED,
                        DNF_STARTED
    DisableableDepends = 1 (from children)
    DevNode 0x81883228 for PDO 0x818838d0
      Parent 0x818a74c8  Sibling 0000000000  Child 0x81819408
      InstancePath is "ACPI_HAL\PNP0C08\0"
      ServiceName is "ACPI"
```

```
Flags (0x000421d8)  DNF_PROCESSED, DNF_ENUMERATED,
                    DNF_ADDED, DNF_HAS_BOOT_CONFIG,
                    DNF_BOOT_CONFIG_RESERVED, DNF_RESOURCE_ASSIGNED,
                    DNF_STARTED
CapabilityFlags (0x000000c0)  UniqueID, SilentInstall
DisableableDepends = 10 (from children)
DevNode 0x81819408 for PDO 0x81891530
  Parent 0x81883228   Sibling 0x818910c8   Child 0000000000
  InstancePath is "ACPI\PNP0C0B\1"
  Flags (0x00040458)  DNF_PROCESSED, DNF_ENUMERATED,
                      DNF_ADDED, DNF_NO_RESOURCE_REQUIRED,
                      DNF_STARTED
  UserFlags (0x00000008)  DNUF_NOT_DISABLEABLE
  CapabilityFlags (0x000001c0)  UniqueID, SilentInstall,
                                RawDeviceOK
  DisableableDepends = 1 (including self)
⋮
```

Information shown for each devnode includes the InstancePath, which is the name of the device's enumeration registry key stored under HKLM\SYSTEM\CurrentControlSet\Enum, and the ServiceName, which corresponds to the device's driver registry key under HKLM\SYSTEM\CurrentControlSet\Services. To see the resources, such as interrupts, ports, and memory assigned to each devnode, specify *0 3* as the command options for the *!devnode* command.

A record of all the devices detected since the system was installed is recorded under the HKLM\SYSTEM\CurrentControlSet\Enum registry key. Subkeys are in the form <Enumerator>\<Device ID>\<Instance ID>, where the enumerator is a bus driver, the device ID is a unique identifier for a type of device, and the instance ID uniquely identifies different instances of the same hardware.

Devnodes

Figure 9-15 shows that a devnode is made up of at least two, and sometimes more, device objects:

- A *physical device object* (PDO) that the PnP manager instructs a bus driver to create when the bus driver reports the presence of a device on its bus during enumeration. The PDO represents the physical interface to the device.

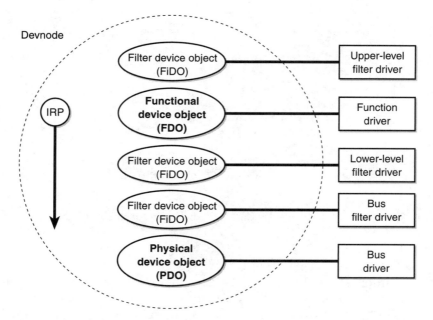

Figure 9-15
Devnode internals

- One or more optional *filter device objects* (FiDOs) that layer between the PDO and the FDO (described next), and that are created by *bus filter drivers*.

- One or more optional FiDOs that layer between the PDO and the FDO (and that layer above any FiDOs created by bus filter drivers) that are created by *lower-level filter drivers*.

- A *functional device object* (FDO) that is created by the driver, which is called a *function driver*, that the PnP manager loads to manage a detected device. An FDO represents the logical interface to a device. A function driver can also act as a bus driver if devices are attached to the device represented by the FDO. The function driver often creates an interface (described earlier) to the FDO's corresponding PDO so that applications and other drivers can open the device and interact with it. Sometimes function drivers are divided into a separate class/port driver and miniport driver that work together to manage I/O for the FDO.

- One or more optional FiDOs that layer above the FDO and that are created by *upper-level filter drivers*.

Devnodes are built from the bottom up and rely on the I/O manager's layering functionality, so IRPs flow from the top of a devnode toward the bottom. However, any level in the devnode can choose to complete an IRP. For example, the function driver can handle a read request without passing the IRP to the bus driver. Only when the function driver requires the help of a bus driver to perform bus-specific processing does the IRP flow all the way to the bottom and then into the devnode containing the bus driver.

Devnode Driver Loading

So far, we've avoided answering two important questions: How does the PnP manager determine what function driver to load for a particular device? and How do filter drivers register their presence so that they are loaded at appropriate times in the creation of a devnode?

The answer to both these questions lies in the registry. When a bus driver performs device enumeration, it reports device identifiers for the devices it detects back to the PnP manager. The identifiers are bus-specific; for a USB bus, an identifier consists of a *vendor ID* (VID) for the hardware vendor that made the device and a *product ID* (PID) that the vendor assigned to the device. (See the DDK for more information on device ID formats.) Together these IDs form what Plug and Play calls a *device ID*. The PnP manager also queries the bus driver for an *instance ID* to help it distinguish different instances of the same hardware. The instance ID can describe either a bus relative location (for example, the USB port) or a globally unique descriptor (for example, a serial number). The device ID and instance ID are combined to form a *device instance ID* (DIID), which the PnP manager uses to locate the device's key in the enumeration branch of the registry (HKLM\SYSTEM\CurrentControlSet\Enum). Figure 9-16 presents an example of a keyboard's enumeration subkey. The device's key contains descriptive data and includes values named Service and ClassGUID (which is obtained from a driver's INF file) that help the PnP manager locate the device's drivers.

Figure 9-16
Keyboard enumeration key

Using the ClassGUID value, the PnP manager locates the device's class key under HKLM\SYSTEM\CurrentControlSet\Control\Class. The keyboard class key is shown in Figure 9-17. The enumeration key and class key supply the PnP manager the information it needs to load the drivers necessary for the device's devnode. Drivers are loaded in the following order:

1. Any lower-level filter drivers specified in the LowerFilters value of the device's enumeration key.

2. Any lower-level filter drivers specified in the LowerFilters value of the device's class key.

3. The function driver specified by the Service value in the device's enumeration key. This value is interpreted as the driver's key under HKLM\SYSTEM\CurrentControlSet\Services.

4. Any upper-level filter drivers specified in the UpperFilters value of the device's enumeration key.

5. Any upper-level filter drivers specified in the UpperFilters value of the device's class key.

In all cases, drivers are referenced by the name of their key under HKLM\SYSTEM\CurrentControlSet\Services.

Figure 9-17
Keyboard class key

> **NOTE** The DDK refers to a device's enumeration key as its *hardware key* and to the class key as the *software key*.

The keyboard device shown in Figure 9-16 and Figure 9-17 has no lower filter drivers. The function driver is the i8042prt driver, and there are two upper filter drivers specified in the keyboard's class key: kbdclass and ctrl2cap.

Driver Installation

If the PnP manager encounters a device for which no driver is installed, it relies on the user-mode PnP manager to guide the installation process. If the device is detected during the system boot, a devnode is defined for the device but the loading process is postponed until the user-mode PnP manager starts. (The user-mode PnP manager is implemented in \Winnt\System32\Umpnpmgr.dll and runs as a service in the Services.exe process.)

The components involved in a driver's installation are shown in Figure 9-18. Shaded objects in the figure correspond to components generally supplied by the system, whereas objects that aren't shaded are included in a driver's installation files. First, a bus driver informs the PnP manager of a device it enumerates using a DIID (1). The PnP manager checks the registry for the presence of a corresponding function driver, and when it doesn't find one, it informs the user-mode PnP manager (2) of the new device by its DIID. The user-mode PnP manager first tries to perform an automatic install without user intervention.

If the installation process involves the posting of dialog boxes that require user interaction and the currently logged-on user has administrator privileges, (3) the user-mode PnP manager launches the Rundll32.exe application (the same application that hosts Control Panel utilities) to execute the Hardware Installation Wizard (\Winnt\System32\Newdev.dll). If the currently logged-on user doesn't have administrator privileges (or if no user is logged on) and the installation of the device requires user interaction, the user-mode PnP manager defers the installation until a privileged user logs on. The Hardware Installation Wizard uses Setup and CfgMgr (Configuration Manager) API functions to locate INF files that correspond to drivers that are compatible with the detected device. This process might involve having the user insert installation media containing a vendor's INF files, or the wizard might locate a suitable INF file in the .cab (Cabinet) file under \Winnt\Driver Cache\i386\Driver.cab that contains drivers that ship with Windows 2000.

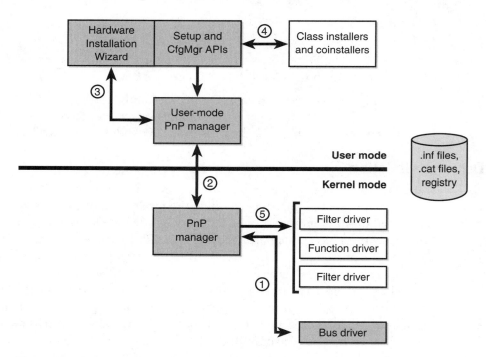

Figure 9-18
Driver installation components

To find drivers for the new device, the installation process gets a list of *hardware IDs* and *compatible IDs* from the bus driver. These IDs describe all the various ways the hardware might be identified in a driver installation file (.inf).

The lists are ordered so that the most specific description of the hardware is listed first. If matches are found in multiple INFs, more precise matches are preferred over less precise matches, digitally signed INFs are preferred over unsigned ones, and newer signed INFs are preferred over older signed ones. If a match is found based on a compatible ID, the Hardware Installation Wizard can choose to prompt for media in case a more up-to-date driver came with the hardware.

The INF file locates the function driver's files and contains commands that fill in the driver's enumeration and class keys, and the INF file might direct the Hardware Installation Wizard to (4) launch class or device coinstaller DLLs that perform class or device-specific installation steps, such as displaying configuration dialog boxes that let the user specify settings for a device.

Before actually installing a driver, the user-mode PnP manager checks the system's driver-signing policy. The policy is stored in the registry key HKLM\SOFTWARE\Microsoft\Driver Signing\Policy if the administrator has designated a systemwide policy and in the key HKCU\Software\Microsoft\Driver Signing\Policy if there are only per-user policies. The policy is configurable using the Driver Signing Options dialog box, accessed from the Hardware tab in the System Control Panel utility, which is shown in Figure 9-19. If the settings specify that the system should block or warn of the installation of unsigned drivers, the user-mode PnP manager checks the driver's INF file for an entry that locates a catalog (a file that ends with the .cat extension) containing the driver's digital signature.

Figure 9-19
Driver-signing policy options

Microsoft's WHQL tests the drivers included with Windows 2000 and those submitted by hardware vendors. When a driver passes the WHQL tests, it is "signed" by Microsoft. This means that WHQL obtains a *hash*, or unique value representing the driver image file, and then cryptographically signs it with Microsoft's private driver-signing key. The signed hash is stored in a catalog file and included on the Windows 2000 installation media or returned to the vendor that submitted the driver for inclusion with its driver.

As it's installing a driver, the user-mode PnP manager extracts the driver's signature from its catalog file, decrypts the signature using the public half of Microsoft's driver-signing private/public key pair, and compares the resulting hash with a hash of the driver file it's about to install. If the hashes match, the driver is verified as having passed WHQL testing. If a driver fails the signature verification, the user-mode PnP manager acts according to the settings of the system driver-signing policy, either failing the installation attempt, warning the user that the driver is unsigned, or silently installing the driver.

> **NOTE** Drivers installed using setup programs that manually configure the registry and copy driver files to a system and driver files that are dynamically loaded by applications aren't checked for signatures. Only drivers installed using INF files are validated against the system's driver-signing policy.

After a driver is installed, the kernel-mode PnP manager (step 5 in Figure 9-18) starts the driver and calls its add-device routine to inform the driver of the presence of the device it was loaded for. The construction of the devnode then continues as described earlier.

I/O Processing

Now that we've covered the structure and types of drivers and the data structures that support them, let's look at how I/O requests flow through the system. I/O requests pass through several predictable stages of processing. The stages vary depending on whether the request is destined for a device operated by a single-layered driver or for a device reached through a multilayered driver. Processing varies further depending on whether the caller specified synchronous or asynchronous I/O, so we'll begin our discussion of I/O types with these two then move on to others.

Types of I/O

Applications have several options for the I/O requests they issue. For example, they can specify synchronous or asynchronous I/O, I/O that maps a device's data into the application's address space for access via application virtual memory rather than I/O APIs, and I/O that transfers data between a device and noncontiguous application buffers in a single request. Furthermore, the I/O manager gives the drivers the choice of implementing a shortcut I/O interface that can often mitigate IRP allocation for I/O processing. In this section, we'll explain each of these I/O variations.

Synchronous I/O and Asynchronous I/O

Most I/O operations that applications issue are *synchronous*; that is, the application waits while the device performs the data transfer and returns a status code when the I/O is complete. The program can then continue and access the transferred data immediately. When used in their simplest form, the Win32 *ReadFile* and *WriteFile* functions are executed synchronously. They complete an I/O operation before returning control to the caller.

Asynchronous I/O allows an application to issue an I/O request and then continue executing while the device transfers the data. This type of I/O can improve an application's throughput because it allows the application to continue with other work while an I/O operation is in progress. To use asynchronous I/O, you must specify the FILE_FLAG_OVERLAPPED flag when you call the Win32 *CreateFile* function. Of course, after issuing an asynchronous I/O operation, the thread must be careful not to access any data from the I/O operation until the device driver has finished the data transfer. The thread must synchronize its execution with the completion of the I/O request by monitoring a handle of a synchronization object (whether that's an event object, an I/O completion port, or the file object itself) that will be signaled when the I/O is complete.

Regardless of the type of I/O request, internally, I/O operations represented by IRPs are performed asynchronously; that is, once an I/O request has been initiated, the device driver returns to the I/O system. Whether or not the I/O system returns immediately to the caller depends on whether the file was opened for synchronous or asynchronous I/O. Figure 9-20 illustrates the flow of control when a read operation is initiated. Notice that if a wait is done, which depends on the overlapped flag in the file object, it is done in kernel mode by the *NtReadFile* function.

Figure 9-20
Control flow for an I/O operation

You can test the status of a pending asynchronous I/O with the Win32 *HasOverlappedIoCompleted* function. If you're using I/O completion ports, you can use the *GetQueuedCompletionStatus* function.

Fast I/O

Fast I/O is a special mechanism that allows the I/O system to bypass generating an IRP and instead go directly to the file system driver or cache manager to complete an I/O request. (Fast I/O is described in detail in Chapters 11 and 12.) A driver registers its fast I/O entry points by entering them in a structure pointed to by the PFAST_IO_DISPATCH pointer in its driver object.

EXPERIMENT: Looking at a Driver's Registered Fast I/O Routines

The *!drvobj* kernel debugger command can list the fast I/O routines that a driver registers in its driver object. However, typically only file system drivers have any use for fast I/O routines. The following output shows the fast I/O table for the NTFS file system driver object:

```
kd> !drvobj \filesystem\ntfs 2
Driver object (ff432670) is for:
 \FileSystem\Ntfs
Dispatch routines:
[00] IRP_MJ_CREATE
 ⋮

Fast I/O routines:
FastIoCheckIfPossible                  be3263ef
Ntfs!NtfsPostUsnChange+0xd8c
FastIoRead                             be31869e
Ntfs!NtfsCreateInternalStreamCommon+0x1b43
FastIoWrite                            be318df9
Ntfs!NtfsCreateInternalStreamCommon+0x229e
FastIoQueryBasicInfo                   be3020fa
Ntfs!NtfsRaiseStatus+0x105a8
FastIoQueryStandardInfo                be317d1e
Ntfs!NtfsCreateInternalStreamCommon+0x11c3
FastIoLock                             be32622d
Ntfs!NtfsPostUsnChange+0xbca
FastIoUnlockSingle                     be326139
Ntfs!NtfsPostUsnChange+0xad6
 ⋮
```

The output shows that NTFS has registered its *NtfsPostUsnChange* routine as the fast I/O table's *FastIoCheckIfPossible* entry. As the name of this fast I/O entry implies, the I/O manager sometimes calls this function before issuing a fast I/O request, giving a driver an opportunity to indicate when fast I/O operations on a file are not feasible.

Mapped File I/O and File Caching

Mapped file I/O is an important feature of the I/O system, one that the I/O system and the memory manager produce jointly. (See Chapter 7 for details on how mapped files are implemented.) *Mapped file I/O* refers to the ability to view a file residing on disk as part of a process's virtual memory. A program can access the file as a large array without buffering data or performing disk I/O. The

program accesses memory, and the memory manager uses its paging mechanism to load the correct page from the disk file. If the application writes to its virtual address space, the memory manager writes the changes back to the file as part of normal paging.

Mapped file I/O is available in user mode through the Win32 *CreateFile-Mapping* and *MapViewOfFile* functions. Within the operating system, mapped file I/O is used for important operations such as file caching and image activation (loading and running executable programs). The other major consumer of mapped file I/O is the cache manager. File systems use the cache manager to map file data in virtual memory to provide better response time for I/O-bound programs. As the caller uses the file, the memory manager brings accessed pages into memory. Whereas most caching systems allocate a fixed number of bytes for caching files in memory, the Windows 2000 cache grows or shrinks depending on how much memory is available. This size variability is possible because the cache manager relies on the memory manager to automatically expand (or shrink) the size of the cache, using the normal working set mechanisms explained in Chapter 7. By taking advantage of the memory manager's paging system, the cache manager avoids duplicating the work that the memory manager already performs. (The workings of the cache manager are explained in detail in Chapter 11.)

Scatter/Gather I/O

Windows 2000 also supports a special kind of high-performance I/O that is called *scatter/gather,* available via the Win32 *ReadFileScatter* and *WriteFile-Gather* functions. These functions allow an application to issue a single read or write from more than one buffer in virtual memory to a contiguous area of a file on disk. To use scatter/gather I/O, the file must be opened for noncached I/O, the user buffers being used have to be page-aligned, and the I/Os must be asynchronous (overlapped). Furthermore, if the I/O is directed at a mass storage device, the I/O must be aligned on a device sector boundary and have a length that is a multiple of the sector size.

I/O Request to a Single-Layered Driver

This section traces a synchronous I/O request to a single-layered kernel-mode device driver. Handling a synchronous I/O to a single-layered driver consists of seven steps:

1. The I/O request passes through a subsystem DLL.

2. The subsystem DLL calls the I/O manager's *NtWriteFile* service.

3. The I/O manager allocates an IRP describing the request and sends it to the driver (a device driver in this case) by calling its own *IoCall-Driver* function.

4. The driver transfers the data in the IRP to the device and starts the I/O operation.

5. The driver signals I/O completion by interrupting the CPU.

6. When the device completes the operation and interrupts the CPU, the device driver services the interrupt.

7. The driver calls the I/O manager's *IoCompleteRequest* function to inform it that it has finished processing the IRP's request, and the I/O manager completes the I/O request.

These seven steps are illustrated in Figure 9-21.

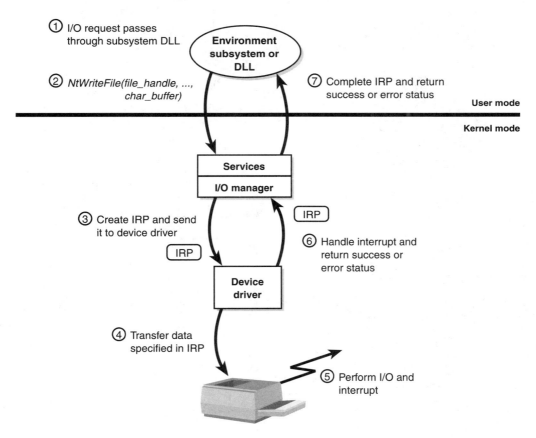

Figure 9-21
Queuing and completing a synchronous request

Now that we've seen how an I/O is initiated, let's take a closer look at interrupt processing and I/O completion.

Servicing an Interrupt

After an I/O device completes a data transfer, it interrupts for service and the Windows 2000 kernel, I/O manager, and device driver are called into action. Figure 9-22 illustrates the first phase of the process. (Chapter 3 describes the interrupt dispatching mechanism, including DPCs. We've included a brief re-cap here because DPCs are key to I/O processing.)

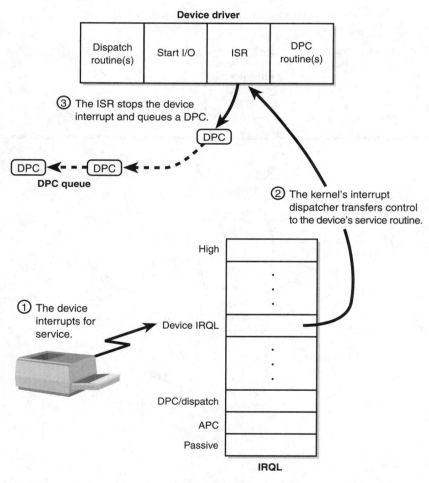

Figure 9-22
Servicing a device interrupt (phase 1)

When a device interrupt occurs, the processor transfers control to the kernel trap handler, which indexes into its interrupt dispatch table to locate the ISR for the device. ISRs in Windows 2000 typically handle device interrupts in two steps. When an ISR is first invoked, it usually remains at device IRQL only long enough to capture the device status and then stop the device's interrupt. It then queues a DPC and exits, dismissing the interrupt. Later, when the DPC routine is called, the device finishes processing the interrupt. When that's done, the device calls the I/O manager to complete the I/O and dispose of the IRP. It might also start the next I/O request that is waiting in the device queue.

The advantage of using a DPC to perform most of the device servicing is that any blocked interrupt whose priority lies between the device IRQL and the DPC/dispatch IRQL is allowed to occur before the lower-priority DPC processing occurs. Intermediate-level interrupts are thus serviced more promptly than they otherwise would be. This second phase of an I/O (the DPC processing) is illustrated in Figure 9-23.

Completing an I/O Request

After a device driver's DPC routine has executed, some work still remains before the I/O request can be considered finished. This third stage of I/O processing is called *I/O completion* and is initiated when a driver calls *IoCompleteRequest* to inform the I/O manager that it is through processing the request specified in the IRP (and the stack location that it owns). The steps I/O completion entails vary with different I/O operations. For example, all the I/O services record the outcome of the operation in an *I/O status block,* a data structure the caller supplies. Similarly, some services that perform buffered I/O require the I/O system to return data to the calling thread.

In both cases, the I/O system must copy some data that is stored in system memory into the caller's virtual address space. If the IRP completed synchronously, the caller's address space is current and directly accessible, but if the IRP completed asynchronously, the I/O manager must delay IRP completion until it can access the caller's address space. To gain access to the caller's virtual address space, the I/O manager must transfer the data "in the context of the caller's thread"—that is, while the caller's thread is executing (which means that caller's process is the current process and has its address space active on the processor). It does so by queuing a kernel-mode asynchronous procedure call (APC) to the thread. This process is illustrated in Figure 9-24.

As explained in Chapter 3, APCs execute in the context of a particular thread, whereas a DPC executes in arbitrary thread context, meaning that the DPC routine can't touch the user-mode process address space. Remember too that DPCs have a higher software interrupt priority than APCs.

Figure 9-23
Servicing a device interrupt (phase 2)

I/O manager

IRP

② The I/O manager queues an APC to complete the I/O request in the caller's context.

① The DPC routine calls the I/O manager to complete the original I/O request.

IRP

APC

Device driver

| Dispatch routine(s) | Start I/O | ISR | DPC routine(s) |

IRP

APC

IRP

APC

Thread's APC queue

Figure 9-24
Completing an I/O request (phase 1)

The next time that thread begins to execute at low IRQL, the pending APC is delivered. The kernel transfers control to the I/O manager's APC routine, which copies the data (if any) and the return status into the original caller's address space, frees the IRP representing the I/O operation, and sets the caller's file handle (and any caller-supplied event or I/O completion port) to the signaled state. The I/O is now considered complete. The original caller or any other threads that are waiting on the file (or other object) handle are released from their waiting state and readied for execution.

Figure 9-25 illustrates the second stage of I/O completion.

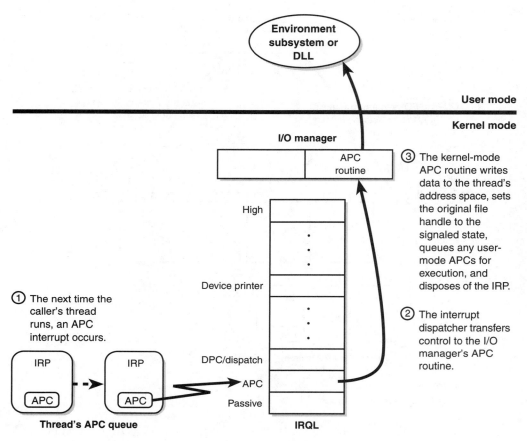

Figure 9-25
Completing an I/O request (phase 2)

A final note about I/O completion: the asynchronous I/O functions *Read-FileEx* and *WriteFileEx* allow a caller to supply a user-mode APC as a parameter. If the caller does so, the I/O manager queues this APC to the caller's thread APC queue as the last step of I/O completion. This feature allows a caller to specify a subroutine to be called when an I/O request is completed or canceled. User-mode APC completion routines execute in the context of the requesting thread and are delivered only when the thread enters an alertable wait state (such as calling the Win32 *SleepEx*, *WaitForSingleObjectEx*, or *WaitForMultipleObjectsEx* function).

I/O Requests to Layered Drivers

The preceding section showed how an I/O request to a simple device controlled by a single device driver is handled. I/O processing for file-based devices or for requests to other layered drivers happens in much the same way. The major difference is, obviously, that one or more additional layers of processing are added to the model.

Figure 9-26 shows how an asynchronous I/O request travels through layered drivers. It uses as an example a disk controlled by a file system.

Once again, the I/O manager receives the request and creates an I/O request packet to represent it. This time, however, it delivers the packet to a file system driver. The file system driver exercises great control over the I/O operation at that point. Depending on the type of request the caller made, the file system can send the same IRP to the disk driver or it can generate additional IRPs and send them separately to the disk driver.

The file system is most likely to reuse an IRP if the request it receives translates into a single straightforward request to a device. For example, if an application issues a read request for the first 512 bytes in a file stored on a floppy disk, the FAT file system would simply call the disk driver, asking it to read one sector from the floppy disk, beginning at the file's starting location.

To accommodate its reuse by multiple drivers in a request to layered drivers, an IRP contains a series of *IRP stack locations* (not to be confused with the stack used by threads to store function parameters and return addresses). These data areas, one for every driver that will be called, contain the information that each driver needs in order to execute its part of the request—for example, function code, parameters, and driver context information. As Figure 9-26 illustrates, additional stack locations are filled in as the IRP passes from one driver to the next. You can think of an IRP as being similar to a stack in the way data is added to it and removed from it during its lifetime. However, an IRP isn't associated with any particular process, and its allocated size doesn't grow and shrink. The I/O manager allocates an IRP from one if its IRP look-aside lists or nonpaged system memory at the beginning of the I/O operation.

After the disk driver finishes a data transfer, the disk interrupts and the I/O completes, as shown in Figure 9-27.

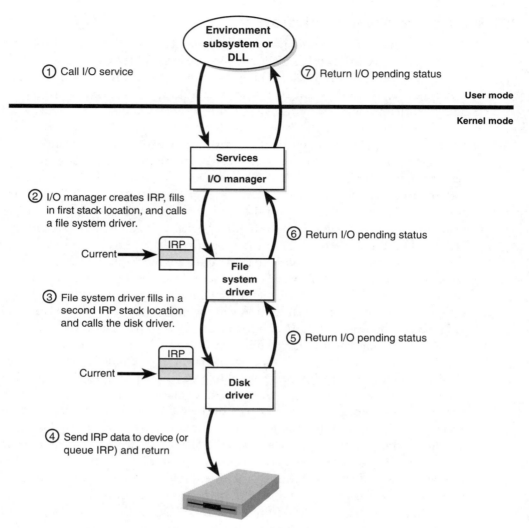

Figure 9-26
Queuing an asynchronous request to layered drivers

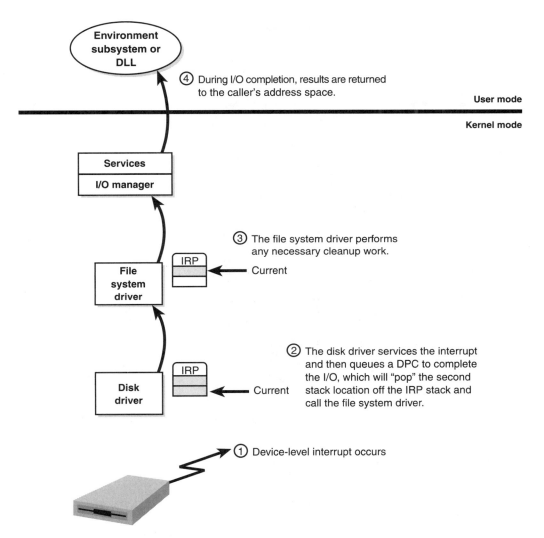

Figure 9-27
Completing a layered I/O request

As an alternative to reusing a single IRP, a file system can establish a group of *associated* IRPs that work in parallel on a single I/O request. For example, if the data to be read from a file is dispersed across the disk, the file system driver might create several IRPs, each of which reads some portion of the request from a different sector. This queuing is illustrated in Figure 9-28.

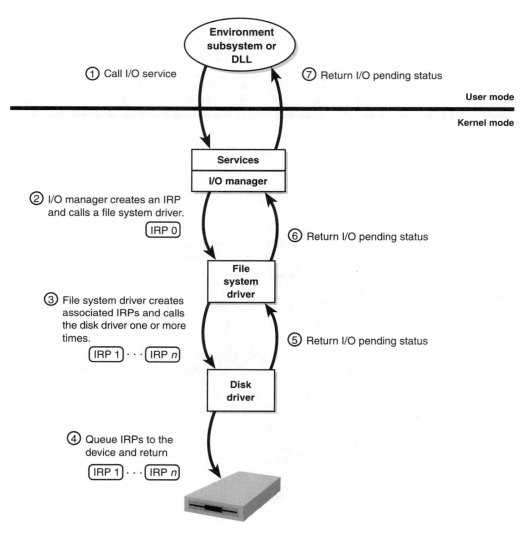

Figure 9-28
Queuing associated IRPs

The file system driver delivers the associated IRPs to the device driver, which queues them to the device. They are processed one at a time, and the file system driver keeps track of the returned data. When all the associated IRPs complete, the I/O system completes the original IRP and returns to the caller, as shown in Figure 9-29.

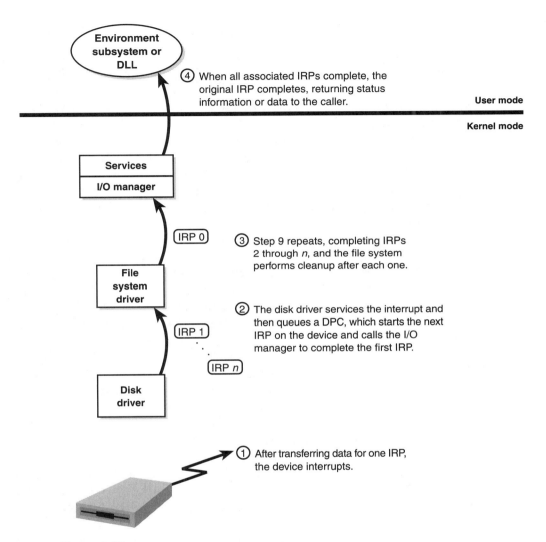

Figure 9-29
Completing associated IRPs

NOTE All Windows 2000 file system drivers that manage disk-based file systems are part of a stack of drivers that is at least three layers deep: the file system driver sits at the top, a volume manager in the middle, and a disk driver at the bottom. In addition, any number of filter drivers can be interspersed above and below these drivers. For clarity, the preceding example of layered I/O requests includes only a file system driver and a disk device driver. See Chapter 10, on storage management, for more information.

I/O Completion Port Operation

Win32 applications create completion ports by calling the Win32 API *CreateIo-CompletionPort* and specifying a NULL completion port handle. This results in the execution of the *NtCreateIoCompletion* system service. The executive's *IoCompletion* object is based on the kernel synchronization object called a *queue*. Thus, the system service creates a completion port object and initializes a queue object in the port's allocated memory. (A pointer to the port also points to the queue object because the queue is at the start of the port memory.) A queue object has a concurrency value that is specified when a thread initializes one, and in this case the value that is used is the one that was passed to *CreateIo-CompletionPort*. *KeInitializeQueue* is the function that *NtCreateIoCompletion* calls to initialize a port's queue object.

When an application calls *CreateIoCompletionPort* to associate a file handle with a port, the *NtSetInformationFile* system service is executed with the file handle as the primary parameter. The information class that is set is *FileCompletion-Information*, and the completion port's handle and the *CompletionKey* parameter from *CreateIoCompletionPort* are the data values. *NtSetInformationFile* dereferences the file handle to obtain the file object and allocates a completion context data structure.

Finally, *NtSetInformationFile* sets the *CompletionContext* field in the file object to point at the context structure. When an asynchronous I/O operation completes on a file object, the I/O manager checks to see whether the *CompletionContext* field in the file object is non-NULL. If it is, the I/O manager allocates a completion packet and queues it to the completion port by calling *KeInsertQueue* with the port as the queue on which to insert the packet. (Remember that the completion port object and queue object are synonymous.)

When a server thread invokes *GetQueuedCompletionStatus*, the system service *NtRemoveIoCompletion* is executed. After validating parameters and translating the completion port handle to a pointer to the port, *NtRemoveIo-Completion* calls *KeRemoveQueue*.

As you can see, *KeRemoveQueue* and *KeInsertQueue* are the engines behind completion ports. They are the functions that determine whether a thread waiting for an I/O completion packet should be activated. Internally, a queue object maintains a count of the current number of active threads and the maximum number of active threads. If the current number equals or exceeds the maximum when a thread calls *KeRemoveQueue*, the thread will be put (in LIFO order) onto a list of threads waiting for a turn to process a completion packet. The list of threads hangs off the queue object. A thread's control block data

structure has a pointer in it that references the queue object of a queue that it's associated with; if the pointer is NULL, the thread isn't associated with a queue.

Windows 2000 keeps track of threads that become inactive because they block on something other than the completion port by relying on the queue pointer in a thread's control block. The scheduler routines that possibly result in a thread blocking (such as *KeWaitForSingleObject*, *KeDelayExecutionThread*, and so on) check the thread's queue pointer. If the pointer isn't NULL, the functions call *KiActivateWaiterQueue*, a queue-related function that decrements the count of active threads associated with the queue. If the resultant number is less than the maximum and at least one completion packet is in the queue, the thread at the front of the queue's thread list is awakened and given the oldest packet. Conversely, whenever a thread that is associated with a queue wakes up after blocking, the scheduler executes the function *KiUnwaitThread*, which increments the queue's active count.

Finally, the *PostQueuedCompletionStatus* Win32 API function results in the execution of the *NtSetIoCompletion* system service. This function simply inserts the specified packet onto the completion port's queue by using *KeInsertQueue*.

Figure 9-30 shows an example of a completion port object in operation. Even though two threads are ready to process completion packets, the concurrency value of 1 allows only one thread associated with the completion port to be active, and so the two threads are blocked on the completion port.

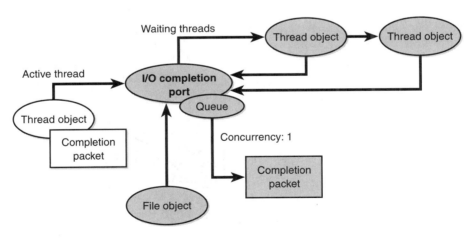

Figure 9-30
I/O completion port operation

Synchronization

Drivers must synchronize their access to global driver data and hardware registers for two reasons:

- The execution of a driver can be preempted by higher-priority threads and time-slice (or quantum) expiration or can be interrupted by interrupts.

- On multiprocessor systems, Windows 2000 can run driver code simultaneously on more than one processor.

Without synchronization, corruption could occur—for example, because device driver code running at a passive IRQL when a caller initiates an I/O operation can be interrupted by a device interrupt, causing the device driver's ISR to execute while its own device driver is already running. If the device driver was modifying data that its ISR also modifies, such as device registers, heap storage, or static data, the data can become corrupted when the ISR executes. Figure 9-31 illustrates this problem.

Figure 9-31
Queuing an asynchronous request to layered drivers

To avoid this situation, a device driver written for Windows 2000 must synchronize its access to any data that the device driver shares with its ISR. Before

attempting to update shared data, the device driver must lock out all other threads (or CPUs, in the case of a multiprocessor system) to prevent them from updating the same data structure.

The Windows 2000 kernel provides special synchronization routines that device drivers must call when they access data that their ISRs also access. These kernel-synchronization routines keep the ISR from executing while the shared data is being accessed. On a single CPU system, these routines raise the IRQL to a specified level before updating a structure. On a multiprocessor system, however, because a driver can execute on two or more processors at once, this technique isn't enough to block other accessors. Therefore, another mechanism, a *spinlock,* is used to lock a structure for exclusive access from a particular CPU. (Spinlocks are explained in the section "Kernel Synchronization" in Chapter 3.)

By now, you should realize that although ISRs require special attention, any data that a device driver uses is subject to being accessed by the same device driver running on another processor. Therefore, it's critical for device driver code to synchronize its use of any global or shared data (or any accesses to the physical device itself). If the ISR uses that data, the device driver must use kernel-synchronization routines; otherwise, the device driver can use a kernel spinlock.

Conclusion

The I/O system defines the model of I/O processing on Windows 2000 and performs functions that are common to or required by more than one driver. Its chief responsibility is to create IRPs representing I/O requests and to shepherd the packets through various drivers, returning results to the caller when an I/O is complete. The I/O manager locates various drivers and devices by using I/O system objects, including driver and device objects. Internally, the Windows 2000 I/O system operates asynchronously to achieve high performance and provides both synchronous and asynchronous I/O capabilities to user-mode applications.

Device drivers include not only traditional hardware device drivers but also file system, network, and layered filter drivers. All drivers have a common structure and communicate with one another and the I/O manager by using common mechanisms. The I/O system interfaces allow drivers to be written in a high-level language to lessen development time and to enhance their portability. Because drivers present a common structure to the operating system, they

can be layered one on top of another to achieve modularity and reduce duplication between drivers. Also, all Windows 2000 device drivers should be designed to work correctly on multiprocessor systems.

Finally, the role of the PnP manager is to work with device drivers to dynamically detect hardware devices and to build an internal device tree that guides hardware device enumeration and driver installation. The power manager works with device drivers to move devices into low-power states when applicable to conserve energy and prolong battery life.

The final four chapters cover additional topics related to the I/O system: storage management, file systems (including details on the NTFS file system), the cache manager, and networking.

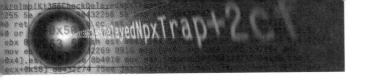

Storage Management

Storage management defines the way that an operating system interfaces with nonvolatile storage devices and media. The term *storage* encompasses many different devices, including tape drives, optical media, CD jukeboxes, floppy diskettes, and hard disks. Microsoft Windows 2000 provides specialized support for each of these classes of storage media. Because our focus in this book is on the kernel components of Windows 2000, in this chapter we'll concentrate on just the fundamentals of the hard disk storage subsystem in Windows 2000. Significant portions of the Windows 2000 support for removable media and remote storage (offline archiving) are implemented in user mode.

In this chapter, we'll define basic and dynamic disks and explain how they are partitioned. We'll then examine how kernel-mode device drivers interface file system drivers to disk media. We'll also go over the implementation of multipartition disk-management features in Windows 2000, including replicating and dividing file system data across physical disks for reliability and for performance enhancement. We conclude the chapter with a look at the process that Windows 2000 uses to assign drive letters and a discussion of how file system drivers mount volumes they are responsible for managing.

The Evolution of Windows 2000 Storage

The evolution of storage management in Windows 2000 begins with MS-DOS, Microsoft's first operating system. As hard disks became larger, MS-DOS needed to accommodate them. To do so, one of the first steps Microsoft took was to let MS-DOS create multiple partitions, or logical disks, on a physical disk. MS-DOS could format each partition with a different file system type (FAT12 or FAT16) and assign each partition a different drive letter. MS-DOS versions 3 and 4 were severely limited in the size and number of partitions they could create, but in MS-DOS 5 the partitioning scheme fully matured. MS-DOS 5 was able to divide a disk into any number of partitions of any size.

Windows NT borrowed the partitioning scheme that evolved in MS-DOS both to provide disk compatibility with MS-DOS and Windows 3.x and to let the Windows NT development team rely on proven tools for disk management. Microsoft extended the basic concepts of MS-DOS disk partitioning in Windows NT to support storage-management features that an enterprise-class operating system requires: disk spanning and fault tolerance. Starting with the first version of Windows NT, version 3.1, systems administrators have been able to create volumes that comprise multiple partitions, which allows large volumes to consist of partitions from multiple physical disks and to implement fault tolerance through software-based data redundancy.

Although this MS-DOS-style partitioning support in versions of Windows NT prior to Windows 2000 is flexible enough to support most storage-management tasks, it suffers from several drawbacks. One drawback is that most disk-configuration changes require a reboot before taking effect. In today's world of servers that must remain on line for months or even years at a time, any reboot—even a planned reboot—is a major inconvenience. Another drawback is that the Windows NT 4 registry stores multipartition disk-configuration information for MS-DOS-style partitions. This arrangement means that moving configuration information is onerous when you move disks between systems, and you can easily lose configuration information when you need to reinstall the operating system. Finally, a requirement that each volume have a unique drive letter in the A through Z range plagues users of all Microsoft operating systems prior to Windows 2000 with an upper limit on the number of possible local and remote volumes they can create.

To fully understand the rest of this chapter, you need to be familiar with some basic terminology:

- *Disks* are a physical storage device such as a hard disk, a 3.5-inch floppy disk, or a CD-ROM.

- A disk is divided into *sectors,* addressable blocks of fixed size. Sector sizes are determined by hardware. All current x86-processor hard disk sectors are 512 bytes, and CD-ROM sectors are typically 2048 bytes. (Future x86 systems might support larger hard disk sector sizes.)

- *Partitions* are collections of contiguous sectors on a disk. A partition table or other disk-management database stores a partition's starting sector, size, and other characteristics.

- *Simple volumes* are objects that represent sectors from a single partition that file system drivers manage as a single unit.

■ *Multipartition volumes* are objects that represent sectors from multiple partitions and that file system drivers manage as a single unit. Multipartition volumes offer performance, reliability, and sizing features that simple volumes do not.

Partitioning

Windows 2000 introduces the concept of *basic* and *dynamic* disks. Windows 2000 calls disks that rely on the MS-DOS-style partitioning scheme basic disks. In a sense, basic disks are Windows 2000 legacy disks. Dynamic disks are new to Windows 2000 and implement a more flexible partitioning scheme than that of basic disks. The fundamental difference between basic and dynamic disks is that dynamic disks support the creation of new multipartition volumes. (Basic disks support only multipartition volumes carried forward from an upgraded Windows NT 4 installation.) Recall from the list of terms in the preceding section that multipartition volumes provide performance, sizing, and reliability features not supported by simple volumes. Multipartition-volume configuration information for basic disks is stored in the registry; storage of multipartition-volume configuration information for dynamic disks is on-disk. Storing multipartition-volume configuration information on-disk rather than in the registry ties the dynamic disk to the storage it describes, so losing configuration data is less likely and moving disks between systems is easier.

Windows 2000 manages all disks as basic disks unless you manually create dynamic disks or convert existing basic disks (with enough free space) to dynamic disks. To encourage administrators to use dynamic disks, Microsoft has imposed some usage limitations on basic disks. For example, you can create new multipartition volumes only on dynamic disks. (If you upgrade a Windows NT 4 system, Windows 2000 will support existing multipartition volumes.) Another limitation is that Windows 2000 lets you dynamically grow NTFS volumes only on dynamic disks. A disadvantage to dynamic disks is that the partitioning format they use is proprietary and incompatible with other operating systems, including all other versions of Windows. Thus, you can't access dynamic disks in a dual-boot environment.

NOTE For a number of reasons, including the fact that laptops usually have only one disk and laptop disks typically don't move easily between computers, Windows 2000 uses only basic disks on laptops. In addition, only fixed disks can be dynamic, and disks located on IEEE 1394 or USB buses as well as on shared cluster server disks are always basic disks.

Basic Partitioning

When you install Windows 2000 on a computer, one of the first things it requires you to do is to create a partition on the system's primary physical disk. Windows 2000 defines the system volume on this partition to store the files that it invokes early in the boot process. In addition, Windows 2000 Setup requires you to create a partition that serves as the home for the boot volume, onto which the setup program installs the Windows 2000 system files and creates the system directory (\Winnt). The system and boot volumes can be the same volume, in which case you don't have to create a new partition for the boot volume. The nomenclature that Microsoft defines for system and boot volumes is somewhat confusing. The system volume is where Windows 2000 places boot files, including the boot loader (Ntldr) and Ntdetect, and the boot volume is where Windows 2000 stores operating system files such as Ntoskrnl.exe, the core kernel file.

The standard BIOS implementations that x86 hardware uses dictate one requirement of the partitioning format in Windows 2000—that the first sector of the primary disk contains the master boot record (MBR). When an x86 processor boots, the computer's BIOS reads the MBR and treats part of the MBR's contents as executable code. The BIOS invokes the MBR code to initiate an operating system boot process after the BIOS performs preliminary configuration of the computer's hardware. In Microsoft operating systems, including Windows 2000, the MBR also contains a *partition table*. A partition table consists of four entries that define the locations of as many as four *primary partitions* on a disk. The partition table also records a partition's type. Numerous predefined partition types exist, and a partition's type specifies which file system the partition includes. For example, partition types exist for FAT32 and NTFS. A special partition type, an *extended partition,* contains another MBR with its own partition table. By using extended partitions, Microsoft's operating systems overcome the apparent limit of four partitions per disk. In general, the recursion that extended partitions permit can continue indefinitely, which means that no upper limit exists to the number of possible partitions on a disk. Figure 4-1 on page 179 shows an example disk-partitioning scenario. The Windows 2000 boot process makes evident the distinction between primary and extended partitions. The system must mark one primary partition of the primary disk as active. The Windows 2000 code in the MBR loads the code stored in the first sector of the active partition (the system volume) into memory and then transfers control to that code. Because of the role in the boot process played by this first sector in the primary partition, Windows 2000 designates the first sector of any partition as the boot sector. Recall from Chapter 4 that every partition formatted

with a file system has a boot sector that stores information about the structure of the file system on that partition.

> **NOTE** Because Windows 2000 doesn't support the creation of multipartition volumes on basic disks, a new basic disk partition (as opposed to a multipartition volume migrated from a Windows NT 4 upgrade) is the equivalent of a volume. For this reason, the Disk Management MMC snap-in uses the term *partition* when you create a volume on a basic disk.

Dynamic Partitioning

As we've stated, dynamic disks are the favored disk format in Windows 2000 and are necessary for creating new multipartition volumes. The Logical Disk Manager (LDM) subsystem in Windows 2000, which consists of user-mode and device driver components, oversees dynamic disks. Microsoft licenses LDM from VERITAS Software, which originally developed LDM technology for UNIX systems. Working closely with Microsoft, VERITAS ported its LDM to Windows 2000 to provide the operating system with more robust partitioning and multipartition volume capabilities. A major difference between LDM's partitioning and MS-DOS-style partitioning is that LDM maintains one unified database that stores partitioning information for all the dynamic disks on a system—including multipartition-volume configuration. LDM's UNIX version incorporates *disk groups*, in which all the dynamic disks that the system assigns to a disk group share a common database. VERITAS's commercial volume-management software for Windows 2000 also includes disk groups, but the Windows 2000 LDM implementation includes only one disk group.

The LDM database resides in a 1-MB reserved space at the end of each dynamic disk. The need for this space is the reason Windows 2000 requires free space at the end of a basic disk before you can convert it to a dynamic disk. Although the partitioning data of a dynamic disk resides in the LDM database, LDM implements an MS-DOS-style partition table so that legacy disk-management utilities, including those that run under Windows 2000 and under other operating systems in dual-boot environments, don't mistakenly believe a dynamic disk is unpartitioned. Because LDM partitions aren't described in the MS-DOS-style partition table of a disk, they are called *soft partitions*; MS-DOS-style partitions are called *hard partitions*.

Another reason LDM creates an MS-DOS-style partition table is so that the Windows 2000 boot code can find the system and boot volumes, even if the volumes are on dynamic disks. (Ntldr, for example, knows nothing about LDM

partitioning.) If a disk contains the system or boot volumes, hard partitions in the MS-DOS partition table describe the location of those volumes. Otherwise, one hard partition begins at the first cylinder of the disk (typically 63 sectors into the disk) and extends to the beginning of the LDM database. LDM marks this partition as type "LDM," an MS-DOS-style partition type new to Windows 2000. The region encompassed by this place-holding MS-DOS-style partition is where LDM creates soft partitions that the LDM database organizes. Figure 10-1 illustrates this dynamic disk layout.

Figure 10-1
Internal dynamic disk organization

The LDM database consists of four regions, which Figure 10-2 shows: a header sector that LDM calls the Private Header, a table of contents area, a database records area, and a transactional log area. (The fifth region shown in Figure 10-2 is simply a copy of the Private Header.) The Private Header sector resides 1 MB before the end of a dynamic disk and anchors the database. As you spend time with Windows 2000, you'll quickly notice that it uses GUIDs to identify just about everything, and disks are no exception. A GUID (globally unique identifier) is a 128-bit value that various components in Windows 2000 use to uniquely identify objects. LDM assigns each dynamic disk a GUID, and the Private Header sector notes the GUID of the dynamic disk on which it resides—hence the Private Header's designation as information that is private to the disk. The Private Header also stores the name of the disk group, which is the name of the computer concatenated with Dg0 (for example, SusanDg0 if the computer's name is Susan), and a pointer to the beginning of the database table of contents. (As mentioned earlier, the Windows 2000 implementation of LDM includes only one disk group, so the disk group name will always end with Dg0.) For reliability, LDM keeps a copy of the Private Header in the disk's last sector.

The database table of contents is 16 sectors in size and contains information regarding the database's layout. LDM begins the database record area immediately following the table of contents with a sector that serves as the

Figure 10-2
LDM database layout

database record header. This sector stores information about the database record area, including the number of records it contains, the name and GUID of the disk group the database relates to, and a sequence number identifier that LDM uses for the next entry it creates in the database. Sectors following the database record header contain 128-byte fixed-size records that store entries that describe the disk group's partitions and volumes.

A database entry can be one of four types: partition, disk, component, and volume. LDM uses the database entry types to identify three levels that describe volumes. LDM connects entries with internal object identifiers. At the lowest level, *partition entries* describe soft partitions, which are contiguous regions on a disk; identifiers stored in a partition entry link the entry to a component and disk entry. A *disk entry* represents a dynamic disk that is part of the disk group and includes the disk's GUID. A *component entry* serves as a connector between one or more partition entries and the volume entry each partition is associated with. A *volume entry* stores the GUID of the volume, the volume's total size and state, and a drive-letter hint. Disk entries that are larger than a database record span multiple records; partition, component, and volume entries rarely span multiple records.

LDM requires three entries to describe a simple volume: a partition, component, and volume entry. The following listing shows the contents of a simple LDM database that defines one 200-MB volume that consists of one partition:

```
Disk Entry          Volume Entry        Component Entry      Partition Entry
Name: Disk1         Name: Volume1       Name: Volume1-01     Name: Disk1-01
GUID: XXX-XX...     ID: 0x408           ID: 0x409            ID: 0x407
Disk ID: 0x404      State: ACTIVE       Parent ID: 0x408     Parent ID: 0x409
                    Size: 200MB                              Disk ID: 0x404
                    GUID: XXX-XX...                          Start: 300MB
                    Drive Hint: H:                           Size: 200MB
```

The partition entry describes the area on a disk that the system assigned to the volume, the component entry connects the partition entry with the volume entry, and the volume entry contains the GUID that Windows 2000 uses internally to identify the volume. Multipartition volumes require more than three entries. For example, a striped volume (striped volumes are described later in the chapter) consists of at least two partition entries, a component entry, and a volume entry. The only volume type that has more than one component entry is a mirror; mirrors have two component entries, each of which represents one-half of the mirror. LDM uses two component entries for mirrors so that when you break a mirror, LDM can split it at the component level, creating two volumes with one component entry each. Because a simple volume requires three entries and the 1-MB database contains space for approximately 8000 entries, the effective upper limit on the number of volumes you can create on a Windows 2000 system is approximately 2500.

The final area of the LDM database is the transactional log area, which consists of a few sectors for storing backup database information as the information is modified. This setup safeguards the database in case of a crash or power failure because LDM can use the log to return the database to a consistent state.

EXPERIMENT: Using DmDiag to View the LDM Database

The Windows 2000 resource kits include a tool named DmDiag that you can use to view detailed information about a system's physical disks, the contents of the LDM database, and the partitioning layout of MS-DOS-style partition tables. In addition to this disk-related data, DmDiag also dumps the mount points defined for a system (mount points are described later in this chapter) and the device objects and symbolic links present in the object manager namespace.

DmDiag takes no command-line options, and its output is usually more than a few screens in size, so you should pipe its output to a file for viewing in a text editor. For example, *dmdiag > disk.txt*. The following figure shows excerpts of DmDiag output. A description of the types of disks present on the system is followed by the listing of the LDM database records that describe a 1-GB simple volume. The volume's database entry is listed as Volume1.

```
C:\>dmdiag
:
:
---------- Physical Disk to disk type ----------

  PhysicalDrive0 \Device\Harddisk0\DR0 (Signature 00008c21) Basic
  PhysicalDrive1 \Device\Harddisk1\DR1 (Signature 082a8a35) Dynami
  PhysicalDrive2 \Device\Harddisk2\DR2 (Signature 8b7c71bf) Dynami
:
:
---------- disk config Harddisk1 ----------

#Config copy 01

#Header nblocks=5924 blksize=128 hdrsize=512
#flags=0x0100 (CLEAN)
#version: 4/10
#timestamp: 125989959415000000
#dgname: SusanDg0  dgid: 6d5ad9b9-a587-41f2-9723-4edcf3508cc5
#config: tid=0.1783 nvol=3 nplex=3 nsd=3 ndm=2 nda=0
#pending: tid=0.1783 nvol=3 nplex=3 nsd=3 ndm=2 nda=0
#
#Block    4: flag=0x0000 ref=11   offset=0    frag_size=59
#Block    5: flag=0x0000 ref=5    offset=0    frag_size=69
#Block    6: flag=0x0000 ref=18   offset=0    frag_size=83
#Block    7: flag=0x0000 ref=3    offset=0    frag_size=48
#Block    8: flag=0x0000 ref=1    offset=0    frag_size=83
#Block    9: flag=0x0000 ref=10   offset=0    frag_size=83
#Block   10: flag=0x0000 ref=7    offset=0    frag_size=48
#Block   11: flag=0x0000 ref=8    offset=0    frag_size=50
#Block   13: flag=0x0000 ref=13   offset=0    frag_size=48
#Block   14: flag=0x0000 ref=14   offset=0    frag_size=50
#Block   21: flag=0x0000 ref=15   offset=0    frag_size=50
#Block   26: flag=0x0000 ref=22   offset=0    frag_size=59
#Record   10: type=0x0251 flags=0x0000 gen_flags=0x0004 size=83
#Blocks: 9
:
:
Volume:    Volume1 rid=0.1763 update=0.1770 mountname=H:
 info:     len=10240000 guid=25a98d75-fe4e-4237-9374-f663ecd7bd0d
 type:     parttype=6 usetype=gen
 state:    state=ACTIVE
 policies: read=SELECT
:
:
```

1-GB volume object

LDM database table of contents

LDM database Private Header

GUID Partition Table Partitioning

As part of an initiative to provide a standardized and extensible firmware platform for operating systems to use during their boot process, Intel has designed the Extensible Firmware Interface (EFI) specification. EFI includes a mini–operating system environment implemented in firmware (typically ROM) that operating systems use early in the system boot process to load system diagnostics and their boot code. One of the first targets of EFI is IA-64, so the 64-bit version of Windows 2000 will use EFI. You can find a complete description of EFI at *developer. intel.com/technology/efi.*

EFI defines a new partitioning scheme, called the GUID Partition Table (GPT), that addresses some of the shortcomings of MS-DOS-style partitioning. For example, the sector addresses that the GPT partition structures use are 64 bits wide instead of 32 bits. A 32-bit sector address is sufficient to access only 2 terabytes (TB) of storage. You don't see storage devices with that capacity today, but the GPT standard is designed with the future in mind. Other advantages of the GPT scheme include the fact that it uses cyclic redundancy checksums (CRC) to ensure the integrity of the partition table, and it maintains a backup copy of the partition table. GPT takes its name from the fact that in addition to storing a 36-byte Unicode partition name for each partition, it assigns each partition a GUID.

The following figure shows an example GPT partition layout. Like basic and dynamic disks in Windows 2000, the first sector of a GPT disk is an MBR. However, the second and last sectors of the disk store the GPT partition tables. With its extensible list of partitions, GPT partitioning doesn't require nested partitions, as MS-DOS-style partitions do.

First usable block

LBA0 LBA1

Start partition End partition

LBA*n*

MBR | Partition table header | 0 1 ... *n*

Partition 1

0 1 ... *n* | Partition table header

Start partition End partition Last usable block

Primary partition table

Backup partition table

Note: LBA = Logical Block Address

Although the GPT partitioning scheme is an improvement over MS-DOS-style partitions, it isn't a replacement for Windows 2000 LDM partitioning. Just as Windows 2000 integrates MS-DOS-style partitions with LDM partitioning areas on dynamic boot and system disks so that the operating system loader can locate Windows 2000 boot and system files, LDM will integrate with the GPT partitioning scheme in 64-bit Windows 2000.

Storage Drivers

As you saw in Chapter 4, Ntldr is the Windows 2000 operating system file that conducts the first portion of the Windows boot process. Ntldr resides on the system volume; the boot-sector code on the system volume executes Ntldr. Ntldr

reads the Boot.ini file from the system volume and presents the computer's boot choices to the user. The partition names that Boot.ini designates are in the form multi(0)disk(0)rdisk(0)partition(1). These names are Advanced RISC Computing (ARC) names because they're part of a standard partition-naming scheme that Alpha firmware and other RISC processors use. Ntldr translates the name of the Boot.ini boot entry that a user selects to the appropriate boot partition and then loads the Windows 2000 system files (starting with the registry, Ntoskrnl.exe, and the boot drivers) into memory to continue the boot process.

Disk Drivers

During initialization, the Windows 2000 I/O manager starts the hard disk storage drivers. Storage drivers in Windows 2000 follow a class/port/miniport architecture, in which Microsoft supplies a storage class driver that implements functionality common to all storage devices and a storage port driver that implements functionality common to a particular bus, such as a Small Computer System Interface (SCSI) bus or an Integrated Devise Electronics (IDE) system, and OEMs supply miniport drivers that plug into the port driver to interface Windows 2000 to a particular implementation.

In the disk storage driver architecture, only class drivers conform to the standard Windows 2000 device driver interfaces. Miniport drivers use a port driver interface instead of the device driver interface, and the port driver simply implements a collection of device driver support routines that interface miniport drivers to Windows 2000. This approach simplifies the role of miniport driver developers and, because Microsoft supplies operating system–specific port drivers, gives miniport drivers binary portability between Microsoft Windows 98, Microsoft Windows Millennium Edition, and Windows 2000.

Windows 2000 includes Disk (\Winnt\System32\Drivers\Disk.sys), a class driver that implements functionality common to disks. Windows 2000 also provides a handful of disk port drivers. For example, Scsiport.sys is the port driver for disks on SCSI buses, and Pciidex.sys is a port driver for IDE-based systems. Windows 2000 ships with several miniport drivers, including one—Aha154x.sys— for Adaptec's 1540 family of SCSI controllers. On systems that have at least one ATAPI-based IDE device, one driver—Atapi.sys—combines port and miniport functionality. Most Windows 2000 installations include one or more of the drivers mentioned.

Device Naming

The Windows 2000 disk class driver creates device objects that represent disks and partitions. Device objects that represent disks have names of the form \Device\ Harddisk*X*\DR*X;* the number that identifies the disk replaces both *X*s. The disk class driver uses the I/O manager's *IoReadPartitionTable* function to identify device objects that represent partitions. As miniport drivers present the disks that they identify early in the boot process to the disk class driver, the disk class driver invokes the *IoReadPartitionTable* function for each disk. *IoReadPartitionTable* invokes sector-level disk I/O that the class, port, and miniport drivers provide to read a disk's MS-DOS-style partition table and construct an internal representation of the disk's hard partitioning. The disk class driver creates device objects to represent each primary partition (including primary partitions within extended partitions) that the driver obtains from *IoReadPartitionTable*. The following is an example partition object name:

 \Device\Harddisk0\DP(1)0x7e000-0x7ff50c00+2

This name identifies the first partition on a system's first disk. The first two hexadecimal numbers (0x7e000 and 0x7ff50c00) designate the start and length of the partition, and the last number is an internal identifier that the class driver assigns.

To maintain compatibility with applications that use the Windows NT 4 naming conventions, the disk class driver creates symbolic links with Windows NT 4–formatted names that refer to the device objects the driver created. For example, the Disk class driver creates the link \Device\Harddisk0\Partition0 to refer to \Device\Harddisk0\DR0, and \Device\Harddisk0\Partition1 to refer to the first partition device object of the first disk. The class driver also creates the same Win32 symbolic links in Windows 2000 that represent physical drives that it created in Windows NT 4 systems. Thus, for example, the link \??\PhysicalDrive0 references \Device\Harddisk0\DR0. Figure 10-3 shows the Winobj utility (available on the companion CD in \Sysint\Winobj.exe) displaying the contents of a Harddisk directory for a basic disk. You can see the physical disk and partition device objects in the right-hand pane.

Figure 10-3
Winobj showing a Harddisk directory of a basic disk

As you saw in Chapter 3, the Win32 API is unaware of the Windows 2000 object manager namespace. Windows 2000 reserves two different namespace subdirectories for Win32 to use, one of which is the \?? subdirectory. (The other is the \BaseNamedObjects subdirectory, which is covered in Chapter 3.) In this subdirectory, Windows 2000 makes available device objects that Win32 applications interact with—including COM and parallel ports—as well as disks. Because disk objects actually reside in other subdirectories, Windows 2000 uses symbolic links to connect names under \?? with objects located elsewhere in the namespace. For each physical disk on a system, the I/O manager creates a \??\PhysicalDrive*X* link that points to \Device\Harddisk*X*\Partition0. (Numbers, starting from 0, replace *X*.) Win32 applications that directly interact with the sectors on a disk open the disk by calling the Win32 *CreateFile* function and specifying the name \\.\PhysicalDrive*X* (in which *X* is the disk number) as a parameter. The Win32 application layer converts the name to \??\PhysicalDrive*X* before handing the name to the Windows 2000 object manager.

Basic Disk Management

The FtDisk driver (\Winnt\System32\Drivers\Ftdisk.sys) creates disk device objects that represent volumes on basic disks. FtDisk is present in Windows NT 4 only when at least one multipartition volume is present; in Windows 2000, FtDisk plays an integral role in managing all basic disk volumes, including simple volumes. For each volume, FtDisk creates a device object of the form \Device\

HarddiskVolumeX, in which X is a number (starting from 1) that identifies the volume. FtDisk uses the basic disk configuration information that the registry key HKLM\SYSTEM\Disk stores to determine what basic volumes, multipartition and otherwise, a system includes. Note that the Disk key is only on Windows 2000 systems that were upgraded from Windows NT 4 (or Windows 98) and that already had a Disk key from previous disk-management activity (such as assigning drive letters to volumes or creating multipartition volumes). To avoid reliance on the registry, FtDisk migrates configuration information from the Disk key to hidden sectors on disk.

FtDisk is actually a bus driver because it's responsible for enumerating basic disks to detect the presence of basic volumes and report them to the Windows 2000 Plug and Play (PnP) manager. To implement this enumeration, FtDisk leverages the PnP manager, with the aid of the partition manager (Partmgr.sys) driver, to determine what basic disk partitions exist. The partition manager registers with the PnP manager so that Windows 2000 can inform the partition manager whenever the disk class driver creates a partition device object. The partition manager informs FtDisk about new partition objects through a private interface and creates filter device objects that the partition manager then attaches to the partition objects. The existence of the filter objects prompts Windows 2000 to inform the partition manager whenever a partition device object is deleted so that the partition manager can update FtDisk. The disk class driver deletes a partition device object when a partition in the Disk Management Microsoft Management Console (MMC) snap-in is deleted. As FtDisk becomes aware of partitions, it uses the basic disk configuration information to determine the correspondence of partitions to volumes and creates a volume device object when it has been informed of the presence of all the partitions in a volume's description.

Windows 2000 volume drive-letter assignment, a process described shortly, creates drive-letter symbolic links under the \?? object manager directory that point to the volume device objects that FtDisk creates. When the system or an application accesses a volume for the first time, Windows 2000 performs a mount operation that gives file system drivers the opportunity to recognize and claim ownership for volumes formatted with a file system type they manage. (Mount operations are described in the section "Volume Mounting" later in this chapter.)

Dynamic Disk Management

The Disk Management MMC snap-in DLL (DMDiskManager, located in Winnt\System32\Dmdskmgr.dll), shown in Figure 10-4, uses the DMAdmin, the LDM Disk Administrator service (Winnt\System32\Dmadmin.exe), to create and change

Figure 10-4
Disk Management MMC snap-in

the contents of the LDM database. When you launch the Disk Management MMC snap-in, DMDiskManager loads into memory and starts DMAdmin, if it's not already running. DMAdmin reads the LDM database from each disk and returns the information it obtains to DMDiskManager. If DMAdmin detects a database from another computer's disk group, it notes that the volumes on the disk are foreign and lets you import them into the current computer's database if you want to use them. As you change the configuration of dynamic disks, DMDiskManager informs DMAdmin of the changes and DMAdmin updates its in-memory copy of the database. When DMAdmin commits changes, it passes the updated database to DMIO, the Dmio.sys device driver. DMIO is the dynamic disk equivalent of FtDisk, so it controls access to the on-disk database and creates device objects that represent the volumes on dynamic disks. When you exit Disk Management, DMDiskManager stops and unloads the DMAdmin service.

DMIO doesn't know how to interpret the database it oversees. DMConfig (Winnt\System32\Dmconfig.dll), a DLL that DMAdmin loads, and another device driver, DMBoot (Dmboot.sys), are responsible for interpreting the database. DMConfig knows how to both read and update the database; DMBoot knows only how to read the database. DMBoot loads during the boot process

if another LDM driver, DMLoad (Dmload.sys), determines that at least one dynamic disk is present on the system. DMLoad makes this determination by asking DMIO, and if at least one dynamic disk is present, DMLoad starts DMBoot, which scans the LDM database. DMBoot informs DMIO of the composition of each volume it encounters so that DMIO can create device objects to represent the volumes. DMBoot unloads from memory immediately after it finishes its scan. Because DMIO has no database interpretation logic, it is relatively small. Its small size is beneficial because DMIO is always loaded.

Like FtDisk, DMIO is a bus driver and creates a device object for each dynamic disk volume with a name in the form \Device\HarddiskDmVolumes\ PhysicalDmVolumes\BlockVolumeX, in which X is an identifier that DMIO assigns to the volume. In addition, DMIO creates another device object that represents raw (unstructured) I/O in a volume named \Device\HarddiskDm-Volumes\PhysicalDmVolumes\RawVolumeX. Figure 10-5 shows the device objects that DMIO created on a system that consists of two dynamic disk volumes. DMIO also creates numerous symbolic links in the object manager namespace for each volume, starting with one link in the form \Device\HarddiskDmVolumes\ *ComputerName*Dg0\VolumeY for each volume. DMIO replaces *ComputerName* with the name of the computer, and replaces Y with a volume identifier (different from the internal identifier that DMIO assigns to the device objects). These links refer to the block-device objects under the PhysicalDmVolumes directory.

Figure 10-5
DMIO driver device objects

Disk Performance Monitoring

Windows 2000 I/O architecture permits the dynamic layering of device objects, which Chapter 9 describes in detail. A device driver can create a device object and attach it to a target device object. The I/O manager routes requests directed at a target device object to that object's attached device object, if one exists. Device drivers use this mechanism to monitor, augment, or change the behavior of device objects that belong to other device drivers. A driver that relies on layering is a *filter driver*, and when a filter driver receives an I/O request packet (IRP) aimed at a target device, the filter driver has full control over the request. The filter driver can fail the request, create new subrequests, or pass the unmodified request to the target device. (IRPs are covered in more detail in Chapter 9.)

Windows 2000 storage drivers commonly use layering in two places. The first place involves file system filter drivers. At the highest level, file system filter drivers attach to the target device objects that represent mounted partitions that file system drivers create. A file system filter driver therefore intercepts requests aimed at mounted volumes so that the driver can implement functionality such as monitoring, encryption, or on-access virus scanning. File Monitor, a utility included on the companion CD under \Sysint\Filemon.exe, is an example of a file system filter driver.

The second place storage drivers commonly use layering is to implement monitoring. Windows 2000 includes a layered storage driver named DiskPerf (Disk Performance driver - \Winnt\System32\Drivers\Diskperf.sys) to do this. DiskPerf attaches to the device objects that represent physical disks (for example, \Device\Harddisk0\Partition0) so that it can generate performance-related statistics for the Performance tool to present. Statistics include bytes read and written per second, transfers per second, and the amount of time spent performing disk I/O.

Multipartition Volume Management

FtDisk and DMIO are responsible for presenting volumes that file system drivers manage and for mapping I/O directed at volumes to the underlying partitions that they're made of. For simple volumes, this process is straightforward: the volume manager ensures that volume-relative offsets are translated to disk-relative offsets by adding the volume-relative offset to the volume's starting disk offset.

Multipartition volumes are more complex because the partitions that make up a volume can be located on discontiguous partitions or even on different disks. Some types of multipartition volumes use data redundancy, so they require more

involved volume–to–disk-offset translation. Thus, FtDisk and DMIO must process all I/O requests aimed at the multipartition volumes they manage by determining which partitions the I/O ultimately affects.

The following types of multipartition volumes are available in Windows 2000:

- Spanned volumes

- Mirrored volumes

- Striped volumes

- RAID-5 volume

After describing multipartition-volume partition configuration and logical operation for each of the multipartition-volume types, we'll cover the way that the FtDisk and DMIO drivers handle IRPs that a file system driver sends to multipartition volumes. The term *volume manager* is used to represent both FtDisk and DMIO throughout the explanation of multipartition volumes because both FtDisk and DMIO support the same multipartition-volume types.

Spanned Volumes

A *spanned volume* is a single logical volume composed of a maximum of 32 free partitions on one or more disks. The Windows 2000 Disk Management MMC snap-in combines the partitions into a spanned volume, which can then be formatted for any of the Windows 2000–supported file systems. Figure 10-6 shows a 100-MB spanned volume identified by drive letter D: that has been created from the last third of the first disk and the first third of the second. Spanned volumes were called *volume sets* in Windows NT 4.

Figure 10-6
Spanned volume

A spanned volume is useful for consolidating small areas of free disk space into one larger volume or for creating a single, large volume out of two or more small disks. If the spanned volume has been formatted for NTFS, it can be extended to include additional free areas or additional disks without affecting the data already stored on the volume. This extensibility is one of the biggest benefits of describing all data on an NTFS volume as a file. NTFS can dynamically increase the size of a logical volume because the bitmap that records the allocation status of the volume is just another file—the bitmap file. The bitmap file can be extended to include any space added to the volume. Dynamically extending a FAT volume, on the other hand, would require the FAT itself to be extended, which would dislocate everything else on the disk.

A volume manager hides the physical configuration of disks from the file systems installed on Windows 2000. NTFS, for example, views volume D: in Figure 10-6 as an ordinary 100-MB volume. NTFS consults its bitmap to determine what space in the volume is free for allocation. It then calls the volume manager to read or write data beginning at a particular byte offset on the volume. The volume manager views the physical sectors in the spanned volume as numbered sequentially from the first free area on the first disk to the last free area on the last disk. It determines which physical sector on which disk corresponds to the supplied byte offset.

Striped Volumes

A *striped volume* is a series of up to 32 partitions, one partition per disk, that combines into a single logical volume. Striped volumes are also known as *RAID level 0* (RAID-0) volumes. Figure 10-7 shows a striped volume consisting of three partitions, one on each of three disks. (A partition in a striped volume need not span an entire disk; the only restriction is that the partitions on each disk be the same size.)

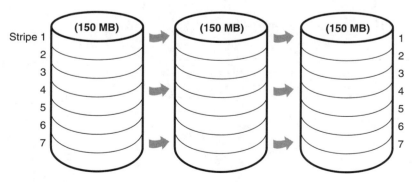

Figure 10-7
Striped volume

To a file system, this striped volume appears to be a single 450-MB volume, but a volume manager optimizes data storage and retrieval times on the striped volume by distributing the volume's data among the physical disks. The volume manager accesses the physical sectors of the disks as if they were numbered sequentially in stripes across the disks, as illustrated in Figure 10-8.

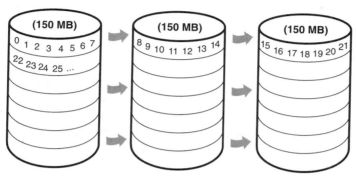

Figure 10-8
Logical numbering of physical sectors on a striped volume

Because each stripe is a relatively narrow 64 KB (a value chosen to prevent individual reads and writes from accessing two disks), the data tends to be distributed evenly among the disks. Stripes thus increase the probability that multiple pending read and write operations will be bound for different disks. And because data on all three disks can be accessed simultaneously, latency time for disk I/O is often reduced, particularly on heavily loaded systems.

Spanned volumes make managing disk volumes more convenient, and striped volumes spread the I/O load over multiple disks. These two volume-management features don't provide the ability to recover data if a disk fails, however. For data recovery, a volume manager implements three redundant storage schemes: mirrored volumes, RAID-5 volumes, and sector sparing. (Sector sparing and NTFS support for sector sparing are described in Chapter 12.) These features are created with the Windows 2000 Disk Management administrative tool.

Mirrored Volumes

In a *mirrored volume,* the contents of a partition on one disk are duplicated in an equal-sized partition on another disk. Mirrored volumes are sometimes referred to as *RAID level 1* (RAID-1). A mirrored volume is shown in Figure 10-9.

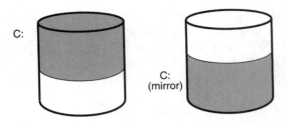

Figure 10-9
Mirrored volume

When a program writes to drive C:, the volume manager writes the same data to the same location on the mirror partition. If the first disk or any of the data on its C: partition becomes unreadable because of a hardware or software failure, the volume manager automatically accesses the data from the mirror partition. A mirror volume can be formatted for any of the Windows 2000–supported file systems. The file system drivers remain independent and are not affected by the volume manager's mirroring activity.

Mirrored volumes can aid in I/O throughput on heavily loaded systems. When I/O activity is high, the volume manager balances its read operations between the primary partition and the mirror partition (accounting for the number of unfinished I/O requests pending from each disk). Two read operations can proceed simultaneously and thus theoretically finish in half the time. When a file is modified, both partitions of the mirror set must be written, but disk writes are done asynchronously, so the performance of user-mode programs is generally not affected by the extra disk update.

Mirrored volumes are the only multipartition volume type supported for system and boot volumes. The reason for this is that the Windows 2000 boot code, including the MBR code and Ntldr, don't have the sophistication required to understand multipartition volumes—mirrored volumes are the exception because the boot code treats them as simple volumes, reading from the half of the mirror marked as the boot or system drive in the MS-DOS-style partition table. Because the boot code doesn't modify the disk, it can safely ignore the other half of the mirror.

EXPERIMENT: Watching Mirrored Volume I/O Operations

Using the Windows 2000 Performance tool, you can verify that write operations directed at mirrored volumes copy to both disks that make up the mirror and that read operations, if relatively infrequent, occur primarily from one half of the volume. This experiment requires three hard disks and Windows 2000 Server, Windows 2000 Advanced Server, or Windows 2000 Datacenter Server. If you don't have three disks or a server system, you can skip the experiment setup instructions and view the Performance tool screen shot in this experiment that demonstrates the experiment's results.

Use the Disk Management MMC snap-in to create a mirrored volume. To do this, perform the following steps:

1. Run Disk Management by starting Computer Management, expanding the Storage tree, and selecting Disk Management (or by inserting Disk Management as a snap-in in an MMC console).

2. Right-click on an unallocated space of a drive, and select Create Volume.

3. Follow the instructions in the Create Volume wizard to create a simple volume. (Make sure there's enough room on another disk for a volume of the same size as the one you're creating.)

4. Right-click on the new volume, and select Add Mirror from the context menu.

Once you have a mirrored volume, run the Performance tool and add counters for the PhysicalDisk performance object for both disk instances that contain a partition belonging to the mirror. Select the Disk Reads/Sec and Disk Writes/Sec counters for each instance. Select a large directory from the third disk (the one that isn't part of the mirrored volume), and copy it to the mirrored volume. The Performance tool output window should look something like the following as the copy operation progresses.

(continued)

EXPERIMENT: Watching Mirrored Volume I/O Operations *continued*

The top two lines, which overlap throughout the timeline, are the Disk Writes/Sec counters for each disk. The bottom two lines are the Disk Reads/Sec lines. The screen shot reveals that the volume manager (in this case DMIO) is writing the copied file data to both halves of the volume but primarily reading from only one. This read behavior occurs because the number of outstanding I/O operations during the copy didn't warrant that the volume manager perform more aggressive read-operation load balancing.

RAID-5 Volumes

A *RAID-5 volume* is a fault tolerant variant of a regular striped volume. RAID-5 volumes implement *RAID level 5*. They are also known as *striped volumes with parity* because they are based on the striping approach taken by striped volumes. Fault tolerance is achieved by reserving the equivalent of one disk for storing parity for each stripe. Figure 10-10 is a visual representation of a RAID-5 volume.

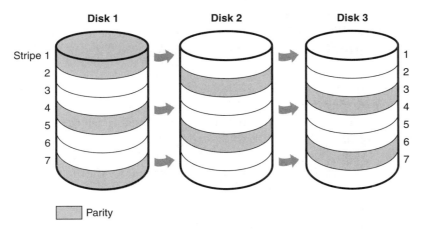

Figure 10-10
RAID-5 volume

In Figure 10-10, the parity for stripe 1 is stored on disk 1. It contains a byte-for-byte logical sum (XOR) of the first stripe on disks 2 and 3. The parity for stripe 2 is stored on disk 2, and the parity for stripe 3 is stored on disk 3. Rotating the parity across the disks in this way is an I/O optimization technique. Each time data is written to a disk, the parity bytes corresponding to the modified bytes must be recalculated and rewritten. If the parity were always written to the same disk, that disk would be busy continually and could become an I/O bottleneck.

Recovering a failed disk in a RAID-5 volume relies on a simple arithmetic principle: in an equation with n variables, if you know the value of $n - 1$ of the variables, you can determine the value of the missing variable by subtraction. For example, in the equation $x + y = z$, where z represents the parity stripe, the volume manager computes $z - y$ to determine the contents of x; to find y, it computes $z - x$. The volume manager uses similar logic to recover lost data. If a disk in a RAID-5 volume fails or if data on one disk becomes unreadable, the volume manager reconstructs the missing data by using the XOR operation (bitwise logical addition).

If disk 1 in Figure 10-10 fails, the contents of its stripes 2 and 5 are calculated by XORing the corresponding stripes of disk 3 with the parity stripes on disk 2. The contents of stripes 3 and 6 on disk 1 are similarly determined by

XORing the corresponding stripes of disk 2 with the parity stripes on disk 3. At least three disks (or rather, three same-sized partitions on three disks) are required to create a RAID-5 volume.

Volume I/O Operations

File system drivers manage data stored on volumes but rely on volume managers to interact with storage drivers to transfer data to and from the disk or disks on which a volume resides. File system drivers obtain references to a volume manager's volume objects through the mount process (described later in this chapter) and then send the volume manager requests via the volume objects. Applications can also send the volume manager requests, bypassing file system drivers, when they want to directly manipulate a volume's data. File-undelete programs are an example of applications that do this, and so is the DiskProbe utility that's part of the Windows 2000 resource kits.

Whenever a file system driver or application sends an I/O request to a device object that represents a volume, the Windows 2000 I/O manager routes the request (which comes in an IRP—a self-contained package) to the volume manager that created the target device object. Thus, if an application wants to read the boot sector of the second volume on the system (which is a simple volume in this example), it opens the device object \Device\HarddiskVolume2 and then sends the object a request to read 512 bytes starting at offset zero on the device. The I/O manager sends the application's request in the form of an IRP to the volume manager that owns the device object, notifying it that the IRP is directed at the HarddiskVolume2 device.

Because partitions are logical conveniences that Windows 2000 uses to represent contiguous areas on a physical disk, the volume manager must translate offsets that are relative to a partition to offsets that are relative to the beginning of a disk. If partition 2 begins 3449 sectors into the disk, the volume manager would adjust the IRP's parameters to designate an offset with that value before passing the request to the disk class driver. The disk class driver uses a miniport driver to carry out physical disk I/O and read requested data into an application buffer designated in the IRP.

Some examples of a volume manager's operations will help clarify its role when it handles requests aimed at multipartition volumes. If a striped volume consists of two partitions, partition 1 and partition 2, that are represented by the device object \Device\HarddiskDmVolumes\PhysicalDmVolumes\BlockVolume3, as Figure 10-11 shows, and an administrator has assigned drive letter D: to the stripe, the I/O manager defines the link \??\D: to reference \Device\Harddisk-DmVolumes*ComputerName*Dg0\Volume3, where *ComputerName* is the name

of the computer. Recall from earlier that this link is also a symbolic link, and it points to the corresponding volume device object in the PhysicalDmVolumes directory (in this case, BlockVolume3). The DMIO device object intercepts file system disk I/O aimed at \Device\HarddiskDmVolumes\PhysicalDmVolumes\ BlockVolume3, and the DMIO driver adjusts the request before passing it to the Disk class driver. The adjustment that DMIO makes configures the request to refer to the correct offset of the request's target stripe on either partition 1 or partition 2. If the I/O spans both partitions of the volume, DMIO must issue two subsidiary I/O requests, one aimed at each disk.

Figure 10-11
DMIO I/O operations

In the case of writes to a mirrored volume, DMIO splits each request so that each half of the mirror receives the write operation. For mirrored reads, DMIO performs a read from half of a mirror, relying on the other half when a read operation fails.

The Volume Namespace

Drive-letter assignment is an aspect of storage management that changed significantly from Windows NT 4 to Windows 2000. Even so, Windows 2000 includes support for migrating drive-letter assignments made in a Windows NT 4 installation that upgrades to Windows 2000. Windows NT 4 drive-letter assignments are stored in HKLM\SYSTEM\Disk. After the upgrade procedure reads and stores the information in Windows 2000–specific locations, the system no longer references the Disk key.

The Mount Manager

A new driver in Windows 2000, the Mount Manager (Mountmgr.sys), assigns drive letters for dynamic disk volumes and for basic disk volumes created after Windows 2000 is installed. Windows 2000 stores all drive-letter assignments under HKLM\SYSTEM\MountedDevices. If you look in the registry under that key, you'll see values with names such as \??\Volume{X} (where X is a GUID) and values such as ??\C:. Every volume has a volume name entry, but a volume doesn't necessarily have an assigned drive letter. Figure 10-12 shows the contents of an example Mount Manager registry key. Note that the MountedDevices key, like the Disk key in Windows NT 4, isn't included in a control set and so isn't protected by the last known good boot option. (See the section "Accepting the Boot and Last Known Good" on page 256 in Chapter 5 for more information on control sets and the last known good boot option.)

The data that the registry stores in values for basic disk volume drive letters and volume names is the Windows NT 4–style disk signature and the starting offset of the first partition associated with the volume. The data that the registry stores in values for dynamic disk volumes includes the volume's DMIO internal GUID. When the Mount Manager initializes during the boot process, it registers with the Windows 2000 Plug and Play subsystem so that it receives notification whenever either FtDisk or DMIO creates a volume. When the

Figure 10-12
Mounted devices listed in the Mount Manager's registry key

Mount Manager receives such a notification, it determines the new volume's GUID or disk signature and then asks either FtDisk or DMIO (whichever created the volume) for a suggested drive-letter assignment. FtDisk doesn't return suggestions (as it does during an upgrade from Windows NT 4 when it queries the Windows NT 4 HKLM\SYSTEM\Disk key), and DMIO looks at the drive-letter hint in the volume's database entry.

If no suggested drive-letter assignment exists for the volume, the Mount Manager uses the volume GUID or signature as a guide and looks in its internal database, which reflects the contents of the registry key. The Mount Manager then determines whether its internal database contains the drive-letter assignment. If it doesn't, the Mount Manager uses the first unassigned drive letter (if one exists), defines a new assignment, creates a symbolic link for the assignment (for example, \??\D:), and updates the MountedDevices registry key. If there are no available drive letters, no drive letter assignment is made. At the same time, the Mount Manager creates a volume symbolic link (that is, \??\Volume{X}) that defines a new volume GUID, if the volume doesn't already have one. This GUID is different from the volume GUIDs that DMIO uses internally.

Mount Points

Mount points, a mechanism new to Windows 2000, let you link volumes through directories on NTFS volumes, which makes volumes with no drive-letter assignment accessible. For example, an NTFS directory that you've named C:\Projects could mount another volume (NTFS or FAT) that contains your project directories and files. If your project volume had a file you named CurrentProject\Description.txt, you could access the file through the path C:\Projects\CurrentProject\Description.txt. What makes mount points possible is *reparse point* technology. (Reparse points are discussed in more detail in Chapter 12.)

A reparse point is a block of arbitrary data with some fixed header data that Windows 2000 associates with an NTFS file or directory. An application or the system defines the format and behavior of a reparse point, including the value of the unique reparse point tag that identifies reparse points belonging to the application or system and specifies the size and meaning of the data portion of a reparse point. (The data portion can be as large as 16 KB.) Reparse points store their unique tag in a fixed segment. Any application that implements a reparse point must supply a file system filter driver to watch for reparse-related return codes for file operations that execute on NTFS volumes, and the driver must take appropriate action when it detects the codes. NTFS returns a reparse status code whenever it processes a file operation and encounters a file or directory with an associated reparse point.

The Windows 2000 NTFS file system driver, the I/O manager, and the object manager all partly implement reparse point functionality. The object manager initiates pathname-parsing operations by using the I/O manager to interface with file system drivers. Therefore, the object manager must retry operations for which the I/O manager returns a reparse status code. The I/O manager implements pathname modification that mount points and other reparse points might require, and the NTFS file system driver must associate and identify reparse point data with files and directories. You can therefore think of the I/O manager as the reparse point file system filter driver for many Microsoft-defined reparse points.

An example of a reparse point application is a Hierarchical Storage Management (HSM) system that uses reparse points to designate files that an administrator moves to offline tape storage. When a user tries to access an offline file, the HSM filter driver detects the reparse status code that NTFS returns, communicates with a user-mode service to retrieve the file from offline storage, deletes the reparse point from the file, and lets the file operation retry after the service retrieves the file. This is exactly how the Windows 2000 Remote Storage Services (RSS) filter driver, Rsfilter.sys, uses reparse points.

If the I/O manager receives a reparse status code from NTFS and the file or directory for which NTFS returned the code isn't associated with one of a handful of built-in Windows 2000 reparse points, no filter driver claimed the reparse point. The I/O manager then returns an error to the object manager that propagates as a "file cannot be accessed by the system" error to the application making the file or directory access.

Mount points are reparse points that store a volume name (\??\Volume{X}) as the reparse data. When you use the Disk Management MMC snap-in to assign or remove path assignments for volumes, you're creating mount points. You can also create and display mount points by using the built-in command-line tool *Mountvol.exe* (\Winnt\System32\Mountvol.exe).

The Mount Manager maintains the Mount Manager remote database on every NTFS volume, in which the Mount Manager records any mount points defined for that volume. The database file, $MountMgrRemoteDatabase, resides in the NTFS root directory. Mount points move when a disk moves from one system to another and in dual-boot environments—that is, when booting between multiple Windows 2000 installations—because of the Mount Manager remote database's existence. NTFS also keeps track of mount points in the NTFS metadata file \$Extend\$Reparse. (NTFS doesn't make any of its metadata files available for viewing by applications.) NTFS stores mount-point information in the metadata file so that Windows 2000 can easily enumerate the mount points defined for a volume when a Win32 application, such as Disk Management, requests mount-point definitions.

EXPERIMENT: Recursive Mount Points

This experiment uses Filemon (available on the companion CD as \Sysint\ Filemon.exe) to show the interesting behavior caused by a recursive mount point. A recursive mount point is a mount point that links to the same volume it's on. Performing a recursive directory listing on a recursive mount point produces file access traces that clearly demonstrate how NTFS treats mount points.

To create and view a mount point, perform the following steps:

1. Open a Command Prompt or Windows Explorer window, and create a directory on an NTFS drive named \Recurse.

2. In the Disk Management MMC snap-in, right-click on the volume and select Change Drive Letter And Path.

3. When the Add/Remove dialog box appears, enter the path to the directory you created (for example, *I:\Recurse*).

4. Start Filemon, and in the Drives menu, uncheck all the volumes except the one on which you created the mount point.

Now you're ready to generate a recursive mount-point trace. Open a Command Prompt, and execute the command *dir /s I:\Recurse*. If you look at all the file accesses that reference Recurse in the Filemon's trace of the subsequent file operations, you'll notice that the Command Prompt first accesses I:\Recurse, then I:\Recurse\Recurse, and so on, recursing deeper and deeper.

The application attempts to perform a directory listing at each level of the recursion, but whenever it encounters the mount point, it digs into it to try another directory listing. NTFS returns a reparse status code, which tells the object manager to back up one level and try again. Finally, when it gets back to the root directory, the application examines the file or directory that it had found deep in the mount-point recursion. The application never receives a reparse code because of the object manager–directed retry activity. The object manager processes the reparse codes as it receives them from NTFS when it performs directory lookups.

Filemon presents request types as their native IRP type, so a directory or file open appears as an *IRP_MJ_CREATE* request. A file or

directory close is *IRP_MJ_CLOSE*, and a directory query is an *IRP_MJ_DIRECTORY_CONTROL* request with *FileBothDirectoryInfo* in Filemon's Other column.

To prevent buffer overflows and infinite loops, both Command Prompt and Windows Explorer halt their recursion when the directory depth reaches 32 or the pathname exceeds 256 characters, whichever comes first.

Volume Mounting

Because Windows 2000 assigns a drive letter to a partition doesn't mean that the partition contains data that has been organized in a file system format that Windows 2000 recognizes. The volume-recognition process consists of a file system claiming ownership for a partition; the process takes place the first time the kernel, a device driver, or an application accesses a file or directory on a partition. After a file system driver signals its responsibility for a partition, the I/O manager directs all IRPs aimed at the partition to the owning driver. Mount operations in Windows 2000 consist of three components: file system driver registration, volume parameter blocks (VPBs), and mount requests.

The I/O manager oversees the mount process and is aware of available file system drivers because all file system drivers register with the I/O manager when they initialize. The I/O manager provides the *IoRegisterFileSystem* function to local disk (rather than network) file system drivers for this registration. When a file system driver registers, the I/O manager stores a reference to the driver in a list that the I/O manager uses during mount operations.

Every device object contains a VPB data structure, but the I/O manager treats VPBs as meaningful only for volume device objects. A VPB serves as the link between a volume device object and the device object that a file system driver creates to represent a mounted file system instance for that volume. If a VPB's file system reference is empty, no file system has mounted the volume. The I/O manager checks a volume device object's VPB whenever an open API that specifies a filename or a directory name on a volume device object executes.

For example, if the mount manager assigns drive letter D to the second volume on a system, it creates a \??\D: symbolic link that resolves to the device object \Device\HarddiskVolume2. A Win32 application that attempts to open the \Temp\Test.txt file on the D: drive specifies the name D:\Temp\Test.txt, which the Win32 subsystem converts to \??\D:\Temp\Test.txt before invoking *NtCreateFile*, the kernel's file-open routine. *NtCreateFile* uses the object manager to parse the name, and the object manager encounters the \Device\ HarddiskVolume2 device object with the path \Temp\Test.txt still unresolved. At that point, the I/O manager checks to see whether \Device\HarddiskVolume2's VPB references a file system. If it doesn't, the I/O manager asks each registered file system driver via a mount request whether the driver recognizes the format of the volume in question as the driver's own.

EXPERIMENT: Looking at VPBs

You can look at the contents of a VPB by using the *!vpb* kernel debugger command. Because the VPB is pointed to by the device object for a volume, you must first locate a volume device object. To do this, you must dump a volume manager's driver object, locate a device object that represents a volume, and display the device object, which reveals its VPB field.

If your system has a dynamic disk, you can use the *!drvobj* driver object viewing command on the DMIO driver; otherwise, you need to specify the FtDisk driver. Here's an example:

```
kd> !drvobj ftdisk
Driver object (818aec50) is for:
 \Driver\Ftdisk
Driver Extension List: (id , addr)

Device Object list:
818a5290  817e96f0  817e98b0  817e9030
818a73b0  818a7810  8182d030
```

The *!drvobj* command lists the addresses of the device objects a driver owns. In this example, there are seven device objects. One of them represents the programmatic interface to the device driver, and the rest are volume device objects. Because the objects are listed in reverse order of the way that they were created and the driver creates the device driver interface object first, you know the first device object listed is that of a volume. Now execute the *!devobj* kernel debugger command on the volume device object address:

```
kd> !devobj 818a5290
Device object (818a5290) is for:
 HarddiskVolume6 \Driver\Ftdisk DriverObject 818aec50
 Current Irp 00000000 RefCount 3 Type 00000007 Flags 00001050
 Vpb 818a5da8 DevExt 818a5348 DevObjExt 818a53f8 Dope 818a50a8
  DevNode 818a5ae8
ExtensionFlags (0xa0000000)
                        Unknown flags 0xa0000000
```

The *!devobj* command shows the VPB field for the volume device object. (The device object shown is named HarddiskVolume6.) Now you're ready to execute the *!vpb* command:

```
kd> !vpb 818a5da8
Vpb at 0x818a5da8
Flags: 0x1 mounted
DeviceObject: 0x850dcac0
RealDevice:   0x818a5290
RefCount: 3
Volume Label:     GAMES
```

The command reveals that the volume device object is mounted by a file system driver that has assigned the volume the name GAMES. The *RealDevice* field in the VPB points back to the volume device object, and the *DeviceObject* field points to the mounted file system device object.

The convention followed by file system drivers for recognizing volumes mounted with their format is to examine the volume's boot record, which is stored in the first sector of the volume. Boot records for Microsoft file systems contain a field that stores a file system format type. File system drivers usually examine this field, and if it indicates a format they manage, they look at other information stored in the boot record. This information usually includes a file system name field and enough data for the file system driver to locate critical

metadata files on the volume. NTFS, for example, will recognize a volume only if the type field is NTFS, the name field is "NTFS", and the critical metadata files described by the boot record are consistent.

If a file system driver signals affirmatively, the I/O manager fills in the VPB and passes the open request with the remaining path (that is, \Test) to the file system driver. The file system driver completes the request by using its file system format to interpret the data that the partition stores. After a mount fills in a partition device object's VPB, the I/O manager hands sub-sequent open requests aimed at the partition to the mounted file system driver. If no file system driver claims a partition, Raw—a file system driver built into Windows 2000—claims the partition and fails all requests to open files on that partition. Figure 10-13 shows a simplified example (that is, the figure omits the file system driver's interactions with the Windows 2000 cache manager) of the path that I/O directed at a mounted partition follows.

Figure 10-13
Mounted volume I/O flow

Instead of having every file system driver loaded, regardless of whether or not they have any volumes to manage, Windows 2000 tries to minimize memory usage by using a surrogate driver named File System Recognizer (Winnt\System32\Drivers\Fs_rec.sys) to perform preliminary file system recognition. File System Recognizer knows enough about each file system format that Windows 2000 supports to be able to examine a boot record and determine whether it's associated with a Windows 2000 file system driver. When the system boots, File System Recognizer registers as a file system driver, and when the I/O manager calls it during a file system mount operation for a new volume, File System Recognizer loads the appropriate file system driver if the boot record corresponds to one that isn't loaded. After loading a file system driver, File System Recognizer forwards the mount IRP to the driver and lets the file system driver claim ownership of the volume.

Aside from the boot volume, which a driver mounts while the kernel is initializing, file system drivers mount most volumes when the Chkdsk file system consistency-checking application runs during a boot sequence. The boot-time version of Chkdsk is a native application (as opposed to a Win32 application) named Autochk.exe (\Winnt\System32\Autochk.exe), and the Session Manager (\Winnt\System32\Smss.exe) runs it because it is specified as a boot-run program in the HKLM\SYSTEM\CurrentControlSet\Control\Session Manager\ BootExecute value. Chkdsk accesses each drive letter to see whether the volume associated with the letter requires a consistency check.

One place in which mounting can occur more than once for the same disk is with removable media. Windows 2000 file system drivers respond to media changes by querying the disk's volume identifier. If they see the volume identifier change, the driver dismounts the disk and attempts to remount it.

Conclusion

In this chapter, we've reviewed the on-disk organization, components, and operation of Windows 2000 disk storage management. In the next chapter, we delve into the cache manager, an executive component integral to the operation of file system drivers that mount the volume types presented in this chapter.

ntkrnlmp!Ki386CheckDelayedNpxTrap+2cf:
80432255 5e pop esi 80432256 5b pop ebx 8
c20800 ret 0x8 8043225b cc int 3 ntkrnlmp
095150 or [ecx+0x50],edx 8043225f 8b4158
push ebx 80432263 56 push esi 80432264 8b
3b10 mov ed 8916 mov [esi
edx+0x4] mov eax,[ea
eax,[ecx ntkrnlmp
80432276 8b60 mov x+0x60] 8043
8043227b 902 mov [edx x 8043227e 895
0b9eb00 r [ecx+0xeb]
eax,[ecx+ jz ntkrnlmp!
80432290 80b byte ptr [eax+0x3],
dx,[eax+0x18] 80432297 8b401c mov eax,[e
eax],edx 8043229c 894204 mov [edx+0x4],e
eax,[ecx+0xe0] 804322a5 85c0 test eax,ea
tkrnlmp!KiUnwaitThread+0x50 (804322ac) 8
eax+0x18] 804322ac 8a5133 mov dl,[ecx+0
,[ecx+0x44] 804322b2 80fa10 cmp dl,0x
tkrnlmp!KiUnwaitThread+0xc2 (8043231e) 8
[ecx+0x6d] 804322ba 84db test bl,bl 8
krnlmp!KiUnwaitThread+0x96 (804322f2) 8
[ecx+0x18] 804322c8 4d dec ebp 804a90
[ecx+0x8] 804a90f1 5f pop edi 804

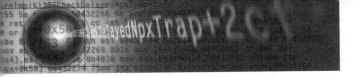

Cache Manager

The Microsoft Windows 2000 cache manager is a set of kernel-mode functions and system threads that cooperate with the memory manager to provide data caching for all Windows 2000 file system drivers (both local and network). In this chapter, we'll explain how the Windows 2000 cache manager, including its key internal data structures and functions, works; how it is sized at system initialization time; how it interacts with other elements of the operating system; and how you can observe its activity through performance counters. We'll also describe the five flags on the Win32 *CreateFile* function that affect file caching.

> **NOTE** None of the cache manager's internal functions are outlined in this chapter beyond the depth required to explain how the cache manager works. The programming interfaces to the cache manager are documented in the *Windows 2000 Installable File System* (IFS) kit. For more information about the IFS kit, see *microsoft.com/ddk/ifskit/*.

Key Features of the Windows 2000 Cache Manager

The Windows 2000 cache manager has several key features:

- Supports all file system types (both local and network), thus removing the need for each file system to implement its own cache management code

- Uses the memory manager to control what parts of what files are in physical memory (trading off demands for physical memory between user processes and the operating system)

■ Caches data on a virtual block basis (offsets within a file)—in contrast to most caching systems, which cache on a logical block basis (offsets within a disk partition)—allowing for intelligent read-ahead and high-speed access to the cache without involving file system drivers. (This method of caching, called *fast I/O*, is described later in this chapter.)

■ Supports "hints" passed by applications at file open time (such as random versus sequential access, temporary file creation, and so on)

■ Supports recoverable file systems (for example, those that use transaction logging) to recover data after a system failure

Although we'll talk more throughout this chapter about how these features are used in the cache manager, in this section we'll introduce you to the concepts behind these features.

Single, Centralized System Cache

Some operating systems rely on each individual file system to cache data, a practice that results either in duplicated caching and memory management code in the operating system or in limitations on the kinds of data that can be cached. In contrast, Windows 2000 offers a centralized caching facility that caches all externally stored data, whether on local hard disks, floppy disks, network file servers, or CD-ROMs. Any data can be cached, whether it's user data streams (the contents of a file and the ongoing read and write activity to that file) or file system *metadata* (such as directory and file headers). As you'll discover in this chapter, the method Windows 2000 uses to access the cache depends on the type of data being cached.

The Memory Manager

One unusual aspect of the Windows 2000 cache manager is that it never knows how much cached data is actually in physical memory. This statement might sound strange, since the purpose of a cache is to keep a subset of frequently accessed data in physical memory as a way to improve I/O performance. The reason the Windows 2000 cache manager doesn't know how much data is in

physical memory is that it accesses data by mapping views of files into system virtual address spaces, using standard *section objects* (*file mapping objects* in Win32 terminology). (Section objects are the basic primitive of the memory manager and are explained in detail in Chapter 7.) As addresses in these mapped views are accessed, the memory manager pages in blocks that aren't in physical memory. And when memory demands dictate, the memory manager pages data out of the cache and back to the files that are open in (mapped into) the cache.

By caching on the basis of a virtual address space using mapped files, the cache manager avoids generating read or write I/O request packets (IRPs) to access the data for files it's caching. Instead, it simply copies data to or from the virtual addresses where the portion of the cached file is mapped and relies on the memory manager to fault in (or out) the data into (or out of) memory as needed. This process allows the memory manager to make global trade-offs on how much memory to give to the system cache versus to the user processes. (The cache manager also initiates I/O, such as lazy writing, which is described later in this chapter; however, it calls the memory manager to write the pages.) Also, as you'll learn in the next section, this design makes it possible for processes that open cached files to see the same data as do those processes mapping the same files into their user address spaces.

Cache Coherency

One important function of a cache manager is to ensure that any process accessing cached data will get the most recent version of that data. A problem can arise when one process opens a file (and hence the file is cached) while another process maps the file into its address space directly (using the Win32 *MapViewOfFile* function). This potential problem doesn't occur under Windows 2000 because both the cache manager and the user applications that map files into their address spaces use the same memory management file mapping services. Because the memory manager guarantees that it has only one representation of each unique mapped file (regardless of the number of section objects or mapped views), it maps all views of a file (even if they overlap) to a single set of pages in physical memory, as shown in Figure 11-1. (For more information on how the memory manager works with mapped files, see Chapter 7.)

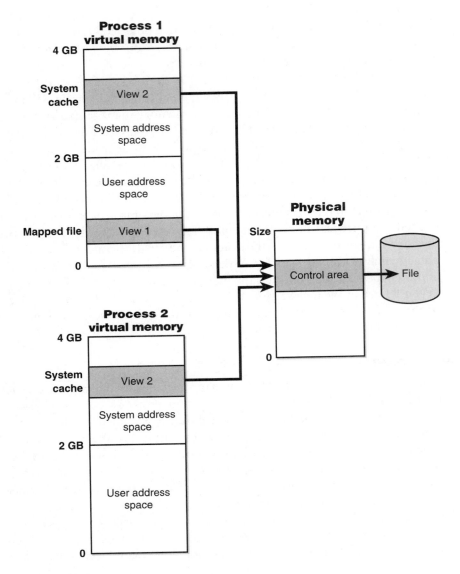

Figure 11-1
Coherent caching scheme

So, for example, if Process 1 has a view (View 1) of the file mapped into its user address space and Process 2 is accessing the same view via the system cache, Process 2 will see any changes that Process 1 makes as they're made, not

as they're flushed. The memory manager won't flush *all* user-mapped pages—only those that it knows have been written to (because they have the modified bit set). Therefore, any process accessing a file under Windows 2000 always sees the most up-to-date version of that file, even if some processes have the file open through the I/O system and others have the file mapped into their address space using the Win32 file mapping functions.

> **NOTE** Cache coherency is somewhat more difficult for network redirectors than for local file systems because network redirectors must implement additional flushing and purge operations to ensure cache coherency when accessing network data. See Chapter 13 for a description of opportunistic locking, the Windows 2000 distributed cache coherency mechanism.

Virtual Block Caching

Most operating system cache managers (including Novell NetWare, OpenVMS, OS/2, and older UNIX systems) cache data on the basis of *logical blocks*. With this method, the cache manager keeps track of which blocks of a disk partition are in the cache. The Windows 2000 cache manager, in contrast, uses a method known as *virtual block caching*, in which the cache manager keeps track of which parts of which *files* are in the cache. The cache manager is able to monitor these file portions by mapping 256-KB views of files into system virtual address spaces, using special system cache routines located in the memory manager. This approach has the following key benefits:

- It opens up the possibility of doing intelligent read-ahead; because the cache tracks which parts of which files are in the cache, it can predict where the caller might be going next.

- It allows the I/O system to bypass going to the file system for requests for data that is already in the cache (fast I/O). Because the cache manager knows which parts of which files are in the cache, it can return the address of cached data to satisfy an I/O request without having to call the file system.

Details of how intelligent read-ahead and fast I/O work are provided later in this chapter.

Stream-Based Caching

The Windows 2000 cache manager is also designed to do *stream caching*, as opposed to file caching. A *stream* is a sequence of bytes within a file. Some file systems, such as NTFS, allow a file to contain more than one stream; the cache manager accommodates such file systems by caching each stream independently. NTFS can exploit this feature by organizing its master file table (described in Chapter 12) into streams and by caching these streams as well. In fact, although the Windows 2000 cache manager might be said to cache files, it actually caches streams (all files have at least one stream of data) identified by both a filename and, if more than one stream exists in the file, a stream name.

Recoverable File System Support

Recoverable file systems such as NTFS are designed to reconstruct the disk volume structure after a system failure. This capability means that I/O operations in progress at the time of a system failure must be either entirely completed or entirely backed out from the disk when the system is restarted. Half-completed I/O operations can corrupt a disk volume and even render an entire volume inaccessible. To avoid this problem, a recoverable file system maintains a log file in which it records every update it intends to make to the file system structure (the file system's metadata) before it writes the change to the volume. If the system fails, interrupting volume modifications in progress, the recoverable file system uses information stored in the log to reissue the volume updates.

NOTE The term *metadata* applies only to changes in the file system structure: file and directory creation, renaming, and deletion.

To guarantee a successful volume recovery, every log file record documenting a volume update must be completely written to disk before the update itself is applied to the volume. Because disk writes are cached, the cache manager and the file system must work together to ensure that the following actions occur, in sequence:

1. The file system writes a log file record documenting the volume update it intends to make.

2. The file system calls the cache manager to flush the log file record to disk.

3. The file system writes the volume update to the cache; that is, it modifies its cached metadata.

4. The cache manager flushes the altered metadata to disk, updating the volume structure. (Actually, log file records are batched before being flushed to disk, as are volume modifications.)

When a file system writes data to the cache, it can supply a *logical sequence number* (LSN) that identifies the record in its log file, which corresponds to the cache update. The cache manager keeps track of these numbers, recording the lowest and highest LSNs (representing the oldest and newest log file records) associated with each page in the cache. In addition, data streams that are protected by transaction log records are marked as "no write" by NTFS so that the modified page writer won't inadvertently write out these pages before the corresponding log records are written. (When the modified page writer sees a page marked this way, it moves the page to a special list that the cache manager then flushes at the appropriate time, such as when lazy writer activity takes place.)

When it prepares to flush a group of dirty pages to disk, the cache manager determines the highest LSN associated with the pages to be flushed and reports that number to the file system. The file system can then call the cache manager back, directing it to flush log file data up to the point represented by the reported LSN. *After* the cache manager flushes the log file up to that LSN, it flushes the corresponding volume structure updates to disk, thus ensuring that it records what it's going to do before actually doing it. These interactions between the file system and the cache manager guarantee the recoverability of the disk volume after a system failure.

Cache Structure

Because the Windows 2000 system cache manager caches data on a virtual basis, it is given a region of system virtual address spaces to manage (instead of a region of physical memory). The cache manager then divides each address space region into 256-KB slots called *views*, as shown in Figure 11-2. (For a detailed description of the layout of system space, see Chapter 7.)

Figure 11-2
System cache address space

At a file's first I/O (read or write) operation, the cache manager maps a 256-KB view of the 256-KB-aligned region of the file that contains the requested data into a free slot in the system cache address space. For example, if 10 bytes starting at an offset of 300,000 bytes were read into a file, the view that would be mapped would begin at offset 262144 (the second 256-KB-aligned region of the file) and extend for 256 KB.

The cache manager maps views of files into slots in the cache's address space on a round-robin basis, mapping the first requested view into the first 256-KB slot, the second view into the second 256-KB slot, and so forth, as shown in Figure 11-3. In this example, File B was mapped first, File A second, and File C third, so File B's mapped chunk occupies the first slot in the cache. Notice that only the first 256-KB portion of File B has been mapped, which is due to the fact that only part of the file has been accessed and that although File C is only 100 KB (and thus smaller than one of the views in the system cache), it requires its own 256-KB slot in the cache.

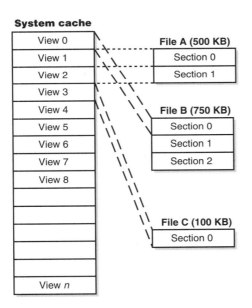

Figure 11-3
Files of varying sizes mapped into the system cache

The cache manager guarantees that a view is mapped only as long as it's active. A view is marked active, however, only during a read or write operation to or from the file. Unless a process opens a file by specifying the FILE_ FLAG_RANDOM_ACCESS flag in the call to *CreateFile*, the cache manager unmaps inactive views of a file as it maps new views for the file. Pages for unmapped

views are sent to the standby or modified lists (depending on whether they have been changed), and because the memory manager exports a special interface for the cache manager, the cache manager can direct the pages to be placed at the end or front of these lists. Pages that correspond to views of files opened with the FILE_FLAG_SEQUENTIAL_SCAN flag are moved to the front of the lists, whereas all others are moved to the end. This scheme encourages the reuse of pages belonging to sequentially accessed files and specifically prevents a large file copy operation from affecting more than a small part of physical memory.

If the cache manager needs to map a view of a file and there are no more free slots in the cache, it will unmap the least recently mapped inactive view and use that slot. If no views are available, an I/O error is returned, indicating that insufficient system resources are available to perform the operation. Given that views are marked active only during a read or write operation, however, this scenario is extremely unlikely because thousands of files would have to be accessed simultaneously for this situation to occur.

Cache Size

In the following sections, we'll explain how Windows 2000 computes the size of the system cache (both virtually and physically). As with most calculations related to memory management, the size of the system cache depends on a number of factors, including memory size and which version of Windows 2000 is running.

Cache Virtual Size

The virtual size of the system cache is a function of the amount of physical memory installed. The default size is 64 MB. If the system has more than 4032 pages (16 MB) of physical memory, the cache size is set to 128 MB plus 64 MB for each additional 4 MB of physical memory. Using this algorithm, the virtual size of the system cache for a computer with 64 MB of physical memory will be:

128 MB + (64 MB − 16 MB) / 4 MB * 64 MB = 896 MB

Table 11-1 shows the minimum and maximum virtual size of the system cache, along with the start and end addresses. If the system calculates a cache virtual size that is greater than 512 MB, the cache is assigned virtual memory from an additional address range known as *cache extra memory*.

Table 11-1 Size and Location of System Data Cache

Platform	Address Range	Minimum/ Maximum Virtual Size
x86 2-GB system space	0xC1000000-E0FFFFFF, 0xA4000000-BFFFFFFF	64–960 MB
x86 1-GB system space	0xC1000000-DBFFFFFF	64–432 MB
x86 1-GB system space with Terminal Services	0xC1000000-DCFFFFFF	64–448 MB

Table 11-2 lists the system variables that contain the virtual size and address of the system cache.

Table 11-2 System Variables for the Virtual Size and Address of the System Cache

System Variable	Description
MmSystemCacheStart	Starting virtual address of cache
MmSystemCacheEnd	Ending virtual address of cache
MiSystemCacheStartExtra	Starting virtual address of cache extra memory if cache size > 512 MB
MiSystemCacheEndExtra	Ending virtual address of cache extra memory if cache size > 512 MB
MmSizeOfSystemCacheInPages	Maximum size of cache in pages

Cache Physical Size

As mentioned earlier, one of the key differences in the design of the Windows 2000 cache manager from that of other operating systems is the delegation of physical memory management to the global memory manager. Because of this, the existing code that handles working set expansion and trimming as well as manages the modified and standby list is also used to control the size of the system cache, dynamically balancing demands for physical memory between processes and the operating system.

The system cache doesn't have its own working set but rather shares a single system set that includes cache data, paged pool, pageable Ntoskrnl code, and pageable driver code. As explained in the section "System Working Set" in Chapter 7 (on page 463), this single working set is called internally the *system cache working set* even though the system cache is just one of the components that contribute to it. For the purposes of this book, we'll refer to this working set simply as the *system working set*.

You can examine the physical size of the system cache compared to that of the total system working set as well as page fault information on the system working set by examining the performance counters or system variables listed in Table 11-3.

Table 11-3 **System Variables for the Physical Size of the System Cache and Page Fault Information**

Performance Counter (in bytes)	System Variable (in pages)	Description
Memory: System Cache Resident Bytes	*MmSystemCachePage*	Physical memory consumed by the system cache.
Memory: Cache Bytes	*MmSystemCacheWs.WorkingSetSize*	Total size of the system working set (including the cache, paged pool, pageable code, and system mapped views). This is *not* the size of the cache (as the name implies)!
Memory: Cache Bytes Peak	*MmSystemCacheWs.Peak*	Peak system working set size.
Memory: Cache Faults/Sec	*MmSystemCacheWs.PageFaultCount*	Page faults in the system working set (not just the cache).

Most utilities that claim to display the size of the system cache (such as Task Manager, Pview, Pstat, Pmon, Perfmtr, and so on) in fact display the total system working set size, not just the cache size. The reason for this inaccuracy is that the performance counter Memory: Cache Bytes (see Table 11-3) returns the

total system working set size, which includes the system cache, paged pool, pageable system code, and system mapped views, even though the name and explanatory text imply that it represents just the cache size. For example, if you start Task Manager (by pressing Ctrl+Shift+Esc) and click the Performance tab, the field named System Cache is actually the system working set size, as you can see in Figure 11-4.

This isn't the size of the system cache.

Figure 11-4
The Windows 2000 Task Manager doesn't report the size of the system cache

A number of internal system variables control working set expansion and trimming, such as *MmWorkingSetReductionMaxCacheWs*, *MmWorkingSet-ReductionMinCacheWs*, *MmWorkingSetVolReductionMaxCacheWs*, and *Mm-PeriodicAgressiveCacheWsMin*. Although we don't cover these variables in detail in this book, in Chapter 7, we do describe the memory manager's general policies for working set management.

EXPERIMENT: Looking at the Cache's Working Set

The *!filecache* debugger command dumps information about the physical memory the cache is using, including the names of files mapped into virtual address control blocks (VACBs), where applicable, as you can see in the following output. (File system drivers cache metadata by using unnamed file streams.)

```
kd> !filecache 3
***** Dump file cache******
File Cache Information
  Current size 6344 kb
  Peak size    14440 kb
  Loading file cache database (131072 PTEs)...
  File cache PTEs loaded, loading PFNs...
  File cache has 278 valid pages
  File cache PFN data extracted
  Building kernel map
  Finished building kernel map

  Usage Summary (in Kb):
Control Valid Standby Dirty Shared Locked PageTables  name
  ff3f5908   20       0     0      0      0        0   No Name for File
  ff3a0328    8       0     0      0      0        0   No Name for File
  fe50ba68   72       0     0      0      0        0   No Name for File
  fe4edd68    4       0     0      0      0        0   No Name for File
  fe4edcc8   88       0     0      0      0        0   No Name for File
  fe4ed7e8   16       0     0      0      0        0   No Name for File
  ff457968    4       0     0      0      0        0   No Name for File
  ff422de8    4       0     0      0      0        0   No Name for File
  ff142208    4       0     0      0      0        0   mapped_file( ias.mdb )
  ff163708    4       0     0      0      0        0   No Name for File
  ff1314c8    4       0     0      0      0        0   No Name for File
  ff0ec448    4       0     0      0      0        0   mapped_file( dnary.mdb )
  ff0f23a8    4       0     0      0      0        0   No Name for File
  fe50bda8    4       0     0      0      0        0   No Name for File
  ff0691a8    4       0     0      0      0        0   No Name for File
  ff071b08    4       0     0      0      0        0   No Name for File
  ff068b28    4       0     0      0      0        0   No Name for File
  ff0564c8    4       0     0      0      0        0   No Name for File
  ff070c48    4       0     0      0      0        0   No Name for File
  ff018d08    4       0     0      0      0        0   No Name for File
  ff013d48    4       0     0      0      0        0   No Name for File
  ff0e5f08    4       0     0      0      0        0   No Name for File
  ff02a628    4       0     0      0      0        0   No Name for File
```

```
ff0f0ba8     4      0    0    0    0    0   No Name for File
ff0e8b28     4      0    0    0    0    0   No Name for File
ff05a628     4      0    0    0    0    0   No Name for File
ff104e08     8      0    0    0    0    0   No Name for File
ff016328     4      0    0    0    0    0   No Name for File
ff06da88     4      0    0    0    0    0   No Name for File
ff2d2e28   692      0    0    0    0    0   mapped_file( ntoskrnl.pdb )
ff0afce8     4      0    0    0    0    0   No Name for File
ff001ae8    12      0    0    0    0    0   No Name for File
feffe308     4      0    0    0    0    0   No Name for File
ff175508    12      0    0    0    0    0   No Name for File
feffd328    12      0    0    0    0    0   No Name for File
feffc408     4      0    0    0    0    0   mapped_file( mshtml.tlb )
fefed788    12      0    0    0    0    0   No Name for File
feff9d28     4      0    0    0    0    0   mapped_file
( relationship[1].gif )
ff03dd08     4      0    0    0    0    0   mapped_file
( emotional[1].gif )
ff059828     4      0    0    0    0    0   mapped_file
( ADSAdClient31[1].htm )
fefe72e8     4      0    0    0    0    0   mapped_file
( comp_medicine[1].gif )
fefe9868    12      0    0    0    0    0   mapped_file
( ADSAdClient31[1].htm )
unable to get subsection fefe4d08
feffd8a8     8      0    0    0    0    0   mapped_file
( ADSAdClient31[1].htm )
fefef008     4      0    0    0    0    0   mapped_file
( 002924Z0001_LG[1].gif )
ff2f64e8     4      0    0    0    0    0   mapped_file( SOFTWARE.LOG )
```

Cache Data Structures

The cache manager uses the following data structures to keep track of cached files:

- Each 256-KB slot in the system cache is described by a VACB.

- Each separately opened cached file has a private cache map, which contains information used to control read-ahead (discussed later in the chapter).

- Each cached file has a single shared cache map structure, which points to slots in the system cache that contain mapped views of the file.

These structures and their relationships are described in the next sections.

Systemwide Cache Data Structures

The cache manager keeps track of the state of the views in the system cache by using an array of data structures called *virtual address control blocks* (VACBs). During system initialization, the cache manager allocates a single chunk of nonpaged pool to contain all the VACBs required to describe the system cache. It stores the address of the VACB array in the variable *CcVacbs*. Each VACB represents one 256-KB view in the system cache, as shown in Figure 11-5. The structure of a VACB is shown in Figure 11-6.

Figure 11-5
System VACB array

Virtual address of data in system cache
Pointer to shared cache map
File offset
Active count

Figure 11-6
VACB structure

As you can see in Figure 11-6, the first field in a VACB is the virtual address of the data in the system cache. The second field is a pointer to the shared cache map structure, which identifies which file is cached. The third field identifies the offset within the file at which the view begins (always based on a 256-KB granularity). Finally, the VACB contains the number of references to the view—that is, how many active reads or writes are accessing the view. During an I/O operation on a file, the file's VACB reference count is incremented and then it's decremented when the I/O operation is over. For access to file system metadata, the active count represents how many file system drivers have the pages in that view locked into memory.

Per-File Cache Data Structures

Each open handle to a file has a corresponding file object. (File objects are explained in detail in Chapter 9.) If the file is cached, the file object points to a *private cache map* structure that contains the location of the last two reads so that the cache manager can perform intelligent read-ahead (described in the section "Intelligent Read-Ahead" on page 669). In addition, all the private cache maps for a file object are linked together.

Each cached file (as opposed to file object) has a *shared cache map* structure that describes the state of the cached file, including its size and (for security reasons) its valid data length. (The function of the valid data length field is explained in the section "Write-Back Caching and Lazy Writing" on page 665.) The shared cache map also points to the *section object* (maintained by the memory manager, and which describes the file's mapping into virtual memory), the list of private cache maps associated with that file, and any VACBs that describe currently mapped views of the file in the system cache. (See page 482 in Chapter 7 for more about section object pointers.) The relationships among these per-file cache data structures are illustrated in Figure 11-7.

When asked to read from a particular file, the cache manager must determine the answers to two questions:

1. Is the file in the cache?
2. If so, which VACB, if any, refers to the requested location?

In other words, the cache manager must find out whether a view of the file at the desired address is mapped into the system cache. If no VACB contains the desired file offset, the requested data isn't currently mapped into the system cache.

Figure 11-7
Per-file cache data structures

To keep track of which views for a given file are mapped into the system cache, the cache manager maintains an array of pointers to VACBs, the *VACB index array*. The first entry in the VACB index array refers to the first 256 KB of the file, the second entry to the second 256 KB, and so on. The diagram in Figure 11-8 shows four different sections from three different files that are currently mapped into the system cache.

When a process accesses a particular file in a given location, the cache manager looks in the appropriate entry in the file's VACB index array to see whether the requested data has been mapped into the cache. If the array entry is nonzero (and hence contains a pointer to a VACB), the area of the file being referenced is in the cache. The VACB, in turn, points to the location in the system cache where the view of the file is mapped. If the entry is zero, the cache manager must find a free slot in the system cache (and therefore a free VACB) to map the required view.

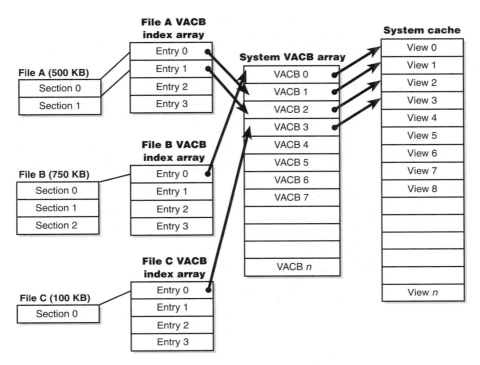

Figure 11-8
VACB index arrays

As a size optimization, the shared cache map contains a VACB index array that is 4 entries in size. Because each VACB describes 256 KB, the entries in this small fixed-size index array can point to VACB array entries that together describe a file of up to 1 MB. If a file is larger than 1 MB, a separate VACB index array is allocated from nonpaged pool, based on the size of the file divided by 256 KB and rounded up in the case of a remainder. The shared cache map then points to this separate structure.

As a further optimization, the VACB index array allocated from nonpaged pool becomes a sparse multilevel index array if the file is larger than 32 GB, where each index array consists of 128 entries. You can calculate the number of levels required for a file with the following formula:

(Number of bits required to represent file size – 18) / 7

Round the result of the equation up to the next whole number. The value 18 in the equation comes from the fact that a VACB represents 256 KB, and 256 KB is 2^{18}. The value 7 comes from the fact that each level in the array has

128 entries and 2^7 is 128. Thus, a file that has a size that is the maximum that can be described with 63 bits (the largest size the cache manager supports) would require only seven levels. The array is sparse because the only branches that the cache manager allocates are ones for which there are active views at the lowest-level index array. Figure 11-9 shows an example of a multilevel VACB array for a sparse file that is large enough to require three levels.

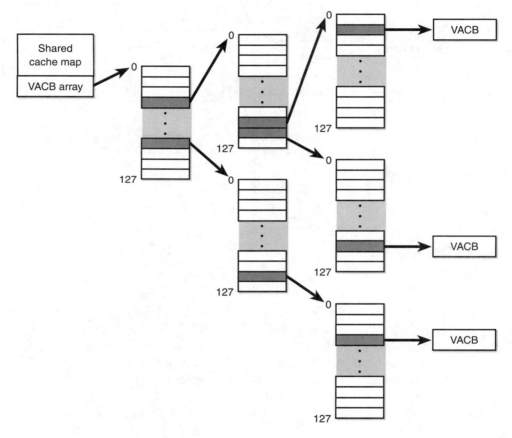

Figure 11-9
Multilevel VACB arrays

This scheme is required to efficiently handle sparse files that might have extremely large file sizes with only a small fraction of valid data because only enough of the array is allocated to handle the currently mapped views of a file.

For example, a 32-GB sparse file for which only 256 KB is mapped into the cache's virtual address space would require a VACB array with three allocated index arrays because only one branch of the array has a mapping and a 32-GB (2^{35} bytes) file requires a three-level array. If the cache manager didn't use the multilevel VACB array optimization for this file, it would have to allocate a VACB array with 128,000 entries, or the equivalent of 1000 index arrays.

Cache Operation

In this section, you'll see how the cache manager implements reading and writing file data on behalf of file system drivers. Keep in mind that the cache manager is involved in file I/O only when a file is opened (for example, using the Win32 *CreateFile* function). Mapped files don't go through the cache manager, nor do files opened with the FILE_FLAG_NO_BUFFERING flag set.

Write-Back Caching and Lazy Writing

The Windows 2000 cache manager implements a write-back cache with lazy write. This means that data written to files is first stored in memory in cache pages and then written to disk later. Thus, write operations are allowed to accumulate for a short time and are then flushed to disk all at once, reducing the overall number of disk I/O operations.

The cache manager must explicitly call the memory manager to flush cache pages because otherwise the memory manager writes memory contents to disk only when demand for physical memory exceeds supply, as is appropriate for volatile data. Cached file data, however, represents nonvolatile disk data. If a process modifies cached data, the user expects the contents to be reflected on disk in a timely manner.

The decision about how often to flush the cache is an important one. If the cache is flushed too frequently, system performance will be slowed by unnecessary I/O. If the cache is flushed too rarely, you risk losing modified file data in the cases of a system failure (a loss especially irritating to users who know that they asked the application to save the changes) and running out of physical memory (because it's being used by an excess of modified pages).

To balance these concerns, once per second a system thread created by the cache manager—the *lazy writer*—queues one-eighth of the dirty pages in the system cache to be written to disk. If the rate at which dirty pages are being produced is greater than the amount the lazy writer had determined it should

write, the lazy writer writes an additional number of dirty pages that it calculates are necessary to match that rate. System worker threads from the systemwide critical worker thread pool actually perform the I/O operations.

NOTE For C2-secure file systems (such as NTFS), the cache manager provides a means for the file system to track when and how much data has been written to a file. After the lazy writer flushes dirty pages to the disk, the cache manager notifies the file system, instructing it to update its view of the valid data length for the file.

You can examine the activity of the lazy writer by examining the cache performance counters or system variables listed in Table 11-4.

Table 11-4 System Variables for Examining the Activity of the Lazy Writer

Performance Counter (frequency)	System Variable (count)	Description
Cache: Lazy Write Flushes/Sec	*CcLazyWriteIos*	Number of lazy writer flushes
Cache: Lazy Write Pages/Sec	*CcLazyWritePages*	Number of pages written by the lazy writer

Calculating the Dirty Page Threshold

The *dirty page threshold* is the number of pages that the system cache keeps in memory before waking up the lazy writer system thread to write out pages back to the disk. This value is computed at system initialization time and depends on physical memory size and the value of the registry value HKLM\SYSTEM\CurrentControlSet\Control\SessionManager\Memory Management\LargeSystemCache. This value is 0 by default on Windows 2000 Professional and 1 on Windows 2000 Server systems. You can adjust this value through the GUI on Windows 2000 Server systems by modifying the properties of the file server service. (Bring up the properties for a network connection, and double-click on File And Printer Sharing For Microsoft Networks.) Even though this service exists on Windows 2000 Professional, its parameters can't be adjusted. Figure 11-10 shows the dialog box you use when modifying the amount of memory allocated for local and network applications in the Server network service.

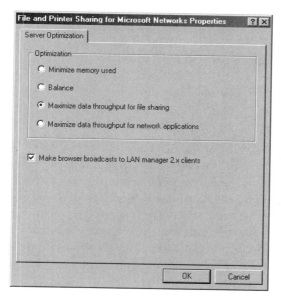

Figure 11-10
File And Printer Sharing For Microsoft Networks Properties dialog box, which is used to modify the properties of the Windows 2000 Server network service

The setting shown in Figure 11-10, Maximize Data Throughput For File Sharing, is the default for Server systems running with Terminal Services installed—the LargeSystemCache value is 1. Choosing any of the other settings will set the LargeSystemCache value to 0. Although each of the four settings in the Optimization section of the File And Printer Sharing For Microsoft Networks Properties dialog box affect the behavior of the system cache, they also modify the behavior of the file server service.

Table 11-5 contains the algorithm used to calculate the dirty page threshold. The calculations in Table 11-5 are overridden if the system maximum working set size is greater than 4 MB—and it often is. (See page 457 in Chapter 7 to find out how the memory manager chooses system working set sizes—that is, how it determines whether the size is small, medium, or large.) When the maximum working set size exceeds 4 MB, the dirty page threshold is set to the value of the system maximum working set size minus 2 MB.

Table 11-5 Algorithm for Calculating the Dirty Page Threshold

System Memory Size	Dirty Page Threshold
Small	Physical pages / 8
Medium	Physical pages / 4
Large	Sum of the above two values

Disabling Lazy Writing for a File

If you create a temporary file by specifying the flag FILE_ATTRIBUTE_TEMPORARY in a call to the Win32 *CreateFile* function, the lazy writer won't write dirty pages to the disk unless there is a severe shortage of physical memory or the file is closed. This characteristic of the lazy writer improves system performance—the lazy writer doesn't immediately write data to a disk that might ultimately be discarded. Applications usually delete temporary files soon after closing them.

Forcing the Cache to Write Through to Disk

Because some applications can't tolerate even momentary delays between writing a file and seeing the updates on disk, the cache manager also supports write-through caching on a per-file basis; changes are written to disk as soon as they're made. To turn on write-through caching, set the FILE_FLAG_WRITE_THROUGH flag in the call to the *CreateFile* function. Alternatively, a thread can explicitly flush an open file, by using the Win32 *FlushFileBuffers* function, when it reaches a point at which the data needs to be written to disk. You can observe cache flush operations that are the result of write-through I/O requests or explicit calls to *FlushFileBuffers* via the performance counters or system variables shown in Table 11-6.

Table 11-6 System Variables for Viewing Cache Flush Operations

Performance Counter (frequency)	System Variable (count)	Description
Cache: Data Flushes/Sec	*CcDataFlushes*	Number of times cache pages were flushed explicitly or because of write through
Cache: Data Flush Pages/Sec	*CcDataPages*	Number of pages flushed explicitly or because of write through

Flushing Mapped Files

If the lazy writer must write data to disk from a view that's also mapped into another process's address space, the situation becomes a little more complicated because the cache manager will only know about the pages it has modified. (Pages modified by another process are known only to that process because the modified bit in the page table entries for modified pages are kept in the process private page tables.) To address this situation, the memory manager informs the cache manager when a user maps a file. When such a file is flushed in the cache (for example, as a result of a call to the Win32 *FlushFileBuffers* function), the cache manager writes the dirty pages in the cache and then checks to see whether the file is also mapped by another process. When the cache manager sees that the file is, the cache manager then flushes the entire view of the section in order to write out pages that the second process might have modified. If a user maps a view of a file that is also open in the cache, when the view is unmapped, the modified pages are marked as dirty so that when the lazy writer thread later flushes the view, those dirty pages will be written to disk. This procedure works as long as the sequence occurs in the following order:

1. A user unmaps the view.

2. A process flushes file buffers.

If this sequence isn't followed, you can't predict which pages will be written to disk.

Intelligent Read-Ahead

The Windows 2000 cache manager uses the principle of spatial locality to perform *intelligent read-ahead* by predicting what data the calling process is likely to read next based on the data that it is reading currently. Because the system cache is based on virtual addresses, which are contiguous for a particular file, it doesn't matter whether they're juxtaposed in physical memory. File read-ahead for logical block caching is more complex and requires tight cooperation between file system drivers and the block cache because that cache system is based on the relative positions of the accessed data on the disk, and of course, files aren't necessarily stored contiguously on disk.

The two types of read-ahead—virtual address read-ahead and asynchronous read-ahead with history—are explained in the next two sections. You can examine read-ahead activity by using the Cache: Read Aheads/Sec performance counter or the *CcReadAheadIos* system variable.

Virtual Address Read-Ahead

Recall from Chapter 7 that when the memory manager resolves a page fault, it reads into memory several pages near the one explicitly accessed, a method called *clustering*. For applications that read sequentially, this *virtual address read-ahead* operation reduces the number of disk reads necessary to retrieve data. The only disadvantage to the memory manager's method is that because this read-ahead is done in the context of resolving a page fault it must be performed synchronously, while the thread waiting on the data being paged back into memory is waiting.

Asynchronous Read-Ahead with History

The virtual address read-ahead performed by the memory manager improves I/O performance, but its benefits are limited to sequentially accessed data. To extend read-ahead benefits to certain cases of randomly accessed data, the cache manager maintains a history of the last two read requests in the private cache map for the file handle being accessed, a method known as *asynchronous read-ahead with history*. If a pattern can be determined from the caller's apparently random reads, the cache manager extrapolates it. For example, if the caller reads page 4000 and then page 3000, the cache manager assumes that the next page the caller will require is page 2000 and prereads it.

> **NOTE** Although a caller must issue a minimum of three read operations to establish a predictable sequence, only two are stored in the private cache map.

To make read-ahead even more efficient, the Win32 *CreateFile* function provides a flag indicating sequential file access: FILE_FLAG_SEQUENTIAL_SCAN. If this flag is set, the cache manager doesn't keep a read history for the caller for prediction but instead performs sequential read-ahead. However, as the file is read into the cache's working set, the cache manager unmaps views of the file that are no longer active and directs the memory manager to place the

pages belonging to the unmapped views at the front of the standby list or modified list (if the pages are modified) so that they will be quickly reused. It also reads ahead three times as much data (192 KB instead of 64 KB, for example) by using a separate I/O operation for each read. As the caller continues reading, the cache manager prereads additional blocks of data, always staying about one read (of the size of the current read) ahead of the caller.

The cache manager's read-ahead is asynchronous because it is performed in a thread separate from the caller's thread and proceeds concurrently with the caller's execution. When called to retrieve cached data, the cache manager first accesses the requested virtual page to satisfy the request and then queues an additional I/O request to retrieve additional data to a system worker thread. The worker thread then executes in the background, reading additional data in anticipation of the caller's next read request. The preread pages are faulted into memory while the program continues executing so that when the caller requests the data it's already in memory.

Although the asynchronous read-ahead with history technique uses more memory than the standard read-ahead, it minimizes disk I/O and further improves the performance of applications reading large amounts of cached sequential data. The Cache: Read Aheads/Sec performance counter indicates sequential access read-ahead operations.

For applications that have no predictable read pattern, the FILE_FLAG_ RANDOM_ACCESS flag can be specified when the *CreateFile* function is called. This flag instructs the cache manager not to attempt to predict where the application is reading next and thus disables read-ahead. The flag also stops the cache manager from aggressively unmapping views of the file as the file is accessed so as to minimize the mapping/unmapping activity for the file when the application revisits portions of the file.

System Threads

As mentioned earlier, the cache manager performs lazy write and read-ahead I/O operations by submitting requests to the common critical system worker thread pool. However, it does limit the use of these threads to one less than the total number of critical worker system threads for small and medium memory systems (two less than the total for large memory systems).

Internally, the cache manager organizes its work requests into two lists (though these are serviced by the same set of executive worker threads):

- The *express queue* is used for read-ahead operations.
- The *regular queue* is used for lazy write scans (for dirty data to flush), write behinds, and lazy closes.

To keep track of the work items the worker threads need to perform, the cache manager creates its own internal *per-processor look-aside list*, a fixed-length list—one for each processor—of worker queue item structures. (Look-aside lists are discussed in Chapter 7.) The number of worker queue items depends on system size: 32 for small-memory systems, 64 for medium-memory systems, 128 for large-memory Windows 2000 Professional systems, and 256 for large-memory Windows 2000 Server systems.

Fast I/O

Whenever possible, reads and writes to cached files are handled by a high-speed mechanism named *fast I/O*. Fast I/O is a means of reading or writing a cached file without going through the work of generating an IRP, as described in Chapter 9. With fast I/O, the I/O manager calls the file system driver's fast I/O routine to see whether I/O can be satisfied directly from the cache manager without generating an IRP.

Because the Windows 2000 cache manager keeps track of which blocks of which files are in the cache, file system drivers can use the cache manager to access file data simply by copying to or from pages mapped to the actual file being referenced without going through the overhead of generating an IRP.

Fast I/O doesn't always occur. For example, the first read or write to a file requires setting up the file for caching (mapping the file into the cache and setting up the cache data structures, as explained earlier in the section "Cache Data Structures" on page 659). Also, if the caller specified an asynchronous read or write, fast I/O isn't used because the caller might be stalled during paging I/O operations required to satisfy the buffer copy to or from the system cache and thus not really providing the requested asynchronous I/O operation. But even on a synchronous I/O, the file system driver might decide that it can't process the I/O operation by using the fast I/O mechanism, say, for example, if the file in question has a locked range of bytes (as a result of calls to the Win32 *LockFile* and *UnlockFile* functions). Because the cache manager doesn't know what parts of which files are locked, the file system driver must check the validity of the read or write, which requires generating an IRP. The decision tree for fast I/O is shown in Figure 11-11.

Figure 11-11
Fast I/O decision tree

These steps are involved in servicing a read or a write with fast I/O:

1. A thread performs a read or write operation.

2. If the file is cached and the I/O is synchronous, the request passes to the fast I/O entry point of the file system driver. If the file isn't cached, the file system driver sets up the file for caching so that the next time, fast I/O can be used to satisfy a read or write request.

3. If the file system driver's fast I/O routine determines that fast I/O is possible, it calls the cache manager read or write routine to access the file data directly in the cache. (If fast I/O isn't possible, the file system driver returns to the I/O system, which then generates an IRP for the I/O and eventually calls the file system's regular read routine.)

4. The cache manager translates the supplied file offset into a virtual address in the cache.

5. For reads, the cache manager copies the data from the cache into the buffer of the process requesting it; for writes, it copies the data from the buffer to the cache.

6. One of the following actions occurs:

 a. For reads, the read-ahead information in the caller's private cache map is updated.

 b. For writes, the dirty bit of any modified page in the cache is set so that the lazy writer will know to flush it to disk.

 c. For write-through files, any modifications are flushed to disk.

NOTE The fast I/O path isn't limited to occasions when the requested data already resides in physical memory. As noted in steps 5 and 6 of the preceding list, the cache manager simply accesses the virtual addresses of the already opened file where it expects the data to be. If a cache miss occurs, the memory manager dynamically pages the data into physical memory.

The performance counters or system variables listed in Table 11-7 can be used to determine the fast I/O activity on the system.

Table 11-7 System Variables for Determining Fast I/O Activity

Performance Counter (frequency)	System Variable (count)	Description
Cache: Sync Fast Reads/Sec	*CcFastReadWait*	Synchronous reads that were handled as fast I/O requests
Cache: Async Fast Reads/Sec	*CcFastReadNoWait*	Asynchronous reads that were handled as fast I/O requests (These are always zero because asynchronous fast reads aren't done in Windows 2000.)
Cache: Fast Read Resource Misses/Sec	*CcFastReadResourceMiss*	Fast I/O operations that couldn't be satisfied because of resource conflicts (This situation can occur with FAT but not with NTFS.)
Cache: Fast Read Not Possibles/Sec	*CcFastReadNotPossible*	Fast I/O operations that couldn't be satisfied (The file system driver decides; for example, files with byte range locks can't use fast I/O.)

Cache Support Routines

The first time a file's data is accessed for a read or write operation, the file system driver is responsible for determining whether some part of the file is mapped in the system cache. If it's not, the file system driver must call the *CcInitialize-CacheMap* function to set up the per-file data structures described in the preceding section.

Once a file is set up for cached access, the file system driver calls one of several functions to access the data in the file. There are three primary methods for accessing cached data, each intended for a specific situation:

■ The copy read method copies user data between cache buffers in system space and a process buffer in user space.

■ The mapping and pinning method uses virtual addresses to read and write data directly to cache buffers.

■ The physical memory access method uses physical addresses to read and write data directly to cache buffers.

File system drivers must provide two versions of the file read operation—cached and noncached—to prevent an infinite loop when the memory manager processes a page fault. When the memory manager resolves a page fault by calling the file system to retrieve data from the file (via the device driver, of course), it must specify this noncached read operation by setting the "no cache" flag in the IRP.

The next three sections explain these cache access mechanisms, their purpose, and how they're used.

Copying to and from the Cache

Because the system cache is in system space, it is mapped into the address space of every process. As with all system space pages, however, cache pages aren't accessible from user mode because that would be a potential security hole. (For example, a process might not have the rights to read a file whose data is currently contained in some part of the system cache.) Thus, user application file reads and writes to cached files must be serviced by kernel-mode routines that copy data between the cache's buffers in system space and the application's buffers residing in the process address space. The functions that file system drivers can use to perform this operation are listed in Table 11-8.

Table 11-8 Kernel-Mode Functions for Copying to and from the Cache

Function	Description
CcCopyRead	Copies a specified byte range from the system cache to a user buffer
CcFastCopyRead	Faster variation of *CcCopyRead* but limited to 32-bit file offsets and synchronous reads (used by NTFS, not FAT)
CcCopyWrite	Copies a specified byte range from a user buffer to the system cache
CcFastCopyWrite	Faster variation of *CcCopyWrite* but limited to 32-bit file offsets and synchronous, non-write-through writes (used by NTFS, not FAT)

You can examine read activity from the cache via the performance counters or system variables listed in Table 11-9.

Table 11-9 System Variables for Examining Read Activity from the Cache

Performance Counter (frequency)	System Variable (count)	Description
Cache: Copy Read Hits %	(*CcCopyReadWait* + *CcCopyReadNoWait*) / (*CcCopyReadWait* + (*CcCopyReadWaitMiss* + *CcCopyReadNoWait*) + *CcCopyReadNoWaitMiss*)	Percentage of copy reads to parts of files that were in the cache (A copy read can still generate paging I/O—the Memory: Cache Faults/Sec counter reports page fault activity for the system working set but includes both hard and soft page faults, so the counter still doesn't indicate actual paging I/O caused by cache faults.)
Cache: Copy Reads/Sec	*CcCopyReadWait* + *CcCopyReadNoWait*	Total copy reads from the cache
Cache: Sync Copy Reads/Sec	*CcCopyReadWait*	Synchronous copy reads from the cache
Cache: Async Copy Reads/Sec	*CcCopyReadNoWait*	Asynchronous copy reads from the cache

Caching with the Mapping and Pinning Interfaces

Just as user applications read and write data in files on a disk, file system drivers need to read and write the data that describes the files themselves (the metadata, or volume structure data). Because the file system drivers run in kernel mode, however, they could, if the cache manager were properly informed, modify data directly in the system cache. To permit this optimization, the cache manager provides the functions shown in Table 11-10. These functions permit the file system drivers to find where in virtual memory the file system metadata resides, thus allowing direct modification without the use of intermediary buffers.

Table 11-10 Functions for Finding Metadata Locations

Function	Description
CcMapData	Maps the byte range for read access
CcPinRead	Maps the byte range for read/write access and pins it
CcPreparePinWrite	Maps and pins the byte range for write access
CcPinMappedData	Pins a previously mapped buffer
CcSetDirtyPinnedData	Notifies the cache manager that the data has been modified
CcUnpinData	Releases the pages so that they can be removed from memory

If a file system driver needs to read file system metadata in the cache, it calls the cache manager's mapping interface to obtain the virtual address of the desired data. The cache manager touches all the requested pages to bring them into memory and then returns control to the file system driver. The file system driver can then access the data directly.

If the file system driver needs to modify cache pages, it calls the cache manager's pinning services, which keep the pages being modified in memory. The pages aren't actually locked into memory (such as when a device driver locks pages for direct memory access transfers). Instead, the memory manager's mapped page writer (explained in Chapter 7) sees that these pages are pinned and doesn't write the pages to disk until the file system driver unpins (releases) them. When the pages are released, the cache manager flushes any changes to disk and releases the cache view that the metadata occupied.

The mapping and pinning interfaces solve one thorny problem of implementing a file system: buffer management. Without directly manipulating cached metadata, a file system must predict the maximum number of buffers it will need when updating a volume's structure. By allowing the file system to access and

update its metadata directly in the cache, the cache manager eliminates the need for buffers, simply updating the volume structure in the virtual memory the memory manager provides. The only limitation the file system encounters is the amount of available memory.

You can examine pinning and mapping activity in the cache via the performance counters or system variables listed in Table 11-11.

Table 11-11 System Variables for Examining Pinning and Mapping Activity

Performance Counter (frequency)	System Variable (count)	Description
Cache: Data Map Hits %	($CcMapDataWait$ + $CcMapDataNoWait$)/ ($CcMapDataWait$ + $CcMapDataNoWait$)+ ($CcMapDataWaitMiss$ + $CcMapDataNoWaitMiss$)	Percentage of data maps to parts of files that were in the cache (A copy read can still generate paging I/O.)
Cache: Data Maps/Sec	$CcMapDataWait$ + $CcMapDataNoWait$	Total data maps from the cache
Cache: Sync Data Maps/Sec	$CcMapDataWait$	Synchronous data maps from the cache
Cache: Async Data Maps/Sec	$CcMapDataNoWait$	Asynchronous data maps from the cache
Cache: Data Map Pins/Sec	$CcPinMappedDataCount$	Number of requests to pin mapped data
Cache: Pin Read Hits %	($CcPinReadWait$ + $CcPinReadNoWait$) / ($CcPinReadWait$ + $CcPinReadNoWait$)+ ($CcPinReadWaitMiss$ + $CcPinReadNoWaitMiss$)	Percentage of pinned reads to parts of files that were in the cache (A copy read can still generate paging I/O.)
Cache: Pin Reads/Sec	$CcPinReadWait$ + $CcPinReadNoWait$	Total pinned reads from the cache
Cache: Sync Pin Reads/Sec	$CcPinReadWait$	Synchronous pinned reads from the cache
Cache: Async Pin Reads/Sec	$CcPinReadNoWait$	Asynchronous pinned reads from the cache

Caching with the Direct Memory Access Interfaces

In addition to the mapping and pinning interfaces used to access metadata directly in the cache, the cache manager provides a third interface to cached data: *direct memory access* (DMA). The DMA functions are used to read from or write to cache pages without intervening buffers, such as when a network file system is doing a transfer over the network.

The DMA interface returns to the file system the physical addresses of cached user data (rather than the virtual addresses, which the mapping and pinning interfaces return), which can then be used to transfer data directly from physical memory to a network device. Although small amounts of data (1 KB to 2 KB) can use the usual buffer-based copying interfaces, for larger transfers, the DMA interface can result in significant performance improvements for a network server processing file requests from remote systems.

To describe these references to physical memory, a *memory descriptor list* (MDL) is used. (MDLs were introduced in Chapter 7.) The four separate functions described in Table 11-12 create the cache manager's DMA interface.

Table 11-12 Functions That Create the DMA Interface

Function	Description
CcMdlRead	Returns an MDL describing the specified byte range
CcMdlReadComplete	Frees the MDL
CcMdlWrite	Returns an MDL describing a specified byte range (possibly containing zeros)
CcMdlWriteComplete	Frees the MDL and marks the range for writing

You can examine MDL activity from the cache via the performance counters or system variables listed in Table 11-13.

Table 11-13 System Variables for Examining MDL Activity from the Cache

Performance Counter (frequency)	System Variable (count)	Description
Cache: MDL Read Hits %	$(CcMdlReadWait + CcMdlReadNoWait) / (CcMdlReadWait + CcMdlReadNoWait) + (CcMdlReadWaitMiss + (CcMdlReadWaitMiss + CcMdlReadNoWaitMiss)$	Percentage of MDL reads to parts of files that were in the cache (References to pages satisfied by an MDL read can still generate paging I/O.)
Cache: MDL Reads/Sec	$CcMdlReadWait + CcMdlReadNoWait$	Total MDL reads from the cache
Cache: Sync MDL Reads/Sec	$CcMdlReadWait$	Synchronous MDL reads from the cache
Cache: Async MDL Reads/Sec	$CcMdlReadNoWait$	Asynchronous MDL reads from the cache

Write Throttling

Windows 2000 must determine whether the scheduled writes will affect system performance and then schedule any delayed writes. First it asks whether a certain number of bytes can be written right now without hurting performance and blocks that write if necessary. Then it sets up callback for automatically writing the bytes when writes are again permitted. Once it's notified of an impending write operation, the cache manager determines how many dirty pages are in the cache and how much physical memory is available. If few physical pages are free, the cache manager momentarily blocks the file system thread that's requesting to write data to the cache. The cache manager's lazy writer flushes some of the dirty pages to disk and then allows the blocked file system thread to continue. This *write throttling* prevents system performance from degrading because of a lack of memory when a file system or network server issues a large write operation.

Write throttling is also useful for network redirectors transmitting data over slow communication lines. For example, suppose a local process writes a large amount of data to a remote file system over a 9600-baud line. The data isn't

written to the remote disk until the cache manager's lazy writer flushes the cache. If the redirector has accumulated lots of dirty pages that are flushed to disk at once, the recipient could receive a network timeout before the data transfer completes. By using the *CcSetDirtyPageThreshold* function, the cache manager allows network redirectors to set a limit on the number of dirty cache pages they can tolerate, thus preventing this scenario. By limiting the number of dirty pages, the redirector ensures that a cache flush operation won't cause a network timeout.

EXPERIMENT: Viewing the Write-Throttle Parameters

The *!defwrites* kernel debugger command dumps the values of the kernel variables the cache manager uses, including the number of dirty pages in the file cache (*CcTotalDirtyPages*) when determining whether it should throttle write operations:

```
kd> !defwrites
*** Cache Write Throttle Analysis ***

        CcTotalDirtyPages:                 758 (    3032 Kb)
        CcDirtyPageThreshold:              770 (    3080 Kb)
        MmAvailablePages:                42255 (  169020 Kb)
        MmThrottleTop:                     250 (    1000 Kb)
        MmThrottleBottom:                   30 (     120 Kb)
        MmModifiedPageListHead.Total:      689 (    2756 Kb)

CcTotalDirtyPages within 64 (max charge) pages of the threshold, writes
    may be throttled

Check these thread(s): CcWriteBehind(LazyWriter)
Check critical workqueue for the lazy writer, !exqueue 16
```

This output shows that the number of dirty pages is close to the number that triggers write throttling (*CcDirtyPageThreshold*), so if a process tried to write more than 12 pages (48 KB) at the time of the experiment, it would be delayed until the lazy writer lowered the number of dirty pages.

Conclusion

The Windows 2000 cache manager provides a high-speed, intelligent mechanism for reducing disk I/O and increasing overall system throughput. By caching on the basis of virtual blocks, the Windows 2000 cache manager can perform intelligent read-ahead. By relying on the global memory manager's mapped file primitive to access file data, the cache manager can provide the special fast I/O mechanism to reduce the CPU time required for read and write operations and also leave all matters related to physical memory management to the single Windows 2000 global memory manager, thus reducing code duplication and increasing efficiency.

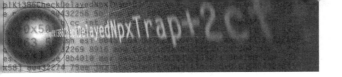

CHAPTER TWELVE

File Systems

In this chapter, we present an overview of the file system formats supported by Microsoft Windows 2000. We then describe the types of file system drivers and their basic operation, including how they interact with other system components such as the memory manager and the cache manager. Windows 2000 includes a native file system format called the NTFS file system. In the balance of the chapter, we focus on the on-disk layout of NTFS volumes and the advanced features of NTFS, such as compression, recoverability, quotas, and encryption.

To fully understand this chapter, you should be familiar with the terminology introduced in Chapter 10, including the terms *volume* and *partition*. You'll also need to be acquainted with these additional terms:

- *Sectors* are hardware-addressable blocks on a storage medium. Hard disks for x86 systems almost always define a 512-byte sector size. Thus, if the operating system wants to modify the 632nd byte on a disk, it must write a 512-byte block of data to the second sector on the disk.

- *File system formats* define the way that file data is stored on storage media and impact a file system's features. For example, a format that doesn't allow user permissions to be associated with files and directories can't support security. A file system format can also impose limits on the sizes of files and storage devices that the file system supports. Finally, some file system formats efficiently implement support for either large or small files or for large or small disks.

■ *Clusters* are the addressable blocks that many file system formats use. Cluster size is always a multiple of the sector size, as shown in Figure 12-1. File system formats use clusters to manage disk space more efficiently; a cluster size that is larger than the sector size divides a disk into more manageable blocks. The potential trade-off of a larger cluster size is wasted disk space, or internal fragmentation, that results because file sizes typically aren't perfect multiples of cluster sizes.

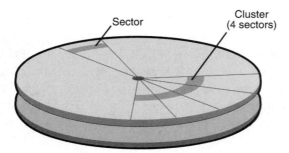

Figure 12-1
Sectors and a cluster on a disk

■ *Metadata* is data stored on a volume in support of file system format management. It isn't typically made accessible to applications. Metadata includes the data that defines the placement of files and directories on a volume, for example.

Windows 2000 File System Formats

Windows 2000 includes support for the following file system formats:

■ CDFS

■ UDF

■ FAT12, FAT16, and FAT32

■ NTFS

Each of these formats is best suited for certain environments, as you'll see in the following sections.

CDFS

CDFS, or CD-ROM file system, is a relatively simple format that was defined in 1988 as the read-only formatting standard for CD-ROM media. Windows 2000 implements ISO 9660-compliant CDFS in \Winnt\System32\Drivers\Cdfs.sys, with long filename support defined by Level 2 of the ISO 9660 standard. Because of its simplicity, the CDFS format has a number of restrictions:

- Directory and file names must be fewer than 32 characters long.
- Directory trees can be no more than eight levels deep.

CDFS is considered a legacy format because the industry has adopted the Universal Disk Format (UDF) as the standard for read-only media.

UDF

The Windows 2000 UDF file system implementation is ISO 13346-compliant and supports UDF versions 1.02 and 1.5. OSTA (Optical Storage Technology Association) defined UDF in 1995 as a format to replace CDFS for magneto-optical storage media, mainly DVD-ROM. UDF is included in the DVD specification and is more flexible than CDFS. UDF file systems have the following traits:

- Filenames can be 255 characters long.
- The maximum path length is 1023 characters.
- Filenames can be upper and lower case.

Although the UDF format was designed with rewritable media in mind, the Windows 2000 UDF driver (\Winnt\System32\Drivers\Udfs.sys) provides read-only support.

FAT12, FAT16, and FAT32

Windows 2000 supports the FAT file system primarily to enable upgrades from other versions of Microsoft Windows, for compatibility with other operating systems in multiboot systems, and as a floppy disk format. The Windows 2000 FAT file system driver is implemented in \Winnt\System32\Drivers\Fastfat.sys.

Each FAT format includes a number that indicates the number of bits the format uses to identify clusters on a disk. FAT12's 12-bit cluster identifier limits a partition to storing a maximum of 2^{12} (4096) clusters. Windows 2000 uses

cluster sizes from 512 bytes to 8 KB in size, which limits a FAT12 volume size to 32 MB. Therefore, Windows 2000 uses FAT12 as the format for all 5¼-inch floppy disks and 3.5-inch floppy disks, which store up to 1.44 MB of data.

FAT16, with a 16-bit cluster identifier, can address 2^{16} (65,536) clusters. On Windows 2000, FAT16 cluster sizes range from 512 bytes (the sector size) to 64 KB, which limits FAT16 volume sizes to 4 GB. The cluster size Windows 2000 uses depends on the size of a volume. The various sizes are listed in Table 12-1. If you format a volume that is less than 16 MB as FAT by using the *format* command or the Disk Management snap-in, Windows 2000 uses the FAT12 format instead of FAT16.

Table 12-1 Default FAT16 Cluster Sizes in Windows 2000

Volume Size	Cluster Size
0–32 MB	512 bytes
33 MB–64 MB	1 KB
65 MB–128 MB	2 KB
129 MB–256 MB	4 KB
257 MB–511 MB	8 KB
512 MB–1023 MB	16 KB
1024 MB–2047 MB	32 KB
2048 MB–4095 MB	64 KB

A FAT volume is divided into several regions, which are shown in Figure 12-2. The file allocation table, which gives the FAT file system format its name, has one entry for each cluster on a volume. Because the file allocation table is critical to the successful interpretation of a volume's contents, the FAT format maintains two copies of the table so that if a file system driver or consistency-checking program (such as Chkdsk) can't access one (because of a bad disk sector, for example) it can read from the other.

Boot sector	File allocation table 1	File allocation table 2 (duplicate)	Root directory	Other directories and all files

Figure 12-2
FAT format organization

Entries in the file allocation table define file-allocation chains (shown in Figure 12-3) for files and directories, where the links in the chain are indexes to the next cluster of a file's data. A file's directory entry stores the starting cluster of the file. The last entry of the file's allocation chain is the reserved value of 0xFFFF for FAT16 and 0xFFF for FAT12. The FAT entries for unused clusters have a value of 0. You can see in Figure 12-3 that FILE1 is assigned clusters 2, 3, and 4; FILE2 is fragmented and uses clusters 5, 6, and 8; and FILE3 uses only cluster 7.

Figure 12-3
Example FAT file-allocation chains

The root directory of FAT12 and FAT16 volumes are preassigned enough space at the start of a volume to store 256 directory entries, which places an upper limit on the number of files and directories that can be stored in the root directory. (There's no preassigned space or size limit on FAT32 root directories.) A FAT directory entry is 32 bytes and stores a file's name, size, starting cluster, and time stamp (last-accessed, created, and so on) information. If a file has a name that is Unicode or that doesn't follow the MS-DOS 8.3 naming convention, additional directory entries are allocated to store the long filename. The supplementary entries precede the file's main entry. Figure 12-4 shows an example directory entry for a file named "The quick brown fox." The system has created a THEQUI~1.FOX 8.3 representation of the name (you don't see a "." in the directory entry because it is assumed to come after the eighth character) and used two more directory entries to store the Unicode long filename. Each row in the figure is made up of 16 bytes.

Figure 12-4
FAT directory entry

FAT32 is the most recently defined FAT-based file system format, and it's included with Windows 95 OSR2, Windows 98, and Windows Millennium Edition. FAT32 uses 32-bit cluster identifiers but reserves the high 4 bits, so in effect it has 28-bit cluster identifiers. Because FAT32 cluster sizes can be as large as 32 KB, FAT32 has a theoretical ability to address 8-terabyte (TB) volumes. Although Windows 2000 works with existing FAT32 volumes of larger sizes (created in other operating systems), it limits new FAT32 volumes to a maximum of 32 GB. FAT32's higher potential cluster numbers let it more efficiently manage disks than FAT16; it can handle up to 128-MB volumes with 512-byte clusters. Table 12-2 shows default cluster sizes for FAT32 volumes.

Table 12-2 Default Cluster Sizes for FAT32 Volumes

Partition Size	Cluster Size
32 MB to 8 GB	4 KB
8 GB to 16 GB	8 KB
16 GB to 32 GB	16 KB
32 GB	32 KB

Besides the higher limit on cluster numbers, other advantages FAT32 has over FAT12 and FAT16 include the fact that the FAT32 root directory isn't stored at a predefined location on the volume, the root directory doesn't have an upper limit on its size, and FAT32 stores a second copy of the boot sector for reliability. A limitation FAT32 shares with FAT16 is that the maximum file size is 4 GB because directories store file sizes as 32-bit values.

NTFS

As we said at the beginning of the chapter, the NTFS file system is the native file system format of Windows 2000. NTFS uses 64-bit cluster indexes. This capacity gives NTFS the ability to address volumes of up to 16 exabytes (16 billion GB); however, Windows 2000 limits the size of an NTFS volume to that addressable with 32-bit clusters, which is 128 TB (using 64-KB clusters). Table 12-3 shows the default cluster sizes for NTFS volumes. (You can override the default when you format an NTFS volume.)

Table 12-3 Default Cluster Sizes for NTFS Volumes

Volume Size	Default Cluster Size
512 MB or less	512 bytes
513 MB–1024 MB (1 GB)	1 KB
1025 MB–2048 MB (2 GB)	2 KB
Greater than 2048 MB	4 KB

NTFS includes a number of advanced features, such as file and directory security, disk quotas, file compression, directory-based symbolic links, and encryption. One of its most significant features is *recoverability*. If a system is halted unexpectedly, the metadata of a FAT volume can be left in an inconsistent state, leading to the corruption of large amounts of file and directory data. NTFS logs changes to metadata in a transactional manner so that file system structures can be repaired to a consistent state with no loss of file or directory structure information. (File data can be lost, however.)

We'll describe NTFS data structures and advanced features in detail later in this chapter.

File System Driver Architecture

File system drivers (FSDs) manage file system formats. Although FSDs run in kernel mode, they differ in a number of ways from standard kernel-mode drivers. Perhaps most significant, they must register as an FSD with the I/O manager and they interact more extensively with the memory manager and the cache manager. Thus, they use a superset of the exported Ntoskrnl functions that standard drivers use. Whereas you need the Windows 2000 DDK in order to build standard kernel-mode drivers, you must have the Windows 2000 Installable File System (IFS) Kit to build file system drivers. (See Chapter 1 for more information on the DDK, and see *www.microsoft.com/ddk/ifskit* for more information on the IFS Kit.)

Windows 2000 has two different types of file system drivers:

- *Local FSDs* manage volumes directly connected to the computer.

- *Network FSDs* allow users to access data volumes connected to remote computers.

Local FSDs

Local FSDs include Ntfs.sys, Fastfat.sys, Udfs.sys, Cdfs.sys, and the Raw FSD (integrated in Ntoskrnl.exe). Figure 12-5 shows a simplified view of how local FSDs interact with the I/O manager and storage device drivers. As we described in the section "Volume Mounting" in Chapter 10, a local FSD is responsible for registering with the I/O manager. Once the FSD is registered, the I/O manager can call on it to perform volume recognition when applications or the system initially access the volumes. Volume recognition involves an examination of a volume's boot sector and often, as a consistency check, the file system metadata.

The first sector of every Windows 2000–supported file system format is reserved as the volume's boot sector. A boot sector contains enough information so that a local FSD can both identify the volume on which the sector resides as containing a format that the FSD manages and locate any other metadata necessary to identify where metadata is stored on the volume.

When a local FSD recognizes a volume, it creates a device object that represents the mounted file system format. The I/O manager makes a connection through the volume parameter block (VPB) between the volume's device

Figure 12-5
Local FSD

object (which is created by a storage device) and the device object that the FSD created. The VPB's connection results in the I/O manager redirecting I/O requests targeted at the volume device object to the FSD device object. (See Chapter 10 for more information on VPBs.)

To improve performance, local FSDs usually use the cache manager to cache file system data, including metadata. They also integrate with the memory manager so that mapped files are implemented correctly. For example, they must query the memory manager whenever an application attempts to truncate a file in order to verify that no processes have mapped the part of the file beyond the truncation point. Windows 2000 doesn't permit file data that is mapped by an application to be deleted either through truncation or file deletion.

Local FSDs also support file system dismount operations, which permit the system to disconnect the FSD from the volume object. A dismount occurs whenever an application requires raw access to the on-disk contents of a volume or the media associated with a volume is changed. The first time an application accesses the media after a dismount, the I/O manager reinitiates a volume mount operation for the media.

Remote FSDs

Remote FSDs consist of two components: a client and a server. A client-side remote FSD allows applications to access remote files and directories. The client FSD accepts I/O requests from applications and translates them into network file system protocol commands that the FSD sends across the network to a server-side remote FSD. A server-side FSD listens for commands coming from a network connection and fulfills them by issuing I/O requests to the local FSD that manages the volume on which the file or directory that the command is intended for resides. Figure 12-6 shows the relationship between the client and server sides of a remote FSD interaction.

Figure 12-6
Remote FSD operation

Windows 2000 includes a client-side remote FSD named LANMan Redirector (redirector) and a server-side remote FSD server named LANMan Server (server). The redirector is implemented as a port/miniport driver combination, where the port driver (\Winnt\System32\Drivers\Rdbss.sys) is implemented as a driver subroutine library and the miniport (\Winnt\System32\Drivers\Mrxsmb.sys) uses services implemented by the port driver. The port/miniport model simplifies redirector development because the port driver, which all remote FSD miniport drivers share, handles many of the mundane details involved with interfacing a client-side remote FSD to the Windows 2000 I/O manager. In addition to the FSD components, both LANMan Redirector and LANMan Server include Win32 services named Workstation and Server, respectively.

Windows 2000 relies on the Common Internet File System (CIFS) protocol to format messages exchanged between the redirector and the server. CIFS is an enhanced version of Microsoft's Server Message Block (SMB) protocol. (For more information on CIFS, go to *www.cifs.com*.)

Like local FSDs, client-side remote FSDs usually use cache manager services to locally cache file data belonging to remote files and directories. However, client-side remote FSDs must implement a distributed cache coherency protocol, called *oplocks* (opportunistic locking), so that the data an application sees when it accesses a remote file is the same as the data applications running on other computers that are accessing the same file see. Although server-side remote FSDs participate in maintaining cache coherency across their clients, they don't cache data from the local FSDs because local FSDs cache their own data. (Oplocks, redirector, and server are described in more detail in the section "Common Internet File System (CIFS)" on page 803 in Chapter 13.)

> **NOTE** A filter driver that layers over a file system driver is called a *file-system filter driver*. The ability to see all file system requests and optionally modify or complete them enables a range of applications, including on-access virus scanners and remote file replication services. Filemon, on the companion CD as \Sysint\Filemon, is an example of a file-system filter driver that is a *pass-through* filter. Filemon displays file system activity in real time without modifying the requests it sees.

EXPERIMENT: Viewing the List of Registered File Systems

When the I/O manager loads a device driver into memory, it typically names the driver object it creates to represent the driver so that it's placed in the \Drivers object manager directory. The driver objects for any driver the I/O manager loads that have a Type attribute value of SERVICE_FILE_SYSTEM_DRIVER (2) are placed in the \FileSystem directory by the I/O manager. Thus, using a tool like Winobj (on the companion CD in \Sysint\Winobj.exe), you can see the file systems that have registered on a system, as shown in the following screen shot. (Note that some file system drivers also place device objects in the \FileSystem directory.)

File System Operation

Applications and the system access files in two ways: directly, via file I/O functions (such as *ReadFile* and *WriteFile*), and indirectly, by reading or writing a portion of their address space that represents a mapped file section. (See Chapter 7 for more information on mapped files.) Figure 12-7 is a simplified diagram that shows the components involved in these file system operations and the ways in which they interact. As you can see, an FSD can be invoked through several paths:

- From a user or system thread performing explicit file I/O
- From the memory manager's modified page writer

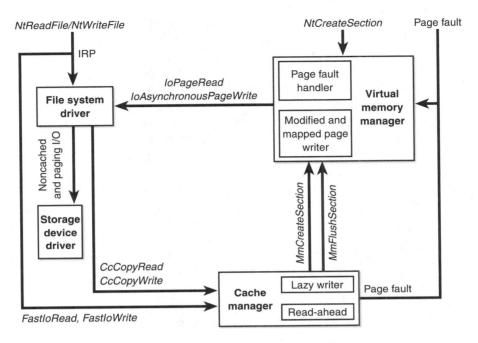

Figure 12-7
Components involved in file system I/O

- Indirectly from the cache manager's lazy writer
- Indirectly from the cache manager's read-ahead thread
- From the memory manager's page fault handler

The following sections describe the circumstances surrounding each of these scenarios and the steps FSDs typically take in response to each one. You'll see how much FSDs rely on the memory manager and the cache manager.

Explicit File I/O

The most obvious way an application accesses files is by calling Win32 I/O functions such as *CreateFile*, *ReadFile*, and *WriteFile*. An application opens a file with *CreateFile* and then reads, writes, or deletes the file by passing the handle returned from *CreateFile* to other Win32 functions. The *CreateFile* function, which is implemented in the Kernel32.dll Win32 client-side DLL, invokes the native function *NtCreateFile*, forming a complete root-relative pathname for

the path that the application passed to it (processing "." and ".." symbols in the pathname) and prepending the path with "\??" (for example, \??\C:\ Susan\Todo.txt).

The *NtCreateFile* system service uses *ObOpenObjectByName* to open the file, which parses the name starting with the object manager root directory and the first component of the path name ("??"). \?? is a subdirectory that contains symbolic links representing volumes that are assigned drive letters (and symbolic links to serial ports and other device objects that Win32 applications access directly), so the "C:" component of the name resolves to the \??\C: symbolic link. The symbolic link points to a volume device object under \Device, so when the object manager encounters the volume object, the object manager hands the rest of the pathname to the parse function that the I/O manager has registered for device objects, *IopParseDevice*. (In volumes on dynamic disks, a symbolic link points to an intermediary symbolic link, which points to a volume device object.) Figure 12-8 shows how volume objects are accessed through the object manager namespace. The figure shows how the \??\C: symbolic link points to the \Device\HarddiskVolume1 volume device object.

Figure 12-8
Drive-letter name resolution

After locking the caller's security context and obtaining security information from the caller's token, *IopParseDevice* creates an I/O request packet (IRP) of type IRP_MJ_CREATE, creates a file object that stores the name of the file being opened, follows the VPB of the volume device object to find the volume's mounted file system device object, and uses *IoCallDriver* to pass the IRP to the file system driver that owns the file system device object.

When an FSD receives an IRP_MJ_CREATE IRP, it looks up the specified file, performs security validation, and if the file exists and the user has permission to access the file in the way requested, returns a success code. The object manager creates a handle for the file object in the process's handle table, and the handle propagates back through the calling chain, finally reaching the application as a return parameter from *CreateFile*. If the file system fails the create, the I/O manager deletes the file object it created for it.

We've skipped over the details of how the FSD locates the file being opened on the volume, but a *ReadFile* function call operation shares many of the FSD's interactions with the cache manager and storage driver. The path into the kernel taken as the result of a call to *ReadFile* is the same as for a call to *CreateFile*, but the *NtReadFile* system service doesn't need to perform a name lookup—it calls on the object manager to translate the handle passed from *ReadFile* into a file object pointer. If the handle indicates that the caller obtained permission to read the file when the file was opened, *NtReadFile* proceeds to create an IRP of type IRP_MJ_READ and sends it to the FSD on which the file resides. *NtReadFile* obtains the FSD's device object, which is stored in the file object, and calls *IoCallDriver*, and the I/O manager locates the FSD from the device object and gives the IRP to the FSD.

If the file being read can be cached (the FILE_FLAG_NO_BUFFERING flag wasn't passed to *CreateFile* when the file was opened), the FSD checks to see whether caching has already been initiated for the file object. The *PrivateCacheMap* field in a file object points to a private cache map data structure (which we described in Chapter 11) if caching is initiated for a file object. If the FSD hasn't initialized caching for the file object (which it does the first time a file object is read from or written to), the *PrivateCacheMap* field will be null. The FSD calls the cache manager *CcInitializeCacheMap* function to initialize caching, which involves the cache manager creating a private cache map and, if another file object referring to the same file hasn't initiated caching, a shared cache map and a section object.

After it has verified that caching is enabled for the file, the FSD copies the requested file data from the cache manager's virtual memory to the buffer that the thread passed to the *ReadFile* function. The file system performs the copy

within a try/except block so that it catches any faults that are the result of an invalid application buffer. The function the file system uses to perform the copy is the cache manager's *CcCopyRead* function. *CcCopyRead* takes as parameters a file object, file offset, and length.

When the cache manager executes *CcCopyRead*, it retrieves a pointer to a shared cache map, which is stored in the file object. Recall from Chapter 11 that a shared cache map stores pointers to virtual address control blocks (VACBs), with one VACB entry per 256-KB block of the file. If the VACB pointer for a portion of a file being read is null, *CcCopyRead* allocates a VACB, reserving a 256-KB view in the cache manager's virtual address space, and maps (using *MmCreateSection* and *MmMapViewOfSection*) the specified portion of the file into the view. Then *CcCopyRead* simply copies the file data from the mapped view to the buffer it was passed (the buffer originally passed to *ReadFile*). If the file data isn't in physical memory, the copy operation generates page faults, which are serviced by *MmAccessFault*.

When a page fault occurs, *MmAccessFault* examines the virtual address that caused the fault and locates the virtual address descriptor (VAD) in the VAD tree of the process that caused the fault. (See Chapter 7 for more information on VAD trees.) In this scenario, the VAD describes the cache manager's mapped view of the file being read, so *MmAccessFault* calls *MiDispatchFault* to handle a page fault on a valid virtual memory address. *MiDispatchFault* locates the control area (which the VAD points to) and through the control area finds a file object representing the open file. (If the file has been opened more than once, there might be a list of file objects linked through pointers in their private cache maps.)

With the file object in hand, *MiDispatchFault* calls the I/O manager function *IoPageRead* to build an IRP (of type IRP_MJ_READ) and sends the IRP to the FSD that owns the device object the file object points to. Thus, the file system is reentered to read the data that it requested via *CcCopyRead*, but this time the IRP is marked as noncached and paging I/O. These flags signal the FSD that it should retrieve file data directly from disk, and it does so by determining which clusters on disk contain the requested data and sending IRPs to the volume manager that owns the volume device object on which the file resides. The volume parameter block (VPB) field in the FSD's device object points to the volume device object.

The virtual memory manager waits for the FSD to complete the IRP read and then returns control to the cache manager, which continues the copy operation that was interrupted by a page fault. When *CcCopyRead* completes, the FSD returns control to the thread that called *NtReadFile*, having copied the requested file data—with the aid of the cache manager and the virtual memory manager—to the thread's buffer.

The path for *WriteFile* is similar except that the *NtWriteFile* system service generates an IRP of type IRP_MJ_WRITE and the FSD calls *CcCopyWrite* instead of *CcCopyRead*. *CcCopyWrite*, like *CcCopyRead*, ensures that the portions of the file being written are mapped into the cache and then copies to the cache the buffer passed to *WriteFile*.

If a file's data is already stored in the system's working set, there are several variants on the scenario we've just described. If a file's data is already stored in the cache, *CcCopyRead* doesn't incur page faults. Also, under certain conditions, *NtReadFile* and *NtWriteFile* call an FSD's fast I/O entry point instead of immediately building and sending an IRP to the FSD. Some of these conditions follow: the portion of the file being read must reside in the first 4 GB of the file, the file can have no locks, and the portion of the file being read or written must fall within the file's currently allocated size.

The fast I/O read and write entry points for most FSDs call the cache manager's *CcFastCopyRead* and *CcFastCopyWrite* functions. These variants on the standard copy routines ensure that the file's data is mapped in the file system cache before performing a copy operation. If this condition isn't met, *CcFastCopyRead* and *CcFastCopyWrite* indicate that fast I/O isn't possible. When fast I/O isn't possible, *NtReadFile* and *NtWriteFile* fall back on creating an IRP. (See the section "Fast I/O" on page 672 in Chapter 11 for a more complete description of fast I/O.)

Memory Manager's Modified and Mapped Page Writer

The memory manager's modified and mapped page writer threads wake up periodically to flush modified pages. The threads call *IoAsynchronousPageWrite* to create IRPs of type IRP_MJ_WRITE and write pages to either a paging file or a file that was modified after being mapped. Like the IRPs that *MiDispatchFault* creates, these IRPs are flagged as noncached and paging I/O. Thus, an FSD bypasses the file system cache and issues IRPs directly to a storage driver to write the memory to disk.

Cache Manager's Lazy Writer

The cache manager's lazy writer thread also plays a role in writing modified pages because it periodically flushes views of file sections mapped in the cache that it knows are dirty. The flush operation, which the cache manager performs by calling *MmFlushSection*, triggers the memory manager to write any modified pages in the portion of the section being flushed to disk. Like the modified and mapped page writers, *MmFlushSection* uses *IoAsynchronousPageWrite* to send the data to the FSD.

Cache Manager's Read-Ahead Thread

The cache manager includes a thread that is responsible for attempting to read data from files before an application, a driver, or a system thread explicitly requests it. The read-ahead thread uses the history of read operations that were performed on a file, which are stored in a file object's private cache map, to determine how much data to read. When the thread performs a read-ahead, it simply maps the portion of the file it wants to read into the cache (allocating VACBs as necessary) and touches the mapped data. The page faults caused by the memory accesses invoke the page fault handler, which reads the pages into the system's working set.

Memory Manager's Page Fault Handler

We described how the page fault handler is used in the context of explicit file I/O and cache manager read-ahead, but it is also invoked whenever any application accesses virtual memory that is a view of a mapped file and encounters pages that represent portions of a file that aren't part of the application's working set. The memory manager's *MmAccessFault* handler follows the same steps it does when the cache manager generates a page fault from *CcCopyRead* or *CcCopyWrite*, sending IRPs via *IoPageRead* to the file system on which the file is stored.

NTFS Design Goals and Features

In the following section, we'll look at the requirements that drove the design of NTFS. Then in the subsequent section, we'll examine the advanced features of NTFS.

High-End File System Requirements

From the start, NTFS was designed to include features required of an enterprise-class file system. To minimize data loss in the face of an unexpected system outage or crash, a file system must ensure that the integrity of the file system's metadata be guaranteed at all times, and to protect sensitive data from unauthorized access, a file system must have an integrated security model. Finally, a file system must allow for software-based data redundancy as a low-cost alternative to hardware-redundant solutions for protecting user data. In this section, you'll find out how NTFS implements each of these capabilities.

Recoverability

To address the requirement for reliable data storage and data access, NTFS provides file system recovery based on the concept of an *atomic transaction*. Atomic transactions are a technique for handling modifications to a database so that system failures don't affect the correctness or integrity of the database.

The basic tenet of atomic transactions is that some database operations, called *transactions*, are all-or-nothing propositions. (A *transaction* is defined as an I/O operation that alters file system data or changes the volume's directory structure.) The separate disk updates that make up the transaction must be executed *atomically*; that is, once the transaction begins to execute, all its disk updates must be completed. If a system failure interrupts the transaction, the part that has been completed must be undone, or *rolled back*. The rollback operation returns the database to a previously known and consistent state, as if the transaction had never occurred.

NTFS uses atomic transactions to implement its file system recovery feature. If a program initiates an I/O operation that alters the structure of an NTFS drive—that is, changes the directory structure, extends a file, allocates space for a new file, and so on—NTFS treats that operation as an atomic transaction. It guarantees that the transaction is either completed or, if the system fails while executing the transaction, rolled back. The details of how NTFS does this are explained in the section "NTFS Recovery Support" on page 746.

In addition, NTFS uses redundant storage for vital file system information so that if a sector on the disk goes bad, NTFS can still access the volume's critical file system data. This redundancy of file system data contrasts with the on-disk structures of both the FAT file system and the HPFS file system (OS/2's native file system format), which have single sectors containing critical file system data. On these file systems, if a read error occurs in one of those sectors an entire volume is lost.

Security

Security in NTFS is derived directly from the Windows 2000 object model. Files and directories are protected from being accessed by unauthorized users. (For more information on Windows 2000 security, see Chapter 8.) An open file is implemented as a file object with a security descriptor stored on disk as a part of the file. Before a process can open a handle to any object, including a file object, the Windows 2000 security system verifies that the process has appropriate authorization to do so. The security descriptor, combined with the requirement that a user log on to the system and provide an identifying password, ensures that no process can access a file unless given specific permission to do so by a system administrator or by the file's owner. (For more information about security descriptors, see the section "Security Descriptors and Access Control" on page 507 in Chapter 8, and for more details about file objects, see the section "File Objects" on page 554 in Chapter 9.)

Data Redundancy and Fault Tolerance

In addition to recoverability of file system data, some customers require that their own data not be endangered by a power outage or catastrophic disk failure. The NTFS recovery capabilities do ensure that the file system on a volume remains accessible, but they make no guarantees for complete recovery of user files. Protection for applications that can't risk losing file data is provided through data redundancy.

Data redundancy for user files is implemented via the Windows 2000 layered driver model (explained in Chapter 9), which provides fault tolerant disk support. NTFS communicates with a volume manager, which in turn communicates with a hard disk driver to write data to disk. A volume manager can *mirror*, or duplicate, data from one disk onto another disk so that a redundant copy can always be retrieved. This support is commonly called *RAID level 1*. Volume managers also allow data to be written in *stripes* across three or more disks, using the equivalent of one disk to maintain parity information. If the data on one disk is lost or becomes inaccessible, the driver can reconstruct the disk's contents by means of exclusive-OR operations. This support is called *RAID level 5*. (See Chapter 10 for more information on striped volumes, mirrored volumes, and RAID-5 volumes.)

Advanced Features of NTFS

In addition to NTFS being recoverable, secure, reliable, and efficient for mission-critical systems, it includes the following advanced features that allow it to support a broad range of applications. Some of these features are exposed as APIs for applications to leverage, and others are internal features:

- Multiple data streams
- Unicode-based names
- General indexing facility
- Dynamic bad-cluster remapping
- Hard links and junctions
- Compression and sparse files
- Change logging
- Per-user volume quotas

- Link tracking
- Encryption
- POSIX support
- Defragmentation

The following sections provide an overview of these features.

Multiple Data Streams

In NTFS, each unit of information associated with a file, including its name, its owner, its time stamps, its contents, and so on, is implemented as a file attribute (NTFS object attribute). Each attribute consists of a single *stream,* that is, a simple sequence of bytes. This generic implementation makes it easy to add more attributes (and therefore more streams) to a file. Because a file's data is "just another attribute" of the file and because new attributes can be added, NTFS files (and file directories) can contain multiple data streams.

An NTFS file has one default data stream, which has no name. An application can create additional, named data streams and access them by referring to their names. To avoid altering the Microsoft Win32 I/O APIs, which take a string as a filename argument, the name of the data stream is specified by appending a colon (:) to the filename. Because the colon is a reserved character, it can serve as a separator between the filename and the data stream name, as illustrated in this example:

```
myfile.dat:stream2
```

Each stream has a separate allocation size (how much disk space has been reserved for it), actual size (how many bytes the caller has used), and valid data length (how much of the stream has been initialized). In addition, each stream is given a separate file lock that is used to lock byte ranges and to allow concurrent access.

One component in Windows 2000 that uses multiple data streams is the Apple Macintosh file server support that comes with Windows 2000 Server. Macintosh systems use two streams per file—one to store data and the other to store resource information, such as the file type and the icon used to represent the file. Because NTFS allows multiple data streams, a Macintosh user can copy an entire Macintosh folder to a Windows 2000 server, and another Macintosh user can copy the folder from the server without losing resource information.

Windows Explorer is another application that uses streams. When you right-click on an NTFS file and select Properties, the Summary tab of the resulting dialog box lets you associate information with the file, such as a title, subject, author, and keywords. Windows Explorer stores the information in an alternate stream it adds to the file, named "Summary Information."

Other applications can use the multiple data stream feature as well. A backup utility, for example, might use an extra data stream to store backup-specific time stamps on files. Or an archival utility might implement hierarchical storage in which files that are older than a certain date or that haven't been accessed for a specified period of time are moved to tape. The utility could copy the file to tape, set the file's default data stream to 0, and add a data stream that specifies the name and location of the tape on which the file is stored.

EXPERIMENT: Looking at Streams

Most Windows 2000 applications aren't designed to work with alternate named streams, but both the *echo* and the *more* commands are. Thus, a simple way to view streams in action is to create a named stream using *echo* and then display it using *more*. The following command sequence creates a file named test with a stream named stream:

```
C:\>echo hello > test:stream
C:\>more < test:stream
hello
C:\>
```

If you perform a directory listing, test's file size doesn't reflect the data stored in the alternate stream because NTFS returns the size of only the unnamed data stream for file query operations, including directory listings.

```
C:\>dir test
 Volume in drive C is WINDOWS
 Volume Serial Number is 3991-3040

 Directory of C:\

08/01/00  02:37p                     0 test
               1 File(s)             0 bytes
                       112,558,080 bytes free
```

Unicode-Based Names

Like Windows 2000 as a whole, NTFS is fully Unicode enabled, using Unicode characters to store names of files, directories, and volumes. Unicode, a 16-bit character-coding scheme, allows each character in each of the world's major languages to be uniquely represented, which aids in moving data easily from one country to another. Unicode is an improvement over the traditional representation of international characters—using a double-byte coding scheme that stores some characters in 8 bits and others in 16 bits, a technique that requires loading various code pages to establish the available characters. Because Unicode has a unique representation for each character, it doesn't depend on which code page is loaded. Each directory and filename in a path can be as many as 255 characters long and can contain Unicode characters, embedded spaces, and multiple periods.

General Indexing Facility

The NTFS architecture is structured to allow indexing of file attributes on a disk volume. This structure enables the file system to efficiently locate files that match certain criteria—for example, all the files in a particular directory. The FAT file system indexes filenames but doesn't sort them, making lookups in large directories slow.

Several NTFS features take advantage of general indexing, including consolidated security descriptors, in which the security descriptors of a volume's files and directories are stored in a single internal stream, have duplicates removed, and are indexed using an internal security identifier that NTFS defines.

Dynamic Bad-Cluster Remapping

Ordinarily, if a program tries to read data from a bad disk sector, the read operation fails and the data in the allocated cluster becomes inaccessible. If the disk is formatted as a fault tolerant NTFS volume, however, the Windows 2000 fault tolerant driver dynamically retrieves a good copy of the data that was stored on the bad sector and then sends NTFS a warning that the sector is bad. NTFS allocates a new cluster, replacing the cluster in which the bad sector resides, and copies the data to the new cluster. It flags the bad cluster and no longer uses it. This data recovery and dynamic bad-cluster remapping is an especially useful feature for file servers and fault tolerant systems or for any application that can't afford to lose data. If the volume manager isn't loaded when a sector goes bad, NTFS still replaces the cluster and doesn't reuse it, but it can't recover the data that was on the bad sector.

Hard Links and Junctions

A hard link allows multiple paths to refer to the same file or directory. If you create a hard link named C:\Users\Documents\Spec.doc that refers to the existing file C:\My Documents\Spec.doc, the two paths link to the same on-disk file and you can make changes to the file using either path. Processes can create hard links with the Win32 *CreateHardLink* function or the *ln* POSIX function.

EXPERIMENT: Creating a Hard Link

Although applications can use the Win32 function *CreateHardLink* to create a hard link, no tools use this function. However, you can create a hard link by using the POSIX *ln* utility in the Windows 2000 resource kits. The POSIX tools can't be installed through the resource kit setup program, so you'll need to copy them manually from the \Apps\Posix directory on the resource kit CDs.

In addition to hard links, NTFS supports another type of redirection called *junctions*. Junctions, also called symbolic links, allow a directory to redirect file or directory pathname translation to an alternate directory. For example, if the path C:\Drivers is a junction that redirects to C:\Winnt\System32\Drivers, an application reading C:\Drivers\Ntfs.sys actually reads C:\Winnt\System\Drivers\Ntfs.sys. Junctions are a useful way to lift directories that are deep in a directory tree to a more convenient depth without disturbing the original tree's structure or contents. The example just cited lifts the drivers directory to the volume's root directory, reducing the directory depth of Ntfs.sys from three levels to one when Ntfs.sys is accessed through the junction. You can't use junctions to link to remote directories—only to directories on local volumes.

Junctions are based on an NTFS mechanism called *reparse points*. (Reparse points are discussed further in the section "Reparse Points" later in this chapter.) A reparse point is a file or directory that has a block of data called *reparse data* associated with it. Reparse data is user-defined data about the file or directory, such as its state or location, that can be read from the reparse point by the application that created the data, a file system filter driver, or the I/O manager. When NTFS encounters a reparse point during a file or directory lookup, it returns a *reparse status code*, which signals file system filter drivers that are attached to the volume, and the I/O manager, to examine the reparse data. Each reparse point type has a unique *reparse tag*. The reparse tag allows the compo-

nent responsible for interpreting the reparse point's reparse data to recognize the reparse point without having to check the reparse data. A reparse tag owner, either a file system filter driver or the I/O manager, can choose one of the following options when it recognizes reparse data:

- The reparse tag owner can manipulate the pathname specified in the file I/O operation that crosses the reparse point and let the I/O operation reissue with the altered pathname. Junctions take this approach to redirect a directory lookup, for example.

- The reparse tag owner can remove the reparse point from the file, alter the file in some way, and then reissue the file I/O operation. The Windows 2000 Hierarchical Storage Management (HSM) system uses reparse points in this way. HSM archives files by moving their contents to tape, leaving reparse points in their place. When a process accesses a file that has been archived, the HSM filter driver (\Winnt\System32\Drivers\Rsfilter.sys) removes the reparse point from the file, reads the file's data from the archival media, and reissues the access. Thus, the retrieval of the offline data is transparent to a process accessing an archived file.

There are no Win32 functions for creating reparse points. Instead, processes must use the FSCTL_SET_REPARSE_POINT file system control code with the Win32 *DeviceIoControl* function. A process can query a reparse point's contents with the FSCTL_GET_REPARSE_POINT file system control code. The FILE_ATTRIBUTE_REPARSE_POINT flag is set in a reparse point's file attributes, so applications can check for reparse points by using the Win32 *GetFileAttributes* function.

EXPERIMENT: Creating a Junction

Windows 2000 doesn't include any tools for creating junctions, but you can create a junction with either the Junction tool on the companion CD (\Sysint\Junction.exe) or the Windows 2000 resource kits tool Linkd. The Linkd tool also lets you view the definition of existing junctions, and Junction lets you view information about junctions and other reparse point tags.

Compression and Sparse Files

NTFS supports compression of file data. Because NTFS performs compression and decompression procedures transparently, applications don't have to be modified to take advantage of this feature. Directories can also be compressed, which means that any files subsequently created in the directory are compressed.

Applications compress and decompress files by passing *DeviceIoControl* the FSCTL_SET_COMPRESSION file system control code. They query the compression state of a file or directory with the FSCTL_GET_COMPRESSION file system control code. A file or directory that is compressed has the FILE_ATTRIBUTE_COMPRESSED flag set in its attributes, so applications can also determine a file or directory's compression state with *GetFileAttributes*.

A second type of compression is known as *sparse files*. If a file is marked as sparse, NTFS doesn't allocate space on a volume for portions of the file that an application designates as empty. NTFS returns 0-filled buffers when an application reads from empty areas of a sparse file. This type of compression can be useful for client/server applications that implement circular-buffer logging, in which the server records information to a file and clients asynchronously read the information. Because the information that the server writes isn't needed after a client has read it, there's no need to store the information in the file. By making such a file sparse, the client can specify the portions of the file it reads as empty, freeing up space on the volume. The server can continue to append new information to the file, without fear that the file will grow to consume all available space on the volume.

As for compressed files, NTFS manages sparse files transparently. Applications specify a file's sparseness state by passing the FSCTL_SET_SPARSE file system control code to *DeviceIoControl*. To set a range of a file to empty, applications use the FSCTL_SET_ZERO_DATA code, and they can ask NTFS for a description of what parts of a file are sparse by using the control code FSCTL_QUERY_ALLOCATED_RANGES. One application of sparse files is the NTFS *change journal*, described next.

Change Logging

Many types of applications need to monitor volumes for file and directory changes. For example, an automatic backup program might perform an initial full backup and then incremental backups based on file changes. An obvious way for an application to monitor a volume for changes is for it to scan the volume, recording the state of files and directories, and on a subsequent scan detect differences. This process can adversely affect system performance, however, especially on computers with thousands or tens of thousands of files.

An alternate approach is for an application to register a directory notification by using the *FindFirstChangeNotification* or *ReadDirectoryChangesW* Win32 functions. As an input parameter, the application specifies the name of a directory it wants to monitor, and the function returns whenever the contents of the directory changes. Although this approach is more efficient than volume scanning, it requires the application to be running at all times. Using these functions can also require an application to scan directories because *FindFirstChangeNotification* doesn't indicate what changed—just that something in the directory has changed. An application can pass a buffer to *ReadDirectoryChangesW* that the FSD fills in with change records. If the buffer overflows, however, the application must be prepared to fall back on scanning the directory.

NTFS provides a third approach that overcomes the drawbacks of the first two: an application can configure the NTFS change journal facility by using the *DeviceIoControl* function's FSCTL_CREATE_USN_JOURNAL file system control code to have NTFS record information about file and directory changes to an internal file called the *change journal*. A change journal is usually large enough to virtually guarantee that applications get a chance to process changes without missing any. Applications use the FSCTL_QUERY_USN_JOURNAL file system control to read records from a change journal, and they can specify that the *DeviceIoControl* function not complete until new records are available.

Per-User Volume Quotas

Systems administrators often need to track or limit user disk space usage on shared storage volumes, so NTFS includes quota-management support. NTFS quota-management support allows for per-user specification of quota enforcement, which is useful for usage tracking and tracking when a user reaches warning and limit thresholds. NTFS can be configured to log an event indicating the occurrence to the system Event Log if a user surpasses his warning limit. Similarly, if a user attempts to use more volume storage then her quota limit permits, NTFS can log an event to the system Event Log and fail the application file I/O that would have caused the quota violation with a "disk full" error code.

NTFS tracks a user's volume usage by relying on the fact that it tags files and directories with the security ID (SID) of the user who created them. (See Chapter 8 for a definition of SIDs.) The logical sizes of files and directories a user owns count against the user's administrator-defined quota limit. Thus, a user can't circumvent his or her quota limit by creating an empty sparse file that is larger than the quota would allow and then filling the file with nonzero data. Similarly, whereas a 50-KB file might compress to 10 KB, the full 50 KB is used for quota accounting.

By default, volumes don't have quota tracking enabled. You need to use the Quota tab of a volume's Properties dialog box, shown in Figure 12-9, to enable quotas, to specify default warning and limit thresholds, and to configure the NTFS behavior that occurs when a user hits the warning or limit threshold. The Quota Entries tool, which you can launch from this dialog box, enables an administrator to specify different limits and behavior for each user. Applications that want to interact with NTFS quota management use COM quota interfaces, including *IDiskQuotaControl*, *IDiskQuotaUser*, and *IDiskQuotaEvents*.

Figure 12-9
Volume Properties dialog box

Link Tracking

Shell shortcuts allow users to place files in their shell namespace (on their desktop, for example) that link to files located in the file system namespace. The Windows 2000 Start menu uses shell shortcuts extensively. Similarly, object linking and embedding (OLE) links allow documents from one application to be transparently embedded in the documents of other applications. The products of the Microsoft Office 2000 suite, including PowerPoint, Excel, and Word, use OLE linking.

Although shell and OLE links provide an easy way to connect files with one another and with the shell namespace, they have in the past been difficult to manage. If a user moves the source of a shell or OLE link (a link source is the file or directory to which a link points) in Windows NT 4, Windows 95, or Windows 98, the link will be broken and the system has to rely on heuristics to attempt to locate the link's source. NTFS in Windows 2000 includes support for a service application called distributed link-tracking, which maintains the integrity of shell and OLE links when link targets move. Using the NTFS link-tracking support, if a link source located on an NTFS volume moves to any other NTFS volume within the originating volume's domain, the link-tracking service can transparently follow the movement and update the link to reflect the change.

NTFS link-tracking support is based on an optional file attribute known as an *object ID*. An application can assign an object ID to a file by using the FSCTL_CREATE_OR_GET_OBJECT_ID (which assigns an ID if one isn't already assigned) and FSCTL_SET_OBJECT_ID file system control codes. Object IDs are queried with the FSCTL_CREATE_OR_GET_OBJECT_ID and FSCTL_GET_OBJECT_ID file system control codes. The FSCTL_DELETE_OBJECT_ID file system control code lets applications delete object IDs from files.

Encryption

Corporate users often store sensitive information on their computers. Although data stored on company servers is usually safely protected with proper network security settings and physical access control, data stored on laptops can be exposed when a laptop is lost or stolen. NTFS file permissions don't offer protection because NTFS volumes can be fully accessed without regard to security by using NTFS file-reading software that doesn't require Windows 2000 to be running. Furthermore, NTFS file permissions are rendered useless when an alternate Windows 2000 installation is used to access files from an administrator account. Recall from Chapter 8 that the administrator account has the take-ownership and backup privileges, both of which allow it to access any secured object by overriding the object's security settings.

NTFS includes a facility called Encrypting File System (EFS), which users can use to encrypt sensitive data. The operation of EFS, as that of file compression, is completely transparent to applications, which means that file data is automatically decrypted when an application running in the account of a user authorized to view the data reads it and is automatically encrypted when an authorized application changes the data.

NOTE NTFS doesn't permit the encryption of files located in the system volume's root directory or under the \Winnt directory because many of the files in these locations are required during the boot process and EFS isn't active during the boot process.

EFS relies on cryptographic services supplied by Windows 2000 in user mode, and so it consists of both a kernel-mode device driver that tightly integrates with NTFS as well as user-mode DLLs that communicate with the Local Security Authority Subsystem (Lsass) and cryptographic DLLs.

Files that are encrypted can be accessed only by using the private key of an account's EFS private/public key pair, and private keys are locked using an account's password. Thus, EFS-encrypted files on lost or stolen laptops can't be accessed using any means (other than a brute-force cryptographic attack) without the password of an account that is authorized to view the data.

Applications can use the *EncryptFile* and *DecryptFile* Win32 API functions to encrypt and decrypt files, and *FileEncryptionStatus* to retrieve a file or directory's EFS-related attributes, such as whether the file or directory is encrypted.

POSIX Support

As explained in Chapter 2, one of the mandates for Windows 2000 was to fully support the POSIX 1003.1 standard. In the file system area, the POSIX standard requires support for case-sensitive file and directory names, traversal permissions (where security for each directory of a path is used when determining whether a user has access to a file or directory), a "file-change-time" time stamp (which is different than the MS-DOS "time-last-modified" stamp), and hard links (multiple directory entries that point to the same file). NTFS implements each of these features.

Defragmentation

A common myth that many people have held since the introduction of NTFS is that it automatically optimizes file placement on disk so as not to fragment the files. A file is fragmented if its data occupies discontiguous clusters. For example, Figure 12-10 shows a fragmented file consisting of three fragments. However, like most file systems (including versions of FAT on Windows 2000), NTFS makes no special efforts to keep files contiguous, other than to reserve a region of disk space known as the master file table (MFT) zone for the MFT. (NTFS lets other files allocate from the MFT zone when volume free space runs low.) Keeping an area free for the MFT can help it stay contiguous, but it, too, can become fragmented. (See the section "Master File Table (MFT)" later in this chapter for more information on MFTs.)

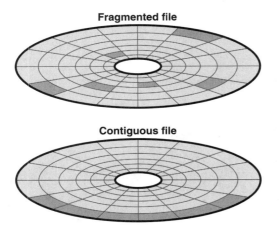

Figure 12-10
Fragmented and contiguous files

To facilitate the development of third-party disk defragmentation tools, Windows 2000 includes a defragmentation API that such tools can use to move file data so that files occupy contiguous clusters. The API consists of file system controls that let applications obtain a map of a volume's free and in-use clusters (FSCTL_GET_VOLUME_BITMAP), obtain a map of a file's cluster usage (FSCTL_GET_RETRIEVAL_POINTERS), and move a file (FSCTL_MOVE_FILE).

Windows 2000 includes a built-in defragmentation tool that is accessible by using the Disk Defragmenter utility (\Winnt\System32\Dfrg.msc). The built-in defragmentation tool has a number of limitations, such as an inability to be run from the command prompt or to be automatically scheduled. Third-party disk defragmentation products typically offer a richer feature set.

NTFS File System Driver

As described in Chapter 9, in the framework of the Windows 2000 I/O system, NTFS and other file systems are loadable device drivers that run in kernel mode. They are invoked indirectly by applications that use Win32 or other I/O APIs (such as POSIX). As Figure 12-11 shows, the Windows 2000 environment subsystems call Windows 2000 system services, which in turn locate the appropriate loaded drivers and call them. (For a description of system service dispatching, see the section "System Service Dispatching" on page 121 in Chapter 3.)

Figure 12-11
Components of the Windows 2000 I/O system

The layered drivers pass I/O requests to one another by calling the Windows 2000 executive's I/O manager. Relying on the I/O manager as an intermediary allows each driver to maintain independence so that it can be loaded or unloaded without affecting other drivers. In addition, the NTFS driver interacts with the three other Windows 2000 executive components, shown in the left side of Figure 12-12, that are closely related to file systems.

The log file service (LFS) is the part of NTFS that provides services for maintaining a log of disk writes. The log file LFS writes is used to recover an NTFS-formatted volume in the case of a system failure. (See the section "Log File Service (LFS)" on page 750 for more information on LFS.)

The cache manager is the component of the Windows 2000 executive that provides systemwide caching services for NTFS and other file system drivers, including network file system drivers (servers and redirectors). All file systems implemented for Windows 2000 access cached files by mapping them into system address space and then accessing the virtual memory. The cache manager provides a specialized file system interface to the Windows 2000 memory manager for this purpose. When a program tries to access a part of a file that isn't

Figure 12-12
NTFS and related components

loaded into the cache (a *cache miss*), the memory manager calls NTFS to access the disk driver and obtain the file contents from disk. The cache manager optimizes disk I/O by using its lazy writer threads to call the memory manager to flush cache contents to disk as a background activity (asynchronous disk writing). (For a complete description of the cache manager, see Chapter 11.)

NTFS participates in the Windows 2000 object model by implementing files as objects. This implementation allows files to be shared and protected by the object manager, the component of Windows 2000 that manages all executive-level objects. (The object manager is described in the section "Object Manager" on page 125 in Chapter 3.)

An application creates and accesses files just as it does other Windows 2000 objects: by means of object handles. By the time an I/O request reaches NTFS, the Windows 2000 object manager and security system have already verified that the calling process has the authority to access the file object in the way it is attempting to. The security system has compared the caller's access token to the entries in the access-control list for the file object. (See Chapter 8 for more information about access-control lists.) The I/O manager has also transformed the file handle into a pointer to a file object. NTFS uses the information in the file object to access the file on disk.

Figure 12-13 shows the data structures that link a file handle to the file system's on-disk structure.

Figure 12-13
NTFS data structures

NTFS follows several pointers to get from the file object to the location of the file on disk. As Figure 12-13 shows, a file object, which represents a single call to the open-file system service, points to a *stream control block* (SCB) for the file attribute that the caller is trying to read or write. In Figure 12-13, a process has opened both the unnamed data attribute and a named stream (alternate data attribute) for the file. The SCBs represent individual file attributes and contain information about how to find specific attributes within a file. All the SCBs for a file point to a common data structure called a *file control block* (FCB). The FCB contains a pointer (actually, a file reference, explained in the section "File Reference Numbers" later in this chapter) to the file's record in the disk-based master file table (MFT), which is described in detail in the following section.

NTFS On-Disk Structure

This section describes the on-disk structure of an NTFS volume, including how disk space is divided and organized into clusters, how files are organized into directories, how the actual file data and attribute information is stored on disk, and finally, how NTFS data compression works.

Volumes

The structure of NTFS begins with a volume. A *volume* corresponds to a logical partition on a disk, and it is created when you format a disk or part of a disk for NTFS. You can also create a RAID volume that spans multiple disks by using the Windows 2000 Disk Management MMC snap-in.

A disk can have one volume or several. NTFS handles each volume independently of the others. Three sample disk configurations for a 150-MB hard disk are illustrated in Figure 12-14.

Figure 12-14
Sample disk configurations

A volume consists of a series of files plus any additional unallocated space remaining on the disk partition. In the FAT file system, a volume also contains areas specially formatted for use by the file system. An NTFS volume, however, stores all file system data, such as bitmaps and directories, and even the system bootstrap, as ordinary files.

Clusters

The cluster size on an NTFS volume, or the *cluster factor*, is established when a user formats the volume with either the *format* command or the Disk Management MMC snap-in. The default cluster factor varies with the size of the

volume, but it is an integral number of physical sectors, always a power of 2 (1 sector, 2 sectors, 4 sectors, 8 sectors, and so on). The cluster factor is expressed as the number of bytes in the cluster, such as 512 bytes, 1 KB, or 2 KB.

Internally, NTFS refers only to clusters. (However, NTFS forms low-level volume I/O operations such that it is sector-aligned and its length is a multiple of the sector size.) NTFS uses the cluster as its unit of allocation to maintain its independence from physical sector sizes. This independence allows NTFS to efficiently support very large disks by using a larger cluster factor or to support nonstandard disks that have a sector size other than 512 bytes. On a larger volume, use of a larger cluster factor can reduce fragmentation and speed allocation, at a small cost in terms of wasted disk space. Both the *format* command available from the Windows 2000 Command Prompt and the Format menu option under the All Tasks option on the Action menu in the Disk Management MMC snap-in choose a default cluster factor based on the volume size, but you can override this size.

NTFS refers to physical locations on a disk by means of *logical cluster numbers* (LCNs). LCNs are simply the numbering of all clusters from the beginning of the volume to the end. To convert an LCN to a physical disk address, NTFS multiplies the LCN by the cluster factor to get the physical byte offset on the volume, as the disk driver interface requires. NTFS refers to the data within a file by means of *virtual cluster numbers* (VCNs). VCNs number the clusters belonging to a particular file from 0 through m. VCNs aren't necessarily physically contiguous, however; they can be mapped to any number of LCNs on the volume.

Master File Table

In NTFS, all data stored on a volume is contained in files, including the data structures used to locate and retrieve files, the bootstrap data, and the bitmap that records the allocation state of the entire volume (the NTFS metadata). Storing everything in files allows the file system to easily locate and maintain the data, and each separate file can be protected by a security descriptor. In addition, if a particular part of the disk goes bad, NTFS can relocate the metadata files to prevent the disk from becoming inaccessible.

The MFT is the heart of the NTFS volume structure. The MFT is implemented as an array of file records. The size of each file record is fixed at 1 KB, regardless of cluster size. (The structure of a file record is described in the "File

Records" section on page 726.) Logically, the MFT contains one record for each file on the volume, including a record for the MFT itself. In addition to the MFT, each NTFS volume includes a set of metadata files containing the information that's used to implement the file system structure. Each of these NTFS metadata files has a name that begins with a dollar sign ($), although the signs are hidden. For example, the filename of the MFT is $Mft. The rest of the files on an NTFS volume are normal user files and directories, as shown in Figure 12-15.

Figure 12-15
File records for NTFS metadata files in the MFT

Usually, each MFT record corresponds to a different file. If a file has a large number of attributes or becomes highly fragmented, however, more than one record might be needed for a single file. In such cases, the MFT first record, which stores the locations of the others, is called the *base file record*.

EXPERIMENT: Viewing the MFT

The Nfi utility included in the OEM Support Tools (part of the Windows 2000 debugging tools and available for download at *support.microsoft. com/support/kb/articles/Q253/0/66.asp*) allows you to dump the contents of an NTFS volume's MFT as well as to translate a volume cluster number or physical-disk sector number (on non-RAID volumes only) to the file that contains it, if it's part of a file. The first 16 entries of the MFT are reserved for metadata files, but optional metadata files (which are present only if a volume uses an associated feature) fall outside this area: \$Extend\$Quota, \$Extend\$ObjId, \$Extend\$UsnJrnl, and \$Extend\$Reparse. The following dump was performed on a volume that uses reparse points (\$Reparse), quotas (\$Quota), and object IDs (\$ObjId):

```
C:\>nfi G:\
NTFS File Sector Information Utility.
Copyright (C) Microsoft Corporation 1999. All rights reserved.

File 0
Master File Table ($Mft)
    $STANDARD_INFORMATION (resident)
    $FILE_NAME (resident)
    $DATA (nonresident)
        logical sectors 32-52447 (0x20-0xccdf)
    $BITMAP (nonresident)
        logical sectors 16-23 (0x10-0x17)

File 1
Master File Table Mirror ($MftMirr)
    $STANDARD_INFORMATION (resident)
    $FILE_NAME (resident)
    $DATA (nonresident)
        logical sectors 2048728-2048735 (0x1f42d8-0x1f42df)

File 2
Log File ($LogFile)
    $STANDARD_INFORMATION (resident)
    $FILE_NAME (resident)
    $DATA (nonresident)
        logical sectors 2048736-2073343 (0x1f42e0-0x1fa2ff)
```

```
File 3
DASD ($Volume)
    $STANDARD_INFORMATION (resident)
    $FILE_NAME (resident)
    $OBJECT_ID (resident)
    $SECURITY_DESCRIPTOR (resident)
    $VOLUME_NAME (resident)
    $VOLUME_INFORMATION (resident)
    $DATA (resident)

File 4
Attribute Definition Table ($AttrDef)
    $STANDARD_INFORMATION (resident)
    $FILE_NAME (resident)
    $SECURITY_DESCRIPTOR (resident)
    $DATA (nonresident)
        logical sectors 512256-512263 (0x7d100-0x7d107)

File 5
Root Directory
    $STANDARD_INFORMATION (resident)
    $FILE_NAME (resident)
    $SECURITY_DESCRIPTOR (resident)
    $INDEX_ROOT $I30 (resident)
    $INDEX_ALLOCATION $I30 (nonresident)
        logical sectors 2073416-2073423 (0x1fa348-0x1fa34f)
    $BITMAP $I30 (resident)

File 6
Volume Bitmap ($BitMap)
    $STANDARD_INFORMATION (resident)
    $FILE_NAME (resident)
    $DATA (nonresident)
        logical sectors 2073424-2073675 (0x1fa350-0x1fa44b)

File 7
Boot Sectors ($Boot)
    $STANDARD_INFORMATION (resident)
    $FILE_NAME (resident)
    $SECURITY_DESCRIPTOR (resident)
    $DATA (nonresident)
        logical sectors 0-15 (0x0-0xf)
```

(continued)

721

EXPERIMENT: Viewing the MFT *continued*

```
File 8
Bad Cluster List ($BadClus)
    $STANDARD_INFORMATION (resident)
    $FILE_NAME (resident)
    $DATA (resident)
    $DATA $Bad (nonresident)

File 9
Security ($Secure)
    $STANDARD_INFORMATION (resident)
    $FILE_NAME (resident)
    $DATA $SDS (nonresident)
        logical sectors 2073932-2074447 (0x1fa54c-0x1fa74f)
        logical sectors 523160-523163 (0x7fb98-0x7fb9b)
    $INDEX_ROOT $SDH (resident)
    $INDEX_ROOT $SII (resident)
    $INDEX_ALLOCATION $SDH (nonresident)
        logical sectors 1876152-1876159 (0x1ca0b8-0x1ca0bf)
    $INDEX_ALLOCATION $SII (nonresident)
        logical sectors 24-31 (0x18-0x1f)
    $BITMAP $SDH (resident)
    $BITMAP $SII (resident)

File 10
Upcase Table ($UpCase)
    $STANDARD_INFORMATION (resident)
    $FILE_NAME (resident)
    $DATA (nonresident)
        logical sectors 2073676-2073931 (0x1fa44c-0x1fa54b)

File 11
Extend Table ($Extend)
    $STANDARD_INFORMATION (resident)
    $FILE_NAME (resident)
    $INDEX_ROOT $I30 (resident)

File 12
(unknown/unnamed)
    $STANDARD_INFORMATION (resident)
    $SECURITY_DESCRIPTOR (resident)
    $DATA (resident)
```

```
File 13
(unknown/unnamed)
    $STANDARD_INFORMATION (resident)
    $SECURITY_DESCRIPTOR (resident)
    $DATA (resident)

File 14
(unknown/unnamed)
    $STANDARD_INFORMATION (resident)
    $SECURITY_DESCRIPTOR (resident)
    $DATA (resident)

File 15
(unknown/unnamed)
    $STANDARD_INFORMATION (resident)
    $SECURITY_DESCRIPTOR (resident)
    $DATA (resident)

File 24
\$Extend\$Quota
    $STANDARD_INFORMATION (resident)
    $FILE_NAME (resident)
    $INDEX_ROOT $O (resident)
    $INDEX_ROOT $Q (resident)

File 25
\$Extend\$ObjId
    $STANDARD_INFORMATION (resident)
    $FILE_NAME (resident)
    $INDEX_ROOT $O (resident)

File 26
\$Extend\$Reparse
    $STANDARD_INFORMATION (resident)
    $FILE_NAME (resident)
    $INDEX_ROOT $R (resident)
```

When it first accesses a volume, NTFS must *mount* it—that is, read metadata from the disk and construct internal data structures so that it can process application file system accesses. To mount the volume, NTFS looks in the boot sector to find the physical disk address of the MFT. The MFT's own file record is

the first entry in the table; the second file record points to a file located in the middle of the disk called the *MFT mirror* (filename $MftMirr) that contains a copy of the first few rows of the MFT. This partial copy of the MFT is used to locate metadata files if part of the MFT file can't be read for some reason.

Once NTFS finds the file record for the MFT, it obtains the VCN-to-LCN mapping information in the file record's data attribute and stores it in memory. Each run has a VCN-to-LCN mapping and a run length because that's all the information necessary to locate an LCN for any VCN. This mapping information tells NTFS where the runs composing the MFT are located on the disk. (Runs are explained later in this chapter in the section "Resident and Nonresident Attributes.") NTFS then processes the MFT records for several more metadata files and opens the files. Next, NTFS performs its file system recovery operation (described in the section "Recovery" on page 756), and finally, it opens its remaining metadata files. The volume is now ready for user access.

As the system runs, NTFS writes to another important metadata file, the *log file* (filename $LogFile). NTFS uses the log file to record all operations that affect the NTFS volume structure, including file creation or any commands, such as *Copy,* that alter the directory structure. The log file is used to recover an NTFS volume after a system failure.

Another entry in the MFT is reserved for the *root directory* (also known as "\"). Its file record contains an index of the files and directories stored in the root of the NTFS directory structure. When NTFS is first asked to open a file, it begins its search for the file in the root directory's file record. After opening a file, NTFS stores the file's MFT file reference so that it can directly access the file's MFT record when it reads and writes the file later.

NTFS records the allocation state of the volume in the *bitmap file* (filename $Bitmap). The data attribute for the bitmap file contains a bitmap, each of whose bits represents a cluster on the volume, identifying whether the cluster is free or has been allocated to a file.

The *security file* (filename $Secure) stores the volumewide security descriptor database. NTFS files and directories have individually settable security descriptors, but to conserve space, NTFS stores the settings in a common file, which allows files and directories that have the same security settings to reference the same security descriptor. In most environments, entire directory trees have the same security settings, so this optimization provides a significant savings.

Another system file, the *boot file* (filename $Boot), stores the Windows 2000 bootstrap code. For the system to boot, the bootstrap code must be located at a specific disk address. During formatting, however, the *format* command defines this area as a file by creating a file record for it. Creating the boot file allows NTFS to adhere to its rule of making everything on the disk a file. The boot file as well as NTFS metadata files can be individually protected by means of the security descriptors that are applied to all Windows 2000 objects. Using this "everything on the disk is a file" model also means that the bootstrap can be modified by normal file I/O, although the boot file is protected from editing.

NTFS also maintains a *bad-cluster file* (filename $BadClus) for recording any bad spots on the disk volume and a file known as the *volume file* (filename $Volume), which contains the volume name, the version of NTFS for which the volume is formatted, and a bit that when set signifies that a disk corruption has occurred and must be repaired by the Chkdsk utility. (The Chkdsk utility is covered in more detail later in the chapter.) The *uppercase file* (filename $UpCase) includes a translation table between lowercase and uppercase characters. NTFS maintains a file containing an *attribute definition table* (filename $AttrDef) that defines the attribute types supported on the volume and indicates whether they can be indexed, recovered during a system recovery operation, and so on.

NTFS stores several metadata files in the *extensions* (directory name $Extend) metadata directory, including the *object identifier file* (filename $ObjId), the *quota file* (filename $Quota), the *change journal file* (filename $UsnJrnl), and the *reparse point file* (filename $Reparse). These files store information related to optional features of NTFS. The object identifier file stores file object IDs, the quota file stores quota limit and behavior information on volumes that have quotas enabled, the change journal file records file and directory changes, and the reparse point file stores information about which files and directories on the volume include reparse point data.

File Reference Numbers

A file on an NTFS volume is identified by a 64-bit value called a *file reference*. The file reference consists of a file number and a sequence number. The file number corresponds to the position of the file's file record in the MFT minus 1 (or to the position of the base file record minus 1 if the file has more than one file record). The file reference sequence number, which is incremented each time an MFT file record position is reused, enables NTFS to perform internal consistency checks. A file reference is illustrated in Figure 12-16.

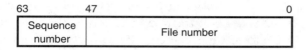

Figure 12-16
File reference

File Records

Instead of viewing a file as just a repository for textual or binary data, NTFS stores files as a collection of attribute/value pairs, one of which is the data it contains (called the *unnamed data attribute*). Other attributes that comprise a file include the filename, time stamp information, and possibly additional named data attributes. Figure 12-17 illustrates an MFT record for a small file.

Figure 12-17
MFT record for a small file

Each file attribute is stored as a separate stream of bytes within a file. Strictly speaking, NTFS doesn't read and write files—it reads and writes attribute streams. NTFS supplies these attribute operations: create, delete, read (byte range), and write (byte range). The read and write services normally operate on the file's unnamed data attribute. However, a caller can specify a different data attribute by using the named data stream syntax.

Table 12-4 lists the attributes for files on an NTFS volume. (Not all attributes are present for every file.)

Table 12-4 **Attributes for NTFS Files**

Attribute	Attribute Name	Description
Volume information	$VOLUME_INFORMATION, $VOLUME_NAME	These attributes are present only in the $Volume metadata file. They store volume version sand label information.
Standard information	$STANDARD_INFORMATION	File attributes such as read-only, archive, and so on; time stamps, including when the file was created or last modified; and how many directories point to the file (its *hard link count*).
Filename	$FILE_NAME	The file's name in Unicode characters. A file can have multiple filename attributes, as it does when a hard link to a file exists or when a file with a long name has an automatically generated "short name" for access by MS-DOS and 16-bit Microsoft Windows applications.
Security descriptor	$SECURITY_DESCRIPTOR	This attribute is present for backward compatibility with previous versions of NTFS. The Windows 2000 version of NTFS stores all security descriptors in the $Secure metadata file, sharing descriptors among files and directories that have the same settings. Previous versions of NTFS stored private security descriptor information with each file and directory.
Data	$DATA	The contents of the file. In NTFS, a file has one default unnamed data attribute and can have additional named data attributes; that is, a file can have multiple data streams. A directory has no default data attribute but can have optional named data attributes.
Index root, index allocation, and index bitmap	$INDEX_ROOT, $INDEX_ALLOCATION, $BITMAP	Three attributes used to implement filename allocation and bitmap indexes for large directories (directories only).

(continued)

Table 12-4 *continued*

Attribute	Attribute Name	Description
Attribute list	$ATTRIBUTE_LIST	A list of the attributes that make up the file and the file reference of the MFT file record in which each attribute is located. This seldom-used attribute is present when a file requires more than one MFT file record.
Object ID	$OBJECT_ID	A 64-byte identifier for a file or directory, with the lowest 16 bytes (128 bits) unique to the volume. The link-tracking service assigns object IDs to shell shortcut and OLE link source files. NTFS provides APIs so that files and directories can be opened with their object ID rather than their filename.
Reparse information	$REPARSE_POINT	This attribute stores a file's reparse point data. NTFS junctions and mount points include this attribute.
Extended attributes	$EA, $EA_INFORMATION	Extended attributes aren't actively used but are provided for backward compatibility with OS/2 applications.
EFS information	$LOGGED_UTILITY_STREAM	EFS stores data in this attribute that's used to manage a file's encryption, such as the encrypted version of the key needed to decrypt the file and a list of users that are authorized to access the file. The word *logged* is in the attribute's name because changes to this attribute are recorded in the volume log file (described later in this chapter) for recoverability.

Table 12-4 shows attribute names; however, attributes actually correspond to numeric type codes, which NTFS uses to order the attributes within a file record. The file attributes in an MFT record are ordered by these type codes (numerically in ascending order), with some attribute types appearing more than once—if a file has multiple data attributes, for example, or multiple filenames.

Each attribute in a file record is identified with its attribute type code and has a value and an optional name. An attribute's value is the byte stream composing the attribute. For example, the value of the $FILE_NAME attribute is the file's name; the value of the $DATA attribute is whatever bytes the user stored in the file.

Most attributes never have names, though the index-related attributes and the $DATA attribute often do. Names distinguish among multiple attributes of the same type that a file can include. For example, a file that has a named data stream has two $DATA attributes: an unnamed $DATA attribute storing the default unnamed data stream and a named $DATA attribute having the name of the alternate stream and storing the named stream's data.

Filenames

Both NTFS and FAT allow each filename in a path to be as many as 255 characters long. Filenames can contain Unicode characters as well as multiple periods and embedded spaces. However, the FAT file system supplied with MS-DOS is limited to 8 (non-Unicode) characters for its filenames, followed by a period and a 3-character extension. Figure 12-18 provides a visual representation of the different file namespaces Windows 2000 supports and shows how they intersect.

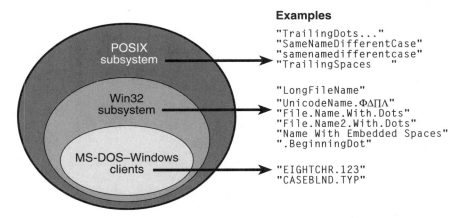

Figure 12-18
Windows 2000 file namespaces

The POSIX subsystem requires the biggest namespace of all the application execution environments that Windows 2000 supports, and therefore the NTFS namespace is equivalent to the POSIX namespace. The POSIX subsystem can create names that aren't visible to Win32 and MS-DOS applications, including names with trailing periods and trailing spaces. Ordinarily, creating a file using the large POSIX namespace isn't a problem because you would do that only if you intended the POSIX subsystem or POSIX client systems to use that file.

The relationship between 32-bit Windows (Win32) applications and MS-DOS Windows applications is a much closer one, however. The Win32 area in Figure 12-18 represents filenames that the Win32 subsystem can create on an NTFS volume but that MS-DOS and 16-bit Windows applications can't see. This group includes filenames longer than the 8.3 format of MS-DOS names, those containing Unicode (international) characters, those with multiple period characters or a beginning period, and those with embedded spaces. When a file is created with such a name, NTFS automatically generates an alternate, MS-DOS-style filename for the file. Windows 2000 displays these short names when you use the /x option with the *dir* command.

The MS-DOS filenames are fully functional aliases for the NTFS files and are stored in the same directory as the long filenames. The MFT record for a file with an autogenerated MS-DOS filename is shown in Figure 12-19.

Figure 12-19
MFT file record with an MS-DOS filename attribute

The NTFS name and the generated MS-DOS name are stored in the same file record and therefore refer to the same file. The MS-DOS name can be used to open, read from, write to, or copy the file. If a user renames the file using either the long filename or the short filename, the new name replaces both the existing names. If the new name isn't a valid MS-DOS name, NTFS generates another MS-DOS name for the file.

NOTE POSIX hard links are implemented in a similar way. When a hard link to a POSIX file is created, NTFS adds another filename attribute to the file's MFT file record. The two situations differ in one regard, however. When a user deletes a POSIX file that has multiple names (hard links), the file record and the file remain in place. The file and its record are deleted only when the last filename (hard link) is deleted. If a file has both an NTFS name and an autogenerated MS-DOS name, however, a user can delete the file using either name.

Here's the algorithm NTFS uses to generate an MS-DOS name from a long filename:

1. Remove from the long name any characters that are illegal in MS-DOS names, including spaces and Unicode characters. Remove preceding and trailing periods. Remove all other embedded periods, except the last one.

2. Truncate the string before the period (if present) to six characters, and append the string "~n" (where n is a number, starting with 1, that is used to distinguish different files that truncate to the same name). Truncate the string after the period (if present) to three characters.

3. Put the result in uppercase letters. MS-DOS is case-insensitive, and this step guarantees that NTFS won't generate a new name that differs from the old only in case.

4. If the generated name duplicates an existing name in the directory, increment the ~n string.

Table 12-5 shows the long Win32 filenames from Figure 12-18 and their NTFS-generated MS-DOS versions. The current algorithm and the examples in Figure 12-18 should give you an idea of what NTFS-generated MS-DOS-style filenames look like. Application developers shouldn't depend on this algorithm, though, because it might change in the future.

Table 12-5 NTFS-Generated Filenames

Win32 Long Name	NTFS-Generated Short Name
LongFileName	LONGFI~1
UnicodeName.ΦΔΠΛ	UNICOD~1
File.Name.With.Dots	FILENA~1.DOT
File.Name2.With.Dots	FILENA~2.DOT
Name With Embedded Spaces	NAMEWI~1
.BeginningDot	BEGINN~1

Resident and Nonresident Attributes

If a file is small, all its attributes and their values (its data, for example) fit in the file record. When the value of an attribute is stored directly in the MFT, the attribute is called a *resident attribute*. (In Figure 12-17, for example, all attributes are resident.) Several attributes are defined as always being resident so that NTFS can locate nonresident attributes. The standard information and index root attributes are always resident, for example.

Each attribute begins with a standard header containing information about the attribute, information that NTFS uses to manage the attributes in a generic way. The header, which is always resident, records whether the attribute's value is resident or nonresident. For resident attributes, the header also contains the offset from the header to the attribute's value and the length of the attribute's value, as Figure 12-20 illustrates for the filename attribute.

Figure 12-20
Resident attribute header and value

When an attribute's value is stored directly in the MFT, the time it takes NTFS to access the value is greatly reduced. Instead of looking up a file in a table and then reading a succession of allocation units to find the file's data (as the FAT file system does, for example), NTFS accesses the disk once and retrieves the data immediately.

The attributes for a small directory, as well as for a small file, can be resident in the MFT, as Figure 12-21 shows. For a small directory, the index root attribute contains an index of file references for the files and the subdirectories in the directory.

Standard information	Filename	Index root	
		Index of files	Empty
		file1, file2, file3, . . .	

Figure 12-21
MFT file record for a small directory

Of course, many files and directories can't be squeezed into a 1-KB fixed-size MFT record. If a particular attribute, such as a file's data attribute, is too large to be contained in an MFT file record, NTFS allocates clusters for the attribute's data separate from the MFT. This area is called a *run* (or an *extent*). If the attribute's value later grows (if a user appends data to the file, for example), NTFS allocates another run for the additional data. Attributes whose values are stored in runs rather than in the MFT are called *nonresident attributes*. The file system decides whether a particular attribute is resident or nonresident; the location of the data is transparent to the process accessing it.

When an attribute is nonresident, as the data attribute for a large file might be, its header contains the information NTFS needs to locate the attribute's value on the disk. Figure 12-22 shows a nonresident data attribute stored in two runs.

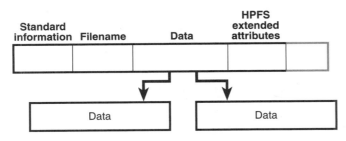

Figure 12-22
MFT file record for a large file with two data runs

Among the standard attributes, only those that can grow can be nonresident. For files, the attributes that can grow are the data and the attribute list (not shown in Figure 12-22). The standard information and filename attributes are always resident.

A large directory can also have nonresident attributes (or parts of attributes), as Figure 12-23 shows. In this example, the MFT file record doesn't have enough room to store the index of files that make up this large directory. A part

Figure 12-23
MFT file record for a large directory with a nonresident filename index

of the index is stored in the index root attribute, and the rest of the index is stored in nonresident runs called *index buffers*. The index root, index allocation, and bitmap attributes are shown here in a simplified form. They are described in more detail in the next section. The standard information and filename attributes are always resident. The header and at least part of the value of the index root attribute are also resident for directories.

When a file's (or a directory's) attributes can't fit in an MFT file record and separate allocations are needed, NTFS keeps track of the runs by means of VCN-to-LCN mapping pairs. LCNs represent the sequence of clusters on an entire volume from 0 through *n*. VCNs number the clusters belonging to a particular file from 0 through *m*. For example, the clusters in the runs of a nonresident data attribute are numbered as shown in Figure 12-24.

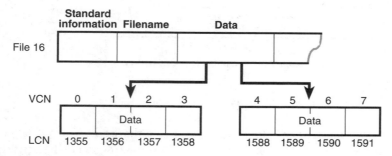

Figure 12-24
VCNs for a nonresident data attribute

If this file had more than two runs, the numbering of the third run would start with VCN 8. As Figure 12-25 shows, the data attribute header contains VCN-to-LCN mappings for the two runs here, which allows NTFS to easily find the allocations on the disk.

Figure 12-25
VCN-to-LCN mappings for a nonresident data attribute

Although Figure 12-25 shows just data runs, other attributes can be stored in runs if there isn't enough room in the MFT file record to contain them. And if a particular file has too many attributes to fit in the MFT record, a second MFT record is used to contain the additional attributes (or attribute headers for nonresident attributes). In this case, an attribute called the *attribute list* is added. The attribute list attribute contains the name and type code of each of the file's attributes and the file reference of the MFT record where the attribute is located. The attribute list attribute is provided for those cases in which a file grows so large or so fragmented that a single MFT record can't contain the multitude of VCN-to-LCN mappings needed to find all its runs. Files with more than 200 runs typically require an attribute list.

Indexing

In NTFS, a file directory is simply an index of filenames—that is, a collection of filenames (along with their file references) organized in a particular way for quick access. To create a directory, NTFS indexes the filename attributes of the files in the directory. The MFT record for the root directory of a volume is shown in Figure 12-26.

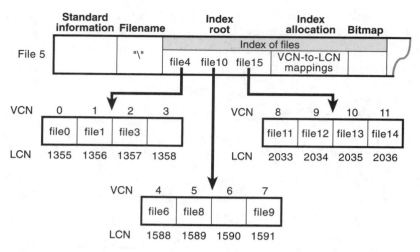

Figure 12-26
Filename index for a volume's root directory

Conceptually, an MFT entry for a directory contains in its index root attribute a sorted list of the files in the directory. For large directories, however, the filenames are actually stored in 4-KB fixed-size index buffers that contain and organize the filenames. Index buffers implement a *b+ tree* data structure, which minimizes the number of disk accesses needed to find a particular file, especially for large directories. The index root attribute contains the first level of the b+ tree (root subdirectories) and points to index buffers containing the next level (more subdirectories, perhaps, or files).

Figure 12-26 shows only filenames in the index root attribute and the index buffers (*file6*, for example), but each entry in an index also contains the file reference in the MFT where the file is described and time stamp and file size information for the file. NTFS duplicates the time stamp and file size information from the file's MFT record. This technique, which is used by FAT and NTFS, requires updated information to be written in two places. Even so, it's a significant speed optimization for directory browsing because it enables the file system to display each file's time stamps and size without opening every file in the directory.

The index allocation attribute maps the VCNs of the index buffer runs to the LCNs that indicate where the index buffers reside on the disk, and the bitmap attribute keeps track of which VCNs in the index buffers are in use and which are free. Figure 12-26 shows one file entry per VCN (that is, per cluster), but filename entries are actually packed into each cluster. Each 4-KB index buffer can contain about 20 to 30 filename entries.

The b+ tree data structure is a type of balanced tree that is ideal for organizing sorted data stored on a disk because it minimizes the number of disk accesses needed to find an entry. In the MFT, a directory's index root attribute contains several filenames that act as indexes into the second level of the b+ tree. Each filename in the index root attribute has an optional pointer associated with it that points to an index buffer. The index buffer it points to contains filenames with lexicographic values less than its own. In Figure 12-26, for example, *file4* is a first-level entry in the b+ tree. It points to an index buffer containing filenames that are (lexicographically) less than itself—the filenames *file0*, *file1*, and *file3*. Note that the names *file1*, *file2*, and so on that are used in this example are not literal filenames but names intended to show the relative placement of files that are lexicographically ordered according to the displayed sequence.

Storing the filenames in b+ trees provides several benefits. Directory lookups are fast because the filenames are stored in a sorted order. And when higher-level software enumerates the files in a directory, NTFS returns already-sorted names. Finally, because b+ trees tend to grow wide rather than deep, NTFS's fast lookup times don't degrade as directories grow.

NTFS also provides general support for indexing data besides filenames. As we stated earlier, a file can have an object ID assigned to it, which is stored in the file's $OBJECT _ID attribute. NTFS provides an API that allows applications to open a file by using the file's object ID instead of its name. NTFS therefore must make the process of translating an object ID to a file's file number an efficient one. To do so, it stores a mapping of all a volume's object IDs to their file reference numbers in the \$Extend\$ObjId metadata file. NTFS sorts the object IDs in the $ObjId's $O index. As are filenames in filename indexes, the object ID index is stored as a b+ tree.

Data Compression and Sparse Files

NTFS supports compression on a per-file, per-directory, or per-volume basis. (NTFS compression is performed only on user data, not file system metadata.) You can tell whether a volume is compressed by using the Win32 *GetVolume-Information* function. To retrieve the actual compressed size of a file, use the Win32 *GetCompressedFileSize* function. Finally, to examine or change the compression setting for a file or directory, use the Win32 *DeviceIoControl* function. (See the FSCTL_GET_COMPRESSION and FSCTL_SET_COMPRESSION file system control codes.) Keep in mind that although setting a file's compression state compresses (or decompresses) the file right away, setting a directory's or volume's compression state doesn't cause any immediate compression or decompression. Instead, setting a directory's or volume's compression state sets a default compression state that will be given to all newly created files and subdirectories within that directory or volume.

The following section introduces NTFS compression by examining the simple case of compressing sparse data. The subsequent sections extend the discussion to the compression of ordinary files and sparse files.

Compressing Sparse Data

Sparse data is often large but contains only a small amount of nonzero data relative to its size. A sparse matrix is one example of sparse data. As described earlier, NTFS uses VCNs, from 0 through m, to enumerate the clusters of a file. Each VCN maps to a corresponding LCN, which identifies the disk location of the cluster. Figure 12-27 illustrates the runs (disk allocations) of a normal, noncompressed file, including its VCNs and the LCNs they map to.

Figure 12-27
Runs of a noncompressed file

This file is stored in 3 runs, each of which is 4 clusters long, for a total of 12 clusters. Figure 12-28 shows the MFT record for this file. As described earlier, to save space, the MFT record's data attribute, which contains VCN-to-LCN mappings, records only one mapping for each run, rather than one for each cluster. Notice, however, that each VCN from 0 through 11 has a corresponding LCN associated with it. The first entry starts at VCN 0 and covers 4 clusters, the second entry starts at VCN 4 and covers 4 clusters, and so on. This entry format is typical for a noncompressed file.

Standard information	Filename	Data		
		Starting VCN	Starting LCN	Number of clusters
		0	1355	4
		4	1588	4
		8	2033	4

Figure 12-28
MFT record for a noncompressed file

When a user selects a file on an NTFS volume for compression, one NTFS compression technique is to remove long strings of zeros from the file. If the file's data is sparse, it typically shrinks to occupy a fraction of the disk space it would otherwise require. On subsequent writes to the file, NTFS allocates space only for runs that contain nonzero data.

Figure 12-29 depicts the runs of a compressed file containing sparse data. Notice that certain ranges of the file's VCNs (16–31 and 64–127) have no disk allocations.

Figure 12-29
Runs of a compressed file containing sparse data

The MFT record for this compressed file omits blocks of VCNs that contain zeros and therefore have no physical storage allocated to them. The first data entry in Figure 12-30, for example, starts at VCN 0 and covers 16 clusters. The second entry jumps to VCN 32 and covers 16 clusters.

Standard information	Filename	Data		
		Starting VCN	Starting LCN	Number of clusters
		0	133	16
		32	193	16
		48	96	16
		128	324	16

Figure 12-30
MFT record for a compressed file containing sparse data

When a program reads data from a compressed file, NTFS checks the MFT record to determine whether a VCN-to-LCN mapping covers the location being read. If the program is reading from an unallocated "hole" in the file, it means that the data in that part of the file consists of zeros, so NTFS returns zeros without accessing the disk. If a program writes nonzero data to a "hole," NTFS quietly allocates disk space and then writes the data. This technique is very efficient for sparse file data that contains a lot of zero data.

Compressing Nonsparse Data

The preceding example of compressing a sparse file is somewhat contrived. It describes "compression" for a case in which whole sections of a file were filled with zeros but the remaining data in the file wasn't affected by the compression. The data in most files isn't sparse, but it can still be compressed by the application of a compression algorithm.

In NTFS, users can specify compression for individual files or for all the files in a directory. (New files created in a directory marked compressed are automatically compressed—existing files must be compressed individually.) When it compresses a file, NTFS divides the file's unprocessed data into *compression units* 16 clusters long (equal to 8 KB for a 512-byte cluster, for example). Certain sequences of data in a file might not compress much, if at all; so for each compression unit in the file, NTFS determines whether compressing the unit will save at least 1 cluster of storage. If compressing the unit won't free up at least 1 cluster, NTFS allocates a 16-cluster run and writes the data in that unit to disk without compressing it. If the data in a 16-cluster unit will compress to 15 or fewer clusters, NTFS allocates only the number of clusters needed to contain the compressed data and then writes it to disk. Figure 12-31 illustrates

Figure 12-31
Data runs of a compressed file

the compression of a file with four runs. The unshaded areas in this figure represent the actual storage locations that the file occupies after compression. The first, second, and fourth runs were compressed; the third run wasn't. Even with one noncompressed run, compressing this file saved 26 clusters of disk space, or 41 percent.

NOTE Although the diagrams in this chapter show contiguous LCNs, a compression unit need not be stored in physically contiguous clusters. Runs that occupy noncontiguous clusters produce slightly more complicated MFT records than the one shown in Figure 12-32.

When it writes data to a compressed file, NTFS ensures that each run begins on a virtual 16-cluster boundary. Thus the starting VCN of each run is a multiple of 16, and the runs are no longer than 16 clusters. NTFS reads and writes at least one compression unit at a time when it accesses compressed files. When it writes compressed data, however, NTFS tries to store compression units in physically contiguous locations so that it can read them all in a single I/O operation. The 16-cluster size of the NTFS compression unit was chosen to reduce internal fragmentation: the larger the compression unit, the less the overall disk space needed to store the data. This 16-cluster compression unit

size represents a trade-off between producing smaller compressed files and slowing read operations for programs that randomly access files. The equivalent of 16 clusters must be decompressed for each cache miss. (A cache miss is more likely to occur during random file access.) Figure 12-32 shows the MFT record for the compressed file shown in Figure 12-31.

Standard information	Filename	Data		
		Starting VCN	Starting LCN	Number of clusters
		0	19	4
		16	23	8
		32	97	16
		48	113	10

Figure 12-32
MFT record for a compressed file

One difference between this compressed file and the earlier example of a compressed file containing sparse data is that three of the compressed runs in this file are less than 16 clusters long. Reading this information from a file's MFT file record enables NTFS to know whether data in the file is compressed. Any run shorter than 16 clusters contains compressed data that NTFS must decompress when it first reads the data into the cache. A run that is exactly 16 clusters long doesn't contain compressed data and therefore requires no decompression.

If the data in a run has been compressed, NTFS decompresses the data into a scratch buffer and then copies it to the caller's buffer. NTFS also loads the decompressed data into the cache, which makes subsequent reads from the same run as fast as any other cached read. NTFS writes any updates to the file to the cache, leaving the lazy writer to compress and write the modified data to disk asynchronously. This strategy ensures that writing to a compressed file produces no more significant delay than writing to a noncompressed file would.

NTFS keeps disk allocations for a compressed file contiguous whenever possible. As the LCNs indicate, the first two runs of the compressed file shown in Figure 12-31 on page 741 are physically contiguous, as are the last two. When two or more runs are contiguous, NTFS performs disk read-ahead, as it does with the data in other files. Because the reading and decompression of con-

tiguous file data take place asynchronously before the program requests the data, subsequent read operations obtain the data directly from the cache, which greatly enhances read performance.

Sparse Files

Sparse files (the NTFS file type, as opposed to files that consist of sparse data, described earlier) are essentially compressed files for which NTFS doesn't apply compression to the file's nonsparse data. However, NTFS manages the run data of a sparse file's MFT record the same way it does for compressed files that consist of sparse and nonsparse data.

Reparse Points

As described earlier in the chapter, a *reparse point* is a block of up to 16 KB of application-defined reparse data and a 32-bit reparse tag that are stored in the $REPARSE_POINT attribute of a file or directory. Whenever an application creates or deletes a reparse point, NTFS updates the \$Extend\$Reparse metadata file, in which NTFS stores entries that identify the file record numbers of files and directories that contain reparse points. Storing the records in a central location enables NTFS to provide interfaces for applications to enumerate all a volume's reparse points or just specific types of reparse points, such as mount points. (See Chapter 10 for more information on mount points.) The \$Extend\$Reparse file uses the general indexing facility of NTFS by collating the file's entries (in an index named $R) by reparse point tags.

The Change Journal File

The change journal file, \$Extend\$UsnJrnl, is a sparse file that NTFS creates only when an application enables change logging. The journal stores change entries in the $J data stream. Entries include the following information about a file or directory change:

- The time of the change
- The change type (delete, rename, size extend, and so on)
- The file or directory's attributes
- The file or directory's name
- The file or directory's file reference number
- The file reference number of the file's parent directory

The journal is sparse so that it never overflows; when the journal's on-disk size exceeds the maximum defined for the file, NTFS simply begins zeroing the file data that precedes the window of change information having a size equal to the maximum journal size, as shown in Figure 12-33. To prevent constant resizing when an application is continuously exceeding the journal's size, NTFS shrinks the journal only when its size is twice an application-defined value over the maximum configured size.

Figure 12-33
Change journal ($UsnJrnl) space allocation

Object IDs

In addition to storing the object ID assigned to a file or directory in the $OBJECT_ID attribute of its MFT record, NTFS also keeps the correspondence between object IDs and their file reference numbers in the $O index of the \$Extend\$ObjId metadata file. The index collates entries by object ID, making it easy for NTFS to quickly locate a file based on its ID. This feature allows applications, using undocumented native API functionality, to open a file or directory using its object ID.

Quota Tracking

The NTFS quota-tracking facility associates an owner ID with each user who creates files and stores the user's owner ID with each file or directory the user creates. To determine whether a user has been assigned an ID, NTFS uses the user's SID as a key to index the $O index of the \$Extend\$Quota metadata file. If an ID isn't located, NTFS allocates a unique ID for the user and records the association in the $O index.

\$Extend\$Quota also contains an index named $Q that NTFS uses to store per-user quota information entries, collating the entries by owner ID. When a user attempts to allocate space on a volume, NTFS uses the owner ID to look up the user's quota entry and determine whether there is sufficient disk space left in the user's quota to allow the allocation.

Consolidated Security

Another example of general indexing is seen in the \$Secure metadata file, which stores security descriptors for all the files and directories on a volume. NTFS assigns each unique security descriptor an NTFS security ID. (These are different than the SIDs described in Chapter 8.)

When a process applies a security descriptor to a file or directory, NTFS obtains a 32-bit hash of the descriptor and looks up the corresponding security ID in an index named $SDH that is stored in the \$Secure file. Multiple security descriptors can hash to the same value, so NTFS compares the security descriptor being applied with any that have the same hash to verify an exact match. If it locates the applied security descriptor in the $SDH index, NTFS assigns the file the associated security ID. Otherwise, it allocates a new security

ID, updates the $SDH index, and adds the security descriptor to the $SII index. The $SII index is collated by security ID so that when a user attempts to open a file or directory, NTFS can quickly locate the file or directory's security descriptor by using the file or directory's security ID.

NTFS Recovery Support

NTFS recovery support ensures that if a power failure or a system failure occurs, no file system operations (transactions) will be left incomplete and the structure of the disk volume will remain intact without the need to run a disk repair utility. The NTFS Chkdsk utility is used to repair catastrophic disk corruption caused by I/O errors (bad disk sectors, electrical anomalies, or disk failures, for example) or software bugs. But with the NTFS recovery capabilities in place, Chkdsk is rarely needed.

As mentioned earlier (in the section "Recoverability" on page 700), NTFS uses a transaction-processing scheme to implement recoverability. This strategy ensures a full disk recovery that is also extremely fast (on the order of seconds) for even the largest disks. NTFS limits its recovery procedures to file system data to ensure that at the very least the user will never lose a volume because of a corrupted file system; however, unless an application takes specific action (such as flushing cached files to disk), NTFS doesn't guarantee user data to be fully updated if a crash occurs. Transaction-based protection of user data is available in most of the database products available for Windows 2000, such as Microsoft SQL Server. The decision not to implement user data recovery in the file system represents a trade-off between a fully fault tolerant file system and one that provides optimum performance for all file operations.

The following sections describe the evolution of file system reliability as a context for an introduction to recoverable file systems, detail the transaction-logging scheme NTFS uses to record modifications to file system data structures, and explain how NTFS recovers a volume if the system fails.

Evolution of File System Design

The development of a recoverable file system was a step forward in the evolution of file system design. In the past, two techniques were common for constructing a file system's I/O and caching support: *careful write* and *lazy write*. The file systems developed for Digital Equipment Corporation's (now Compaq's) VAX/VMS and for some other proprietary operating systems employed a careful write algorithm, while OS/2 HPFS and most older UNIX file systems used a lazy write file system scheme.

The next two subsections briefly review these two types of file systems and their intrinsic trade-offs between safety and performance. The third subsection describes NTFS's recoverable approach and explains how it differs from the other two strategies.

Careful Write File Systems

When an operating system crashes or loses power, I/O operations in progress are immediately, and often prematurely, interrupted. Depending on what I/O operation or operations were in progress and how far along they were, such an abrupt halt can produce inconsistencies in a file system. An inconsistency in this context is a file system corruption—a filename appears in a directory listing, for example, but the file system doesn't know the file is there or can't access the file. The worst file system corruptions can leave an entire volume inaccessible.

A careful write file system doesn't try to prevent file system inconsistencies. Rather, it orders its write operations so that, at worst, a system crash will produce predictable, noncritical inconsistencies, which the file system can fix at its leisure.

When any kind of file system receives a request to update the disk, it must perform several suboperations before the update will be complete. In a file system that uses the careful write strategy, the suboperations are always written to disk serially. When allocating disk space for a file, for example, the file system first sets some bits in its bitmap and then allocates the space to the file. If the power fails immediately after the bits are set, the careful write file system loses access to some disk space—to the space represented by the set bits—but existing data isn't corrupted.

Serializing write operations also means that I/O requests are filled in the order in which they are received. If one process allocates disk space and shortly thereafter another process creates a file, a careful write file system completes the disk allocation before it starts to create the file because interleaving the suboperations of the two I/O requests could result in an inconsistent state.

NOTE The FAT file system uses a *write-through* algorithm that causes disk modifications to be immediately written to the disk. Unlike the careful write approach, the write-through technique doesn't require the file system to order its writes to prevent inconsistencies.

The main advantage of a careful write file system is that in the event of a failure the volume stays consistent and usable without the need to immediately run a slow volume repair utility. Such a utility is needed to correct the

predictable, nondestructive disk inconsistencies that occur as the result of a system failure, but the utility can be run at a convenient time, typically when the system is rebooted.

Lazy Write File Systems

A careful write file system sacrifices speed for the safety it provides. A lazy write file system improves performance by using a *write-back* caching strategy; that is, it writes file modifications to the cache and flushes the contents of the cache to disk in an optimized way, usually as a background activity.

The performance improvements associated with the lazy write caching technique take several forms. First, the overall number of disk writes is reduced. Because serialized, immediate disk writes aren't required, the contents of a buffer can be modified several times before they are written to disk. Second, the speed of servicing application requests is greatly increased because the file system can return control to the caller without waiting for disk writes to be completed. Finally, the lazy write strategy ignores the inconsistent intermediate states on a file volume that can result when the suboperations of two or more I/O requests are interleaved. It is thus easier to make the file system multithreaded, allowing more than one I/O operation to be in progress at a time.

The disadvantage of the lazy write technique is that it creates intervals during which a volume is in too inconsistent a state to be corrected by the file system. Consequently, lazy write file systems must keep track of the volume's state at all times. In general, lazy write file systems gain a performance advantage over careful write systems—at the expense of greater risk and user inconvenience if the system fails.

Recoverable File Systems

A recoverable file system such as NTFS tries to exceed the safety of a careful write file system while achieving the performance of a lazy write file system. A recoverable file system ensures volume consistency by using logging techniques (sometimes called *journaling*) originally developed for transaction processing. If the operating system crashes, the recoverable file system restores consistency by executing a recovery procedure that accesses information that has been stored in a log file. Because the file system has logged its disk writes, the recovery procedure takes only seconds, regardless of the size of the volume.

The recovery procedure for a recoverable file system is exact, guaranteeing that the volume will be restored to a consistent state. In NTFS, none of the inadequate restorations associated with lazy write file systems can happen.

A recoverable file system incurs some costs for the safety it provides. Every transaction that alters the volume structure requires that one record be written to the log file for each of the transaction's suboperations. This logging overhead is ameliorated by the file system's *batching* of log records—writing many records to the log file in a single I/O operation. In addition, the recoverable file system can employ the optimization techniques of a lazy write file system. It can even increase the length of the intervals between cache flushes because the file system can be recovered if the system crashes before the cache changes have been flushed to disk. This gain over the caching performance of lazy write file systems makes up for, and often exceeds, the overhead of the recoverable file system's logging activity.

Neither careful write nor lazy write file systems guarantee protection of user file data. If the system crashes while an application is writing a file, the file can be lost or corrupted. Worse, the crash can corrupt a lazy write file system, destroying existing files or even rendering an entire volume inaccessible.

The NTFS recoverable file system implements several strategies that improve its reliability over that of the traditional file systems. First, NTFS recoverability guarantees that the volume structure won't be corrupted, so all files will remain accessible after a system failure.

Second, although NTFS doesn't guarantee protection of user data in the event of a system crash—some changes can be lost from the cache—applications can take advantage of the NTFS write-through and cache-flushing capabilities to ensure that file modifications are recorded on disk at appropriate intervals. Both *cache write-through*—forcing write operations to be immediately recorded on disk—and *cache flushing*—forcing cache contents to be written to disk—are efficient operations. NTFS doesn't have to do extra disk I/O to flush modifications to several different file system data structures because changes to the data structures are recorded—in a single write operation—in the log file; if a failure occurs and cache contents are lost, the file system modifications can be recovered from the log. Furthermore, unlike the FAT file system, NTFS guarantees that user data will be consistent and available immediately after a write-through operation or a cache flush, even if the system subsequently fails.

Logging

NTFS provides file system recoverability by means of a transaction-processing technique called *logging*. In NTFS logging, the suboperations of any transaction that alters important file system data structures are recorded in a log file

before they are carried through on the disk. That way, if the system crashes, partially completed transactions can be redone or undone when the system comes back on line. In transaction processing, this technique is known as *write-ahead logging*. In NTFS, transactions include writing to the disk or deleting a file and can be made up of several suboperations.

Log File Service (LFS)

The log file service (LFS) is a series of kernel-mode routines inside the NTFS driver that NTFS uses to access the log file. Although originally designed to provide logging and recovery services for more than one client, the LFS is used only by NTFS. The caller—NTFS in this case—passes the LFS a pointer to an open file object, which specifies a log file to be accessed. The LFS either initializes a new log file or calls the Windows 2000 cache manager to access the existing log file through the cache, as shown in Figure 12-34.

Figure 12-34
Log file service (LFS)

The LFS divides the log file into two regions: a *restart area* and an "infinite" *logging area*, as shown in Figure 12-35.

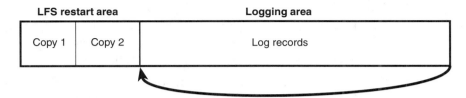

LFS restart area **Logging area**

| Copy 1 | Copy 2 | Log records |

Figure 12-35
Log file regions

NTFS calls the LFS to read and write the restart area. NTFS uses the restart area to store context information such as the location in the logging area at which NTFS will begin to read during recovery after a system failure. The LFS maintains a second copy of the restart data in case the first becomes corrupted or otherwise inaccessible. The remainder of the log file is the logging area, which contains transaction records NTFS writes in order to recover a volume in the event of a system failure. The LFS makes the log file appear infinite by reusing it circularly (while guaranteeing that it doesn't overwrite information it needs). The LFS uses *logical sequence numbers* (LSNs) to identify records written to the log file. As the LFS cycles through the file, it increases the values of the LSNs. NTFS uses 64 bits to represent LSNs, so the number of possible LSNs is so large as to be virtually infinite.

NTFS never reads transactions from or writes transactions to the log file directly. The LFS provides services NTFS calls to open the log file, write log records, read log records in forward or backward order, flush log records up to a particular LSN, or set the beginning of the log file to a higher LSN. During recovery, NTFS calls the LFS to perform the following actions: read forward through the log records to redo any transactions that were recorded in the log file but weren't flushed to disk at the time of the system failure; read backward through the log records to undo, or roll back, any transactions that weren't completely logged before the crash; and set the beginning of the log file to a record with a higher LSN when NTFS no longer needs the older transaction records in the log file.

Here's how the system guarantees that the volume can be recovered:

1. NTFS first calls the LFS to record in the (cached) log file any transactions that will modify the volume structure.

2. NTFS modifies the volume (also in the cache).

3. The cache manager prompts the LFS to flush the log file to disk. (The LFS implements the flush by calling the cache manager back, telling it which pages of memory to flush. Refer back to the calling sequence shown in Figure 12-34 on page 750.)

4. After the cache manager flushes the log file to disk, it flushes the volume changes (the metadata operations themselves) to disk.

These steps ensure that if the file system modifications are ultimately unsuccessful, the corresponding transactions can be retrieved from the log file and can be either redone or undone as part of the file system recovery procedure.

File system recovery begins automatically the first time the volume is used after the system is rebooted. NTFS checks whether the transactions that were recorded in the log file before the crash were applied to the volume, and if they weren't, it redoes them. NTFS also guarantees that transactions not completely logged before the crash are undone so that they don't appear on the volume.

Log Record Types

The LFS allows its clients to write any kind of record to their log files. NTFS writes several types of records. Two types, *update records* and *checkpoint records*, are described here.

Update records Update records are the most common type of record NTFS writes to the log file. Each update record contains two kinds of information:

- **Redo information** How to reapply one suboperation of a fully logged ("committed") transaction to the volume if a system failure occurs before the transaction is flushed from the cache

- **Undo information** How to reverse one suboperation of a transaction that was only partially logged ("not committed") at the time of a system failure

Figure 12-36 shows three update records in the log file. Each record represents one suboperation of a transaction, creating a new file. The redo entry in each update record tells NTFS how to reapply the suboperation to the volume, and the undo entry tells NTFS how to roll back (undo) the suboperation.

LFS restart area

Logging area

Redo: Allocate/initialize an MFT file record
Undo: Deallocate the file record

Redo: Set bits 3–9 in the bitmap
Undo: Clear bits 3–9 in the bitmap

Redo: Add the filename to the index
Undo: Remove the filename from the index

Figure 12-36
Update records in the log file

After logging a transaction (in this example, by calling the LFS to write the three update records to the log file), NTFS performs the suboperations on the volume itself, in the cache. When it has finished updating the cache, NTFS writes another record to the log file, recording the entire transaction as complete—a suboperation known as *committing* a transaction. Once a transaction is committed, NTFS guarantees that the entire transaction will appear on the volume, even if the operating system subsequently fails.

When recovering after a system failure, NTFS reads through the log file and redoes each committed transaction. Although NTFS completed the committed transactions before the system failure, it doesn't know whether the cache manager flushed the volume modifications to disk in time. The updates might have been lost from the cache when the system failed. Therefore, NTFS executes the committed transactions again just to be sure that the disk is up to date.

After redoing the committed transactions during a file system recovery, NTFS locates all the transactions in the log file that weren't committed at failure and rolls back (undoes) each suboperation that had been logged. In Figure 12-36, NTFS would first undo the $T1_c$ suboperation and then follow the backward pointer to $T1_b$ and undo that suboperation. It would continue to follow the backward pointers, undoing suboperations, until it reached the first suboperation in the transaction. By following the pointers, NTFS knows how many and which update records it must undo to roll back a transaction.

Redo and undo information can be expressed either physically or logically. Physical descriptions specify volume updates in terms of particular byte ranges on the disk that are to be changed, moved, and so on. Logical descriptions

express updates in terms of operations such as "delete file A.dat." As the lowest layer of software maintaining the file system structure, NTFS writes update records with physical descriptions. Transaction-processing or other application-level software might benefit from writing update records in logical terms, however, because logically expressed updates are more compact than physically expressed ones. Logical descriptions necessarily depend on NTFS to understand what operations such as deleting a file involve.

NTFS writes update records (usually several) for each of the following transactions:

- Creating a file
- Deleting a file
- Extending a file
- Truncating a file
- Setting file information
- Renaming a file
- Changing the security applied to a file

The redo and undo information in an update record must be carefully designed because although NTFS undoes a transaction, recovers from a system failure, or even operates normally, it might try to redo a transaction that has already been done or, conversely, to undo a transaction that never occurred or that has already been undone. Similarly, NTFS might try to redo or undo a transaction consisting of several update records, only some of which are complete on disk. The format of the update records must ensure that executing redundant redo or undo operations is *idempotent*, that is, has a neutral effect. For example, setting a bit that is already set has no effect, but toggling a bit that has already been toggled does. The file system must also handle intermediate volume states correctly.

Checkpoint records In addition to update records, NTFS periodically writes a checkpoint record to the log file, as illustrated in Figure 12-37.

Figure 12-37
Checkpoint record in the log file

A checkpoint record helps NTFS determine what processing would be needed to recover a volume if a crash were to occur immediately. Using information stored in the checkpoint record, NTFS knows, for example, how far back in the log file it must go to begin its recovery. After writing a checkpoint record, NTFS stores the LSN of the record in the restart area so that it can quickly find its most recently written checkpoint record when it begins file system recovery after a crash occurs.

Although the LFS presents the log file to NTFS as if it were infinitely large, it isn't. The generous size of the log file and the frequent writing of checkpoint records (an operation that usually frees up space in the log file) make the possibility of the log file's filling up a remote one. Nevertheless, the LFS accounts for this possibility by tracking several numbers:

- The available log space

- The amount of space needed to write an incoming log record and to undo the write, should that be necessary

- The amount of space needed to roll back all active (noncommitted) transactions, should that be necessary

If the log file doesn't contain enough available space to accommodate the total of the last two items, the LFS returns a "log file full" error and NTFS raises an exception. The NTFS exception handler rolls back the current transaction and places it in a queue to be restarted later.

To free up space in the log file, NTFS must momentarily prevent further transactions on files. To do so, NTFS blocks file creation and deletion and then requests exclusive access to all system files and shared access to all user files.

Gradually, active transactions either are completed successfully or receive the "log file full" exception. NTFS rolls back and queues the transactions that receive the exception.

Once it has blocked transaction activity on files as just described, NTFS calls the cache manager to flush unwritten data to disk, including unwritten log file data. After everything is safely flushed to disk, NTFS no longer needs the data in the log file. It resets the beginning of the log file to the current position, making the log file "empty." Then it restarts the queued transactions. Beyond the short pause in I/O processing, the "log file full" error has no effect on executing programs.

This scenario is one example of how NTFS uses the log file not only for file system recovery but also for error recovery during normal operation. You'll find out more about error recovery in the following section.

Recovery

NTFS automatically performs a disk recovery the first time a program accesses an NTFS volume after the system has been booted. (If no recovery is needed, the process is trivial.) Recovery depends on two tables NTFS maintains in memory:

- The *transaction table* keeps track of transactions that have been started but aren't yet committed. The suboperations of these active transactions must be removed from the disk during recovery.

- The *dirty page table* records which pages in the cache contain modifications to the file system structure that haven't yet been written to disk. This data must be flushed to disk during recovery.

NTFS writes a checkpoint record to the log file once every 5 seconds. Just before it does, it calls the LFS to store a current copy of the transaction table and of the dirty page table in the log file. NTFS then records in the checkpoint record the LSNs of the log records containing the copied tables. When recovery begins after a system failure, NTFS calls the LFS to locate the log records containing the most recent checkpoint record and the most recent copies of the transaction and dirty page tables. It then copies the tables to memory.

The log file usually contains more update records following the last checkpoint record. These update records represent volume modifications that occurred after the last checkpoint record was written. NTFS must update the transaction

and dirty page tables to include these operations. After updating the tables, NTFS uses the tables and the contents of the log file to update the volume itself.

To effect its volume recovery, NTFS scans the log file three times, loading the file into memory during the first pass to minimize disk I/O. Each pass has a particular purpose:

1. Analysis

2. Redoing transactions

3. Undoing transactions

Analysis Pass

During the *analysis pass,* as shown in Figure 12-38, NTFS scans forward in the log file from the beginning of the last checkpoint operation to find update records and use them to update the transaction and dirty page tables it copied to memory. Notice in the figure that the checkpoint operation stores three records in the log file and that update records might be interspersed among these records. NTFS therefore must start its scan at the beginning of the checkpoint operation.

Figure 12-38
Analysis pass

Most update records that appear in the log file after the checkpoint operation begins represent a modification to either the transaction table or the dirty page table. If an update record is a "transaction committed" record, for example, the transaction the record represents must be removed from the transaction table. Similarly, if the update record is a "page update" record that modifies a file system data structure, the dirty page table must be updated to reflect that change.

Once the tables are up to date in memory, NTFS scans the tables to determine the LSN of the oldest update record that logs an operation that hasn't been carried out on disk. The transaction table contains the LSNs of the noncommitted (incomplete) transactions, and the dirty page table contains the LSNs of records in the cache that haven't been flushed to disk. The LSN of the oldest update record that NTFS finds in these two tables determines where the redo pass will begin. If the last checkpoint record is older, however, NTFS will start the redo pass there instead.

Redo Pass

During the *redo pass*, as shown in Figure 12-39, NTFS scans forward in the log file from the LSN of the oldest update record, which it found during the analysis pass. It looks for "page update" records, which contain volume modifications that were written before the system failure but that might not have been flushed to disk. NTFS redoes these updates in the cache.

Figure 12-39
Redo pass

When NTFS reaches the end of the log file, it has updated the cache with the necessary volume modifications and the cache manager's lazy writer can begin writing cache contents to disk in the background.

Undo Pass

After it completes the redo pass, NTFS begins its *undo pass*, in which it rolls back any transactions that weren't committed when the system failed. Figure 12-40 shows two transactions in the log file; transaction 1 was committed before the power failure, but transaction 2 wasn't. NTFS must undo transaction 2.

Figure 12-40
Undo pass

Suppose that transaction 2 created a file, an operation that comprises three suboperations, each with its own update record. The update records of a transaction are linked by backward pointers in the log file because they are usually not contiguous.

The NTFS transaction table lists the LSN of the last-logged update record for each noncommitted transaction. In this example, the transaction table identifies LSN 4049 as the last update record logged for transaction 2. As shown from right to left in Figure 12-41, NTFS rolls back transaction 2.

Figure 12-41
Undoing a transaction

After locating LSN 4049, NTFS finds the undo information and executes it, clearing bits 3 through 9 in its allocation bitmap. NTFS then follows the backward pointer to LSN 4048, which directs it to remove the new filename

from the appropriate filename index. Finally, it follows the last backward pointer and deallocates the MFT file record reserved for the file, as the update record with LSN 4046 specifies. Transaction 2 is now rolled back. If there are other noncommitted transactions to undo, NTFS follows the same procedure to roll them back. Because undoing transactions affects the volume's file system structure, NTFS must log the undo operations in the log file. After all, the power might fail again during the recovery, and NTFS would have to redo its undo operations!

When the undo pass of the recovery is finished, the volume has been restored to a consistent state. At this point, NTFS flushes the cache changes to disk to ensure that the volume is up to date. NTFS then writes an "empty" LFS restart area to indicate that the volume is consistent and that no recovery need be done if the system should fail again immediately. Recovery is complete.

NTFS guarantees that recovery will return the volume to some preexisting consistent state, but not necessarily to the state that existed just before the system crash. NTFS can't make that guarantee because, for performance, it uses a "lazy commit" algorithm, which means that the log file isn't immediately flushed to disk each time a "transaction committed" record is written. Instead, numerous "transaction committed" records are batched and written together, either when the cache manager calls the LFS to flush the log file to disk or when the LFS writes a checkpoint record (once every 5 seconds) to the log file. Another reason the recovered volume might not be completely up to date is that several parallel transactions might be active when the system crashes and some of their "transaction committed" records might make it to disk whereas others might not. The consistent volume that recovery produces includes all the volume updates whose "transaction committed" records made it to disk and none of the updates whose "transaction committed" records didn't make it to disk.

NTFS uses the log file to recover a volume after the system fails, but it also takes advantage of an important "freebie" it gets from logging transactions. File systems necessarily contain a lot of code devoted to recovering from file system errors that occur during the course of normal file I/O. Because NTFS logs each transaction that modifies the volume structure, it can use the log file to recover when a file system error occurs and thus can greatly simplify its error handling code. The "log file full" error described earlier is one example of using the log file for error recovery.

Most I/O errors a program receives aren't file system errors and therefore can't be resolved entirely by NTFS. When called to create a file, for example, NTFS might begin by creating a file record in the MFT and then enter the new

file's name in a directory index. When it tries to allocate space for the file in its bitmap, however, it could discover that the disk is full and the create request can't be completed. In such a case, NTFS uses the information in the log file to undo the part of the operation it has already completed and to deallocate the data structures it reserved for the file. Then it returns a "disk full" error to the caller, which in turn must respond appropriately to the error.

NTFS Bad-Cluster Recovery

The volume managers included with Windows 2000, FtDisk (for basic disks) and Logical Disk Manager (LDM, for dynamic disks), can recover data from a bad sector on a fault tolerant volume, but if the hard disk doesn't use the SCSI protocol or runs out of spare sectors, a volume manager can't perform sector sparing to replace the bad sector. (See Chapter 10 for more information on the volume managers.) When the file system reads from the sector, the volume manager instead recovers the data and returns the warning to the file system that there is only one copy of the data.

The FAT file system doesn't respond to this volume manager warning. Moreover, neither these file systems nor the volume managers keep track of the bad sectors, so a user must run the Chkdsk or Format utility to prevent a volume manager from repeatedly recovering data for the file system. Both Chkdsk and Format are less than ideal for removing bad sectors from use. Chkdsk can take a long time to find and remove bad sectors, and Format wipes all the data off the partition it's formatting.

In the file system equivalent of a volume manager's sector sparing, NTFS dynamically replaces the cluster containing a bad sector and keeps track of the bad cluster so that it won't be reused. (Recall that NTFS maintains portability by addressing logical clusters rather than physical sectors.) NTFS performs these functions when the volume manager can't perform sector sparing. When a volume manager returns a bad-sector warning or when the hard disk driver returns a bad-sector error, NTFS allocates a new cluster to replace the one containing the bad sector. NTFS copies the data that the volume manager has recovered into the new cluster to reestablish data redundancy.

Figure 12-42 shows an MFT record for a user file with a bad cluster in one of its data runs as it exited before the cluster went bad. When it receives a bad-sector error, NTFS reassigns the cluster containing the sector to its bad-cluster file. This prevents the bad cluster from being allocated to another file. NTFS

Figure 12-42
MFT record for a user file with a bad cluster

then allocates a new cluster for the file and changes the file's VCN-to-LCN mappings to point to the new cluster. This bad-cluster remapping (introduced earlier in this chapter) is illustrated in Figure 12-43. Cluster number 1357, which contains the bad sector, is replaced by a new cluster, number 1049.

Bad-sector errors are undesirable, but when they do occur, the combination of NTFS and volume managers provides the best possible solution. If the bad sector is on a redundant volume, the volume manager recovers the data and replaces the sector if it can. If it can't replace the sector, it returns a warning to NTFS and NTFS replaces the cluster containing the bad sector.

If the volume isn't configured as a redundant volume, the data in the bad sector can't be recovered. When the volume is formatted as a FAT volume and the volume manager can't recover the data, reading from the bad sector yields indeterminate results. If some of the file system's control structures reside in the bad sector, an entire file or group of files (or potentially, the whole disk) can be lost. At best, some data in the affected file (often, all the data in the file beyond the bad sector) is lost. Moreover, the FAT file system is likely to reallocate the bad sector to the same or another file on the volume, causing the problem to resurface.

Like the other file systems, NTFS can't recover data from a bad sector without help from a volume manager. However, NTFS greatly contains the

Figure 12-43
Bad-cluster remapping

damage a bad sector can cause. If NTFS discovers the bad sector during a read operation, it remaps the cluster the sector is in, as shown in Figure 12-43. If the volume isn't configured as a redundant volume, NTFS returns a "data read" error to the calling program. Although the data that was in that cluster is lost, the rest of the file—and the file system—remains intact; the calling program can respond appropriately to the data loss, and the bad cluster won't be reused in future allocations. If NTFS discovers the bad cluster on a write operation rather than a read, NTFS remaps the cluster before writing and thus loses no data and generates no error.

763

The same recovery procedures are followed if file system data is stored in a sector that goes bad. If the bad sector is on a redundant volume, NTFS replaces the cluster dynamically, using the data recovered by the volume manager. If the volume isn't redundant, the data can't be recovered and NTFS sets a bit in the volume file that indicates corruption on the volume. The NTFS Chkdsk utility checks this bit when the system is next rebooted, and if the bit is set, Chkdsk executes, fixing the file system corruption by reconstructing the NTFS metadata.

In rare instances, file system corruption can occur even on a fault tolerant disk configuration. A double error can destroy both file system data and the means to reconstruct it. If the system crashes while NTFS is writing the mirror copy of an MFT file record, of a filename index, or of the log file, for example, the mirror copy of such file system data might not be fully updated. If the system were rebooted and a bad-sector error occurred on the primary disk at exactly the same location as the incomplete write on the disk mirror, NTFS would be unable to recover the correct data from the disk mirror. NTFS implements a special scheme for detecting such corruptions in file system data. If it ever finds an inconsistency, it sets the corruption bit in the volume file, which causes Chkdsk to reconstruct the NTFS metadata when the system is next rebooted. Because file system corruption is rare on a fault tolerant disk configuration, Chkdsk is seldom needed. It is supplied as a safety precaution rather than as a first-line data recovery strategy.

The use of Chkdsk on NTFS is vastly different from its use on the FAT file system. Before writing anything to disk, FAT sets the volume's dirty bit and then resets the bit after the modification is complete. If any I/O operation is in progress when the system crashes, the dirty bit is left set and Chkdsk runs when the system is rebooted. On NTFS, Chkdsk runs only when unexpected or unreadable file system data is found and NTFS can't recover the data from a redundant volume or from redundant file system structures on a single volume. (The system boot sector is duplicated, as are the parts of the MFT required for booting the system and running the NTFS recovery procedure. This redundancy ensures that NTFS will always be able to boot and recover itself.)

Table 12-6 summarizes what happens when a sector goes bad on a disk volume formatted for one of the Windows 2000–supported file systems according to various conditions we've described in this section.

Table 12-6 Summary of NTFS Data Recovery Scenarios

Scenario	With a SCSI disk that has spare sectors	With a non-SCSI disk or a disk with no spare sectors*
Fault tolerant volume**	1. Volume manager recovers the data. 2. Volume manager performs sector sparing (replaces the bad sector). 3. File system remains unaware of the error.	1. Volume manager recovers the data. 2. Volume manager sends the data and a bad-sector error to the file system. 3. NTFS performs cluster remapping.
Non-fault-tolerant volume	1. Volume manager can't recover the data. 2. Volume manager sends a bad-sector error to the file system. 3. NTFS performs cluster remapping. Data is lost†.	1. Volume manager can't recover the data. 2. Volume manager sends a bad-sector error to the file system. 3. NTFS performs cluster remapping. Data is lost†.

* In neither of these cases can a volume manager perform sector sparing: (1) hard disks that don't use the SCSI protocol have no standard interface for providing sector sparing; (2) some hard disks don't provide hardware support for sector sparing, and SCSI hard disks that do provide sector sparing can eventually run out of spare sectors if a lot of sectors go bad.

** A fault tolerant volume is one of the following: a mirror set or a RAID-5 set.

† In a write operation, no data is lost: NTFS remaps the cluster before the write.

If the volume on which the bad sector appears is a fault tolerant volume (a mirrored or RAID-5 volume) and if the hard disk is one that supports sector sparing (and that hasn't run out of spare sectors), which file system you're using—FAT or NTFS—doesn't matter. The volume manager replaces the bad sector without the need for user or file system intervention.

If a bad sector is located on a hard disk that doesn't support sector sparing, the file system is responsible for replacing (remapping) the bad sector or—in the case of NTFS—the cluster in which the bad sector resides. The FAT file

system doesn't provide sector or cluster remapping. The benefits of NTFS cluster remapping are that bad spots in a file can be fixed without harm to the file (or harm to the file system, as the case may be) and that the bad cluster won't be reallocated to the same or another file.

Encrypting File System Security

EFS security relies on Windows 2000 cryptography support, which Microsoft introduced in Windows NT 4. The first time a file is encrypted, EFS assigns the account of the user performing the encryption a private/public key pair for use in file encryption. Users can encrypt files via Windows Explorer by opening a file's Properties dialog box, pressing Advanced, and selecting the Encrypt Contents To Secure Data option, as shown in Figure 12-44. Users can also encrypt files via a command-line utility named *cipher*. Windows 2000 automatically encrypts files that reside in directories that are designated as encrypted directories. When a file is encrypted, EFS generates a random number for the file that EFS calls the file's file encryption key (FEK). EFS uses the FEK to encrypt the file's contents with a stronger variant of the Data Encryption Standard (DES) algorithm—DESX. EFS stores the file's FEK with the file but encrypts the file with the user's EFS public key by using the RSA public key–based encryption algorithm. After EFS completes these steps, the file is secure: other users can't decrypt the data without the file's decrypted FEK, and they can't decrypt the FEK without the private key.

Figure 12-44
Encrypt files by using the Advanced Attributes dialog box

EFS uses a private/public key algorithm to encrypt FEKs. To encrypt file data, EFS uses DESX because DESX is a *symmetric encryption algorithm,* which means it uses the same key to encrypt and decrypt data. Symmetric encryption algorithms are typically very fast, which makes them suitable for encrypting large amounts of data, such as file data. However, symmetric encryption algorithms have a weakness: you can bypass their security if you obtain the key. If multiple users want to share one encrypted file protected only by DESX, each user would require access to the file's FEK. Leaving the FEK unencrypted would obviously be a security problem, but encrypting the FEK once would require all the users to share the same FEK decryption key—another potential security problem.

Keeping the FEK secure is a difficult problem, which EFS addresses with the public key–based half of its encryption architecture. Encrypting a file's FEK for individual users who access the file lets multiple users share an encrypted file. EFS can encrypt a file's FEK with each user's public key and can store each user's encrypted FEK with the file. Anyone can access a user's public key, but no one can use a public key to decrypt the data that the public key encrypted. The only way users can decrypt a file is with their private key, which the operating system must access and typically stores in a secure location. A user's private key decrypts the user's encrypted copy of a file's FEK. Windows 2000 stores private keys on a computer's hard disk (which isn't terribly secure), but subsequent releases of the operating system will let users store their private key on portable media such as smart cards. Public key–based algorithms are usually slow, but EFS uses these algorithms only to encrypt FEKs. Splitting key management between a publicly available key and a private key makes key management a little easier than symmetric encryption algorithms do and solves the dilemma of keeping the FEK secure.

Several components work together to make EFS work, as the diagram of EFS architecture in Figure 12-45 shows. As you can see, EFS is implemented as a device driver that runs in kernel mode and is tightly connected with the NTFS file system driver. Whenever NTFS encounters an encrypted file, NTFS executes functions in the EFS driver that the EFS driver registered with NTFS when EFS initialized. The EFS functions encrypt and decrypt file data as applications access encrypted files. Although EFS stores an FEK with a file's data, users' public keys encrypt the FEK. To encrypt or decrypt file data, EFS must decrypt the file's FEK with the aid of cryptography services that reside in user mode.

Figure 12-45
EFS architecture

The Local Security Authority Subsystem (Lsass - \Winnt\System32\Lsass.exe) manages logon sessions but also handles EFS key management chores. For example, when the EFS driver needs to decrypt an FEK in order to decrypt file data a user wants to access, the EFS driver sends a request to Lsass. EFS sends the request via a local procedure call (LPC). The KSecDD (\Winnt\System32\ Drivers\Ksecdd.sys) device driver exports functions for other drivers that need to send LPC messages to Lsass. The Local Security Authority Server (Lsasrv - \Winnt\System32\Lsasrv.dll) component of Lsass that listens for remote procedure call (RPC) requests passes requests to decrypt an FEK to the appropriate EFS-related decryption function, which also resides in Lsasrv. Lsasrv uses functions in Microsoft CryptoAPI (also referred to as CAPI) to decrypt the FEK, which the EFS driver sent to Lsass in encrypted form.

CryptoAPI comprises cryptographic service provider (CSP) DLLs that make various cryptography services (such as encryption/decryption and hashing) available to applications. The CSP DLLs manage retrieval of user private and

public keys, for example, so that Lsasrv doesn't need to concern itself with the details of how keys are protected or even with the details of the encryption algorithms. After Lsasrv decrypts an FEK, Lsasrv returns the FEK to the EFS driver via an LPC reply message. After EFS receives the decrypted FEK, EFS can use DESX to decrypt the file data for NTFS. Let's look at the details of how EFS integrates with NTFS and how Lsasrv uses CryptoAPI to manage keys.

Registering Callbacks

NTFS doesn't require the EFS driver's (Winnt\System32\Drivers\Efs.sys) presence to execute, but encrypted files won't be accessible if the EFS driver isn't present. NTFS has a plug-in interface for the EFS driver, so when the EFS driver initializes, it can attach itself to NTFS. The NTFS driver exports several functions for the EFS driver to use, including one that EFS calls to notify NTFS both of the presence of EFS and of the EFS-related APIs EFS is making available.

Encrypting a File for the First Time

The NTFS driver calls only the EFS functions that register when NTFS encounters an encrypted file. A file's attributes record that the file is encrypted in the same way that a file records that it is compressed (discussed earlier in this chapter). NTFS and EFS have specific interfaces for converting a file from nonencrypted to encrypted form, but user-mode components primarily drive the process. Windows 2000 lets you encrypt a file in two ways: by using the *cipher* command-line utility or by checking the Encrypt Contents To Secure Data check box in the Advanced Attitudes dialog box for a file in Windows Explorer. Both Windows Explorer and the *cipher* command rely on the *EncryptFile* Win32 API that the Advapi32.dll (Advanced Win32 APIs DLL) exports. Advapi32 loads another DLL, Feclient.dll (File Encryption Client DLL), to obtain APIs that Advapi32 can use to invoke EFS interfaces in Lsasrv via LPCs.

When Lsasrv receives an LPC message from Feclient to encrypt a file, Lsasrv uses the Windows 2000 impersonation facility to impersonate the user that ran the application (either *cipher* or Windows Explorer) that is encrypting the file. This procedure lets Windows 2000 treat the file operations that Lsasrv performs as if the user who wants to encrypt the file is performing them. Lsasrv usually runs in the System account. (The System account is described in Chapter 8.) In fact, if it doesn't impersonate the user, Lsasrv usually won't have permission to access the file in question.

Lsasrv next creates a log file in the volume's System Volume Information directory into which Lsasrv records the progress of the encryption process. The log file usually has the name Efs0.log, but if other files are undergoing encryption, increasing numbers replace the 0 until a unique log file name for the current encryption is created.

CryptoAPI relies on information that a user's registry profile stores, so Lsasrv next uses the *LoadUserProfile* API function of Userenv.dll (User Environment DLL) to load the profile into the registry of the user it is impersonating. Typically, the user profile is already loaded because Winlogon loads a user's profile when a user logs on. However, if a user uses the Windows 2000 *RunAs* command to log on to a different account, when you try to access encrypted files from that account, the account's profile might not load.

Lsasrv then generates an FEK for the file by using the RSA encryption facilities of the Microsoft Base Cryptographic Provider 1.0 CSP.

Constructing Key Rings

At this point, Lsasrv has an FEK and can construct EFS information to store with the file, including an encrypted version of the FEK. Lsasrv reads the HKEY_CURRENT_USER\Software\Microsoft\Windows NT\CurrentVersion\EFS\CurrentKeys\CertificateHash value of the user performing the encryption to obtain the user's public key signature. (Note that this key doesn't appear in the registry until a file or folder is encrypted.) Lsasrv uses the signature to access the user's public key and encrypt FEKs.

Lsasrv can now construct the information that EFS stores with the file. EFS stores only one block of information in an encrypted file, and that block contains an entry for each user sharing the file. These entries are called *key entries,* and EFS stores them in the Data Decryption Field (DDF) portion of the file's EFS data. A collection of multiple key entries is called a *key ring* because, as mentioned earlier, EFS lets multiple users share encrypted files.

Figure 12-46 shows a file's EFS information format and key entry format. EFS stores enough information in the first part of a key entry to precisely describe a user's public key. This data includes the user's security ID (SID), the container name in which the key is stored, the cryptographic provider name, and the private/public key pair certificate hash. The second part of the key entry contains an encrypted version of the FEK. Lsasrv uses the CryptoAPI to encrypt the FEK with the RSA algorithm and the user's public key.

EFS information

Header	Version
	Checksum
	Number of DDF key entries

Data decryption field: DDF key entry 1 / DDF key entry 2

Data recovery field: Number of DRF key entries / DRF key entry 1

Key entry

User SID
(S-1-5-21-...)

Container name
(ee341-2144-55ba...)

Provider name
(Microsoft Base Cryptographic Provider 1.0)

EFS certificate hash
(cb3e4e...)

Encrypted FEK
(03fe4f3c...)

Figure 12-46
Format of EFS information and key entries

Next, Lsasrv creates another key ring that contains recovery key entries. EFS stores information about recovery key entries in a file's Data Recovery Field (DRF). The format of DRF entries is identical to the format of DDF entries. The DRF's purpose is to let designated accounts, or Recovery Agents, decrypt a user's file when administrative authority must have access to the user's data. For example, suppose a company employee used a CryptoAPI that let him store his private key on a smart card, and then he lost the card. Without Recovery Agents, no one could recover his encrypted data.

Recovery Agents are defined with the Encrypted Data Recovery Agents security policy of the local computer or domain. This policy is available from the Group Policy MMC snap-in, as shown in Figure 12-47. When you use the Recovery Agent Wizard (by right-clicking on Encrypted Data Recovery Agents and selecting Encrypted Recovery Agent from the New option), you can add Recovery Agents and specify which private/public key pairs (designated by their certificates) the Recovery Agents use for EFS recovery. Lsasrv interprets the recovery policy when it initializes and when it receives notification that the recovery policy has changed. EFS creates a DRF key entry for each Recovery Agent by using the cryptographic provider registered for EFS recovery. The default Recovery Agent provider is the RSA encryption facility of Base Cryptographic Provider 1.0—the same provider Lsasrv uses for user keys.

Figure 12-47
Encrypted Data Recovery Agents group policy

In the final step in creating EFS information for a file, Lsasrv calculates a checksum for the DDF and DRF by using the MD5 hash facility of Base Cryptographic Provider 1.0. Lsasrv stores the checksum's result in the EFS information header. EFS references this checksum during decryption to ensure that the contents of a file's EFS information haven't become corrupted or been tampered with.

Encrypting File Data

Figure 12-48 illustrates the flow of the encryption process. After Lsasrv constructs the necessary information for a file a user wants to encrypt, it can begin encrypting the file. Lsasrv creates a backup file, Efs0.tmp, for the file undergoing encryption. (Lsasrv uses higher numbers in the backup filename if other backup files exist.) Lsasrv creates the backup file in the directory that contains the file undergoing encryption. Lsasrv applies a restrictive security descriptor to the backup file so that only the System account can access the file's contents. Lsasrv next initializes the log file that it created in the first phase of the encryption process. Finally, Lsasrv records in the log file that the backup file has been created. Lsasrv encrypts the original file only after the file is completely backed up.

Lsasrv next sends the EFS device driver, through NTFS, a command to add to the original file the EFS information that it just created. NTFS receives this command, but because NTFS doesn't understand EFS commands, NTFS calls the EFS driver. The EFS driver takes the EFS information that Lsasrv sent and uses exported NTFS functions to apply the information to the file. The exported NTFS functions let EFS add the $LOGGED_UTILITY_STREAM

Figure 12-48
Flow of EFS

attribute to NTFS file. Execution returns to Lsasrv, which copies the contents of the file undergoing encryption to the backup file. When the backup copy is complete, including backups of all alternate data streams, Lsasrv records in the log file that the backup file is up to date. Lsasrv then sends another command to NTFS to tell NTFS to encrypt the contents of the original file.

When NTFS receives the EFS command to encrypt the file, NTFS deletes the contents of the original file and copies the backup data to the file. After NTFS copies each section of the file, NTFS flushes the section's data from the file system cache, which prompts the cache manager to tell NTFS to write the file's data to disk. Because the file is marked as encrypted, at this point in the file-writing process, NTFS calls EFS to encrypt the data before NTFS writes the data

773

to disk. EFS uses the unencrypted FEK that NTFS passes it to perform DESX encryption of the file, one sector (512 bytes) at a time.

On Windows 2000 versions approved for export outside the United States, the EFS driver implements a 56-bit key DESX encryption. For the U.S.-only version of Windows 2000, the key is 128 bits long.

After EFS encrypts the file, Lsasrv records in the log file that the encryption was successful and deletes the file's backup copy. Finally, Lsasrv deletes the log file and returns control to the application that requested the file's encryption.

Encryption Process Summary

The following list summarizes the steps EFS performs to encrypt a file:

1. The user profile is loaded if necessary.

2. A log file is created in the System Volume Information directory with the name Efs*x*.log, where *x* is a unique number (for example, Efs0.log). As subsequent steps are performed, records are written to the log so that the file can be recovered in case the system fails during the encryption process.

3. Base Cryptographic Provider 1.0 generates a random 128-bit FEK for the file.

4. A user EFS private/public key pair is generated or obtained. HKEY_ CURRENT_USER\Software\Microsoft\Windows NT\CurrentVersion\ EFS\CurrentKeys\CertificateHash identifies the user's key pair.

5. A DDF key ring is created for the file that has an entry for the user. The entry contains a copy of the FEK that has been encrypted with the user's EFS public key.

6. A DRF key ring is created for the file. It has an entry for each Recovery Agent on the system, with each entry containing a copy of the FEK encrypted with the agent's EFS public key.

7. A backup file with a name in the form Efs0.tmp is created in the same directory as the file to be encrypted.

8. The DDF and DRF key rings are added to a header and augment the file as its EFS attribute.

9. The backup file is marked encrypted, and the original file is copied to the backup.

10. The original file's contents are destroyed, and the backup is copied to the original. This copy operation results in the data in the original file being encrypted because the file is now marked as encrypted.

11. The backup file is deleted.

12. The log file is deleted.

13. The user profile is unloaded (if it was loaded in step 1).

If the system crashes during the encryption process, either the original file remains intact or the backup file contains a consistent copy. When Lsasrv initializes after a system crash, it looks for log files under the System Volume Information subdirectory on each NTFS volume on the system. If Lsasrv finds one or more log files, it examines their contents and determines how recovery should take place. Lsasrv deletes the log file and the corresponding backup file if the original file wasn't modified at the time of the crash; otherwise, Lsasrv copies the backup file over the original, partially encrypted file and then deletes the log and backup. After Lsasrv processes log files, the file system will be in a consistent state with respect to encryption, with no loss of user data.

The Decryption Process

The decryption process begins when a user opens an encrypted file. NTFS examines the file's attributes when opening the file and then executes a callback function in the EFS driver. The EFS driver reads the $LOGGED_UTILITY_ STREAM attribute associated with the encrypted file. To read the attribute, the driver calls EFS support functions that NTFS exports for EFS's use. NTFS completes the necessary steps to open the file. The EFS driver ensures that the user opening the file has access privileges to the file's encrypted data (that is, that an encrypted FEK in either the DDF or DRF key rings corresponds to a private/public key pair associated with the user). As EFS performs this validation, EFS obtains the file's decrypted FEK to use in subsequent data operations the user might perform on the file.

EFS can't decrypt an FEK and relies on Lsasrv (which can use CryptoAPI) to perform FEK decryption. EFS sends an LPC message by way of the Ksecdd.sys driver to Lsasrv that asks Lsasrv to obtain the decrypted form of the encrypted FEK in the $LOGGED_UTILITY_STREAM attribute data (the EFS data) that corresponds to the user who is opening the file.

When Lsasrv receives the LPC message, Lsasrv executes the Userenv.dll (User Environment DLL) *LoadUserProfile* API function to bring the user's profile into the registry, if the profile isn't already loaded. Lsasrv proceeds through each key field in the EFS data, using the user's private key to try to decrypt each FEK. For each key, Lsasrv attempts to decrypt a DDF or DRF key entry's FEK. If the certificate hash in a key field doesn't refer to a key the user owns, Lsasrv moves on to the next key field. If Lsasrv can't decrypt any DDF or DRF key field's FEK, the user can't obtain the file's FEK. Consequently, EFS denies access to the application opening the file. However, if Lsasrv identifies a hash as corresponding to a key the user owns, it decrypts the FEK with the user's private key using CryptoAPI.

Because Lsasrv processes both DDF and DRF key rings when decrypting an FEK, it automatically performs file recovery operations. If a Recovery Agent that isn't registered to access an encrypted file (that is, it doesn't have a corresponding field in the DDF key ring) tries to access a file, EFS will let the Recovery Agent gain access because the agent has access to a key pair for a key field in the DRF key ring.

Decrypted FEK Caching

Traveling the path from the EFS driver to Lsasrv and back can take a relatively long time—in the process of decrypting an FEK, CryptoAPI uses results in more than 2000 registry API calls and 400 file system accesses on a typical system. The EFS driver, with the aid of NTFS, uses a cache to try to avoid this expense.

Decrypting File Data

After an application opens an encrypted file, the application can read from and write to the file. NTFS calls the EFS driver to decrypt file data as NTFS reads the data from the disk and before NTFS places the data in the file system cache. Similarly, when an application writes data to a file, the data remains in unencrypted form in the file system cache until the application or the cache manager uses

NTFS to flush the data back to disk. When an encrypted file's data writes back from the cache to the disk, NTFS calls the EFS driver to encrypt the data.

As stated earlier, the EFS driver performs encryption and decryption in 512-byte units. The 512-byte size is the most convenient for the driver because disk reads and writes occur in multiples of the 512-byte sector.

Backing Up Encrypted Files

An important aspect of any file encryption facility's design is that file data is never available in unencrypted form except to applications that access the file via the encryption facility. This restriction particularly affects backup utilities, in which archival media store files. EFS addresses this problem by providing a facility for backup utilities so that the utilities can back up and restore files in their encrypted states. Thus, backup utilities don't have to be able to decrypt file data, nor do they need to decrypt file data in their backup procedures.

Backup utilities use the new EFS API functions *OpenEncryptedFileRaw*, *ReadEncryptedFileRaw*, *WriteEncryptedFileRaw*, and *CloseEncryptedFileRaw* in Windows 2000 to access a file's encrypted contents. The Advapi32.dll library provides these API functions, which all use LPCs to invoke corresponding functions in Lsasrv. For example, after a backup utility opens a file for raw access during a backup operation, the utility calls *ReadEncryptedFileRaw* to obtain the file data. The Lsasrv function *EfsReadFileRaw* issues control commands (which the EFS session key encrypts with DESX) to the NTFS driver to read the file's EFS attribute first and then the encrypted contents.

EfsReadFileRaw might have to perform multiple read operations to read a large file. As *EfsReadFileRaw* reads each portion of such a file, Lsasrv sends an RPC message to Advapi32.dll that executes a callback function that the backup program specified when it issued the *ReadEncryptedFileRaw* API function. *EfsReadFileRaw* hands the encrypted data it just read to the callback function, which can write the data to the backup media. Backup utilities restore encrypted files in a similar manner. The utilities call the *WriteEncryptedFileRaw* API function, which invokes a callback function in the backup program to obtain the unencrypted data from the backup media while Lsasrv's *EfsWriteFileRaw* function is restoring the file's contents.

EXPERIMENT: Viewing EFS Information

EFS has a handful of other API functions that applications can use to manipulate encrypted files. For example, applications use the *AddUsersToEncryptedFile* API function to give additional users access to an encrypted file and *RemoveUsersFromEncryptedFile* to revoke users' access to an encrypted file. Applications use the *QueryUsersOnEncryptedFile* function to obtain information about a file's associated DDF and DRF key fields. *QueryUsersOnEncryptedFile* returns the SID, certificate hash value, and display information that each DDF and DRF key field contains. The following output is from the EFSDump utility, included on the companion CD under \Sysint\Efsdump.exe, when an encrypted file is specified as a command-line argument:

```
C:\>efsdump test.txt
EFS Information Dumper v1.02
Copyright (C) 1999 Mark Russinovich
Systems Internals - http://www.sysinternals.com

test.txt:
DDF Entry:
     SUSANCOMP\Joe:
          CN=Joe,L=EFS,OU=EFS File Encryption Certificate
DRF Entry:
     SUSANCOMP\Administrator
          OU=EFS File Encryption Certificate, L=EFS, CN=Administrator
```

You can see that the file test.txt has one DDF entry for user Joe and one DRF entry for Administrator, which is the only Recovery Agent currently registered on the system.

Conclusion

As you saw in the introduction to this chapter, the overriding goal for NTFS was to provide a file system that wasn't only reliable but also fast. The performance of Windows 2000 disk I/O isn't due solely to the implementation of NTFS, however. It comes in large measure from synergy between NTFS and the Windows 2000 cache manager. Together, NTFS and the cache manager achieve respectable I/O performance while providing an unprecedented level of reliability and high-end data storage features for both workstation and server systems.

Networking

Microsoft Windows 2000 was designed with networking in mind, and it includes broad networking support that is integrated with the I/O system and the Win32 API. The four basic types of networking software are services, APIs, protocols, and network adapter device drivers, and each is layered on the next to form a network stack. Windows 2000 has well-defined interfaces for each layer, so in addition to using the wide variety of different APIs, protocols, and adapter device drivers that ship with Windows 2000, third parties can extend the operating system's networking capabilities by developing their own.

In this chapter, we take you from the top of the Windows 2000 networking stack to the bottom. First, we present the mapping between the Windows 2000 networking software components and the Open Systems Interconnection (OSI) reference model. Then we briefly describe the networking APIs available on Windows 2000 and explain how they are implemented. You'll learn how network-resource name resolution works and how protocol drivers are implemented. After looking at the implementation of network adapter device drivers, we examine *binding*, which is the glue that connects protocols to network adapters. Finally, we briefly describe layered networking services included with Windows 2000, such as Active Directory directory service and File Replication service (FRS).

The OSI Reference Model

The goal of network software is to take a request (usually an I/O request) from an application on one machine, pass it to another machine, execute the request on the remote machine, and return the results to the first machine. In the course of this process, the request must be transformed several times along the way. A high-level request, such as "read *x* number of bytes from file *y* on machine *z*," requires software that can determine how to get to machine *z* and what communication software that machine understands. Then the request must be altered for transmission across a network—for example, divided into short packets of information. When the request reaches the other side, it must be checked for completeness, decoded, and sent to the correct operating system component for execution. Finally, the reply must be encoded for sending back across the network.

To help different computer manufacturers standardize and integrate their networking software, in 1974 the International Organization for Standardization (ISO) defined a software model for sending messages between machines. The result is the *Open Systems Interconnection* (OSI) *reference model*. The model defines seven layers of software, as shown in Figure 13-1.

Figure 13-1
OSI reference model

The OSI reference model is an idealized scheme that few systems implement precisely, but it's often used to frame discussions of networking principles. Each layer on one machine assumes that it is "talking to" the same layer on the other

machine. Both machines "speak" the same language, or protocol, at the same level. In reality, however, a network transmission must pass down each layer on the client machine, be transmitted across the network, and then pass up the layers on the destination machine until it reaches a layer that can understand and implement the request.

OSI Layers

The purpose of each layer in the OSI model is to provide services to higher layers and to abstract how the services are implemented at lower layers. Detailing the purpose of each layer is beyond the scope of this book, but here are some brief descriptions of the various layers:

- **Application layer** Handles information transfer between two network applications, including functions such as security checks, identification of the participating machines, and initiation of the data exchange.

- **Presentation layer** Handles data formatting, including issues such as whether lines end in carriage return/line feed (CR/LF) or just carriage return (CR), whether data is to be compressed or encoded, and so forth.

- **Session layer** Manages the connection between cooperating applications, including high-level synchronization and monitoring of which application is "talking" and which is "listening."

- **Transport layer** On the client, this layer divides messages into packets and assigns them sequence numbers to ensure that they are all received in the proper order. On the destination, it assembles packets that have been received. It also shields the session layer from the effects of changes in hardware.

- **Network layer** Creates packet headers and handles routing, congestion control, and internetworking. It is the highest layer that understands the network's *topology,* that is, the physical configuration of the machines in the network, any limitations in bandwidth, and so on.

- **Data-link layer** Transmits low-level data frames, waits for acknowledgment that they were received, and retransmits frames that were lost over unreliable lines.

- **Physical layer** Passes bits to the network cable or other physical transmission medium.

The dashed lines in Figure 13-1 represent protocols used in transmitting a request to a remote machine. As stated earlier, each layer of the hierarchy assumes that it is speaking to the same layer on another machine and uses a common protocol. The collection of protocols through which a request passes on its way down and back up the layers of the network is called a *protocol stack*.

Windows 2000 Networking Components

Figure 13-2 provides an overview of the components of Windows 2000 networking, showing how each component fits into the OSI reference model and which protocols are used between layers. The mapping between OSI layers and networking components isn't precise, which is the reason that some components cross layers. The various components include the following:

- *Networking APIs* provide a protocol-independent way for applications to communicate across a network. Networking APIs can be implemented in user mode or in both user mode and kernel mode, and in some cases are wrappers around another networking API that implements a specific programming model or provides additional services. (Note that the term *networking API* also describes any programming interfaces provided by networking-related software.)

- *Transport Driver Interface* (TDI) *clients* are kernel-mode device drivers that usually implement the kernel-mode portion of a networking API's implementation. TDI clients get their name from the fact that the I/O request packets (IRPs) they send to protocol drivers are formatted according to the Windows 2000 Transport Driver Interface standard (documented in the DDK). This standard specifies a common programming interface for kernel-mode device drivers. (See Chapter 9 for more information about IRPs.)

■ *TDI transports,* also known as *transports, Network Driver Interface Specification* (NDIS) *protocol drivers,* and *protocol drivers,* are kernel-mode protocol drivers. They accept IRPs from TDI clients and process the requests these IRPs represent. This processing might require network communications with a peer, prompting the TDI transport to add protocol-specific headers (such as TCP, UDP, IPX) to data passed in the IRP and to communicate with adapter drivers using NDIS functions (also documented in the DDK). TDI transports generally facilitate application network communications by transparently performing message operations such as segmentation and reassembly, sequencing, acknowledgment, and retransmission.

■ The *NDIS library* (Ndis.sys) provides encapsulation for adapter drivers, hiding from them specifics of the Windows 2000 kernel-mode environment. The NDIS library exports functions for use by TDI transports as well as support functions for adapter drivers.

■ *NDIS miniport drivers* are kernel-mode drivers that are responsible for interfacing TDI transports to particular network adapters. NDIS miniport drivers are written so that they are wrapped by the Windows 2000 NDIS library. The encapsulation provides cross-platform compatibility with Microsoft Consumer Windows. NDIS miniport drivers don't process IRPs; rather, they register a call-table interface to the NDIS library that contains pointers to functions corresponding to ones that the NDIS library exports to TDI transports. NDIS miniport drivers communicate with network adapters by using NDIS library functions that resolve to hardware abstraction layer (HAL) functions.

As the figure shows, the OSI layers don't correspond to actual software. TDI transports, for example, frequently cross several boundaries. In fact, the bottom four layers of software are often referred to collectively as "the transport." Software components residing in the upper three layers are referred to as "users of the transport."

Figure 13-2
OSI model and Windows 2000 networking components

In the remainder of this chapter, we'll examine the networking components shown in Figure 13-2 (as well as others not shown in the figure), looking at how they fit together and how they relate to Windows 2000 as a whole.

Networking APIs

Windows 2000 implements multiple networking APIs to provide support for legacy applications and compatibility with industry standards. In this section, we'll briefly look at the networking APIs and describe how applications use them.

It's important to keep in mind that the decision about which API an application uses depends on characteristics of the API, such as which protocols the API can layer over, whether the API supports reliable or bidirectional communication, and the API's portability to other Windows platforms the application might run on. We'll discuss the following networking APIs:

- Named pipes and mailslots
- Windows Sockets (Winsock)
- Remote procedure call (RPC)
- Common Internet File System (CIFS)
- NetBIOS

In addition, we'll briefly describe several APIs that build on the APIs listed here and that are widely used on a typical Windows 2000 system.

Named Pipes and Mailslots

Named pipes and mailslots are programming APIs that Microsoft originally developed for OS/2 LAN Manager and then ported to Windows NT. Named pipes provide for reliable bidirectional communications, whereas mailslots provide unreliable unidirectional data transmission. An advantage of mailslots is that they support broadcast capability. In Windows 2000, both APIs take advantage of Windows 2000 security, which allows a server to control precisely which clients can connect to it.

The names servers assign to named pipes and clients conform to the Windows 2000 Universal Naming Convention (UNC), which is a protocol-independent way to identify resources on a Windows network. The implementation of UNC names is described later in the chapter.

Named Pipe Operation

Named pipe communication consists of a named pipe server and a named pipe client. A named pipe server is an application that creates a named pipe to which clients can connect. A named pipe's name has the format \\Server\Pipe\PipeName. The *Server* component of the name specifies the computer on which the named pipe server is executing (a named pipe server can't create a named pipe on a

remote system), and the name can be a DNS name (for example, *mspress. microsoft.com*), a NetBIOS name (*mspress*), or an IP address (255.0.0.0). The *Pipe* component of the name must be the string "Pipe", and *PipeName* is the unique name assigned to a named pipe. The unique portion of the named pipe's name can include subdirectories; an example of a named pipe name with a subdirectory is \\MyComputer\Pipe\MyServerApp\ConnectionPipe.

A named pipe server uses the *CreateNamedPipe* Win32 function to create a named pipe. One of the function's input parameters is a pointer to the named pipe name, in the form\\.\Pipe\PipeName. The "\\.\" is a Win32-defined alias for "this computer." Other parameters the function accepts include an optional security descriptor that protects access to the named pipe, a flag that specifies whether the pipe should be bidirectional or unidirectional, a value indicating the maximum number of simultaneous connections the pipe supports, and a flag specifying whether the pipe should operate in *byte mode* or *message mode*.

Most networking APIs operate only in byte mode, which means that a message sent with one send function might require the receiver to perform multiple receives, building up the complete message from fragments. Named pipes operating in message mode simplify the implementation of a receiver because there is a one-to-one correspondence between sends and receives. A receiver therefore obtains an entire message each time it completes a receive and doesn't have to concern itself with keeping track of message fragments.

The first call to *CreateNamedPipe* for a particular name creates the first instance of that name and establishes the behavior of all named pipe instances having that name. A server creates additional instances, up to the maximum specified in the first call, with additional calls to *CreateNamedPipe*. After creating at least one named pipe instance, a server executes the *ConnectNamedPipe* Win32 function, which enables the named pipe the server created to establish connections with clients. *ConnectNamedPipe* can be executed synchronously or asynchronously, and it doesn't complete until a client establishes a connection with the instance (or an error occurs).

A named pipe client uses the Win32 *CreateFile* or *CallNamedPipe* function, specifying the name of the pipe a server has created, to connect to a server. If the server has performed a *ConnectNamedPipe* call, the client's security profile and the access it requests to the pipe (read, write) are validated against the named pipe's security descriptor. (See Chapter 8 for more information on the security-check algorithms Windows 2000 uses.) If the client is granted access to a named pipe, it receives a handle representing the client side of a named pipe connection and the server's call to *ConnectNamedPipe* completes.

After a named pipe connection is established, the client and server can use the *ReadFile* and *WriteFile* Win32 functions to read from and write to the pipe. Named pipes support both synchronous and asynchronous operation for message transmittal. Figure 13-3 shows a server and client communicating through a named pipe instance.

Figure 13-3
Named pipe communications

A unique characteristic of the named pipe networking API is that it allows a server to impersonate a client by using the *ImpersonateNamedPipeClient* function. See the section "Impersonation" on page 504 in Chapter 8 for a discussion of how impersonation is used in client/server applications.

Mailslot Operation

Mailslots provide an unreliable unidirectional broadcast mechanism. One example of an application that can use this type of communication is a time synchronization service, which might broadcast a source time across the domain every few seconds. Receiving the source-time message isn't crucial for every computer on the network and is therefore a good candidate for the use of mailslots.

Like named pipes, mailslots are integrated with the Win32 API. A mailslot server creates a mailslot by using the *CreateMailslot* function. *CreateMailslot* accepts a name of the form "\\.\Mailslot\MailslotName" as an input parameter. Again like named pipes, a mailslot server can create mailslots only on the machine it's executing on, and the name it assigns to a mailslot can include subdirectories. *CreateMailslot* also takes a security descriptor that controls client access to the mailslot. The handles returned by *CreateMailslot* are *overlapped*, which means that operations performed on the handles, such as sending and receiving messages, are asynchronous.

Because mailslots are unidirectional and unreliable, *CreateMailslot* doesn't take many of the parameters that *CreateNamedPipe* does. After it creates a mailslot, a server simply listens for incoming client messages by executing the *ReadFile* function on the handle representing the mailslot.

Mailslot clients use a naming format similar to that used by named pipe clients but with variations that make it possible to broadcast messages to all the mailslots of a given name within the client's domain or a specified domain. To send a message to a particular instance of a mailslot, the client calls *CreateFile*, specifying the computer-specific name. An example of such a name is "\\Server\Mailslot\MailslotName". (The client can specify "\\.\" to represent the local computer.) If the client wants to obtain a handle representing all the mailslots of a given name on the domain it's a member of, it specifies the name in the format "*\Mailslot\MailslotName", and if the client wants to broadcast to all the mailslots of a given name within a different domain, the format it uses is "\\DomainName\Mailslot\MailslotName".

After obtaining a handle representing the client side of a mailslot, the client sends messages by calling *WriteFile*. Because of the way mailslots are implemented, only messages smaller than 425 bytes can be broadcast. If a message is larger than 425 bytes, the mailslot implementation uses a reliable communications mechanism that requires a one-to-one client/server connection, which precludes broadcast capability. Also, a quirk of the mailslot implementation causes messages of 425 or 426 bytes to be truncated to 424 bytes. These limitations make mailslots generally unsuitable for messages larger than 424 bytes. Figure 13-4 shows an example of a client broadcasting to multiple mailslot servers within a domain.

Figure 13-4
Mailslot broadcast

Named Pipe and Mailslot Implementation

As evidence of their tight integration with Win32, named pipe and mailslot functions are all implemented in the Kernel32.dll Win32 client-side DLL. *ReadFile* and *WriteFile*, which are the functions applications use to send and

receive messages using named pipes and mailslots, are the primary Win32 I/O routines. The *CreateFile* function, which a client uses to open either a named pipe or a mailslot, is also a standard Win32 I/O routine. However, the names specified by named pipe and mailslot applications specify file system namespaces managed by the named pipe file system driver (\Winnt\System32\Drivers\Npfs.sys) and the mailslot file system driver (\Winnt\System32\Drivers\Msfs.sys), as shown in Figure 13-5. The named pipe file system driver creates a device object named \Device\NamedPipe and a symbolic link to that object named \??\Pipe, and the mailslot file system driver creates a device object named \Device\Mailslot and a symbolic link named \??\Mailslot that points to that object. (See Chapter 3 for an explanation of the \?? object manager directory.) Names passed to *CreateFile* of the form \\.\Pipe\... and \\.\Mailslot\... have their prefix of \\.\ translated to \??\ so that the names resolve through a symbolic link to a device object. The special functions *CreateNamedPipe* and *CreateMailslot* use the corresponding native functions *NtCreateNamedPipeFile* and *NtCreateMailslotFile*.

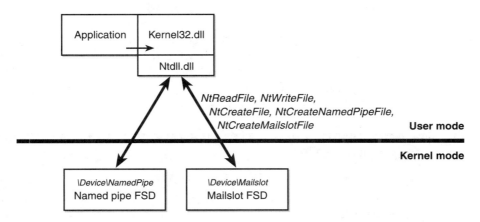

Figure 13-5
Named pipe and mailslot implementation

Later in the chapter, we'll discuss how the redirector file system driver is involved when a name that specifies a remote named pipe or mailslot resolves to a remote system. However, when a named pipe or mailslot is created by a server or opened by a client, the appropriate file system driver (FSD) on the machine where the named pipe or mailslot is located is eventually invoked. There

are several reasons why FSDs in kernel mode implement named pipes and mailslots, the main one being that they integrate with the object manager namespace and can use file objects to represent opened named pipes and mailslots. This integration results in several benefits:

- The FSDs use kernel-mode security functions to implement standard Windows 2000 security for named pipes and mailslots.

- Applications can use *CreateFile* to open a named pipe or mailslot because FSDs integrate with the object manager namespace.

- Applications can use Win32 functions such as *ReadFile* and *WriteFile* to interact with named pipes and mailslots.

- The FSDs rely on the object manager to track handle and reference counts for file objects representing named pipes and mailslots.

- The FSDs can implement their own named pipe and mailslot namespaces, complete with subdirectories.

Because named pipes and mailslot name resolution uses the redirector FSD to communicate across the network, they indirectly rely on the CIFS protocol (described later). CIFS works by using the IPX, TCP/IP, and NetBEUI protocols, so applications running on systems that have at least one of these in common can use named pipes and mailslots.

EXPERIMENT: Listing the Named Pipe Namespace and Watching Named Pipe Activity

It's not possible to use the Win32 API to open the root of the named pipe FSD and perform a directory listing, but you can do this by using native API services. The PipeList tool (on the companion CD as \Sysint\Pipelist.exe) shows you the names of the named pipes defined on a computer as well as the number of instances that have been created for a name and the maximum number of instances as defined by a server's call to *CreateNamedPipe*. Here's an example of PipeList output:

```
C:\>pipelist
PipeList v1.01
by Mark Russinovich
```

```
http://www.sysinternals.com

Pipe Name                                Instances      Max Instances
------------------
InitShutdown                                 2               -1
lsass                                        3               -1
ntsvcs                                      32               -1
scerpc                                       2               -1
net\NtControlPipe1                           1                1
DhcpClient                                   1               -1
net\NtControlPipe2                           1                1
Winsock2\CatalogChangeListener-184-0         1                1
net\NtControlPipe3                           1                1
spoolss                                      2               -1
net\NtControlPipe4                           1                1
net\NtControlPipe5                           1                1
net\NtControlPipe0                           1                1
net\NtControlPipe6                           1                1
net\NtControlPipe7                           1                1
winreg                                       2               -1
Winsock2\CatalogChangeListener-208-0         1                1
atsvc                                        2               -1
net\NtControlPipe8                           1                1
SecondaryLogon                               1               10
SfcApi                                       2               -1
ProfMapApi                                   2               -1
winlogonrpc                                  2               -1
Winsock2\CatalogChangeListener-d8-0          1                1
epmapper                                     2               -1
POLICYAGENT                                  2               -1
WMIEP_e4                                      2               -1
WMIEP_1d4                                     2               -1
tapsrv                                        2               -1
ROUTER                                        9               -1
WMIEP_3c4                                      2               -1
WMIEP_3d0                                      2               -1
WMIEP_3ec                                      2               -1
```

(continued)

EXPERIMENT: Listing the Named Pipe Namespace and Watching Named Pipe Activity *continued*

It's clear from this output that several system components use named pipes as their communications mechanism. For example, the *InitShutdown* pipe is created by Winlogon to accept remote shutdown commands, and the *SecondaryLogon* pipe is created by the Runas service to perform logon operations on behalf of the Runas utility. You can determine what process has each of these pipes open by using the object search facility in HandleEx (on the companion CD as \Sysint\ Handleex.exe). Note that a Max Instances value of −1 means that there is no upper limit on the number of instances for the given name.

The Filemon file system filter driver (on the companion CD as \Sysint\Filemon.exe) is able to attach to either the Npfs.sys or Msfs.sys file system drivers and to therefore see all named pipe or mailslot activity occurring on a system. Select the Named Pipes or Mail Slots menu entries from Filemon's Drives menu to have Filemon attach to the corresponding driver. The following screen shot shows Filemon capturing the named pipe activity generated when the My Network Places icon on the desktop was opened. Notice the messages transmitted through the Lsass and workstation service named pipes.

Windows Sockets

Windows Sockets (Winsock) is Microsoft's implementation of BSD (Berkeley Software Distribution) Sockets, a programming API that became the standard by which UNIX systems have communicated over the Internet since the 1980s. Support for sockets on Windows 2000 makes the task of porting UNIX networking applications to Windows 2000 relatively straightforward. Winsock includes most of the functionality of BSD Sockets but also includes Microsoft-specific enhancements, which continue to evolve. Winsock supports reliable-connection-oriented communication as well as unreliable-connectionless communication. Windows 2000 provides Winsock 2.2, which is also either included with or available as an add-on for all versions of Consumer Windows.

Winsock includes the following features:

- Support for scatter-gather and asynchronous application I/O.

- Quality of service (QoS) conventions so that applications can negotiate latency and bandwidth requirements when the underlying network supports QoS.

- Extensibility so that Winsock can be used with protocols other than those Windows 2000 requires it to support.

- Support for integrated namespaces other than those defined by a protocol an application is using with Winsock. A server can publish its name in Active Directory, for example, and using namespace extensions, a client can look up the server's address in Active Directory.

- Support for multipoint messages where messages transmit to multiple receivers simultaneously.

We'll examine typical Winsock operation and then describe ways that Winsock can be extended.

Winsock Operation

After initializing the Winsock API with a call to an initialization function, the first step a Winsock application takes is to create a *socket* that will represent a communications endpoint. A socket must be *bound* to an address on the local computer, so binding is the second step the application performs. Winsock is a protocol-independent API, so an address can be specified for any protocol

installed on the system over which Winsock operates (NetBEUI, TCP/IP, IPX). After binding is complete, the steps taken by a server and client diverge, as do steps for connection-oriented and connectionless socket operation.

A connection-oriented Winsock server performs a *listen* operation on the socket, indicating the number of connections that it can support for the socket. Then it performs an *accept* operation to allow a client to connect to the socket. If there is a pending connection request, the accept call completes immediately; otherwise, it completes when a connection request arrives. When a connection is made, the *accept* function returns a new socket that represents the server's end of the connection. The server can perform receive and send operations by using functions such as *recv* and *send*.

Connection-oriented clients connect to a server by using the Winsock *connect* function that specifies a remote address. When a connection is established, the client can send and receive messages over its socket. Figure 13-6 shows connection-oriented communication between a Winsock client and server.

Figure 13-6
Connection-oriented Winsock operation

After binding an address, a connectionless server is no different from a connectionless client: it can send and receive messages over the socket simply by specifying the remote address with each message. When using connectionless messages, which are also called *datagrams,* a sender learns that a message wasn't received when the sender obtains an error code the next time a receive operation is performed.

Winsock Extensions

A powerful feature from a Windows programming point of view is that the Winsock API is integrated with Windows messages. A Winsock application can take advantage of this feature to perform asynchronous socket operations and receive notification of an operation's completion via a standard Windows mes-

sage or through the execution of a callback function. This capability simplifies the design of a Windows application because the application doesn't need to be multithreaded or manage synchronization objects to both perform network I/O and respond to user input or requests from the window manager to update the application windows. The names of message-based versions of BSD-style Winsock functions usually begin with the prefix *WSA*—for example, *WSAAccept*.

In addition to supporting functions that correspond directly to those implemented in BSD Sockets, Microsoft has added a handful of functions that aren't part of the Winsock standard. Two of these functions, *AcceptEx* and *TransmitFile*, are worth describing because many Web servers on Windows 2000 use them to achieve high performance. *AcceptEx* is a version of the *accept* function that, in the process of establishing a connection with a client, returns the client's address and the client's first message. With this function, a Web server avoids executing multiple Winsock functions that would otherwise be required.

After establishing a connection with a client, a Web server usually sends a file, such as a Web page, to the client. The *TransmitFile* function's implementation is integrated with the Windows 2000 cache manager so that a client can send a file directly from the file system cache. Sending data in this way is called *zero-copy* because the server doesn't have to touch the file data to send it; it simply specifies a handle to a file and the ranges of the file to send. In addition, *TransmitFile* allows a server to prepend or append data to the file's data so that the server can send header information, which might include the name of the Web server and a field that indicates to the client the size of the message the server is sending. Internet Information Services (IIS) 5.0, which is bundled with Windows 2000, uses both *AcceptEx* and *TransmitFile*.

Extending Winsock

Winsock is an extensible API on Windows 2000 because third parties can add a *transport service provider* that interfaces Winsock with other protocols as well as a *namespace service provider* to augment Winsock's name-resolution facilities. Service providers plug in to Winsock using the Winsock *service provider interface* (SPI). When a transport service provider is registered with Winsock, Winsock uses the transport service provider to implement socket functions, such as *connect* and *accept*, for the address types that the provider indicates it implements. There are no restrictions on how the transport service provider implements the functions, but the implementation usually involves communicating with a transport driver in kernel mode.

A requirement of any Winsock client/server application is for the server to make its address available to clients so that the clients can connect to the server. Standard services that execute on the TCP/IP protocol use "well-known addresses" to make their addresses available. As long as a browser knows the name of the computer a Web server is running on, it can connect to the Web server by specifying the well-known Web server address (the IP address of the server concatenated with :80, the port number used for HTTP). Namespace service providers make it possible for servers to register their presence in other ways. For example, one namespace service provider might on the server side register the server's address in Active Directory, and on the client side look up the server's address in Active Directory. Namespace service providers supply this functionality to Winsock by implementing standard Winsock name-resolution functions such as *gethostbyaddr*, *getservbyname*, and *getservbyport*.

EXPERIMENT: Looking at Winsock Service Providers

The Windows Sockets Configuration utility (Sporder.exe) included with the Platform SDK shows the registered Winsock transport and namespace providers and allows you to change the order in which transport service providers are enumerated. For example, if there are two TCP/IP transport service providers, the first one listed is the default provider for Winsock applications using the TCP/IP protocol. Here's a screen shot from Sporder showing the registered transport service providers:

Winsock Implementation

Winsock's implementation is shown in Figure 13-7. Its application interface consists of an API DLL, Ws2_32.dll (\Winnt\System32\Ws2_32.dll), which provides applications access to Winsock functions. Ws2_32.dll calls on the services of namespace and transport service providers to carry out name and message operations. The Msafd.dll library acts as a transport service provider for the protocols Microsoft provides support for in Winsock, and Msafd.dll uses *Winsock Helper* libraries that are protocol specific to communicate with kernel-mode protocol drivers. For example, Wshtcpip.dll is the TCP/IP helper, and Wshnetbs.dll is the NetBEUI helper. Mswsock.dll (\Winnt\System32\Mswsock.dll) implements the Microsoft Winsock extension functions, such as *TransmitFile*, *AcceptEx*, and *WSARecvEx*. Windows 2000 ships with helper DLLs for TCP/IP, NetBEUI, AppleTalk, IPX/SPX, ATM, and IrDA (Infrared Data Association) and namespace service providers for DNS (TCP/IP), Active Directory, and IPX/SPX.

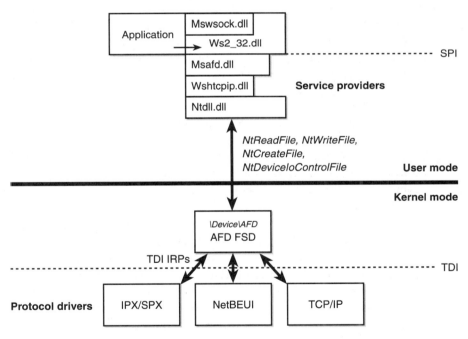

Figure 13-7
Winsock implementation

Like the named pipe and mailslot APIs, Winsock integrates with the Win32 I/O model and uses file handles to represent sockets. This support requires the aid of a kernel-mode file system driver, so Msafd.dll uses the services of the Ancillary Function Driver (AFD - \Winnt\System32\Drivers\Afd.sys) to implement socket-based functions. AFD is a TDI client and executes network socket operations, such as sending and receiving messages, by sending TDI IRPs to protocol drivers. AFD isn't coded to use particular protocol drivers; instead, Msafd.dll informs AFD of the name of the protocol used for each socket so that AFD can open the device object representing the protocol.

Remote Procedure Call

Remote procedure call (RPC) is a network programming standard originally developed in the early 1980s. The Open Software Foundation (now The Open Group) made RPC part of the distributed computing environment (DCE) distributed computing standard. Although there is a second RPC standard, SunRPC, the Microsoft RPC implementation is compatible with the OSF/DCE standard. RPC builds on other networking APIs, such as named pipes or Winsock, to provide an alternate programming model that in some sense hides the details of networking programming from an application developer.

RPC Operation

An RPC facility is one that allows a programmer to create an application consisting of any number of procedures, some that execute locally and others that execute on remote computers via a network. It provides a procedural view of networked operations rather than a transport-centered view, thus simplifying the development of distributed applications.

Networking software is traditionally structured around an I/O model of processing. In Windows 2000, for example, a network operation is initiated when an application issues a remote I/O request. The operating system processes it accordingly by forwarding it to a *redirector*, which acts as a remote file system by making the client interaction with the remote file system invisible to the client. The redirector passes the operation to the remote file system, and after the remote system fills the request and returns the results, the local network card interrupts. The kernel handles the interrupt, and the original I/O operation completes, returning results to the caller.

RPC takes a different approach altogether. RPC applications are like other structured applications, with a main program that calls procedures or procedure libraries to perform specific tasks. The difference between RPC applications and

regular applications, however, is that some of the procedure libraries in an RPC application execute on remote computers, as shown in Figure 13-8, whereas others execute locally.

Figure 13-8
RPC operation

To the RPC application, all the procedures appear to execute locally. In other words, instead of making a programmer actively write code to transmit computational or I/O-related requests across a network, handle network protocols, deal with network errors, wait for results, and so forth, RPC software handles these tasks automatically. And the Windows 2000 RPC facility can operate over any available transports loaded into the system.

To write an RPC application, the programmer decides which procedures will execute locally and which will execute remotely. For example, suppose an ordinary workstation has a network connection to a Cray supercomputer or to a machine designed specifically for high-speed vector operations. If the programmer were writing an application that manipulated large matrices, it would make sense from a performance point of view to offload the mathematical calculations to the remote computer by writing the program as an RPC application.

RPC applications work like this: As an application runs, it calls local procedures as well as procedures that aren't present on the local machine. To handle the latter case, the application is linked to a local static-link library or DLL that contains *stub procedures*, one for each remote procedure. For simple applications, the stub procedures are statically linked with the application, but for bigger components the stubs are included in separate DLLs. In DCOM, covered later in the chapter, the latter method is typically used. The stub procedures have the same name and use the same interface as the remote procedures, but instead of

performing the required operations, the stub takes the parameters passed to it and *marshals* them for transmission across the network. Marshaling parameters means ordering and packaging them in a particular way to suit a network link, such as resolving references and picking up a copy of any data structures that a pointer refers to.

The stub then calls RPC run-time procedures that locate the computer where the remote procedure resides, determine which transport mechanisms that computer uses, and send the request to it using local transport software. When the remote server receives the RPC request, it *unmarshals* the parameters (the reverse of marshaling them), reconstructs the original procedure call, and calls the procedure. When the server finishes, it performs the reverse sequence to return results to the caller.

In addition to the synchronous function-call-based interface described here, Windows 2000 RPC also supports *asynchronous RPC*. Asynchronous RPC lets an RPC application execute a function but not wait until the function completes to continue processing. Instead, the application can execute other code and later, when a response has arrived from the server, the RPC run time signals an event object the client associates with the asynchronous call. The client can use standard Win32 functions, such as *WaitForSingleObject*, to learn of the function's completion.

Besides the RPC run time, Microsoft's RPC facility includes a compiler, called the *Microsoft Interface Definition Language* (MIDL) compiler. The MIDL compiler simplifies the creation of an RPC application. The programmer writes a series of ordinary function prototypes (assuming a C or C++ application) that describe the remote routines and then places the routines in a file. The programmer then adds some additional information to these prototypes, such as a network-unique identifier for the package of routines and a version number, plus attributes that specify whether the parameters are input, output, or both. The embellished prototypes form the developer's *Interface Definition Language* (IDL) file.

Once the IDL file is created, the programmer compiles it with the MIDL compiler, which produces both client-side and server-side stub routines, mentioned previously, as well as header files to be included in the application. When the client-side application is linked to the stub routines file, all remote procedure references are resolved. The remote procedures are then installed, using a similar process, on the server machine. A programmer who wants to call an existing RPC application need only write the client side of the software and link the application to the local RPC run-time facility.

The RPC run time uses a generic *RPC transport provider interface* to talk to a transport protocol. The provider interface acts as a thin layer between the RPC facility and the transport, mapping RPC operations onto the functions provided by the transport. The Windows 2000 RPC facility implements transport provider DLLs for named pipes, NetBIOS, and TCP/IP. You can write new provider DLLs to support additional transports. In a similar fashion, the RPC facility is designed to work with different network security facilities.

Most of the Windows 2000 networking services are RPC applications, which means that both local processes and processes on remote computers can call them. Thus, a remote client computer can call the server service to list shares, open files, write to print queues, or activate users on your server, or it can call the messenger service to direct messages to you (all subject to security constraints, of course).

Server name publishing, which is the ability of a server to register its name in a location accessible for client lookup, is in RPC and is integrated with Active Directory. If Active Directory isn't installed, the RPC name locator services fall back on NetBIOS broadcast. This behavior ensures interoperability with Windows NT 4 systems and allows RPC to function on stand-alone servers and workstations.

RPC Security

Windows 2000 RPC includes integration with security support providers (SSPs) so that RPC clients and servers can use authenticated or encrypted communications. When an RPC server wants secure communication, it must register its SSP-specific *principal name* with an SSP. A client registers its security credentials when it *binds* to a server, specifying the server's principal name. At the time of the binding, the client also specifies the *authentication level* it wants. Various authentication levels exist to ensure that only authorized clients connect to a server, verify that each message a server receives originates at an authorized client, check the integrity of RPC messages to detect manipulation, and even encrypt RPC message data. Obviously, higher authentication levels require more processing.

An SSP handles the details of performing network communication authentication and encryption, not only for RPC but also for Winsock. Windows 2000 includes a number of built-in SSPs, including a Kerberos SSP to implement Kerberos version 5 authentication, and Secure Channel (SChannel), which implements Secure Sockets Layer (SSL), Transport Layer Security (TLS) protocol, and private communication technology (PCT). In the absence of a specified SSP, RPC software uses the built-in security of named pipes.

Another feature of RPC security is the ability of a server to impersonate the security identity of a client with the *RpcImpersonateClient* function. After a server has finished performing impersonated operations on behalf a client, it returns to its own security identity by calling *RpcRevertToSelf* or *RpcRevertToSelfEx*. (See Chapter 8 for more information on impersonation.)

RPC Implementation

RPC implementation is depicted in Figure 13-9, which shows that an RPC-based application links with the RPC run-time DLL (\Winnt\System32\Rpcrt4.dll). The RPC run-time DLL provides marshaling and unmarshaling functions for use by an application's RPC function stubs as well as functions for sending and receiving marshaled data. The RPC run-time DLL includes support routines to handle RPC over a network as well as a form of RPC called *local RPC*. Local RPC can be used for communication between two processes located on the same system, and the RPC run-time DLL uses the local procedure call (LPC) facilities in kernel mode as the local networking API. (See Chapter 3 for more information on LPCs.) When RPC is based on nonlocal communication mechanisms, the RPC run-time DLL uses the Winsock, named pipe, or Message Queuing (described shortly) APIs.

Figure 13-9
RPC implementation

For name registry and lookup, RPC applications link with the RPC name services DLL (\Winnt\System32\Rpcns4.dll). The DLL communicates with the RPC Subsystem (RPCSS - \Winnt\System32\Rpcss.dll), which is implemented as a Win32 service. RPCSS is itself an RPC application that communicates with instances of itself on other systems to perform name lookup and registration. (For clarity, Figure 13-9 doesn't show RPCSS link with the RPC run–time DLL.)

Common Internet File System (CIFS)

Common Internet File System (CIFS) is an enhanced form of the Server Message Block (SMB) protocol, which is the protocol Windows 2000 uses to implement file sharing. Because applications access remote files using standard Win32 file I/O functions, applications don't directly use the CIFS protocol, but the protocol is used to process the I/O request. CIFS defines printer-sharing conventions, so Windows 2000 uses CIFS for that as well. Although CIFS isn't itself an API, we cover it in this section because file and printer sharing is built on CIFS and is exposed to applications via the Win32 API.

CIFS is a published Microsoft standard (documented in the Platform SDK) that allows third parties to interoperate with Windows 2000 file servers and with Windows 2000 file sharing clients. For example, the Samba shareware suite allows UNIX systems to serve files to Windows 2000 clients and for UNIX applications to access files served by Windows 2000 systems. Other platforms that support CIFS include DEC VMS and Apple Macintosh.

File sharing on Windows 2000 is based on a redirector FSD (redirector, for short) executing on a client machine that communicates with a server FSD executing on the server. The redirector FSD intercepts Win32 file I/O directed at files residing on the server and transmits CIFS messages to the server file system to execute client requests. The server receives CIFS messages and translates them back to I/O operations that it issues to local FSDs, such as NTFS, running on the server. Figure 13-10 shows a redirector and server communicating with one another.

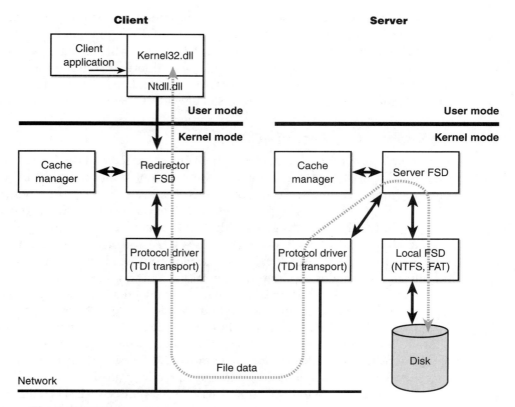

Figure 13-10
CIFS file sharing

Because they are integrated with the Windows 2000 I/O system, redirector and server FSDs have several advantages over alternate user-space implementations of file servers:

- They can interact directly with TDI transports and local FSDs.
- They can integrate with the cache manager to seamlessly cache server file data on client systems. (The caching protocol Windows 2000 uses is described shortly.)
- Applications can use standard Win32 file I/O functions, such as *CreateFile*, *ReadFile*, and *WriteFile* to access remote files.

Windows 2000 redirector and server FSDs rely on standard network-resource naming conventions that all kernel-mode file servers and client software use. If a remote file share is connected using a drive letter, network file names are specified in the same way as local names. However, redirector also supports UNC names. Network-resource name resolution is described in the section "Network-Resource Name Resolution" later in this chapter.

CIFS Implementation

The redirector FSD on Windows 2000 is implemented in a port/miniport model common to many other device driver types. (See Chapter 9 for information on device drivers.) Microsoft provides a redirector library named \Winnt\System32\ Drivers\Rdbss.sys to which developers can write a redirector miniport. The redirector library hides many details of implementing a redirector, such as integrating with the cache manager, the memory manager, and TDI transports. The CIFS miniport driver is named \Winnt\System32\Drivers\Mrxsmb.sys.

Rdbss uses the cache manager services described in Chapter 11 and Chapter 12 to cache file data and to take advantage of intelligent read-ahead. The CIFS miniport driver sends CIFS commands to a remote server by way of the TDI API. It can use any transport that supports the TDI interface, such as NetBEUI, NetBT (NetBIOS over TCP/IP), and TCP/IP.

On a system acting as a file server, the server (\Winnt\System32\Drivers\ Srv.sys) FSD listens for CIFS commands originating on client machines and acts as a surrogate interface to the local FSD on which accessed files reside. The server FSD uses file system interfaces implemented by native Windows 2000 FSDs to implement zero-copy send capability. The interfaces allow for the server FSD to obtain a memory descriptor list (MDL) description of a file's data residing in the file system cache of the server and to pass the MDL to a TDI transport for transmission across the network using a network adapter driver. (See Chapter 7 for more information on MDLs.) Without the support of local FSDs and the cache manager, the server FSD would have to copy file data into its own buffers that it would subsequently pass to TDI transports.

Both the server FSD and the redirector have corresponding Win32 services, *Server* and *Workstation*, that execute in the service control manager (SCM) process to provide administrative management interfaces to the drivers.

Distributed File Caching

If a single client accesses a file on a server, it's obvious that the client can safely cache the file's data on the client system. When two clients access the same file, however, steps must be taken to provide a consistent view of the file between the two clients and the server. The Windows 2000 solution to this problem, which is known as *distributed cache coherency*, is implemented through a mechanism called an *opportunistic lock* (oplock). When a client wants to access a server file, it must first request an oplock. The type of oplock that the server grants the client dictates the kind of caching that the client can perform.

There are three main types of oplock:

- A Level I oplock is granted when a client has exclusive access to a file. A client holding this type of oplock for a file can cache both reads and writes on the client system.

- A Level II oplock represents a shared file lock. Clients that hold a Level II oplock can cache reads, but writing to the file invalidates the Level II oplock.

- A Batch oplock is the most permissive kind of oplock. A client with this oplock can cache both reads and writes to the file as well as open and close the file without requesting additional oplocks. Batch oplocks are typically used only to support the execution of batch files, which can open and close a file repeatedly as they execute.

If a client has no oplock, it can cache neither read nor write data locally and instead must retrieve data from the server and send all modifications directly to the server.

An example, shown in Figure 13-11, will help illustrate oplock operation. The server automatically grants a Level I oplock to the first client to open a server file for access. The redirector on the client caches the file data for both reads and writes in the file cache of the client machine. If a second client opens the file, it too requests a Level I oplock. However, because there are now two clients accessing the same file, the server must take steps to present a consistent view of the file's data to both clients. If the first client has written to the file, as is the case in Figure 13-11, the server revokes its oplock and grants neither client an oplock. When the first client's oplock is revoked, or *broken*, the client flushes any data it has cached for the file back to the server.

If the first client hadn't written to the file, the first client's oplock would have been broken to a Level II oplock, which is the same type of oplock the server grants to the second client. Now both clients can cache reads, but if either writes to the

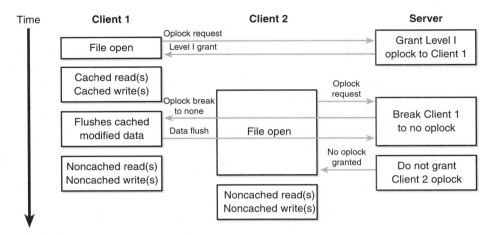

Figure 13-11
Oplock example

file, the server revokes their oplocks so that noncached operation commences. Once oplocks are broken, they aren't granted again for the same open instance of a file. However, if a client closes a file and then reopens it, the server reassesses what level of oplock to grant the client based on what other clients have the file open and whether or not at least one of them has written to the file.

NetBIOS

Until the 1990s, the Network Basic Input/Output System (NetBIOS) programming API had been the most widely used programming API on PCs. NetBIOS allows for both reliable-connection-oriented and unreliable-connectionless communication. Windows 2000 supports NetBIOS for its legacy applications. Microsoft discourages application developers from using NetBIOS because other APIs, such as named pipes and Winsock, are much more flexible and portable. NetBIOS is supported by the TCP/IP, NetBEUI, and IPX/SPX protocols on Windows 2000.

NetBIOS Names

NetBIOS relies on a naming convention whereby computers and network services are assigned a 16-byte name called a NetBIOS name. The 16th byte of a NetBIOS name is treated as a modifier that can specify a name as unique or as part of a group. Only one instance of a unique NetBIOS name can be assigned to a network, but

multiple applications can assign the same group name. A client can broadcast messages by sending them to a group name.

To support interoperability with Windows NT 4 systems as well as Consumer Windows, Windows 2000 automatically defines a NetBIOS name for a domain that is the first 15 bytes of the Domain Name System (DNS) name that an administrator assigns to the domain. For example, if a domain were named *mspress.microsoft.com*, the NetBIOS name of the domain would be *mspress*. Similarly, Windows 2000 requires an administrator to assign each computer a NetBIOS name at the time of installation.

Another concept used by NetBIOS is that of LAN adapter (LANA) numbers. A LANA number is assigned to every NetBIOS-compatible protocol that layers above a network adapter. For example, if a computer has two network adapters and TCP/IP and NetBEUI can use either adapter, there would be four LANA numbers. LANA numbers are important because a NetBIOS application must explicitly assign its service name to each LANA through which it's willing to accept client connections. If the application listens for client connections on a particular name, clients can access the name only via protocols on the network adapters for which the name is registered.

A networking service called *Windows Internet Name Service* (WINS) maintains the mapping between NetBIOS names and TCP/IP protocol addresses. If WINS isn't installed, NetBIOS uses name broadcasting to propagate names within a Windows network. Note that NetBIOS names are secondary to DNS names; computer names are registered and resolved first through DNS, with Windows 2000 falling back on NetBIOS names only if DNS name resolution fails. (DNS name resolution is described in the section "Network-Resource Name Resolution" later in this chapter.)

NetBIOS Operation

A NetBIOS server application uses the NetBIOS API to enumerate the LANAs present on a system and assign a NetBIOS name representing the application's service to each LANA. If the server is connection oriented, it performs a NetBIOS listen command to wait for client connection attempts. After a client is connected, the server executes NetBIOS functions to send and receive data. Connectionless communication is similar, but the server simply reads messages without establishing connections.

A connection-oriented client uses NetBIOS functions to establish a connection with a NetBIOS server and then executes further NetBIOS functions to send and receive data. An established NetBIOS connection is also known as a *session*. If the client wants to send connectionless messages, it simply specifies the NetBIOS name of the server with the send function.

NetBIOS consists of a number of functions, but they all route through the same interface: *Netbios*. This routing scheme is the result of a legacy left over from the time when NetBIOS was implemented on MS-DOS as an MS-DOS interrupt service. A NetBIOS application would execute an MS-DOS interrupt and pass a data structure to the NetBIOS implementation that specified every aspect of the command being executed. As a result, the *Netbios* function in Windows 2000 takes a single parameter, which is a data structure that contains the parameters specific to the service the application requests.

EXPERIMENT: Using Nbtstat to See NetBIOS Names

You can use the *Nbtstat* command, which is included with Windows 2000, to list the active sessions on a system, the NetBIOS-to-TCP/IP name mappings cached on a computer, and the NetBIOS names defined on a computer. Here's an example of the *Nbtstat* command with the −*n* option, which lists the NetBIOS names defined on the computer:

```
C:\>nbtstat -n
Local Area Connection:
Node IpAddress: [10.0.0.5] Scope Id: []

                NetBIOS Local Name Table

        Name              Type         Status
    ---------------------------------------------
        MARKLAP       <00>  UNIQUE      Registered
        MARKLAP       <20>  UNIQUE      Registered
        MARK          <00>  GROUP       Registered
        MARK          <1E>  GROUP       Registered

\Device\NetBT_Tcpip_{0A546AD9-3AD1-4A89-858B-1ADBF9AC5620}:
Node IpAddress: [32.100.225.5] Scope Id: []

                NetBIOS Local Name Table

        Name              Type         Status
    ---------------------------------------------
        MARKLAP       <00>  UNIQUE      Registered
        MARK          <00>  GROUP       Registered
        MARK          <1E>  GROUP       Registered
```

NetBIOS API Implementation

The components that implement the NetBIOS API are shown in Figure 13-12. The *Netbios* function is exported to applications by \Winnt\System32\Netapi32. dll. Netapi32.dll opens a handle to the kernel-mode driver named the *NetBIOS emulator* (\Winnt\System32\Drivers\Netbios.sys) and issues Win32 *DeviceIo-Control* file commands on behalf of an application. The NetBIOS emulator translates NetBIOS commands issued by an application into TDI commands that it sends to protocol drivers.

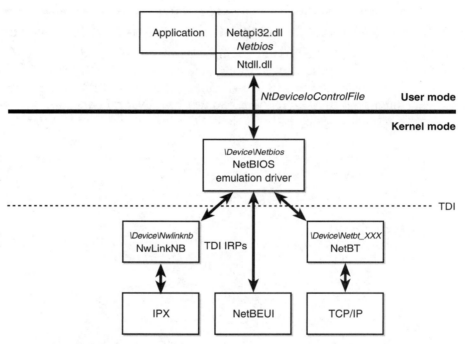

Figure 13-12
NetBIOS API implementation

If an application wants to use NetBIOS over the TCP/IP protocol, the NetBIOS emulator requires the presence of the NetBT driver (\Winnt\System32\ Drivers\Netbt.sys). NetBT is known as the NetBIOS over TCP/IP driver and is responsible for supporting NetBIOS semantics that are inherent to the NetBEUI protocol (described later in this chapter), but not the TCP/IP protocol. For

example, NetBIOS relies on NetBEUI's message-mode transmission and NetBIOS name resolution facilities, so the NetBT driver implements them on top of the TCP/IP protocol. Similarly, the NwLinkNB driver implements NetBIOS semantics over the IPX/SPX protocol.

Other Networking APIs

Windows 2000 includes other networking APIs that are used less frequently or are layered on the APIs already described (and outside the scope of this book). Three of these, however, Telephony API (TAPI), Distributed Component Object Model (DCOM), and Message Queuing, are important enough to the operation of a Windows 2000 system and many applications to merit brief descriptions.

Telephony API

Telephony integrates computers with communications devices such as telephones and modems. In Windows 2000, telephony also encompasses applications such as Voice over Internet Protocol (VoIP), multicast multimedia conferencing, and real-time collaboration (RTC). Windows 2000 includes the Telephony API (TAPI) for applications that want to communicate over telephony-supported devices. TAPI abstracts the details of device management so that TAPI applications can work over different devices without change. Windows 2000 ships with two versions of TAPI, TAPI 2.2 for C applications, and TAPI 3.0 for COM applications.

TAPI can be broken down into subset APIs for device, session, and media control. Device control interfaces allow TAPI to communicate device characteristics and changes to those characteristics to a TAPI application and for a TAPI application to query the device's characteristics. Characteristics include lines, address identifiers, device events, and media types. Session control interfaces let an application establish a connection between two or more addresses. Session control operations are similar to the ones supported by sophisticated telephones and include session initiation, answer, accept, forward, park, transfer, and drop. Finally, media control interfaces allow a TAPI application to perform operations such as tone-detection and dialing.

The Microsoft Telephony architecture, shown in Figure 3-13, is centered on the TAPI service (\Winnt\System32\Tapisrv.dll), which runs as a Win32 service in a Service Host process. (See Chapter 5 for more information on Win32 services.) TAPI applications use the TAPI client-side DLL (\Winnt\System32\Tapi32.dll) to communicate via RPCs with the TAPI service.

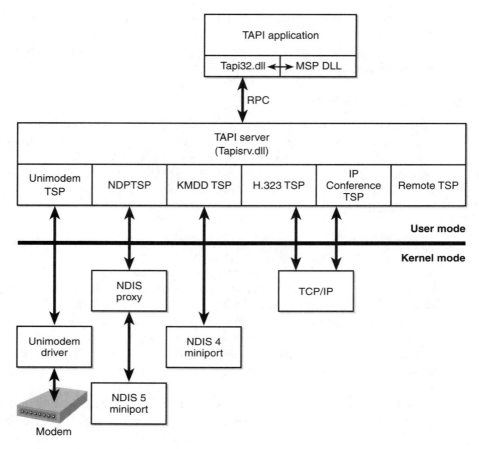

Figure 13-13
TAPI architecture

To support device abstraction, the TAPI service loads TAPI service providers (TSPs) that provide interfaces to a particular device or class of devices. For example, the Unimodem TSP interfaces the TAPI service with most types of modems. TAPI also includes Media Service Providers (MSPs) that allow a TAPI application enhanced media-specific control over a medium. An MSP DLL loaded by the application has a corresponding TSP in the TAPI server. Other TSPs that come with Windows 2000 include the following:

- Remote TSP provides access to remote communications resources such as modem pools.

- H.323 TSP allows TAPI applications to make and receive video and audio calls according to the H.323 telephony protocol.

- NDIS Proxy TSP (NDPTSP) presents NDIS 5 miniports (described later in the chapter) as TAPI lines.

- Kernel-Mode Device Driver (KMDD) TSP presents legacy NDIS 4 miniports for WAN devices as TAPI lines.

- IP Conference TSP supports conferencing over TCP/IP connections.

The TAPI architecture and documentation also make it possible for third parties to develop their own TAPI TSPs.

DCOM

Microsoft's COM API lets applications consist of different components, each component being a replaceable self-contained module. A COM object exports an object-oriented interface to methods for manipulating the data within the object. Because COM objects present well-defined interfaces, developers can implement new objects to extend existing interfaces and dynamically update applications with the new support.

DCOM extends COM by letting an application's components reside on different computers, which means that applications don't need to be concerned that one COM object might be on the local computer and another might be across the LAN. DCOM thus provides location transparency, which simplifies developing distributed applications. DCOM isn't a self-contained API but relies on RPC to carry out its work.

Message Queuing

Microsoft's newest networking service, Message Queuing, was introduced in Windows NT 4 Enterprise Edition. Message Queuing is a general-purpose platform for developing distributed applications that take advantage of loosely coupled messaging. Message Queuing is therefore an API and a messaging infrastructure. Its flexibility comes from the fact that its queues serve as message repositories in which senders can queue messages for receivers, and receivers can dequeue the messages at their discretion. Senders and receivers do not need to establish connections to use Message Queuing, nor do they even need to be executing at the same time, which allows for disconnected asynchronous message exchange.

A notable feature of Message Queuing is that it is integrated with Microsoft Transaction Server (MTS) and SQL Server, so it can participate in Microsoft Distributed Transaction Coordinator (MS DTC) coordinated transactions. Using MS DTC with Message Queuing allows you to develop reliable transaction functionality to three-tier applications.

Network-Resource Name Resolution

Applications can examine or access resources on remote systems in two ways. One way is by using the UNC standard with Win32 functions to directly address a remote resource; a second way is by using the Windows Networking (WNet) API to enumerate computers and resources that those computers export for sharing. Both these approaches use the capabilities of a redirector to find their way to the network. As we stated earlier, to access CIFS servers from a client, Microsoft supplies a CIFS redirector, which has a kernel-mode component called the redirector FSD and a user-mode component called the Workstation service. Microsoft also makes available a redirector that can access resources shared by Novell NetWare servers, and third parties can add their own redirectors to Windows 2000. In this section, we'll examine the software that decides which redirector to invoke when remote I/O requests are issued. Here are the responsible components:

- *Multiple provider router* (MPR) is a DLL that determines which network to access when an application uses the Win32 WNet API for browsing remote file systems.

- *Multiple UNC Provider* (MUP) is a driver that determines which network to access when an application uses the Win32 I/O API to open remote files.

We'll conclude this section by describing Domain Name System (DNS), the heart of computer name resolution in Windows 2000.

Multiple Provider Router

The Win32 WNet functions allow applications (including the Windows Explorer My Network Places) to connect to network resources, such as file servers and printers, and to browse the contents of any type of remote file system. Because the WNet API can be called to work across different networks using different transport protocols, software must be present to send the request correctly over the network and to understand the results that the remote server returns. Figure 13-14 shows the redirector software responsible for these tasks.

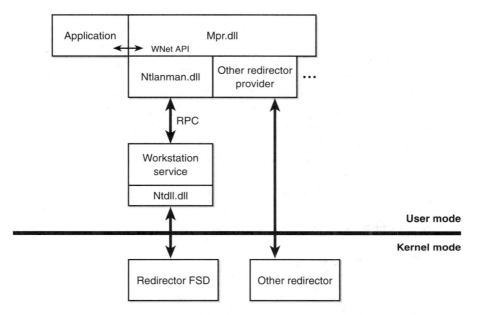

Figure 13-14
MPR components

A *provider* is software that establishes Windows 2000 as a client of a remote network server. Some of the operations a WNet provider performs include making and breaking network connections, printing remotely, and transferring data. The built-in WNet provider includes a DLL, the Workstation service, and the redirector. Other network vendors need to supply only a DLL and a redirector.

When an application calls a WNet routine, the call passes directly to the MPR DLL. MPR takes the call and determines which WNet provider recognizes the resource being accessed. Each provider DLL beneath MPR supplies a set of standard functions collectively called the *provider interface*. This interface allows MPR to determine which network the application is trying to access and to direct the request to the appropriate WNet provider software. The redirector's provider is \Winnt\System32\Ntlanman.dll, as directed by the ProviderPath value under the HKLM\SYSTEM\CurrentControlSet\Services\lanmanworkstation\ NetworkProvider registry key.

When called by the *WNetAddConnection* API function to connect to a remote network resource, MPR checks the HKLM\SYSTEM\CurrentControlSet\Control\NetworkProvider\Order\ProviderOrder registry value to determine which network providers are loaded. It polls them one at a time in the order in which they're listed in the registry until a redirector recognizes the resource or until all available providers have been polled. You can change the ProviderOrder by using the Advanced Settings dialog box, shown in Figure 13-15. (Only one provider is installed on the system from which the screen shot was taken.) This dialog box is accessible from the Advanced menu of the Network And Dial-Up Connections application. You can access the Network And Dial-Up Connections application by right-clicking the My Network Places icon on the desktop and selecting Properties from the pop-up menu or by selecting it from the Settings option from the Start menu.

Figure 13-15
The provider order editor

The *WNetAddConnection* function can also assign a drive letter or device name to a remote resource. When called to do so, *WNetAddConnection* routes the call to the appropriate network provider. The provider, in turn, creates a symbolic-link object in the object manager namespace that maps the drive letter being defined to the redirector (that is, the remote FSD) for that network.

Figure 13-16 shows the \?? directory, where you can see several driver letters representing connections to remote file shares. The figure shows that the redirector creates a device object named \Device\LanmanRedirector and that the additional text included in the symbolic link's value indicates to the redirector which remote resource the drive letter corresponds to. When a user opens X:\Book\Chap13.doc, the redirector is passed the unparsed portion of the path that resolves through the symbolic link, which is ";X:0\dual\e\Book\Chap13.doc". The redirector notes that the resource being accessed is located on the E share of server *dual*.

Figure 13-16
Resolving a network resource name

Like the built-in redirector, other redirectors create a device object in the object manager namespace when they are loaded into the system and initialized. Then, when the WNet or other API calls the object manager to open a resource on a different network, the object manager uses the device object as a jumping-off point into the remote file system. It calls an I/O manager parse method associated with the device object to locate the redirector FSD that can handle the request. (See Chapter 12 for more information on file system drivers.)

Multiple UNC Provider

The Multiple UNC Provider (MUP) is a networking component similar to MPR. It fields I/O requests destined for a file or a device that has a UNC name (names beginning with the characters \\, indicating that the resource exists on the network). MUP takes such requests and, like MPR, determines which local

redirector recognizes the remote resource. Unlike MPR, MUP is a device driver (loaded at system boot time) that issues I/O requests to lower-layer drivers, in this case to redirectors, as shown in Figure 13-17.

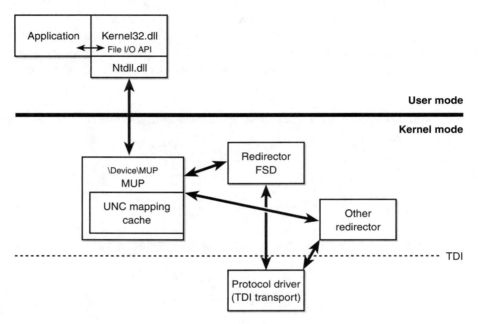

Figure 13-17
Multiple UNC Provider (MUP)

The MUP driver is activated when an application first attempts to open a remote file or device by specifying a UNC name (instead of a redirected drive letter, as described earlier). When the Win32 client-side DLL Kernel32.dll (which is the DLL that exports file-I/O-related APIs) receives such a request, the subsystem appends the UNC name to the string \??\UNC and then calls the *NtCreateFile* system service to open the file. This object name is the name of a symbolic link that resolves to \Device\Mup, a device object that represents the MUP driver.

The MUP driver receives the request and sends an IRP asynchronously to each registered redirector, waiting for one of them to recognize the resource name and reply. When a redirector recognizes the name, it indicates how much of the name is unique to it. For example, if the name is \\WIN2KSERVER\ PUBLIC\insidew2k\chap13.doc, the redirector recognizes it and claims the string \\WIN2KSERVER\PUBLIC as its own. The MUP driver caches this information and thereafter sends requests beginning with that string directly to the

redirector, skipping the polling operation. The MUP driver's cache has a timeout feature, so after a period of inactivity, a string's association with a particular redirector expires. If more than one redirector claims a particular resource, the MUP driver uses the registry's ProviderOrder value's list of loaded redirectors to determine which redirector takes precedence.

Domain Name System

Domain Name System (DNS) is a standard by which Internet names (such as *www.microsoft.com*) are translated to their corresponding IP addresses. A network application that wants to resolve a DNS name to an IP address sends a DNS lookup request using the TCP/IP protocol to a DNS server. DNS servers implement a distributed database of name/IP address pairs that are used to perform translations, and each server maintains the translations for a particular *zone*. Describing the details of DNS are outside the scope of this book, but DNS is the foundation of naming in Windows 2000 and so it is the primary Windows 2000 name resolution protocol.

The Windows 2000 DNS server is implemented as a Win32 service (\Winnt\ System32\Dns.exe) that is included in server versions of Windows 2000. Standard DNS server implementation relies on a text file as the translation database, but the Windows 2000 DNS server can be configured to store zone information in Active Directory.

Protocol Drivers

Networking API drivers must take API requests and translate them into low-level network protocol requests for transmission across the network. The API drivers rely on transport protocol drivers in kernel mode to do the actual translation. Separating APIs from underlying protocols gives the networking architecture the flexibility of letting each API use a number of different protocols. The protocol drivers that Windows 2000 includes are Data Link Control (DLC), NetBEUI, TCP/IP, and NWLink, although other protocols might be present as options, such as the AppleTalk protocol installed with Services For Macintosh on Windows 2000 servers. Here's a brief description of each protocol:

- DLC is a relatively primitive protocol that some IBM mainframes as well as some Hewlett-Packard network printers use. It is a "raw" protocol in the sense that no networking APIs can use it; applications that want to use DLC must interface directly to the DLC transport protocol device driver.

■ IBM and Microsoft introduced NetBEUI in 1985, and Microsoft adopted NetBEUI as the default protocol for LAN Manager and the NetBIOS API. Microsoft has since enhanced NetBEUI, but the protocol is limited because it's not routable and performs poorly on WANs. NetBEUI (NetBIOS Extended User Interface) was so named because it is tightly integrated with the NetBIOS API, but the protocol Microsoft's NetBEUI protocol driver implements is NetBIOS Frame (NBF) format. Windows 2000 includes NetBEUI solely for interoperability with legacy Windows systems (Windows NT 4 and Consumer Windows).

■ The Internet's explosive growth and reliance on the TCP/IP protocol has made TCP/IP the preeminent protocol in Windows 2000. The Defense Advanced Research Projects Agency (DARPA) developed TCP/IP in 1969 specifically as the foundation for the Internet; therefore, TCP/IP has WAN-friendly characteristics such as routability and good WAN performance. TCP/IP is the preferred Windows 2000 protocol and is the only one installed by default.

■ NWLink consists of Novell's IPX and SPX protocols. Windows 2000 includes NWLink for interoperability with Novell NetWare servers.

TDI transports in Windows 2000 generally implement all the protocols associated with their primary protocol. For example, the TCP/IP driver (\Winnt\ System32\Drivers\Tcpip.sys) implements TCP, UDP, IP, ARP, ICMP, and IGMP. A TDI transport generally creates device objects that represent particular protocols so that clients can obtain a file object representing a protocol and issue network I/O to the protocol by using IRPs. The TCP/IP driver creates three device objects that represent various TDI-client accessible protocols: \Device\Tcp, \Device\Udp, and \Device\Ip.

So that networking API drivers don't need to employ various interfaces for each transport protocol they might want to use, Microsoft established the Transport Driver Interface (TDI) standard. As mentioned earlier in this chapter, a TDI interface is essentially a convention for the way network requests format into IRPs and for the way network addresses and communications are allocated. Transport protocols that adhere to the TDI standard export the TDI interface to their clients, which include networking API drivers such as AFD and the redirector. A transport protocol implemented as a Windows 2000 device driver is known as a TDI transport. Because TDI transports are device drivers, they format requests they receive from clients as IRPs.

Support functions in the \Winnt\System32\Drivers\Tdi.sys library, along with definitions developers include in their drivers, make up the TDI interface. The TDI programming model is very similar to that of Winsock. A TDI client executes the following steps to establish a connection with a remote server:

1. The client allocates and formats an *address open* TDI IRP to allocate an address. The TDI transport returns a file object, which is known as an *address object*, that represents the address. This step is the equivalent of using the *bind* Winsock function.

2. The client then allocates and formats a *connection open* TDI IRP, and the TDI transport returns a file object, which is known as a *connection object*, that represents the connection. This step is the equivalent of the use of the Winsock *socket* function.

3. The client associates the connection object to the address object with an *associate address* TDI IRP. (There's no equivalent to this step in Winsock.)

4. A TDI client that accepts remote connections issues a *listen* TDI IRP specifying the number of connections supported for a connection object and then issues an *accept* TDI IRP, which completes when a remote system establishes a connection (or an error occurs). These operations are equivalent to the use of the Winsock *listen* and *accept* functions.

5. A TDI client that wants to establish a connection with a remote server issues a *connect* TDI IRP, specifying the connection object, that the TDI transport completes when a connection is established (or an error occurs). Issuing a *connect* TDI IRP is the equivalent of using the *connect* Winsock function.

TDI also supports connectionless communications for connectionless protocols such as UDP. In addition, TDI provides a means whereby a TDI client can register *event callbacks* (that is, functions that are directly invoked) with TDI transports. When it receives data from across the network, a TDI transport can invoke a registered client receive callback, for example. This event-based callback feature of TDI allows the TDI transport to notify its clients of network events, and clients that rely on event callbacks don't need to preallocate resources such as buffers when receiving network data because they can view the contents of the buffers supplied by a TDI protocol driver.

EXPERIMENT: Watching TDI Activity

TDImon, a utility included on the companion CD as \Sysint\Tdimon.exe, is a form of filter driver that attaches to the \Device\Tcp and \Device\Udp device objects that the TCP/IP driver creates. After attaching, TDImon sees every IRP that TDI clients issue to these protocols. By intercepting TDI client event callback registration, it also monitors event callbacks. The TDImon driver sends information about the TDI activity for display in its GUI, where you can see the time of an operation, the type of TDI activity that took place, the local and remote addresses of a TCP connection or the local address of a UDP endpoint, the resulting status code of the IRP or event callback, and additional information such as the number of bytes sent or received. Here's a screen shot of TDImon watching the TDI activity that is generated when Microsoft Internet Explorer browses a Web page:

As evidence that TDI operations are inherently asynchronous, the PENDING codes in the Result column indicate that an operation initiated but that the IRP defining the operation hasn't yet completed. To accurately show the order of completions with respect to the start of other operations, the issuing of each IRP or event callback is tagged with a sequence number. If other IRPs are issued or completed before an IRP completes, the IRP's completion is also tagged with a sequence number that is shown in the Result column. For example, the IRP that was tagged with sequence number 1278 in the screen shot completed after the one tagged with 1279 was issued, so you see 1280 in the Result column for IRP 1278.

NDIS Drivers

When a protocol driver wants to read or write messages formatted in its protocol's format from or to the network, the driver must do so using a network adapter. Because expecting protocol drivers to understand the nuances of every network adapter on the market (proprietary network adapters number in the thousands) isn't feasible, network adapter vendors provide device drivers that can take network messages and transmit them via the vendors' proprietary hardware. In 1989, Microsoft and 3Com jointly developed the Network Driver Interface Specification (NDIS), which lets protocol drivers communicate with network adapter drivers in a device-independent manner. Network adapter drivers that conform to NDIS are called NDIS drivers or NDIS miniport drivers. The version of NDIS that ships with Windows 2000 is NDIS 5.

On Windows 2000, the NDIS library (\Winnt\System32\Drivers\Ndis.sys) implements the NDIS boundary that exists between TDI transports (typically) and NDIS drivers. As is Tdi.sys, the NDIS library is a helper library that NDIS driver clients use to format commands they send to NDIS drivers. NDIS drivers interface with the library to receive requests and send back responses. Figure 13-18 shows the relationship between various NDIS-related components.

Figure 13-18
NDIS components

One of Microsoft's goals for its network architecture was to let network adapter vendors easily develop NDIS drivers and take driver code and move it between Consumer Windows and Windows 2000. Thus, instead of merely providing the NDIS boundary helper routines, the NDIS library provides NDIS drivers an entire execution environment. NDIS drivers aren't genuine Windows 2000 drivers because they can't function without the encapsulation the NDIS library gives them. This insulation layer wraps NDIS drivers so thoroughly that NDIS drivers don't accept and process IRPs. Rather, the NDIS library receives IRPs from TDI servers and translates the IRPs into calls into the NDIS driver. NDIS drivers also don't have to worry about reentrancy, in which the NDIS library invokes an NDIS driver with a new request before the driver has finished servicing a previous request. Exemption from reentrancy means that NDIS driver writers don't need to worry about complex synchronization, which is made even more tricky because of the parallel execution possible on a multiprocessor.

NOTE The NDIS library hides from both TDI transports and NDIS miniport drivers the fact that it uses IRPs to represent network requests. It does so by requiring TDI transports to allocate an NDIS packet by calling *NdisAllocatePacket* and then passing the packet to an NDIS miniport by calling an NDIS library function (*NdisSend*, for example). On Windows 2000, the NDIS library uses IRPs to implement NDIS packets, but on Consumer Windows, it doesn't.

Although the NDIS library's serialization of NDIS drivers simplifies development, serialization can hamper multiprocessor scalability. Standard NDIS 4 drivers (the Windows NT 4 version of the NDIS library) don't scale well for certain operations on multiprocessors. Microsoft gave developers a deserialized operation option in NDIS 5. NDIS 5 drivers can indicate to the NDIS library that they don't want to be serialized; the NDIS library will then forward requests to the driver as fast as it receives the IRPs that describe the requests. Responsibility for queuing and managing multiple simultaneous requests falls on the NDIS driver, but deserialization confers the benefit of higher multiprocessor performance.

NDIS 5 also includes the following features:

- NDIS drivers can report whether or not their network medium is active, which allows Windows 2000 to display a network connected/disconnected icon on the taskbar. This feature also allows protocols and other applications to be aware of this state and react accordingly. The TCP/IP transport, for example, will use this information to determine when it should reevaluate addressing information it receives from DHCP.

- TCP/IP task offloading allows a miniport to use advanced features of a network adapter to perform operations such as packet checksums and Internet Protocol security (IPSec). This task offloading can improve system performance by relieving the CPU from these operations.

- Fast packet forwarding allows the network adapter hardware to route packets not destined for a computer to remote systems without ever delivering them to the CPU.

- Wake-on-LAN allows a wake-on-LAN-capable network adapter to bring Windows 2000 out of a suspend power state. Events that can trigger the network adapter to signal the system include media connections (such as plugging a network cable into the adapter), the receipt of protocol-specific patterns registered by a protocol (the TCP/IP transport asks to be woken for Address Resolution Protocol [ARP] requests), and, for Ethernet adapters, the receipt of a *magic* packet (a network packet that contains 16 contiguous copies of the adapter's Ethernet address).

- Connection-oriented NDIS allows NDIS drivers to manage connection-oriented media such as Asynchronous Transfer Mode (ATM) devices. (Connection-oriented NDIS is described in more detail shortly.)

The interfaces that the NDIS library provides for NDIS drivers to interface with network adapter hardware are available via functions that translate directly to corresponding functions in the HAL.

EXPERIMENT: Listing the Loaded NDIS Miniports

The Ndiskd kernel debugger extension library includes the *!miniports* and *!miniport* commands, which let you list the loaded miniports using a kernel debugger and, given the address of a miniport block (a data structure Windows 2000 uses to track miniports), see detailed information about the miniport driver. The following example shows the *!miniports* and *!miniport* commands being used to list all the miniports and then specifics about the miniport responsible for interfacing the system to a PCI Ethernet adapter. (Note that WAN miniport drivers work with dial-up connections.)

```
kd> .load ndiskd
Loaded ndiskd extension DLL

kd> !miniports
Driver verifier level: 0
Failed allocations: 0
Miniport Driver Block: 817aa610
  Miniport: 817b1130 RAS Async Adapter
Miniport Driver Block: 81a1ef30
  Miniport: 81a1ea70 Direct Parallel
Miniport Driver Block: 81a21cd0
  Miniport: 81a217f0 WAN Miniport (PPTP)
Miniport Driver Block: 81a22650
  Miniport: 816545f0 WAN Miniport (NetBEUI, Dial Out)
  Miniport: 81a21130 WAN Miniport (IP)
Miniport Driver Block: 81a23290
  Miniport: 81a22130 WAN Miniport (L2TP)
Miniport Driver Block: 81a275f0
  Miniport: 81a25130 Intel 8255x-based PCI Ethernet Adapter (10/100)

kd> !miniport 81a25130
  Miniport 81a25130 : Intel 8255x-based PCI Ethernet Adapter (10/100)
    Flags         : 20413208
                    BUS_MASTER, INDICATES_PACKETS, IGNORE_REQUEST_QUEUE
                    IGNORE_TOKEN_RING_ERRORS, NDIS_5_0,
                    RESOURCES_AVAILABLE, DESERIALIZED, MEDIA_CONNECTED,
                    NOT_SUPPORTS_MEDIA_SENSE,
    PnPFlags      : 00010021
                    PM_SUPPORTED, DEVICE_POWER_ENABLED, RECEIVED_START
    CheckforHang interval: 2 seconds
      CurrentTick   : 0001
      IntervalTicks : 0001
```

```
      InternalResetCount : 0000
      MiniportResetCount : 0000

      References: 3
      UserModeOpenReferences: 0

      PnPDeviceState : PNP_DEVICE_STARTED
      CurrentDevicePowerState : PowerDeviceD0
      Bus PM capabilities
      DeviceD1:                  1
      DeviceD2:                  1
      WakeFromD0:                0
      WakeFromD1:                1
      WakeFromD2:                0
      WakeFromD3:                0

      SystemState                DeviceState
      PowerSystemUnspecified     PowerDeviceUnspecified
      S0                         D0
      S1                         D1
      S2                         PowerDeviceUnspecified
      S3                         PowerDeviceUnspecified
      S4                         D3
      S5                         D3
      SystemWake: S1
      DeviceWake: D1

  WakeupMethodes Enabled 6:
      WAKE_UP_PATTERN_MATCH  WAKE_UP_LINK_CHANGE
  WakeUpCapabilities of the miniport
      MinMagicPacketWakeUp: 4
      MinPatternWakeUp: 4
      MinLinkChangeWakeUp: 4

      Current PnP and PM Settings:        : 00000030
                  DISABLE_WAKE_UP, DISABLE_WAKE_ON_RECONNECT,

      Allocated Resources:
          Memory: f4100000, Length: 1000
          IO Port: 1440, Length: 40
          Memory: f4000000, Length: 100000
          Interrupt Level: 9, Vector: 9
      Translated Allocated Resources:
          Memory: f4100000, Length: 1000
          IO Port: 1440, Length: 40
```

(continued)

EXPERIMENT: Listing the Loaded NDIS Miniports *continued*

```
           Memory: f4000000, Length: 100000
           Interrupt Level: 12, Vector: 39
MediaType        : 802.3
DeviceObject     : 81a25030, PhysDO : 81a93cd0  Next DO: 81a63030
MapRegisters     : 819fc000
FirstPendingPkt: 0
SingleWorkItems:
  [0]: 81a254e8 [1]: 81a254f4 [2]: 81a25500 [3]: 81a2550c
  [4]: 81a25518 [5]: 81a25524
DriverVerifyFlags       : 00000000
Miniport Open Block Queue:
  8164b888: Protocol 816524a8 = NBF, ProtocolContext 81649030
  8191f628: Protocol 81928d88 = TCPIP, ProtocolContext 8191f728
 Miniport Interrupt 81a00970
```

The Flags field for the miniport that was examined indicates that the miniport supports deserialized operation (DESERIALIZED), that the media is currently active (MEDIA_CONNECTED), and that it is an NDIS 5 miniport driver (NDIS_5_0). Also listed are the adapter's system-to-device power-state mappings and the bus resources that the Plug and Play manager assigned to the adapter. (See the section "The Power Manager" on page 546 in Chapter 9 for more information on power-state mappings.)

Variations on the NDIS Miniport

The NDIS model also supports hybrid TDI transport-NDIS drivers, called *NDIS intermediate drivers*. These drivers lie between TDI transports and NDIS drivers. To an NDIS driver, an NDIS intermediate driver looks like a TDI transport; to a TDI transport, an NDIS intermediate driver looks like an NDIS driver. NDIS intermediate drivers can see all network traffic taking place on a system because the drivers lie between protocol drivers and network drivers. Software that provides fault tolerant and load balancing options for network adapters, such as Microsoft's Network Load Balancing Provider, are based on NDIS intermediate drivers. The packet scheduler that is part of Microsoft's Quality of Service (QoS) implementation is another example of an NDIS intermediate driver.

Connection-Oriented NDIS

NDIS 5 introduces a new type of NDIS driver—a connection-oriented NDIS miniport driver. Support for connection-oriented network hardware (for example, ATM) is therefore native in Windows 2000, which makes connection management and establishment standard in the Windows 2000 network architecture. Connection-oriented NDIS drivers use many of the same APIs that standard NDIS drivers use; however, connection-oriented NDIS drivers send packets through established network connections rather than place them on the network medium.

In addition to miniport support for connection-oriented media, NDIS 5 includes definitions for drivers that work to support a connection-oriented miniport driver:

- Call managers are NDIS drivers that provide call setup and teardown services for connection-oriented clients (described shortly). A call manager uses a connection-oriented miniport to exchange signaling messages with other network entities such as network switches or other call managers. A call manager supports one or more signaling protocols, such as ATM User-Network Interface (UNI) 3.1.

- An integrated miniport call manager (MCM) is a connection-oriented miniport driver that also provides call manager services to connection-oriented clients. An MCM is essentially an NDIS miniport driver with a built-in call manager.

- A connection-oriented client uses the call setup and teardown services of a call manager or MCM and the send and receive services of a connection-oriented NDIS miniport driver. A connection-oriented client can provide its own protocol services to higher levels in the network stack, or it can implement an emulation layer that interfaces connectionless legacy protocols and connection-oriented media. An example of an emulation layer fulfilled by a connection-oriented client is a LAN emulation (LANE), which hides the connected-oriented characteristics of ATM and presents a connectionless media (such as Ethernet) to protocols above it.

Figure 13-19 shows the relationships between these components.

Figure 13-19
Connection-oriented NDIS drivers

EXPERIMENT: Using Network Monitor to Capture Network Packets

Windows 2000 Server comes with a tool named Network Monitor that lets you capture packets that flow through one or more NDIS miniport drivers on your system by installing an NDIS intermediate driver. Before you can use Network Monitor, you need to have the Windows 2000 Network Monitor Tools installed on your system. To install these tools, open Add/Remove Programs in Control Panel, and select Add/Remove Windows Components. Select Management And Monitoring Tools, click Details, select Network Monitor Tools, and click OK.

After you've installed Network Monitor Tools, you install Network Monitor by following these steps:

1. Bring up the Network And Dial-Up Connections application by right-clicking on the My Network Places icon on the desktop and selecting Properties, or by selecting Network And Dial-Up Connections from the Settings option on the Start menu.

2. Right-click on a local adapter, select Properties, and click the Install button in the Local Area Connection Properties dialog box.

3. Select Protocol, and click the Add button.

4. Choose Network Monitor Driver, and click OK

After the Network Monitor driver has installed, you can launch Network Monitor by selecting it from the Programs, Administrative Tools folder in the Start menu.

Network Monitor might ask you which network connection you want to monitor. After selecting one, begin monitoring by pressing the Start Capture button in the toolbar. Perform operations that generate network activity on the connection you're monitoring, and after you see that Network Monitor has captured packets, stop monitoring by clicking the Stop And View Capture button (the stop button that has glasses next to it). Network Monitor will present a view of the capture data like the following:

(continued)

EXPERIMENT: Using Network Monitor to Capture Network Packets *continued*

The screen shot shows the SMB (CIFS) packets that Network Monitor captured as remote files were accessed from the system. If you double-click on a line, Network Monitor will switch to a view of the packet that breaks it apart to show various layered application and protocol headers as shown in the following screen shot:

Network Monitor also includes a number of other features, such as capture triggers and filters, that make it a powerful tool for troubleshooting network problems.

Binding

The final piece in the Windows 2000 networking architecture puzzle is the way in which the components at the various layers—networking API layer, TDI transport driver layer, NDIS driver layer—locate one another. The name of the process that connects the layers is *binding*. You've witnessed binding taking place if you've changed your network configuration by adding or removing a component using Network Properties.

When you install a networking component, you must supply an INF file for the component. (INF files are described in Chapter 9.) This file includes directions that setup API routines must follow to install and configure the component, including binding dependencies or binding relationships. A developer can specify

binding dependencies for a proprietary component so that the SCM will not only load the component in the correct order but will also load the component only if other components the proprietary component depends on are present on the system. Binding relationships, which the bind engine determines with the aid of additional information in a component's INF file, establish connections between components at the various layers. The connections specify which components a network component on one layer can use on the layer beneath it.

For example, the Workstation service (redirector) will automatically bind to the NBF (NetBEUI) and TCP/IP protocols if they are both present on a system. The order of the binding, which you can examine on the Adapters And Bindings tab in the Advanced Settings dialog box, shown in Figure 13-20, determines the priority of the binding. (See the section "Network-Resource Name Resolution" on page 814 for instructions on how to launch the Advanced Settings dialog box.) When the redirector receives a request to access a remote file, it submits the request to both protocol drivers simultaneously. When the response comes, the redirector waits until it has also received responses from any higher-priority protocol drivers. Only then will the redirector return the result to the caller. Thus, it can be advantageous to reorder bindings so that bindings of high priority are also the most performance efficient or applicable to most of the computers in your network. You can also manually remove bindings with the Advanced Settings dialog box.

Figure 13-20
Editing bindings with the Advanced Settings dialog box

The Bind value, in the Linkage subkey of a network component's registry configuration key, stores binding information for that component. For example, if you examine HKLM\SYSTEM\CurrentControlSet\Services\LanmanWorkstation\Linkage\Bind, you'll see the binding information for the Workstation service.

Layered Network Services

Windows 2000 includes network services that build on the APIs and components we've presented in this chapter. Describing the capabilities and detailed internal implementation of these services is outside the scope of this book, but this section provides a brief overview of remote access, Active Directory, Network Load Balancing, File Replication service (FRS), and Distributed File System (DFS). In addition, Windows 2000 supports several services that are based on extensions to the TCP/IP protocol. These include network address translation (NAT), Internet Protocol security (IPSec), and Quality of Service (QoS), and we conclude with a look at each.

Remote Access

Remote access, which is available with Windows 2000 Server, allows remote access clients to connect to remote access servers and access network resources such as files, printers, and network services as if the client were physically connected to the remote access server's network. Windows 2000 provides two types of remote access:

- Dial-up remote access is used by clients that connect to a remote access server via a telephone or other telecommunications infrastructure. The telecommunications medium is used to create a temporary physical or virtual connection between the client and the server.

- Virtual private network (VPN) remote access lets a VPN client establish a virtual point-to-point connection to the server over an IP network such as the Internet.

Remote access differs from remote control solutions because remote access acts as a proxy connection to a Windows 2000 network, whereas remote control software executes applications on a server, presenting a user interface to the client.

Active Directory

Active Directory is the Windows 2000 implementation of Lightweight Directory Access Protocol (LDAP) directory services. Active Directory is based on a database that stores objects representing resources defined by applications in a Windows 2000 network. For example, the structure and membership of a Windows 2000 domain, including the user account and password information, are stored in Active Directory.

Object classes and the attributes that define properties of objects are specified by a *schema*. The objects in the Active Directory schema are hierarchically arranged, much like the registry's logical organization, where container objects can store other objects, including other container objects. (See Chapter 8 for more information on container objects.)

Active Directory supports a number of APIs that clients can use to access objects within an Active Directory database:

- The LDAP C API is a C language API that uses the LDAP networking protocol. Applications written in C or C++ can use this API directly, and applications written in other languages can access the APIs through translation layers.

- Active Directory Service Interfaces (ADSI) is a COM interface to Active Directory that abstracts the details of LDAP programming. ADSI supports multiple languages, including Microsoft Visual Basic, C, and Microsoft Visual C++. ADSI can also be used by Microsoft Windows Script Host (WSH) applications.

- Messaging API (MAPI) is supported for compatibility with Microsoft Exchange client and Outlook Address Book client applications.

- Security Account Manager (SAM) APIs are built on top of Active Directory to provide an interface to logon authentication packages such as MSV1_0 (\Winnt\System32\Msv1_0.dll, which is used for legacy NT LAN Manager authentication) and Kerberos (\Winnt\System32\Kdcsvc.dll).

- Windows NT 4 networking APIs (Net APIs) are used by Windows NT 4 clients to gain access to Active Directory through SAM.

Active Directory is implemented as a database file that is named \Winnt\Ntds\Ntds.dit, and that is replicated across the domain controllers in a domain. The Active Directory directory service, which is a Win32 service that executes in

835

the Local Security Authority Subsystem (Lsass) process, manages the database, using DLLs that implement the on-disk structure of the database as well as provide transaction-based updates to protect the integrity of the database. The Active Directory database store is based on a version of the Extensible Storage Engine (ESE) database that is used by Microsoft Exchange Server version 5.5 client/server messaging and groupware. Figure 13-21 shows the Active Directory architecture.

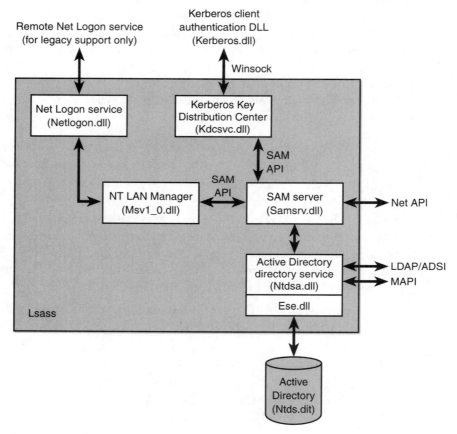

Figure 13-21
Active Directory architecture

Network Load Balancing

As we stated earlier in the chapter, Network Load Balancing, which is included with Windows 2000 Advanced Server, is based on NDIS intermediate-driver technology. Network Load Balancing allows for the creation of a cluster containing up to 32 computers, which are called *cluster hosts* in Network Load Balancing. The cluster maintains a single virtual IP address that is published for access by clients, and client requests go to all the computers in the cluster. However, only one cluster host responds to the request. The Network Load Balancing NDIS drivers effectively partition the client space among available cluster hosts in a distributed manner. This way, each host handles its portion of incoming client requests and every client request always gets handled by one and only one host. The cluster host that determines it should handle a client request allows the request to propagate up to the TCP/IP protocol driver and eventually a server application; the other cluster hosts don't. If a cluster host fails, the rest of the cluster realizes that the cluster host is no longer a candidate for processing requests and redistributes the incoming client requests to the remaining cluster hosts. No new client requests are sent to the downed cluster host. Another cluster host can be added to the cluster as a replacement, and it will then seamlessly start handling client requests.

Network Load Balancing isn't a general-purpose clustering solution because the server application that clients communicate with must have certain characteristics: the first is that it must be TCP/IP-based, and the second is that it must be able to handle client requests on any system in a Network Load Balancing cluster. This second requirement typically means that an application that must have access to shared state in order to service client requests must manage the shared state itself—Network Load Balancing doesn't include services for automatically distributing shared state across cluster hosts. Applications that are ideally suited for Network Load Balancing include a Web server that serves static content, Windows Media Server, and Terminal Services. Figure 13-22 shows an example of a Network Load Balancing operation.

Figure 13-22
Network Load Balancing operation

File Replication Service

File Replication service (FRS) is included with Windows 200 Server. Its primary purpose is to replicate the contents of a domain controller's \SYSVOL directory, which is where Windows 2000 domain controllers store logon scripts and group policies. (Group policies permit administrators to define usage and security policies for the computers that belong to a domain.) In addition, FRS can be used to replicate Distributed File System (DFS) shares between systems. FRS allows for distributed multimaster replication, which enables any server to perform replication activity. When a replicated directory or file is changed, the changes are propagated to the other domain controllers.

The fundamental concept in FRS is a *replica set*, which consists of two or more systems that replicate between themselves the contents of a directory tree according to an administratively defined schedule and topology. Only directories on NTFS volumes can be replicated because FRS relies on the NTFS change

journal to detect changes to files in directories in a replica set. Because FRS is based on multimaster replication, it can theoretically support hundreds or even thousands of systems as part of a replica set, and the computers of a replica set can be connected with arbitrary network topologies (such as ring, star, or mesh). Computers can also be members of multiple replica sets.

FRS is implemented as a Win32 service (\Winnt\System32\Ntfrs.exe) that uses authenticated RPC with encryption to communicate between instances of itself running on different computers. In addition, because Active Directory contains its own replication capabilities, FRS uses Active Directory APIs to retrieve FRS configuration information from a domain's Active Directory.

Distributed File System

Distributed File System (DFS) is a service that layers on top of the Workstation service to connect together file shares into a single namespace. The file shares can reside on the same or on different computers, and DFS provides client access to the resources in a location-transparent manner. The root of a DFS namespace must be a file share defined on a Windows 2000 server.

In addition to delivering a unified network-resource namespace, DFS provides other benefits through DFS replica sets, which are based on FRS replica sets. An administrator can create DFS replica sets from two or more shares so that FRS copies data between the shares of a replica set to keep their contents synchronized. DFS provides a limited form of load balancing by randomly selecting a member of a replica set to fulfill a client request for data on the replica set. In addition, DFS achieves high availability by routing requests to the working member or members of a replica set when a member becomes unavailable.

The components that make up the DFS architecture are shown in Figure 13-23. The server-side implementation of DFS consists of a Win32 service (\Winnt\System32\Dfssvc.exe) and a device driver (\Winnt\System32\Drivers\Dfs.sys). The DFS service is responsible for exporting DFS topology management interfaces and maintaining the DFS topology in either the registry (on non–Active Directory systems) or Active Directory. The DFS driver performs topology lookups when it receives a client request so that it can direct the client to the system where the file it is requesting resides.

Figure 13-23
DFS components

On the client side, the implementation of DFS relies on support from the MUP driver and the NetWare and CIFS redirector. When a client issues a file I/O request that specifies a file in the DFS namespace, the MUP driver on the client communicates with a DFS server by using the appropriate redirector.

TCP/IP Extensions

Other Windows 2000 networking services extend basic networking features of the TCP/IP protocol driver by relying on add-on drivers that integrate with the TCP/IP protocol driver using private interfaces. These include network address translation (NAT), Internet Protocol security (IPSec), and Quality of Service (QoS).

Network Address Translation

Network address translation (NAT) is a routing service that allows multiple local IP addresses to map to a single IP address. Without NAT, each computer of a LAN must be assigned a public IP address to communicate across the Internet. NAT allows one computer of the LAN to be assigned an IP address and the other computers to be connected to the Internet through that computer. NAT translates between LAN addresses and the public IP address as necessary, routing packets from the Internet to the appropriate LAN computer.

NAT components on Windows 2000 consist of a NAT device driver that interfaces with the TCP/IP stack as well as editors that an administrator uses to define address translations. NAT can be installed as a protocol with the Routing And Remote Access MMC snap-in or by configuring Internet connection sharing using the Network And Dial-Up Connections tool (though NAT is much more configurable when installed using the Routing And Remote Access MMC snap-in).

Internet Protocol Security

Internet Protocol security (IPSec), which is integrated with the Windows 2000 TCP/IP stack, provides protection for IP data against snooping and manipulation and defends against IP-based attacks. Both goals are met through cryptography-based protection services, security protocols, and dynamic key management. IPSec-based communication includes these properties:

- Authentication verifies the origin and integrity of an IP message.

- Integrity protects IP data from being modified in transit without being detected.

- Confidentiality uses encryption to ensure that only valid recipients of a message can decipher the contents of the message.

- Antireplay ensures that each packet is unique and can't be reused. This property prevents a snooper from replying to captured messages to establish a session or gain unauthorized access to data.

IPSec on Windows 2000 relies on group policies that are stored in Active Directory for configuration, and it uses Active Directory's Kerberos version 5 authentication to authenticate computers that participate in IPSec message exchange. IPSec uses private/public keys pairs based on the Windows 2000 CryptoAPI certificate services for encrypting and decrypting IPSec message data and passwords as part of its authentication process. (See the section "Encrypting File System Security" on page 766 in Chapter 12 for more information on CryptoAPI.)

IPSec's implementation consists of an IPSec device driver (\Winnt\System32\Drivers\Ipsec.sys) that integrates with the TCP/IP protocol driver. In user space, a policy agent obtains IPSec configuration information from Active Directory and passes IPSec filtering information (IP address filters for which

IPSec communications should be used) to the IPSec driver and security settings to an Internet Key Exchange (IKE) module. The IKE module waits for security association requests from the IPSec driver and negotiates the requests, passing the results back to the IPSec driver for use during authentication and encryption.

Quality of Service

If no special measures are taken, IP traffic is delivered over a network on a first-come-first-serve basis. Applications have no control over the priority of their messages and can experience *bursty* network behavior, where they occasionally obtain high throughput and low latencies but otherwise receive poor network performance. Although this level of service is acceptable in most situations, an increasing number of network applications demand more consistent service levels, or *Quality of Service* (QoS) guarantees. Video conferencing, media streaming, and enterprise resource planning (ERP) are examples of applications that require good network performance. QoS allows an application to specify minimum bandwidth and maximum latencies, which can be satisfied only if every networking software and hardware component between a sender and receiver supports QoS standards such as IEEE 802.1p, an industry standard that specifies the format of QoS packets and how OSI layer 2 devices (switches and network adapters) respond to them.

Windows 2000 QoS support is based on a handful of Microsoft-defined Winsock APIs that allow an application to request QoS for traffic over their Winsock sockets. For example, an application uses *WSCInstallQOSTemplate* to install a QoS template that specifies desired bandwidth and latency. (Only applications with administrative privileges can use QoS.) A second API, the traffic control (TC) API, lets an administrative application more precisely control the traffic flow over networks attached to the computer.

The heart of the Windows 2000 QoS implementation is the Resource Reservation Setup Protocol (RSVP) Win32 service (\Winnt\System32\Rsvp.exe), as shown in Figure 13-24. The RSVP Winsock service provider (\Winnt\System32\Rsvp.dll) communicates application QoS requests via RPC to the RSVP service. The RSVP service in turn uses the TC API to control traffic flow. The TC API, which is implemented in \Winnt\System32\Traffic.dll, sends I/O control commands to the Generic Packet Classifier (GPC) driver (\Winnt\System32\Drivers\Msgpc.sys). The GPC driver communicates closely with the QoS packet scheduler NDIS intermediate driver (\Winnt\System32\Drivers\

Psched.sys) to control the flow of packets to the network from the computer so that the QoS levels promised to particular applications can be met and to ensure that appropriate QoS headers can be placed on packets for which QoS is desired.

Figure 13-24
QoS architecture

Conclusion

The Windows 2000 network architecture provides a flexible infrastructure for networking APIs, network protocol drivers, and network adapter drivers. The Windows 2000 networking architecture takes advantage of I/O layering to give

networking support the extensibility to evolve as computer networking evolves. When new protocols appear, developers can write a TDI transport to implement the protocol on Windows 2000. Similarly, new APIs can interface to existing Windows 2000 protocol drivers. Finally, the range of networking APIs implemented on Windows 2000 affords network application developers a range of possible implementations, each with different programming models and protocol support.

GLOSSARY

access-control list (ACL) The part of a security descriptor that enumerates who has what access to an object. The owner of an object can change the object's ACL to allow or disallow others access to the object. An ACL is made up of an ACL header and zero or more access-control entry (ACE) structures. An ACL with zero ACEs is called a null ACL and indicates that no user has access to the object.

access token A data structure that contains the security identification of a process or a thread, which includes its security ID (SID), the list of groups that the user is a member of, and the list of privileges that are enabled and disabled. Each process has a primary access token that it inherits by default from its creating process.

add-device routine A routine implemented by drivers that supports Plug and Play. The Plug and Play manager sends a driver notification via this routine whenever a device for which the driver is responsible is detected. In this routine, a driver typically allocates a device object to represent the device.

Address Windowing Extensions (AWE) A mechanism in Windows 2000 that allows a 32-bit application to allocate up to 64 GB of physical memory and then map views, or windows, into its 2-GB virtual address space. Using AWE puts the burden of managing mappings of virtual-to-physical memory on the programmer but solves the immediate need of being able to directly access more physical memory than can be mapped at any one time in a 32-bit process address space.

affinity mask A bitmask that specifies the processors on which the thread is allowed to run. The initial thread affinity mask is inherited from the process affinity mask.

aging A process performed on a page that increments a count indicating that the page hasn't been referenced since the last working set trim scan. On a single-processor system, the working set manager tries to remove pages that haven't been accessed recently. It does this by first clearing the accessed bit in the hardware page table entry (PTE) and then later checking the bit to see whether the page has been accessed. If the bit remains clear, the page wasn't accessed between scans and is aged. Later, the age of pages is used to locate candidate pages to remove from the working set.

alertable wait state A thread state that the thread enters either by waiting on an object handle and specifying that its wait is alertable (with the Win32 *WaitForMultipleObjectsEx* function) or by testing directly whether it has a pending APC (using *SleepEx*). In both cases, if a user-mode APC is pending, the kernel interrupts (alerts) the thread, transfers control to the APC routine, and resumes the thread's execution when the APC routine completes. User-mode APCs are delivered to a thread only when it's in an alertable wait state.

allocation granularity The granularity with which virtual memory is allocated. Windows 2000 aligns each region of reserved process address space to begin on an integral boundary defined by the system allocation granularity value, which can be retrieved from the Win32 *GetSystemInfo* function. Currently, this value is 64 KB. This size was chosen so

that if support were added for future processors with large page sizes (for example, up to 64 KB), the risk of requiring changes to applications that made assumptions about allocation alignment would be reduced. (Windows 2000 kernel-mode code isn't subject to the same restrictions; it can reserve memory on a single-page granularity.)

alternative hive A hive that acts as a backup to the crucial SYSTEM hive. The alternate hive is stored in \Winnt\System32\Config as System.alt. Whenever a hive sync flushes dirty sectors to the SYSTEM hive, the hive sync also updates the System.alt hive. If the configuration manager detects that the SYSTEM hive is corrupt when the system boots, the configuration manager attempts to load the alternate hive. If that hive is usable, it then uses that alternate to update the original SYSTEM hive.

APC queue A queue in which asynchronous procedure calls (APCs) waiting to execute reside. The APC queues (one for user mode and one for kernel mode) are thread-specific—each thread has its own APC queues (unlike the DPC queue, which is processor-wide).

asymmetric multiprocessing (ASMP) A system of processing on a multiprocessor system that typically selects one processor to execute operating system code while other processors run only user code.

asynchronous I/O An I/O model that allows an application to issue an I/O request and then continue executing while the request is completed. This type of I/O can improve an application's throughput because it allows the application to continue with other work while an I/O operation is in progress.

asynchronous procedure call (APC) A function that provides a way for user programs and system code to execute code in the context of a particular user thread (and hence a particular process address space). An APC can be either kernel mode or user mode. (Kernel-mode APCs don't require "permission" from a target thread to run in that thread's context, as user-mode APCs do.)

atomic transaction A technique for handling modifications to a database so that system failures don't affect the correctness or integrity of the database. The basic tenet of atomic transactions is that some database operations, called transactions, are all-or-nothing propositions. The separate disk updates that make up the transaction must be executed atomically; that is, once the transaction begins to execute, all its disk updates must be completed. If a system failure interrupts the transaction, the part that has been completed must be undone, or rolled back. The rollback operation returns the database to a previously known and consistent state, as if the transaction had never occurred. *See also* transaction.

attribute list A special kind of file attribute in an NTFS file header that contains additional attributes. The attribute list is created if a particular file has too many attributes to fit in the master file table (MFT) record. The attribute list attribute contains the name and type code of each of the file's attributes and the file reference of the MFT record where the attribute is located.

authentication packages Dynamic-link libraries (DLLs) that run in the context of the Lsass process and that implement Windows 2000 authentication policy. An authentication DLL is responsible for checking whether a given username and password match, and if so, returning to Lsass information detailing the user's security identity. Windows 2000 authentication packages include Kerberos and MSV1_0.

automatic working set trimming A technique the memory manager uses when physical memory runs low to increase the amount of free memory available in the system.

bad-cluster file A system file (filename $BadClus) that records any bad spots on the disk volume.

balance set manager A system thread that wakes up once per second to check and possibly initiate various scheduling and memory management–related events.

basic disk A disk that relies on the MS-DOS-style partitioning scheme. *See also* dynamic disk.

bitmap file A system file (filename $Bitmap) in which NTFS records the allocation state of the volume. The data attribute for the bitmap file contains a bitmap, each of whose bits represents a cluster on the volume, identifying whether the cluster is free or has been allocated to a file.

boot code Instructions executed when a system is booted.

boot device drivers Device drivers necessary to boot the system.

boot file A system file (filename $Boot) that stores the Windows 2000 bootstrap code.

boot partition The partition that contains core operating system files. The boot partition is identified by the system at startup. The code in a master boot record (MBR) scans the primary partition table until it locates a partition containing a flag that signals the partition is bootable. When the MBR finds at least one such flag, it reads the first sector from the flagged partition into memory and transfers control to code within the partition.

bus driver Driver that services a bus controller, adapter, bridge, or any device that has child devices. Bus drivers are required drivers, and Microsoft generally provides them; each type of bus (such as PCI, PCMCIA, and USB) on a system has one bus driver.

cache manager The component of the Windows 2000 executive that provides systemwide caching services for NTFS and other file system drivers, including network file system drivers (servers and redirectors).

careful write A technique for constructing a file system's I/O and caching support. *See also* write-through.

change journal An internal file where an NTFS file system can record information that allows applications to efficiently monitor file and directory changes. A change journal is usually large enough to virtually guarantee that applications get a chance to process changes without missing any.

checked build A special debug version of Windows 2000 Professional that is available only as part of the MSDN Professional (or Universal) subscription. (No checked build is available for Windows 2000 Server.) The checked build is created by compiling the Windows 2000 sources with the compile-time flag DEBUG set to TRUE.

checkpoint record A record that helps NTFS determine what processing would be needed to recover a volume if a crash were to occur immediately. This record also includes redo and undo information.

class driver A type of kernel-mode device driver that implements the I/O processing for a particular class of devices, such as disk, tape, or CD-ROM.

clock algorithm A working set page replacement policy implemented on uniprocessor systems, similar to a least recently used policy (as implemented in most versions of UNIX).

clock interrupt handler A system routine that updates the system time and then decrements a counter that tracks how long the current thread has run.

cluster factor The cluster size on a volume, which is established when a user formats the volume with either the *format* command or the Disk Management Microsoft Management Console (MMC) snap-in.

cluster remapping A process in which NTFS dynamically retrieves good data from a cluster with a bad sector, allocates a new cluster, and copies the data to the new cluster.

clustering A method by which the memory manager resolves a page fault by reading into memory several pages near the page explicitly accessed.

clusters Same-size allocation units into which a volume is divided. Each cluster must be uniquely numbered using 16 bits.

collided page fault A fault that occurs when another thread or process faults a page that is currently being in-paged.

commitment The process by which the memory manager keeps track of private committed memory usage on a global basis.

common model A set of classes in the Common Information Model (CIM) that represent objects that are specific to management areas of a system but independent of a particular implementation. These classes are considered an extension of the CIM core model. *See also* core model.

complete memory dump A memory dump that contains all of physical memory at the time of the crash. This type of dump requires that a page file be at least the size of physical memory. Because it can require an inordinately large page file on large memory systems, this type of dump file is the least common. Windows NT 4 supported only this type of crash dump file.

completion port A mechanism to deliver I/O completion notification to threads. Once a file is associated with a completion port, any asynchronous I/O operations that complete on the file result in a completion packet being queued to the completion port. A thread can wait for any outstanding I/Os to complete on multiple files simply by waiting for a completion packet to be queued to the completion port. With completion ports, concurrency, or the number of threads that an application has actively servicing client requests, is controlled with the aid of the system.

configuration manager A major component of the executive that's responsible for implementing and managing the system registry.

container object A namespace object that can hold other objects, including other container objects. Examples of containers are directories in the file system namespace and keys in the registry namespace.

context switch The procedure of saving the volatile machine state associated with a running thread, loading another thread's volatile state, and starting the new thread's execution.

control objects A set of kernel objects that establishes semantics for controlling various operating system functions. This set includes the kernel process object, the asynchronous procedure call (APC) object, the deferred procedure call (DPC) object, and several objects the I/O system uses, such as the interrupt object.

core model A set of classes in the Common Information Model (CIM) provided as part of the WBEM standard. These classes are CIM's basic language and represent objects that apply to all areas of management. *See also* common model.

deferred procedure call (DPC) A routine that performs most of the work involved in handling a device interrupt after the interrupt service routine (ISR) executes. The DPC routine executes at an interrupt request level (IRQL) that is lower than that of the ISR to avoid blocking other interrupts unnecessarily. A DPC routine initiates I/O completion and starts the next queued I/O operation on a device.

deferred procedure call (DPC) object A kernel control object that describes a request to defer interrupt processing to DPC/dispatch level. (See interrupt request levels (IRQLs).) This object isn't visible to user-mode programs but is visible to device drivers and other system code. The most important piece of information the DPC object contains is the address of the system function that the kernel will call when it processes the DPC interrupt.

demand-paging policies A fetch policy that loads a page into physical memory only when a page fault occurs. In a demand-paging system, a process incurs many page faults when its threads first begin executing because the threads reference the initial set of pages they need to get going. Once this set of pages is loaded into memory, the paging activity of the process decreases.

device drivers Loadable kernel-mode modules (typically ending in .sys) that interface between the I/O system and the relevant hardware. Device drivers on Windows 2000 don't manipulate hardware devices directly, but rather they call parts of the hardware application layer (HAL) to interface with the hardware.

device ID A device identifier reported to the Plug and Play manager. The identifiers are bus-specific; for a USB bus, an identifier consists of a vendor ID (VID) for the hardware vendor that made the device and a product ID (PID) that the vendor assigned to the device.

device instance ID (DIID) An identifier consisting of a device ID and an instance ID that the Plug and Play manager uses to locate the device's key in the enumeration branch of the registry (HKLM\SYSTEM\CurrentControlSet\Enum).

device object A data structure that represents a physical, logical, or virtual device on the system and describes its characteristics, such as the alignment it requires for buffers and the location of its device queue to hold incoming I/O request packets.

device tree An internal tree the Plug and Play manager creates that represents the relationships between devices. Nodes in the tree are called devnodes. *See also* devnode.

devnode A node in a device tree. A devnode contains information about the device objects that represent the device as well as other Plug and Play–related information the Plug and Play manager stores. *See also* device tree.

dirty page threshold The number of pages that the system cache keeps in memory before waking up the cache manager's lazy writer system thread to write out pages back to the disk. This value is computed at system initialization time and depends on physical memory size and the value of the registry value HKLM\SYSTEM\CurrentControlSet\Control\ Session Manager\Memory Management\LargeSystemCache.

disk group Dynamic disks that share a common database. VERITAS's commercial volume-management software for Windows 2000 includes disk groups, but the Windows 2000 Logical Disk Manager (LDM) implementation includes only one disk group.

dispatch code Instructions of assembly language code stored in an interrupt object when it is initialized. When an interrupt occurs, this code is executed.

dispatch routines The main functions that a device driver provides. Some examples of dispatch routines are open, close, read, and write, and any other capabilities the device, file system, or network supports. When called on to perform an I/O operation, the I/O manager generates an IRP and calls a driver through one of the driver's dispatch routines.

dispatcher A set of routines in the kernel that implement Windows 2000 scheduling. Windows 2000 doesn't have a single "scheduler" module or routine—the code is spread throughout the kernel in which scheduling-related events occur.

dispatcher database A set of data structures the kernel maintains to make thread-scheduling decisions. The dispatcher database keeps track of which threads are waiting to execute and which processors are executing which threads. *See also* dispatcher ready queue.

dispatcher header A data structure that contains the object type, the signaled state, and a list of the threads waiting on that object.

dispatcher objects A set of kernel objects that incorporate synchronization capabilities and alter or affect thread scheduling. The dispatcher objects include the kernel thread, mutex (called *mutant* internally), event, kernel event pair, semaphore, timer, and waitable timer.

dispatcher ready queue The most important structure in the dispatcher database (located at *KiDispatcherReadyListHead*). The dispatcher ready queue is really a series of queues, one queue for each scheduling priority. The queues contain threads that are in the ready state, waiting to be scheduled for execution.

display driver Driver that translates device-independent graphics requests into device-specific requests. The device-specific requests are then paired with a kernel-mode video miniport driver to complete video display support. A display driver is responsible for implementing drawing operations, either by writing directly to the frame buffer or by communicating with the graphics accelerator chip on the controller.

driver object Data structure that represents an individual driver in the system and records for the I/O manager the address of each of the driver's dispatch routines (entry points).

driver support routines Routines that device drivers call to accomplish their I/O requests.

dynamic disk A disk that supports multipartition volumes, providing a more flexible partitioning scheme than that of a basic disk. *See also* basic disk.

dynamic-link library (DLL) A set of callable subroutines linked as a binary image that can be dynamically loaded by applications that use them.

environment subsystems User processes that expose the native operating system services to user applications, thus providing an operating system environment, or personality. Windows 2000 ships with three environment subsystems: Win32, POSIX, and OS/2 1.2.

event An object with a persistent state (signaled or not signaled) that can be used for synchronization; also, a system occurrence that triggers an action.

exception A synchronous condition that results from the execution of a particular instruction. Running a single program with the same data under the same conditions can reproduce exceptions.

exception dispatcher A kernel module that services all exceptions, except those simple enough to be resolved by the trap handler. The exception dispatcher's job is to find an exception handler that can "dispose of" the exception.

executive The upper layer of Ntoskrnl.exe. (The kernel is the lower layer.) The executive contains the base operating system services, such as the process and thread manager, the virtual memory manager, the memory manager, the security reference monitor, the I/O system, and the cache manager. *See also* kernel.

executive objects Objects implemented by various components of the executive (such as the process manager, memory manager, I/O subsystem, and so on). The executive objects and object services are primitives that the environment subsystems use to construct their own versions of objects and other resources. Because executive objects are typically created either by an environment subsystem on behalf of a user application or by various components of the operating system as part of their normal operation, many of them contain (encapsulate) one or more kernel objects. *See also* kernel objects.

executive resources Resources that provide both exclusive access (such as a mutex) as well as shared read access (multiple readers sharing read-only access to a structure). Because executive resources are available only to kernel-mode code, they aren't accessible from the Win32 API.

extended partition A special partition type that contains a master boot record (MBR) with its own partition table. By using extended partitions, Microsoft's operating systems overcome the apparent limit of four partitions per disk. In general, the recursion that extended partitions permit can continue indefinitely, which means that no upper limit exists to the number of possible partitions on a disk. *See also* partition.

fast I/O A means of reading or writing a cached file without going through the work of generating an I/O request packet (IRP).

fast LPC A special interprocess communication facility used to send messages between threads.

file mapping objects Win32 API underlying primitives in the memory manager that are used to implement shared memory (called *section objects* internally). *See also* section object.

file reference A 64-bit value that identifies a file on an NTFS volume. The file reference consists of a file number and a sequence number. The file number corresponds to the position of the file's file record in the master file table minus 1 (or to the position of the base file record minus 1 if the file has more than one file record).

file system driver (FSD) A type of kernel-mode device driver that accepts I/O requests to files and satisfies the requests by issuing its own, more explicit, requests to physical device drivers. *See also* local file system driver (FSD), network file system driver (FSD).

file system filter driver A type of kernel-mode device driver that intercepts I/O requests, performs additional processing, and passes them on to lower-level drivers.

file system format Defines the way that file data is stored on storage media and impacts a file system's features. For example, a format that doesn't allow user permissions to be associated with files and directories can't support security. A file system format can also impose limits on the sizes of files and storage devices that the file system supports.

filter device object (FiDO) A device object that can be part of a devnode. One or more optional FiDOs can layer either between the physical device object (PDO) and the functional device object (FDO) or above the FDO. *See also* devnode, functional device object (FDO), physical device object (PDO).

filter driver *See* file system filter driver.

foreground application The process that owns the thread that owns the window that's in focus.

free build The version of the Windows 2000 system that can be purchased as a retail product. It is built with full compiler optimizations turned on and has internal symbol table information stripped out from the images. *See also* checked build.

function driver The main device driver that provides the operational interface for its device. It is a required driver unless the device is used raw (an implementation in which I/O is done by the bus driver and any bus filter drivers, such as SCSI PassThru). A function driver is the driver that knows the most about a particular device and is usually the only driver that accesses device-specific registers.

functional device object (FDO) A device object that is a required part of a devnode. The function driver that the Plug and Play manager loads to manage a detected device creates the FDO. An FDO represents the logical interface to a device. *See also* devnode, filter device object (FiDO), physical device object (PDO).

Graphical Identification and Authentication (GINA) A user-mode DLL that runs in the Winlogon process and that Winlogon uses to obtain a user's name and password or smart card PIN. The standard GINA is \Winnt\System32\Msgina.dll.

handle An object identifier. A process receives a handle to an object when it creates or opens an object by name. Referring to an object by its handle is faster than using its name because the object manager can skip the name lookup and find the object directly.

handle table A table that contains pointers to all the objects that the process has opened a handle to. Handle tables are implemented as a three-level scheme, similar to the way that the x86 memory management unit implements virtual-to-physical address translation.

hardware abstraction layer (HAL) A loadable kernel-mode module (Hal.dll) that provides the low-level interface to the hardware platform on which Windows 2000 is running. The HAL hides hardware-dependent details such as I/O interfaces, interrupt controllers, and multiprocessor communication mechanisms—any functions that are architecture-specific and machine-dependent.

hash A statistically unique value that is generated from a block of data (for example, a file) using cryptographic algorithms. Because different data results in different hashes, hashes can be used to detect changes to data from corruption or tampering. The Windows 2000 driver signing facility uses hashes.

heap A region of one or more pages that can be subdivided and allocated in smaller chunks by a set of functions provided by the heap manager.

heap manager A set of functions that allocate and deallocate variable amounts of memory (not on a page-size granularity). The heap manager functions exist in two places: Ntdll.dll and Ntoskrnl.exe. The subsystem APIs (such as the Win32 heap APIs) use the copy in Ntdll, and various executive components and device drivers use the copy in Ntoskrnl.

hive One of a number of files stored on disk that contain registry information. Each hive contains a registry tree, which has a key that serves as the root or starting point of the tree.

hyperspace A special region used to map the process working set list and to temporarily map other physical pages for such operations as zeroing a page on the free list (when the zero list is empty and a zero page is needed), invalidating page table entries in other page tables (such as when a page is removed from the standby list), and on process creation setting up a new process's address space.

I/O completion routine A routine implemented by a layered driver that will notify the driver when a lower-level driver finishes processing an I/O request packet (IRP). For example, the I/O manager calls a file system driver's I/O completion routine after a device driver finishes transferring data to or from a file. The completion routine notifies the file system driver about the operation's success, failure, or cancellation, and it allows the file system driver to perform cleanup operations.

I/O request packet (IRP) A data structure that controls how the I/O operation is processed at each stage. Most I/O requests are represented by an IRP, which travels from one I/O system component to another.

I/O subsystem API The internal executive system services (such as *NtReadFile* and *NtWriteFile*) that subsystem DLLs call to implement a subsystem's documented I/O functions.

I/O system The Windows 2000 executive component that accepts I/O requests (from both user-mode and kernel-mode callers) and delivers them, in a different form, to I/O devices.

ideal processor The preferred processor that a particular thread should run on.

idle summary A bitmask (*KiIdleSummary*) in which each set bit represents an idle processor.

impersonation A capability that allows threads to have a different access token than that of the process.

initialization routine A driver routine that the I/O manager executes when it loads the driver into the operating system. The initialization routine creates system objects that the I/O manager uses to recognize and access the driver.

in-paging I/O A condition that occurs when a read operation must be issued to a file (paging or mapped) to satisfy a page fault. The in-page I/O operation is synchronous— the thread waits on an event until the I/O completes—and isn't interruptible by asynchronous procedure call (APC) delivery.

instancing The term for making separate copies of the same parts of a namespace. Instancing \DosDevices makes it possible for each user to have different drive letters and Win32 objects such as serial ports.

intelligent file read-ahead A technique that predicts what data the calling thread is likely to read next based on the data it's currently reading.

inter-processor interrupt (IPI) An interrupt the kernel issues to request that another processor perform an action, such as dispatching a particular thread for execution or updating its translation look-aside buffer cache.

interrupt An asynchronous event (one that can occur at any time) that is unrelated to what the processor is executing. Interrupts are generated primarily by I/O devices, processor clocks, or timers, and they can be enabled or disabled.

interrupt dispatch table (IDT) A data structure that Windows 2000 uses to locate the routine that will handle a particular interrupt. The interrupt request level (IRQL) of the interrupting source serves as a table index, and table entries point to the interrupt-handling routines.

interrupt dispatcher A submodule of the kernel's trap handler that responds to interrupts.

interrupt object A kernel control object that allows device drivers to register interrupt service routines (ISRs) for their devices. An interrupt object contains all the information the kernel needs to associate a device ISR with a particular level of interrupt, including the address of the ISR, the interrupt request level (IRQL) at which the device interrupts, and the entry in the kernel's interrupt dispatch table with which the ISR should be associated.

interrupt request (IRQ) A value identifying an interrupt. On x86 systems, external I/O interrupts come into one of the lines on an interrupt controller. The controller in turn interrupts the processor on a single line. Once the processor is interrupted, it queries the controller to get the interrupt request (IRQ). The interrupt controller translates the IRQ to an interrupt number, uses this number as an index into the interrupt dispatch table (IDT), and transfers control to the appropriate interrupt dispatch routine. At system boot time, Windows 2000 fills in the IDT with pointers to the kernel routines that handle each interrupt and exception.

interrupt request levels (IRQLs) An interrupt priority scheme imposed by Windows 2000. The kernel represents IRQLs internally as a number from 0 through 31, with higher numbers representing higher-priority interrupts. Although the kernel defines the standard set of IRQLs for software interrupts, the HAL maps hardware-interrupt numbers to the IRQLs.

interrupt service routine (ISR) A device driver routine that the kernel's interrupt dispatcher transfers control to when a device issues an interrupt. In the Windows 2000 I/O model, ISRs run at a high device interrupt request level (IRQL), so they perform as little work as possible to avoid blocking lower-level interrupts unnecessarily. An ISR queues a deferred procedure call (DPC), which runs at a lower IRQL, to execute the remainder of interrupt processing. Only drivers for interrupt-driven devices have ISRs; a file system, for example, doesn't have one.

job object A nameable, securable, shareable object in Windows 2000 that controls certain attributes of processes associated with the job. A job object's basic function is to allow groups of processes to be managed and manipulated as a unit. The job object also records basic accounting information for all processes associated with the job and for all processes that were associated with the job but have since terminated.

journaling A logging technique originally developed for transaction processing that a recoverable file system such as NTFS uses to ensure volume consistency.

kernel The lowest layer in Ntoskrnl.exe. The kernel, a component of the executive, determines how the operating system uses the processor or processors and ensures that they are used prudently. The kernel provides thread scheduling and dispatching, trap handling and exception dispatching, interrupt handling and dispatching, and multiprocessor synchronization. *See also* executive.

kernel debugger A tool used to debug drivers, troubleshoot hung systems, and examine crash dumps. It is also a useful tool for investigating Windows 2000 internals because it can display internal Windows 2000 system information not visible through any standard utility. (The LiveKd tool on the companion CD allows the use of the standard kernel debuggers on a live system.)

kernel handle table A table (referenced internally with the name *ObpKernelHandleTable*) whose handles are accessible only from kernel mode and in any process context. A kernel-mode function can reference the handles in this table in any process context with no performance impact.

kernel memory dump A type of memory dump (the default on Windows 2000 Server systems) that contains only the kernel-mode read/write pages present in physical memory at the time of the crash. A kernel memory dump doesn't contain pages belonging to user processes. Because only kernel-mode code can directly cause Windows 2000 to crash, however, it's unlikely that user process pages are necessary to debug a crash. There is no way to predict the size of a kernel memory dump because its size depends on the amount of kernel-mode memory allocated by the operating system and drivers present on the machine.

kernel mode A privileged mode of code execution in a processor in which all memory is totally accessible and all CPU instructions can be issued. Operating system code (such as system services and device drivers) runs in kernel mode. *See also* user mode.

kernel objects A primitive set of objects implemented by the Windows 2000 kernel. These objects aren't visible to user-mode code but are created and used only within the executive. Kernel objects provide fundamental capabilities, such as synchronization, on which executive objects are built. *See also* executive objects.

kernel streaming filter drivers Kernel-mode drivers chained together to perform signal processing on data streams, such as recording or displaying audio and video.

kernel-mode device driver The only type of driver that can directly control and access hardware devices.

kernel-mode graphics driver A Win32 subsystem display or print device driver that translates device-independent graphics (GDI) requests into device-specific requests.

key A mechanism to refer to data in the registry. Although keys appear in the object manager namespace, the registry manages them in a way similar to how it manages file objects. Zero or more key values are associated with a key object; key values contain data about the key.

key control block A structure that stores the full pathname of a registry key, includes the cell index of the key node that the control block refers to, and contains a flag that notes whether the configuration manager needs to delete the key cell that the key control block refers to when the last handle for the key closes. In Windows 2000, all key control blocks are in an alphabetized binary tree to enable quick searches for existing key control blocks by name. A key object points to its corresponding key control block, so if two applications open the same registry key, each will receive a key object and both key objects will point to a common key control block.

key object An object type the configuration manager defines to integrate the registry's namespace with the kernel's general namespace.

last known good control set A copy of the critical boot-time information under the registry key HKLM\SYSTEM\CurrentControlSet, made when a user successfully logs on. The last known good control set can be selected at boot time in case configuration changes made to the registry result in the system not being able to boot successfully.

lazy IRQL A performance optimization that avoids Programmable Interrupt Controller (PIC) accesses. When the interrupt request level (IRQL) is raised, the HAL notes the new IRQL internally instead of changing the interrupt mask. If a lower-priority interrupt subsequently occurs, the HAL sets the interrupt mask to the settings appropriate for the first interrupt and postpones the lower-priority interrupt until the IRQL is lowered. Thus, if no lower-priority interrupts occur while the IRQL is raised, the HAL doesn't need to modify the PIC.

lazy writer A set of system threads that call the memory manager to flush cache contents to disk as a background activity (asynchronous disk writing). The cache manager optimizes disk I/O by using its lazy writer.

legacy drivers Device drivers written for Microsoft Windows NT but that run unchanged on Windows 2000. They are differentiated from other Windows 2000 drivers in that they don't support power management or work with the Windows 2000 Plug and Play manager.

local file system driver (FSD) A driver that manages volumes directly connected to the computer. *See also* file system driver.

local procedure call (LPC) An interprocess communication facility for high-speed message passing (not available through the Win32 API but rather through an internal mechanism available only to Windows 2000 operating system components). LPCs are

typically used between a server process and one or more client processes of that server. An LPC connection can be established between two user-mode processes or between a kernel-mode component and a user-mode process.

local security authority (LSA) server A user-mode process running the image \Winnt\ System32\Lsass.exe that is responsible for the local system security policy (such as which users are allowed to log on to the machine, password policies, privileges granted to users and groups, and the system security auditing settings), user authentication, and sending security audit messages to the Event Log. The LSA service (Lsasrv - \Winnt\System32\ Lsasrv.dll), a library that Lsass loads, implements most of this functionality.

local security authority (LSA) server policy database A database (stored in the registry under HKLM\SECURITY) that contains the system security policy settings. This database includes such information as what domains are trusted to authenticate logon attempts, who has permission to access the system and how (interactive, network, and service logons), who is assigned which privileges, and what kind of security auditing is to be performed.

log file A metadata file (filename $LogFile) NTFS uses to record all operations that affect the NTFS volume structure, including file creation or any commands, such as *Copy*, that alter the directory structure. The log file is used to recover an NTFS volume after a system failure.

log hive A registry hive the configuration manager uses to make sure that a nonvolatile registry hive (one with an on-disk file) is always in a recoverable state. Each nonvolatile hive has an associated log hive, which is a hidden file with the same base name as the hive and a .log extension. *See also* hive.

logging A transaction-processing technique NTFS uses to maintain file system integrity in case of system crashes or other failures. In NTFS logging, the suboperations of any transaction that alters important file system data structures are recorded in a log file before they are carried through on the disk so that if the system crashes, partially completed transactions can be redone or undone when the system comes back on line.

logical cluster numbers (LCNs) The numbers of all clusters from the beginning of the volume to the end with which NTFS refers to physical locations on a disk. To convert an LCN to a physical disk address, NTFS multiplies the LCN by the cluster factor to get the physical byte offset on the volume, as the disk driver interface requires.

logical sequence numbers (LSNs) The numbers that NTFS uses to identify records written to the log file.

logon process A user-mode process running Winlogon.exe that is responsible for capturing the username and password, sending them to the local security authority server for verification, and creating the initial process in the user's session.

look-aside list A fast memory allocation mechanism that contains only fixed-sized blocks. Look-aside lists can be either pageable or nonpageable, so they are allocated from paged or nonpaged pool.

mapped file I/O The ability to view a file residing on disk as part of a process's virtual memory. A program can access the file as a large array without buffering data or performing disk I/O. The program accesses memory, and the memory manager uses its

paging mechanism to load the correct page from the disk file. If the application writes to its virtual address space, the memory manager writes the changes back to the file as part of normal paging.

mask The process whereby interrupts wait for an executing thread to lower the IRQL before the interrupt is processed. Interrupts from a source with an IRQL above the current level interrupt the processor, whereas interrupts from sources with IRQLs equal to or below the current level are masked until an executing thread lowers the IRQL.

master file table (MFT) The heart of the NTFS volume structure. The MFT is implemented as an array of file records. The size of each file record is fixed at 1 KB, regardless of cluster size.

memory manager The Windows 2000 executive component that implements demand-paged virtual memory, giving each process the illusion that it has a 4-GB 32-bit address space (while mapping a subset of that address space to physical memory).

metadata Data that describes the files on a disk; also called *volume structure data*.

metadata files A set of files in each NTFS volume that contains the information used to implement the file system structure.

MFT mirror An NTFS metadata file (filename $MFTMirr) located in the middle of the disk called that contains a copy of the first few rows of the master file table.

miniport driver A type of kernel-mode device driver that maps a generic I/O request to a type of port into an adapter type, such as a specific SCSI adapter.

mirrored volume A volume on which the contents of a partition on one disk are duplicated in an equal-sized partition on another disk. Mirrored volumes are sometimes referred to as RAID level 1 (RAID-1).

mirror set A technique by which the contents of a partition on one disk are duplicated in an equal-size partition on another disk.

modified page writer A thread in the virtual memory manager that is responsible for limiting the size of the modified page list by writing pages to their backing store locations when the list becomes too big. The modified page writer consists of two system threads: one to write out modified pages (*MiModifiedPageWriter*) to the paging file and a second one to write modified pages to mapped files (*MiMappedPageWriter*).

mount A technique NTFS uses when it first accesses a volume; in this context, to mount means to prepare the volume for use. To mount the volume, NTFS looks in the boot file to find the physical disk address of the master file table.

mount points A mechanism that permits the linking of volumes through directories on NTFS volumes, which makes volumes accessible with no drive-letter assignment. Reparse points in NTFS make mount points possible.

MSDN Microsoft Developer Network, Microsoft's support program for developers. MSDN offers three CD-ROM subscription programs: MSDN Library, Professional, and Universal. For more information, see *msdn.microsoft.com*.

multipartition volumes Objects that represent sectors from multiple partitions and that file system drivers manage as a single unit. Multipartition volumes offer performance, reliability, and sizing features that simple volumes don't.

mutant Internal name for a mutex.

mutex A synchronization mechanism used to serialize access to a resource.

name retention The first phase of object retention, which the object manager implements. Name retention is controlled by the number of open handles to an object that exist. Every time a process opens a handle to an object, the object manager increments the open handle counter in the object's header. As processes finish using the object and close their handles to it, the object manager decrements the open handle counter. When the counter drops to 0, the object manager deletes the object's name from its global namespace. This deletion prevents new processes from opening a handle to the object.

native application An application that uses only system service APIs provided by Ntdll and that isn't a client of the Win32 subsystem. Smss (Session Manager) is an example of a native application.

network file system driver (FSD) A driver that allows users to access data volumes connected to remote computers. *See also* file system driver.

network logon service A user-mode service inside the Services.exe process that responds to network logon requests. Authentication is handled as local logons are, by sending them to the Lsass process for verification.

network redirectors and servers File system drivers that transmit remote I/O requests to a machine on the network and receive such requests, respectively.

nonpaged pool Memory pool that consists of ranges of system virtual addresses that are guaranteed to be resident in physical memory at all times and thus can be accessed from any address space without incurring paging I/O. Nonpaged pool is created at system initialization and is used by kernel-mode components to allocate system memory.

Ntdll.dll A special system-support library primarily for the use of subsystem DLLs that contains System service dispatch stubs to Windows 2000 executive system services and internal support functions used by subsystems, subsystem DLLs, and other native images.

Ntkrnlmp.exe The executive and kernel for multiprocessor systems.

Ntoskrnl.exe The executive and kernel for uniprocessor systems.

object In the Windows 2000 executive, a single, run-time instance of a statically defined object type.

object attribute A field of data in an object that partially defines the object's state.

object directory A container object for other objects. The object directory is used to implement the hierarchical namespace within which other object types are stored.

object handle An index into a process-specific handle table, pointed to by the executive process (EPROCESS) block.

object manager The Windows 2000 executive component responsible for creating, deleting, protecting, and tracking objects. The object manager centralizes resource control operations that would otherwise be scattered throughout the operating system.

object methods The means for manipulating objects, usually to read or change the object attributes. For example, the *open* method for a process would accept a process identifier as input and return a pointer to the object as output.

object reuse protection A means of preventing users from seeing data that another user has deleted or from accessing memory that another user previously used and then released. Object reuse protection prevents potential security holes by initializing all objects, including files and memory, before they are allocated to a user.

object type A system-defined data type, including services that operate on instances of the data type and a set of object attributes; sometimes called an *object class*.

page directory A page the memory manager creates to map the location of all page tables for that process. Each process has a single page directory.

page directory entries (PDEs) The page directory is composed of PDEs, each of which is 4 bytes long and describes the state and location of all the possible page tables for that process.

page fault A reference to an invalid page. The kernel trap handler dispatches this kind of fault to the memory manager fault handler (*MmAccessFault*) to resolve.

page file backed section A section object that is mapped to committed memory.

page file quota A limit on the number of committed pages a process can consume—not necessarily page file space.

page frame database A database that describes the state of each page in physical memory. Pages are in one of eight states: active (also called *valid*), transition, standby, modified, modified-no-write, free, zeroed, or bad.

page frame number (PFN) database Describes the state of each page in physical memory.

page table A page of mapping information (made up of an array of page table entries) the operating system constructs that describes the location of the virtual pages in a process address space. Because Windows 2000 provides a private address space for each process, each process has its own set of process page tables to map that private address space because the mappings will be different for each process. The page tables that describe system space are shared among all processes.

page table entry (PTE) An entry in a process's page table that contains the address to which the virtual address is mapped. The page can be in physical memory or it can be on disk.

paged pool A region of virtual memory in system space that can be paged in and out of the system process's working set. Paged pool is created at system initialization and is used by kernel-mode components to allocate system memory. Uniprocessor systems have two paged pools; multiprocessor systems have four. Having more than one paged pool reduces the frequency of system code blocking on simultaneous calls to pool routines.

paging The process of moving memory contents to disk, freeing physical memory so that it can be used for other processes or for the operating system itself. Because most systems have much less physical memory than the total virtual memory in use by the running processes (2 GB or 3 GB for each process), the memory manager transfers, or pages, some of the memory contents to disk.

partition A discrete area of the hard disk in Microsoft operating systems. File systems (such as FAT and NTFS) format each partition into a volume. A hard disk can contain up to four primary partitions. *See also* extended partition.

partition table A part of the master boot record (MBR) that consists of four entries that define the locations of as many as four primary partitions on a disk. The partition table also records a partition's type. Numerous predefined partition types exist, and a partition's type specifies which file system the partition includes.

Physical Address Extension (PAE) A memory-mapping mode included in all Intel x86 processors since the Pentium Pro. With the proper chipset, the PAE mode allows access to up to 64 GB of physical memory. When the x86 executes in PAE mode, the memory management unit (MMU) divides virtual addresses into four fields.

physical device object (PDO) A device object that's a required part of a devnode. The PDO represents the physical interface to a device. *See also* devnode.

Plug and Play (PnP) manager A major component of the executive that determines which drivers are required to support a particular device and loads those drivers. The PnP manager retrieves the hardware resource requirements for each device during enumeration. Based on the resource requirements of each device, the PnP manager assigns the appropriate hardware resources such as I/O ports, IRQs, DMA channels, and memory locations. It is also responsible for sending proper event notification for device changes (addition or removal of a device) on the system.

port driver A type of kernel-mode device driver that implements the processing of an I/O request specific to a type of I/O port, such as SCSI.

port object A single executive object a local procedure call (LPC) exports to maintain the state needed for communication.

power manager A major component of the executive that coordinates power events and generates power management I/O notifications to device drivers. When the system is idle, the power manager can be configured to reduce power consumption by putting the CPU to sleep. Changes in power consumption by individual devices are handled by device drivers but are coordinated by the power manager.

printer driver A driver that translates device-independent graphics requests to printer-specific commands. These commands are then typically forwarded to a kernel-mode port driver such as the parallel port driver (Parport.sys) or the USB printer port driver (Usbprint.sys).

private cache map A structure that contains the location of the last two reads so that the cache manager can perform intelligent read-ahead.

process The virtual address space and control information necessary for the execution of a set of thread objects.

process ID A unique identifier for a process (internally called a *client ID*).

process working set The subset of a process's virtual address space that is resident and owned by the running process. *See also* system working set.

processor affinity The set of processors a thread is permitted to run on.

processor control register (PCR) A data structure that along with its extension, the processor control block (PRCB), contains information about the state of each processor in the system, such as the current interrupt request level (IRQL), a pointer to the hardware interrupt dispatch table (IDT), the currently running thread, and the next thread selected to run. The kernel and the HAL use this information to perform architecture-specific and machine-specific actions. Portions of the PCR and PRCB structures are defined publicly in the Windows 2000 Device Driver Kit (DDK) header file Ntddk.h.

protected-mode A state during the boot process in which no virtual-to-physical translation occurs but a full 32 bits of memory becomes accessible. After the system is in protected-mode, Ntldr can access all of physical memory.

protocol driver A driver that implements a networking protocol such as TCP/IP, NetBEUI, or IPX/SPX.

prototype page table entries (prototype PTEs) A software structure the memory manager relies on to map potentially shared pages when a page can be shared between two processes. An array of prototype PTEs is created when a section object is first created.

quality of service (Qos) A networking technology that ensures that critical network applications receive highest priority.

quantum The length of time a thread is allowed to run before Windows 2000 interrupts the thread to find out whether another thread at the same priority level is waiting to run or whether the thread's priority needs to be reduced.

quantum unit A value that represents how long a thread can run until its quantum expires. This value is an integer value, not a length of time.

queue A method for threads to enqueue and dequeue notifications of the completion of I/O operations (called an *I/O completion port* in the Win32 API).

queued spinlock A special type of spinlock that is used only by the kernel and not exported for executive components or device drivers. A queued spinlock scales better on multiprocessor systems than a standard spinlock does. *See also* spinlock.

quota charges In the Windows 2000 object manager, the record of how much the object manager subtracts from a process's allotted paged and/or nonpaged pool quota when a thread in the process opens a handle to the object.

RAID-5 volume A fault tolerant variant of a regular stripe volume. Fault tolerance is achieved by reserving the equivalent of one disk for storing parity for each stripe. Also called *stripe volume with parity*.

ready summary A 32-bit mask (*KiReadySummary*) that Windows 2000 maintains to speed up the selection of which thread to run or preempt.

real-mode An operating mode in which no virtual-to-physical translation of memory addresses occurs, which means that programs that use the memory addresses interpret them as physical addresses and that only the first 1 MB of the computer's physical memory is accessible. Simple MS-DOS programs execute in a real-mode environment.

recoverability An advanced feature of NTFS that allows a system to recover from an unexpected system halt. If a system is halted unexpectedly, the metadata of a FAT volume can be left in an inconsistent state, leading to the corruption of large amounts of file and directory data. NTFS implements recoverability by logging changes to metadata in a transactional manner so that file system structures can be repaired to a consistent state with no loss of file or directory structure information. (File data can be lost, however.)

redo information Information included in the NTFS checkpoint record that explains how to reapply one suboperation of a fully logged (*committed*) transaction to the volume if a system failure occurs before the transaction is flushed from the cache.

reference count The object manager's record of how many object pointers it has dispensed to operating system processes. The object manager increments a reference count for an object each time it gives out a pointer to the object; when kernel-mode components finish using the pointer, they call the object manager to decrement the object's reference count.

reparse data User-defined data about the file or directory, such as its state or location, that can be read from the reparse point by the application that created the data, a file system filter driver, or the I/O manager.

reparse point An NTFS file or directory that has a block of data called *reparse data* associated with it.

resident attribute An attribute that is stored directly in the master file table. (If a file is small, all its attributes and their values [its data, for example] fit in the file record.)

resource arbitration A process by which the Plug and Play (PnP) manager optimally assigns hardware resources so that each device meets the requirements necessary for its operation. Because hardware devices can be added to the system after boot-time resource assignment, the PnP manager must also be able to reassign resources to accommodate the needs of dynamically added devices.

restricted token A token created from a primary or impersonation token using the *CreateRestrictedToken* function. The restricted token is a copy of the token it's derived from, with some possible modifications: Privileges can be removed from the token's privilege array. SIDs in the token can be marked as *deny-only*. SIDS in the token can be marked as *restricted*.

ring A privilege level defined in the Intel x86 processor architecture to protect system code and data from being overwritten either inadvertently or maliciously by code of lesser privilege. Windows 2000 uses privilege level 0 (or ring 0) for kernel mode and privilege level 3 (or ring 3) for user mode.

safe mode A boot configuration that consists of the minimal set of device drivers and services. By relying on only the drivers and services that are necessary for booting, Windows 2000 avoids loading third-party and other nonessential drivers that might crash.

SAM database A database (stored in the registry under HKLM\SAM) that contains the defined users and groups, along with their passwords and other attributes.

scatter/gather I/O A kind of high-performance I/O Windows 2000 supports, available via the Win32 *ReadFileScatter* and *WriteFileGather* functions. These functions allow an application to issue a single read or write from more than one buffer in virtual memory to a contiguous area of a file on disk. To use scatter/gather I/O, the file must be opened for noncached I/O, the user buffers being used have to be page-aligned, and the I/Os must be asynchronous (overlapped).

section object An object that represents a block of memory that two or more processes can share. A section object can be mapped to the paging file or to another file on disk. The executive uses section objects to load executable images into memory, and the cache manager uses them to access data in a cached file. In the Win32 subsystem, a section object is called a *file-mapping object*.

section object pointers Structure for each open file (represented by a file object) that is the key to maintaining data consistency for all types of file access as well as to providing caching for files. The section object pointers structure points to one or two control areas. One control area is used to map the file when accessed as a data file, and one is used to map the file when it is run as an executable image.

sector A hardware-addressable portion of a physical disk. A hard disk sector on an IBM-compatible PC is typically 512 bytes. Utilities that prepare hard disks for the definition of logical drives, including the MS-DOS Fdisk utility or the Windows 2000 Setup program, write a sector of data called a master boot record (MBR) to the first sector on a hard disk. The MBR includes a fixed amount of space that contains executable instructions (called boot code) and a partition table with four entries that define the locations of the primary partitions on the disk. *See also* boot code, partition table.

secure attention sequence (SAS) A keystroke combination that when entered notifies Winlogon of a user logon request.

Security Accounts Manager (SAM) service A set of subroutines responsible for managing the database that contains the usernames and groups defined on the local machine or for a domain (if the system is a domain controller). The SAM runs in the context of the Lsass process.

security auditing A way in which Windows 2000 detects and records important security-related events or any attempts to create, access, or delete system resources. Logon identifiers record the identities of all users, making it easier to trace anyone who performs an unauthorized action.

security identifier (SID) A means of uniquely identifying entities that perform actions in a system. A SID is a variable-length numeric value that consists of a SID structure revision number, a 48-bit identifier authority value, and a variable number of 32-bit subauthority or relative identifier (RID) values.

security reference monitor (SRM) A component in the Windows 2000 executive (Ntoskrnl.exe) that enforces security policies on the local computer. It guards operating system resources, performing run-time object protection and auditing.

semaphore A counter that provides a resource gate by allowing some maximum number of threads to access the resources protected by the semaphore.

server processes User processes that are Windows 2000 services, such as the Event Log and Schedule services. Many add-on server applications, such as Microsoft SQL Server and Microsoft Exchange Server, also include components that run as Windows 2000 services.

session Consists of the processes and other system objects (such as the window station, desktops, and windows) that represent a single user's workstation logon session. Each session has a session-specific paged pool area used by the kernel-mode portion of the Win32 subsystem (Win32k.sys) to allocate session-private GUI data structures. In addition, each session has its own copy of the Win32 subsystem process (Csrss.exe) and logon process (Winlogon.exe).

session space A component of system space used to map information specific to a user session. (Windows 2000 supports multiple user sessions when Terminal Services is installed.) The session working set list describes the parts of session space that are resident and in use.

shared cache map A structure that describes the state of a cached file, including its size and (for security reasons) its valid data length.

shared memory Memory visible to more than one process or that is present in more than one virtual address space.

signal state The state of a synchronization object.

simple volume A set of objects that represent sectors from a single partition that file system drivers manage as a single unit.

single sign-on The ability for logon information to be simultaneously authenticated on more than one system. For example, a user logging on to a Windows 2000 system might simultaneously be authenticated on a UNIX server. That user would then be able to access resources of the UNIX server from the machine running Windows 2000 without requiring additional authentication.

small memory dump A small memory dump (the default on Windows 2000 Professional, 64 KB in size) containing the stop code and parameters, the list of loaded device drivers, the data structures that describe the current process and thread (called the EPROCESS and ETHREAD), and the kernel stack for the thread that caused the crash.

spanned volume A single logical volume composed of a maximum of 32 free partitions on one or more disks. The Windows 2000 Disk Management Microsoft Management Console (MMC) snap-in combines the partitions into a spanned volume, which can then be formatted for any of the file systems that Windows 2000 supports.

sparse files Files, often large, that contain only a small amount of nonzero data relative to their size.

spinlock The locking mechanism the kernel uses to achieve multiprocessor mutual exclusion. The spinlock gets its name from the fact that the kernel (and thus, the processor) is held in limbo, "spinning," until it gets the lock. Spinlocks, like the data structures they protect, reside in global memory. *See also* queued spinlock.

stack frame Information, representing the activation of a procedure, that is pushed onto the stack when a procedure is invoked. A stack frame can have one or more exception handlers associated with it, each of which protects a particular block of code in the source program.

stream A sequence of bytes within a file.

striped volume Series of up to 32 partitions, one partition per disk, that combines into a single logical volume. Striped volumes are also known as RAID level 0 (RAID-0) volumes. A partition in a striped volume need not span an entire disk; the only restriction is that the partitions on each disk be the same size.

structured exception handling A type of exception handling that allows applications to gain control when exceptions occur. The application can then fix the condition and return to the place the exception occurred, unwind the stack (thus terminating execution of the subroutine that raised the exception), or declare back to the system that the exception isn't recognized, and continue searching for an exception handler that might process the exception.

subsection A structure that describes the mapping information for each section of the file (read-only, read-write, copy-on-write, and so on).

subsystem dynamic-link libraries (DLLs) DLLs that translate a documented function into the appropriate undocumented Windows 2000 system service calls. This translation might or might not involve sending a message to the environment subsystem process that is serving the user application.

symbolic link A mechanism for referring to an object name indirectly.

symmetric encryption algorithm An algorithm that uses the same key to encrypt and decrypt data. Symmetric encryption algorithms are typically very fast, which makes them suitable for encrypting large amounts of data, such as file data. They do have a weakness, however; their security can be bypassed if their key is obtained.

symmetric multiprocessing (SMP) A multiprocessing operating system in which there is no master processor—the operating system as well as user threads can be scheduled to run on any processor. All the processors share just one memory space.

synchronization A thread's ability to synchronize its execution by waiting for an object to change from one state to another. A thread can synchronize with executive process, thread, file, event, semaphore, mutex, and timer objects. Section, port, access token, object directory, symbolic-link, profile, and key objects don't support synchronization.

synchronous I/O A model for I/O in which a device performs a data transfer and returns a status code when the I/O is complete. The program can then access the transferred data immediately. When used in their simplest form, the Win32 *ReadFile* and *WriteFile* functions are executed synchronously. They complete an I/O operation before returning control to the caller.

system access-control list (SACL) Specifies which operations by which users should be logged in the security audit log.

system audit ACE An access-control entry (ACE) contained by a system access-control list (SACL) that, along with the system audit-object ACE, specifies which operations performed on the object by specific users or groups should be audited. System audit-object ACEs specify a GUID indicating the types of objects or subobjects that the ACE applies to and an optional GUID that controls propagation of the ACE to particular child object types. If an SACL is null, no auditing takes place on the object.

system cache Pages used to map files open in the system cache.

system page table entries (PTEs) Pool of system PTEs used to map system pages such as I/O space, kernel stacks, and memory descriptor lists.

system service dispatch table Table in which each entry contains a pointer to a system service rather than to an interrupt handling routine.

system services (or executive system services) Native functions in the Windows 2000 operating system that are callable from user mode. For example, *NtCreateProcess* is the internal system service the Win32 *CreateProcess* function calls to create a new process.

system support processes User processes, such as the logon process and the Session Manager, that are not Windows 2000 services (that is, not started by the service controller).

system thread A kind of thread that runs only in kernel mode. System threads always reside in the System process (always process ID 2). These threads have all the attributes and contexts of regular user-mode threads (such as a hardware context, priority, and so on) but run only in kernel-mode executing code loaded in system-space code, whether that be in Ntoskrnl.exe or in any other loaded device driver. System threads don't have a user process address space and hence must allocate any dynamic storage from operating system memory heaps, such as paged or nonpaged pool.

system worker threads Threads created in the System process during system initialization that exist solely to perform work on behalf of other threads.

system working set The physical memory being used by the system cache, paged pool, pageable code in Ntoskrnl.exe, and pageable code in device drivers. *See also* process working set.

thread An entity within a process that Windows 2000 schedules for execution. A thread includes the contents of a set of volatile registers representing the state of the processor; two stacks, one for the thread to use while executing in kernel mode and one for executing in user mode; a private storage area for use by subsystems, run-time libraries, and DLLs; and a unique identifier called a *thread ID* (also internally called a *client ID*).

thread context A thread's volatile registers, the stacks, and the private storage area. Because this information is different for each machine architecture that Windows 2000 runs on, this structure is architecture-specific. In fact, the CONTEXT structure returned by the Win32 *GetThreadContext* function is the only public data structure in the Win32 API that is machine-dependent.

timer A mechanism that notifies a thread when a fixed period of time elapses.

transaction An I/O operation that alters file system data or changes the volume's directory structure. The separate disk updates that make up the transaction must be executed atomically; that is, once the transaction begins to execute, all its disk updates must be completed. If a system failure interrupts the transaction, the part that has been completed must be undone, or rolled back. The rollback operation returns the database to a previously known and consistent state, as if the transaction had never occurred.

transaction table A table that keeps track of transactions that have been started but that aren't yet committed. The suboperations of these active transactions must be removed from the disk during recovery.

transition A kind of invalid page table entry (PTE) in which the desired page is in memory on either the standby, modified, or modified-no-write list. The page is removed from the list and added to the working set.

translation look-aside buffer A CPU cache of recently translated virtual page numbers.

trap A processor's mechanism for capturing an executing thread when an exception or an interrupt occurs, switching it from user mode into kernel mode, and transferring control to a fixed location in the operating system. In Windows 2000, the processor transfers control to the kernel's trap handler.

trap frame A data structure in which the execution state of the interrupted thread is stored. This information allows the kernel to resume execution of the thread after handling the interrupt or the exception. The trap frame is usually a subset of a thread's complete context.

trap handler A module in the kernel that acts as a switchboard, fielding exceptions and interrupts detected by the processor and transferring control to code that handles the condition.

type object An internal system object that contains information common to each instance of the object.

Unicode An international character set standard that defines unique 16-bit values for most of the world's known character sets.

update records The most common type of record NTFS writes to the log file. Each update record contains the information needed to redo an operation that updated the file system structure.

user mode The nonprivileged processor mode that applications run in. A limited set of interfaces is available in this mode, and the access to system data is limited. *See also* kernel mode.

view The portion of the section object requires by a process. A section object can refer to files that are much larger than can fit in the address space of a process. (If the paging file backs a section object, sufficient space must exist in the paging file to contain it.) To access a very large section object, a process can map only a view of the section by calling the *MapViewOfFile* function and then specifying the range to map. Mapping views permits processes to conserve address space because only the views of the section object needed at the time must be mapped into memory. *See also* section object.

virtual address descriptors (VADs) Data structures the memory manager maintains that keep track of which virtual addresses have been reserved in the process's address space. VADs are structured as a self-balancing binary tree to make lookups efficient.

virtual address space A set of virtual memory addresses that a process can use.

virtual block caching A method the Windows 2000 cache manager uses to keep track of which parts of which files are in the cache.

virtual cluster numbers (VCNs) VCNs number the clusters belonging to a particular file from 0 through *m*. VCNs aren't necessarily physically contiguous, but they can be mapped to any number of logical cluster numbers (LCNs) on a volume.

virtual device drivers (VDDs) Drivers used to emulate 16-bit MS-DOS applications. They trap what an MS-DOS application thinks are references to I/O ports and translate them into native Win32 I/O functions. Because Windows 2000 is a fully protected operating system, user-mode MS-DOS applications can't access hardware directly and thus must go through a real kernel-mode device driver.

virtual memory manager Implements virtual memory, a memory management scheme that provides a large, private address space for each process that can exceed available physical memory.

volume One or more logical disk partitions that are treated as a single unit.

volume file A system file (filename $Volume) that contains the volume name, the version of NTFS for which the volume is formatted, and a bit that when set signifies that a disk corruption has occurred and must be repaired by the Chkdsk utility.

volume manager A term used to represent both FtDisk and DMIO because both FtDisk and DMIO support the same multipartition-volume types.

volume set A single logical volume composed of a maximum of 32 areas of free space on one or more disks.

wait block A data structure that represents a thread waiting on an object. Each thread that is in a wait state has a list of the wait blocks that represent the objects the thread is waiting on. Each dispatcher object has a list of the wait blocks that represent which threads are waiting on the object.

wait hint A value indicating how long a service should wait before informing the system a shutdown is complete.

WDM drivers Device drivers that adhere to the Windows Driver Model (WDM). WDM includes support for Windows 2000 power management, Plug and Play, and Windows Management Instrumentation (WMI). WDM is implemented on Windows 2000, Windows 98, and Windows Millennium Edition, so WDM drivers are source compatible between these operating systems and in many cases are also binary compatible. There are three types of WDM drivers: bus drivers, function drivers, and filter drivers.

Win32 application programming interface (API) The primary programming interface to the Microsoft Windows operating system family, including Windows NT 4, Windows 2000, Microsoft Windows 95, Windows 98, Windows Millennium Edition, and Microsoft Windows CE.

Win32 services A mechanism to start processes at system startup time that provide services not tied to an interactive user. Services are similar to UNIX daemon processes and often implement the server side of client/server applications.

window station A window station contains desktops, and desktops contain windows. Only one window station can be visible on a console and receive user mouse and keyboard input. In a Terminal Services environment, one window station per session is visible, but services all run as part of the console session.

Windows 2000 drivers Device drivers that integrate with the Windows 2000 power manager and Plug and Play manager, when required. They include drivers for mass storage devices, protocol stacks, and network adapters.

Windows Management Instrumentation (WMI) manager A component of the executive that enables device drivers to publish performance and configuration information and receive commands from the user-mode WMI service. Consumers of WMI information can be on the local machine or remote across the network.

work item A unit of work placed on a queue dispatcher object when a device driver or an executive component requests a system worker thread's services by calling the executive functions *ExQueueWorkItem* or *IoQueueWorkItem*. Work items include a pointer to a routine and a parameter that the thread passes to the routine when it processes the work item. The routine is implemented by the device driver or executive component that requires passive-level execution.

working set A subset of virtual pages resident in physical memory. There are two kinds of working sets—process working sets and the system working set.

working set manager A routine that runs in the context of the balance set manager system thread to initiate automatic working set trimming to increase the amount of free memory available in the system. Although Windows 2000 attempts to keep memory available by writing modified pages to disk, when modified pages are being generated at a very high rate, more memory is required to meet memory demands. The working set manager is called when physical memory runs low (when *MmAvailablePages* is less than *MmMinimumFreePages*).

write-back A caching strategy the lazy write file system uses to improve performance. In write-back, the file system writes file modifications to the cache and flushes the contents of the cache to disk in an optimized way, usually as a background activity.

write-through An algorithm the FAT file system uses that causes disk modifications to be immediately written to the disk. Unlike the careful-write approach, the write-through technique doesn't require the file system to order its writes to prevent inconsistencies. *See also* careful write.

zero page thread A kernel-mode system thread (thread 0 in the System process). A zero page thread zeros out pages on the free list so that a cache of zero pages is available to satisfy future demand-zero page faults.

INDEX

Note: Italicized page references indicate figures, tables, or code listings.

M

mailslots. *See* named pipes and mailslots

Managed Object Format (MOF) language, 269–72, *270*

 management mechanisms. *See* registry; services; Windows Management Instrumentation (WMI)

mapped file I/O, 589–90

mapped files

 flushing, 669

 section objects and, 380 (*see also* section objects)

 shared memory and, 393–95, *393*

mapped page writer, 381

 file system operation and, 699

mapping

 AWE and memory, 401–2, *402*

 cache manager mapping interface, 677–78, *677, 678*

 dynamic bad-cluster remapping, 705

 interrupts to IRQLs, 100–101

 system-to-device power, *550*

 VCN-to-LCN, 724, 734–35, *734, 735*

 virtual memory to physical memory, 8–9, *9,* 430–31, *430* (*see also* address translation)

 Win32 to Windows 2000 device names, 560–61

masked interrupts, 99, 156

master boot record (MBR), 179–80

master file table (MFT), NTFS, 718–25, *719*

memory descriptor list (MDL), 679, *680*

memory management, 379–486

 address space layout (*see* address space layout)

 address translation (*see* address translation)

 components and services (*see* memory manager)

 crash dumps (*see* crash dumps)

 job and process memory limit, 376

 page fault handling, 443–52, *444*

 page frame number (PFN) database, 465–78, *466, 467, 468*

 real-mode vs. protected mode, 181

 section objects, 478–86, *479, 480, 482*

 stacks (*see* stacks)

memory management, *continued*

 system memory pools, 403–17, *404*

 virtual address descriptors (VADs), 452–54, *453*

 virtual address space and processes, 4

 virtual address space in Consumer Windows, 419

 virtual memory, 7–9, *8, 9,* 379–80

 working sets, 455–65

memory manager, 380–402

 accounting for physical memory use, 387–89

 Address Windowing Extensions (AWE), 401–2, *402*

 allocation granularity and, 392

 cache manager and, 646–47

 components, 380–82

 configuring, 382–84, *382–83, 384*

 copy-on-write page protection, 398–99, *398, 399*

 determining system memory size, 384

 examining memory usage, 385–89

 executive and, 63

 file system operation and, 699, 700

 heap functions, 400

 initialization, 191

 locking memory, 392

 protecting memory, 10, 395–97, *396–97*

 reserving and committing pages, 390–91

 services, 389–402

 shared memory and mapped files, 393–95, *393*

 viewing system memory information, 385–87

menu, boot-selection, 181, 188, 196

Message Queuing, 813–14

metadata, 650, 684

 locations, *677*

 NTFS files, *719*

 recoverability and, 689

methods, object, 14, 135–37, *135*

MFT. *See* master file table (MFT), NTFS

microkernel-based system, Windows 2000 as, 31

Microsoft Developer Network (MSDN), 2, 24

Microsoft kernel debuggers, 21–23. *See also* kernel debuggers

David Solomon

David Solomon, president of David Solomon Expert Seminars (*www.solsem.com*), has been teaching seminars on Microsoft Windows NT and Microsoft Windows 2000 internals and systems programming since 1992. His clients include all the major software and hardware companies, including Microsoft.

Formerly a consulting software engineer at Digital Equipment Corporation, David worked for over nine years as a project leader and developer in the VMS operating system development group. He left DEC to focus on evangelizing Windows NT to the VMS customer base. His first book, *Windows NT for OpenVMS Professionals* (Digital Press/Butterworth Heinemann, 1996), was based on his initial classes that explained Windows NT to VMS-knowledgeable programmers and system managers.

In addition to organizing and teaching seminars, David is a regular speaker at industry events such as Microsoft TechEd, Microsoft PDCs, WinDev, and Software Development. He has also served as technical chair for several Windows NT conferences. When he's not researching Windows 2000, David enjoys sailing, reading, and Star Trek.

Mark Russinovich

Mark Russinovich is chief software architect and cofounder of Winternals Software (*www.winternals.com*), a company that specializes in advanced systems software for Microsoft Windows NT, Microsoft Windows 2000, and Microsoft Consumer Windows. He is a contributing editor for *Dr. Dobb's Journal* (*www.ddj.com*) and *Windows 2000 Magazine,* and he writes the monthly "Internals" column for *Windows 2000 Magazine* (*www.win2000mag.com*). He is also a frequent speaker at major industry conferences such as WinDev, Software Development, and WinSummit, where he speaks on Windows 2000 internals and device driver and file system driver development.

Mark has a B.S. from Carnegie Mellon University and an M.S. from Rennselear Polytechnic Institute, both in computer engineering. In 1994, he earned a Ph.D. from Carnegie Mellon University, also in computer engineering. After working briefly at NuMega Technologies (now Compuware NuMega Laboratories), Mark worked for two and a half years at IBM's Thomas J. Watson Research Center in New York, where he participated in the research and development of kernel-mode Web server–accelerator technologies.

Founder of the highly trafficked Sysinternals Web site (*www.sysinternals .com*), Mark has authored or coauthored dozens of popular freeware tools for Windows 2000 and Consumer Windows, including Filemon, Regmon, NTFSDOS (an NTFS file system driver for MS-DOS), and HandleEx. When Mark isn't writing tools or researching Windows 2000 internals, he enjoys hiking; biking; watching movies with his wife, Susan; and driving fast cars.

The manuscript for this book was prepared and submitted to Microsoft Press in electronic form. Text files were prepared using Microsoft Word 2000. Pages were composed by Microsoft Press using Adobe PageMaker 6.52 for Windows, with text in Galliard and display type in Helvetica bold. Composed pages were delivered to the printer as electronic prepress files.

Cover Graphic Designer
Girvin | Strategic Branding & Design

Cover Illustrator
Glenn Mitsui

Interior Graphic Artist
Jim Kramer

Principal Compositor
Gina Cassill

Principal Proofreader/Copy Editor
Holly M. Viola

Technical Copy Editor
Shawn Peck

Indexer
Shane-Armstrong Information Systems

If you liked the book,
you'll love the seminar

MICROSOFT LICENSE AGREEMENT

Book Companion CD

IMPORTANT—READ CAREFULLY: This Microsoft End-User License Agreement ("EULA") is a legal agreement between you (either an individual or an entity) and Microsoft Corporation for the Microsoft product identified above, which includes computer software and may include associated media, printed materials, and "online" or electronic documentation ("SOFTWARE PRODUCT"). Any component included within the SOFTWARE PRODUCT that is accompanied by a separate End-User License Agreement shall be governed by such agreement and not the terms set forth below. By installing, copying, or otherwise using the SOFTWARE PRODUCT, you agree to be bound by the terms of this EULA. If you do not agree to the terms of this EULA, you are not authorized to install, copy, or otherwise use the SOFTWARE PRODUCT; you may, however, return the SOFTWARE PRODUCT, along with all printed materials and other items that form a part of the Microsoft product that includes the SOFTWARE PRODUCT, to the place you obtained them for a full refund.

SOFTWARE PRODUCT LICENSE

The SOFTWARE PRODUCT is protected by United States copyright laws and international copyright treaties, as well as other intellectual property laws and treaties. The SOFTWARE PRODUCT is licensed, not sold.

1. **GRANT OF LICENSE.** This EULA grants you the following rights:

 a. **Software Product.** You may install and use one copy of the SOFTWARE PRODUCT on a single computer. The primary user of the computer on which the SOFTWARE PRODUCT is installed may make a second copy for his or her exclusive use on a portable computer.

 b. **Storage/Network Use.** You may also store or install a copy of the SOFTWARE PRODUCT on a storage device, such as a network server, used only to install or run the SOFTWARE PRODUCT on your other computers over an internal network; however, you must acquire and dedicate a license for each separate computer on which the SOFTWARE PRODUCT is installed or run from the storage device. A license for the SOFTWARE PRODUCT may not be shared or used concurrently on different computers.

 c. **License Pak.** If you have acquired this EULA in a Microsoft License Pak, you may make the number of additional copies of the computer software portion of the SOFTWARE PRODUCT authorized on the printed copy of this EULA, and you may use each copy in the manner specified above. You are also entitled to make a corresponding number of secondary copies for portable computer use as specified above.

 d. **Sample Code.** Solely with respect to portions, if any, of the SOFTWARE PRODUCT that are identified within the SOFTWARE PRODUCT as sample code (the "SAMPLE CODE"):

 i. **Use and Modification.** Microsoft grants you the right to use and modify the source code version of the SAMPLE CODE, *provided* you comply with subsection (d)(iii) below. You may not distribute the SAMPLE CODE, or any modified version of the SAMPLE CODE, in source code form.

 ii. **Redistributable Files.** Provided you comply with subsection (d)(iii) below, Microsoft grants you a nonexclusive, royalty-free right to reproduce and distribute the object code version of the SAMPLE CODE and of any modified SAMPLE CODE, other than SAMPLE CODE, or any modified version thereof, designated as not redistributable in the Readme file that forms a part of the SOFTWARE PRODUCT (the "Non-Redistributable Sample Code"). All SAMPLE CODE other than the Non-Redistributable Sample Code is collectively referred to as the "REDISTRIBUTABLES."

 iii. **Redistribution Requirements.** If you redistribute the REDISTRIBUTABLES, you agree to: (i) distribute the REDISTRIBUTABLES in object code form only in conjunction with and as a part of your software application product; (ii) not use Microsoft's name, logo, or trademarks to market your software application product; (iii) include a valid copyright notice on your software application product; (iv) indemnify, hold harmless, and defend Microsoft from and against any claims or lawsuits, including attorney's fees, that arise or result from the use or distribution of your software application product; and (v) not permit further distribution of the REDISTRIBUTABLES by your end user. Contact Microsoft for the applicable royalties due and other licensing terms for all other uses and/or distribution of the REDISTRIBUTABLES.

2. **DESCRIPTION OF OTHER RIGHTS AND LIMITATIONS.**

 - **Limitations on Reverse Engineering, Decompilation, and Disassembly.** You may not reverse engineer, decompile, or disassemble the SOFTWARE PRODUCT, except and only to the extent that such activity is expressly permitted by applicable law notwithstanding this limitation.

 - **Separation of Components.** The SOFTWARE PRODUCT is licensed as a single product. Its component parts may not be separated for use on more than one computer.

 - **Rental.** You may not rent, lease, or lend the SOFTWARE PRODUCT.

 - **Support Services.** Microsoft may, but is not obligated to, provide you with support services related to the SOFTWARE PRODUCT ("Support Services"). Use of Support Services is governed by the Microsoft policies and programs described in the

user manual, in "online" documentation, and/or in other Microsoft-provided materials. Any supplemental software code provided to you as part of the Support Services shall be considered part of the SOFTWARE PRODUCT and subject to the terms and conditions of this EULA. With respect to technical information you provide to Microsoft as part of the Support Services, Microsoft may use such information for its business purposes, including for product support and development. Microsoft will not utilize such technical information in a form that personally identifies you.

- **Software Transfer.** You may permanently transfer all of your rights under this EULA, provided you retain no copies, you transfer all of the SOFTWARE PRODUCT (including all component parts, the media and printed materials, any upgrades, this EULA, and, if applicable, the Certificate of Authenticity), **and** the recipient agrees to the terms of this EULA.

- **Termination.** Without prejudice to any other rights, Microsoft may terminate this EULA if you fail to comply with the terms and conditions of this EULA. In such event, you must destroy all copies of the SOFTWARE PRODUCT and all of its component parts.

3. **COPYRIGHT.** All title and copyrights in and to the SOFTWARE PRODUCT (including but not limited to any images, photographs, animations, video, audio, music, text, SAMPLE CODE, REDISTRIBUTABLES, and "applets" incorporated into the SOFTWARE PRODUCT) and any copies of the SOFTWARE PRODUCT are owned by Microsoft or its suppliers. The SOFTWARE PRODUCT is protected by copyright laws and international treaty provisions. Therefore, you must treat the SOFTWARE PRODUCT like any other copyrighted material **except** that you may install the SOFTWARE PRODUCT on a single computer provided you keep the original solely for backup or archival purposes. You may not copy the printed materials accompanying the SOFTWARE PRODUCT.

4. **U.S. GOVERNMENT RESTRICTED RIGHTS.** The SOFTWARE PRODUCT and documentation are provided with RESTRICTED RIGHTS. Use, duplication, or disclosure by the Government is subject to restrictions as set forth in subparagraph (c)(1)(ii) of the Rights in Technical Data and Computer Software clause at DFARS 252.227-7013 or subparagraphs (c)(1) and (2) of the Commercial Computer Software—Restricted Rights at 48 CFR 52.227-19, as applicable. Manufacturer is Microsoft Corporation/One Microsoft Way/Redmond, WA 98052-6399.

5. **EXPORT RESTRICTIONS.** You agree that you will not export or re-export the SOFTWARE PRODUCT, any part thereof, or any process or service that is the direct product of the SOFTWARE PRODUCT (the foregoing collectively referred to as the "Restricted Components"), to any country, person, entity, or end user subject to U.S. export restrictions. You specifically agree not to export or re-export any of the Restricted Components (i) to any country to which the U.S. has embargoed or restricted the export of goods or services, which currently include, but are not necessarily limited to, Cuba, Iran, Iraq, Libya, North Korea, Sudan, and Syria, or to any national of any such country, wherever located, who intends to transmit or transport the Restricted Components back to such country; (ii) to any end user who you know or have reason to know will utilize the Restricted Components in the design, development, or production of nuclear, chemical, or biological weapons; or (iii) to any end user who has been prohibited from participating in U.S. export transactions by any federal agency of the U.S. government. You warrant and represent that neither the BXA nor any other U.S. federal agency has suspended, revoked, or denied your export privileges.

DISCLAIMER OF WARRANTY

NO WARRANTIES OR CONDITIONS. MICROSOFT EXPRESSLY DISCLAIMS ANY WARRANTY OR CONDITION FOR THE SOFTWARE PRODUCT. THE SOFTWARE PRODUCT AND ANY RELATED DOCUMENTATION ARE PROVIDED "AS IS" WITHOUT WARRANTY OR CONDITION OF ANY KIND, EITHER EXPRESS OR IMPLIED, INCLUDING, WITHOUT LIMITATION, THE IMPLIED WARRANTIES OF MERCHANTABILITY, FITNESS FOR A PARTICULAR PURPOSE, OR NONINFRINGEMENT. THE ENTIRE RISK ARISING OUT OF USE OR PERFORMANCE OF THE SOFTWARE PRODUCT REMAINS WITH YOU.

LIMITATION OF LIABILITY. TO THE MAXIMUM EXTENT PERMITTED BY APPLICABLE LAW, IN NO EVENT SHALL MICROSOFT OR ITS SUPPLIERS BE LIABLE FOR ANY SPECIAL, INCIDENTAL, INDIRECT, OR CONSEQUENTIAL DAMAGES WHATSOEVER (INCLUDING, WITHOUT LIMITATION, DAMAGES FOR LOSS OF BUSINESS PROFITS, BUSINESS INTERRUPTION, LOSS OF BUSINESS INFORMATION, OR ANY OTHER PECUNIARY LOSS) ARISING OUT OF THE USE OF OR INABILITY TO USE THE SOFTWARE PRODUCT OR THE PROVISION OF OR FAILURE TO PROVIDE SUPPORT SERVICES, EVEN IF MICROSOFT HAS BEEN ADVISED OF THE POSSIBILITY OF SUCH DAMAGES. IN ANY CASE, MICROSOFT'S ENTIRE LIABILITY UNDER ANY PROVISION OF THIS EULA SHALL BE LIMITED TO THE GREATER OF THE AMOUNT ACTUALLY PAID BY YOU FOR THE SOFTWARE PRODUCT OR US$5.00; PROVIDED, HOWEVER, IF YOU HAVE ENTERED INTO A MICROSOFT SUPPORT SERVICES AGREEMENT, MICROSOFT'S ENTIRE LIABILITY REGARDING SUPPORT SERVICES SHALL BE GOVERNED BY THE TERMS OF THAT AGREEMENT. BECAUSE SOME STATES AND JURISDICTIONS DO NOT ALLOW THE EXCLUSION OR LIMITATION OF LIABILITY, THE ABOVE LIMITATION MAY NOT APPLY TO YOU.

MISCELLANEOUS

This EULA is governed by the laws of the State of Washington USA, except and only to the extent that applicable law mandates governing law of a different jurisdiction.

Should you have any questions concerning this EULA, or if you desire to contact Microsoft for any reason, please contact the Microsoft subsidiary serving your country, or write: Microsoft Sales Information Center/One Microsoft Way/Redmond, WA 98052-6399.

PN 097-0002296

OWNER REGISTRATION CARD

Register Today!

0-7356-1021-5

Return the bottom portion of this card to register today.

Inside Microsoft® Windows® 2000, **Third Edition**

FIRST NAME MIDDLE INITIAL LAST NAME

INSTITUTION OR COMPANY NAME

ADDRESS

CITY STATE ZIP

()

E-MAIL ADDRESS PHONE NUMBER

U.S. and Canada addresses only. Fill in information above and mail postage-free.
Please mail only the bottom half of this page.

For information about Microsoft Press®
products, visit our Web site at
mspress.microsoft.com